Capturing, Analyzing, and Managing Word-of-Mouth in the Digital Marketplace

Sumangla Rathore
Sir Padampat Singhania University, India

Avinash Panwar
Sir Padampat Singhania University, India

A volume in the Advances in Marketing, Customer Relationship Management, and E-Services (AMCRMES) Book Series

BUSINESS SCIENCE Reference
An Imprint of IGI Global

Managing Director: Lindsay Johnston
Managing Editor: Keith Greenberg
Director of Intellectual Property & Contracts: Jan Travers
Acquisitions Editor: Kayla Wolfe
Production Editor: Christina Henning
Cover Design: Jason Mull

Published in the United States of America by
Business Science Reference (an imprint of IGI Global)
701 E. Chocolate Avenue
Hershey PA, USA 17033
Tel: 717-533-8845
Fax: 717-533-8661
E-mail: cust@igi-global.com
Web site: http://www.igi-global.com

Library of Congress Cataloging-in-Publication Data

Capturing, analyzing, and managing word-of-mouth in the digital marketplace / Sumangla Rathore and Avinash Panwar, editors.
pages cm
Includes bibliographical references and index.
ISBN 978-1-4666-9449-1 (hardcover : alk. paper) -- ISBN 978-1-4666-9450-7 (ebook) 1. Telemarketing. 2. Online social networks. I. Rathore, Sumangla, 1978- editor. II. Panwar, Avinash, 1977- editor.
HF5415.1265C3627 2016
658.8'72--dc23
2015028183

This book is published in the IGI Global book series Advances in Marketing, Customer Relationship Management, and E-Services (AMCRMES) (ISSN: 2327-5502; eISSN: 2327-5529)

British Cataloguing in Publication Data
A Cataloguing in Publication record for this book is available from the British Library.

For electronic access to this publication, please contact: eresources@igi-global.com.

Advances in Marketing, Customer Relationship Management, and E-Services (AMCRMES) Book Series

Eldon Y. Li
National Chengchi University, Taiwan & California Polytechnic State University, USA

ISSN: 2327-5502
EISSN: 2327-5529

Mission

Business processes, services, and communications are important factors in the management of good customer relationship, which is the foundation of any well organized business. Technology continues to play a vital role in the organization and automation of business processes for marketing, sales, and customer service. These features aid in the attraction of new clients and maintaining existing relationships.

The Advances in Marketing, Customer Relationship Management, and E-Services (AMCRMES) Book Series

addresses success factors for customer relationship management, marketing, and electronic services and its performance outcomes. This collection of reference source covers aspects of consumer behavior and marketing business strategies aiming towards researchers, scholars, and practitioners in the fields of marketing management.

Coverage

- Customer retention
- CRM in financial services
- Cases on CRM Implementation
- Legal Considerations in E-Marketing
- Social Networking and Marketing
- Customer Relationship Management
- CRM strategies
- Relationship marketing
- Telemarketing
- Electronic Services

IGI Global is currently accepting manuscripts for publication within this series. To submit a proposal for a volume in this series, please contact our Acquisition Editors at Acquisitions@igi-global.com or visit: http://www.igi-global.com/publish/.

Titles in this Series

For a list of additional titles in this series, please visit: www.igi-global.com

Strategic Customer Relationship Management in the Age of Social Media
Amir Khanlari (University of Tehran, Iran)
Business Science Reference • copyright 2015 • 333pp • H/C (ISBN: 9781466685864) • US $200.00 (our price)

Maximizing Commerce and Marketing Strategies through Micro-Blogging
Janée N. Burkhalter (Saint Joseph's University, USA) and Natalie T. Wood (Saint Joseph's University, USA & Edith Cowan University, Australia)
Business Science Reference • copyright 2015 • 354pp • H/C (ISBN: 9781466684089) • US $225.00 (our price)

Analyzing the Cultural Diversity of Consumers in the Global Marketplace
Juan Miguel Alcántara-Pilar (University of Granada, Spain) Salvador del Barrio-García (University of Granada, Spain) Esmeralda Crespo-Almendros (University of Granada, Spain) and Lucia Porcu (University of Granada, Spain)
Business Science Reference • copyright 2015 • 404pp • H/C (ISBN: 9781466682627) • US $200.00 (our price)

Engaging Consumers through Branded Entertainment and Convergent Media
Jose Marti Parreno (Universidad Europea de Valencia, Spain) Carla Ruiz Mafe (Universidad de Valencia, Spain) and Lisa Scribner (University of North Carolina Wilmington, USA)
Business Science Reference • copyright 2015 • 354pp • H/C (ISBN: 9781466683426) • US $205.00 (our price)

Handbook of Research on Integrating Social Media into Strategic Marketing
Nick Hajli (Newcastle University Business School, UK)
Business Science Reference • copyright 2015 • 440pp • H/C (ISBN: 9781466683532) • US $310.00 (our price)

Customer Relationship Management Strategies in the Digital Era
Süphan Nasır (Istanbul University, Turkey)
Business Science Reference • copyright 2015 • 322pp • H/C (ISBN: 9781466682313) • US $200.00 (our price)

Handbook of Research on Effective Advertising Strategies in the Social Media Age
Nurdan Öncel Taşkıran (Ondokuz Mayıs University, Turkey) and Recep Yılmaz (Ondokuz Mayıs University, Turkey)
Business Science Reference • copyright 2015 • 509pp • H/C (ISBN: 9781466681255) • US $335.00 (our price)

Understanding Consumer Behavior and Consumption Experience
Rajagopal (EGADE Business School, Tecnologico de Monterrey, Mexico) and Raquel Castaño (EGADE Business School, Tecnologico de Monterrey, Mexico)
Business Science Reference • copyright 2015 • 303pp • H/C (ISBN: 9781466675186) • US $185.00 (our price)

Editorial Advisory Board

Table of Contents

Detailed Table of Contents

In the present era of technology enabled markets, social media marketing is gaining increasing importance through the process of gaining website traffic or attention with the use of social media websites. To most of the entrepreneurs, social media marketing is the "next big thing". It is a powerful tool that must be taken advantage of. In a very short span of time, social media marketing has become one of the most loved media for the youths today. Social Media Marketing (SMM) is the hottest new marketing concept and every business owner wants to know the way in which social media can generate value for their business. Businesses today are using SMM for grabbing attention, stimulating interest, creating desire and promoting action. It has become a panacea for communication, visibility, promotion, brand building and everything. This chapter attempts to highlight the significance of e-WOM on social media as a tool for brand building and creating value to business. It also discusses its role, benefits and challenges.

From technology focused conceptual perspectives, the Unified Theory of Acceptance and Use of Technology (UTAUT) as a theory of technology acceptance postulates four identified constructs as: performance expectancy, effort expectancy, social influence and facilitating conditions (Venkatesh, Morris, Davis, & Davis, 2003). This study concentrates on digital storytelling as a form of eWOM for tourism promotion within the UTAUT capacities in selected 'developing' tourism market perspectives. Results outline that in almost every aspects and contexts, appropriate technology application is supportive for tourism promotion where institutionalisation of market structures is relatively weaker.

Online social networks (oSNS) enable users to construct strong relationships with friends, family, as well as strangers. They also enable users to share information concerning experiences and opinions about products, brands and companies via electronic word of mouth (eWOM). The unique nature of oSNS-eWOM relationship forms the basis of this research. The authors report the results of a research investigating six motivational factors for engaging in eWOM communication, investigated under three dimensions; producing, consuming and forwarding of content on oSNSs. Results reveal that eWOM production behavior on oSNS is mainly motivated by altruism, self enhancement, electronic social interaction and exhibitionism. The motivating factors of eWOM forwarding behavior showed up as electronic social interaction and exhibitionism, whereas the motivating factors for eWOM consumption behavior are altruism, electronic social interaction and need for intellectual engagement. Aversion of cognitive activities appeared to have a negative effect on consumption of eWOM communication.

This chapter takes fashion blogs as a case to explain motivations behind becoming a blogger and then to keep being one on the long-term. It wraps up past research findings before presenting the result of an original study conducted recently with authors of successful blogs as interviewees. It presents the typology of motivations but also the nature of potential brand-blogger relationships. Understanding such points is key to successfully use blogs as part of a useful WoM communication strategy. Findings generalizable across other sectors of activity conclude the chapter.

Electronic Word-of-Mouth (eWOM) has been identified and proven to be one of the major factors affecting online buying behaviour of the consumers. A growing number of sellers are shifting to online business channels in order to attract the online consumer. The consumers are also utilizing online platforms for sharing their product related experiences and thereby influencing other consumers. Thus, it is critical for businesses to recognize the important factors affecting eWOM. This chapter deals with different elements that conceptualize the phenomenon of eWOM and analyze what may be the possible ways for service marketers to influence this recommendation-based communication among online consumers. This study investigates factors affecting the eWOM behaviour of consumers by using of qualitative and quantitative research.

Through Social Media, like social networking sites, wikis, web forums or blogs, people can debate and influence each other. Due to this reason, the analysis of online conversations has been recognized to be relevant to organizations. In the chapter we introduce two strategic tools to monitor and analyze online conversations, Sentiment Text Analysis (STA) and Network Text Analysis (NTA). Finally, we propose one empirical example in which these tools are integrated to analyze Word-of-Mouth regarding products and services in the Digital Marketplace.

Netnography is a specialized form of ethnographic research that has been adapted to the unique contingencies of various types of computer-mediated social interaction. With the tremendous growth in the number of Internet users in India, the potential of utilizing netnography to study various aspects of management and business has also increased. Several e-Commerce companies have started operating in India since 2007. Over time, the number of online consumers has also increased in India. Therefore it is important to know the online consumer behaviour towards e-Commerce companies operating in India. Keeping the above facts in view, this chapter proposes Netnogrpahy as an effective research method to assess online consumer behavior. The chapter not only helps in providing future agenda for research, but also presents a framework that may be adopted to carry out Netnogrpahy of e-commerce related websites in India.

Marketing concept has progressed through different phases of evolution in the past. At the moment, customer relationship management is considered as the last era of marketing development. The main purpose of this approach is to build long-term oriented profitable relationships with customers. So, companies should know better their customers. This knowledge can be created through a deeper analysis of companies' data with data mining tools. Companies which are able to use data mining tools will gain strong competitive advantages for their strategic decisions. Hotel industry is selected in this study, since it provides a warehouse of customer comments from which precious knowledge can be obtained if text mining as a data mining tool is used appropriately. Thus, this study attempts to explain the stages of text mining with the use of Rapidminer. As a result, different approaches according to the customer satisfaction/dissatisfaction are discussed to build competitive advantages.

Though the concept of experience was propounded decades ago, the terms such as Customer Experience Management, Brand Experience etc. have started gaining currency only recently. Renewed focus on the concept is the result of positive impacts of brand experience as evidenced by researches. Emergence of Social Media has provided the organizations with supplementary platforms to enhance customer experiences. The experiences of customers with various social media platforms may rub on to their experiences with the brands being promoted through these. Accordingly, present research studies the experience of select social media platforms in Indian context. Result revealed that the experience of Facebook was significantly favorable in comparison to the rest three platforms; however, a scope of improvement is evident. Result is important for platform developers as it helps them to improve their platforms and for Marketing managers as it guides them to associate their brands with the more favourable platforms in order to reap concomitant benefits.

The domination of Word of mouth (WOM) has been applauded for many years as key influence on consumer purchases. Associating WOM with the internet usually called electronic-WOM (e-WOM) makes transmission of messages much easier, wider and faster. As e-WOM is not restricted to strong social tie groups thus the message itself plays a critical role in building purchase intention. The present study, first attempts to investigate messages efficacy on identified constructs. The study recognized credibility of message as a sole component that could moderate the discord between level of involvement and expected intention for online purchase.

In the global era, Electronic Word of Mouth (E-WOM) has become an important emerging business strategy in the marketing and consumer environment. Along with the growth of digital connectivity and E-WOM, new ongoing challenges have also emerged for online users, businesses, and services. The chapter mainly aims to look closer upon how Electronic Word of Mouth faced challenges related to social, personal, psychological and human appeal in FMCG sector which influence customers as well as firms. The study used survey method to approach the respondents. The primary data was collected from 250 respondents and descriptive statistics and F-test ANOVA were used to test the significant of the association / non-association between variables. It was found that mostly customers have positive attitude towards E-WOM phenomenon. The study could help the FMCG Company in taking such steps that could make improvements in their business processes and expand their business without spending lot of money.

Social media has been found to have created a paradigm shift in the digital marketplace by giving a new technological face to marketing, highlighting on brand awareness and effectiveness. In this digital marketplace, emotions lead users to like or dislike, share or not to share messages, thus evoking, influencing and shifting public opinions on everything from political parties to corporate reputations, brands, products etc. It is important to understand how emotions and content relevance make these messages go viral. To explore this relationship, in-depth interviews with people of Generation Y were

Preface

Word of Mouth (WOM) remains an extensively researched marketing paradigm since 1960's with incessant evolution in its forms and definitions. The growth of Information technology and Internet in particular, has led to the emergence of new forms of communication channels and platforms, which are not only user-friendly, but also highly interactive and provide several means to create and exchange user-generated content. In the context of growing usage of Internet and social media as a preferred channel of communication, WOM may be "e-defined" as 'eWOM' or online Word of Mouth, which covers all Internet-mediated informal communications directed at consumers about the ownership, usage, or characteristics of particular goods, services or their sellers where the communicator is perceived to be free of any commercial influence. This new phenomenon is creating an inevitable impact on marketing tactics and strategies adopted by the companies. Hence, in order to ride this wave of change, a clear understanding of the various factors that influence the WOM in online world is essential.

This edited book was conceptualised with an objective of covering various aspects of electronic WOM and social media. The chapters describing its meaning, growth, recent trends, practices, issues and main challenges were sought from academicians, researchers and practitioners. Special emphasis was given on describing the online word of mouth phenomenon in the form of conceptual and empirical research articles and/or case studies, both in international and Indian context.

This book provides relevant theoretical frameworks and the latest empirical research findings in the area so as to contribute substantially to the body of knowledge on online word of mouth. It has been written for academicians, students as well as marketing professionals who wish to enhance their understanding of the subject. This shall help the marketers to plan their marketing strategies more effectively and to tap the potential benefits from this highly pervasive and influential tool of communication.

The book has been organised into following sections:

Section 1: Electronic Word of Mouth: concepts and practices.
Section 2: Precursors to electronic word of mouth.
Section 3: Capturing and analysing electronic word of mouth.
Section 4: Studies in Indian context.

The first Chapter of the book is an attempt to organise the fragmented literature related to eWOM. The authors have drawn attention to the fact that fragmentation of the research on eWOM can be traced back to a lack of conceptualization of the term eWOM. Therefore, this chapter highlights the great impact of eWOM on consumer's behavior and sheds light on this concept. The chapter first introduces the context of eWOM, defines the concept and distinguishes it from other close concepts like traditional word of mouth, buzz marketing and viral marketing. At the end, the last section of the chapter focuses on the importance given by consumers to eWOM.

Chapter 2 explains the strategic importance of electronic word-of-mouth (eWOM) for organisations. This chapter discusses the genesis of eWOM from word-of-mouth and the differences between the traditional word of mouth and the eWOM. The chapter also presents a literature review to explain what motivates consumers to share their consumption experience through eWOM. The author has described the various eWOM marketing techniques, a criticism of eWOM and the fields yet to be explored in eWOM research.

Social media marketing is gaining increasing importance and businesses worldwide are aiming at gaining website traffic or attention with the use of social media websites. In a very short span of time, social media has become one of the most loved media for the youths today and every business owner wants to know the way in which social media can generate value for their business. Social media marketing is being used for grabbing attention, stimulating interest, creating desire and promoting action. It has become a panacea for communication, visibility, promotion, brand building and everything. In this context, the third chapter of the book highlights the significance of e-WOM on social media as a tool for brand building and creating value to business. It also discusses its role, benefits and challenges.

Chapter 4 describes the significance of Unified Theory of Acceptance and Use of Technology (UTAUT) as a theory of technology acceptance to propose a conceptual model for eWOM in tourism industry. The author has emphasized upon application of digital storytelling as a form of eWOM for tourism promotion within the UTAUT capacities in selected 'developing' tourism markets.

The growing popularity of Online Social Networks(oSNS) has been a primary reason behind the eWOM phenomena. The oSNSs enable users to construct strong relationships with friends, family, as well as strangers. They also enable users to share information concerning experiences and opinions about products, brands and companies via electronic word of mouth (eWOM). This unique nature of relationship between Online social networks (oSNS) and eWOM forms the basis of Chapter 5. The authors report the results of a research investigating six motivational factors for engaging in eWOM communication, investigated under three dimensions; producing, consuming and forwarding of content on oSNSs. The study reveals that eWOM production behavior on oSNS is mainly motivated by altruism, self enhancement, electronic social interaction and exhibitionism. The motivating factors of eWOM forwarding behavior include electronic social interaction and exhibitionism, whereas the motivating factors for eWOM consumption behavior are altruism, electronic social interaction and need for intellectual engagement. Aversion of cognitive activities appeared to have a negative effect on consumption of eWOM communication.

Chapter 6 takes fashion blogs as a case to explain motivations behind becoming a blogger and continuing being one on the long-term. The authors present a review of past research findings and discussed the results of a study conducted with authors of successful blogs as interviewees. The chapter highlights the typology of motivations and the nature of potential brand-blogger relationships. The findings described in the chapter are useful for planning successful eWoM strategies using blogs as the media of communication especially in the case of fashion industry.

Chapter 7 is based on a research study conducted by the author to investigate the factors that affect electronic word of mouth. The chapter deals with different elements that conceptualize the phenomenon of eWOM and analyze what may be the possible ways for service marketers to influence this recommendation-based communication among online consumers.

The social networks and other forms of electronic communication on Internet have created enormous amount of online data regarding customer opinions and their preferences. These data sources and consumer networks can provide significant and noteworthy insights about the consumer behaviour, and thus must be gathered and analysed using various tools and techniques.

Chapter 8 highlights the role of Social Media, like social networking sites, wikis, web forums or blogs and their relevance for organizations. In the chapter the authors have introduced two strategic tools to monitor and analyse online conversations, Sentiment Text Analysis (STA) and Network Text Analysis (NTA). An empirical example in which these tools are integrated to analyse word-of-mouth regarding products and services in the digital marketplace is also presented.

Another approach for analysing consumer opinions shared on online platforms has been described in Chapter 9. Authors of the chapter have described qualitative research approach that is termed as Netnography. Netnography is a specialized form of ethnographic research that has been adapted to the unique contingencies of various types of computer-mediated social interaction. This chapter proposes Netnogrpahy as an effective research method to assess online consumer behavior. The chapter not only helps in providing future agenda for research, but also presents a framework that may be adopted to carry out Netnogrpahy of e-commerce related websites in India.

Chapter 10 describes the application of a text mining tool, Rapidminer. Text mining is appropriate for analysing textual data in the online environments, and especially for electronic word-of-mouth. The author has explained the practical application of Rapidminer with the help of description of specific steps and screen shots.

According to 2014 statistics published on www.internetlivestats.com, India is ranked third in terms of number of Internet users, after China and USA at first and second rank respectively, with a 14% one year growth in number of users. This is much higher than that of China and United States. With this tremendous and fast growth in the number of Internet users and the rise of e-commerce companies in India, the world of business has been completely transformed. The proliferation of Internet enabled devices coupled with the changing demographics and life style of middle class population of the country has helped in creation of a huge market full of endless business opportunities for online marketers. The shopping preferences of the consumers are also changing and a large number of Indian consumers are now buying online. They are not only sharing their shopping experiences online, but also referring to information shared by other consumers for making their purchase related decisions. Hence, it is imperative to understand the role played by the online reviews and electronic word of mouth in shaping online consumer behavior and their opinions towards e-Commerce companies in Indian context.

Chapter 11 highlights the significance of Social Media being used by organisations as a supplementary platform to enhance customer experiences. The authors have emphasised in this chapter that experiences of customers with various social media platforms may rub on to their experiences with the brands being promoted through these. The chapter describes a research undertaken to study the experience of select social media platforms in Indian context. The findings indicated in the chapter are important for platform developers as it helps them to improve their platforms and for marketing managers as it guides them to associate their brands with the more favourable platforms in order to reap concomitant benefits.

Chapter 12 is based on the notion that e-WOM is not restricted to strong social tie groups and thus the role of message itself in building purchase intentions is critical. The author of the chapter attempts to investigate messages efficacy on identified constructs and has recognized credibility of message as a sole component that could moderate the discord between level of involvement and expected intention for online purchase.

Chapter 13 looks closer upon how Electronic Word of Mouth faced challenges related to social, personal, psychological and human appeal in FMCG sector which influence customers as well as firms. The authors have presented the results of a study that was undertaken in India. The chapter explains the association among various variables and concludes that mostly customers have positive attitude towards E-WOM phenomenon.

In the digital marketplace, emotions lead users to like or dislike, share or not to share messages, thus evoking, influencing and shifting public opinions on everything from political parties to corporate reputations, brands, products etc. It is important to understand how emotions and content relevance make these messages go viral. To explore this relationship, the author of Chapter 14 conducted in-depth interviews with people of Generation Y, who were shown two videos that have gone viral. The chapter described the findings of the study that focus on how the content of these videos and emotions generated will lead the respondents to share them online. The chapter also proposes an Emo-Cog (emotion –cognition) induced decision tree model which the generation Y consumers might frequently be using to decide on whether to share the videos or not. An extensive literature review on related topics has also been presented in the chapter.

Internet has enabled today's consumer to transform himself from passive to an active and an informed consumer who can share his experiences, opinions about product or services with an infinite number of consumers around the globe. These reviews or opinions are further used by potential buyers of that particular product or service via electronic Word of Mouth (e-WOM). The Chapter 15 is based on a study carried out on Indian academicians to assess the impact of one type of e-WOM, i.e., the online consumer reviews, on purchasing decisions of electronic products. This empirical study also focuses on the relationship between reviews and purchasing behaviour. The authors have demonstrated the causal impact of customer reviews on product selection and consumer purchasing behaviour.

To summarize, this publication is an attempt to encompass various aspects of electronic word of mouth and will serve as a ready reference for the Marketing practitioners, academicians and students to understand the notion of online Word of Mouth and Social Technologies.

Acknowledgment

We would like to acknowledge the contribution of all the people involved in this project who have directly or indirectly helped in making this book a reality. A sincere note of gratitude is extended to the members of the editorial advisory board and the reviewers, whose constructive suggestions have led to making significant improvements in the quality, coherence and content of this book.

We would also like to thank each one of the authors for their contributions and their roles as reviewers.

Above all, we would like to thank our parents, family and friends who blessed, supported and encouraged us throughout this endeavour. Thanks to our loving son, Suyash for cheering us in spite of all the time it took us away from him.

Sumangla Rathore
Sir Padampat Singhania University, India

Avinash Panwar
Sir Padampat Singhania University, India

Section 1

Electronic Word of Mouth:
Concepts and Practices

Chapter 1
Electronic Word of Mouth: Definitions and Concepts

Rym Srarfi Tabbane
University of Manouba, Tunisia

Mohsen Debabi
University of Manouba, Tunisia

ABSTRACT

Because of its great impact on the consumer's behavior, electronic Word Of Mouth (eWOM) has become an important concept for the researchers and during the last decade, a great deal of attention was paid to the concept of eWOM. However, despite the growing number of studies on the subject, related literature remains fragmented, possibly affecting the long term development of the eWOM research. Fragmentation of this research can be traced back to a lack of conceptualization of the term eWOM. Therefore, this chapter proposes to highlight the great impact of eWOM on consumer's behavior and to shed light on this concept. Then, this chapter will first introduce the context in which eWOM takes place, define the concept and distinguish it from other close concepts like traditional word of mouth, buzz marketing and viral marketing. At the end, the last section will focus on the importance given by consumers to eWOM.

INTRODUCTION

Electronic Word of Mouth or eWOM is a particular form of communication that has emerged with the development of Internet and especially with the advent and evolution of social media as well as user-generated content (UGC).

During the last decade, both researchers and practitioners placed a great deal of attention to eWOM (Dwyer, 2007) and several studies examined this concept. However, despite the increasing number of studies on eWOM, research on the subject remains relatively fragmented (Cheung & Thadani, 2012), which could - on the long run- hinder the development of the concept itself. The reasons for this fragmentation are many and various.

DOI: 10.4018/978-1-4666-9449-1.ch001

Indeed, these reasons may relate to how researchers label eWOM phenomenon, as well as to how researchers use different terms such as Web of mouse, internet word of mouth, word of modem, online references, etc. to designate eWOM (Shin, 2008).

The great number of eWOM definitions that are suggested by researchers may represent a second reason to this fragmentation. In fact, the research trend on eWOM being somewhat new, thus it is possible to find within literature several definitions that describe the phenomenon.

The proximity of eWOM to other concepts such as the conventional WOM, buzz marketing, user-generated content, or viral marketing, has created some confusion in the use of the term eWOM, often confound with these concepts and used in synonymous ways. This represents a third reason to the fragmentation of research on eWOM.

The purpose of this chapter is, then, to identify and analyze - through a review of the literature - the main reasons leading to the fragmentation of eWOM research. Emphasis will also be placed on the issues around the development of research in this field as well as its impact on consumer behavior.

The chapter is structured into four sections. The first one tries to determine the reasons which led to the emergence of eWOM. The second aims at better understanding eWOM by defining it, explaining its different communication channels and by listing its different features. The third section tries to position the concept in relation to similar concepts which are often regarded as its synonyms. The last section argues the reasons why consumers prefer eWOM as a communication model.

THE ADVENT OF eWOM

As explained by Dellarocas (2003), the advent of Internet has generated an evolution in the way communication is made between individuals. Since the early 2000's, the second generation of Internet-based applications (also known as Web 2.0) has emerged. Thanks to the opportunities that Web 2.0 offers, as well as the emergence of user-generated media, internet users have been enabled to generate information and control communication. Since then, this user-generated media are not anymore limited to be used as distribution channels, but used to facilitate the development and communication between Internet users. As a result marketing managers have lost control on marketing communication (Miller & Lammas, 2010).

Thanks to the shifting landscape of information and communication technology, users have begun to electronically exchange information about products and make known of their preferences and their consumption experiences through the technology offered by web 2.0 (Huang, Cai, Tsang, & Zhou, 2011). This marks the emergence of a new form of communication: the eWOM. Indeed, with the advent of Internet, consumers are gradually moving towards computer-mediated communication to obtain the information they need to make purchase decisions (Dellarocas, 2003; Kozinets, 2002).

In what follows, an overview of the different concepts that are at the origin of eWOM will be presented. These concepts include Web 2.0, user-generated content and social media. The second part will focus on the emergence of eWOM.

Web 2.0

Kaplan and Haenlein (2010) define Web 2.0 as a term used to describe a new way with which software developers and end users access the Web. It refers to a platform in which the content and applications are no longer created and posted by some individuals only. With the advent of Web 2.0, content can be continuously modified by all users in a participatory and collective manner. In fact, Web 2.0 does not refer to a new version of the Web, but rather it denotes a set of features necessary for its operation. It is possible then to consider it as a platform which allowed the evolution of social media. According to Chen, Yen, and Hwang (2012), Web 2.0 does not have real clear-cut barriers, but it revolves around the following core values: interaction, participation and sharing. The emergence of Web 2.0 can be apprehended through the growth of blogs as well as social networking sites.

Social Media

Kaplan and Haenlein (2010, p. 61) define social media as "a group of Internet-based applications that build on the ideological and technological foundations of Web 2.0, and that allow the creation and exchange of User Generated Content".

Social media includes a variety of online information-sharing formats such as social networking sites (like Facebook, MySpace, etc.), sites for sharing creative work (like Youtube or Flickr), collaborative websites (Wikipedia) and microblogging sites (Twitter). Social media has given consumers the opportunity to express themselves. In fact, these consumers are no longer passive respondents when dealing with brands as was the case in the past. Instead of that, they are now active members in brand communities.

User Generated Content -UGC-

In the literature, several researchers have tried to define user-generated content (UGC). Among these definitions, a few were able to obtain consensus among researchers. Kaplan and Haenlein (2010, p. 61) define UGC as "the sum of all ways in which people make use of Social Media… it is generally applied to describe the various forms of media content that are publicly available and created by end-users".

The Organization for Economic Co-operation and Development [OECD] (2007) set three criteria used to determine "user generated content": being published online and available to the public (on a web site or a social networking site). Moreover, the content should display a certain level of creativity, and therefore it cannot be considered as any user-generated content replicating existing content. Finally, the creation of this content should take place in the context of a hobby or outside any professional routine, thus a content that was created with a commercial purpose is excluded.

As noted by Krishnamurthy and Dou (2008), thanks to user-generated content, consumers produce, design, edit or publish content that makes this latter vivid and attractive. These authors propose a typology of UGC determined by the main purpose for which users participate in UGC activities and the level of community involvement in the creation of UGC. As for the main factors behind participating in UGC, we distinguish two types of motivations: rational motives and emotional motives. Rational motivation includes sharing knowledge and the recommendation of a particular position on a particular issue. Emotional motivation may include the development of social relationships with friends, relatives or other users, or entertainment. It is therefore possible to define user-generated content as any form of original content, available online and published by users whose motivations are devoid of any commercial purposes. In conclusion, it is possible to consider Web 2.0 as a platform in which social media evolve. UGC then designates all the ways by which users use these social media platforms.

Emergence of eWOM

With the development of Internet and particularly the evolution of information and communication technology, consumers have witnessed a transition from Web 1.0 to Web 2.0, the emergence of UGC as well as social media. All this led to the emergence and development of a new way to communicate online: the peer-to-peer electronic communication, which has become an important phenomenon. This new form of communication has enabled users to share information and opinions with other users (Hennig-Thurau, Gwinner, Walsh, & Gremler, 2004) and this in a much easier way than before. More particularly, in the field of consumer products and services, Web 2.0 has given the opportunity and the power to consumers to influence other consumers through the use of a variety of platforms, and the posting of content regarding their consumption experiences: it is the emergence of the eWOM phenomenon.

Consequently, this latter use had an impact on consumers and allowed for the emergence of new behaviors. The act of sending an eWOM message or being exposed to it, represents a manifestation of eWOM behaviors. Indeed, thanks to the development in technology, consumers are no longer limited to expressing their opinions about products and services and to describe their consumption experiences directly to their surroundings by oral route, but instead they started using social media and UGC to communicate electronically in a way their views can reach a large number of unknown users. The latter makes their communication more powerful, since it can reach a larger number of receivers. This new opportunity to communicate views on a large scale has had a great impact on consumer behavior, which makes eWOM a very popular topic (Shen, Maceli, Zhao, Baack, & Bacon, 2014) and justifies the usefulness of investigating its scope for electronic Marketing.

Having presented the circumstances under which eWOM developed, the next section will be dedicated to defining eWOM, presenting its different channels and its various features and characteristics.

WHAT IS eWOM?

This section will review the different definitions proposed in the literature to determine eWOM, its various components and the communication channels adopted by eWOM users to convey their opinions.

Definition of eWOM

The significant amount of research on eWOM that has emerged during the last decade suggested a number of terminologies to describe this phenomenon. Indeed, to refer to eWOM, researchers have often used the following terms: word of mouse, Web of mouse, Internet word of mouth, consumer reviews, online references, word of modem, online Word of Mouth. Researchers also proposed many terminologies for the different definitions describing the phenomenon. In order to see our way through this multitude of terms, a literature review was conducted, which allowed us to expose the great number of terms given to eWOM and the different definitions proposed by researchers. Table 1 presents a summary of all the terms found.

In Table 1, it is possible to notice that some of the proposed definitions such as that of Litvin et al. (2008), include in their definition of eWOM not only communication among consumers, but also communications taking place between producers and consumers. Such definitions are not consistent with the eWOM concept on which most researchers agree that it is an interpersonal communication

Table 1. The Definitions of eWOM in the Literature

Naming	Definition	Reference
Virtual Word of mouth	"Virtual Word-of-Mouth involves virtual communication between consumers who have never met in real life."	(Parry, Kawakami, & Kishiya, 2012, p. 952)
Internet Word of Mouth	"Internet Word of mouth is a boundless dialogue with a potentially unlimited number of Net users."	(Stauss, 1997, p. 28)
Internet customer communication	"Internet customer communication occurs when customers report/interact about consumption-relevant circumstances on the Internet."	(Stauss, 2000, p. 243)
Online Feedback mechanisms	"Online feedback mechanisms are using the Internet's bi-directional communication capabilities in order to artificially engineer large-scale word-of-mouth networks in which individuals share opinions and experiences on a wide range of topics, including companies, products, services, and even world events."	(Dellarocas, 2003, p. 2)
Electronic Referral Marketing	"The goal of Electronic Referral Marketing is to use consumer-consumer (or peer-to-peer) communications, as opposed to company-consumer communications, to disseminate information about a product or service, hence leading to its rapid and cost effective market adoption."	(De Bruyn & Lilien, 2004, p. 4)
Electronic Word of mouth	"Any positive or negative statement made by potential, actual or former customers about a product or a company, which is made available to a multitude of people and institutions via the Internet."	(Hennig-Thurau et al., 2004, p. 39)
	"Any positive or negative statements made about a product, company, or media personality that are made widely available via the Internet."	(Thorson & Rodgers, 2006, p. 40)
	"All informational communications directed at consumers through Internet-based technology related to the usage or characteristics of particular goods and services, or their sellers. This includes communication between producers and consumers as well as those between consumers themselves."	(Litvin, Goldsmith, & Pan, 2008, p. 461)
	"eWOM involves consumer's comments about products and services posted on the Internet."	(Bronner & de Hoog, 2011, p. 15)
	"eWOM refers to any statement based on positive, neutral, or negative experiences made by potential, actual or former consumers about a product, service, brand, or company, which is made available to a multitude of people and institutions via the Internet (through web sites, social networks, instant messages, news feed,…)."	(Kietzmann & Canhoto, 2013, pp. 147-148)
	"It is a new kind of word of mouth communication that is based on Consumer-created information: new information presented from the perspective of consumers who have purchased and used the product. It includes their experiences, evaluations and opinions."	(Park, Lee, & Han, 2007, p. 125)

taking place between people, and in which professionals (sellers, manufacturers, marketing managers) can in no way intervene. The influence and power exercised by eWOM on Internet users largely stems from the fact that unlike professionals, communication conveyed by internet users about products and services is void from any commercial interest, and therefore their communication is more reliable than that provided by companies.

Therefore, comparing the different definitions proposed therein, it is possible to use the definition that has been proposed by Hennig-Thurau et al. (2004): "Any positive or negative statement made by potential, actual or former customers about a product or a company, which is made available to a multitude of people and institutions via the Internet." (p. 39)

The choice of the above definition was motivated by two main reasons. On the one hand, this definition is almost unanimous among a lot of researchers who have adopted it (Wang & Rodgers, 2011). On the other hand, this definition is consistent with the eWOM concept as any communication taking place exclusively between users, and is not in any way subject to actions of marketers. This definition is also coherent with the definitions proposed in the literature about traditional WOM as a verbal form of communication between consumers. In a study dealing with WOM in a non-virtual environment, Buttle (1998, p. 243) reached the conclusion that the only specific characteristic of WOM could be the fact that "WOM is uttered by sources who are assumed by receivers to be independent of corporate influence".

Finally, in terms of the terminology used, it is possible to note that most of the current studies consistently use the term eWOM (Barnes & Jacobsen, 2014; Daugherty & Hoffman, 2014; Reichelt, Sievert, & Jacob, 2014); It would be wise, in order to align research together, to use this terminology, and overlook other terms proposed in past research.

Having proposed a terminology and a definition of eWOM, it would be helpful, to better understand the concept of eWOM, to present the channels that are used most by consumers in their eWOM communication and to introduce the different components of the eWOM concept.

Types of Channels Used for eWOM Communication

EWOM communication takes place through the Internet, and it is based on different media or different communication channels that will influence the way in which eWOM communication is realized. And, as noted by Rejón-Guardia and Martínez-López (2014), eWOM can be understood separately through the channels it uses. Consumers have indeed different ways to communicate online with each other to share information and feelings about products and brands.

These channels can take the form of: opinion platforms, forums, discussion groups (Hennig-Thurau et al., 2004), e-mail, discussion forums (Goldsmith & Horowitz, 2006) unique Web 2.0-based platforms such as personal blogs and business blogs (Hung & Yiyan Li, 2007), general social networks like Facebook (Leivadiotou & Markopoulos, 2010), specialized social networks such as tourism, or micro blogging (Jansen, Zhang, Sobel, & Chowdury, 2009).

Litvin et al. (2008) attempted to propose a typology of media used by eWOM based on two dimensions: the scope of communication and the level of interactivity.

- The scope of communication

The scope of communication relates to the number of people involved in communication. This can vary between a communication involving a single sender and a single receiver (e-mail-based communication), a communication involving a sender and multiple receivers (such as communication that takes place through review sites) or a communication involving multiple senders and multiple receivers (as it is the case with communication based on online communities as channels, for example).

- The level of interactivity

The level of interactivity relates to the degree of the synchronization of the communication. Communication can indeed vary between asynchronous communication in which transmission and reception of communication does not happen at the same time (An example is online review sites) to a perfectly synchronous communication in which the presence of the sender and receiver at the same time is necessary for communication to take place (e.g. instant messaging). In what follows, we will present some of the channels that are the most often studied in the literature on eWOM and the most used by consumers to obtain and disseminate information on products and services. These are: discussion forums, blogs and online review sites that can include retail sites, social networking sites and online review platforms.

Online Discussion Forums

As indicated by Evans, Wedande, Ralston, and Hul (2001) online chatting provides an online "avenue" allowing users to share their opinions as consumers over the Internet. Indeed, discussion forums, present an opportunity for participants to share with other forum members their experiences, opinions and the expertise they dispose of on specific subjects. Moreover, discussion forums can cover various subjects on any product or service of interest to consumers. Thus, participants in discussion forums may have comments on almost any type of purchase decision (Fong & Burton, 2006).

In discussion forums, participants can both read and post messages that can be ordered by date and subject, and they also have in addition the opportunity to respond to the different lines of the discussion. The impact of the use of forums during eWOM has got the interest of a number of researchers. For example, some studies have used forums to study the size and dispersion of eWOM (Godes & Mayzlin, 2004), while other studies used a qualitative approach to study consumer attitudes towards online interaction in virtual communities (Evans et al., 2001).

In fact, discussion forums have the advantage of broad exposure and impact because they often gather participants who share the same interests (Nelson & Otnes, 2005). Previous eWOM studies indicated that discussion forums present an opportunity for individuals with similar interests to meet and share their opinions. The opinions and information presented from a potentially credible eWOM source might influence other participants in the discussion forums (Fong & Burton, 2006).

Blogs

The act of blogging (to "blog") is to just continually post their own ideas, opinions, internet links or any other item on their own site called "web blog" and often abbreviated as "blog" (Smudde, 2005). Blogs are then online journals in which content is classified in a chronological order (Blood, 2002). The OECD (2007) defined blogs as one of the oldest forms of social media, which represent specific Web sites that usually display information entries that display dates in a reverse chronological order. These blogs can take different forms ranging from personal blogs describing the life of the author to summaries of any relevant information dealing with a particular subject. By defining blogs as Web sites in the form of newspaper that generally provide reviews and information listed in a chronological order and allow readers to leave recommendation comments and links, Johnson and Kaye (2004) summarize the main elements of the proposed OECD definition adding that blogs allow for posting readers' feedback. This possibility of interaction is emphasized by Kaplan and Haenlein (2010): "Blogs are usually managed by one person only, but provide the possibility of interaction with others through the addition of comments" (p. 63) .It is possible to classify blogs into two groups: blogs generated by businesses, and blogs generated by consumers. Corporate blogs are blogs owned and managed by the company. They are a way to deliver content to customers. Blogs generated by consumers do not report to marketers, but they are run by and targeted to consumers. The blog is the place where consumers can express their own opinions and describe their own experiences with brands, products and/or services (Morimoto & Trimble, 2012).

When consumers use blogs to communicate to brand-related information, this latter should appear in different forms. They can take the form of a description of bloggers' evaluation of their personal experience, or of a sponsorship blog in which information related to brands is communicated through posts and finally of an advertising blog in which information on brands is distinct from posts.

Nardi, Schiano, Gumbrecht, and Swartz (2004) found several reasons of why bloggers engage in a blogging activity. For example, thanks to a "daily events" chronicle, they update others on their lives, express opinions that could influence others and then look for others' opinions and feedback. Armstrong (2006) notes that half of bloggers provide information on brands and this at least once a week, and that 77% of bloggers get an idea of the brand from other blogs and consider blogging as a useful way to get information about brands before making their own purchases. Johnson and Kaye (2004) compare the credibility of blogs and traditional media, as assessed by bloggers, and showed that bloggers perceive blogs as more credible than traditional media. Moreover, brand-targeting messages on blogs are perceived as highly credible as bloggers remain independent of corporate interests (Chu & Kamal, 2008).

Online Review Sites

With technological developments, Internet has become a place where consumers share comments about products. Indeed, one of the greatest advantages of Internet as seen by consumers has been the emergence of a large number of websites where consumers can read comments or speak about their discontent or their opinions about products or services (Bailey, 2004; Chatterjee, 2001). These review-based Web sites can be developed either by consumers or even by private business marketers. Therefore, the consumer accumulates a large number of product information that can take place either before or after purchasing the product. Information, which takes the form of online reviews, is a form of eWOM that may influence buying online. Indeed, consumers generally place a great importance to online reviews. Bailey (2005), studying the impact of online reviews on consumers, showed that many consumers consult these sites and place great importance to the information and opinions found in them.

It is possible to classify sites using online reviews into three broad categories: commercial, social networking sites, and sites that combine both elements of social networking and elements for profit-making (Williams, van der Wiele, van Iwaarden, & Eldridge, 2010).

Commercial Websites

Shopping sites are also known as branded or commercial websites. Although these commercial websites often dispose of a passive communication medium, they can be used in order to stimulate internet users to engage in eWOM (Litvin et al., 2008). This is achieved by providing users access to the opinions and reviews of other consumers, and enabling them in turn to comment on the company's products. This allows the company to create traffic to its site, helping customers make their purchasing decisions and getting an idea about consumers' opinions about the products. Indeed, online reviews often allow companies to get an idea about the way by which they can improve their products and services while remaining in constant contact with their customers. It is for these reasons that many commercial sites voluntarily adopt online reviews from consumers. Reviews may also be owned by the site, or it may be owned by a specialized reviews provider.

Social Networking Sites

Social networking sites are applications that allow users to connect by creating personal information profiles, invite friends and colleagues to access their profiles and to send e-mail and instant messages to each other. Users of social networking sites can post any type of information including, for example, photos, videos, audio and blogs. These social networking sites are often used by companies to create or assist in the creation and development of brand communities.

Social networking sites are particularly popular, and we can also find eWOM reviews in social networking sites such as YouTube, Facebook or Twitter. Indeed, allowing a high level of self-disclosure and social presence, social networks have become the most popular online activity, and have enabled consumers to connect with others by sharing information, opinions and thoughts about products and brands (Shu-Chuan & Yoojung, 2011).

Consumer Opinion Platforms

These are combined sites that act both as facilitators and social networking sites in which information and advice can be obtained to assist in decision making.

These platforms allow consumers to read other consumers' opinions and experiences related to different consumption areas. Those who consult the platform also have the opportunity to write their own contributions (Hennig-Thurau & Walsh, 2003). These consumer opinion platforms have the advantage of requiring less expertise in Internet use than would other similar media such as forums, for example.

In general, these opinion platforms score some minor differences among them, yet most of them have common basic functions. These platforms enable consumers to read other consumers' opinions and experiences about a wide range of product categories and services. The relative contributions of opinion platforms generally include both a verbal description of the consumer experience with the product and a formal product rating. Readers also have the opportunity to assess the quality and reliability of the contributions of users as their rating is visible to other users. Moreover, consumer opinion platforms can sometimes support the decision making process through links to commercial websites (Hennig-Thurau & Walsh, 2003). Business models platforms are often similar and their revenues generally come from banner ads and search services. Furthermore, some revenues may come from sales commissions which could offset the reliability of the platform (Hennig-Thurau & Walsh, 2003).

A large number of eWOM studies use online consumer opinion platforms. This can be explained by several reasons (Hennig-Thurau et al., 2004). The first is that online opinion platforms are the most widely used among all eWOM formats. The second is that eWOM is built around web-based consumer opinion platforms that may have a greater impact on consumers than eWOM conveyed through other means, because unlike focus groups, such platforms are relatively easy to use and require consumers to have less internet knowledge to obtain information. The third and final reason is that consumer opinion platforms provide information on almost all areas of consumption.

Having chosen a definition of eWOM and presented the main channels of this type of communication, the next two parts will focus on the reasons that motivate the consumer to engage in a eWOM communication and on the different eWOM characteristics.

Why Do Consumers Engage in eWOM Communication?

The reasons why users choose to engage in eWOM are many and varied. It is possible to combine these reasons according to the type of behavior in which the user engages. Indeed, the literature distinguishes between two different behaviors: a transmission behavior of eWOM and an exposure behavior to eWOM.

Motivations for a Transmission Behavior of eWOM

Many researchers tried to determine the different reasons that may affect users' behavior of generating eWOM messages.

Based on previous research, it is possible to bring together all the reasons as follows:

- Support for other consumers

This comes from the desire to make an altruistic act to help another consumer to make a purchase decision. In this case, the eWOM message can be either positive or negative (Sundaram, Mitra, & Webster, 1998). Transmitters of eWOM messages wishing to support others will use their experience to help other consumers achieve the maximum benefit during their purchase decision process. Support for other consumers is the most frequently cited by users to explain their eWOM behavior.

- Pleasure and Fun

This type of motivation often relates to the following concepts: fun, fun to share information, entertainment, need to relax and escape from daily responsibilities and extension of experience (Dholakia, Bagozzi, & Pearo, 2004; Okazaki, 2009; Stöckl, Rohrmeier, & Hess, 2008; Walsh, Gwinner, & Swanson, 2004). And in this case engaging in eWOM communication can help the transmitter to experience pleasure and fun and to escape from daily problems and responsibilities.

- Economic Incentives

Sometimes eWOM behavior is not totally insensitive to economic incentives. EWOM transmitters will be economically motivated by receiving remuneration or financial incentives against generating an eWOM message (Hennig-Thurau et al., 2004; Stöckl et al., 2008).

- Social relationships

In this case, users will be motivated by benefits of building and developing a social bond. In particular, it is possible to acquire the following advantages: being part of a group, developing a sense of belonging, developing a relationship with this group, maintaining interconnectivity between individuals, contact, attachment and commitment to the group, and meeting friends (Dholakia et al., 2004; Hennig-Thurau et al., 2004; Ho & Dempsey, 2010; Wetzer, Zeelenberg, & Pieters, 2007).

- Reprisal to the company

This type of motivation emerges when consumers are not satisfied with their consumption experience and when the company with which they have been involved did not stand up to their expectations resulting therefore in a sense of dissatisfaction with the company. Then, the consumer will seek revenge by issuing a negative eWOM message.

- Expressing feelings

Consumers who felt positive or negative feelings during their shopping experience will tend to want to communicate them to others by generating positive and negative messages. Particularly, in the case of an unsatisfactory experience, consumers seek to disseminate their negative feelings by expressing them through eWOM, allowing them to lessen the frustration resulting from their unhappy experience (Hennig-Thurau et al., 2004).

- Support to companies

Individuals experiencing this type of motivation will try, through the issuance of generally positive eWOM messages, to stimulate business success by encouraging other people to opt for a particular company as they consider it a good one and good companies should be supported (Hennig-Thurau et al., 2004).

Motivations for an Exposure Behavior to eWOM

Several studies investigated the reasons that might lead consumers to expose themselves to eWOM messages. It is possible to present the following reasons:

- Information about the product:

It is the desire to collect information about the product and shopping experiences so that consumers will be able to form their own opinion about the product and therefore to make a good purchase decision.

- Save time and reduce efforts seeking information during the decision making process.

In fact, information gathered through eWOM communication can help consumers to collect the information they need to make their choice in a more rapid and less expensive way.

- Risk reduction and the desire to optimize the purchasing decision

Thanks to the information collected by being exposed to eWOM, the consumer will be able to make an informed purchase decision and to reduce risks of experiencing unsatisfactory consumption.

- The reduction of dissonance

Having completed the purchase, consumers may in some cases feel a dissonance because they might have chosen one product over another or because of an interaction with other people. In this case, in order to reduce this dissonance, consumers may use neutral and unbiased information like eWOM messages to reduce the tension felt following this dissonance (Hennig-Thurau & Walsh, 2003).

- Fun

Utilitarian motivation and the fact of making the best purchase is not the only reason that may incite consumers to seek eWOM messages. Hedonic motivation may also push a consumer looking for fun and entertainment to consult eWOM messages.

EWOM Characteristics

The literature has highlighted a number of elements that characterize the eWOM concept. These features are numerous and can affect consumer behavior in a different manner. These characteristics can be classified according to:

Argument Quality or Argument Strength

Regarding argument quality and strength discussed in eWOM literature, the researchers presented two concepts often related and sometimes used synonymously. Argument strength relates to the quality of the information received (Cacioppo, Petty, & Morris, 1983). In this case, the eWOM receivers will try to determine if and to what degree the argument of the message is valid and convincing to support their position. Argument is understood as a quality argument when the received message is perceived to be valid. Argument quality can be translated in terms of four concepts: relevance, timeliness, accuracy and comprehensiveness (Awad & Ragowsky, 2008; Cheung, Lee, & Rabjohn, 2008; Cheung, Luo, Sia, & Chen, 2009; Chu & Kamal, 2008; Lee, Park, & Han, 2008; Park et al., 2007; Sher & Lee, 2009; Zhang & Watts, 2008).

- Relevance: Refers to the degree to which messages are applicable and useful for decision making.
- Timeliness: How the messages are presented and updated, in a timely manner. Updated information is usually preferred by consumers.
- Accuracy for the reliability of messages or arguments: This denotes the receiver's perception that the conveyed information is correct (Wixom & Todd, 2005).
- Comprehensiveness: Comprehensiveness of messages refers to information completeness.

Having no standard format, quality of online reviews depends on its length (from short to long), and on the objective and subjective nature of its content (Chatterjee, 2001). Therefore, each consumer's online review will be different.

Park et al. (2007), in an attempt to sort reviews according to their quality, compared messages containing logical, persuasive reviews that proposed fact-based arguments to messages with emotional, subjective and empty reviews that do not offer factual information and simply provide recommendations. The former are described as high-quality reviews while the latter are qualified as low quality reviews by respondents.

Therefore, we see from the above that there is no real consensus on determining arguments quality. The difference in their conceptualization probably results from the fact that studies of the concept combine two different areas, namely marketing on one side and information systems management on the other. Despite this inconsistency, all researchers agree on the idea that quality of online reviews plays an important role and may influence consumer behavior. Indeed, quality of message may influence the perceived credibility of the message since a message perceived as high-quality is also seen as reliable and trustworthy. High quality of the message may also influence the attitude toward the product. If receivers perceive information as having valid arguments, they will develop a favorable attitude towards this information. Otherwise, when receivers perceive information as invalid they will develop a negative attitude toward this information.

Valence of Messages

Valence of a message is the tendency of the message to carry either positive or negative information about the product or service being assessed (Chu & Kamal, 2008). Positive valence focuses on the strengths and benefits of the product while an eWOM with a negative valence focuses on the weaknesses or problems in relation with the product or service (Grewal, Gotlieb, & Marmorstein, 1994).

Through the elaboration of an eWOM message, the sender will try to impact the receiver's choices. This will contribute to the formation of consumer attitudes and purchase decisions. A positive message will tend to develop a positive attitude while a message with a rather negative valence will result in an unfavorable attitude.

Several previous studies have indicated that information with negative valence greatly influences receivers than information with a positive valence (Kanouse, 1984; Weinberger, Allen, & Dillon, 1981). Indeed, this could be partly explained by the fact that a negative message reduces the possibility that the information is being posted by the company or by someone who wished to promote the product. This could also be explained by the fact that individuals tend to avoid taking risks. Believing in a negative eWOM message in this way could help consumers avoid making a bad purchase decision (Cheung et al., 2009).

Recommendation Sidedness

A biased message (also called unilateral message) denotes the positive or even the negative aspects of the product or service being assessed, but not both simultaneously. However, a bilateral and an impartial message highlights both the positive and negative aspects of the product or service being assessed. In the past, marketing research has focused on the effect of attitudinal biased messages (unilateral) more than unbiased messages (bilateral) in communication. Receiving information about the two aspects of a product through an eWOM could highlight completeness of the information provided, since each product has generally strengths and weaknesses (Cheung & Thadani, 2012), which could potentially increase the credibility of the information and the perceived quality of the message.

Source Credibility

According to Duhan, Johnson, Wilcox, and Harrell (1997), recommendations through eWOM can be classified according to the degree of closeness of the relationship between the decision maker and source of the recommendation. These authors suggest that the greater the emotional closeness, the greater is the likelihood of following the sources with whom receivers have a strong connection when looking for recommendations.

Several key variables may influence perceived credibility of eWOM source. Specifically, it is relevant to mention that expertise, trustworthiness and attractiveness are the most common source credibility dimensions (Ohanian, 1991).

- Expertise

It refers to "perceived ability of the source to make valid assertions" (McCracken, 1989, p. 311). In other words, it is about the degree to which the issuer is qualified to provide valid and accurate information or discuss a specific topic (Chu & Kamal, 2008).

- Trustworthiness

McCracken (1989) defines the trustworthiness of the source as the "perceived willingness of the source to make valid assertions" (p. 311). Chu and Kamal (2008) indicate that the reliability of the source refers to the fact that the receiver of the message believes that the transmitter (the source) of the information is honest, fair and sincere.

- Attractiveness

The third dimension of source credibility is attractiveness (Choi, Lee, & Kim, 2005). The Attractiveness of the source indicates all the elements that can describe the perceived social value of the source: the physical appearance, the personality, the social status of the source transmitting the information, and the source's similarity with the receiver (McCroskey & McCain, 1974). However, as noted by Chu and Kamal (2008) when it comes to eWOM, the attractiveness of the source cannot be easily visible.

In the case of an eWOM-based communication, source credibility could be represented by the reputation of the issuer's credibility (Chu & Kamal, 2008). This reputation may be witnessed by either other eWOM users who assess and rate the issuers of messages based on message history or the site's administrator who, using the issuer's past contributions, assigns a credibility assessment. Finally, virtual reputation systems also may evaluate the reputation of eWOM issuers. Indeed, the study of Ba and Pavlou (2003) on the effects of virtual reputation systems has found that virtual credibility could have an important influence on changes in attitudes towards received information.

Recommendation Consistency

Recommendation consistency indicates the degree to which the current eWOM message is consistent with other contributions made by users while assessing the same product or service (Zhang & Watts, 2003). In the event that an eWOM-based review is consistent with other reviews, readers will tend to perceive the comment as coherent and credible. However, if the receiver is exposed to an eWOM recommendation that is not coherent with most of the other recommendations, he/she will feel confused and assesses the views of the current eWOM as inconsistent and therefore less credible (Cheung, Luo, Sia, & Chen, 2007).

Information Volume

In the literature on traditional WOM, the impact of information volume (i.e. the amount of information transmitted in a WOM) on consumer behavior has been particularly studied by researchers.

In the case of eWOM, information volume is measured by the number of comments posted by consumers for a given product. A number of studies examining volume of reviews indicated that there was a significant relationship between reviews volume and product sales evaluated at an eWOM communication instance (Berger, Sorensen, & Rasmussen, 2010; Liu, 2006). Duan, Gu, and Whinston (2008) argued that customer reviews are able to communicate about the existence of the product and therefore help create and develop an awareness of the existence of the product.

Moreover, the number of online reviews of a product (the number of comments) could be considered an indicator of the popularity of products. In fact, it is reasonable to assume that the number of comments depends on the number of consumers who have purchased the product (Chatterjee, 2001; Chen & Xie, 2008; Park et al., 2007). Furthermore, Berger et al. (2010) showed that even negative eWOM reviews are able to increase the likelihood of purchase, and concluded eventually that "any publicity is good publicity" (p. 816), whatever its valence (positive or negative).

Classification of Messages

Classification of messages denotes the overall assessment by other users of a particular eWOM message (Cheung et al., 2007). For example, online discussion forums allow users to rate eWOM posts. They can rank a post based on their perception of the message. Thus, the overall ranking of a message provides information on the manner with which readers reacted to this comment. Several researchers showed that this rating could significantly influence the way receivers perceive the message. If most of the other users give high rating to a message, this means that most users agree with the message.

CONCEPTS RELATED TO eWOM

Finally, to better understand the concept of eWOM, and to understand its limits, we need to define the concepts that are sometimes wrongly confused with it, namely traditional WOM, Viral Marketing and Buzz Marketing.

Traditional WOM

Marketing research has begun to address the concept of traditional WOM since the mid-20th century, and several definitions have been proposed to better understand the concept. Drawing on different proposals, it is possible to claim that traditional WOM is any form of interpersonal, informal communication devoid of any business interest and resulting from an exceptional experience with a product, service, or linked to the company that sells them.

Several studies approach eWOM as a similar concept to traditional WOM and treat it as if it was a continuation. Indeed, eWOM, as a message of opinion from other consumers, is sometimes considered similar to traditional WOM (Chatterjee, 2001; Chen & Xie, 2008), and some authors even confuse the two concepts defining them under the term WOM (Chen, Liu, Fang, & Lin, 2013). However, it is noteworthy that despite the similarity between electronic and traditional WOM, they are actually two different concepts. The differences between traditional WOM and eWOM are numerous and result from the very specificity of eWOM. These are as follows:

Communication Involving a Much Larger Network

EWOM communication network is greater than that of traditional WOM. Indeed, the influence of traditional WOM is typically limited to a local social network (Brown & Reingen, 1987). However, the impact of eWOM may exceed the local community because consumers all over the world can access online reviews (Chen & Xie, 2008). Characterized by a greater number of contributors and a wider audience, the scope of eWOM extends indeed beyond some personal connections to a larger number of connections in the virtual world. Moreover, eWOM channels offer a variety of ways with which consumers can share information that contributes to an increase in the number of senders and receivers.

Communication Allowing Adaptability and Rapid Diffusion of Information

EWOM has a great adaptability and rapidity of diffusion, which is not the case for traditional WOM (Cheung & Thadani, 2012). In fact, thanks to social media the information transferred through eWOM communication can easily and rapidly reach a great number of cyber consumers which allows a rapid diffusion of information.

An Asynchronous and Permanent Communication

EWOM breaks restrictions of time and place. Indeed, in the case of traditional WOM, information sharing occurs synchronically between small groups of individuals. Accordingly, information is usually exchanged in private conversations, and it is relatively difficult to access information if no one is present at the time and place where information is being exchanged (Cheung & Thadani, 2012). However, in the case of eWOM, information exchange is done asynchronously. Discussions that take the form of eWOM do not need to be exchanged at the same time when all communication agents are present. These asynchronous discussions are usually kept for some time in order to enable users to participate or read messages safely later on (Hoffman and Novak, 1997). Therefore, eWOM is more persistent and accessible than traditional WOM. Most of the information conveyed through eWOM is archived online and is made available for an indefinite period of time.

Communication Involving a Large Number of Anonymous Participants

Being free from the geographical and time constraints mentioned above, Internet transforms into a global community standing in parallel with the local and physical community. This global community is particularly characterised by the large number of participants. Internet users tend to be exposed to comments from a large number of other users who are often unknown to them. This anonymous aspect is a particular feature of eWOM as traditional WOM usually involves transmitters known by the receiver of the message. Indeed, in traditional WOM sources of information are usually family members or friends, or by anyone familiar, while eWOM messages come from unknown users (Ratchford, Talukdar, & Lee, 2001). In conclusion, it can be said that online anonymity and privacy are among the many characteristics that are unique to eWOM.

A Measurable Communication

EWOM is more measurable than traditional WOM. In fact, the presentation format, the volume and persistence of eWOM communication constitute observable elements. Information available online is far more voluminous in quantity compared to information obtained as a result of traditional WOM communication.

Buzz Marketing

Buzz marketing is a new marketing strategy that uses WOM. Indeed, buzz marketing plays an important role in channeling WOM communication (Salzman, Matathia, & O'Reilly, 2004, p. 30). The aim of buzz marketing is to develop a relationship between brands and individuals in view of influencing their purchase decisions and establishing loyalty to a particular brand (Salzman et al., 2004).

In terms of how to implement buzz marketing strategies, it is possible to distinguish two different trends in the literature.

The first trend assumes that buzz marketing is a form of communication in which the identity of one of the parties is visible and identifiable to the other participants. Indeed, in a study of buzz marketing, Carl (2006) puts forward the idea that it is possible to distinguish between two types of WOM: an "everyday" WOM and an "institutional" WOM. "Everyday" WOM is defined by the author as any "informal, evaluative communication (positive or negative) between at least two conversational participants about characteristics of an organization and/or a brand, product, or service that could take place online or offline" (p. 605). However, institutional WOM or buzz marketing is used to refer to: "WOM communication where the institutional identity or corporate affiliation of at least one participant may be salient and/or where the object being discussed (i.e., an organization, brand, product, or service) is part of an organized WOM campaign" (p. 605).

The second trend adopts "everyday" WOM and favors the idea that buzz marketing is structured so that individuals who communicate through WOM do not suspect the involvement of the company. In contrast to eWOM, which is a form of spontaneous communication taking place between users, buzz marketing intervenes in communication and tries to encourage people to speak favorably to each other of a product or service. In this case, WOM communication is not achieved spontaneously. However, when buzz marketing is done effectively, some illusion of spontaneity takes place, and therefore, consumers will not suspect a company is behind this transmission of information. Goyette, Ricard, Bergeron, and Marticotte (2010) define buzz marketing as “a catalyst for a WOM conversion to occur in person or online derived from a formal corporate strategy with a view to creating an illusion of spontaneity”(p. 9).

Based on these two views, it is possible to define buzz marketing like any business strategy that aims at influencing consumers by means of WOM communication in which the role of the company in this communication is more or less apparent.

Viral Marketing

The concept of viral marketing relates also to WOM through online media. Internet represents the central component of viral marketing (Goyette et al., 2010). Without Internet, there is no viral marketing as this latter can take place only in an online environment. The term “viral” refers to a virus, an epidemic or further to a viral idea that propagates across a segment of the population. Being such a transferable disease, the idea that spreads virally will aim at influencing individuals who will then be affected (Godin, 2001, p. 17). Viral marketing can be defined as: “a rapidly spreading informal online communication between individuals regarding a service or a good” (Goyette et al., 2010, p. 9).

Sometimes the concepts of buzz marketing and viral marketing are confused and used interchangeably. However, there is indeed a difference between these two concepts. Contrary to viral marketing, buzz marketing is not uniquely associated with Internet or any other electronic communication media (Goyette et al., 2010).

Moreover, researchers often confound viral marketing with eWOM and use these two terms in interchangeably (Stanbouli, 2003). However, despite the fact that these two concepts are evolving in the same electronic sphere, viral marketing is different from eWOM. Viral marketing is generally understood as a marketing technique or method that can be used by the company as a communication tool to improve business performance (Stanbouli, 2003).

Viral marketing is actually a tool of marketing mix which uses eWOM and allows the company to communicate with its customers and targets. Specifically, viral marketing aims at using eWOM to obtain at “a minimum cost” an exponentially fast advertising campaign (Stanbouli, 2003, p. 100). In the case of a viral marketing campaign, companies will try to engage prescribers of a segment so that they communicate about the product, service or company.

It is therefore possible to define viral marketing as a tool in the marketing mix taking place in an online environment whose aim is to provide information about products, services or the company. This is achieved in a rapid and extended way so that a significant number of individuals may be exposed.

Having developed the differences that may exist between eWOM, traditional WOM, buzz marketing and viral marketing, the next section will highlight the importance of eWOM compared to traditional WOM or any other institutional communication made by the company.

IMPORTANCE OF eWOM TO CONSUMERS

A number of studies have shown that eWOM might influence consumers more significantly than could traditional WOM or any institutional communication.

Thanks to its characteristics, eWOM is often perceived as being more powerful than traditional WOM. Indeed, eWOM is a mode of immediate communication because it is always available to information seeker, it has significant scope because eWOM communication can reach a large number of internet users, it is credible In fact, it is usually perceived as reliable by internet users and finally, it is available to everyone (anyone with an internet connection can have access to eWOM communication).

Supremacy of eWOM is not only expressed towards traditional WOM, but this it also seems to prevail when dealing with other sources of institutional communication (communication from vendors, companies or marketing managers). For example, Bickart and Schindler (2001) showed through a twelve week experimentation that individuals who collected product information through consumer-generated forums have expressed greater interest in the product category than individuals who have collected information through different forms of professionals-generated information such as company websites. Although vendors are sources of information for the consumer who provide also information about the product, this information is perceived by the user less favorably than information given by means of eWOM. This can be explained by a number of reasons. Indeed, information provided through eWOM is often perceived as more credible, more consumer-oriented, and does not have a standardized form and therefore it allows for greater adaptation of information to the needs of users.

- EWOM-generated information is more credible

EWOM is perceived more reliable than information provided by professionals. The reliability of an information source often relates positively to information credibility (Bickart & Schindler, 2001). Past studies indicated that information created by the consumer is more credible than that presented by the seller (Dellarocas, 2003). When sellers provide information about products, they tend to hide the product's weaknesses and develop its strengths. However, consumers provide honest assessments of a product's strengths and weaknesses, and this from the consumer's perspective. Therefore, consumers online reviews are more likely to be reliable than information generated by the seller.

- EWOM-generated information is consumer-oriented

Bickart and Schindler (2001) emphasized the fact that consumer-generated information is more likely to be consumer-oriented than seller-generated information. Seller-generated information is product-oriented and is often objective. This type of information focuses on product attributes that are generally aimed to several unspecified consumers. This will mean that company-provided information is geared more towards the product and its characteristics. Consumer-provided information, on the other hand, describes the usage and benefits of products from the consumer perspective. It is more understandable and familiar because it reflects personal feelings or consumer satisfaction about the used products (Chen & Xie, 2008). We can then say that contrary to information provided through an institutional communication, information conveyed through eWOM is oriented towards the consumer.

- EWOM-generated information has no standardized form

Information generated by the seller is represented in a standardized and structured format, yet information generated by consumer is not. This latter qualifies as subjective information, consisting largely of emotional output, or it may be as well objective information the same as information created by the seller. Furthermore, it may consist of a few words or a larger number of words.

CONCLUSION

As it appears in this chapter, eWOM represents an important concept in the research on the consumer's behavior. In fact, studying eWOM communication can help understand both the consumer's behavior that generates eWOM messages and the consumer's developed reactions after being exposed to eWOM. More precisely, eWOM communication has the capability to influence different elements of the consumer's behavior such as consumers purchase decisions, their purchase intentions, their potential re-purchase intentions and the development of future approach.

Hence, the concept of eWOM communication can be considered as a central concept in marketing research and, as such, it should be better studied and focused on in order to improve the understanding of the various reactions of the cyber consumer involved in eWOM communication.

This study has been particularly interested in surveying the great role that eWOM can play on the consumer's behavior and the importance of digging deeper into this research topic. Moreover, this chapter has focused on determining some sources behind the current fragmentation of research on eWOM.

In response to this need, a new terminology, definition and a distinction between eWOM and other related concepts like traditional WOM, buzz marketing and viral marketing have been put forward. However, it is possible to notice that the current divergence on the eWOM concept may come from the fact that those researchers interested in the concept, belong to various research fields.

Indeed, these researchers, who may have been operating in the areas of e-marketing, services, marketing, or information systems management, showed a particular interest in eWOM and used therefore different theories, thus explaining the fragmentation of eWOM research.

It would make sense therefore to conduct a meta-analysis of all the research undertaken in order to determine which theories are most suitable to investigate eWOM.

This could be a first step towards the merger of the used theories and would allow us to recommend ways to conduct more coherent research on eWOM.

REFERENCES

Armstrong, S. (2006). Bloggers for hire. *New Statesman (London, England)*, *135*(4807), 26–27.

Awad, N. F., & Ragowsky, A. (2008). Establishing Trust in Electronic Commerce Through Online Word of Mouth: An Examination Across Genders. *Journal of Management Information Systems*, *24*(4), 101–121. doi:10.2753/MIS0742-1222240404

Ba, S., & Pavlou, P. A. (2003). Evidence of the Effect of Trust Building Technology in Electronic Markets: Price Premiums and Buyer Behavior. *Management Information Systems Quarterly*, *26*(3), 243–268. doi:10.2307/4132332

Bailey, A. A. (2004). Thiscompanysucks. com: The use of the Internet in negative consumer-to-consumer articulations. *Journal of Marketing Communications*, *10*(3), 169–182. doi:10.1080/1352726042000186634

Bailey, A. A. (2005). Consumer Awareness and Use of Product Review Websites. *Journal of Interactive Advertising*, *6*(1), 90–108. doi:10.1080/15252019.2005.10722109

Barnes, N. G., & Jacobsen, S. L. (2014). Missed eWOM opportunities: A cross-sector analysis of online monitoring behavior. *Journal of Marketing Communications*, *20*(1-2), 147–158. doi:10.1080/13527266.2013.797788

Berger, J., Sorensen, A. T., & Rasmussen, S. J. (2010). Positive Effects of Negative Publicity: When Negative Reviews Increase Sales. *Marketing Science*, *29*(5), 815–827. doi:10.1287/mksc.1090.0557

Bickart, B., & Schindler, R. M. (2001). Internet forums as influential sources of consumer information. *Journal of Interactive Marketing*, *15*(3), 31–40. doi:10.1002/dir.1014

Blood, R. (2002). *The weblog handbook: Practical advice on creating and maintaining your blog*. Basic Books.

Bronner, F., & de Hoog, R. (2011). Vacationers and eWOM: Who Posts, and Why, Where, and What? *Journal of Travel Research*, *50*(1), 15–26. doi:10.1177/0047287509355324

Brown, J. J., & Reingen, P. H. (1987). Social ties and Word-of-Mouth referral behavior. *The Journal of Consumer Research*, *14*(3), 350–362. doi:10.1086/209118

Buttle, F. A. (1998). Word of mouth: Understanding and managing referral marketing. *Journal of Strategic Marketing*, *6*(3), 241–254. doi:10.1080/096525498346658

Cacioppo, J. T., Petty, R. E., & Morris, K. J. (1983). Effects of need for cognition on message evaluation, recall, and persuasion. *Journal of Personality and Social Psychology*, *45*(4), 805–818. doi:10.1037/0022-3514.45.4.805

Carl, W. J. (2006). What's all the buzz about? Everyday communication and the relational basis of word-of-mouth and buzz marketing practices. *Management Communication Quarterly*, *19*(4), 601–634. doi:10.1177/0893318905284763

Chatterjee, P. (2001). Online reviews: Do consumers use them? *Advances in Consumer Research. Association for Consumer Research (U. S.)*, *28*(1), 129–133.

Chen, S.-C., Yen, D. C., & Hwang, M. I. (2012). Factors influencing the continuance intention to the usage of Web 2.0: An empirical study. *Computers in Human Behavior*, *28*(3), 933–941. doi:10.1016/j.chb.2011.12.014

Chen, Y., Liu, F., Fang, C.-H., & Lin, T. M. (2013). Understanding the effectiveness of word-of-mouth: An elasticity perspective. *Journal of Research in Interactive Marketing*, *7*(1), 57–77. doi:10.1108/17505931311316743

Chen, Y., & Xie, J. (2008). Online Consumer Review: Word-of-Mouth as a New Element of Marketing Communication Mix. *Management Science*, *54*(3), 477–491. doi:10.1287/mnsc.1070.0810

Cheung, C. M. K., Lee, M. K. O., & Rabjohn, N. (2008). The impact of electronic word-of-mouth: The adoption of online opinions in online customer communities. *Internet Research*, *18*(3), 229–247. doi:10.1108/10662240810883290

Cheung, C. M. K., & Thadani, D. R. (2012). The impact of electronic word-of-mouth communication: A literature analysis and integrative model. *Decision Support Systems*, *54*(1), 461–470. doi:10.1016/j.dss.2012.06.008

Cheung, M. Y., Luo, C., Sia, C. L., & Chen, H. (2007). *How do People Evaluate Electronic Word-Of-Mouth? Informational and Normative Based Determinants of Perceived Credibility of Online Consumer Recommendations in China*. Paper presented at the 11th Pacific-Asia Conference on Information Systems, Auckland, New Zealand.

Cheung, M. Y., Luo, C., Sia, C. L., & Chen, H. (2009). Credibility of Electronic Word-of-Mouth: Informational and Normative Determinants of On-line Consumer Recommendations. *International Journal of Electronic Commerce*, *13*(4), 9–38. doi:10.2753/JEC1086-4415130402

Choi, S. M., Lee, W.-N., & Kim, H.-J. (2005). Lessons from the rich and famous: A cross-cultural comparison of celebrity endorsement in advertising. *Journal of Advertising*, *34*(2), 85–98. doi:10.1080/00913367.2005.10639190

Chu, S.-C., & Kamal, S. (2008). The Effect of Perceived Blogger Credibility and Argument Quality on Message Elaboration and Brand Attitudes: An Exploratory Study. *Journal of Interactive Advertising*, *8*(2), 1–31. doi:10.1080/15252019.2008.10722140

Daugherty, T., & Hoffman, E. (2014). eWOM and the importance of capturing consumer attention within social media. *Journal of Marketing Communications*, *20*(1-2), 82–102. doi:10.1080/13527266.2013.797764

De Bruyn, A., & Lilien, G. L. (2004). *A multi-stage model of word of mouth through electronic referrals*. eBusiness Research Center, Working Paper.

Dellarocas, C. (2003). The digitization of word of mouth: Promise and challenges of online feedback mechanisms. *Management Science*, *49*(10), 1407–1424. doi:10.1287/mnsc.49.10.1407.17308

Dholakia, U. M., Bagozzi, R. P., & Pearo, L. K. (2004). A social influence model of consumer participation in network-and small-group-based virtual communities. *International Journal of Research in Marketing*, *21*(3), 241–263. doi:10.1016/j.ijresmar.2003.12.004

Duan, W., Gu, B., & Whinston, A. B. (2008). Do online reviews matter?—An empirical investigation of panel data. *Decision Support Systems*, *45*(4), 1007–1016. doi:10.1016/j.dss.2008.04.001

Duhan, D., Johnson, S., Wilcox, J., & Harrell, G. (1997). Influences on consumer use of word-of-mouth recommendation sources. *Journal of the Academy of Marketing Science*, *25*(4), 283–295. doi:10.1177/0092070397254001

Dwyer, P. (2007). Measuring the value of electronic word of mouth and its impact in consumer communities. *Journal of Interactive Marketing, 21*(2), 63-79.

Evans, M., Wedande, G., Ralston, L., & Hul, S. (2001). Consumer Interaction in the Virtual Era: Some Qualitative Insights. *Qualitative Market Research*, *4*(3), 150–159. doi:10.1108/13522750110393053

Fong, J., & Burton, S. (2006). Electronic Word-of-Mouth: A Comparison of Stated and Revealed Behavior on Electronic Discussion Boards. *Journal of Interactive Advertising*, *6*(2), 61–70. doi:10.1080/15252019.2006.10722119

Godes, D., & Mayzlin, D. (2004). Using Online Conversations to Study Word-of-Mouth Communication. *Marketing Science*, *23*(4), 545–560. doi:10.1287/mksc.1040.0071

Godin, S. (2001). *Les secrets du marketing viral: le bouche- à- oreille à la puissance 10!* Paris Maxima Laurent Du Mesnil Éditeur.

Goldsmith, R. E., & Horowitz, D. (2006). Measuring Motivations for Online Opinion Seeking. *Journal of Interactive Advertising*, *6*(2), 1–16. doi:10.1080/15252019.2006.10722114

Goyette, I., Ricard, L., Bergeron, J., & Marticotte, F. (2010). e-WOM Scale: Word-of-Mouth Measurement Scale for e-Services Context. *Canadian Journal of Administrative Sciences*, *27*(1), 5–23. doi:10.1002/cjas.129

Grewal, D., Gotlieb, J., & Marmorstein, H. (1994). The Moderating Effects of Message Framing and Source Credibility on the Price-perceived Risk Relationship. *The Journal of Consumer Research*, *21*(1), 145–153. doi:10.1086/209388

Hennig-Thurau, T., Gwinner, K. P., Walsh, G., & Gremler, D. D. (2004). Electronic word-of-mouth via consumer-opinion platforms: What motivates consumers to articulate themselves on the Internet? *Journal of Interactive Marketing*, *18*(1), 38–52. doi:10.1002/dir.10073

Hennig-Thurau, T., & Walsh, G. (2003). Electronic Word-of-Mouth: Motives for and Consequences of Reading Customer Articulations on the Internet. *International Journal of Electronic Commerce*, *8*(2), 51–74.

Ho, J. Y., & Dempsey, M. (2010). Viral marketing: Motivations to forward online content. *Journal of Business Research*, *63*(9), 1000–1006. doi:10.1016/j.jbusres.2008.08.010

Huang, M., Cai, F., Tsang, A. S. L., & Zhou, N. (2011). Making your online voice loud: The critical role of WOM information. *European Journal of Marketing*, *45*(7/8), 1277–1297. doi:10.1108/03090561111137714

Hung, K. H., & Yiyan Li, S. (2007). The Influence of eWOM on Virtual Consumer Communities: Social Capital, Consumer Learning, and Behavioral Outcomes. *Journal of Advertising Research*, *47*(4), 485–495. doi:10.2501/S002184990707050X

Jansen, B. J., Zhang, M., Sobel, K., & Chowdury, A. (2009). *Micro-blogging as online word of mouth branding*. Paper presented at the CHI'09 Extended Abstracts on Human Factors in Computing Systems. doi:10.1145/1520340.1520584

Johnson, T. J., & Kaye, B. K. (2004). Wag the blog: How reliance on traditional media and the Internet influence credibility perceptions of weblogs among blog users. *Journalism & Mass Communication Quarterly*, *81*(3), 622–642. doi:10.1177/107769900408100310

Kanouse, D. E. (1984). Explaining Negativity Biases in Evaluation and Choice Beavior: Theory and Reserach. *Advances in Consumer Research. Association for Consumer Research (U. S.)*, *11*(1), 703–708.

Kaplan, A. M., & Haenlein, M. (2010). Users of the world, unite! The challenges and opportunities of Social Media. *Business Horizons*, *53*(1), 59–68. doi:10.1016/j.bushor.2009.09.003

Kietzmann, J., & Canhoto, A. (2013). Bittersweet! Understanding and Managing Electronic Word of Mouth. *Journal Of Public Affairs*, *13*(2), 146–159. doi:10.1002/pa.1470

Kozinets, R. V. (2002). The field behind the screen: Using netnography for marketing research in online communities. *JMR, Journal of Marketing Research*, *39*(1), 61–72. doi:10.1509/jmkr.39.1.61.18935

Krishnamurthy, S., & Dou, W. (2008). Note From Special Issue Editors: Advertsing With User-Generated Content: A Framework and Research Agenda. Journal of Interactive Advertising, 8(2), 1-4.

Lee, J., Park, D.-H., & Han, I. (2008). The effect of negative online consumer reviews on product attitude: An information processing view. *Electronic Commerce Research and Applications*, *7*(3), 341–352. doi:10.1016/j.elerap.2007.05.004

Leivadiotou, E., & Markopoulos, D. (2010). Cyber communities and Electronic Word-of-Mouth: The use of Facebook in the promotion of hospitality services. *MIBES Transactions*, *4*(1), 138–151.

Litvin, S. W., Goldsmith, R. E., & Pan, B. (2008). Electronic word-of-mouth in hospitality and tourism management. *Tourism Management*, *29*(3), 458–468. doi:10.1016/j.tourman.2007.05.011

Liu, Y. (2006). Word of mouth for movies: Its dynamics and impact on box office revenue. *Journal of Marketing*, *70*(3), 74–89. doi:10.1509/jmkg.70.3.74

McCracken, G. (1989). Who is the celebrity endorser? Cultural foundations of the endorsement process. *The Journal of Consumer Research*, *16*(3), 310–321. doi:10.1086/209217

McCroskey, J. C., & McCain, T. A. (1974). *The measurement of interpersonal attraction*. Academic Press.

Miller, R., & Lammas, N. (2010). Social media and its implications for viral marketing. *Asia Pacific Public Relations Journal*, *11*, 1–9.

Morimoto, M., & Trimble, C. S. (2012). Consumer's Use of Blogs as Product Information Sources: From Nee-for-Cognition Perspective. *Marketing Management Journal*, *22*(2), 45–60.

Nardi, B. A., Schiano, D. J., Gumbrecht, M., & Swartz, L. (2004). Why we blog. *Communications of the ACM*, *47*(12), 41–46. doi:10.1145/1035134.1035163

Nelson, M. R., & Otnes, C. C. (2005). Exploring cross-cultural ambivalence: A netnography of intercultural wedding message boards. *Journal of Business Research*, *58*(1), 89–95. doi:10.1016/S0148-2963(02)00477-0

OECD. (2007). *Participative web and user-created content: Web 2.0, wikis, and social networking*. Paris: Organisation for Economic Co-operation and Development.

Ohanian, R. (1991). The impact of celebrity spokespersons' perceived image on consumers' intention to purchase. *Journal of Advertising Research.*

Okazaki, S. (2009). Social influence model and electronic word of mouth PC versus mobile internet. *International Journal of Advertising*, *28*(3), 439–472. doi:10.2501/S0265048709200692

Park, D.-H., Lee, J., & Han, I. (2007). The Effect of On-Line Consumer Reviews on Consumer Purchasing Intention: The Moderating Role of Involvement. *International Journal of Electronic Commerce*, *11*(4), 125–148. doi:10.2753/JEC1086-4415110405

Parry, M. E., Kawakami, T., & Kishiya, K. (2012). The Effect of Personal and Virtual Word-of-Mouth on Technology Acceptance. *Journal of Product Innovation Management*, *29*(6), 952–966. doi:10.1111/j.1540-5885.2012.00972.x

Ratchford, B. T., Talukdar, D., & Lee, M.-S. (2001). A model of consumer choice of the Internet as an information source. *International Journal of Electronic Commerce*, *5*, 7–22.

Reichelt, J., Sievert, J., & Jacob, F. (2014). How credibility affects eWOM reading: The influences of expertise, trustworthiness, and similarity on utilitarian and social functions. *Journal of Marketing Communications*, *20*(1-2), 65–81. doi:10.1080/13527266.2013.797758

Rejón-Guardia, F., & Martínez-López, F. J. (2014). *The Pervasive Influence of Electronic Word of Mouth (eWOM) on Today's Social Consumer Handbook of Strategic e-Business Management* (pp. 821–839). Springer.

Salzman, M., Matathia, I., & O'Reilly, A. (2004). *Buzz . . . Le marketing du bouche-à-oreille*. Paris: Village Mondial.

Shen, W., Maceli, K. M., Zhao, Y., Baack, D. W., & Bacon, D. R. (2014). *The Impact Of Gender and National Culture On Electronic Word Of Mouth Communication*. Paper presented at the Annual Meeting of the Association of Collegiate Marketing educators, Dallas.

Sher, P., & Lee, S. (2009). Consumer Skepticism and Online Reviews: An Elaboration Likehihood Model Perspective. *Social Behavior and Personality*, *37*(1), 137–144. doi:10.2224/sbp.2009.37.1.137

Shin, D. H. (2008). Understanding purchasing behaviors in a virtual economy: Consumer behavior involving virtual currency in Web 2.0 communities. *Interacting with Computers*, *20*(4), 433–446. doi:10.1016/j.intcom.2008.04.001

Shu-Chuan, C., & Yoojung, K. (2011). Determinants of consumer engagement in electronic word-of-mouth (eWOM) in social networking sites. *International Journal of Advertising*, *30*(1), 47–75. doi:10.2501/IJA-30-1-047-075

Smudde, P. M. (2005). Blogging, ethics and public relations: A proactive and dialogic approach. *Public Relations Quarterly*, *50*(3), 34–38.

Stanbouli, K. (2003). Marketing Viral et Publicité. *Revue Française du Marketing*(192), 97-106.

Stauss, B. (1997). Global Word of Mouth. *Marketing Management*, *6*, 28–30.

Stauss, B. (2000). In T. Hennig-Thurau & U. Hansen (Eds.), *Relationship Marketing* (pp. 233–253). Berlin: Springer. doi:10.1007/978-3-662-09745-8_13

Stöckl, R., Rohrmeier, P., & Hess, T. (2008). *Why customers produce user generated content Web 2.0* (pp. 271–287). Springer.

Sundaram, D. S., Mitra, K., & Webster, C. (1998). Word-of-Mouth Communications: A Motivational Analysis. *Advances in Consumer Research. Association for Consumer Research (U. S.)*, *25*(1), 527–531.

Thorson, K. S., & Rodgers, S. (2006). Relationships between Blogs as eWOM and Interactivity, Perceived Interactivity, and Parasocial Interaction. *Journal of Interactive Advertising*, *6*(2), 39–50. doi:10.1080/15252019.2006.10722117

Walsh, G., Gwinner, K. P., & Swanson, S. R. (2004). What makes mavens tick? Exploring the motives of market mavens' initiation of information diffusion. *Journal of Consumer Marketing*, *21*(2), 109–122. doi:10.1108/07363760410525678

Wang, Y., & Rodgers, S. (2011). Electronic Word of Mouth and Consumer Generated Content In Handbook of Research on Digital Media and Advertising: User Generated Content (pp. 212-231). Academic Press.

Weinberger, M. G., Allen, C. T., & Dillon, W. R. (1981). Negative Information: Perspectives and Research Directions. *Advances in Consumer Research. Association for Consumer Research (U. S.)*, *8*(1), 398–404.

Wetzer, I. M., Zeelenberg, M., & Pieters, R. (2007). "Never eat in that restaurant, I did!": Exploring why people engage in negative word-of-mouth communication. *Psychology and Marketing*, *24*(8), 661–680. doi:10.1002/mar.20178

Williams, R., van der Wiele, T., van Iwaarden, J., & Eldridge, S. (2010). The importance of user-generated content: The case of hotels. *The TQM Journal*, *22*(2), 117–128. doi:10.1108/17542731011024246

Wixom, B. H., & Todd, P. A. (2005). A Theoretical Integration of User Satisfaction and Technology Acceptance. *Information Systems Research*, *16*(1), 85–102. doi:10.1287/isre.1050.0042

Zhang, W., & Watts, S. (2003). *Knowledge adoption in online communities of practice*. Paper presented at the 24th International Conference on Information Systems, Atlanta, GA.

Zhang, W., & Watts, S. A. (2008). Capitalizing on Content: Information Adoption in Two Online communities. *Journal of the Association for Information Systems*, *9*(2), 72–93.

KEY TERMS AND DEFINITIONS

Buzz Marketing: Any form of marketing strategy using WOM to influence consumer choices and loyalty by means of creating a relationship between brands and individuals.

Social Media: Internet applications using Web 2.0 and allowing the creation and exchange of information by users.

Traditional WOM: Any form of interpersonal and informal communication, devoid of any business interests and motivated by an exceptional experience with a product, service or a company that sells them.

User-Generated Content: Any form of original content, available online and published by users whose motivations are devoid of commercial purposes.

Valence of an E-WOM Message: The tendency of the message to carry either positive or negative information about the product or service being assessed.

Viral Marketing: A tool in the marketing mix taking place in an online environment, exploiting E-WOM and aimed at disseminating information about products, services or the company and this in a rapid and extended way so that a significant number of individuals may be exposed.

Web 2.0: A platform that allows all users to participate in the creation and publication of information on the Internet.

Chapter 2
eWOM Marketing Techniques for Competitive Advantage

Arijit Bhattacharya
Lala Lajpatrai Institute of Management, India

ABSTRACT

In today's dynamic marketing world, it is critical to understand the strategic importance of electronic word-of-mouth (eWOM). This chapter discusses the genesis of eWOM from word-of-mouth, difference between the two and what marketing literature says about eWOM's different aspects - both pros and cons. The chapter also tries to explain what motivates consumers to share their consumption experience through eWOM route with the help of literature review. The chapter also discusses present eWOM marketing techniques adopted and also the criticism of eWOM. Lastly, the author points out fields yet to be explored in eWOM research.

INTRODUCTION

Traditionally, word-of-mouth (WOM) has significant impact as a potent marketing tool, especially in the field of consumer behavior. Many research studies have shown that compared to traditional forms of advertising, personal influence, if rightly used, has a more significant impact on customers which will lead to large-scale product diffusion.

With advent of information technology, specifically the Internet and online social groups, electronic word-of-mouth (eWOM), has changed online information transmission and exchange. eWOM facilitates the peer-to-peer information exchange of WOM manifold by enabling a consumer to transmit information to multiple recipients simultaneously. This can be done using various eWOM communications e.g. online discussion forums, blogs, review sites, virtual brand communities and social networking sites. Using this channel, customers share information and experience about product and services, both positive and negative which ultimately impacts consumer's decision making, adoption of products and consumer loyalty. Consequently, electronic word-of-mouth (eWOM) is considered a cost-effective marketing tool which no marketer can afford to ignore and researchers take keen interest in why customers are influenced by eWOM and by how much. Many brands, both global and Indian have successfully taken eWOM route to gain brand visibility, brand differentiation and to build lasting consumer connect.

DOI: 10.4018/978-1-4666-9449-1.ch002

Studies have been conducted in several sub-domains within marketing especially service industry where due to intangibility of the service offering it is difficult to evaluate before consumption. Few examples include:

- Effect of eWOM on movie revenue
- Effect of micro-blogging (tweeter post) to share opinions concerning brands through postings containing branding comments
- Sentiments and opinion concerning travel and tourism industry, low cost airline industry
- Restaurant review
- Book review in Amazon

An AC Nielson survey (2007) has found that most consumers perceive that online opinion expression is as credible as brand websites and in today's dynamic and highly competitive marketing world many experts propose that instead of focusing only on traditional advertising, firms should focus on forming online communities around their brand/product/service to gain sustainable competitive advantage.

BACKGROUND

Genesis of WOM

In the social psychology domain, interpersonal communication assumes a significant role (Cheun & Thadani, 2010). Over the years, several consumer behavior studies have shown that interpersonal influences, through word-of-mouth (WOM), influence individual purchase decision making. The sole purpose of this type of communication is to pass negative or positive acknowledgement about a product and/or services from an individual (the "sender") to other individual/s (the "receiver"). A study done in 1950s has documented that WOM communication took place among neighbors to exchange information about new product offerings in neighborhood stores (Whyte, 1954). Later research showed that word-of mouth was nine times more effective than advertising in influencing consumer attitudes (Day, 1971) and "other people's recommendations" were thrice more effective across 60 different product types viz-a-viz traditional advertising (Morin, 1983).

Based on the literature review, few noteworthy definitions of WoM are: "oral, person to person communication between a receiver and a communicator whom the receiver perceives as non-commercial, concerning a brand, a product or a service" (Arndt, 1967); "In a postpurchase context, consumer word-of-mouth transmissions consist of informal communications directed at other consumers about the ownership, usage, or characteristics of particular goods and services and/or their sellers." (Haywood, 1989); "Positive and negative word-of-mouth are examples of exit behaviors exhibited by consumers at the conclusion of a service encounter." (File, Judd, & Prince, 1992). WOM is also termed as "buzz" in some literature and the term is defined as a "WOM effect, a transfer of information through social networks. It frequently occurs in a spontaneous manner…" (Salzman, Matathia, & O'Reilly, 2004). Thus, the concept of buzz marketing, a marketing strategy, has its root in conventional word-of-mouth (Goyette, 2010).

Research has shown that consumers rely on WOM to reduce their perceived risk derived from the uncertainty inherent in service purchase decisions (Murray, 1991). As this mode of communication has been gaining popularity over the years among marketers who treat WOM as a useful source of business intelligence, the researches related to WOM also flourished which included WOM's effect on purchase intention, consumption experience, post-purchase attitudes, why and how WOM was created and its impact on organization's reputation. WOM is considered as a non-commercial source of information having more persuasive effect on consumer purchase decisions than traditional marketing tools (conventional advertising, sales promotions, personal selling, and public relations) (Cheung, Lee Mathew, & Rabjohn, 2008). Since the receiver of WOM considers the message as not commercially motivated, WOM has higher credibility and trustworthiness as compared to traditional advertisements. This view is further corroborated in an AC Nielson study (Trust In Advertising, 2013) where it has been found that when respondents were asked "to what extent do you trust the following forms of advertising", 'recommendations from people I know' tops the list for both 2013 (84%) and 2007 (78%) survey findings when compared with paid advertising channels e.g. TV and newspapers, magazines, radio, search engine ads, banner ads and mobile.

Research has found that consumers do not belong to a single homogeneous group with reference to their WOM motivations and they can be segregated into separate groups based on their motives. Following is a typology of different drivers of WOM behaviors (Hennig-Thurau, Gwinner, & Gremle, 2004):

- Product involvement: a customer feels so strongly about the product that a pressure builds up in wanting to do something about it; recommending the product to others reduces the tension caused by the consumption experience.
- Self-involvement: the product serves as a means through which the speaker can gratify certain emotional needs
- Other-involvement: word-of-mouth activity addresses the need to give something to the receiver
- Message-involvement: refers to discussion which is stimulated by advertisements, commercials, or public relations
- Involvement: level of interest or involvement in the topic under consideration serves to stimulate discussion
- Self-enhancement: recommendations allow person to gain attention, show connoisseurship, suggest status, give the impression of possessing inside information, and assert superiority
- Concern for others: a genuine desire to help a friend or relative make a better purchase decision
- Message intrigue: entertainment resulting from talking about certain ads or selling appeals
- Dissonance reduction: reduces cognitive dissonance (doubts) following a major purchase decision
- Altruism (positive WOM): the act of doing something for others without anticipating any reward in return
- Product involvement: personal interest in the product, excitement resulting from product ownership and product use
- Self-enhancement: enhancing images among other consumers by projecting themselves as intelligent shoppers
- Helping the company: desire to help the company
- Altruism (negative WOM): to prevent others from experiencing the problems they had encountered
- Anxiety reduction: easing anger, anxiety, and frustration
- Vengeance: to retaliate against the company associated with a negative consumption experience
- Advice seeking: obtaining advice on how to resolve problems

In a book titled, *Word of mouth marketing: How Smart Companies get People Talking*, it is pointed out that "happy customers are your biggest advertisers" (Sernovitz, 2009). The author of this book, Andy Sernovitz, coined this as "C to C marketing" where a customer talks positively to a customer about an organization's product or service. According to him, the four rules of word-of-mouth marketing are:

1. Be interesting – as customers tend to talk about a something interesting, compared to a "boring" company, product or an advertising.
2. Make People Happy – by creating amazing products, excelling service or going the extra mile compelling the customer to be excited and energized to share it with his or her network of friends.
3. Earn Trust and Respect – by communicating with customers on a regular basis, treating them as smart and fulfilling their product or service related needs efficiently.
4. Make it Easy – in word-of-mouth marketing instead of focusing on formal brand statement or product statement is wiser to stress on a simple topic that is easy to repeat.

This book further probed the reasons why people want to talk to a company. These are:

1. 'You': Customers like the company and its staff and since they find a connection based on mutual respect, they want to support the company
2. 'Them': Talking makes people feel good about themselves as they feel smart, connected, in the know, and important. Also, people feel good when they can provide relevant information about a problem-solving.
3. 'Us': They feel connected to the group as being passionate makes them feel like part of a team or a family.

Also, this book proposed 5Ts of word-of-mouth marketing, which are:

1. Talkers: Find the customers who like to talk about what the company is doing and give them necessary information to talk about.
2. Topics: Give them a reason to talk. It could be about "a special sale, good service, a new furniture, a better flavor, a funny package".
3. Tools: Help the message spread faster and farther by handing out samples, including posters and stickers in the box in the package, creating a chat room or blog conversation or sending thank-you notes.
4. Taking Part: Join the conversation by replying to e-mails or commenting on blogs.
5. Tracking: Measure and understand what people are saying as it is the best form of feedback that an organization can receive because it is the "authentic voice" of the consumer.

Evolution of eWOM

During the peak of dotcom boom and subsequent rise of electronic commerce of 1990s, research studies began to propose that WOM can be effectively mediated through electronic means and as a result, gradually, electronic-word-of-mouth (eWOM) gained acceptance in the marketing domain and went on to become a significant market force. The importance of word-of-mouth communication in the context of marketing increased manifold with the advent of the Internet, a highly interactive medium of communication. Using this medium, it was possible for consumers to interactively share their thoughts and experiences about products, brands, celebrities. Also, due to the huge scale and scope of customer's eWOM communication marketers recognized the market power of eWOM. Eventually, eWOM became a much researched topic in consumer and marketing research and e-WOM's rapid proliferation in recent years can be attributed to popularity of user-generated content that include blogs (WordPress.com), social networking sites (Facebook), wikis (Wikipedia), podcasting (Archive.org), web sites allowing feedback (Amazon.com) and review sites (Mouthshut.com).

Due to the above-mentioned paradigm shift, in today's Web connected world, the traditional marketing communication model is challenged and the dependence on mass advertising is losing its edge day by day. Marketing literature has pointed out few reasons for this change (Heyne, 2009):

- Increased marketing literacy of the consumer: As the today's consumer is shifting from a passive receiver to an active player in the marketing communications process she has become more critical and skeptical of marketing claims through traditional media and has started questing its trustworthiness.
- Advertising Clutter: As the customer is bombarded with an overdose of advertising her senses become numb instead of receptive leading to dislike of this form of communication. As a result, it has become increasingly difficult for marketers to break through the clutter and grab attention.
- Media Fragmentation: with proliferation of new media, audience is getting divided very rapidly. As a result, the effectiveness of commercials in traditional advertising media (TV, newspapers, magazines, radio etc.) has lost its sheen. Also, it is observed that the target audience of advertising is busy with multitasking during the exposure leading to divided attention – another cause of concern for marketers.
- Ad-blockers: This 'consumer-empowering' technology (e.g. TiVo DVR) which enables consumer to skip or avoid unsolicited marketing messages and interruptive advertising has given consumers control over their viewing experience but has become a nightmare for many marketers.
- Legal Restrictions on Advertising: For certain product categories (e.g. tobacco) many forms of traditional advertising are not possible due to government regulations and worldwide protest against 'visual pollutions' caused by outdoor advertising are getting stronger.

As a result of the factors discussed above, globally, the Return on Investment (ROI) for traditional advertising is showing a downward trend. According to a PricewaterhouseCoopers report, global marketing spend was $ 400bn in 2006, however the actual ROI was only 4% (Heyne, 2009) .

With such radical change taking place in the marketing domain, it makes sense to understand the concept of eWOM in more detail. In this context, an accepted definition of eWOM is, "any positive or negative statement made by potential, actual or former customers about a product or company, which is made available to a multitude of people and institutions via the Internet"(Hennig-Thurau, Gwinner, & Gremle, 2004). So, in other words, eWOM, which is also known as Online Word of Mouth (OWOM) and can be described as all online statements about products, brands or even a certain lifestyle that are exchanged between consumers.

With the advancement in Internet and Communications Technology (ICT) and advent of eWOM, traditional marketing and specifically marketing communications strategy, have gone through a sea change. Worldwide, 40% of populations has internet connection, whereas nearly 20 years back, in 1995, it was just 1%. India had more than 243 million internet users in 2014 and the figure represents the fact that

1 out of 5 Indians is a user of the Internet. It ranks third in terms of Internet population, behind China and United States (Internet World Stats, 2014). 75% of India's online population is under the age of 35 years. 86% Indian web users visit a social networking site.

In this networked world of individuals, how to handle consumer trust effectively has become a serious concern for modern marketers. Studies have shown that compared to marketer-generated sources of information e.g. company websites and online advertising, eWOM communications have greater credibility and relevance for today's technology savvy customers. Also, due to digital convergence customer felt more in control as new communication platforms like blogs, online reviews, social networks, brand communities empowered them to create consumer generated content and took part in brand building through co-creation. Today's marketers have understood the importance of eWOM in the context of Internet environment as a significant market force and a trust-building marketing tool which influences each step of consumer buying decisions process from pre-purchase attitudes to reducing post-purchase dissonance. As a result, companies spend significant resources to influence what is being talked about them online. As today's customers are technology-savvy and frequent Internet users, to browse information about related product/service brand they give lesser importance to traditional modes of advertising and hence marketers are forced to search for an alternative strategy to communicate as part of the marketing mix which will also serve as a feedback mechanism to the firm and will create a brand community where customers can relate to each other based on shared values. Research has shown that eWOM is more impactful that traditional WOM on consumer's decision-making process because of its interactive nature – the marketer can take immediate corrective measures if a campaign it is not doing well. However, it is to be kept in mind that traditional advertising can be controlled, while eWOM cannot by controlled by the marketer.

Difference between WOM and eWOM

Despite few basic similarities between WOM and eWOM communications, eWOM is unique in many ways. It has the power of immediate reach and scalability and high speed of diffusion among networked individuals. Another difference is, WOM is sharing of information between small groups of individuals in synchronous or real-time mode. However, eWOM involves multi-way exchanges of information in asynchronous mode (Cheung & Thadani, 2010). In contrast with traditional WOM, eWOM communications are publicly available and easy to access at any point of time and are available for an indefinite period of time. eWOM communications can be easily measured compared to traditional WOM.

Why Consumers Share Consumption?

To identify eWOM communication motives on consumer-opinion platforms Hennig-Tharau, Gwiner, and Gremle proposed a framework (2004). Building on the works of previous researchers they proposed five consumer utility types to assign motives for engaging in eWOM communication on Web-based consumer-opinion platforms. These are: (a) focus-related utility, approval utility, (b) consumption utility, (c) approval utility, (d) moderator-related utility and (e) homeostase utility. Each utilities are described below:

Focus related utility: It is the utility the consumer receives when adding value to the community through his or her contributions.

a) *Concern for other consumers*: Initiated because of a desire to help other consumers with their buying decisions, to save others from negative experiences, or both. It is closely related to the concept of altruism (or pro-social behavior).

b) *Helping the company:* It is the result of a consumer's satisfaction with a product and his or her subsequent desire to help the company by giving "something in return". In this scenario, the customer is motivated to spread positive WOM about the company as a social institution. According to literature, this behavior is also supported by equity theory (Oliver & Swan, 1989) which suggests that every company-customer exchange is characterized by an output/input ratio. In an ideal situation, both the numerator and denominator should be equal. However, if a customer feels that she has received more (output; in form of customer satisfaction) than what she has invested (input; in the form of money, time, effort) then she will give back to the company in the form of positive WOM to make the ratio equal.

c) *Social benefits:* Through eWOM consumers participate in and belong to a virtual community which help in identification and social integration. Writing comments on such a forum enables them to reap social benefit from community membership (McWilliam, 2000).

d) *Exerting of (collective) power over companies:* eWOM can cause a shift of power from companies to customers as negative word-of-mouth can influence the way a company and its image are perceived, thus such public articulation make customers more empowered.

Consumption Utility: It refers to consumers obtaining value through "direct consumption of the contributions of other community constituents" (Balasubramanian & Mahajan, 2001) manifested through reading product reviews and comments of others on a Web-based opinion platform by a consumer. Such writings may describe consumer experience with a product or service and sometimes ask for problem-solving information and help to get more customized, tailored feedback.

Approval Utility: It is concerned with a consumer's satisfaction that comes "when other constituents consumer and approve of the constituent's own contributions" (Balasubramanian & Mahajan, 2001). In eWOM context, such approvals are of two types: (a) informal approval: when a contributor receives group/private messages praising his/her contribution, and (b) formal approval: Used by websites where product reviews are evaluated and ranked by other users based on its helpfulness.

Motives Associated with Approval Utility:

a) *Self enhancement motivation* (Engel & Miniard, 1993): It is driven by one's desire for positive recognition from others. In eWOM context, this self-related need is fulfilled when someone is given a special status by others by naming him/her a "consumption expert" or "intelligent shopper". Electronic communication that is read by others allows consumers to signal a level of social status that can become important to one's self concept.

b) *Economic rewards*: In some cases, the eWOM information provider may receive remuneration from the web-platform operator. Literature shows economic rewards are significant drivers of human behavior and in eWOM context it is considered as a source of significant sign of appreciation (Lawler, 1984).

Moderator-Related Utility: It is derived when a third party makes the complaining act convenient and provides problem-solving support for the customer who has dissatisfying experience. In a research study involving content analysis of messages of unhappy United Airline customers through United.com it was found convenience of complaining was crucial to consumer's decision of where to vent (Harrison-Walker, 2001). Another motivating factor could be the customer's hope of getting active support from third-party web-platforms "perhaps replacing other third-party institutions (e.g. attorneys, consumer advocacy groups, and news media" (Hennig-Thurau, Gwinner, & Gremle, 2004).

Homeostase Utility

It is based on the notion that people have a basic desire for balance in their lives (Zajonc, 1971). Also according to balance theory, if a balanced state is unbalanced, humans will always endeavor to restore equilibrium (Newcomb, 1953). In the context of WOM, the source of unbalance comes from either a strong positive or negative consumption experience.

Two motives are linked to homeostase utility:

Expressing positive emotions: The reason behind the consumer's need to express positive emotions is that the consumer's positive consumption experiences contribute to a psychological tension inside him or her because of a strong desire to want to share the joy of the experience with someone. That tension may be reduced by writing comments on Web-based opinion platforms, a behavior that allows the consumer to share the experience with many others (Sundaram & Mitra, 1998).

Venting negative feelings: Sharing bad consumption experiences can help to reduce frustration and anxiety related to the incident (Sundaram & Mitra, 1998). Similarly, this desire for catharsis is also observed when a customer shares a negative consumption experience in online context to reduce his/her negative feelings related to the incident.

Moderators of the eWOM Impact

eWOM effect is increased or decreased based on other factors. They are as follows:

i) Positive predispositions towards a brand,
ii) Prior information about a brand,
iii) Expert level of the communicator,
iv) Presence of negative information along with positive information,
v) Written from a first-person perspective,
vi) Perceived similarity between writer and receiver,
vii) Source's perceived trustworthiness,
viii) Vividness of the message.

Negative vs. Positive eWOM

A negative eWOM is related to communicating a dissatisfying experience with a bad product or service. It can happen due to: customer dissatisfaction because a product failed to meet expectation, unexpected product failures, negative eWOM from competitors or critics. They are extremely harmful for a brand or company as they can spread rapidly to a large number of people connected with each other. Also, the written record is permanent and anyone can access it in future. Researches have shown that unfavorable eWOM about a brand or service is more potent in its impact than positive eWOM, spreads more quickly and spreads further than positive eWOM within social networks. Customers are more distrustful and skeptical toward positive information but more receptive to and find easier to relate to negative information. Also many consumers believe that the sender of positive eWOM has personal gain by spreading the message. Bloggers being paid to spread positive eWOM is well documented in marketing research literature (Lee & Youn, 2009). Thus motivated by a genuine desire to prevent others from making dissatisfying product or service decisions, people spread eWOM. A related concept to negative eWOM is, *Streisand Effect*, where a company or individual try to remove information etc. from the web but it generates further interest and the information is widely published (Canton, 2005) and has maximum impact on potential customers (López & Sicilia, 2014). Cross-national cultural difference in the processing of eWOM information and eWOM research that are not product class specific are potentially challenging field of study in this domain that need more focus (Christodoulides, Michaelidou, & Argyriou, 2012). Examining cross-national differences in the context of e-WOM can be insightful as online behavior is not homogeneous across the Web but may get influenced by national culture (Fong, 2008).

The Social Technographics Profile

According to research carried out by Forrester Research, there are 6 different types of online social media users: (Li, 2007); *Creators:* own websites, blogs, upload YouTube videos; *Critics:* comment on blogs, post ratings and reviews; *Collectors:* use RSS feed, tag web pages; *Joiners:* use social networking sties; *Spectators:* only consume the content of social media platforms - read blogs, watch peer-generated video and *Inactives:* none of these activities.

Few eWOM Marketing Techniques

There are several forms of eWOM or "viral marketing" techniques. All these methods are related to spreading the word-of-mouth through electronic media (Goyette, 2010). The term "viral marketing" was coined by Juvertson and Draper in 1997 to describe Hotmail's free email service (Cruz, 2008) and involves passing on or referring news, information or entertainment to another person. Research has shown above-the-line media has been very effective in creating awareness in marketing among the target group and is a highest rated technique not only for getting relevant information but also for making buying decision (Pruden, 2004). Different other terminologies are used to describe eWOM e.g. "Interactive Marketing", "Internet word-of-mouth", "word-of-mouse", "stealth marketing" and "referral marketing" (Cruz, 2008).

In the marketing literature, viral marketing has been compared to a living biological virus. A commentator has characterized viral marketing as a "digitized sneeze" that leads to release of "millions of tiny particles that can infect others who come into contact with them" (Knight, 1999) and it is defined as "any strategy that encourages individuals to pass on a marketing message to others, creating the potential for exponential growth in the message's exposure and influence" (Wilson, 2000). However, apart from benefits to marketers, viral marketing poses few challenges in the form of unpredictability and lack of message control (Fattah, 2000).

Following is a discussion on few of the techniques:

- *Viral video*: Marketers can use this technique to launch a new product to create awareness and 'buzz' around it. In 2012, the launch of the song 'Kolaveri D' in YouTube was an example of this. Famebox, a company promoted by Malaysia's Astro group, is in the business of making viral videos which gets at least a million hits, a number necessary to make profit. It promotes and shares revenues with catchy videos made by amateurs on social media platforms like Facebook and Twitter. Another site following the revenue sharing model is You Tube on the basis of sponsorships from brands looking to grab attention on this platform. Medium like You Tube, with a user base of over 60 million in India, pays approximately INR 100 (USD 1.61) per 1,000 hits in India and keeps 45 per cent of the revenue made through ad sales on the video. Recently, an Indian video titled "I'm not a Woman" and with a strong social message has received 230,000 hits. The co-creator Kunal Rao describes this as an effective use of viral video to spread a message: "There is also a tremendous reach when you look at videos created just for Internet. … if the content is good, it can spread like wildfire on social media.". (Khosl, 2014)

- *Brand or company profile* on a social networking site (e.g. Facebook, Twitter): Firms do this for better 'brand connect' with the customer so that it will translate into possible buying decision catalysed by positive eWOM. Also, such forums act as a feedback mechanism. Nowadays, many companies have started to realize the need for an in-house social media strategist as it is lot easier to create new brands using social media as compared to conventional way and to measure the brand value (Uboweja, 2015).
- *Brand communities*: Such communities are formed due to users' emotional attachment with the brand. It is perceived that belonging to such a community is a form of self-expression of the consumer. Example: Harley-Davidson Owner Group (HOG). In 1983, Harley-Davidson almost faced bankruptcy. Now, the company boasts a top-50 global ranking and is valued at $7.8 billion. The key strategy for Harley's turnaround was its commitment to building a brand community: a group of ardent consumers organized around the lifestyle, activities, and ethos of the brand. It happened as people are more interested in the social links that come from the brand affiliations than in the brands themselves. Brand communities in online context also serve valuable community functions (Fournie & Lee, 2009) .
- *Crowdsourcing:* It is defined as a "process of needed services, ideas, or content by soliciting contributions from large sums of people and especially online communities" (Maher, 2014). Outsourcing the creating of ideas, content, solution to the crowd in social media where customers provide creative input (new ideas, test new products, how to improve existing services/products etc.) to the company in making of advertising or marketing communications. It is cost-effective way to promote a brand and also increasing brand-connect with the consumer in the process. Example: Nissan Projct 370Z and Lego Ideas.
- *Chat Rooms and Message Boards:* These opinion-based forums are meant for free expression of consumers about their feelings and associated emotions about a consumption experience. A firm can use these to find new customers or to gain insights from existing customers. As each forum or message board has a personality of its own expressed through its opinionated and influential group members, concerned marketer needs to treat this subculture carefully (Beliclove, 2012). Also, the firm should not shy away from honestly and immediately addressing criticisms, complaints, comments, and questions on such forums as it may dent the company or the brand reputation in the long run (Ionel, 2012).
- *Blogging:* Blog, a shorter version of the world 'weblog' has been extensively used to spread eWOM by the marketer. This form of content marketing is especially useful in case of creating awareness and positive opinion about high involvement technology product by using blogs of opinion leaders and is preferred over direct marketing (Elizabeth, 2015). A successful blog can be a great eWOM marketing tool because: a) it can direct online traffic to the main website, b) can

generate more sales, c) can create extra advertising revenue, and d) can be a great tool to connect with the customer (Gehl, 2006). As a result, marketing firms are wooing famous bloggers with huge online followings to write about their products or services as opinions of such consumers will make their products visible and memorable amidst marketing clutter. However, many people suspect credibility of such commercial blogging and see it as kickbacks (Joshi, 2009).

Unethical eWOM Marketing Tactics

The biggest threat to eWOM marketing in specific and to social media marketing in general is the unethical use of the medium by unscrupulous marketers to mislead the customer and that, experts say, may cause serious brand damage and eventually alienate the brand or company from the consumers instead of endearing it.

Some of the unethical marketing techniques are:

a) Manipulating user's newsfeeds: In an article titled "Experimental Evidence of Massive-Scale Emotional Contagion through Social Networks" published in the journal Proceedings of the National Academy of Sciences of the United States of America it is revealed that Facebook conducted a massive psychological experiment on 689,003 users manipulating their news feeds to assess the effects on their emotions without customer consent (McNeal, 2014).
b) Using Search Engine Optimization (SEO) techniques to hide negative results, deleting negative reviews, posts and comments: Using different 'Online Reputation Management' tools, companies push negative online comments to the second page of the search results or even lower (Quipp, 2008)
c) Paying for 'likes' or writing positive reviews about a product/service: As the number of 'likes' on a Facebook page has become an indicator of popularity and profitability, few niche companies, known as 'like farms' have specialized in boosting page like artificially. They are doing brisk business by using a network of profiles to fraud protection algorithms (De Cristofaro, 2014)
d) Creating 'fake' followers on social media: According to StatusPeople.com, a Twitter-auditing tool, out of 3.6 million Twitter followers of Hillary Clinton at least 15% are fake. Also, the 2016 US presidential candidate is also accused of having Facebook followers from Baghdad, Iraq than any US city (Martosko, 2015).
f) Sending spam mails without receivers' permission: Unsolicited Bulk Commercial E-mail (UBCE), popularly called spam, are a major problem among the users of the Internet. According to an estimate nearly 66 per cent of emails are spams. These unsolicited emails also carry harmful viruses, Trojans and worms to wreck computers and steal valuable personal information (Spam: Internet menace on the prowl, 2013).

SOLUTIONS AND RECOMMENDATIONS

To counter the above-mentioned eWOM marketing menace, there is rising pressure on the business to have a clear benchmark that will mirror the organization's core values. To bridge the gap between what the marketers and consumers think 'right' the Chartered Institute of Marketing has initiated *Keep Social Honest* campaign where certain guidelines are proposed for the companies:

a) Define and capture right policies for your organization,
b) Appoint and empower a champion and ambassadors,
c) Embed social media policies internally,
d) Share company's social media position publicly,
e) Adopt social media compliance as a professional development priority,
f) Involve employees in social media, but signpost their affiliation,
g) Take active role in the debate (Keep Social Honest, n.d.)

FUTURE RESEARCH DIRECTIONS

The marketing literature shows researchers have probed various aspects of eWOM marketing. However, future researchers can focus on areas yet to be explored in-depth. Instead of focusing on single product category/brand research can be carried out across multiple products and industries. Also, for a research question, data collection can be done from multiple social platforms like social networking sites, blogs, micro-blogs, online forums to increase robustness (Das D., 2013). Further researches can be carried out to find out what combinations of traditional advertising and eWOM is best for the marketer in a particular industry or how can eWOM reinforce the image of a brand that already has some recognition in traditional channels. In eWOM research, typically data are collected retrospectively (i.e. considerable time elapsed between the response and actual buying activity), however, future research can ask for responses while shoppers are in the process of seeking other's opinions or just after buying. Another interesting area of research in this field would be whether source characteristics affect source credibility. With the advent of social media it would be beneficial for firms to know which type of platform (e.g. social networking sites, blogs, virtual communities WOM) is a more credible source of information than traditional firm-driven communication is not abundant (Christodoulides, Michaelidou, & Argyriou, 2012). Furthermore, more research can be carried out to probe the effects of eWOM on brand image across brands and different product categories.

CONCLUSION

eWOM has radically transformed the traditional one-way, top-down marketing communication to a two-way dialogue. eWOM is most effective to counter challenges like ad clutter and media fragmentation in today's rapidly changing dynamic marketing ecosystem. However, this tool needs to be handled with caution and needs more in-depth research to be more effective in marketing application.

REFERENCES

Addley, E. (2014, March 7). *Ellen's Oscars selfie most retweeted ever – and more of us are taking them.* Retrieved August 30, 2014, from http://www.theguardian.com: http://www.theguardian.com/media/2014/mar/07/oscars-selfie-most-retweeted-ever

Are marketers spending wisely on social media? (n.d.). Retrieved Sept 18, 2014, from http://economictimes.indiatimes.com/slideshows/advertising-marketing/are-marketers-spending-wisely-on-social-media/slideshow/17956181.cms

Arndt, J. (1967). Word of Mouth Advertising: A Review of the Literature. *Advertising Research Foundation*, 3.

Balasubramanian, S., & Mahajan, V. (2001). The Economic Leverage of the Virtual Community. *International Journal of Electronic Commerce*, *5*(Spring), 103–138.

Beliclove, M. E. (2012). *8 Do's and Don'ts for Marketing on Online Forums and Message Boards*. Retrieved from http://www.entrepreneur.com/article/223900

Brown, T. (2014, Sept 8). *Are your tweets trusted or tainted? The realities of social media #fails*. Retrieved from http://www.theguardian.com/media/2014/sep/08/tweets-trusted-tainted-social-media-fails

Business Today. (n.d.). Retrieved from businesstoday.intoday.in/story/kolaveri-di-success-case-study/1/22957.htmlbusinesstoday.intoday.in/story/kolaveri-di-success-case-study/1/22957.html

Cheun, & Thadani. (n.d.). Retrieved Oct 6, 2014, from https://domino.fov.uni-mb.si/proceedings.nsf/0/7d01f166eebae8e3c1257757003c5e98/$FILE/24_cheung.pdf

Cheung, C. M., Lee Mathew, K. O., & Rabjohn, N. (2008). The impact of electronic word-of mouth: The adoption of online opinions in online customer communities. *Internet Research*, 18.

Cheung, C. M., & Thadani, D. R. (2010). The Effectiveness of Electronic Word-of-Mouth communication: A Literature Analysis. In *23rd Bled eConference eTrust: Implications for the Individual, Enterprises and Society*, 331.

Christodoulides, G., Michaelidou, N., & Argyriou, E. (2012). Cross-national differences in e-WOM influence. *European Journal of Marketing*, *46*(11/12), 1689–1707. doi:10.1108/03090561211260040

Cordelia Jenkins, S. A. (2011, December 8). *How 'Kolaveri Di' went viral*. Retrieved August 30, 2014, from http://www.livemint.com: http://www.livemint.com/Consumer/x7AZWkwVBjr7MbqrTyuChM/How-8216Kolaveri-Di8217-went-viral.html

Cruz, D., & Fill, C. (2008). Evaluating viral marketing: Isolating the key criteria. *Marketing Intelligence & Planning*, *26*(7), 743–758. doi:10.1108/02634500810916690

Das, A. (2014, May). *How 'likes' bring votes – Narendra Modi's campaign on Facebook*. Retrieved August 30, 2014, from http://scroll.in/article/664756/How-%27likes%27-bring-votes-%E2%80%93-Narendra-Modi%E2%80%99s-campaign-on-Facebook

Das, D. (2013, May 20). *Evolution, rapid growth & future of research on electronic word of mouth (eWOM): A scientific review*. Retrieved from http://papers.ssrn.com: http://papers.ssrn.com/sol3/papers.cfm?abstract_id=2287134

Day, G. (1971). Attitude change, media, and word of mouth. *Journal of Advertising Research*, *11*(6), 31–40.

De Cristofaro, E. F. (2014). Paying for Likes?: Understanding Facebook Like Fraud Using Honeypots. In *Proceedings of the 2014 Conference on Internet Measurement Conference* (pp. 129-136). ACM.

Elizabeth, S. (2015). *Online tech startups dumping direct marketing for content marketing*. Retrieved from http://articles.economictimes.indiatimes.com/2015-02-17/news/59232653_1_content-marketing-direct-marketing-customers

Engel, J. B., & Miniard, P. (1993). *Cosnumer Behavior* (8th ed.). Fort Worth, TX: Dryden Press.

Fattah, H. (2000). Viral marketing is nothing new. *Technology Marketing Intelligence*, *20*(10), 1–3.

File, K., Judd, B., & Prince, R. (1992). Interactive Marketing: The Influence of Participation. *Journal of Services Marketing*, *6*(4), 5–14. doi:10.1108/08876049210037113

Fong, J., & Burton, S. (2008). A cross cultural comparison of electronic word-of-mouth and country-of-origin effects. *Journal of Business Research*, *61*(3), 233–242. doi:10.1016/j.jbusres.2007.06.015

Fournie, S., & Lee, R. (2009). *Getting Brand Communities Right*. Retrieved 4 15, 2015, from https://hbr.org: https://hbr.org/2009/04/getting-brand-communities-right

Gehl, D. (2006). *How to Harness the Marketing Power of Blogs*. Retrieved from http://www.entrepreneur.com: http://www.entrepreneur.com/article/84232

Global digital music market to top $9 billion in 2014. (n.d.). Retrieved from http://articles.economictimes.indiatimes.com/keyword/digital-marketing/recent/3

Goyette, I. R. (2010). e-WOM Scale: Word-of_Mouth Measurement Scale for e-Services Context. *Canadian Journal of Administrative Sciences/Revue Canadienne des Sciences de l'Administration*, *27*(1), 5-23.

Harrison-Walker, L. (2001). E-complaining: A Content Analysis of an Internet Complaint Forum. *Journal of Services Marketing*, *15*(5), 397–412. doi:10.1108/EUM0000000005657

Haywood, K. (1989). Managing Word of Mouth Communications. *Journal of Services Marketing*, *3*(2), 55–67. doi:10.1108/EUM0000000002486

Hennig-Thurau, T., Gwinner, K., & Gremle, D. (2004). Electronic-word-of-mouth via consumer-opinion platforms: What motivates customers to articulate themselves on the Internet? *Journal of Interactive Marketing*, *18*(1), 38–52. doi:10.1002/dir.10073

Heyne, L. (2009). *Electronic Word of Mouth - a New Marekting Tool? A Practical Approach to the Opportunities and Perils of Consumer Generated Online Content.* Academic Press.

How IKEA uses social media to emerge a marketing success. (n.d.). Retrieved Sept 18, 2014, from http://articles.economictimes.indiatimes.com/2014-03-03/news/47859301_1_largest-home-furnishing-retailer-catalogue-own-friends-day

Internet World Stats. (2014, Sept 24). Retrieved from http://www.internetlivestats.com: http://www.internetlivestats.com/internet-users/

Ionel, O. (2012). *Effective Online Marketing with Forums and Message Boards*. Retrieved from http://kikolani.com/effective-online-marketing-with-forums-and-message-boards.html

Joshi, P. (2009). *Approval by a Blogger May Please a Sponsor*. Retrieved from http://www.nytimes.com/2009/07/13/technology/internet/13blog.html?_r=0

Keep Social Honest. (n.d.). Retrieved from http://www.keepsocialhonest.com/: http://www.keepsocial-honest.com/

Khosl, V. R. (2014). *Social media sites like Facebook, Twitter in grip of viral videos*. Retrieved 4 15, 2015, from http://articles.economictimes.indiatimes.com/2014-08-16/news/52873607_1_video-online-social-media-viral

Knight, C. (1999). Viral marketing – defy traditional methods for hyper growth. *Broadwatch Magazine*, *13*(11), 50-3.

Kotler, K., & Jha. (2013). Marketing Management: A South Asian Perspective. Pearson.

Kumar, K. (2014, August 5). *The untold stories of Narendra Modi's social media plan in Lok Sabha polls*. Retrieved August 30, 2014, from http://articles.economictimes.indiatimes.com/2014-08-05/news/52471092_1_bjp-team-it-cell-the-bjp

Lawler, E. I. (1984). The Strategic Desing of Reward Systems. *Strategic Human Resource Management*, 127-147.

Lee, M., & Youn, S. (2009). Electronic Word of Mouth (eWOM). *Journal of Advertising*, *28*(3), 473–499. doi:10.2501/S0265048709200709

Li, C. (2007, April 23). *Forrester's new Social Technographics report*. Retrieved from http://forrester.typepad.com: http://forrester.typepad.com/groundswell/2007/04/forresters_new_.html

López, M., & Sicilia, M. (2014). Determinants of E-WOM Influence: The Role of Consumers' Internet Experience. *Journal of Theoretical and Applied Electronic Commerce Research*, *9*(1), 28-43.

Madhavan, N. (2012, April 1). *As if by Magic*. Retrieved August 30, 2014, from http://businesstoday.intoday.in/story/kolaveri-di-success-case-study/1/22957.html

Maher, G. (2014). *Breaking Tradition! Using Crowdsourcing As Part Of Your Social Media Marketing Strategy*. Retrieved 4 15, 2015, from http://www.business2community.com/social-media/breaking-tradition-using-crowdsourcing-part-social-media-marketing-strategy-01090556

Martosko, D. (2015). *More than 2 MILLION of Hillary Clinton's Twitter followers are fake or never tweet – and she's already under fire for 'buying' fake Facebook fans*. Retrieved from http://www.dailymail.co.uk/news/article-3038621/More-2-MILLION-Hillary-Clinton-s-Twitter-followers-fake-never-tweet.html

McNeal, G. S. (2014). *Facebook Manipulated User News Feeds To Create Emotional Responses*. Retrieved from http://www.forbes.com/sites/gregorymcneal/2014/06/28/facebook-manipulated-user-news-feeds-to-create-emotional-contagion/

McWilliam, G. (2000). Building Stronger Brands Through Online Communities. *Sloan Management Review*, *41*(Spring), 43–54.

Misra, B. (2014, February 22). *How IKEA uses social media to emerge a marketing success*. Retrieved August 30, 2014, from http://retail.economictimes.indiatimes.com/news/home-and-decor/furniture-and-decor/how-ikea-uses-social-media-to-emerge-a-marketing-success/30857725

Morin, S. (1983, February 28). Influentials advising their friends to sell lots of high-tech gadgetry. *Wall Street Journal*, 30.

Murray, K. (1991). A Test of Services Marketing Theory: Consumer Information Acquisition Activities. *Journal of Marketing*, *55*(1), 10–25. doi:10.2307/1252200

Newcomb, T. (1953). An Approance to the Study of Communicative Acts. *Psycholigical Reveiw*, *60*(6), 393–404. doi:10.1037/h0063098 PMID:13112341

Oliver, R., & Swan, J. (1989). Consumer Perceptions of Interpersonal Equity and Satisfaction in Transactions: A Field Survey Approach. *Journal of Marketing*, *53*(2), 21–35. doi:10.2307/1251411

Online retailers ready to utilise social media's reach. (n.d.). Retrieved from http://articles.economictimes.indiatimes.com/2014-08-13/news/52768005_1_amazon-india-ravi-vora-social-media

Pande, S. (2014, June 8). *Just the Right Image*. Retrieved August 30, 2014, from http://businesstoday.intoday.in/story/case-study-strategy-tactics-behind-creation-of-brand-narendra-modi/1/206321.html

Pruden, D. a. (2004). Controlling the grapevine: How to measure and manage word-of-mouth. *Marketing Management*, *13*(4), 24–30.

Quipp, J. (2008). *50+ Sites To Help You Bury Negative Posts About You or Your Company!* Retrieved from http://www.searchenginepeople.com/blog/50-sites-to-help-you-bury-negative-posts-about-you-or-your-company.html

Rooney, J. (2012, September 25). *In Dell Social-Media Journey, Lessons For Marketers About The Power Of Listening*. Retrieved August 30, 2014, from http://www.forbes.com/sites/jenniferrooney/2012/09/25/in-dell-social-media-journey-lessons-for-marketers-about-the-power-of-listening/

Salzman, M., Matathia, I., & O'Reilly, A. (2004). *Buzz...Le marketing du bouche -a-oreille*. Paris: Village Mondial.

Sernovitz, A. (2009). *Word of mouth marketing: How smart companies get people talking*. New York: Kaplan.

Spam: Internet menace on the prowl. (2013). Retrieved from http://economictimes.indiatimes.com/slideshows/tech-life/spam-internet-menace-on-the-prowl/spam-facts-and-figures/slideshow/20044279.cms

Steinkuehler, C., & Williams, D. (2006). Where everybody knows your (screen) name: Online games as "third places". *Journal of Computer-Mediated Communication*, *11*(4), 885–909. doi:10.1111/j.1083-6101.2006.00300.x

Sundaram, D., & Mitra, K. W. (1998). Word-of-Mouth Communications: A Motivational Analysis. *Advances in Consumer Research. Association for Consumer Research (U. S.)*, *25*, 527–531.

Svensson, A. (n.d.). *Facebook - the Social Newspaper that Never Sleeps. A Study of Facebook eWOM's persuasiveness on the receivers*. Academic Press.

Svensson, A. E. (n.d.). *Facebook - The Social Newspaper That Never Sleeps. A Study of Facebook eWOM's persuasiveness on the receivers*. Retrieved Sept 14, 2014, from https://gupea.ub.gu.se/bitstream/2077/26249/1/gupea_2077_26249_1.pdf

Trust In Advertising. (2013). Retrieved from http://www.nielsen.com/us/en/insights/news/2013/under-the-influence-consumer-trust-in-advertising.html

Uboweja, S. (2015). *How to build a brand using social media*. Retrieved 4 15, 2015, from http://articles.economictimes.indiatimes.com/2015-04-08/news/60942975_1_social-media-brand-equity/2

US company says FB, Twitter ads fail to deliver. (n.d.). Retrieved from http://articles.economictimes.indiatimes.com/2014-04-16/news/49185111_1_ads-facebook-google

Whyte, W. J. (1954). The web of Word of Mouth. *Fortune*, *50*(5), 140–143.

Wilson, R. (2000). The six simple principles of viral marketing. *Wilson, R.F*, *70*, 1-3.

Zajonc, R. (1971). The Concepts of Balance, Congruity, and Dissocance. In Attitude Change (pp. 63-85). Chicago: Aldine-Atherton.

Zhang, B. J. (2009). Twitter Power:Tweets as ElectronicWord of Mouth. *Journal of the American Society for Information Science and Technology*, *60*(11), 2169–2188. doi:10.1002/asi.21149

KEY TERMS AND DEFINITIONS

Blog: A web page/site meant for personal written expression by an individual.
Buzz Marketing: Another name of spreading WOM to achieve marketing objectives.
Crowdsourcing: Outsourcing specific decision making to the social media user by a company.
Micro-Blog: Social media platform where users write frequent, short posts.
Social Media: Websites or applications where networked users create and share web-based contents.
Spam: Unsolicited marketing e-mail about a product.
Viral Marketing: Using eWOM techniques to achieve marketing goal.

Chapter 3
Word of Mouth on Social Media: A Potent Tool for Brand Building

Disha Mathur
Sir Padampat Singhania University, India

Dipin Mathur
Advent Institute of Management, India

ABSTRACT

In the present era of technology enabled markets, social media marketing is gaining increasing importance through the process of gaining website traffic or attention with the use of social media websites. To most of the entrepreneurs, social media marketing is the "next big thing". It is a powerful tool that must be taken advantage of. In a very short span of time, social media marketing has become one of the most loved media for the youths today. Social Media Marketing (SMM) is the hottest new marketing concept and every business owner wants to know the way in which social media can generate value for their business. Businesses today are using SMM for grabbing attention, stimulating interest, creating desire and promoting action. It has become a panacea for communication, visibility, promotion, brand building and everything. This chapter attempts to highlight the significance of e-WOM on social media as a tool for brand building and creating value to business. It also discusses its role, benefits and challenges.

INTRODUCTION OF SOCIAL MEDIA AS A MARKETING PLATFORM

John Moore, the marketer for Starbucks and Whole Foods says, ***"If people are not talking about you, they are forgetting about you."***

In the present era of technology enabled markets, social media marketing is gaining increasing importance through the process of gaining website traffic or attention with the use of social media websites. The social media marketing programs are usually attempted to create content that attracts buyers' attention and encourages them to share it across their social networks.

To most of the entrepreneurs, social media marketing is the "next big thing". It is a powerful tool that must be taken advantage of. With the rise of the internet, social media and mobile technology, it has led to dramatic increases in the accessibility of information about companies and the experiences they provide.

DOI: 10.4018/978-1-4666-9449-1.ch003

The resulting electronic word of mouth (e-WOM) refers to any statement consumers share via the internet, e.g., web sites, social networks, instant messages, news feeds, etc. about an event, product, service, brand or company. When the underlying message spreads from user to user, it presumably resonates because it appears to come from a trusted, third-party source, as opposed to the brand or company itself. Therefore, this form of marketing results in earned media rather than paid media **(wiki, 2015).**

The statistics, illustrate the following;

- According to Hubspot, 92% of marketers in 2014 claimed that social media marketing was important for their business, with 80% indicating their efforts increased traffic to their websites **(DeMers, 2014).**
- According to Social Media Examiner, 97% of marketers are currently participating in social media but 85% of participants are not sure what social media tools are the best to use. This demonstrates a huge potential for social media marketing to increase sales **(DeMers, 2014).**

RADICAL SHIFT IN BUSINESS IN INDIA

Over the past 40 years, India has experienced a radical shift in the way the business is conducted, drifting at a fast pace towards technology driven ideas and the way, people interact with each other. With introduction of e-commerce, there has been a tremendous impact on how business operates. The social media technology is accelerating and as new technologies become available; businesses that learn to use new technologies gain greater benefits. Some of the best known examples include companies such as Microsoft, eBay, Amazon, Google, Snapdeal, etc.

In a very short span of time, social media marketing has become one of the most loved media for the Indian youths today. Social Media Marketing (SMM) is the hottest new marketing concept and every business owner wants to know the way in which social media can generate value for their business. The fact is that people are social by nature and collecting & sharing information is important to them. SMM is about understanding on how technology can make it easier for people to socially connect with their social networks and profit from that understanding. Today more & more of customers use social media for personal purpose, business to consumer (B2C) purpose or business to business (B2B) purpose.

PURPOSE OF SOCIAL MEDIA MARKETING (SMM)

One of the main purposes in employing social media in marketing is to use it as a communications tool that makes the companies accessible to those interested in their product and make them visible to those, who have no knowledge of their products.

e-WOM is at its heart, using happy customers to promote your business. The aim in e-WOM is to provide customers with an unbelievably amazing, life-affirming product or service so that they cannot help but share their experience with friends, family, co-workers, and the random person, who sits at the bus stop every day. Out of the top 10 factors that correlate with a strong Google organic search, 7 are social media dependent, i.e. if brands are less or non active on social media, they tend to show up less on Google searches

Various social platforms e.g. Twitter, Facebook, Google +, etc. register an increasing number of monthly users. However, the visual-media-sharing based mobile platforms garner a higher interaction rate in comparison and have registered the fastest growth and have also changed the ways, in which consumers engage with brand content. Instagram has an interaction rate of 1.46% with an average of 130 million users monthly as opposed to Twitter, which has a .03% interaction rate with an average of 210 million monthly users **(wiki, 2015).**

ROLE OF SOCIAL MEDIA MARKETING (SMM) IN BUSINESS

There are some ways in which social media marketing can improve the business and these are as follows:

1. **Increased Brand Recognition:** Every opportunity to syndicate content and increasing visibility is valuable in business. SMM is a channel for brand's voice, content & is important because it simultaneously makes it easier, more accessible for new customers and familiar, recognizable for existing customers.
2. **Improved brand loyalty:** The brands who engage on social media channels enjoy higher loyalty from their customers. The companies nowadays take advantage of the tools that social media gives them, when it comes to connecting with their audience. A strategic and open social media plan could prove influential in morphing consumers into being brand loyal.
3. **More Opportunities to Convert:** Every post that companies make on a social media platform is an opportunity for customers to convert. When they build a following, they simultaneously have access to new customers, recent customers, old customers, and they will be able to interact with all of them. Every blog post, image, video, or comment shared is a chance for someone to react, and every reaction could lead to a site visit, and eventually a conversion. Every positive interaction increases the likelihood of an eventual conversion. Even if the click-through rates are low, the sheer number of opportunities on social media is significant **(Benefits of Social Media (n.d)).**
4. **Higher conversion rates:** SMM results in higher conversion rates in a few distinct ways. The most significant is its humanization element, i.e. the fact that brands become more humanized by interacting in social media channels. Social media is a place, where brands can act like people do, and this is important because people like doing business with other people; not with companies. The social media has a 100% higher lead-to-close rate than outbound marketing, and a higher number of social media followers tend to improve trust and credibility in the brand, representing social proof.
5. **Higher Brand Authority:** Interacting with the customers regularly is a show of good faith for other customers. When people go to compliment or brag about a product or service, they turn to social media. And when they post a brand name, new audience members will want to follow that brand for updates. The more people that are talking about a brand on social media, the more valuable and authoritative that brand will seem to new users.
6. **Increased Inbound Traffic:** Without social media, company's inbound traffic is limited to people already familiar with a brand and individuals searching for keywords. Every social media profile is another path leading back to brand website, and every piece of content a brand syndicate on those profiles is another opportunity for a new visitor. The more quality content brand syndicates on social media, the more inbound traffic is generated.

7. **Decreased Marketing Costs:** It is found that if a company can lend just one hour a day to developing their content and syndication strategy, they could start seeing the results of their efforts. Even paid advertising through Facebook and Twitter is relatively cheap.
8. **Better Search Engine Rankings:** SEO is the best way to capture relevant traffic from search engines, but the requirements for success are always changing, i.e. regularly update your blog, ensure optimized title tags, meta descriptions, and distribute links pointing back to website. Google and other search engines calculate rankings using social media presence as a significant factor, because of the fact that strong brands almost always use social media. Being active on social media could act as a "brand signal" to search engines that a brand is legitimate, credible, and trustworthy. Therefore, if a brand wants to rank for a given set of keywords, having a strong social media presence is almost mandatory.
9. **Richer Customer Experiences:** Social media, at its core, is a communication channel like email or phone calls. Every customer interaction on social media is an opportunity to publicly demonstrate customer service level and enrich relationship with customers. For example, if a customer complains about a product on Twitter, the company can immediately address the comment, apologize publicly, and take action to make it right. Or, if a customer compliments a company, it can thank them and recommend additional products. It is a personal experience that lets customers know that company cares about them.
10. **Improved Customer Insights:** Social media also gives an opportunity to gain valuable information about customers' interests and their behaviour via social listening. For example, companies can monitor user comments to see what people think of their business directly. They can segment content syndication lists based on topic to see which types of content generate the most interest and then produce more of that type of content. They can also measure conversions based on different promotions posted on various social media channels and eventually find a perfect combination to generate revenue **(DeMers, 2014).**

ELECTRONIC WORD OF MOUTH (E-WOM) MARKETING

Electronic Word of Mouth (eWOM) is a form of buzz marketing and it can become viral, if the message is persuasive or funny enough. In e-WOM, the focus is on person-to-person contacts over internet, which includes electronic recommendations. Appraisals is a convenient manner to have a product promoted via consumer-to-consumer interactions. An example of e-WOM can be; an online hotel review. The hotel company can have two possible outcomes based on their service. A good service would result in a positive review, which gets the hotel free advertising via social media, however a poor service will result in a negative consumer review, which can potentially harm the company's reputation.

According to a study by Lithium Social Welfare, the following statistics were presented;

- **92% of consumers trust recommendations from friends and family** more than any other form of advertising.
- **20 to 50% of purchases** are the result of a word-of-mouth recommendation.
- **Only 10% of consumers** trust brands.

- **70% of consumers read online customer reviews** when considering a brand.
- **81% of consumers are influenced** by their friends' social media posts **(Nine Big Reasons For Serious Womm, (n.d)).**

Today the top business leaders, entrepreneurs & marketing companies realize the need to keep up with the changing pace of business. Those days are gone, when a pure bricks business model used to thrive well in the market scenario. In order to survive the competition, it is practically impossible to design a marketing strategy without considering social networks. Social media has become a very important aspect in today's marketing mix in general and promotion mix in particular. Adapting some form of online marketing through social media is a key node for most of the businesses, especially in an industry where trends constantly change, i.e. fashion, handicrafts, etc. It is vitally important to understand the effectiveness of social media as a marketing tool, as it helps consumers in buying decision making.

REASONS OF POPULARITY OF E-WOM MARKETING

1. **People like to share:** The need of people to share explains the success of consumer review sites, discussion forums and social media sites, such as Facebook, Twitter, etc. There are several psychological explanations for this sharing behaviour from the need to connect and belong, the need to help others and the need to be perceived as someone with the right connections and knowledge. One person reaches several others and each of them can share the message with their network of friends and so on. This explains the viral potential of e-WOM.
2. **People seek advice online:** There is a natural tendency that whenever someone plans to make a purchase, he/she first would like to get informed about the subject online. Online reviews are used as important information source, shape consumer attitudes towards a product and influence sales.
3. **People trust other people:** Most people trust the opinion of a real person more than they trust advertising, news by the traditional media or information on a corporate website. This is called 'social proof'. E-WOM has a large effect on consumer buying decisions and people can be influenced positively or negatively accordingly.

e-WOM is more powerful marketing tool these days because it reaches more people, it lives forever on the internet and can be monitored.

IMPORTANT WORDS IN E-WOM

1. **Buzz:** Marketing buzz or simply "buzz" is a term used in e-WOM marketing, which is the interaction of consumers of a product or service to amplify the original marketing message. It can be a form of hype among consumers, i.e. excitement or anticipation about a product or service.
2. **Viral effects:** Viral marketing and viral advertising are buzzwords, referring to e-WOM marketing techniques, that use pre-existing social networks to enhance brand awareness or to achieve other marketing objectives, i.e. product sales through self-replicating viral processes, analogous to the spread of computer viruses. It can be word-of-mouth delivered or enhanced by the network effects of the Internet **(wiki, 2015).**

The internet has already overtaken television as the largest advertising market. The websites often include banner or pop-up ads. Social networking sites often have ads & products have entire pages and are able to interact with users. Therefore, in order to capture attention, TV commercials often end with a spokesperson asking viewers to check out the product website for more information. Print ads are also starting to include QR codes on them, which can be scanned by cell phones and computers, sending viewers to the product website. Advertising is beginning to move viewers from the traditional outlets to the electronic ones very rapidly.

THREE E'S IN E-WOM MARKETING

e-WOM Marketing has been identified as the most valuable form of marketing, as the consumers trust other consumers more above all others and it is primarily the most important fact, which is likely to drive sales for company.

In order to succeed, the marketers need to focus on the three E's: Engage, Equip, Empower and if they can master these three E's, they can become the most beloved and talked about product in their category, which will ultimately lead to increased sales **(Whitler, 2014).** These can be elaborated as follows;

1. **Engaging with Customers:** Listening to them & being a part of the conversation about their brand.
2. **Equipping & giving them reasons to talk** about products, service, insider knowledge, social elevation, incredible stories, unbelievable facts or even funny disclosures. It depends on company's understanding of consumers & their needs.
3. **Empowering consumers with different ways to talk and share**: Letting them know that they are important to you and that sharing their opinions is important to you. Helping them find ways to share within their circles and finding ways to help move their conversations around.

Figure 1 Three E's: Engage, Equip, Empower

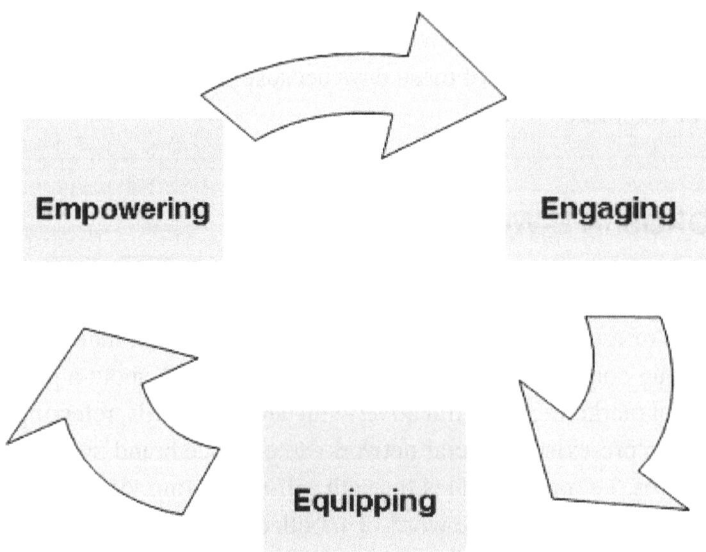

IMPORTANCE OF E-WOM MARKETING

According to a survey by Nielsen, 92% of consumers believed recommendations from friends and family over all forms of advertising. In a recent study, 64% of marketing executives indicated that they believe word of mouth is the most effective form of marketing. However, only 6% say they have mastered it. The technological advancements have made it easier than ever for consumers to access information about other customers' experiences and to share their own. The combination of e-WOM and mobile technology has given everyone a mouthpiece to share this information from anywhere, as soon as the experience happens. Now, 88% of consumers read online reviews to determine the quality of local businesses, according to a recent Bright Local survey. The survey also found that 88% of consumers trust online reviews just as much as personal recommendations. Mobile technology and social media have also increased the impact that one's own experience has on future spending, by reducing the search costs and risk of moving to a competitor. A customer who has had a bad experience will be more likely to let it influence future purchasing behaviour, if they know how easy it is to find an alternative **(Consumer Trust in Online Social and Mobile Advertising Grows, 2012).**

The radio cab company Ola offers another example of this approach. Despite the attention they receive for value for money, most of their resources are spent developing and fine-tuning an app that is directly targeted to customers' needs. Their persistent collection of user feedback after every ride allows them to continuously improve their customer experience. Again, a great experience allows them to leverage satisfied customers to be their marketing machine. During a period of particularly explosive growth in a very short span of time, Ola is benefitted because of e-WOM recommendations.

POPULAR WAYS OF E-WOM MARKETING

Apart from the customer testimonials and message forums, there are some of the popular ways of e-WOM marketing, which may be enlisted as follows:

1. **Twitter:** Twitter allows companies to promote their products in short messages limited to 140 characters, which appear on followers' home pages. The messages can link to the product's website, Facebook profile, photos, videos, etc.
2. **Facebook (FB):** The FB pages are far more detailed than Twitter accounts and these allow the users to upload videos, photos, longer descriptions, testimonials, etc. on product pages, which can be seen by others and the followers can comment on the product pages for others to see. Facebook can link back to the product's Twitter page as well as send out event reminders. A study from year 2011 attributed 84% of engagement or clicks to 'Likes' that are linked to Facebook advertising. In year 2014, Facebook had restricted the content published from businesses' and brands' pages. The adjustments in Facebook algorithms have reduced the audience for non-paying business pages having at least 500,000 "Likes" from 16 percent in 2012 down to 2 percent in February 2014.
3. **Google+:** Google+ is also able to integrate with the Google search engine, Google Adwords & Google Maps. With the development of Google Personalized Search and other location-based search services, Google+ allows for targeted advertising methods, navigation services, and other forms of location-based marketing and promotion. Google+ is also beneficial for other digital marketing

campaigns & social media marketing. Google+ authorship is known to have a significant benefit on a website's search engine optimization (SEO). It is one of the fastest growing social media networks and can benefit almost any business.

4. **LinkedIn:** It is a professional business-related networking site, allowing companies to create professional profiles for themselves as well as their business to network and meet others. Through the use of widgets, members can promote their social networking activities, i.e. Twitter stream, blog entries of their product pages, onto their LinkedIn profile page. LinkedIn provides its members the opportunity to generate sales leads and business partners. The members can use "Company Pages" similar to Facebook pages to create an area that allow business owners to promote their products or services and be able to interact with their customers. Due to spread of spam mail sent to job seeker, leading companies prefer to use LinkedIn for employee's recruitment instead of using different job portals. Additionally, companies have voiced a preference for the amount of information that can be gleaned from LinkedIn profile, versus a limited email.
5. **Yelp & Amazon:** Yelp consists of a comprehensive online index of business profiles. The businesses are searchable by location, similar to Yellow Pages. The website is operational in seven different countries. The business account holders are allowed to create, share, and edit business profiles. They may post information such as the business location, contact information, pictures, and service information. The Yelp & Amazon websites further allow individuals to write, post reviews about businesses and rate them on a five-point scale. The messaging and talk features are further made available for general members of the website, serving to guide thoughts and opinions.
6. **Foursquare:** It is a location based social networking website, where users can check into locations via a Swarm app on their smart phones. The Foursquare allows businesses to create a page or create a new/claim an existing venue. A good marketing strategy for businesses to increase foot traffic or retain loyal customers includes offering incentives such as discounts or free food/beverages for people checking into their location.
7. **Instagram:** Instagram's goal is to help companies to reach their respective audiences through captivating imagery in a rich, visual environment. It provides a platform, where user and company can communicate publicly and directly, making itself an ideal platform for companies to connect with their current and potential customers. Many brands are now heavily using this mobile app to boost their visual marketing strategy. Instagram can be used to gain the necessary momentum needed to capture the attention of the market segment that has an interest in the product offering or services. As Instagram is supported by Apple and android system, it can be easily accessed by smart phone users. Thus, the marketers see it as a potential platform to expand their brands e.g. Starbucks, MTV, Nike, Marc Jacobs, Red Bull, etc. to the public, especially the younger target group. According to a study by Simply Measured, 71 percent of the world's largest brands are now using Instagram as a marketing channel.
8. **YouTube:** YouTube is a popular avenue, where advertisements are done in a way to suit the target audience. The type of language used in the commercials and the ideas used to promote the product reflect the audience's style and taste. The ads on this platform are usually in sync with the content of the video requested. The promotional opportunities, such as sponsoring a video is also possible on YouTube, with sponsored videos from related companies in results along with other videos.
9. **Social Bookmarking Sites:** The websites such as Digg, Slashdot, Reddit, Delicious, etc. are popular social bookmarking sites used in social media promotion. Each of these sites is dedicated to the collection, curation, and organization of links to other websites. This process is crowd sourced,

allowing members to sort and prioritize links by relevance and general category. Due to the large user bases of these websites, any link from one of them to another, smaller website usually results in a flash crowd. In addition to user generated promotion, these sites also offer advertisements within individual user communities and categories. Because ads can be placed in designated communities with a very specific target audience and demographic, they have far greater potential for traffic generation than ads selected simply through cookie and browser history. Additionally, some of these websites have also implemented measures to make ads more relevant to users by allowing users to vote on which ones will be shown on pages they frequently browse. The ability to redirect large volumes of web traffic and target specific, relevant audiences makes social marketing websites a valuable asset for social media marketers.

10. **Blogs:** The companies that recognize the need for information, originality, and accessibility employ blogs to make their products popular and unique, and ultimately reach out to consumers who are privy to social media. The blogs can allow a product or company to provide longer descriptions of products or services, can include testimonials and can link to and from other social network and blog pages. Blogs can be updated frequently and are promotional techniques for keeping customers and also for acquiring followers and subscribers who can then be directed to social network pages.
11. **Tumblr:** Tumblr requires advertisers to create a Tumblr blog, so the content of those blogs can be featured through the site. It spread so wonderfully that just in the formative year 2012, four native ad formats were created on web and mobile, and had more than 100 brands advertising on Tumblr with 500 cumulative sponsored posts.

(Source: http://en.wikipedia.org/wiki/Social_media_marketing)

ADVANTAGES OF E-WOM MARKETING

The e-WOM marketing can make or break the business. If the word of mouth marketing is right, then the company does not need much of an advertisement budget. Rather, the customers will share stories of sublime service & product quality at dinner parties across the country, and certainly, it is better than any billboard. The popularity of sites like Flipkart, Amazon, Snapdeal, Groupon, etc., shows how important the e-WOM is.

The e-WOM marketing through social media has various benefits, which may be enlisted as follows:

1. **Influences customers' buying decisions:** The companies use social media to create buzz and target customers, while learning & improving from their candid feedbacks. It is the only form of marketing that can impact consumers at each and every stage of the consumer decision journey.
2. **Low Cost:** Unlike traditional media that are mostly cost-prohibitive to many companies, a social media strategy does not require astronomical budgeting, in contrast to the use of traditional print/TV/radio advertisements, at a fraction of the cost, attributed to the fact that most social networking sites can be used at no cost. Once the company becomes established, relying on word-of-mouth marketing becomes an inexpensive marketing tool to increase business. Compared to the thousands or even millions of rupees required to run a consistent ad campaign in print, on television or on

radio, a referral costs almost nothing. Adding inexpensive email marketing promotions and viral marketing campaigns using free or low-cost social networking sites to the marketing mix drops the cost to land new customers even more.

3. **Reach to much wider audience:** Today, companies make use of platforms such as Facebook, Twitter, You Tube and Instagram, in order to reach audiences, at much wider range.
4. **Interaction with customers**: e-WOM has changed the ways, in which companies interact & approach its customers, as a substantial percentage of consumer interactions are now being carried out over online platforms with much higher visibility.
5. **Reviews of Products & Services:** Customers can now post reviews of products and services, rate customer service and ask questions or voice concerns directly to companies through social media platforms.
6. **Building trust:** The buyers tend to trust someone who gives them a referral because they assume the person was happy with the services or products, and is unbiased. e-WOM is used by businesses in order to build relationships of trust with consumers. In order to aim this, companies also hire personnel to specifically handle these social media interactions. Handling these interactions in a satisfactory manner result in an increase of consumer trust. According to Nielsen's Global Trust in Advertising report, 92 percent of consumers say they trust recommendations from friends and family above all other forms of advertising. Encouraging and facilitating word-of-mouth marketing helps in breaking down trust barriers by relying on influential customers, who are willing to talk about the company **(Consumer Trust in Online Social and Mobile Advertising Grows, 2012).**
7. **Self Evaluation:** To allow firms to measure their standing in the corporate world, various sites like Glassdoor enable their employees to place evaluations of their companies, which is a unique way in itself in today's world.
8. **Increase in ROI:** With the rise of e-WOM poised to continue, the return on investments that improve customer experience will continue to increase relative to the return on traditional marketing expenditures.
9. **Counteracts Cold Calling:** Many people are listed on the 'Do Not Call' registry, eliminating a potential source of sales for many companies. Using word-of-mouth marketing to reach these consumers through social networking and referral programs gives businesses a way to reach this otherwise fading source of prospects.
10. **Long-Term Value:** The customers, who purchase products or services based on a referral are more likely to buy more than people who find the company through traditional marketing methods. Referred customers also tend to stick with the company longer than people, who find the business by other means. Plus, as happy referred customers direct their friends and family, the value of the first referral grows exponentially.
11. **Builds Brand:** Building a brand is critical, but it is often difficult for a small business to do, especially when larger competitors have already established well-known brands. Using word-of-mouth marketing helps build positive feelings about products and services, and that helps build company's brand. Providing resources, such as tips, information and articles gives the customers an easy means of sharing information about the company, while establishing the brand **(Chaney, 2012).**

To aim and fix the public's perception of a company, there are some critical steps, which should be taken in order to; address consumer concerns, identifying the extent of the social chatter, engaging the influencers to help, and developing a proportional response. The online communities can enable a business to reach the clients of other businesses using various online platforms. To maintain an advantage in a business-consumer relationship, businesses have to be aware of four key assets that consumers maintain: information, involvement, community, and control. Therefore the businesses should opt for integrating social media platforms into their traditional marketing regimen.

DISADVANTAGES OF E-WOM MARKETING

Though the social media marketing provides organizations with a way to connect with their customers, still organizations can suffer a loss due to this. The organisations must protect their information as well as closely watch comments and concerns on the social media that they use.

1. **Manipulated & faked reviews:** While anonymous e-WOM is plentiful, savvy users are aware of how reviews can be manipulated and faked.
2. **Lack of Message Control:** When a business creates an advertisement, the business controls the marketing message that it sends to prospects and customers. In e-WOM marketing, the customer controls the message by telling others about a personal experience. If the message is negative or incorrect, it can create a bad image for the product, service or business.
3. **Lasting Negative Effects:** e-WOM marketing is one of the most credible forms of advertising because a customer's reputation is at stake, when he talks positively or negatively about a product. The negative e-WOM advertising can have lasting effects on a company. It can cause the company to experience a decline in sales and damage the company brand.
4. **Fast Spreads:** If a customer has a bad experience, the company may lose repeat business from the customer. If that customer tells everyone he knows about the bad experience, that can hurt the company in attracting new customers. Some companies spark e-WOM advertising by participating on social media networks. The social media networking groups tend to be close-knit, so when a message goes out, it reaches thousands of individuals very quickly.
5. **Matter of chance:** The customer's rave reviews about product or service comes at customer's good will and his memory. The companies cannot make it happen, nor can they count on a customer remembering to refer it to prospective clients in positive way, when an opportunity presents itself. They could even be afraid of ruining the business, if they get too popular and their best-kept secret gets out. Unlike paid advertising, through which companies can choose the channel, the audience, and the timing of messages, e-WOM marketing is largely a product of chance.
6. **Impersonal:** The electronic version of word of mouth reaches an audience faster but is more impersonal than the traditional method.
7. **Tracking Issue:** It is almost impossible to thoroughly track the amount of business generated by e-WOM. While the incoming customers may be asked, if they have been referred and, in general, how they heard about the company, this gives only information about people, who responded positively and the information is generally scant. The companies need complete information to know how successful the marketing has been, so marketing plans can be made accordingly.
8. **No "Off" Button and Poor Content Control:** In e-WOM Marketing, the companies cannot control or censor what their customers say about them. e-WOM marketing shows its downsides, when a single unsatisfied customer, with choruses from ruthless competitors, take to air waves to bash

product or service. Even with positive e-WOM marketing, there is little control over an important marketing pillar, i.e. positioning. The satisfied customers may peg them as being the greatest and most affordable supplier of a service, when marketing plans are called for going after the luxury, high-end portion of market.

9. **Negative Feedback Effect with less opportunity to make amends:** A hard truth about e-WOM marketing is when a customer tells others about a bad experience with particular business. The company may not be aware, when this occurs, unless the unhappy customer informs that the opinion is being shared with others. This is of particular concern because it does not give company the opportunity to make amends and satisfy the client.
10. **Potential for Abuse:** There may be unscrupulous practices to generate buzz about a business. For example, paying people to talk positively about a product, or negatively about a competitor's product, without revealing the agreement, i.e. shilling, which is unethical. Some small business owners can go as far as creating fake identities and posting product promotions on websites to generate talk. In the extreme, some companies have retaliated against customers for vocal complaints.
11. **Sustaining Buzz:** e-WOM marketing can't be relied upon as a primary source of marketing for any business. Once the buzz stops, interest and knowledge of the product can come to a complete standstill. Rather, e-WOM works well when it supplements a full-scale marketing effort that tells the complete story of the company through multiple outlets.

SOME INSTANCES OF E-WOM MARKETING MISHAPS

- A flash poll done on 1225 IT executives from 33 countries revealed that social media mishaps caused organizations a combined $4.3 million in damages in 2010. The top three social media incidents an organization faced during the previous year included employees sharing too much information in public forums, loss or exposure of confidential information, and increased exposure to litigation. Due to the viral nature of the internet, a mistake by a single employee has in some cases shown to result in devastating consequences for organizations.
- Kenneth Cole's Twitter mishap in 2011: When Kenneth Cole tweeted, "Millions are in uproar in #Cairo. Rumor is they heard our new spring collection is now available online at Kenneth Cole's website". This has reference to the 2011 Egyptian Revolution drew objection from the public and it was widely objected to on the Internet.
- In 2012 during Hurricane Sandy, Gap sent out a tweet to its followers telling them to stay safe but encouraged them to shop online and offered free shipping. The tweet was deemed insensitive and Gap eventually took it down and apologized.
- A YouTube video of a Domino's Pizza employee violating health code standards, which went viral on the internet and later resulted in felony charges against two employees.
- A Twitter hashtag posted by McDonald's in 2012 attracting attention due to numerous complaints and negative events customers experienced at the chain store.
- A 2011 tweet posted by a Chrysler Group employee that no one in Detroit knows how to drive.

- When the Link REIT opened a Facebook page to recommend old-style restaurants, the page was flooded by furious comments criticising the REIT for having forced a lot of restaurants and stores to shut down; it had to terminate its campaign early amid further deterioration of its corporate image.

(Source: http://en.wikipedia.org/wiki/Social_media_marketing)

CHALLENGES IN ETHICAL E-WOM MARKETING

The code of ethics that is affiliated with traditional marketing can also be applied to social media, however with social media being so personal and international, there is a list of complications and challenges that comes along with being ethical online. The general concept of being ethical while marking on social network sites is to be honest with the intentions of the campaign, avoid false advertising, be aware of user privacy conditions, i.e. not using consumers' private information for gain, respect the dignity of persons in the shared online community, and claim responsibility of any mistakes or mishaps that are results of the marketing campaign

With the invention of social media, the marketer no longer has to focus solely on the basic demographics and psychographics given from television and magazines, but now they can see what consumers like to hear from advertisers, how they engage online, and what their needs and wants are. While it is ethical to use social networking websites to spread a message to people who are genuinely interested, many people game the system with auto-friend adding programs, spam messages and bulletins.

In addition, social media platforms have become extremely aware of their users and collect information about their viewers to connect with them in various ways. Social-networking web site Facebook Inc. is quietly working on a new advertising system that would let marketers target users with ads based on the massive amounts of information people reveal on the site about themselves. This may be an unethical or ethical feature to some individuals. Some people may react negatively because they believe it is an invasion of privacy. On the other hand, some individuals may enjoy this feature because their social network recognizes their interests and sends them particular advertisements pertaining to those interests. Consumers like to network with people who have interests and desires that are similar to their own. Individuals who agree to have their social media profile public, should be aware that advertisers have the ability to take information that interests them to be able to send them information and advertisements to boost their sales. Managers invest in social media to foster relationships and interact with customers. This is an ethical way for managers to send messages about their advertisements and products to their consumers.

Internet and social networking leaks are one of the issues, as video and print ads are often leaked to the world via the Internet earlier than they are scheduled to premiere. Social networking sites allow those leaks to go viral and be seen by many users more quickly.

Time difference is also a problem facing traditional advertisers. When social events occur and are broadcasted on television, there is often a time delay between airings on different parts of the world. Social networking sites have become a hub of comment and interaction concerning the event. This allows individuals watching the event on time-delayed zone to know the outcome before it airs. For example, the 2011 Grammy Awards highlighted this problem, as the viewers on the west coast learned, who won different awards based on comments made on social networking sites by individuals watching live on the east coast. Since viewers knew who won already, many tuned out and ratings were lower. All the advertisement and promotion put into the event was lost because viewers didn't have a reason to watch.

SOME EXAMPLES OF COMPANIES USING E-WOM MARKETING SUCCESSFULLY

A frequent social media user could hear about a company for the first time only after stumbling upon it in a newsfeed. An otherwise apathetic customer might become better acquainted with a brand after seeing their presence on multiple networks.

- Nike Support is a prime example of customer service done well. They constantly respond to followers on Twitter, whether it is about their apparel, Fuel Band or other products. Every few minutes, they respond to someone new.
- Apple revolutionizes technological devices and delivers amazing products to its consumers, allowing them to naturally raze about the newest iPhone.
- Lay's is an excellent example to highlight how they empowered their fans to "Do Us a Flavor," and allowed consumers to create a new flavor of potato chips to hit store shelves. Over 3.8 million submissions were sent in the year 2013, making it one of the biggest marketing campaigns for PepsiCo owned Frito-Lay.
- Epic Split video by Volvo featuring Jean-Claude Van Damme was released on YouTube on 14th November' 2013, and on the first day the film was viewed over 6.5 million times and shared over 32 thousand times. Then, in four weeks it was shared over 6 million times across social networks. It quickly became the most shared film on YouTube. The clip has received extensive media coverage from all over the world as well, and has been the subject of approximately 20,000 editorial pieces online thus far.
- Zeno Group received an Engagement award for their Seattle's Best "Black Friday Coffee Break" campaign, focused on a segment of the target, i.e. retail workers by offering free coffee to those working on Black Friday. Consumers leveraged the program through an interactive Facebook application. New fans were encouraged to "like" the page. The brand received 125 million total impressions in two weeks and 6 million YouTube impressions.

CONCLUSION

Since the last decade, e-WOM communication has been increasingly receiving considerable attention in business across India & internationally as well. Numerous studies have been conducted to examine the effectiveness of e-WOM communication. The impact of e-WOM communication is largely focussed on consumer behaviour and is related to the major elements of the social communication. In today's times, the longer a company waits to establish e-WOM communication, the more they have to lose. The SMM, when done right can lead to more customers, more traffic and more conversions. Therefore, the companies need to emphasize the use of relationship marketing through e-WOM communication to maximize the positive word of mouth about their products. The advertisers must also take social relationship factors into account and develop personalized marketing communication strategies to fulfil user's needs.

REFERENCES

Benefits of Social Media. (n.d.). Retrieved from http://rlcomputing.com/Blog/TabId/112/ArtMID/491/ArticleID/8/Benefits-of-Social-Media.aspx

Chaney, P. (2012). *Word Of Mouth Still Most Trusted Resource Says Nielsen; Implications For Social Commerce*. Retrieved in February 2015 from http://digitalintelligencetoday.com

Consumer Trust in Online Social and Mobile Advertising Grows. (2012) Retrieved from http://www.nielsen.com/us/en/insights/news/2012/ consumer-trust-in-online-social-and-mobile-advertising-grows.html

DeMers, J. (2014). *Forbes Top 10 Benefits Of Social Media Marketing*. Retrieved February 2015 from www. infuseddigital.com

Nine Big Reasons For Serious Womm. (n.d.). Retrieved from http://www.lithium.com/pdfs/infographic/lithium_nine_big_reasons_for_serious_WOMM.pdf

Social Media. (2014). Retrieved from http://westshoreconsultants.com/social-media/

Social Media Marketing. (2015). In *Wikipedia*. Retrieved February, 2015, from http://en.wikipedia.org/wiki/Social_Media_Marketing

Whitler, K. A. (2014). *Why Word Of Mouth Marketing is the Most Important Social Media*. Retrieved from http://www.forbes.com

KEY TERMS AND DEFINITIONS

Brand: A brand is a name, term, design or other feature that distinguishes one seller's product from those of others.

Brand Building: It involves all those activities that are necessary to nurture a brand into regular and healthy cash flows for the company after its launch.

Online Community: An online community is a virtual community whose members interact with each other primarily via the Internet. One needs membership of specific sites to be able to post comments and share experiences. It acts as an information system where members can post, comment on discussions, give advice or collaborate.

Social Media: It is internet-based software and interfaces that allow individuals to interact with one another, content-sharing and collaboration.

Social Media Marketing (SMM): Social media marketing refers to the process of gaining traffic or attention through social media sites.

Social Networking Websites: Social networking websites allow individuals to interact with one another and build relationships. When companies join these social channels, consumers can interact with them directly. This type of interaction is more personal than advertising.

Word of Mouth Marketing (WOMM): Oral or written recommendation by a satisfied customer to the prospective customers of a good or service.

Chapter 4
Electronic Word-of-Mouth: An Industry Tailored Application for Tourism Promotion

Azizul Hassan
The Tourism Society, UK

ABSTRACT

From technology focused conceptual perspectives, the Unified Theory of Acceptance and Use of Technology (UTAUT) as a theory of technology acceptance postulates four identified constructs as: performance expectancy, effort expectancy, social influence and facilitating conditions (Venkatesh, Morris, Davis, & Davis, 2003). This study concentrates on digital storytelling as a form of eWOM for tourism promotion within the UTAUT capacities in selected 'developing' tourism market perspectives. Results outline that in almost every aspects and contexts, appropriate technology application is supportive for tourism promotion where institutionalisation of market structures is relatively weaker.

INTRODUCTION

Electronic word-of-mouth (eWOM) is mostly viewed as a type of buzz marketing that goes viral by nature. Internet acts as the core platform for eWOM where person based contacts remain as facilitator. Word-of-mouth is gradually taking specific shapes within both its traditional and electronic format that result in the concept of electronic word-of-mouth (eWOM). This is a relatively useful form of marketing. Also, this has been encompassing attentions and concerns over the last few decades as far as access and availability of electronic interfaces are concerned. In a simple meaning, based on person to person connections, electronic word-of-mouth as a process involves information sharing that can take place in any time and any circumstances depending on access to electronic platforms. Electronic word-of-mouth can render importance to business enterprises as each individual customer can be involved in different ways to help a business, both intentionally and unintentionally. From communication perspective, this is a form of advertising that plausibly acts as a part of reputation sharing of a business through recommendations by existing consumers. This is very unlikely that such recommendations can always be positive and bring effective results for a particular business or any personal gain of an identified customer is involved with

DOI: 10.4018/978-1-4666-9449-1.ch004

such recommendation. This functions not only as experience partaking within like minded peoples but also helps to turn them as potential consumers for the identified business. In order to share specific product or services experiences, storytelling can appear as one of the most typical form of eWOM. Storytelling on electronic platforms and forums can become powerful and influential if adopted and delivered with appeals known as digital storytelling. This is way that passes on a particular message in a more meaningful, impressive and entertaining way. Storytelling is featured as audience attention grabbing when, the message or contents are solid, reliable and transmitted professionally. From theoretical understanding as relevant to both electronic word-of-mouth and storytelling, the Unified Theory of Acceptance and Use of Technology (UTAUT) as offered by Venkatesh, Morris, Davis, & Davis (2003), becomes a familiar model of technology acceptance. Basic constructs of this theory are: performance expectancy, effort expectancy, social influence and facilitating conditions. Following this theory, the first three constructs are direct determinants for use intention and behaviour whereas, the last is the direct determinant of use behaviour. This theory suggests that performance expectancy, effort expectancy and social influence foretell behavioral intention that leads towards the acceptance of information technology. Also, the theory proposes that facilitating conditions and behavioural intention predicts use behaviour for information technology acceptance. Soon after its inception, this theory has been playing crucial role in assessing applications use and is viewed as the dè factor model for measuring user acceptance (Taiwo & Downe, 2013). As electronic word-of-mouth and digital storytelling visibly relates to each other, this study offers insights from selected tourism markets in relation to the UTAUT. The identified tourism markets are generally tagged as 'developing' in terms of technology acceptance. The study critically analyzes all of three notions as: electronic word-of-mouth, digital storytelling and Unified Theory of Acceptance and Use of Technology (UTAUT) symmetrically, as concerned with tourism promotion.

Word-of-Mouth and Electronic Word-of-Mouth: The Background

According to Silverman (2011), word-of-mouth and psychology has very close interaction that was revealed with momentous contributions of his own. This psychologist as viewed as a pioneer in researching word-of-mouth developed the notion, '*teleconferenced peer influence groups*'. This group was created with an aim to involve physicians for discussing pharmaceutical products that were identified as new. Silverman observed a fascinating fact while he was in the process of performing focus groups with selected physicians during the early 70s. From this discussion, this was summarized that physicians with positive experiences on a selected drug tend to influence the cynicism of an entire group. Even, they might also affect those ex-prescribers with negative experiences. This was possible mainly by positive experience that they managed to generate. In fact, emergence of Web 2.0 has radicalized the entire online system where, existing websites started using buzz marketing through integrating social networks that they have created. Examples include YouTube, Facebook, Digg, MySpace and many more (Forbes, 2014). As internet was established as the solid base of communication, use of word-of-mouth appeared as more static, strong and constructive for both marketers and consumers. These in turn accelerated the shift towards electronic word-of-mouth.

Electronic word-of-mouth marketing has been in constructive use for several decades supported by technological development. This certainly supports the general understanding that, typical electronic word-of-mouth is gradually taking place of word-of-mouth through electronic formats as internet supported facilities. Electronic platforms and gadgets are becoming more supported and improved to appear as proven grounds to alter word-of-mouth. Electronic word-of-mouth in recent time becomes more mobile due to mobile electronic gadgets. Institutionalised form of such marketing has evolved over many years. Introduction of paid electronic word-of-mouth is an example. There is a constant demand that activities and performances of such marketers have to align with ethical concerns. There should be a consumerist approach for products or services promotion or marketing on behalf of a specific business establishment. In certain cases, involvement of the government is much desired to explore and inspect circumstances where, the interrelationships between electronic word-of-mouth marketer and consumers become disrupted, in terms of selling, promoting or marketing specific products of services. In given situations, the basic statutory rights of consumers are ignored where profitability becomes predominant to serve interests of a represented business organisation. Also, in some cases, a sort of ambiguity persists while revealing relationships between an electronic word-of-mouth marketer and a consumer (Wu & Wang, 2011). This mostly hampers an agreed and mutual understanding. Status and outcomes of established relationship between a business establishment and consumer vary on many facts or cases. This is related to influential unethical issues where, a strict control needs to be functional. In violated cases where consumer rights are overlooked, civil penalties, fines, property cease or desist orders have to be applied.

Business organisations are constantly pouring funding in electronic word-of-mouth. PQ media, a research firm working on this area has revealed that the amount of funding is multi billion each year whereas conventional advertising or marketing are relatively less funded (PQ Media, 2014). The affectivity of electronic word-of-mouth on electronic platforms is becoming established with continual supports from market research firms. The Ehrenberg-Bass Institute for Marketing Science has outlined that business brands need to rely on online avenues to support their business functionalities where, each brand necessarily has to create electronic word-of-mouth fan groups on social and other media (The Ehrenberg-Bass Institute for Marketing Science, 2014). However, marketers need to diversify the bases and origins of such fan groups to many other printed platforms. This argument is supported by research firm findings as Deloite believes that *'most advocacy takes place offline'*, rather this takes place within personal and individual capacities (Deloite, 2014). Research result reveals that, only 10% conversations concerned with consumer experiences happen on internet, while, 75% happen on face-to-face meetings and 15% over the telephone (Keller Fay Group, 2014). This result was supported by a specialist WOM marketing firm, Keller Fay as this outlined that television advertising creates most of the brand as part of word-of-mouth where, the trend is then followed by public relations (Keller Fay Group, 2014). However, in none of the statements, conversations on social, emotional or business networking sites have been mentioned that possibly can be the most significant part of electronic form of word-of-mouth. Advertising and experience sharing have never been as easy as they are on electronic formats.

Electronic Word-of-Mouth Marketing: The Conventional Meaning

Electronic word-of-mouth is seemingly uncontrollable as this leads to electronic word-of-mouth marketing on three selected avenues as: creating a solid word-of-mouth base through considerable development of levels of promise, reliance and contentment. Electronic word-of-mouth is often referred to as a form of advertising. This is also termed as the Electronic Word-of-mouth Marketing (eWOMM) that is involved with individual networking, regular engagement with consumers and agent involvements. Electronic word-of-mouth marketing is outlined as a useful tool of marketing having numerous applications and commercially viable usage. This can have affectivity by creating consumer interests as naturally reproduced in daily conversations or dialogues between consumers, stakeholders or parties which are involved with a business establishment. Electronic word-of-mouth marketing is normally persuaded by diverse actions or activities as performed by consumers and marketers of a selected business establishment. These typically create more opportunities for a business to support activities or initiatives by both a business establishment and general consumers.

eWOMM normally functions within blog, buzz, viral, social, or relationship marketing. Emotional bindings between a consumer and a business establishment mostly generate from product or service satisfaction that serve both commercial and emotional aspects. These allow them to become responsible and to follow an identified business establishment. This allows businesses to employ representatives for marketing their services or products. Adequate feedback over communication means as electronic or telephony normally helps. A kind of interaction thus develops between an identified business organization and consumers in terms of event, service or product promotion to help stimulating recommendations, discussions or conversations. Both direct and indirect management of eWOMM renders challenge. This is important and significant as effective involvement and control of marketers are required to incur reasonable outcomes. Direct eWOMM management normally relates to increased control level mainly through paid eWOM agents or even schemes like the '*friend get friend*'. In many cases, effective eWOMM is represented and directed by campaigns like teaser, controversial and clubs with customer memberships. Numerous features tend to increase richness of a useful electronic word-of-mouth marketing campaign such as generosity, kinetic and architectural features. These act as core elements to make an effective electronic word-of-mouth campaign. Again, a convenient and successful eWOMM campaign relies on financial budget for experience delivery. This is crucial that experiences are presented meaningfully to potential consumer audiences to help them get attracted and create interests for a certain product or service (Azim & Hassan, 2013).

Electronic word-of-mouth marketing in certain cases becomes incremental with unexpected and increased expenses for consumers. In such circumstances, this necessitates capital investment as levied for covering advertisement costs over a certain period of time. Spending patterns in electronic word-of-mouth marketing create some sort of alignment with traditional advertisement approaches as part with both conventional and unconventional means of products or services promotion. Also, advertisement qualities as lined with experience delivery are concerned that is important to apply electronic word-of-mouth appropriately. The application and expansion of electronic word-of-mouth marketing as part of advertisement and products or services delivery process requires proper concentration in the entire process. This is quite natural that consumers will attempt to explore reasons that attract them for a certain product or service with or without the use of an advertisement. Both existing and potential consumers are required to be contacted in appropriate manners to improve their experiences. The use of electronic word-of-mouth marketing can hardly be generalised to offer only positive commitments to help reducing the risks of negative publicities. Also, there should be opportunities to convert consumers into product or service representatives of a business establishment.

Electronic Word-of-Mouth Marketing: The Concept

The word '*Buzz*' is very often termed as '*marketing buzz*'. '*Buzz*' is very often described as hype within consumers. This is a word employed in electronic word-of-mouth marketing to outline the interaction between product or service and consumer. This is used to provide or expand messages related to marketing, in its authentic nature followed by expectation, enthusiasm or affirmative relationship about an identified service or product. '*Buzz*' can take shape of both positive and negative nature. In a '*positive buzz*' the main goal persists with advertisement, public relations or viral marketing on online platform as web 2.0 media. The term represents a set of marketing techniques that consequently create goodwill. Examples of '*Buzz*' are numerous with product examples like Beanie Babies, Pokémon, the Volkswagen New Beetle, the Harry Potter and the Blair Witch Project.

Viral advertising indicate techniques of marketing that employ networks of pre-existing type to generate brand awareness. These help to gain marketing objectives by self-duplicating viral processes analogues to computer viruses or viruses. Viral marketing is also extensively in use in marketing campaigns in areas of promotion, advertisement, shopping practices and many related areas. This in certain instances acts as enthusiasm to offer or deliver enhanced experiences supported by network effects of internet use. The core substance of viral marketing in promotional shape embraces video clips, advergames, eBooks, interactive flash games, images, brandable software or text message on mobile phone devices. The aim of general marketers is mostly lodged in building effective marketing programmes in order to identify persons having soaring Social Networking Potential (SNP). This also offers increased likeliness to be acquisitioned by different contestants to create viral messages for tempting specific consumer segments.

Diverse factors are associated with electronic word-of-mouth analysis for helping to promote emotional, functional or social aspects. Some common factors to enhance effects of electronic word-of-mouth are: complexity, brand knowledge, differentiation, brand relevance, brand quality, visibility, premium, brand age, product/service types, excitement, perceived risks, involvement and satisfaction. Electronic word-of-mouth analysis endorses of different brands as they are accepted by consumers of many types.

Digital Storytelling

Storytelling normally appears in shapes of words, visuals or images and delivered mainly as narratives. This can appear as an important element of educational or functional activities. The history of storytelling dates back hundreds of years where, its relevancy gradually increased from decades to decades. Storytelling is the transmission of message into an entertaining mode for target audience. The word 'memorable' often incorporates with storytelling that is; listeners will place their full attention while listening to a story and will remember it. The defining criteria of communication have changed and people have relatively less available time to make choice. This is where technologies have importance as these have enabled audiences to listen, experience and do that they could not do before. Consumer audiences will spend less time to interrupt through passing messages than making engagements with innovative ideas. Storytelling on electronic formats is way to express these ideas with better potentials.

Digital storytelling is a solid and powerful mode for making communications mainly because these are relatively easy to memorize, evocative and let a specific business enterprise to create some sort of emotional bond with both consumers and employees. A tricky storytelling capacity helps in encouraging and facilitating audiences to receive specific messages. This stimulates word-of-mouth as the messages to share and remember by not limiting to simple words. 'Third Party Storytelling' is about stories that are told about an identified person or a brand rather than the person or brand talking about them. Third Party Storytelling allows a story to become more focused, reliable and thus ready to make comments and share.

Not all stories can have similar acceptabilities, influences and effects. Rather, a good story appears with some specific features as 'adhesiveness'. This is also related to the delivery of a story that will make people remember it by avoiding excessive complex words and unnecessary information. This turns the audience to learn more about the story by themselves and to become more attached to it. 'Individual' is an element of a good story in a sense that, the story should speak about an individual's experiences not necessarily about a brand or a company. Also, details of this have to be avoided as these can become boring. This may possibly result into the story being perceived as an advertisement. A well accepted story should outline an individual and his involvement with a brand or a business enterprise. 'Trueness' is important as a story by nature can contain unreal facts. However, in a corporate environment stories need to be true and not full of fantasies. Obviously, facts can be added to make them more interesting but, the core content needs to be purely true. 'Appropriateness' means that a story needs to be adjusted in accordance with demands of the audiences. Relevant aspects are required to be included and covered in a story as designed to be delivered in a relevant setting. 'Wow-factor' is the key element of a successful story to grab attention of a group of audience. The background, contents, tone and delivery of a story should reach the desired level to make the audience feel 'wow' about it.

However, use of storytelling in business or corporate environments are relatively new and cannot be viewed as generalized where, more practices and applications are required to turn this as more effective and useful tool to serve specific purposes. Evidently, storytelling in corporate environment is in use to outline and spread electronic word-of-mouth to target audiences and is aimed to grasp its full potentials. Business and corporate world is getting more diverse to embrace technologies in every possible ways. Technology is an inseparable part of business or corporate world and hence, is gaining massive importance. This is natural that technology will be passed over from one generation to the other while getting familiar with technological advancements is on top of all priorities. The necessity to incorporate mainstream business areas as part of technology acceptance is important. These activities also remain relevant in any other business enterprise. Thus, the interrelationships between both eWOM and storytelling become crucial and will have wider importance in years to come. In a natural meaning, a good leadership results good storytelling capacities; that is, a good leader is a good story teller. In corporate industry leadership, the identification of issues or drawbacks is essential to gauze the plausibility or laggards of a business enterprise. This is thus necessary that business enterprises in any sector including tourism can realize their potentials and problems to advance business activities to a desired level. Organisational skills are much desired for a business enterprise to grow and flourish. This also becomes relevant that each of the business enterprises is able to identify the necessities that they require to reach a success level by means of developing capacities where, storytelling can appear as a means.

Tourism as an industry requires good leadership and workforce with expertise in relevant areas. Storytelling can definitely appear as a medium to serve this purpose. Different industries have dissimilar capacities and potentials. Thus, what exist in other business enterprises can be absent in a certain business enterprise like tourism. However, accessibilities and capacities also differ from stages to stages in a sense that, one stage is different from the other while; each advanced stage has some sort of added features than previous ones. Growth of certain sub-sectors within the tourism industry also demands more attention. This outlines that storytelling can perform in two ways: supporting the process of identification of a tourism business enterprise and secondly, helping in marketing communications through experience sharing. Tourism industry is mainly dependent on experience gathering and sharing. As a general proposition, experiences in tourism render necessities and this is where, storytelling can appear as a possible solution to serve specific purposes. Such practices in tourism are relevant and beneficial for an entire set of activities to reach the set objectives. Tourism experiences are shared on both online and offline platforms where, online platforms are becoming more powerful in recent years. This outlines the necessity and relevance that tourism activities need to embrace reliable technological stands. In tourism, recommendations from others play significant roles in helping positive decision making process. Technologies thus have wider importance in tourism through their applications and acceptabilities.

Storytelling on digital formats is a non-conventional method of electronic word-of-mouth, to some extent. As traditional form of word-of-mouth is getting more diverged into electronic form, this is very essential that the perceived benefits are exploited to the maximum. In certain situations, eWOM remains a dilemma, to understand digital storytelling as a way to explore its potentials. The patterns within which marketing communications are made are dispersed into two types as: online and offline. Online platforms feature with social networking sites, blogs and so on while, offline platforms include published articles or similar. Thus evidently, storytelling can have better capacities to perform both online and offline and to help in market communications as well as spreading goodwill of a tourism business enterprise to grow.

The Unified Theory of Acceptance and Use of Technology (UTAUT)

In the last few decades, development, design and acceptance of information technologies have managed to attain considerable attentions. From the consumer perspective, many theories or models have been proposed where, the Unified theory of adoption and use of technology (UTAUT) by Venkatesh, Morris, Davis, & Davis (2003) is the most recent addition. Empirically, this model has been applied in diverse domains of knowledge and business.

Figure 1. The unified theory of acceptance and use of technology (UTAUT) (Venkatesh, Morris, Davis, & Davis, 2003)

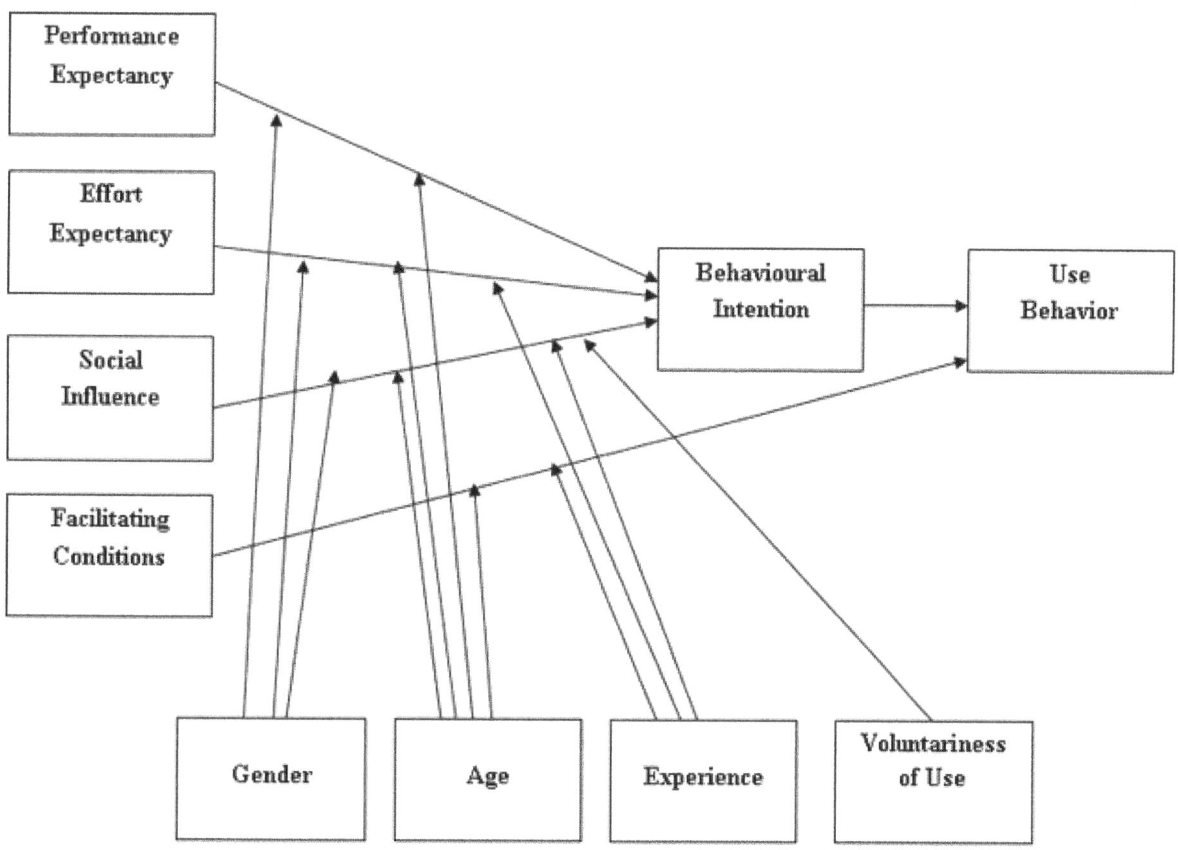

The Unified theory of adoption and use of technology (UTAUT) developed by Venkatesh, Morris, Davis, & Davis (2003) is based on social cognitive theory with a total of eight theories or models in areas of information technology acceptance. The author analyzed predictive validity of eight models which are The Theory of reasoned action (TRA), The theory of Planned behavior (TPB), The technology acceptance model (TAM), The motivational Model (MM), A model combining the technology acceptance model and the theory of planned behavior (C-TAM-TPB), The model of PC Utilization (MPCU), The innovation diffusion theory (ID) and Socio Cognitive Theory (SCT) (Foon & Fah, 2011).

The Unified theory of acceptance and use of technology (UTAUT) is a model of technology acceptance published in 'User acceptance of information technology: Toward a unified view'. This model outlines user intentions for using information system and succeeding usage behaviour. Four key constructs of this model as performance expectancy, effort expectancy, social influence and facilitating conditions. The first three constructs act as direct determinants of usage intention and behaviour where, the last is the direct determinant of use behaviour. Age, gender, experience and voluntariness of use moderate the consequences of these four key constructs on usage intention and behaviour. In a longitudinal study, Venkatesh, Morris, Davis, & Davis (2003) found subsequent validation accounting to 70% variance in behavioural intention and almost 50% in genuine use. This model is taken as more robust than any other existing theories or models in predicting or evaluating technology acceptance. Even the model is extensively used in different areas of knowledge, the significance, magnitude and direction remains as inconclusive in relation to outcome of empirical studies within models (van Raaij & Schepers, 2008).

Electronic Word-of-Mouth, Digital Storytelling, the UTAUT and the Tourism Industry

More updated researches in tourism show that effects of both negative and positive electronic word-of-mouth marketing on tourism products and services among diverse nationalities can be immense and broader. Researchers like Morgan, Pritchard, & Piggott (2003) argued that negative electronic word-of-mouth may have devastating effects on a specific destination's representation or image. This is mainly because, dissatisfied visitor moves with displeasure and makes negative comments all over his journey places based on his experiences. Study on the Caribbean by Crick (2003) as related to previous example also alerted that hostile attitude of the locals to tourists certainly leads to negative electronic word-of-mouth and thus, push the tourism industry to downturn consequences. Díaz-Martín, Iglesias, Vázquez, & Ruiz (2000) in their studies on the Spanish tourists explored that affirmative electronic word-of-mouth boosts expectations as well as makes it more complicated to satisfy such anticipations. Shanka, Ali-Knight, & Pope (2002), in their destination selection method study revealed that, the majority of decisions to travel Western Australia were generated from electronic word-of-mouth communications. O'Neill, Palmer, & Charters, (2002) deliberated their studies on the Australian wine tourism and explored that this form of tourism with wine sales was significantly helped by electronic word-of-mouth recommendations. This happens mainly when these tourists as vacationing opinion leaders return homes and recommend their experiences to others.

In another study with the participation of sample tourists from Brazil, Germany, Japan, Taiwan and the United Kingdom in a cross cultural pattern, Crotts and Erdmann (2000) opined that complaint behaviour was persistent within all sample tourists. This in fact, supported the theory of Cultural Dimension as offered by Hofstede (1991) for explaining the likeliness that those diverse cultures will move along the complaints through electronic word-of-mouth to interested tourists. Farmer and Atchison (2001) in a Power Point presentation analysed facts as related to '*Yours is a Very Bad Hotel*', a website with a facility for offering reviews, feedbacks or comments. They revealed that the creators of this website actually had unexpected and poor experiences at a Houston Doubletree hotel property. Farmer and Atchinson remained very conscious for not allowing people to make their presentation as public. However, this went on to general visitors though electronic communications that created huge response in a very rapid form and simultaneously reached to academics, researchers and business travellers across the world. This generated huge response with four thousand more emails to Farmers and Atchinson with the creation of huge negative 'buzz' for the hotel chain and that particular property. This incident actually revealed the power of electronic word-of-mouth on both online and offline platforms.

Tourism studies as an independent academic discipline has produced considerable number of seminal concepts or theories. The '*drifter, explorer, mass tourist*' typology of Cohen (1972), '*theory of allocentricity and psychocentricity*' of Plog (1974) and '*tourist area life cycle model*' of Butler (1980) relied on observation and thought generation. In each of these theories, the concept of innovation and discovering new products, services or destinations appeared as central themes. Adventure seeking tourists later on turned into opinion leaders through sharing their experiences which were followed by their '*less intrepid cousins*' (Dearden & Harron, 1992). The entire process as whole thus help in building marketing momentum and diffusing new innovative tourism products or services and destinations.

Technology acceptance and decision making process are related to each other and these have importance in a given business environment. Consumers are the most crucial element of a business enterprise regardless of their origin and development. The decision making process of consumers rely on diverse factors as relevant to technology acceptance. Imminent process of technology adoption can be accompanied by word-of-mouth either on conventional or electronic format. Consumer behaviour in online context is an element of a comprehensive form of technology acceptance that beholds the notion to create word-of-mouth and storytelling on electronic format. Possibly, electronic word-of-mouth (eWOM) as an advanced form of oral communication can have better information sharing capacities in the present hyper technology supported socio-cultural context. Electronic word-of-mouth is relevant in areas of technology acceptance when, the entire process is rooted in technology and development. There are also ways where, technology acceptance can help to promote tourism. A consumer is normally influenced by digital word-of-mouth that certainly acts as a facilitator. This is not only restricted within certain business enterprises or organizations rather, this is a process of allowing consumers to become more familiar and getting used to with specific means of technological application.

Functionalities and applications of electronic word-of-mouth are spread in diverse sub-sectors of the tourism industry. Tourism as an industry is huge with many ancillary facilities involved. In this identified industry, interpersonal contacts are respected as one of the most significant elements of communication. Electronic word-of-mouth is important in accessing information about a product or service to purchase. This concept becomes more popular with the ongoing development of technologies as part of moving from one step of advancement to another. The relevancy of electronic word-of-mouth in tourism is unprecedented while, the usage is moving forward consistently and with faster rhythm than ever before. This concept is attached with consumer decision making process and hence, a strong interrelationship is active between this and electronic word-of-mouth. At a certain stage when, technology needs assistance and support from concerned parties, the relevance to adopt specific technology becomes crucial. In tourism or any other business enterprises, this becomes evident that consumers demand maximum outcome from a specific service or product. Consumer decision making process is involved with the ways they are offered access to information and data sources. This is where the importance of electronic word-of-mouth actually lies.

The conceptualisation of digital storytelling in a developing tourism market place can no longer be left without having effects of digitalisation where, the outcomes appear in tourism promotion. Its importance and values of business, educational, moral and cultural preservation can hardly be ignored. Evidently, in many cultures storytelling has dominance as a popular medium of learning and entertainment with the Australian aboriginals as an example. However, this is interesting to explore digital storytelling being used as a form of eWOM to promote tourism on social media and in blogs (Sotiriadis, 2013). Also, this is relevant to see positive results with closer engagement of service providers and tourists.

Theoretically, technology acceptance and marketing concepts are constantly altered with increasing modification and replacement of conceptual notions. There is very low likeliness that a certain idea will remain the same for next several decades. However, this is signs of advancement of ideologies and thoughts as concerned with business. In reality, marketers remain in constant move to adopt and apply technologies to ensure and bring out the maximum from an existing and conventional business and in particular from a tourism market. The Unified Theory of Acceptance and Use of Technology (UTAUT) acts within four identified constructs as: performance expectancy, effort expectancy, social influence and facilitating conditions (Venkatesh, Morris, Davis, & Davis, 2003). The influence of internet and digitalized interfaces mostly has turned as very common. Both marketers and consumers tend to search for managing and harnessing details of a tourism product or service by accepting and using technology more convincingly (Figure 2).

Digital storytelling is a form of electronic word-of-mouth as becoming more influential on electronic platforms. Also, when technology and consumer move together, the understanding of technology acceptance becomes more valid. Electronic word-of-mouth can appear in shapes like both verbal and non verbal discussions in forms of recommendations, discussions, attitudes of behaviours towards a certain business establishment and many more. Electronic word-of-mouth in its generic form has been influenced by technological advancements where, concept of digital storytelling and electronic word-of-mouth appear on the scene. This is a non-conventional form of electronic word-of-mouth on internet or electronic surfaces where the discussions or recommendations are made on digital formats.

Electronic word-of-mouth is provocative particularly when, the consumer experiences move beyond the level of expectation. This happens only when a consumer experiences more than expectations. However, this renders challenges for a business enterprise in terms of products or services offer to bring up to a certain level of standard. This is mostly annoying when employees are desired to make consumers feel that they have received the most excellent services. In fact, consumer experiences are a comprehensive process where, diverse factors are involved because experiences by nature can be sporadic. Not necessarily, each of the consumers who receive exceptional services would make recommendations as part of word-of-mouth. Still, there is a possibility that such experience may be shared in discussions where, personal experiences mostly remain as an individual subject matter on the discussion table. This outlines that the UTAUT is in practice related to tourism promotion in given tourism market context. General business features have also been diverging towards technology use with the effective interaction of technology and business activities. Technologies are turning to have been used to generate more advantages for the business itself and also to devise the overall business performance leading to positive outcomes. When, electronic word-of-mouth and digital storytelling is related to performance and appeal,

Figure 2. The unified theory of acceptance and use of technology (UTAUT) in tourism (modified from Venkatesh, Morris, Davis, & Davis, 2003)

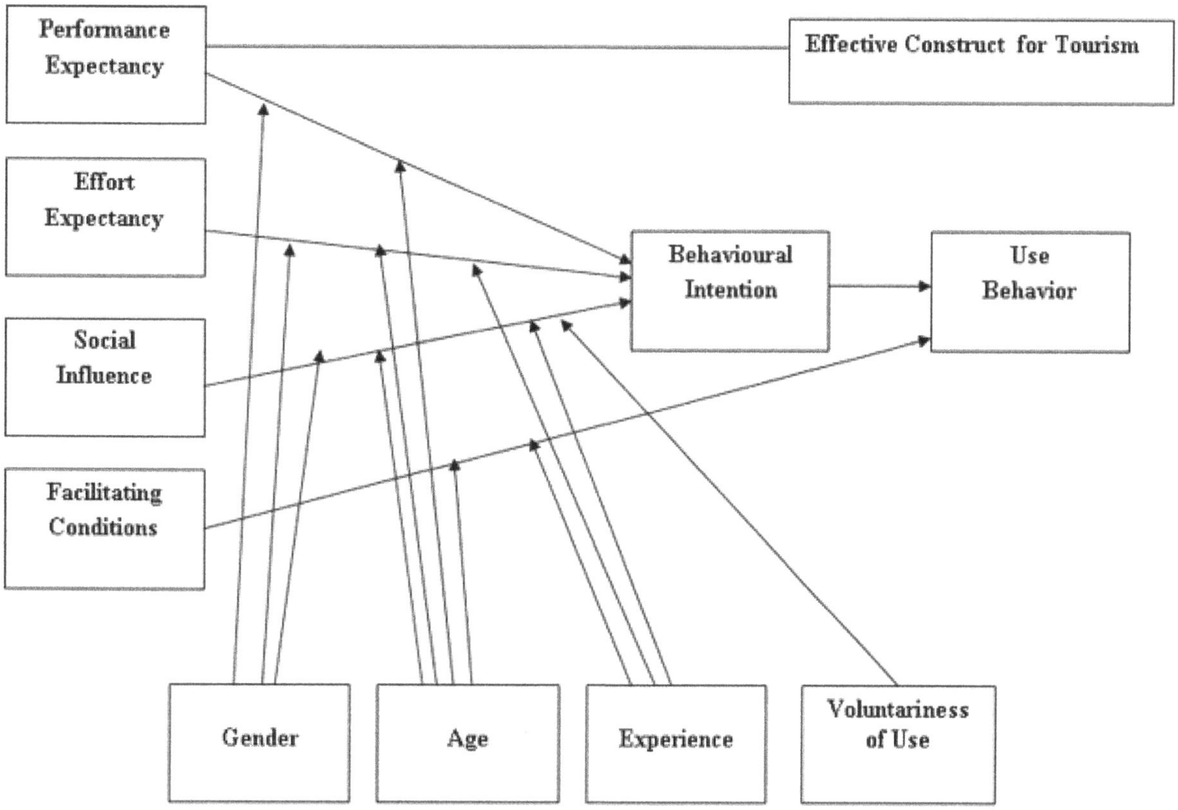

the performance expectancy as a construct of the UTAUT appears as the most effective for tourism. Market settings and capacities of technology acceptance are different across the world with many factors involved. Electronic word-of-mouth and digital storytelling becomes more appealing when the electronic formats are available and accessible.

The African Experience: Business in Africa has always been challenging and to understand consumer patterns. Residents of each country are different in their media preference, attitude and purchase behaviours. Nielsen (2014) stressed on looking both mass and niche audience in order to initiate business in Africa as significant improvement took place in this region over the last few decades. This is the outcome of better wages and living standard supported by upgraded consumption level where, consumers have turned as savvier in selecting brands or service requirements for their consumption. On the basis of demographic, attitudinal, lifestyle and purchasing behaviours backed by media consumption key patterns of 15 sub-Saharan countries were identified. The classification was made into three groups of media consumers as: savvy, selective and simple (Figure 3).

In every category, conversation power both digitally and in person remains powerful. Even, electronic and print media performs well, word-of-mouth stays as the most influential factor in purchase decision making. Result of the survey clearly demonstrated that, respondents rely primarily on recommendations of friends and families than advertisements. The increasing influence of social media is increasing,

Figure 3. Three identified consumer groups in Africa (Nielsen, 2014)

still electronic word-of-mouth stays as the most powerful. When fully adapted by consumer segments, electronic word-of-mouth will appear as the single most powerful element of consumer decision making process (Nielsen, 2014).

The Bangladesh experiences: Case of Bangladesh rectifies that even after having necessary infrastructures with relatively considerable tele-density, institutionalized efforts are necessary to promote tourism services. This asserts to conduct more researches in areas of electronic word-of-mouth where, tourism market is expanding mainly for capacity expansions of middle class of populations. Spending capacities of this social class has helped to expand tourism marketing in Bangladesh. No known research or study has been conducted to reveal existing facts and thus to show future guidelines. Digital storytelling as electronic word-of-mouth has become very popular and common in Bangladesh where, the availability and access to internet facilities is considerable. Tourism as an industry is getting a strong position in the national economy of Bangladesh. The country is experiencing high volume of tourist influx backed by both private and public sector investments. Numerous tourist spots have been developed around the country over the decades and this industry has witnessed a growth of infrastructure development. Still, there are so many opportunities left to develop this sector, systematically and in accordance with consumer demands. Technology is accepted in Bangladesh tourism market and expressed through digital storytelling particularly on social media and blogs.

CONCLUSION

In technology penetrated businesses where, technology is evolving and pushing the advancement process to a certain height, there are very little or no scopes at all to ignore influences and usability of technologies. This is very normal that technology helped to turn traditional word-of-mouth into electronic format. That is, conventional word-of-mouth has modified into non-conventional and more technology focused. The existence of electronic word-of-mouth is certain but, the application and areas will change. As believed that tourism is all about experience generation and sharing, this is also granted that, the platforms for these have moved towards becoming more technology oriented. Instead of traditional manner, word-of-mouth has merged with technology where, consumers share their experiences on blogs or social media. As technological excellences are unstoppable, the shift from traditionalist to non-traditionalist becomes more certain. Thus the channels have changed from conventional to hyper-conventional mainly due to technological advancements.

In tourism, electronic word-of-mouth has a strong ground to support and develop business activities that has relevancies in promoting and advancing the entire consumer decision making process. The acceptance and use of technologies are phenomenal and there is almost no scope to ignore its importance within a given business framework. Technology application in tourism and in particular, electronic word-of-mouth becomes the central focus; this is evident that technologies are merged with traditionalism. That is, electronic word-of-mouth is blended with digital storytelling that creates a newer notion of technology application in tourism industry. Electronic word-of-mouth and tourism promotion activities are part of a comprehensive process of tourism industry and consumer decision making with examples in Sub-Saharan countries and Bangladesh. Hence, this renders useful and possible outcomes. Electronic word-of-mouth on electronic format appears as crucial as any relevant format of consumer decision making in tourism industry. This is a process that outlines the necessity and potentials of a given business communication network. In a technology penetrated social structure where, consumers enjoy more freedom than ever before, the decision making process becomes more validated. Entrepreneurs and business persons become keener to participate in an acceptable mode of decision making and tourism promotion. The relevance of accepting technologies is situation demanding that is, consumers expect better return as they relate to their proposed investments. Aim of this chapter was to focus on digital storytelling as a growingly important element of electronic word-of-mouth. The other focus was to consider the given framework of the UTAUT in relation to tourism promotion in developing tourism market contexts. In relation to both conceptual and practical framework, this study asserts that digital storytelling as an element of electronic word-of-mouth is getting more indulged in tourism promotion. Tourism is also getting more exposed to technology application, particularly in experience generation and sharing. In future, studies on how technology supported electronic word-of-mouth are getting indulged in tourism can appear as a promising research area.

REFERENCES

Azim, R., & Hassan, A. (2013). Impact analysis of wireless and mobile technology on business management strategies. *Journal of Information and Knowledge Management*, *2*(2), 141–150.

Butler, R. W. (1980). The concept of a tourist area cycle evolution: Implications for management of resources. *Canadian Geographer*, *24*(1), 5–12. doi:10.1111/j.1541-0064.1980.tb00970.x

Cohen, E. (1972). Toward a sociology of international tourism. *Social Research*, *39*(1), 164–183.

Crick, A. P. (2003). Internal marketing of attitudes in Caribbean tourism. *International Journal of Contemporary Hospitality Management*, *15*(3), 161–166. doi:10.1108/09596110310470202

Crotts, J. C., & Erdmann, R. (2000). Does national culture influence consumers' evaluation of travel services? A test of Hofstede's model of cross-cultural differences. *Managing Service Quality*, *10*(6), 410–419. doi:10.1108/09604520010351167

Dearden, P., & Harron, S. (1992). Case study: Tourism and the Hilltribes of Thailand. In B. Weiler & B. M. Hall (Eds.), Special Interest Tourism. London: Belhaven Press.

Deloitte. (2014, September 11). *A new breed of brand advocates Social networking redefines consumer engagement*. Retrieved from: http://bit.ly/1tAnCrN

Díaz-Martín, A. M., Iglesias, V., Vázquez, R., & Ruiz, A. V. (2000). The use of quality expectations to segment a service market. *Journal of Services Marketing*, *14*(2), 132–146. doi:10.1108/08876040010320957

Farmer, T., & Atchison, S. (2014, September 10). *Yours is a very bad hotel*. Retrieved from: http://bit.ly/WPT7ni

Foon, Y. S., & Fah, B. C. Y. (2011). Internet banking adoption in Kuala Lumpur: An application of UTAUT model. *International Journal of Business and Management*, *6*(4), 161–167.

Forbes (2014, September 11). *Here's is how Facebook and Google might completely disappear in the next 5 years*. Retrieved from: http://onforb.es/WMjF8J

Hofstede, G. (1991). *Cultures and organizations: Intercultural cooperation and its importance for survival: software of the mind*. London: McGraw-Hill.

Keller Fay Group. (2014, September 11). *The social power of television: what's in it for television*. Retrieved from: http://bit.ly/1qMT4mT

Media, P. Q. (2014, September 11). *Word-of-mouth forecast 2009-2013*. Retrieved from: http://bit.ly/1unFPLX

Morgan, N. J., Pritchard, A., & Piggott, R. (2003). Destination branding and the role of the stakeholders: The case of New Zealand. *Journal of Vacation Marketing*, *9*(3), 285–299. doi:10.1177/135676670300900307

Nielsen. (2014, September 11). *Why word-of- mouth is loudest in Africa*. Retrieved from: http://bit.ly/1lY1dG4

O'Neill, M., Palmer, A., & Charters, S. (2002). Wine production as a service experience – the effects of service quality on wine sales. *Journal of Services Marketing*, *16*(4), 342–362. doi:10.1108/08876040210433239

Plog, S. C. (1974). Why destination areas rise and fall in popularity. *The Cornell H.R. AQ (Balmain, N.S.W.)*, *4*(4), 55–58.

Shanka, T., Ali-Knight, J., & Pope, J. (2002). Intrastate travel experiences of international students and their perceptions of Western Australia as a tourist destination. *Tourism and Hospitality Research*, *3*(3), 245–256.

Silverman, G. (2011). *Secrets of Word-of-mouth Marketing: How to Trigger Exponential Sales through Runaway Word-of-mouth*. New York: American Management Association.

Sotiriadis, M. D. (2013). Electronic word-of-mouth and online reviews in tourism services: The use of twitter by tourists. *Journal Electronic Research*, *13*(1), 103–124.

Taiwo, A. A., & Downe, A. G. (2013). The theory of User acceptance of information technology (UTAUT): A meta-analytic review of empirical findings. *Journal of Theoretical and Applied Information Technology*, *49*(1), 48–58.

The Ehrenberg-Bass Institute for Marketing Science. (2014, September 11). *News and press release*. Retrieved from: http://bit.ly/1pajBXi

van Raaij, E. M., & Schepers, J. J. L. (2008). The acceptance and use of a virtual learning environment in China. *Computers & Education*, *50*(3), 838–852. doi:10.1016/j.compedu.2006.09.001

Venkatesh, V., Morris, M. G., Davis, G. B., & Davis, F. D. (2003). User acceptance of information technology: Toward a unified view. *Management Information Systems Quarterly*, *27*(3), 425–478.

Wu, P. C. S., & Wang, Y.-C. (2011). The influences of electronic word-of-mouth message appeal and message source credibility on brand attitude. *Asia Pacific Journal of Marketing and Logistics*, *23*(4), 448–472. doi:10.1108/13555851111165020

KEY TERMS AND DEFINITIONS

Digital Storytelling: Storytelling normally appears in shapes of words, visuals or images and delivered mainly as narratives. This can appear as an important element of educational or functional activities. Internet: Internet is a network having billions of computers connected globally.

Tourism Promotion: Activities which are conducted for promoting tourism in a particular destination.

The Unified Theory of Acceptance and Use of Technology (UTAUT): A theory of technology acceptance, includes four identified constructs as: performance expectancy, effort expectancy, social influence and facilitating conditions. The first three are taken as direct determinants for use intention and behaviour; where, the last is the direct determinant of use behaviour.

Web 2.0: This is a term given for the second generation World Wide Web to allow people to share and collaborate information.

Word-of-Mouth: Information passing from one person to another by oral communication.

Section 2

Precursors to Electronic Word of Mouth

Chapter 5
Electronic Word-of-Mouth Communication in Online Social Networks:
The Motivational Antecedents of Electronic Word-of-Mouth (eWOM) Engagement in Online Social Networks

Tuğçe Ozansoy Çadırcı
Yıldız Technical University, Turkey

Ayşegül Sağkaya Güngör
Işık University, Turkey

ABSTRACT

Online social networks (oSNS) enable users to construct strong relationships with friends, family, as well as strangers. They also enable users to share information concerning experiences and opinions about products, brands and companies via electronic word of mouth (eWOM). The unique nature of oSNS-eWOM relationship forms the basis of this research. The authors report the results of a research investigating six motivational factors for engaging in eWOM communication, investigated under three dimensions; producing, consuming and forwarding of content on oSNSs. Results reveal that eWOM production behavior on oSNS is mainly motivated by altruism, self enhancement, electronic social interaction and exhibitionism. The motivating factors of eWOM forwarding behavior showed up as electronic social interaction and exhibitionism, whereas the motivating factors for eWOM consumption behavior are altruism, electronic social interaction and need for intellectual engagement. Aversion of cognitive activities appeared to have a negative effect on consumption of eWOM communication.

DOI: 10.4018/978-1-4666-9449-1.ch005

INTRODUCTION

Online social networks (oSNSs) are facing a rapid growth around the world. They help users build and maintain personal relationships with friends, family and as well as strangers (Kim, Sohn & Choi, 2011). As a web based service oSNSs help individuals to construct a public profile, communicate with others and also to follow the content that is provided by other users (Boyd & Ellison, 2008). The main objective of SNS users is social interaction and connection with peers (Cheung, Chiu & Lee, 2010).

As a new construct oSNSs attract many researchers around the world. Most studies concerning oSNSs emphasize the motives behind the use (Bolar, 2009; Cheung, Chiu and Lee, 2010; Kim, Sohn & Choi, 2011; Kraeuter et al., 2011; Lin & Lu, 2010; Peeling et al., 2009). People use and engage in oSNSs for many reasons. The most significant reasons are self-reflection (Bolar, 2009; Peeling et al., 2009), utility (Bolar, 2009; Kim, Sohn & Choi, 2011; Lin & Lu, 2010), information seeking and gathering (Bolar, 2009; Kim, Sohn & Choi, 2011), entertainment (Cheung, Chiu & Lee, 2010; Kim, Sohn & Choi, 2011; Lin & Lu, 2010), peer influence (Bolar, 2009; Kraeuter et al., 2011), social enhancement (Cheung, Chiu, & Lee, 2010; Kim, Sohn & Choi, 2011), social support (Kim, Sohn & Choi, 2011), and belongingness (Peeling et al., 2009). The motives behind the engagement with social networks also provide an insight about the eWOM communication of the users. Two of the most important motives concerning oSNS use and eWOM tendencies are seeking social support and fulfilling information needs(Kim, Sohn, & Choi, 2011).

The rapid growth of oSNSs provides users to construct strong relationships between users and these relationships have a strong effect on consumer behavior and attitudes (Quinton & March, 2010). As an example, according to Ipsos OTX survey (June 2012), 22% of respondents (N=12,000) state that they would buy a brand because a friend 'likes' or follows a brand on a social network. As a communication platform, oSNSs also enables users to share information about brands and products more rapidly than any other online platform. Internet technology and oSNSs provide a possibility for consumers to share information concerning experiences and opinions about products, brands and companies via electronic word of mouth (eWOM) (Jalilvand et al., 2011). OSNSs provide a communication channel for consumers and, are an effective channel for building consumer-brand relationships (Chu & Kim, 2011).

eWOM may include positive and negative comments about a product or brand that is shared between actual and potential consumers via the Internet (Jalilvand et al., 2011). eWOM is seen as more effective than traditional WOM and should get more attention from practitioners due to their great reach potential (Dellarocas & Narayan, 2006; Sache & Mangold, 2010; Zhang et al., 2010).

There are differences between traditional WOM and eWOM communication. First, traditional WOM consists of face-to-face interpersonal communication. The main motivation behind that communication is to warn and help others about products and brands (Kozinets et al., 2010). As a result, it acts as a means for opinion leaders. But eWOM not only helps opinion leaders to help others, it also helps opinion seekers to search for relative information about their purchases (Sun et al., 2006). Second, eWOM is considered more influential when compared to traditional WOM, as the messages are shared more quickly, the opinion seekers can reach to information more easily and messages can reach to a higher number of people. Finally, traditional WOM messages are shared privately while eWOM messages are shared more publicly (Andreassen & Streukens, 2009). Although the spread of information is quick and the number of shared information is high, the monitoring and control capabilities of the marketers are higher.

eWOM communications are exchanged and coproduced among members of the oSNSs (Kozinets et al., 2010). The eWOM communication in oSNSs are shared, transferred and coproduced more rapidly than any other media like emails, blogs etc. and are seen more effective than other media due to social interaction between the members. The strength of ties and size of the network impact the effectiveness of eWOM communication (Andreassen & Streukens, 2009). Also demographic similarities and personal affinity are expected to generate a greater interest for eWOM communication (Bruyn & Lilien, 2008).

oSNSs are expected to facilitate and structure eWOM communication (Chu & Kim, 2011). The unique nature of oSNS-eWOM relationship forms the basis for our research question. In view of the existing gaps in the eWOM literature, the purpose of this study is to investigate the motivational factors for engaging in eWOM communication, which is investigated under three dimensions; producing, consuming and forwarding of content on oSNSs. An understanding of the motivations of eWOM in oSNSs will provide valuable information especially for e-marketing strategies.

STUDY BACKGROUND

The Evolution of the Motivational Theory Concerning Word-of-Mouth (WOM)

WOM is considered to be the most effective medium for affecting consumers' decisions (Keller, 2007). WOM messages are considered to be more powerful than company generated messages (Brown & Reingen, 1987; Murray, 1991; Godes & Mayzlin, 2004). In one of the leading publications concerning WOM, Arndt (1967) defines WOM as *an oral person-to-person communication between a receiver and a communicator whom the receiver perceives as non-commercial, concerning a brand, product or service.*

Due to its power WOM has been the scope of many studies throughout the years. These studies have proven direct and indirect effects of WOM on diffusion of new offerings (Arndt, 1967; Czepiel, 1974), driving sales (Chevalier & Mayzln, 2006; Liu, 2006), increasing confidence in a purchasing decision (Harris & Gupta, 2008), affecting the cross buying decisions and churn (Diekres, Bichler & Krishnan, 2011). Aside from its positive effects WOM can become destructive for a brand or a company in terms of customer dissatisfaction and complaint (Richins, 1983; Sundaram, Mitra & Webster, 1998).

Some of the attempts to understand WOM theory were focused on defining the characteristics (Engel, Kegerris & Blackwell, 1969; Wright, 1974; Scott & Tybout, 1981) of influential people known as opinion leaders and the motivations (Dichter, 1966; Scott & Tybout, 1981; Richins & Root-Shaffer, 1988; Engel, Blackwell & Miniard, 1993; Sundaram, Mitra & Webster, 1998; Anderson, 1998) that lead them to engage in WOM communication.

Dichter (1969)'s study is the first one that focused on the motivational theory of WOM. In his study Dichter (1969) identified four motivational constructs concerning WOM production and transmission. These were *product involvement, self-involvement, other involvement* and *message involvement*. Product involvement referred to the need of the consumer to share with others about his/hers consumption experience. Self involvement was mostly about consumer's psychological needs like gaining attention, feeling like a pioneer or an insider, achieving status, displaying connoisseurship and conforming personal judgments. Other involvement was related to altruistic tendencies, which were driven by the need to give something or provide information to the receiver of the WOM message. The last motivational factor which is message involvement, referred to the discussion that was stimulated by company's communication efforts.

Richins and Root-Shaffer (1988) described the relationship between involvement and consumers' WOM tendencies. They stated that situational involvement with a product category encouraged people to give advice about products. The results of their study revealed a strong relationship between WOM leadership and enduring involvement. As consumers of a given product category become product enthusiasts they become more eager to discuss certain subject in a given product category. Consumers with higher involvement in a product category engage in two-way communications with others. They both produce and receive WOM information and compare their opinions with others.

Engel, Blackwell and Miniard (1993) renamed the original motivational categories in Dichter (1969)'s study and also included a new motive that was entitled "dissonance reduction". Their motivational model included *involvement, self-enhancement, concern for others, message intrigue* and *dissonance reduction*. The new motivational construct dissonance reduction was related to the need of the consumer to reduce the cognitive dissonance following a purchase decision.

Sundaram, Mitra & Webster (1998) have adopted a more detailed approach towards the motivational theory of WOM. They included the effect of the valence of the message. They stated that people engage in positive and negative WOM communications with different motivational factors. Positive WOM was driven by the need to help others *(altruism)*, personal interest in a given product category (*product involvement*), desire to enhance the personal image of the consumer (*self-enhancement*), willingness *to help the company*. Negative WOM motivators included *altruism, anxiety reduction, vengeance* and *advice seeking*. The results of the study have proven the difference between positive and negative WOM tendencies.

Electronic Word-of-Mouth (eWOM)

eWOM is the sharing of information via internet technology. Most of the time eWOM is referred as viral marketing due to transmission of information between acquaintances through different online communication channels (Subramani & Rajagopalan, 2003; DeBruyn & Lilien, 2008; Ho & Dempsey, 2010; Kaplan & Haenlein, 2011). Regardless of the form, the focus is on sharing of information about consumers experience and thoughts about marketing offerings (Steffes & Burgee, 2009).

In this study, deriving from Hennig-Thurau et al. (2004), we refer eWOM communication as *any positive or negative statement made by potential, actual or former customers about a product, brand or company, which is made available to a multitude of people and institutions via the Internet.* These three behaviors are regarded as the constituent parts of eWOM. In this study, eWOM behavior is investigated under these three different behaviors. Each is defined as the following:

- *Production of online content (Producer/initiator).* A person who initiates eWOM either by posting the content for the first time on oSNS or writing content to express his/her feelings about a brand/product/company.
- *Consumption of online content (Consumer).* A person who reads about the content on oSNS. He/she can either forward it or keep it to him/herself.
- *Forwarding of online content (Forwarder).* A person who forwards the content to others on oSNS or makes it visible to others at his/her profile page.

There is not a clear difference between people exhibiting these types of behavior. A person could exhibit all three types of behavior, or only consumes the content and nothing follows. The nature of the

Internet lets the opinion seeker to become an opinion leader or can convert an ordinary customer into an eWOM consumer. The quality, authenticity and originality of an eWOM message affect both the acceptance and forwarding behavior regardless of the valence of the message. eWOM messages hold the opportunity of co-creation. After reading and accepting the statements of an eWOM message consumers can become forwarders and sometimes even producers of eWOM (Huang, Cai, Tsang & Zhou, 2011). Motivations for these behaviors could be same or different.

Viewing eWOM as a conversation between two parties implies a need to understand the motivations leading to each specific behavior. In broad sense, eWOM communication differs from traditional WOM. Traditional WOM is an intimate face-to-face communication between two acquaintances. eWOM is mediated by online media like e-mails, blogs and oSNSs (Jeong, Cheong & Jang, 2011). In traditional WOM, the conversation mostly happens between two people. In eWOM communication with the help of Internet one consumer can share the product information with more than one people. In traditional WOM the receiver knows the sender. Most eWOM information is from strangers whom the receivers have never met. In most cases, the messengers of eWOM are anonymous to receivers. However in oSNSs it's easier to make assumptions of message and source credibility and quality (Lee & Koo, 2012). The impact of eWOM messages is higher than traditional WOM messages, due to two different reasons. The first reason is eWOM leads to both electronic and conventional word-of-mouth communications. The second reason behind eWOMs impact power is the fact that eWOM messages can be stored online for future references (Andreassen & Streukens, 2009).

MAIN FOCUS OF THE CHAPTER

Motivational Antecedents of eWOM Communications in oSNSs

Mostly in traditional WOM, the sender acts with altruistic motives (Kozinets et al., 2010). However in eWOM communications, motives of the sender might be more profit-oriented due to the applications like affiliate marketing. In general, motives concerning both types of WOM communications present same motivational characteristics. Studies have shown that eWOM communication can be motivated by enjoyment (Phelps et.al, 2004), altruism (Yoo & Sanders, 2013; Phelps et al., 2004; Hennig-Thurau et.al, 2004; Wu & Sukoco, 2010), self-enhancement, (Yoo & Sanders, 2013; Hennig-Thurau et.al, 2004; Wu & Sukoco, 2010) electronic social interaction (Yoo & Sanders, 2013; Hennig-Thurau et.al, 2004; Wolny & Mueller, 2013), need for cognition (Wu & Sukoco, 2010) and trust (Wu & Sukoco, 2010; Chu & Kim, 2011; Hsu & Tran, 2013; Hansen & Lee, 2013). Trust has been found to facilitate exchange of information when the partner as an information source is trusted in a social relationship (Robert et al., 2008). Referring the characteristic of oSNSs, to be formed with familiar people mostly, it is possible to say that oSNSs are expected to exert a stronger impact on consumers, and increase the likelihood of eWOM to be distributed to multitude of people. Therefore they gain a significant importance in eWOM context. That's the main reason why this study focuses on oSNSs. Furthermore, although oSNSs are growing in importance, there is not much study concerning motivations. Therefore, it makes sense to do a study on this issue, which has not been studied before.

For the purpose of this study, oSNS is defined as "a virtual community that exists online and whose members interact with each other constantly". Interaction could be in the form of following content (consumption), writing/posting content for others to read (production), sending the content to others (forwarding).

According to Andreasen and Streukens (2009) eWOM communications that occur in oSNSs has different properties. oSNSs are an important source for product information, they own the benefits of social interaction and influence and also they provide the decision makers important indications for credibility assessment.

An initial ten motives pool was constructed on the basis of literature review. They are egoism, altruism, need for cognition, collectivism, self-enhancement, electronic social interaction, vengeance, entertainment, economic incentives, exhibitionism. Following focus group analysis and deleting non-motivating items, five motives were selected that are described below. Their hypothesized effect on the action of producing, consuming and forwarding of electronic content are discussed in the following section.

The Need to Help Others – Altruism

According to Hennig-Thurau et al (2004), one of the four motives that explain WOM communication is altruism. Altruism motivates people for dissemination of both positive and negative information. Therefore, two different definitions appear in the literature. In the form of positive WOM; altruism is defined as the motivation to provide a value to a party without anticipating any reward in return (Sundaram, Mitra & Webster, 1998). On the other hand, regarding negative WOM, it is defined as to prevent others from experiencing the problems they had encountered (Sundaram, Mitra & Webster, 1998). Dichter (1966) suggested that once dissatisfaction occurs, a desire to prevent others from experiencing a similar fate prompts one to engage in negative WOM communication. It is believed that an individual is responsible for the welfare of people nearby thus relating his or her purchase experience in the form of recommendations or warnings (Dichter, 1966). Whether negative or positive, while disseminating information, altruistic personality feels responsible in securing the safety and wellbeing of another.

There are studies of altruism as a motive for WOM communication in traditional environments. Referring to the study of Sundaram, Mitra & Webster (1998); about 28.7 percent of the offline positive WOM conversations, altruistic motives were found to guide people to share consumption experiences with others. These individuals had the intention of aiding the receiver to make a satisfying purchase decision. In the case of negative WOM, however, the motive was to help others by warning them about negative consequences of a particular action (Sundaram, Mitra & Webster, 1998).

Altruism has also found ground on the studies of WOM in online environments. In their study of the responses and motivations to pass along e-mail, Phelps et al. (2004) provides support for the premise that consumers are often driven by altruistic motives in online environments. Hennig-Thurau et al. (2004) suggested that applying the work of Engel et al. (1993, p. 158), "eWOM communication on Web-based opinion platforms may be initiated because of a desire to help other consumers with their buying decisions, to save others from negative experiences, or both". Thus, they argued, such communication can include both positive and negative consumer experiences with a product or company. This *"concern for other consumers"* motive is closely related to the concept of altruism. Batson (1994) defined altruism as a motivation with an ultimate goal of increasing the welfare of one or more individuals other than oneself.

Individuals acting on altruistic goals are willing to volunteer themselves to contribute their knowledge to online consumer reviews without expecting direct rewards in return. For example, consumers may share purchasing experience just because others have a need for it (Kollock, 1999).

Although there is no apparent compensation, people can still obtain intrinsic enjoyment by helping others through sharing their knowledge in virtual communities (Kollock, 1999). It may raise an inside satisfaction. On oSNSs, eWOM may be initiated by a desire to help other consumers with their buying decisions, to save others from negative experiences or both. In either case, altruism is thought to motivate people for producing and forwarding online content to others. Therefore, it is proposed that:

H1. Altruism is a predictive motive for (a) producing and (b) forwarding content on oSNSs.

The Need for Self-enhancement

Self- enhancement is defined as recommendations to allow person to gain attention, show connoisseurship, suggest status, give the impression of possessing inside information, and assert superiority (Engel, Black & Miniard, 1993). It is the tendency to seek experiences that improve or bolster the self-concept (Sirgy, 1982; Baumeister, 1998). The self is "an abstract representation of past experience with personal data" (Rogers, Kuiper & Kirker, 1977, p. 677) that provides a framework for interpreting incoming data. To reinforce a sense of self and express self-identities, consumer use possessions, products, and brands (Belk, 1988; McCracken, 1988; Kleine, Kleine & Allen, 1995), to which they assign meanings. When consumers perceive these meanings as consistent with their self-concepts, they transfer the meaning to their own identity (Levy, 1959).

The tendency to self-enhance is a fundamental and one of the most dominant human social motivations (Fiske, 2001). People like to be recognized positively by others, the main drive of self-enhancement (Hennig-Thurau et al., 2004), and present themselves in ways that enhance such impression. An important aspect of a person's self-enhancement involves managing his or her representation of the self in social interactions to create good impressions and gain positive recognition from others (Berger & Schwartz, 2011). What people talk about and what they say impact how others see them and how they see themselves. Self-enhancement occurs if the consumer believes the good he has purchased is recognized publicly and classified in a manner that supports and matches his self-concept (Grubb & Grathwohl, 1967). Even without consuming a product or brand, and only by discussing about it, consumers may shift inherent meanings from the brand or product to their self-concepts (Taylor, Strutton & Thompson, 2012).

Prior research has suggested that consumers often consider the marketplace as a route to self-express and fulfill psychological needs (Sirgy, 1982; Belk, 1988; Berger & Heath, 2007). In a similar manner, the research on WOM verified that the social networks are one of the best places that people can display their self to public (Taylor, Strutton & Thompson, 2012). oSNSs act as a medium for consumers to express feelings about their good buys, thus regarded as intelligent and expert shoppers. Much of the marketing literature describes self-enhancement as a motive for engaging in traditional WOM, arguing that consumers' motivation to self-enhance their expertise is a critical factor in understanding their WOM propensities (Wojnicki & Godes 2008). By producing and publicly disseminating information/experience about a brand, product or service, consumers can use the symbolic value of the brand, product or service to express their self-concepts (Taylor, Strutton & Thompson, 2012). Moreover, in oSNSs, there is a high probability that the ones that the person knows in addition to the ones that s/he does not know are following the content produced. It may be taken as a cue for the person, initiating eWOM communication in oSNSs, to reveal him/her-self as smart, expert and intelligent to others as enhancing the status and further bolstering the self.

Lampel and Bhalla (2007) suggested that status seeking; a reflection of self-enhancement is the main reason people post online reviews. Chung and Darke (2006) concluded people are more likely to talk about products that convey an impression of being "with-it". People appeared to have the need to share their consumption experiences through WOM communication in an effort to enhance their image among others (Engel et al., 1993; Sundaram, Mitra & Webster, 1998). Irrespective of the information being positive or negative, any information that will bolster the self-identity could initiate eWOM (Pescher, Reichhart & Span, 2014).

As can be understood from the current literature, there are researches, which studied self-enhancement as a motivator, specifically, to *forward* online content (Wojnicki & Godes, 2008; De Angelis et al., 2012; Ho & Dempsey, 2010; Taylor, Strutton & Thompson, 2012). It is identified as a psychological motive to generate referrals, especially, in traditional environments (De Angelis et al., 2012; Wojnicki & Godes, 2008). To our knowledge, the present research is the first to examine the self-enhancement as a motivator to *initiate* eWOM. Thus, the following hypothesis is developed:

H2. Self-enhancement is a predictive motive for producing content on oSNSs.

Electronic Social Interaction

Technology emerges as a support for the satisfaction of social connection, a transformation of the communication between people and making it much more dynamic and transparent (Pereira et al., 2014). The recent adoption of online communication by many consumers has facilitated a fundamental change to the structure of many WOM interactions by exposing consumers to eWOM from virtual strangers (Steffes & Burgee, 2009). In most of the online environments, received information is from complete strangers.

Sun and associates (2006) introduce the construct of "Internet social connection", which (although they do not explicitly define) entails the number and strength of online social ties, as well as the desire to fulfill social needs through Internet connections. Consumers with more online contacts and stronger ties to those contacts will have a greater likelihood of engaging in eWOM communication. The existing literature on social ties and WOM communication finds that active information seeking is more likely to occur from strong tie than from weak tie sources (Brown & Reingen, 1987). As Steffes and Burgee (2014) put it, strong tie relationships more frequently result in eWOM referrals of information that is well-aligned with the recipient's wants and needs. Referring to their study, it can be argued that as the interpersonal knowledge increases, which implies stronger ties, the desire to share increases. Thus, social interaction becomes one of the reasons that motivates people for eWOM communication. As an example, as Phelps et al. (2004) envisaged; the desire to get connected and share ideas has been shown to motivate people to pass along e-mails.

Strong links appear to exist between the use of a social network and the accumulation of online social capital[1] apart from the level of Internet usage (Ellison et al., 2007). Evidence from WOM literature supports the idea that consumers are often driven by the need for social interaction in publishing their experiences on online forums (Hennig-Thurau et al., 2004). As more people rely on the Internet to fulfill their social needs; and the friends being the thrustwortiest source of information, it is surmised that people will share their experiences through online channels in an increasing rate.

While the power of social ties on eWOM communication has been well developed in literature, a non-existing research in eWOM is the impact of electronic social ties on three different aspects of eWOM communication. Therefore, it is proposed that:

H3. People with more strong ties on oSNSs are more likely to engage in eWOM, specifically (a) producing, (b) forwarding, and (c) consuming content on oSNSs.

The Need for Cognition

Need for cognition refers to a stable individual difference in tendency to engage in, and enjoy, effortful cognitive activity (Lin et al., 2011). It is the personality factor that is most commonly used as a means of defining and measuring individuals' tendencies towards information (Amichai-Hamburger et al., 2007), and, therefore, is adopted in the present study as a motivator in consuming the content on oSNSs.

According to Tuten and Bosjnak (2011), individuals with low need for cognition do not enjoy cognitive effort and prefer to rely on others' (preferably experts') opinions when dealing with complicated issues. They do not want to engage in any cognitive effort to interpret the content. Therefore, their effort to reach information is minimal. On the other hand, those high in need for cognition have more cognitive resources available and are more likely to use systematic rules to process information. They are naturally motivated to seek and acquire information (Lin et al., 2011).

Need for cognition has a significant effect on time spent reading and reviewing eWOM messages. People having a higher need for cognition tend to spent more time reading eWOM messages, and they also tend to view multiple eWOM messages. They analyze their product choices and recommendations concerning those products more thoroughly (Gupta & Harris, 2010). Need for cognition affects both the need for information search and the need to share information regarding products, brands and companies (Mowen, Park & Zablah, 2007).

oSNSs, being an important source of information, the following is proposed:

H4. Need for cognition is a predictive motive for consuming content on oSNSs.

Exhibitionism

oSNSs are great places that enable people to share information, video, photos, etc. with a mass of people. While many people are watching, people feel forced to appear smart to others, which in turn causes to develop an "other-directed" personality (Riesman, 1961). It is actually trying to exhibit a positive self to others.

In a very broad sense, exhibitionism is displaying self to public with the aim of perceived to be smart, to gain status, or for any other inherent reason[2]. Holbrook (2001) defines exhibitionism as the impression management. While studying advertising appeals, Pollay (1983) considered exhibitionism as a form of status along with prestige, trend-setting and to seek compliments. Exhibitionism is considered by Schmitt (1999) as a way to manipulate one's own social image. It is the individual self-relating to the broader social and cultural context reflected in a brand (Schmitt, 1999). For the purpose of the study, relating refers to the phenomenon wherein consumers share their feelings/experiences about a product, brand or company on oSNSs as signals to express their actual, desired or ideal self-concepts to others, a definition adopted from Holbrook (2001). In other words, via consumption, one is manipulating his/her own social image, displaying relevant identity cues to lay claim to a certain self-concept (Schmitt, 1999).

Exhibitionism implies the need for someone to watch (Holbrook, 2001). That's the reason oSNSs being the best place for expressing the desired-self; it could be actual or ideal self; while friends, as well as the strangers, are watching. This phenomenon will certainly lead to the production of the electronic content so that the positive impression can be successfully managed. Another aspect is to forward the useful information so that while people are not watching, they still have the opportunity to display smart self to others. To our knowledge, this study is the first to empirically examine exhibitionism, as a motivator in the context of eWOM. With the limited literature findings, the following hypothesis is proposed:

H5. Exhibitionism is a predictive motive for (a) producing, and (b) forwarding content on oSNSs.

METHOD

Subjects and Sampling

The motives for eWOM communication are examined using an online sample of Turkish SNS users. An online questionnaire was developed and announced on Facebook and Twitter which are the most popular oSNSs in Turkey. The data was collected in 3 weeks. The questionnaire link was sent to the prospective respondents via newsfeeds, walls and personal messaging through Facebook and Twitter. Participants were informed that the purpose of the project was to develop an understanding of the motivations to engage in eWOM on oSNSs. They were asked to complete the online questionnaire. A total number of 252 people completed the questionnaire. Due to missing data, 8 of them were eliminated. A sample size of 244 was obtained. There were 122 males and 122 females who completed the questionnaire. The average age of the sample was 28 years old. The average age was low due to oSNSs common user profile in Turkey. All of the subjects had experience with oSNSs. Descriptive statistics concerning online SNS usage and membership of the subjects are summarized in Table 1.

Survey Instrument and Measures

As the research model indicates, the main measures used in this study were altruism, self-enhancement, electronic social interaction, need for cognition and exhibitionism. Also measures concerning production, consumption and forwarding of eWOM messages were used. All of the items used were scored on five point scales from 1 (strongly disagree) to 5 (strongly agree).

In this study, altruism and self-enhancement are measured with the scales developed by Hennig-Thurau et al. (2004). The results of the previous study (Hennig-Thurau et al., 2004) indicated that both altruism and self-enhancement were strongly related to production and consumption of eWOM. Altruism and self-enhancement scales consist of 4 items each.

We measured electronic social interaction by the help of a scale by Taylor (2010), which was adopted, from Boyd and Ellison (2008). The scale asked participants to report their level of agreement with 6 statements.

Exhibitionism implies someone to watch (Hollbrook, 2001) so that s/he can display him/herself. Exhibitionism was measured by asking the subjects their reasons to initiate eWOM communication (e.g.

Table 1 oSNS usage and membership behavior of the subjects

Variables	Frequencies
SNS visit duration/day	
Less than an hour	142 (58.7%)
1-3 hours	85 (34.8%)
4 - 6 hours	9 (3.7%)
More than 6 hours	6 (2.5%)
Number of SNSs. (Membership)	
1	82 (33.6%)
2	76 (31.1%)
3	51 (20.9%)
More than 3	33 (13.5%)
Number of SNSs visited daily	
0-1	140 (57.3%)
2-3	95 (38.9%)
4-5	3 (0.01%)
More than 5	6 (0.02%)

"for attention" and "for fame and notoriety"). To measure exhibitionism Hoolenbaugh's (2011) blogging motives scale and Foster et al.'s (2010) social network motives scale were used. The exhibitionism scale used in this study included 5 items, 2 of which were selected from Hollenbaugh's (2011) study. The other 3 was selected from Foster et al.'s (2010) participation concerns (anti exhibitionism) items.

Another motive measured in this study was need for cognition (NFC). NFC is expected to have a relationship with eWOM tendencies. To measure this construct the scale developed by Cacioppo and Petty (1982) was used. The 18 items from the original study were adopted.

Production of eWOM was measured with two separate scales. The first scale that was used to measure production was the Feick and Price's (1987) "market maven" scale. The scale was used to discover the tendencies of the subject to send market and product related information. The other questions concerning production, consumption and forwarding of eWOM content were adapted from Chu and Kim (2011). The items from the scales were adopted by Chu and Kim (2011) from Flynn's (1996) –production and consumption - and Sun et al.'s (2006) – forwarding - scales. The online survey also included demographic questions like gender, age, education level and income. In addition to demographics, SNS usage and membership profile of the subjects were discovered by 6 questions. The sample statements from the measures used in this study are summarized in Table 2.

Preliminary Analysis

As the study uses a variety of multi item measures, data reduction was required. As a result prior to regression analysis, principal component and factor analysis were conducted separately on multi item measures. To achieve a simpler factor pattern Varimax rotation was used. While conducting the factor

Table 2 Sample statements from the scales

Scales	Statements
Altruism	"I write comments on online *social networks* to…"
	Warn others about bad products
	Help others with positive experiences
Self-Enhancement	"I write comments on online *social networks* because…" This way I can express my joy about a good buy
	I can tell others about a great experience
Electronic Social Interaction	Communicating with others electronically is part of my everyday activity.
	I have many friends with whom I communicate electronically.
Need For Cognition	I like to have the responsibility of handling a situation that requires a lot of thinking.
	I only think as hard as I have to.
Exhibitionism	"I write comments on online *social networks* …" For attention
	For fame and notoriety
Production of eWOM	I like introducing new brands and products to others. I often persuade my contacts on SNS to buy products that I like
Consumption of eWOM	When I consider new products, I ask my contacts on SNS for advice
	I like to get my contacts' opinions on SNS before I buy new products
Forwarding eWOM	When I receive product related information or opinion from a friend, I will pass it along to my other contacts on SNS
	I tend to pass along my contacts' positive reviews of products to other contacts on SNS

analysis eigenvalues were also taken into consideration. Besides factor analysis, reliability analysis was also conducted. To assess the consistency of the scales Cronbach alpha coefficient was used.

Altruism, self-enhancement, electronic social interaction, exhibitionism, production, consumption and forwarding scales were expected to have uni-dimensional structures. As expected, the principal component analysis of these measures led to the extraction of a single factor solution. The eigenvalues for all these factors were greater than one. The KMO measures, cumulative variance and reliability statistics of these variables are summarized in Table 3.

Table 3 Summary of factor and reliability analysis

Scales	KMO Measure	Cumulative Variance Explained (%)	Cronbach Alpha
Altruism	.859	88.582	.957
Self-Enhancement	.861	86.587	.948
Electronic Social Interaction	.866	63.386	.903
Exhibitionism	.715	63.556	.854
Production of eWOM	.895	67.471	.946
Consumption of eWOM	.777	93.351	.964
Forwarding eWOM	.773	93.556	.965

An important aspect in interpreting factor analysis is the factor loadings. Expectations about factor loadings differ according to the sample size of a study. The sample size of the following study is fairly high as a result factor loadings are expected to exceed 0.50. Loadings exceeding .70 are considered as an indicator of a well-defined structure. The factor loadings of the items in the altruism scale were between .864 and .915. The loadings for self-enhancement were between .903 and .948. Electronic social interaction's loadings were between .718 and .843. The highest loading for exhibitionism scale was .837 and the lowest loading was .776. The lowest factor loadings for production, consumption and forwarding of eWOM messages were .763; .962; .957 respectively.

The alpha coefficient for each factor is higher than the expected level of .70. The results of the reliability analysis confirm that the study has internal consistency.

The last principal component analysis that was executed was for 'need for cognition' measure. Need for cognition is expected to be a uni-dimensional construct. However, the results of the analysis led to a two-factor solution, which explained 57% of the total variance. In the single factor solution the factor loadings, extraction scores and the percentage of variance explained were fairly low. As a result, two-factor solution, which showed statistically better results, was accepted. This problem could be due to online questionnaire and/or the geographical origin of the study.

The KMO measure for the analysis was .735. The eigenvalues for both factors were greater than one. Cronbach alpha coefficients were calculated for both factors, and were higher than .70. The reliability measure for the first factor was .810 and for the second was .798 (Table 4).

Before the interpretation of the factor analysis, the factor loadings should be interpreted for both statistical and practical significance. To determine practical significance factor loadings should be examined. The loadings above .50 denote that 25% of the variance is accounted for by the factor and are considered to be practically significant. For statistical significance the loadings should be interpreted with relation to the sample size. For a sample size larger than 250 a loading of .35 is enough for factor analysis to be statistically significant (Hair et al., 2006). As a result these loadings can be considered both practically and statistically significant.

The factors were named as:

Factor 1 - *Need for Intellectual Engagement:* This factor relates to engagement of effortful cognitive activities. It indicates a tendency to seek, acquire, think about and reflect back on information. People in need for intellectual engagement have much fun with thinking, like more complex problems and deliberations, and prefer more difficult problems.

Factor 2 - *Aversion of Cognitive Activities:* This factor indicates avoiding complex thinking and problems, preferring short-term tasks and projects.

Need for cognition refers to a stable individual difference in tendency to engage in, and enjoy, effortful cognitive activity (Lin et al., 2011) and is measured as by individuals' tendencies towards information (Amichai-Hamburger et al., 2007). Individuals disliking cognitive activities do not enjoy cognitive effort to interpret the content (Tuten & Bosjnak, 2011). On the other hand, those in need for intellectual engagement have more cognitive resources, and are naturally motivated to seek and acquire information (Lin et al., 2011).

As need for cognition is known as a uni-dimensional construct, the discriminant validity of the two factors were examined using interfactor correlations and average variance extracted estimates. The average

Table 4 Factor loadings for need for cognition measure

Items	Factor 1	Factor 2
Factor 1: **Need for Intellectual Engagement** – *Reliability: .810*		
I would prefer complex to simple problems.	.742	
I like to have the responsibility of handling a situation that requires a lot of thinking.	.802	
I find satisfaction in deliberating hard and for long hours.	.744	
The idea of relying on thought to make my way to the top appeals to me.	.706	
I really enjoy a task that involves coming up with new solutions to problems.	.796	
Learning new ways to think does not excite me very much.	.753	
I prefer my life to be filled with puzzles that I must solve.	.625	
The notion of thinking abstractly is appealing to me.	.577	
I would prefer a task that is intellectual, difficult, and important to one that is somewhat important but does not require much thought.	.569	
I feel relief rather than satisfaction after completing a task that required a lot of mental effort.	.543	
Factor 2: **Aversion of Cognitive Activities** – *Reliability: .798*		
I usually end up deliberating about issues even when they do not affect me personally.		.540
Thinking is not my idea of fun.		.709
I would rather do something that requires little thought than something that is sure to challenge my thinking abilities.		.577
I try to anticipate and avoid situations where there is a likely chance I will have to think in depth about something.		.669
I only think as hard as I have to.		.657
I prefer to think about small, daily projects than long term ones.		.705
I like tasks that require little thought once I've learned them.		.784
It's enough for me that something gets the job done; I do not care how or why it works.		.545

variance extracted estimates of Factor 1(0,90) and Factor 2(0.85) were greater than the squared interfactor correlation (r^2=0.036) between the two constructs. As a results, the tests support the discriminant validity of these two factors.

As the need for cognition appeared as two factors, H4 is divided into two parts as follows:

H4 (a): *Need for intellectual engagement increases the likelihood to consume content on oSNSs.*
H4 (b): Aversion of cognition activities decreases the likelihood to consume content on oSNSs.

RESULTS

To determine the ability of the different motives to predict the production, consumption and forwarding behavior of eWOM, we conducted multiple regression analysis with behaviors as dependent variables and the hypothesized motives as the independent variables. Factor scores for each of the six eWOM motive factors were calculated from the principle component analysis and they are used as independent variables in the regression analysis.

Analysis of Motive Importance for eWOM Production Behavior

To predict the motivating factors of eWOM production behavior, taking the four motives, namely self-enhancement, altruism, electronic social interaction and exhibitionism, as independent variables, a multiple regression analysis was performed. The regression function was highly significant ($p<0.001$), and it explained 67% of eWOM production behavior. The multiple-regression model also requires the additional assumption that the predictor variables are not correlated among themselves (Churchill, 1991, p. 841). This assumption is known as multicollinearity assumption and analyzed by Variance Inflation Factor (VIF), which is 1/Tolerance. Values of VIF that exceeds 10 are often regarded as indicating multicollinearity (Neter et al., 1985). Among the calculated values, the highest VIF value was 2.02, thus there was no multicollinearity found among the independent variables. The results of the regression model indicated that all four motives had a positive and significant effect on eWOM production behavior ($p\leq0.01$). Among four, the strongest motive was self enhancement (β=.403), followed by exhibitionism (β=.280), then altruism (β=.199) and electronic social interaction (β=.195) (Table 5). With these results, we had support for H1 (a), H2, H3 (a) and H5 (a).

Analysis of Motive Importance for eWOM Consumption Behavior

To predict the importance of the variables in consumption behavior, regression coefficients for electronic social interaction, altruism, need for intellectual engagement and aversion of cognitive activities were calculated. According to the results, the regression function was highly significant ($p<0.001$) and explained the 49% of the eWOM consumption behavior. To test multicollinearity, VIFs were calculated. The highest VIF value was 1.13, for altruism. As a result, we can conclude that; no multicollinearity was found among the independent variables. All the variables were significant ($p<0.001$). Moreover, electronic social interaction was the strongest motive (β=.427), followed by altruism (β=.297), aversion of cognitive activities (β=-.243), and need for intellectual engagement (β=.169) (Table 6). It is not a surprise to find the coefficient of aversion of cognitive activities negative (β=-.243). It suggests that consumers that are averse of cognitive activities are less likely to consume online content. Thus, we found support for H1c, H3c, H4a and H4b.

Table 5 Motive analysis results for eWOM production behavior

	Standardized Coefficients				
	Beta	**Estimate of Std. Error**	**df**	**F**	**Sig.**
Electronic Social Interaction	0.195	0.072	2	7.340	0.001
Self-enhancement	0.403	0.125	2	10.480	0.000
Exhibitionism	0.280	0.115	2	5.900	0.003
Altruism	0.199	0.085	2	5.480	0.005

Table 6 Motive analysis results for eWOM consumption behavior

	Standardized Coefficients				
	Beta	**Estimate of Std. Error**	**df**	**F**	**Sig.**
Electronic Social Interaction	0.427	0.061	2	48.387	0.000
Altruism	0.297	0.063	3	22.089	0.000
Need for Intellectual Engagement	0.169	0.056	4	9.120	0.000
Aversion of Cognitive Activities	-0.243	0.059	2	17.152	0.000

Analysis of Motive Importance for eWOM Forwarding Behavior

Regression coefficients to analyze the importance of motives on forwarding behavior were calculated by taking altruism, electronic social interaction and exhibitionism as independent variables. The regression function was highly significant ($p<0.001$) and explained 65% of forwarding behavior. To test multicollinearity, VIFs were calculated for independent variables as 1/Tolerance. The highest VIF value was 1.29. Thus, we can conclude that multicollinearity was not a problem with this model. Standardized regression coefficients were positive and significant ($p<0.001$) for two of the three variables. We failed to find any significant effect of altruism with eWOM forwarding behavior ($\beta=.241$, $p>0.05$). By far, the strongest motive for forwarding online content is exhibitionism ($\beta=.485$), followed by electronic social interaction ($\beta=.36$) (Table 7). Thus, we had support for H3b, H5b but not for H1b.

SOLUTIONS AND RECOMMENDATIONS

The review of existing literature indicated that almost none is known about the motivators of eWOM communication on oSNSs. The current study supplies an empirical contribution through conceptualizing, and verifying, a model of the motivators of eWOM production, consumption and forwarding motivators of oSNS users. Moreover, the study identifies the prediction power of each variable for different behavior. In this sense, the findings of significant links between such factors and consumers' intention of engagement of eWOM provide useful insights for both theory and practice.

Table 7 Motive analysis results for eWOM forwarding behavior

	Standardized Coefficients				
	Beta	**Estimate of Std. Error**	**df**	**F**	**Sig.**
Electronic Social Interaction	0.360	0.102	3	12.407	0.000
Exhibitionism	0.485	0.100	3	23.415	0.000
Altruism	0.241	0.169	1	2.031	0.155

Theoretical Implications

This research fulfills an identified need to understand the motivating factors of oSNS users to engage in eWOM behavior. To our knowledge, online SNSs are studied for the first time in the context of eWOM. There are other studies concerning oSNSs, and most of them focused on motives to use (Bolar, 2009; Cheung, Chiu & Lee, 2010; Kim, Sohn & Choi, 2011; Kraeuter et al., 2011; Lin & Lu, 2010; Peeling et al., 2009).

Results of the study are one of the contributions to the marketing literature. Results show that, self-enhancement, exhibitionism, altruism and electronic social interaction are motivating factors, in sequence of power, for producing eWOM on oSNSs. Furthermore, consumption behavior of eWOM is motivated by electronic social interaction, altruism and need for intellectual engagement, from strongest to weakest. Aversion of cognitive activities appeared as the least strong variable, with a negative regression coefficient, suggesting that it decreases the motivation of content consumption. What is more, exhibitionism and electronic social interaction are found two motivators of forwarding electronic content. There is no support found for altruism acting as a motivator for forwarding eWOM. Production, consumption and forwarding equations of regression indicate that the factors studied explain 67 per cent, 49 per cent and 65 per cent of behavior, respectively.

It is not surprising to realize that electronic social interaction is a strong motive for all three types of eWOM engagement behavior. Sun and associates (2006) reached a similar conclusion, stating that internet social connection is a motive for online forwarding in their study of WOM in the context of music-related communication. Also, evidence from WOM literature supports the idea that consumers are often driven by the need for social interaction in publishing their experiences on online forums (Hennig-Thurau et al., 2004), engaging in eWOM production. In addition to results of previous studies, this study found that electronic social interaction is the strongest motive for eWOM consumption behavior, meaning that people with more strong ties and more desire to get connected are driven by this motive.

It is not expected to find altruism having no effect on eWOM forwarding behavior. It is found that altruistic people are likely to engage in production and consumption of content but do not have any concern for forwarding. They post the content for others to see, furthermore they read others' posts, but do not have any action for forwarding. They keep the information for themselves. This result may stem from the characteristics of altruistic people in Turkey. They may prefer to post what they read in their own account, in that way they share the information, but not forward to others.

Introduction of exhibitionism as a motivating factor of eWOM is considered as another contribution of this research to the marketing literature. Literature review reveals that exhibitionism is not a much studied construct in marketing, although it may imply much for the subjects of marketing. The two studies encountered were by Pollay (1983), in advertising appeals, and Schmitt (1999) in social image and brand relationship. In our study, regression analysis indicated that exhibitionism is a significant and one of the strongest motives to predict production and forwarding of eWOM communication. The results are consistent with the nature of exhibitionism. People exhibitionist in nature like to display their self to public with the aim of perceived to be smart, to gain status, or for any other inherent reason. Production and forwarding of eWOM communication about products/brands or companies could be the ways to display how smart they are.

Another theoretical contribution of this research is the investigation of eWOM in three dimensions. Producing, communicating and forwarding of eWOM were treated as different behavior, and motivating factors of each behavior were investigated separately. There are other studies, investigating eWOM in two dimensions (e.g., Mowen et al., 2007; Phelps et al., 2004; Wu & Sukoco, 2010), but to our knowledge, it is the first time that the motivating factors are studied for three different dimensions of eWOM.

Managerial Implications

As eWOM is a conversation between two parties, there is a need to understand the motivations in order to practice it successfully as a marketing strategy.

eWOM is a valuable tool for digital marketers to promote the brand, product or company in digital channels. For digital marketers, understanding what kind of people are the prime candidates for eWOM communication is particularly pertinent in terms of targeted marketing efforts and marketing communication strategy. In that way, resources are used more effectively and it leads to achievement of objectives. The results of the study provide the comprehensive account of user's eWOM communication motives.

eWOM communication starts with production. Brand advocates are the most potential group for eWOM production. Results of the study reveal that self-enhancement and exhibitionism are two of the potential motivations for eWOM production. Therefore, those people can be cultivated by meeting their need for self-enhancement and exhibitionism. Asking for their feelings/experiences about the brand/product as a company may further bolster their self, and make them feel smart and gain prestige.

Electronic social interaction is another motivational factor for eWOM production. It indicates that people with more online contacts and strong ties have a greater likelihood of engaging both eWOM production and forwarding. This construct is interrelated with altruism in a way that people with strong ties have a greater tendency to warn others of bad experiences or to help others with positive experiences by producing content. The implication for online marketing practitioners for these motives is to give active people, with high number of connections on oSNSs, a reason for eWOM initiation. Stating a good reason why company's brand should be used, or a problem that the brand could solve may be the starting point.

Consumption of online content is another step that has to be taken, in addition to production, for forwarding content. According to results of the study, consumption of eWOM is motivated by the need to help others, need for intellectual engagement and strong online ties. Thus, people who enjoy intellectually demanding activities should be the target of companies for eWOM consumption. Approaching these people with information that requires an intellectual effort (Cacioppo and Petty, 1982) or asking them for a solution of a complex problem (Cacioppo and Petty, 1982) may be two suggestions to engage these people to eWOM. Furthermore, people with high number of contacts should also be targeted for content consumption.

FUTURE RESEARCH DIRECTIONS

Besides contributions to marketing literature this study also has limitations. The first limitation of this study is that it examines the possible relationships between personal characteristics and eWOM behavior of Turkish social media users. There may be differences between consumers from other cultures and Turkey. Future research should explore whether there are any important differences in motivating factors of oSNSs users in different cultural contexts. This will not only diversify the implications about eWOM communication but also help marketers to target oSNS users more effectively. Another limitation is that this study only discovers the motivating personal characteristics of oSNSs' users. The users of blogs and other media can have different motivators for the production, forwarding and consumption of eWOM. This area needs to be explored in this context. Only six constructs are investigated as motivators in this study. Further research is required to advance these findings with exploring new motivators for eWOM engagement.

CONCLUSION

In conclusion, we have identified six constructs that appear to motivate users of oSNSs' for eWOM communication. We found that there are different motivational factors that cause people to initiate, consume and forward online content. There are still gaps that need to be fulfilled in the context of eWOM communication. It is sure that these are not the only variables of motivation. More needs to be understood about the other motivators and differences between the different cultural contexts. We have provided some initial directions for future research. We hope that our key findings will be helpful and be expanded with future research.

REFERENCES

Amichai-Hamburger, Y., Kaynar, O., & Fine, A. (2007). The effects of need for cognition on Internet use. *Computers in Human Behavior*, *23*(1), 880–891. doi:10.1016/j.chb.2006.03.002

Anderson, E. W. (1998). Customer satisfaction and word of mouth. *Journal of Service Research*, *1*(August), 5–17. doi:10.1177/109467059800100102

Andreassen, T. W., & Streukens, S. (2009). Service innovation and electronic word-of-mouth: Is it worth listening to? *Managing Service Quality*, *19*(3), 249–265. doi:10.1108/09604520910955294

Arndt, J. (1967). The role of product related conversasions in the diffusion of a new product. *JMR, Journal of Marketing Research*, *4*(3), 291–295. doi:10.2307/3149462

Barker, V. (2009). Older adolescents' motivations for social network site use: The influence of gender, group identity, and collective self-esteem. *Cyberpsychology & Behavior*, *12*(2), 209–213. doi:10.1089/cpb.2008.0228 PMID:19250021

Batson, C. D. (1994). Why act for the public good? Four answers. *Personality and Social Psychology Bulletin*, *20*(5), 603–610. doi:10.1177/0146167294205016

Baumeister, R. F. (1998). The Self. In S. Giblert, T. Fiske, & G. Lindzey (Eds.), *The Handbook of Social Psychology* (Vol. 1, pp. 680–740). NJ: John Wiley & Sons.

Belk, R. W. (1988). Possessions and the extended self. *The Journal of Consumer Research*, *15*(2), 139–168. doi:10.1086/209154

Berger, J., & Heath, C. (2007). Where consumers diverge from others: Identity signaling and product domains. *The Journal of Consumer Research*, *34*(2), 121–134. doi:10.1086/519142

Berger, J., & Schwartz, E. (2011). What drives immediate and ongoing wordof- mouth? *JMR, Journal of Marketing Research, 48*(5), 869–880. doi:10.1509/jmkr.48.5.869

Bolar, K. P. (2009). Motives behind the use of social networking sites: An empirical study. *The ICFAI Journal of Management Research, 8*(1), 75–84.

Bourdieu, P., & Wacquant, L. (1992). *An invitation to reflexive sociology*. Chicago: University of Chicago Press.

Boyd, D. M., & Ellison, N. B. (2008). Social network sites: Definition, history, and scholarship. *Journal of Computer-Mediated Communication, 13*(1), 210–230. doi:10.1111/j.1083-6101.2007.00393.x

Brown, J. J., & Reingen, P. H. (1987). Social ties and word-of-mouth referral behavior. *The Journal of Consumer Research, 14*(3), 350–362. doi:10.1086/209118

Bruyn, A., & Lilien, G. L. (2008). A multi-stage of word of mouth influence through viral marketing. *International Journal of Research in Marketing, 25*(3), 151–163. doi:10.1016/j.ijresmar.2008.03.004

Cacioppo, J. T., & Petty, R. E. (1982). The need for cognition. *Journal of Personality and Social Psychology, 42*(1), 116–131. doi:10.1037/0022-3514.42.1.116

Cheung, C. M. K., Chui, P. Y., & Lee, M. K. O. (2011). Online social networks: Why do students use facebook? *Computers in Human Behavior, 27*(4), 1337–1343. doi:10.1016/j.chb.2010.07.028

Chevalier, J. A., & Mayzlin, D. (2006). The Effect of Word-of-Mouth on sales: Online book reviews. *JMR, Journal of Marketing Research, 43*(3), 345–354. doi:10.1509/jmkr.43.3.345

Chu, S. C., & Kim, Y. (2011). Determinants of consumer engagement in electronic word-of-mouth (eWOM) in social networking sites. *International Journal of Advertising, 30*(1), 47–75. doi:10.2501/IJA-30-1-047-075

Chung, C., & Darke, P. (2006). The consumer as advocate: Self-relevance, culture, and word-of-mouth. *Marketing Letters, 17*(4), 269–279. doi:10.1007/s11002-006-8426-7

Churchill, G. A. (1991). *Marketing research: Methodological foundations* (5th ed.). USA: Dryden Press.

Czepiel, J. A. (1974). Word-of-mouth process in the diffusion process of a major technological innovation. *JMR, Journal of Marketing Research, 11*(2), 172–180. doi:10.2307/3150555

De Angelis, M., Bonezzi, A., Peluso, A. M., Rucker, D. D., & Costabile, M. (2012, August). On braggards and gossip: A self-enhancement account of word-of-mouth generation and transmission. *JMR, Journal of Marketing Research, XLXI*(4), 551–563. doi:10.1509/jmr.11.0136

DeBruyn, A., & Lilien, G. L. (2008). A multistage model of word-of-mouth influence through viral marketing. *International Journal of Research in Marketing, 25*(3), 151–163. doi:10.1016/j.ijresmar.2008.03.004

Dellarocas, C., & Narayan, R. (2006). A statistical measure of a population's propensity to engage in post-purchase online word-of-mouth. *Statistical Science, 21*(2), 277–285. doi:10.1214/088342306000000169

Dichter, E. (1966). How word of mouth advertising works. *Harvard Business Review, 44*(6), 147–166.

Dierkes, E., Bichler, M., & Krishnan, R. (2011). Estimating the effect of word of mouth on churn and cross buying decisions in the mobile phone market with markov logic networks. *Decision Support Systems*, *51*(3), 361–371. doi:10.1016/j.dss.2011.01.002

Ellison, N. B., Steinfield, C., & Lampe, C. (2007). The benefit of Facebook friends: Capital and college students use of online social network sites. *Journal of Computer-Mediated Communication*, *12*(4), 1143–1168. doi:10.1111/j.1083-6101.2007.00367.x

Engel, J. F., Blackwell, R. D., & Miniard, P. W. (1993). *Consumer behavior* (8th ed.). Fort Worth: Dryden-Press.

Engel, J. F., Kegerris, R. J., & Blackwell, R. D. (1969). Word of mouth communication by the innovator. *Journal of Marketing*, *33*(3), 15–19. doi:10.2307/1248475

Fiske, S. T. (2001), Five core social motives, plus or minus five, In S. Spencer, S. Fein, M. Zanna & J. Olsen (Eds.), *Motivated Social Perception: The Ontario Symposium*, vol.9, Psychology Press.

Foster, M. K., Francescucci, A., & West, B. C. (2010). Why users participate in online social networks. *International Journal of Business and Management*, *4*(1), 3–19.

Godes, D., & Mayzlin, D. (2004). Using online conversations to study word-of-mouth communications. *Marketing Science*, *23*(4), 545–560. doi:10.1287/mksc.1040.0071

Grubb, E. L., & Grathwohl, H. L. (1967). Consumer self-concept, symbolism and marketing behavior: A theoretical approach. *Journal of Marketing*, *31*(4), 22–27. doi:10.2307/1249461

Gupta, P., & Harris, J. (2010). How eWOM recommandations influence product consideration and quality of choice: A motivation to process information perspective. *Journal of Business Research*, *63*(9-10), 1041–1049. doi:10.1016/j.jbusres.2009.01.015

Hair, J. F., Black, W. C., Babin, B. B., & Anderson, R. E. (2006). *Multivariate data analysis*. New Jersey: Prentice Hall.

Hansen, S. S., & Lee, J. K. (2013). What drives consumers to pass along marketer generated eWOM in social network games? Social and game factors. *Journal of Theoretical And Applied Electronic Commerce*, *8*(1), 53–68.

Harris, J., & Gupta, P. (2008). You Should Buy This One! The Influences of Online Reccomandations on Product Attitudes and Choice Confidence. *Journal of Electronic Marketing and Retailing*, *2*(2), 176–189. doi:10.1504/IJEMR.2008.019816

Hennig-Thurau, T., Gwinner, K. P., Walsh, G., & Gremler, D. D. (2004, Winter). Electronic word-of-mouth via consumer opinion platforms: What motivates consumers to articulate themselves on the Internet. *Journal of Interactive Marketing*, *18*(1), 38–52. doi:10.1002/dir.10073

Ho, J. Y. C., & Dempsey, M. (2010). Viral marketing: Motivations to forward online content. *Journal of Business Research*, *63*(9-10), 1000–1006. doi:10.1016/j.jbusres.2008.08.010

Holbrook, M. B. (2001). The millennial consumer in the texts of our times: Exhibitionism. *Journal of Macromarketing*, *21*(1), 81–95. doi:10.1177/0276146701211008

Hollenbaugh, E. E. (2011). Motives for maintaining personal journal blogs. *Cyberpsychology, Behavior, and Social Networking*, *14*(1-2), 13–20. doi:10.1089/cyber.2009.0403 PMID:21329438

Hsu, Y., & Tran, T. H. C. (2013). Social relationship factors influence on eWOM behaviors in social networking sites: an empirical study: Taiwan and Vietnam. *International Journal of Business. Human Technology*, *3*(3), 22–31.

Huang, M., Cai, F., Tsang, A. S. L., & Zhou, N. (2011). Making online voice loud: The critical role of WOM information. *European Journal of Marketing*, *45*(7/8), 1277–1297. doi:10.1108/03090561111137714

Ipsos, O. T. X. Ipsos Global @dvisor Survey (2012, June 26). *Socialogue*. Retrieved from http://www.ipsos-na.com/news-polls/pressrelease.aspx?id=5671

Jalilvand, M. R., Esfahani, S. S., & Samiei, N. (2011). Electronic word-of-mouth: Challenges and opportunities. *Procedia Computer Science*, *3*, 42–46. doi:10.1016/j.procs.2010.12.008

Jeong, E., Cheong, S., & Jang, S. (2011). Restaurant experiences triggering positive electronic word of mouth (eWOM) motivations. *International Journal of Hospitality Management*, *30*(2), 356–366. doi:10.1016/j.ijhm.2010.08.005

Kaplan, A. M., & Haenlein, M. (2011). Two hearts in three-quarter time: How to waltz the social media/viral marketing dance. *Business Horizons*, *54*(3), 253–263. doi:10.1016/j.bushor.2011.01.006

Keller, E. (2007). Unleashing the power of word of mouth: Creating brand advocacy to drive growth. *Journal of Advertising Research*, *47*(4), 448–452. doi:10.2501/S0021849907070468

Kim, B. (2011). Understanding antecedents of continuance intention in social-networking services. *Cyberpsychology, Behavior, and Social Networking*, *14*(4), 199–205. doi:10.1089/cyber.2010.0009 PMID:21192764

Kim, Y., Sohn, D., & Choi, S. M. (2011). Cultural difference in motivations for using social network sites: A comparative study of American and Korean college students. *Computers in Human Behavior*, *27*(1), 365–372. doi:10.1016/j.chb.2010.08.015

Kleine, S. S., Kleine, R. E., & Allen, C. T. (1995, December). How is a possession 'me' or 'not me?' characterizing types and an antecedent of material possession attachment. *The Journal of Consumer Research*, *22*(3), 327–343. doi:10.1086/209454

Kollock, P. (1999). The economies of online cooperation: Gifts, and public goods in cyberspace. In M. A. Smith & P. Kollock (Eds.), *Communities in Cyberspace* (pp. 220–239). New York: Routledge.

Kozinets, R. V., Valck, K., Wojnicki, A. C., & Wilner, S. J. S. (2010). Networked narratives: Understanding word-of-mouth marketing in online communities. *Journal of Marketing*, *74*(2), 71–89. doi:10.1509/jmkg.74.2.71

Kraeuter, S. G., & Waiguny, M. (2011). *Why users stay in online social networks: Perceptions of value, trust, subjective norm, and the moderating influence of duration of use. 11th AMA Winter Educators' Conference, Winter 2011*. Chicago: American Marketing Association.

Lampel, J., & Bhalla, A. (2007). The role of status seeking in online communities: Giving the gift of experience. *Journal of Computer-Mediated Communication, 12*(2), 434–455. doi:10.1111/j.1083-6101.2007.00332.x

Lee, K. T., & Koo, D. M. (2013). Effects of Attribute and Valence of eWOM on message adaptation: Moderating roles of subjective knowledge and regulatory focus. *Computers in Human Behavior, 28*(5), 1974–1984. doi:10.1016/j.chb.2012.05.018

Levy, S. J. (1959, July-August). Symbols for sale. *Harvard Business Review, 37*, 117–124.

Lin, C. H., Lee, S. H., & Horng, D. J. (2011). The effects of online reviews on purchasing intention: The moderating role of need for cognition. *Social Behavior and Personality, 39*(1), 71–82. doi:10.2224/sbp.2011.39.1.71

Lin, K. Y., & Lu, H. P. (2011). Why people use social networking sites: An empirical study integrating network externalities and motivations theory. *Computers in Human Behavior, 27*(3), 1152–1161. doi:10.1016/j.chb.2010.12.009

Liu, Y. (2006). Word-of-mouth for movies: Its dynamics and impact on box office revenue. *Journal of Marketing, 70*(3), 74–89. doi:10.1509/jmkg.70.3.74

McCracken, G. (1986). Culture and consumption: A theoretical account of the structure: A theoretical account of the structure and movement of the cultural meaning of consumer goods. *The Journal of Consumer Research, 13*(1), 71–84. doi:10.1086/209048

Mowen, J. C., Park, S., & Zablah, A. (2007). Toward a theory of motivation and personality with application to word-of-mouth communications. *Journal of Business Research, 60*(6), 590–596. doi:10.1016/j.jbusres.2006.06.007

Murray, K. B. (1997). A test for services marketing theory: Consumer information acquisition activities. *Journal of Marketing, 55*(1), 10–25. doi:10.2307/1252200

Neter, J., Wasserman, W., & Kutner, M. H. (1985). *Applied linear statistical models: Regression, analysis of variance, and experimental design*. Homewood: Irwin.

Peeling, E. L., & White, K. M. (2009). The theory of planned behavior applied to young people's use of social networking web sites. *Cyberpsychology & Behavior, 12*(2), 755–759. doi:10.1089/cpb.2009.0109 PMID:19788377

Pereira, P.A., Irene, C., Medina, G., Fabiola, Z., Romo, G., & Contreras-Espinosa, R.S. (2014). The importance of Facebook as an online social networking tool for companies. *International Journal of Accounting & Information Management, 22* (4).

Pescher, C., Reichhart, P., & Spann, M. (2014). Consumer decision-making processes in mobile viral marketing campaigns. *Journal of Interactive Marketing, 28*(1), 43–54. doi:10.1016/j.intmar.2013.08.001

Phelps, J. E., Lewis, R., Mobilio, L., & Perry, D. (2004, December). Viral marketing or electronic word-of-mouth advertising: Examining consumer responses and motivations to pass along e-mail. *Journal of Advertising Research, 44*(4), 333–348.

Pollay, R. W. (1983). Measuring the cultural values manifest in advertising. In J. H. Leigh & C. R. Martin Jr., (Eds.), *Current Issues and Research in Advertising* (pp. 72–92). Ann Arbor, MI: Graduate School of Business, Division of Research, University of Michigan.

Quinton, S., & March, S. H. (2010). Relationships in online communities. *Journal of Research in Interactive Marketing*, *4*(1), 59–73. doi:10.1108/17505931011033560

Raskin, R., & Terry, H. (1988). A principal-components analysis of the narcissisti personality inventory and further evidence of its construct validity. *Journal of Personality and Social Psychology*, *54*(5), 890–902. doi:10.1037/0022-3514.54.5.890 PMID:3379585

Richins, M. L. (1983). Negative word-of-mouth by dissatisfied consumers: A pilot study. *Journal of Marketing*, *47*(1), 68–78. doi:10.2307/3203428

Richins, M. L., & Root-Shaffer, T. (1988). The role of involvement and opinion leadership in consumer word of mouth: An implicit made explicit. *Advances in Consumer Research. Association for Consumer Research (U. S.)*, *15*(1), 32–36.

Riesman, D., Glazer, N., & Denney, R. (1961). *The lonely crowd: A study of the changing American character*. New Haven, CT: Yale University Press.

Robert, L. P. Jr, Dennis, A. R., & Ahuja, M. K. (2008). Social capital and knowledge integration in digitally enabled teams. *Information Systems Research*, *19*(3), 314–334. doi:10.1287/isre.1080.0177

Rogers, T. B., Kuiper, N. A., & Kirker, W. S. (1977). Self-reference and the encoding of personal information. *Journal of Personality and Social Psychology*, *35*(9), 677–688. doi:10.1037/0022-3514.35.9.677 PMID:909043

Sachse, S. B., & Mangold, S. (2011). Brand equity dilution through negative online word-of-mouth communication. *Journal of Retailing and Consumer Services*, *18*(1), 38–45. doi:10.1016/j.jretconser.2010.09.003

Schmitt, B. H. (1999). *Experiential marketing: How to get customers to sense, feel, think, act, and relate to your company and brands. NewYork.* Free Press.

Scott, C. A., & Tybout, A. M. (1981). Theoretical perspectives on the impact of negative information: Does valence matter? *Advances in Consumer Research. Association for Consumer Research (U. S.)*, *8*, 408–409.

Sirgy, M. J. (1982). Self-concept in consumer behavior: A critical review. *The Journal of Consumer Research*, *9*(3), 287–300. doi:10.1086/208924

Stefanone, M. A., Lackaff, D., & Rosen, D. (2011). Contingencies of self-worth and social networking site behavior. *Cyberpsychology, Behavior, and Social Networking*, *14*(1-2), 41–49. doi:10.1089/cyber.2010.0049 PMID:21329442

Steffes, E. M., & Burgee, L. E. (2009). Social ties and online word of mouth. *Internet Research*, *19*(1), 42–59. doi:10.1108/10662240910927812

Subramani, M. R., & Rajagopalan, B. (2003). Knowledge Sharing and Influence in Online Social Networks Via Viral Marketing. *Communications of the ACM*, *46*(12), 300–307. doi:10.1145/953460.953514

Sun, T., Youn, Y., Wu, G., & Kuntaraporn, M. (2006). Online word-of-mouth (or mouse): An exploration of its antecedents and consequences. *Journal of Computer-Mediated Communication*, *11* (4). Retrieved from http://jcmc.indiana,edu/vol11/issue4/sun.html

Sundaram, D. S., Mitra, K., & Webster, C. (1998). Word of mouth communications: A motivational analysis. *Advances in Consumer Research. Association for Consumer Research (U. S.)*, *25*, 527–531.

Taylor, D. G. (2010). *I speak, therefore I am: Identity and self-construction as motivation to engage in electronic word of mouth.* (Unpublished doctoral dissertation). University of North Texas.

Taylor, D. G., Strutton, D., & Thompson, K. (2012). Self-enhancement as a motivation for sharing online advertisement. *Journal of Interactive Advertising*, *12*(2), 13–28. doi:10.1080/15252019.2012.10722193

Tuten, T., & Bosnjak, M. (2001). Understanding differences in web usage: The role of need for cognition and the five factor model of personality. *Social Behavior and Personality: An International Journal*, *29*(4), 391–398. doi:10.2224/sbp.2001.29.4.391

Wojnicki, A. C. (2006). Word-of-mouth and word-of-web: Talking about products, talking about me. *Advances in Consumer Research. Association for Consumer Research (U. S.)*, *33*(1), 573–575.

Wojnicki, A.C., & Godes, D. (2008). Word-of-mouth as self-enhancement. *Social Science Research Network*. Retrieved from http://ssrn.com/paper=908999

Wolny, J., & Mueller, C. (2013). Analysis of fashion consumers' motives to engage in electronic word-of-mouth communication through social media. *Journal of Marketing Management*, *29*(5-6), 562–583. doi:10.1080/0267257X.2013.778324

Wright, P. (1974, October). The harassed decision maker: Time pressures, distractions, and use of evidence. *The Journal of Applied Psychology*, *59*(5), 555–561. doi:10.1037/h0037186

Wu, W., & Sukoco, B. M. (2010, Summer). Why should I share? Examining consumers' motives and trust on knowledge sharing. *Journal of Computer Information Systems*, 11–19.

Zhang, J. Q., Craciun, G., & Shin, D. (2010). When does electronic word-of-mouth matter? A study of consumer product reviews. *Journal of Business Research*, *63*(12), 1336–1341. doi:10.1016/j.jbusres.2009.12.011

KEY TERMS AND DEFINITIONS

Electronic Word of Mouth: Sharing of information about consumers' experiences, idea, thoughts on marketing offerings with each other via electronic channels.

Exhibitionism: A personality trait to display self to public with the aim of perceived to be smart, intelligent in order to gain status, or for any other inherent reason.

Online Social Networks: A web based platform to form social relationships among people who have similar interests, activities, backgrounds or real-life connections.

Personal Characteristics: Distinguishing qualities or traits of an individual that shapes the person in question.

Social Media: Tools, mostly computer-mediated, that allow people to create user generated content, share or exchange experiences, information, idea, pictures and videos with each other in virtual networks.

ENDNOTES

1 Social capital is defined as "the sum of the resources, actual or virtual, that accrue to an individual or a group by virtue of possessing a durable network of more or less institutionalized relationships of mutual acquaintance and recognition" (Bourdieu and Wacquant 1992, p 14).

2 Examining the definitions, it may be difficult to distinguish between exhibitionism and self-enhancement. The main difference between two is that exhibitionism harbors a feeling of narcissism (Raskin & Terry, 1988), something inside the person; while self enhancement asks for status seeking, gain attention, show connoisseurship, something person wants others to see.

Chapter 6
Motivations behind Becoming a Blogger and Their Business Implications:
The Case of Fashion

Anne-Flore Maman Larraufie
SemioConsult, France & ESSEC, France

Fabien Sommer
INSEEC, France

ABSTRACT

This chapter takes fashion blogs as a case to explain motivations behind becoming a blogger and then to keep being one on the long-term. It wraps up past research findings before presenting the result of an original study conducted recently with authors of successful blogs as interviewees. It presents the typology of motivations but also the nature of potential brand-blogger relationships. Understanding such points is key to successfully use blogs as part of a useful WoM communication strategy. Findings generalizable across other sectors of activity conclude the chapter.

INTRODUCTION

They [Fashion bloggers] are not passing themselves off as journalists. Instead, they're brand stars whose voices are subjective to what they do or don't like at the moment — often times dependent on which companies will pay them the most. (WDD, 12-06-2014)

Around 2,000 news blogs would be created each year, on the French blogosphere only. Their authors can earn up to 20,000€ per month thanks to a range of side activities bringing them notoriety and hence revenue. They have completely reframed the fashion universe. As a proof, some bloggers have been the target of legal cases, with Vogue or Glamour suing them for a breach of competitive fairness… Their

DOI: 10.4018/978-1-4666-9449-1.ch006

importance and influence is no more discussed and they are now active components of marketing and image campaigns conducted by brands. As we will see later on in this chapter, their influence on their readers is also very important and the content of their blog is subject to word-of-mouth. According to a recent Novius study, 2.3 billions of people have accessed the Internet in 2012-2013. 1.5 billion among them are social media users, 30% more than in 2011. 77% of Internet users acknowledge reading blogs. This e-trend is particularly true in the fashion sector, with fashion brands embracing the web 2.0 and fashion bloggers influencing others or even brands themselves. The nature of a blog is intrinsically connected to word-of-mouth, and their authors are acknowledged as potential influencers, due to their status of credible opinion leaders. They catch stylists' attention, and are offered front-row seats during the catwalks (Corcoran, 2010). Hence their potential business interest is recognized and the word-of-mouth they initiate is more and more catching marketers' attention, for high-street brands or for luxury ones. It is a recognized fact in the psychology community (practitioners & academics) that human beings have a tendency to believe people just like them (Cialdini, 2007). This is particularly true in cultures displaying a low level of power-distance in Hofstede's five dimensions model to classify and specify cultures. In France, for instance, (ranking average on the dimension) it is quite expectant. Besides, the principle of homophily (Dennen & Myers, 2012) explains the interpersonal virtual bound between a blogger and his/her readers: human beings tend to gather with people who share their interests, beliefs, education, gender and social status, creating more or less long-lasting bonds with them. Trusting bloggers and engaging in some kind of relationship with them, they are likely to act as spokespersons and spread the word around the blog content. This is the definition of word-of-mouth, indeed.

This chapter aims at providing readers with both theoretical and practical knowledge on the blogosphere, taking as a case for observation the fashion sector. It is organized in three parts. The first one summarizes the importance of blogs in the fashion system and presents the state of knowledge accumulated by academic research on fashion bloggers, especially regarding their profiles. The second part presents the findings of a recent and original study conducted in-between January and June 2014, aiming at deciphering the hidden motivations for fashion bloggers to engage in their blogging activity. This exploratory study has been conducted through qualitative research, using semi-structured interview as a data collection method (14 interviewees, carefully chosen for their representativeness). Data has been analyzed using content analysis. The third and last part deals with managerial takeaway, making clear for practitioners how they can reuse the knowledge presented on fashion bloggers' motivations to cleverly take advantage of it and to avoid pitfalls, especially when trying to get in touch with them. It points out specifically the traits that are not exclusive to fashion, to make the chapter useful for non-fashion-oriented business people.

BACKGROUND: THE PLACE OF BLOGS IN THE FASHION SECTOR

Defining Blogs and Fashion Blogs

The word 'blog' comes from the contraction of the words web and log. It stands for specific websites on which individuals write to express their thoughts, on a regular basis (Detterbeck, LaMoreaux, & Sciangula, 2012). They usually follow a chronological display and may include texts, videos, pictures and sounds. Such media offers a two-way communication process (Zhang, 2010) as readers are usually invited to react through comments in dedicated areas. The blog audience is the guarantor of the blog image, and the more qualitative it sounds, the more important it becomes in the so-called blogosphere. Blogs usually focus on one topic, such as sports, fashion, or politics (Detterbeck et al., 2012).

A key moment in the history of digital fashion came with the creation of the first fashion blogs in the early XXIst century. *Nogoodform* was launched among the first, in 2003.

Fashion blogs can be of three types (A. Marwick, 2011; Rocamora, 2011):

1. a personal-style blog, close to the author's photo album concerning his/her clothing habits;
2. a conservative blog, which displays the author's opinion on fashion products, fashion trends, or on the last catwalks;
3. a street-style blog, gathering pictures shot in the street by the author, showing other people's fashion style and outfit.

In order to become 'useful', a blog must pay attention to several key parameters (Fandrich, 2007). The most essential one is its content, which should raise readers' interest. Besides, blogs should be unconventional, if not disruptive; this second parameter enables them to create a differentiated world from traditional fashion magazines. Lastly, immediacy is vital: a blog should be able to be the first to provide criticisms and reports on fashion developments (Fandrich, 2007). Fashion itself is based on fast-paced changes. Indeed, content exclusivity and newness lead to immediacy.

On top of usefulness, authenticity is necessary for fashion blogs to be considered qualitative by their readers (A. Marwick, 2011). This feature is what differentiates them from mainstream blogs. To sound authentic, fashion bloggers should be accessible and engage with their readers by answering questions, paying attention to their tweets, etc. They are simultaneously addicted to fashion while caring about their readers.

The Place of Blogs in the Fashion and Digital Universes

Around twenty million fashion blogs were counted in 2013 on the blogosphere. This makes such type of blogs the most numerous one. Millions of readers follow them on a daily basis. Their authors have gained more and more weight, turning from simple opinion-sharers into real opinion-leaders (Mendoza, 2010). People seek for their advice, as fashion and style are factors which can lead to social group acceptance or rejection (Kaner, 2013). Thus, fashion bloggers act in some way as private style consultants.

Their existence cannot be ignored, given the sustainable and long-term impact they have on the fashion industry (Fandrich, 2007). They are an intrinsic component of the so-called fast-fashion industry: with fast collections roll-out comes fast-reactions and comments. Blogs would have a direct impact on fashion consumption, acting as indirect advertising and triggers for purchase (A. Marwick, 2011).

Some bloggers have been raised to the status of **fashion brand ambassadors** by their readers, and brands now court them like they court Hollywood stars. Some brands even use them as inspiration sources and display them on pieces of garment (Manga, 2011). Chanel has casted Peony Lim in an ad campaign and Louis Vuitton has tapped Kristina Bazan for its Gstaad opening (see: http://fashionpost.jp/archives/11938?lang=en) .

Besides this opportunistic re-use of bloggers, brands find other business interests in this unusual communication tool:

1. Blogs are a **segmentation tool**. As previously stated, blogs deal with specific topics, and only interested Internet users read them. Therefore, a psychographic segmentation based on audience-interests is automatically done (Mendoza, 2010). Fashion brands active on such blogs are certain to reach a pre-defined target. It has thus become key for them to identify the relevant bloggers, consistent with their brand and corporate image (Zhang, 2010). This is particularly important as a recent study has shown that 40% of consumers say that they use blogs among the top three sources of information to decide upon a purchase (Source: Fashionbi, 2014).
2. Blogs are **new marketing tools**.
   a. Blogs are **market research tools**. Fashion brands use them to **listen to the market**, especially to its reactions to new product introduction, etc. Influent bloggers are invited in the brands' showrooms to grasp new collections and to quickly write about them. Readers' comments are a good way to pre-assess the success or failure of this collection (Zhang, 2010).
   b. Blogs are **communication tools**. Some fashion brands use them as media support for their communication campaign. They buy advertising space on qualitative blogs. For example, American Apparel is used to doing so on Garance Doré's blog, "The Sartorialist". With 10,000 impressions a day, it is a cost-efficient communication tool (Zhang, 2010). For smaller brands, it is even the cheapest way to get good and large exposure and to enhance brand awareness.
   c. Fashion blogs are a **brand image-building tool**. They help brands display a human face (Hill, 2005). The values of authenticity, transparence and honesty are transferred to the brands, through a mental association effect. Besides, they affect the brand reputation and brand awareness. For instance, Mulberry has co-edited a video with Tanya Burr and Jim Chapman showing how the label's bags fit into her daily life (see: http://www.mulberry.com/journal/a-day-in-the-life/). Tanya & Jim are faces consumers can relate to, turning the brand into a more accessible one in the eyes of prospects.
   d. Fashion brands can use blogs to communicate and engage with consumers. Thus, blogs are a **CRM[1]-building tool**, accessible to anyone connected to the Internet.
   e. Blogs are **SEO[2] tools**. They use the proper keywords, and their ongoing content updates ensure high visibility on search engines.

Thus, fashion brands need to attract bloggers and build some long-term relationships with them, based on trust. Fashion bloggers are not celebrity endorsers (who get paid for supporting a brand), nor journalists (who have editing constraints related to the journal they write for, and are used to get press releases). They are neither famous nor professional writers, but can simply be "the guy next door" (Zhang, 2010). As normal people, they gain readers' trust and confidence. Hence, brands need to approach them in a specific way.

There is a real and legitimate questioning around the reason why blogs should be taking into consideration in a digital-driven communication campaign and not only in a PR-driven campaign. A recent study conducted by Fashionbi found that bloggers have in general a larger audience on other social media sites (e.g. Instagram) than traditional online magazines. The reason might be that consumers feel more concerned when images are shared by bloggers instead as when it is text. For instance on Instagram, Chiara Feragni (Italian blogger, blog name *The Blond Salad*) has 2.9 million followers at the time we write this chapter. It is far ahead from all fashion magazines, the closest one being Vogue (2.8 million followers). However, what is even more interesting in the study is the fact that even when following bloggers on Instagram, Facebook or Twitter, 69% of respondents claim they visit the blogs per se at least once a week. We have a real snowballing effect happening here.

Profiles of Fashion Bloggers

Fashion bloggers consider themselves as narcissistic, superficial and disrupting individuals (A. E. Marwick, 2013). They are passionate about fashion and differentiate themselves from the crowd thanks to a distinct 'style'. They first consider themselves as consumers, closely followed by opinion leaders (A. Marwick, 2011).

Detterbeck et al. (2012) conducted a study to understand better their profile. The authors identified a population mainly composed of individuals from 19 to 29 years old, living in big cities or more specifically, where fashion-related information are usually released first. Most of them are women, who find their inspiration in fashion news/trends first, then in everyday life, personal style and entertainment/pop culture. They consider pictures as key sources of information, followed by historical trend information, the Internet, and links to brand sites. They need good-quality sources of such information, which they usually find on the Internet and in the streets, and last in news with the industry professionals.

Bloggers are proud of their blogs and seek large networks to enhance the originality of their blog content. They consider themselves as very distinct from traditional media, for their blogs are interactive, relay the information at a super-speed pace and display independent content thanks to editorial freedom. This is is key to them in order to sound authentic. And, as already stated, authenticity is synonymous with 'power' in the fashion universe.

TOWARDS AN UNDERSTANDING OF THE MOTIVATIONS TO BECOME A FASHION BLOGGER

As the reader must have noticed, even if researchers have been able to identify fashion bloggers' profiles, they have never really tried to uncover the reasons why they once made the decision to engage into the activity, i.e. their motivations.

This is the main concern of the study that is hereafter presented. More specifically, two questions are addressed:

- What are fashion bloggers' motivations to start blogging (the triggers)?
- What are the reasons/factors that make them engage into fashion blogging intensively and extensively (the LT and sustainable engagement in blogging)?

Research Methodology and Method for Analyzing Data

Because nothing is known on the topic, and rough data is needed to decipher the answers to the questions under investigation, qualitative exploratory research sounded the most appropriate. It would actually enable bloggers to share their feelings, attitudes, emotions, hence leading to deeper richness of data compared to quantitative methods (Gordon, 1999). Besides, to get rid of social desirability bias as much as possible, interviewing was more relevant than focus groups.

Interviewed bloggers were theoretically selected according to the following criteria: male and female, 19-39 years old and 'visible' on the blogosphere. Interviews were conducted online, using the chat function of Facebook or another instant messaging interface. Given the digital-nature of the topic under investigation, it was important to use the same medium of communication as the one bloggers are accustomed to. Besides, it was again another way to keep the social desirability bias away as much as possible. All semi-directed interviews were transcribed, with notes on nuances, tone used, etc. (Corbin & Strauss, 2008). They were analyzed right after to refine the next interview guide, using content analysis. The traditional four types of data were identified (Elo & Kyngäs, 2008):

1. General or specific data, easy to check with no need to be proven: informative data, enabling to set the stage of the topic under investigation.
2. Value judgments, opinions, explanations and point of views: deeper data, enabling to get the blogger's real perspective and feelings toward the topic under investigation.
3. Contextual data relative to the blogger's identity: useful data to understand where data expressed in point 2 may come from (personal history or bias) and to clarify whether this is trustable data or the expression of a social construct the blogger would have heard about.
4. Historical data regarding how and when the blog was created: data linked to the blogger's personal trajectory.

Data was collected until the semantic saturation was reached. This happened after seven interviews. Table 1 below summarizes sample data.

Results of the Study: Fashion Bloggers' Motivations and Concerns

With this study, we aimed at answering two basic questions, one related to the triggers to initially start blogging, and the second one dealing with the reasons for sustainable and long-term investment in a blogging activity.

The Four Triggers for the Creation of a Fashion Blog

1. On the Spur of the Moment

Table 1. Sample Characteristics

Blogger	Blog	Age	Gender	Job
Laura	http://www.lauralovesclothes.fr	22	F	Graphic designer
Séverine	http://www.enmodebonheur.fr	24	F	In-house communication agency
Anouck	http://www.enmodebonheur.fr	23	F	Student
Florent-Alexis	http://sodandy.com	28	M	Product manager
Foucaud	http://thefashionweekcoffee.com	26	M	Unemployed
Katia	http://leblogdekatykat.com	26	F	Journalist
Tanya	http://ellecommelui.fr	26	F	Consultant

Creating a blog following a sudden impulse, on the spur of the moment would be the most frequent way of entering the fashion blogging system. It is an unplanned action, without a well-thought strategy and long-term orientation, at least at the beginning. Creating a blog is a true emotion-led behavior, matching a somewhat carefree temper:

In the end little things drove us to open this blog. We did it without getting worked up, in a 'well, let's see what happens' fashion. We did not think the blog would persist over time! (Anouck)

However, this 'impulse' is only a trigger to blog-creation. As Séverine keeps saying, the desire and willingness to engage into fashion blogging have always been here, latently. The difficult point was to jump-in:

Personally I've always been a heavy blog-reader. Mainly with fashion. The other girls as well [Note: Séverine created a blog with other friends of her]. All along the second year of school, it was some kind of a joke, you know. Saying 'we should open a blog [be]cause we go out all the time and like discovering spots,... And we were at journalist school so we thought we were not such bad writers in the end. (Séverine)

2. Take Advantage of

Another trigger for building one's own blog is related to the context. Some authors admit they simply took advantage of a specific happening event, such as the naming of Marseille as European Capital of Culture in 2013 for Séverine and her co-bloggers. Others consider the environment and the piling up of facts as responsible for their becoming of fashion bloggers, as in the case of Foucaud:

I knew how to create websites and I had a cousin, she already had her blog. At the same time, I did a student internship during the Fashion Week, in the backstage of the catwalks. So I thought: why not combing web and fashion. I was already reading a lot of blogs, not necessarily dedicated to fashion because I thought they were more for a feminine audience ... (Foucaud)

Therefore, bloggers should not be taken out of their context: they are 'social animals', as defined by Jean-Jacques Rousseau. The influence that others and the environment have on them is fundamental to the creation of their blog.

3. A Complement to One's Professional Activity

Some authors decided to open their fashion blogs to reinforce and complement their professional activity, especially when not related to fashion. For instance, someone with a professional life in media planning and passionate about fashion might design his/her fashion blog as a natural combined extension of both. This was the case for Kate for instance:

Through this blog I wanted to launch a web-program. I was a radio host, passionate about radio and TV. It's actually a short program, which deals with specific topics, different each time: heels, patterns, how to look young... (Kate)

4. To Fill a Gap and Leave One's Mark

The last trigger is more knowledge-oriented, focused on providing information to other readers and on becoming 'somebody' as an influent person online. Usually, such authors just happened to be once looking for some information on fashion and could not find what they wanted. So they decided to fill-in the gap. This is the case of the 'Sodandy' blog's authors, dedicated to masculine fashion:

GQ was not on the market yet. We had a vision of a man more fashionable, living with his times. We could not find him and street style was booming. So we decided to be the first to write about that. (Florent-Alexis)

Of course, this last trigger is less and less frequently found: with the proliferation of fashion blogs, gaps are harder to identify…

Ongoing Engagement and Sources of Inspiration

As the first part of this chapter recalled, the content is key for a blog to be source of interest and to capture readers' attention. It is a prerequisite to becoming an influent blog within the blogosphere. As explained in the methodological note, this study deliberately selected authors of successful and influential blogs, so it means they have found at least some of the best practices for designing their blog content. Their sources of inspiration are therefore of high importance to brands who want to take advantage of their influence on the Internet in a pull-communication strategy.

Three main sources of inspiration have been identified: fashion and trends in general, catwalks and other fashion events, and other blogs.

1. Fashion & Trends as Muses

In the end, for fashion bloggers, the simplest and most favored source for daily inspiration is made of fashion itself (as a concept) and trends (as a social phenomenon). This is a reason for keeping engaged with one's blog, as both are ontologically dynamic and at the same-time sociologically and historically embedded. Therefore, non-traditional media sources are relevant and appreciated, such as books dedicated to a brand's history, films related to a designer, exhibitions displaying private historical pieces of one Maison[3], etc. For instance, Katia admits not considering anything in fashion without looking back and forth, trying to identify how brands and their iconic products/consumers have shaped the concept of fashion:

I want to grasp a trend origin. I interpret styles in my own way, looking at brands and at new comers in fashion simultaneously. (Katia)

2. The Fever of Fashion Events

Fashion events, and especially the Fashion Weeks and their catwalks are some kind of a drug for fashion bloggers. It makes them write in-between two 'seasons' and provides them with enough material to do so. They particularly feel they have reached the Holy Grail when invited to attend a show. This does not only turn them into fans, but also into brand-believers. Hence, they are the best possible advocates of a brand and ambassador for a designer.

Besides catwalks, appreciated fashion events are open houses, such as LVMH's 'Les journées particulières'.[4] Getting in is often some kind of assault course, so better be an influent invited fashion blogger! Such events enable to build relationships with fashion bloggers, at very limited cost.

3. Blogs Inspire Bloggers

Fashion bloggers are also blog-readers. They admit that they also get inspired by their counterparts in the blogosphere, and by official blogs from the brands. However, they pay attention to the content displayed, and systematically assess its relevance and legitimacy. That helps them understand whether they are reliable sources of information or not:

I've been quite inspired by Zoé Macaron and Tokyo Banhbao, girls who seem authentic and diversify their content. Plus I identify myself more to girls like them than Bettys from the Blog of Betty. I'm addicted to good shopping tips, trends, etc., discovering new confidential brands and follow their evolution. (Annouck)

In the previous quote, it is also clear that there is some kind of self-identification process happening in the blogs' selection. Trying to understand whether this finding holds for non-bloggers is a potential future source of research for the scientific community.

Some other fashion bloggers started reading blogs for professional purposes, and they have never stopped. It has become some kind of addiction to them.

How Do They See Their Relationship with Fashion Brands

As stated in the literature, fashion brands consider bloggers as relevant and useful resources all along their strategic marketing plan: from R&D[5] to communication, including market research. So naturally, the topic of their relationship with brands appeared in bloggers' verbatims.

The Power of Being a Blogger

Some fashion bloggers are quite conscious of their power in the fashion industry: their opinion counts, as they are all authors of successful and influential blogs. And as previously identified, some of them engaged in blogging in the first place to leave their mark in the history of fashion. Such power actually depends on the blog, its number of readers, and on what fashion brands really seek in their brand-blogger relationship. However, what matters is not to become big headed:

At the same time you have to know how not being exploited by a brand, not to become an advertising tool for them. It must me a win-win relationship, if possible long-time oriented. (Annouck)

Any Relationship is Dangerous

Fashion brands know how to attract and resisting such temptation is often hard:

Well it's difficult with all these gifts and invitations. Sometimes you're tempted to sacrifice your editorial line just to be nice, or because you're afraid not to obey to the 'devil'. (Florent-Alexis)

The issue is that readers are not ignorant and quickly identify sponsored content. If this happens, fashion bloggers lose their credibility and authenticity, two key components of successful and influential blogs.

Types of Relationships

Based on the study, the following types of brand-fashion bloggers relationships were identified. The type is identified from Fournier in its labeling (Fournier, 1998).

1. Partnership: A long-term relationship, in the shape of a win-win strategy. Brands provide content and court the authors who get interesting source of information to share on their blog content. They do not feel like betraying the brand modifying the content nor harming the brand image with negative word: either they speak of a brand in good terms or they do not.
2. Weddings: There is 100% commitment of the blogger with a brand, often with strong financial or emotional incentives. Passion is there at the beginning but content sounds repetitive after a while.
3. Arranged marriage: Some relationships that happened due to financial reasons. This means very commercial blogs that do not sound that much authentic to their readers. It is a short-term oriented relationship: the blogger will switch brand depending on how much the money involved is.
4. Good friends: The blogger shares content about a specific brand because he trusts this one. He is usually the target of non-financial Public Relations activities. The blogger will seek his own new information about the brand.
5. Lovers: A relationship based on passion from the blogger perspective. The problem is that after a while, deception might overpass passion and anger and resentment will appear. This is especially the case if the brand courts other fashion bloggers, perceived as rivals, hence as a betrayal.

A Relationship with Brands?

After analyzing the various types of relationships and fashion bloggers' verbatim, it sounds like there is virtually no relationship with actual brands but more with their Public Relations departments and people working in them:

It's not a real relationship with brands, but more with people. They are the one depending on me, not really the brand they work for... (Foucaud)

Whatever the brand name is, its image, its personality, there will be a human interface between the brand and the blogger. Therefore, picking the right employee will be of high importance to shape the relationship.

About Motivation

Based on the various types of relationships identified, it sounds clear that two clusters of bloggers co-exist, the one motivated by money and the one that are not.

Motivated by Money

Some fashion bloggers, even if not initially motivated by moneymaking, now consider it as an opportunity to develop their blog, or as the welcomed reward for their blog success. Generating money has become part of their blog business model, turning them into small companies far away from their initial "crafty" nature. It is considered necessary in order to maintain a good position in the blogosphere in the future:

Since we created Sodandy, we are eager to share our taste for masculine fashion. When we began none of us thought we could generate revenues thanks to the blog. To consider maintaining a long-term presence and to increase our blog quality, the question of monetization cannot be ignored. (Florent-Alexis)

However, such bloggers still show ethical and authenticity concerns. Their primary focus remains the editorial line, not its monetary impact. This is a non-negotiable point and they make it clear to the reader:

In a transparency concern, we wanted to detail the various actions which can lead to some financial compensation. (Florent-Alexis)

Other fashion bloggers do not include moneymaking in their business model yet, but consider it as an option in the future. For them, it cannot be a motivation for writing a fashion blog. It is more of an opportunity to seize if it arises. They do not seek for monetization but would not turn it down if offered.

Non-Monetary Motivations

Other psychological or emotional features motivate all bloggers, even those also motivated by money:

1. The editorial line is by far the most important motivator. Special attention is paid by bloggers to its ethics and authenticity.
2. Pleasure would be another motivator through the pleasure of writing, sharing and getting feedback from readers (engaging with them). Handling a fashion blog has to be a hedonic experience for bloggers, otherwise they would leave it aside. They invest a lot of time in this activity so they feel that they deserve such pleasant retribution.
3. Encounters and social events would be another shared motivator to keep writing a blog. Being the author of a successful and influential blog leads to meeting Public Relations people, exchanging perspectives with readers, participating in fashion events, etc.
4. The feeling to contribute to enhancing knowledge is motivating fashion bloggers. Some authors fill the gap they found online regarding one aspect of fashion. They feel like collaborating to enhance the social knowledge on fashion, making the Internet a better place to surf.

Discussion and Recommendations

The study presented in this chapter is replicating results from previous research (as presented in the background part) while also providing new insights to both academics and practitioners.

Authenticity and content originality remain key for fashion bloggers and this study demonstrates that ethics and the editorial line also matter to them. Therefore, bloggers do not want to be associated with any type of brand if they face the risk of losing their editorial line and thus of sounding like 'commissioned by the brand'. Such conclusion is consistent with Fandrich (2008) who wrote that originality/authenticity should be the proxies to use to assess blogs relevance, and with Marwick who considered that a lot of bloggers understood the value of authenticity and of its impact on the quality of their blog.

The study also replicated one finding from Detterbeck et al. (2012), which stated that the main source of inspiration for fashion bloggers were trends and fashion newness. However, here the respondents made clear that they find themselves inspired by the longitudinal aspect of fashion, not only its new developments. History and past milestones of both brands and fashion in general are used to clarify and explain new trends. On top of that topic, three additional sources of information were identified: fashion events, catwalks and other blogs.

In a more discovery perspective, this study unwrapped the initial triggers to becoming a fashion blogger. More specifically, four triggers were identified, one very emotional and impulsive, on the spur of the moment; one contextual, taking advantage of an ongoing external event; one rational, related to one's professional activity; and a last one more conative, with the idea of filling a gap on the Internet and leaving one's mark.

The study also explored how fashion bloggers relate to brands. Five types of brand-blogger relationships have been identified and in most cases, bloggers feel empowered by them. They acknowledge the risk of losing their heart in a relationship, along with their credibility if the relationship affects the editorial line of their blog. It is highly important to notice that whatever the type of relationship bloggers hold with a fashion brand, it is always mediated by a human being (usually PR person). Therefore, brand-blogger relationship turns more into being a brand PR-blogger relationship.

Finally, this study presents the authors' motivations in writing a fashion blog: self-pleasure, establishing social links, meeting brands intimately and for some bloggers, generating revenues.

As previously stated, blogs play an increasing role in corporate and brand communication strategies. It is an alternative tool to traditional media advertising that may be more expensive and more difficult to reach in some cases. Such features make blogs highly courted by brands, which see in them the best tools to reach pre-segmented audiences trusting their authors. Then word-of-mouth spreads the message. However, members of the Public Relations departments have the tendency to focus on quantity instead of quality, while the quality of a blog cannot be assessed through its readership rate, but through its content authenticity. Authentic content being free of brand's direct impact, most fashion bloggers of good-quality blogs are not interested in brands' compensation proposals. Approaching them this way might even be a deterrent, with authors fearing some 'dictated' content and modification of their editorial line.

A second important conclusion is that if bloggers feel motivated differently, they should be approached in a same differentiated way. If brands want word-of-mouth to happen through them, they have to optimize the process and conduct more research on the fashion bloggers they would like to seduce.

Ways to Enhance the Brand-Blogger Relationship

Bloggers are as much important as journalists: both are information spreaders. They display different editorial lines, depending on the topic-orientation of their publication and have different reasons for maintaining an ongoing interest in blogging. For these two reasons, they favor some brands over others and resort to various sources to seek for information. As clearly shown in the study, they do not all expect the same things from blogging, even if one common point between them seems to be their unusual relationship with financial remuneration. Even if it is part of the business model of some blogs, it should never substitute freedom of speech, content independence and quality. Therefore **trying to attract fashion bloggers with compensation plans is not a good idea.** Confidence and trust should primarily be established. This can happen only after unfolding bloggers' centers of interest, inspirations, and attitude towards one's brand. Public relation departments should conduct more market research and apply a somewhat customized approach to each blogger who has been identified as relevant to spread the word (in a positive or objective way) on the brand. **Good quality word-of-mouth** should be sought for instead of rollout quantity:

1. Because bloggers do not cherish all brands, Public Relations people should identify those who are interested with and/or passionate about the brand they represent.
2. With each blogger willing to be the author of a blog differentiated from other ones in the blogosphere, they look for new content and exclusive information. A good brand-blogger relationship is based on sharing secrets. **Public Relations should share such exclusive content with their best bloggers** (i.e. brand passionate/interested in, with authentic and original content, with an editorial line consistent with the brand image, with a readership of interest as a brand audience).
3. Bloggers invest a lot of time and personal money in their blog. They expect some personal reward from doing it, which might be of different nature, but most of the time emotional-led. **Public Relations should pay attention at communicating with bloggers in a personalized and human way.** Bloggers will therefore feel pleased of not being in the anonymous crowd.

FUTURE RESEARCH DIRECTIONS

This chapter chose the fashion industry as an illustrative topic to decipher some key points related to a specific group of individuals' sources of word-of-mouth, namely bloggers. However, most findings did not appear as being exclusive to the fashion industry and could be extended to other industry-focused blogs and bloggers in general. Therefore, all managerial recommendations previously presented can be used in a B2C environment. It is key for brands to master the content in word-of-mouth processes and particularly important to understand the various information sources that bloggers use to craft their blog content. If brands cannot control the content itself, they can influence information sources bloggers use.

For instance, bloggers get inspired by:

1. Industry related news from the past and present, including iconic moments, brands and people associated with the brands. Therefore, brands that include in their corporate branding strategy communication on such topics are more likely to succeed in influencing some blog content.
2. Brand events and industry events. Organizing brand events and industry events such as shows (not professional ones, but general public ones) in a brand-blogger relationship building perspective should be of concern.
3. Other blogs. Public Relations departments should think of bloggers as an interconnected network of individuals and not independent atoms. Identifying the most influential ones is fundamental, but quality should be favored instead of quantity, as a proxy for quality of blog content.

Additional research could be conducted to refine the previous points, for example regarding the nature of influence that bloggers have on their counterparts: informative, normative or comparative? Besides, if this chapter helped identify three sources of information, the weight of each in the writing process remains a mystery. It might depend on the brand-blogger type of relationship, on bloggers' demographics or personality, or simply be the result of chance.

Another future research opportunity would be to try to further understand one point raised during the study process, which could be the key to a brand blogging management strategy: the congruence between the blog personality, the blogger personality, the brand personality and the reader personality. From what was said in this chapter, the hypothesis would be that the three should be aligned as a win-win strategy for all parties. Such blogs would then happen to be the 'best' ones in the blogosphere.

On top of these two, a third research project would be to conduct discourse analysis on top of content analysis. While analyzing the data, it appears that two lexical fields were used as metaphors: religion and addiction. Taking such analysis a step further and confronting it with metaphors theory (Lakoff & Johnson, 2008) could help brand not only identify which content they should provide to bloggers and how to do it, but also the exact words to be used to tell the story. In the end, communication is not only about what and with which media, but also when and how (Lasswell, 1948).

REFERENCES

Cialdini, R. (2007). *Influence: The psychology of persuasion*. New York: HarperCollins.

Corbin, J., & Strauss, A. (2008). Basics of Qualitative Research (3rd ed.). Thousand Oaks, CA: Sage.

Corcoran, C. T. (2010, February 17). 2010). Fashion's New Fever: Bloggers in Spotlight As They Aim for Fame. *Women's Wear Daily*, *199*, 18.

Dennen, V., & Myers, J. (2012). *Virtual Professional Development and Informal Learning via Social Networks*. IGI Global. doi:10.4018/978-1-4666-1815-2

Detterbeck, K., LaMoreaux, N., & Sciangula, M. (2012). Style and Substance: The Information Seeking Behavior of Fashion Bloggers. New-York: SUNNY.

Elo, S., & Kyngäs, H. (2008). The qualitative content analysis process. *Journal of Advanced Nursing*, *62*(1), 107–115. doi:10.1111/j.1365-2648.2007.04569.x PMID:18352969

Fandrich, M. W. (2007). *La Dernière Mode: Blogging Fashion*. Paper presented at the extremefashion - Pushing the boundaries of design, technology and business, Ryserson University.

Fournier, S. (1998). Consumers and their brands: Developing relationship theory in consumer research. *The Journal of Consumer Research*, *24*(4), 343–353. doi:10.1086/209515

Gordon, W. (1999). *Good Thinking: A Guide to Qualitative Research*. Henley-on-Thames, UK: Admap Publications.

Hill, J. (2005). *The voice of the blog: the attitudes and experiences of small business bloggers using blogs as a marketing and communications tool*. (MBA Thesis). The University of Liverpool, Liverpool, UK.

Kaner, G. (2013). *Consumer as an Institution in the Fashion System and the Participatory Role of New Media Technologies*. (New Media and Digital Culture Academic Master Master thesis). Universitat Utrecht, Utrecht, The Netherlands.

Lakoff, G., & Johnson, M. (2008). *Metaphors we live by*. University of Chicago press.

Lasswell, Harold D. (1948). The structure and function of communication in society. *The Communication of Ideas, 37*.

Manga, X. (2011). *Les blogs mode seraient-ils devenus des modèles d'inspiration pour ZARA?* Paper presented at the Colloque Web social, communautés virtuelles et consommation 79e congrès international ACFAS, Université Bishop's et Université de Sherbrooke.

Marwick, A. (2011). *Conspicuous and Authentic: Fashion Blogs, Style, and Consumption* Paper presented at the 61st Annual ICA Conference, Boston, MA.

Marwick, A. E. (2013). *"They're really profound women, they're entrepreneurs": Conceptions of Authenticity in Fashion Blogging*. Paper presented at the 7th International AAAI Conference on Weblogs and Social Media, Boston, MA.

Mendoza, M. (2010). I Blog. You Buy. How bloggers are creating a new generation of product endorsers. *Digital Research & Publishing*, *7*, 114–122.

Rocamora, A. (2011). Personal fashion blogs: Screens and mirrors in digital self-portraits. *Fashion Theory*, *15*(4), 407–424. doi:10.2752/175174111X13115179149794

Zhang, C. (2010). Fashion Blogs: The new member in fashion industry. *Journal of Digital Research & Publishing*, *3*(1), 25–32.

KEY TERMS AND DEFINITIONS

Blog Content: The nature and closeness of a relationship that an individual holds with a given brand. It is usually built with time, and has direct and indirect impacts on various variables such as attitude towards the brand, purchase intention, willingness to recommend the brand, etc.

Blog: A specific type of website often looking like a diary. It is composed of articles written by the so-called bloggers, which are displayed with the most recent one first.

Brand Ambassador: A person working as an advocate for a brand he has a close and intense relationship with. He might be paid for that but this is not the motivation for becoming an ambassador. He believes in the brand and not only represents it for advertising purposes. Hence a brand ambassador should be distinguished from a celebrity endorser.

Brand Image Management: The strategic and tactic activities a company uses to handle the perception and attitude that the public holds of its commercial or corporate brand.

Editorial line: The set of choices and decisions made by a communication initiator to conform to some ethical and moral principles they impose on themselves.

Motivation: The reasons, interests, elements that drive individuals towards some specific kind of action.

ENDNOTES

1. CRM ~ Consumer Relationship Management
2. SEO ~ Search Engine Optimization
3. In the Luxury universe, people prefer the French word 'Maison' to Company, to describe the business structure behind a given brand.
4. Launched in 2011 by the LVMH group, 'Les Journées Particulières' aims at opening the craft-places behind the brands belonging to the group. Visitors are invited to visit the so-called 'Ateliers' of Louis Vuitton, Guerlain etc., and to meet artisans face to face. It is very hard to get-in as places are limited. Hence, the 'Open-Day' is in the end opened to lucky people or invited ones.
5. R&D ~ Research and Development

Chapter 7
Investigating Factors Affecting Electronic Word-of-Mouth

Vineet Chouhan
Sir Padampat Singhania University, India

ABSTRACT

Electronic Word-of-Mouth (eWOM) has been identified and proven to be one of the major factors affecting online buying behaviour of the consumers. A growing number of sellers are shifting to online business channels in order to attract the online consumer. The consumers are also utilizing online platforms for sharing their product related experiences and thereby influencing other consumers. Thus, it is critical for businesses to recognize the important factors affecting eWOM. This chapter deals with different elements that conceptualize the phenomenon of eWOM and analyze what may be the possible ways for service marketers to influence this recommendation-based communication among online consumers. This study investigates factors affecting the eWOM behaviour of consumers by using of qualitative and quantitative research.

INTRODUCTION

There are various factors affecting a consumer's purchasing behaviour and decision-making. Social information shared by other consumers' has been considered by various consumers as an important source of information for decision making Especially, when social network services are readily available for consumers in the online context, consumers can easily exchange their purchasing experiences with others. Many potential buyers use other consumers' information, their opinion, comments, and experiences for taking their purchase decisions. This trend is called Word-of-Mouth (WOM) that is regarded as influential in determining customers' purchasing behavior and decision-making (Richins & Root-Shaffer 1988). WOM means interpersonal communication concerning the evaluation about products or service of interest (Arndt, 1967). The Internet is the context of online WOM to share information on products, services, transactions and other experiences. Eric (1988) regarded electronic WOM (eWOM) as a tool for consumers to exchange information with each other. eWOM may be defined as an individual's information sharing and communication activities for others in online context, i.e., online market.

DOI: 10.4018/978-1-4666-9449-1.ch007

An analysis of previous research indicates that WOM is key factor in affecting trust and online sales as an online feedback mechanism (Chevalier & Mayzlin 2006; Dellarocas 2003; Pavlou & Dimoka 2006; Zhu & Zhang 2010). WOM about target product or service reduces uncertainties about the target product and the associated risks in purchasing and using it; this form of reassurance may then affect development of customer trust in the product Based on the trust, customers may decide to proceed to purchase the product or service. For this reason, previous research on WOM regarded the WOM-based marketing approach much more effective in the promotion of sales, compared with advertising or individual sales activities (Katz & Lazardfeld 1955). Chevalier & Mayzlin (2006) found that WOM has an effect on online sales. It is thus one of the most influential sources of marketplace information for customers (Dellarocas 2003). It is created and spread through online WOM platforms such as product review websites, retailers' websites, brands' websites, personal blogs, message boards, and social networking sites (Lee and Youn 2009). It was observed that most of the previous research conducted on eWOM is focused on the online word of mouth pertaining to online shopping malls with single vendor (Lee et al. 2011). There has been, however, lack of research on the factors affecting eWOM among students.

In Internet enabled market, several online vendors provide the products or services to potential customers through online means. For example, there are several vendors selling products in Flipkart. Flipkart manages the online market by selecting and allowing such vendors to do their business through its online market platform. Customers are given space to share their experiences and information about those vendors as well as about those products and services which they have experienced. It is important for potential customers to check the vendors as well as the products and services they are considering in the online market. In order to develop a deeper understanding of the phenomenon related to eWOM a sequential combination of qualitative and quantitative research methods were used, where findings from the qualitative study empirically inform the later quantitative study. Qualitative data were collected by conducting a questionnaire based survey of students who experienced eWOM to explore what motivates them to go for and take decision on the basis of eWOM. The questionnaire thus substantiated the basic premise of the research model. The survey also assisted in the interpretation of specific survey results with 291 respondents. Then quantitative data were collected through online surveys to identify the factors effecting eWOM. This study contributes to research by adding to the broader literature on eWOM. Moreover, the study can inform Internet vendors and internet market providers on how to promote and manage eWOM activities for their online business.

Son, Kim and Jang (2012) have also conducted a similar study by adopting an interview approach with experienced eWOM customers as a qualitative research method to explore potential factors affecting eWOM. Although the interview approach has weaknesses such as response bias, subjective interpretation, and reflexivity, it has several strengths such as the capability to focus directly on the research topic and to deliver perceived causal inferences (Yin 2003). The researchers had conducted structured interviews with 31 randomly selected experienced eWOM customers. The interviewees were mainly asked the factors that affected their decision to do eWOM activities in the open market context. Due to limitations of the interview method this research was conducted with questionnaire method by taking a few variables of eWOM.

Objective of the Study

The objectives of this study are as under:

1. To propose the factors responsible for eWOM by analysing the literature and
2. To identify the common effect of the variables as proposed in previous studies.

REVIEW OF LITERATURE

Traditional eWOM

The concept of word-of-mouth (WOM) has been under the spotlight for decades by academics and practitioners (Lee & Youn 2009). WOM is described as 'oral, person-to-person communication between a receiver and a communicator whom the receiver perceives as non-commercial, regarding a brand, product, or service' (Arndt 1967, p. 3). In 1966, Dichter thought WOM to be a marketing force that is often acknowledged as very powerful but is infrequently utilized. Similarly, Arndt (1967) expressed that favorable word-of-mouth increases the probability of a purchase. Decades later, the phenomenon is described much in the same way. Word-of-mouth is present when one individual communicates to another any kind of information about a target object (Brown et al. 2005). That is, consumers' communication topics are a much wider concept than Arndt's (1967) definition suggests. Customers perceive WOM as credible and custom-tailored information source because the communication is expected to be generated without any commercial interest (e.g. Arndt 1967, Wirtz & Chew 2002, Kozinets et al. 2010). Due to the higher perceived credibility in the face-to-face interaction, the WOM communication often has a strong impact on product judgments (Herr et al. 1990).

Product Perception

An experimental study was conducted by Cordell, (1991) for analysing product choices in which country of origin, competitive context (information on the hierarchical relationship of products in a choice set), price and financial risk were manipulated. He suggested that consumers are more unconvinced of products from less developed countries when the financial risk is higher and when seeking a product with superior tangible attributes. However, within a given product category, price did not produce interaction effects with country of origin.

A conjoint analysis has conducted by Lee, et al. (1992) to identify the relative importance of price, warranty and country of origin information in an experimental design. They found that the price factor have the maximum relative importance, with the warranty second and country of origin, though still significant, they also investigating COO effects on overall customer beliefs and behavior conclude that 35 buying intentions are influenced by factors such as the source country's economic and political maturity, historical events and relationships, traditions, level of industrialisations and economic development and degree of technological virtuosity. In the similar study conjoint analysis was also used by Okechuku, (1994) to investigate the relative importance of the country of origin of product categories including television sets and car radios, to consumers in the US, Canada, Germany, and the Netherlands. The other cues were brand, price, quality and warranty. The results of the study showed that, in all four consuming countries, country of origin is consistently ranked as one of the top three attributes in product evaluations. It was often as important as, or more so than, the brand name and the price.

Elliot and Cameron, (1994) also found country of origin to be significantly less important as a choice determinant than other cues, in this case quality and price. Nevertheless, they observed that, when these other factors are equivalent, the fact that a product is locally made has a positive influence on product choice.

Loyalty

Sirdeshmukh et al. (2002) defined Loyalty as an intention to perform a diverse set of behaviors that signal a motivation to maintain a relationship with the focal firm, including allocating a higher share of the category wallet to the specific service provider, engaging in positive word of mouth (WOM), and repeat purchasing. Engel, Kollat, and Blackwell (1982) defined brand loyalty as the preferential, attitudinal and behavioral response toward one or more brands in a product category expressed over a period of time by a consumer. Jacoby (1971) expressed the view that loyalty is a biased behavioral purchase process that results from a psychological process. Other researchers like Assael (1992) and Keller (1993) have defined loyalty as a favorable attitude toward a brand resulting in consistent purchase of the brand over time. Keller suggested that loyalty is present when favorable attitudes for the brand are manifested in repeat buying behavior. Gremler (1995) suggested that both attitudinal and behavioral dimensions needed to be incorporated in measuring loyalty. Therefore, for present research purposes, loyalty is defined as the customer's favor-able attitude toward an electronic business resulting in repeat buying behavior. Bloemer et al. (1999); Jones and Sasser (1995); Jones and Taylor (2007); Lam et al. (2004); Zeithaml et al. (1996) revealed that this considers positive WOM as a component of loyalty. Sirdeshmukh et al. (2002) also found that it was employed in 40 studies reviewed in meta-analysis. These studies could not, however, be included because they did not present specific results for the WOM construct.

However, a recent study by Söderlund (2006) has questioned this cocktail approach in which loyalty is measured by an aggregated mix of items that form different components of loyalty. He further states that this approach is commonly used to include repatronage intentions and WOM intentions as items of a unidimensional loyalty construct. Blodgett et al. (1993), Gruen et al. (2006), Jones and Reynolds (2006), Maxham (2001), and Maxham and Netemeyer (2002) and Dick and Basu (1994) revealed that there is a need to investigate the influence of loyalty on WOM. Since a very few studies have empirically tested the unidirectional effect of loyalty on WOM (Carpenter and Fairhurst 2005; Gounaris and Stathakopoulos 2004; Reynolds and Arnold 2000; and Sichtmann 2007). Arnett et al. (2003); Gremler and Gwinner (2000); Jones and Reynolds (2006); Macintosh (2007); Maxham and Netemeyer (2002 & 2003); Price and Arnould (1999); Reynolds and Beatty (1999); Söderlund (1998) have measured the bi-directional association (correlation) between these two constructs when considering them as behavioral outcomes, especially of customer satisfaction. Thus, they observed correlations between loyalty and WOM, they have hypothesized Loyalty as an antecedent of WOM to the extent customers are more loyal to a given provider, they are also more likely to (1) give positive recommendations of the company to the individuals in their reference group (friends and relatives), (2) have greater motivation for processing new information about the company, and (3) have stronger resistance to being persuaded by contrary information (Dick and Basu 1994) Wangenheim (2005) moreover analysed a disloyalty situation, in which customers switch providers, they are also likely to spread negative WOM about the provider in order to reduce their cognitive dissonance. Richins (1984) and Sweeney et al. (2005) tried to convince about their decision by convincing others, which is one of the strategies often used for reducing post-decision dissonance. As mentioned before, customers might also engage in negative WOM for other reasons such as to release negative emotions, to warn others, and/or to retaliate.

CUSTOMER SATISFACTION

Oliver (1980) has analysed expectancy disconfirmation theory and develop dominant model for conceptualizing and measuring customer satisfaction. This view holds that customers evaluate a product or service performance and compare their evaluation with their expectations prior to purchase or consumption. In his second paper (Oliver, 1981) analysed to satisfaction as a post-choice evaluative judgment regarding a specific purchase selection, satisfaction is understood by its transaction specific component. Bolton and Drew (1991) developed another approach to measure satisfaction as the customers' evaluations of multiple experiences by taking the same product or service provider over time, Westbrook and Oliver (1991) also have revealed that this cumulative construct incorporates previous experiences, the cumulative satisfaction construct will contain an element of customer attitude. Subsequent studies conducted by Liljander and Strandvik (1997); Oliver and Westbrook (1993); Straus and Neuhaus (1997) have demonstrated thatcustomer satisfaction, in addition to the cognitive view, also contains emotional components. Martin et al. (2008) with Zeelenberg and Pieters (2004) agreed that emotional based satisfaction is a stronger predictor of future behavioral intentions than traditional cognitive measures.

Bearden and Teel (1983); Maxham and Netemeyer (2002); Oliver (1980); Ranaweera and Prabhu (2003) and Richins (1983) revealed that the level of customer satisfaction has an influence on two purchase behaviors, namely, repurchase intentions and WOM. Specially, the likelihood of customers spreading WOM will depend on their satisfaction level for the extent to which the product or service performance exceeds the customer's expectations might motivate him or her to tell others about his or her positive experience. Anderson (1998); Oliver (1997); Richins (1984) and Sweeney et al. (2005) revealed that in the context of service recovery, for instance, the salience and recency of the experience might explain why satisfaction with the recovery prompts customers to tell family and friends about their positive experience (Maxham and Netemeyer (2002). To the extent that the customer's expectations are not fulfilled, possibly creating a customer regret experience, this customer will engage in WOM behavior as a form of "venting" his or her negative emotions, such as anger and frustration, reducing anxiety, warning others, and/or seeking retaliation.

Azar (2008) analyses that the tipping would improve service quality and increase economic efficiency as tips are incentives to provide best service and consequently allow avoiding costly supervision of workers. His study argued that the common notion cannot be proven. He examined the reasons for the increased interest in tipping and concludes that the concerned firms benefit from better understanding of various issues related tipping and also, tipping has become a social norm and a form of consumer behaviour. The author has exposed the inconsistency between the two market characteristics, i.e. tips are hardly affected by service quality and service quality is ranked as being high by customers. This research concluded that tips are not directly proportional to service quality and additional measures should be employed to warrant good service quality.

Lee et al (2006) measured the customer value and marketing effect with reference to direct financial contributions and the potential risk of misleading the marketing managers. By taking the word-of-mouth (WOM) and the customer lifetime value (CLV) they conducted an empirical investigation for measuring the effect of WOM in estimating CLV. Data was collected from 1,493 customers through survey and transaction measures using a 10-point scale. The survey was inclusive of level of customer overall satisfaction and WOM, i.e., willingness to recommend. They revealed that direct financial contributions are alone incorporated in CLV estimation, companies run the risk of missing the latent aspect of customer value and thus there exists a possibility to misjudge customers' true lifetime value. They further expected that the indirect effects of WOM should also be evaluated to maximise the lifetime value of customers and based on this investments can be made accordingly to augment the customers' attitude to generate positive WOM.

Cohen (1997) revealed the term 'WOW' effect which encompasses all the efforts that are being taken by the top management to keep the customers and employees fresh and exciting. He discusses the five WOW aspects viz. WOW yourself; WOW your employees: WOW your customers; WOW your community; and WOW your competition. The aspect WOW yourself concerns about the managers having an environment to think as strategists and futurists and to WOW themselves with creative ideas, WOW the employees aspect is empowerment of employees through financial and psychological ownership, WOW your customers is explained by the author as doing things the right way, and it applies just as much to service as to food. WOW your community, the effective community reach i.e. learning about the diverse communities, their needs etc., and WOW your competition through innovative ideas and concepts i.e. not copying the successful new ideas that is usually being followed in the market.

Forges (2007) argue that value of customers is one of the important intangible assets of any business. The fundamental methodologies for valuing customers are explained and their limitations are included in his study. The value of customer is broadly defined as 'the value that customers generate for the businesses and alternatively, the 'value of relationships'. The study suggests that Porter's value chain can be used to analyse how customer relationships create value. The author claims that there are delicate differences using brand value as a substitute for the value of customer even though they seems to appear similar. The study suggests the common approaches for valuing the customer related intangible assets including Cost approach; Market approach; and Income approach. The cost approach is based on the level of cost to be incurred to create value. The second approach measures the open market expenses, while the income approach is based on the level of income the asset would generate. The study also illustrates the limitations of all the three approaches. The cost approach is distorted by time value of money and the evolvement of the competitive environment. The availability of sufficiently comparable transactions is identified as the primary weakness of the market approach. The income approach is complicated to carryout. The study concludes that since customers are the reason for the existence of a business, skill for managing their customers profitably is crucial.

Shang and Hooker (2006) have conducted a survey which was carried out through email. Their survey data have been used to determine consumer preferences among a set of four alternative food labels which report such plant level performance scores. The authors study the product label reports of food producers' hygiene performance and explore consumer preferences for the 'right' amount of information and how to present this information. The authors carried out the study to verify the hypotheses that in terms of presentation format, consumers prefer number system than other visual or verbal systems, Among the three different levels of information volume sets, consumers don't always prefer the largest volume set, and no matter what their preferences are, consumers are consistent with their information volume preferences.

Consumer's Engagement

Brown et al. (2005) argue that academic understanding of the antecedents affecting WOM is still incomplete. However, the exchange theory has been applied to understand why consumers engage in the word-of-mouth communication (e.g. Wirtz & Chew, 2002, Hennig-Thurau et al., 2004, Ryu and Feick, 2007). According to Ryu and Feick (2007), engaging in WOM depends on perceived costs and benefits of the exchange. Consumers expect to gain something, or that they implicitly satisfy a desire when providing others with WOM (Wirtz & Chew 2002). By engaging in word-of-mouth communication, participants may seek social support for the purchased object (Arndt 1967). Consumers may want to reduce post-purchase dissonance or control others' impressions of them (Ryu & Feick 2007). WOM is a social behavior, where the consumer interacts with various people from friends and family to acquaintances (Wirtz & Chew 2002) helping them to make better choices (Ryu & Feick 2007). The similarity between the message sender and the receiver may be especially important when new attitudes towards brands are formed (Godes & Mayzin 2009).

Consumers' commitment, satisfaction and identification with retailers exert the influence on positive WOM intentions (Brown et al. 2005). Anderson (1998) finds empirical evidence that there is a U-shaped relationship to the consumer satisfaction and the likelihood of engaging in WOM activities. That is, word-of-mouth activity increases as either the satisfaction and/or dissatisfaction increases. Once WOM is generated, Wirtz & Chew (2002) find that the valence of WOM is related to the consumer's experience.

Market Force

In addition to being an effective influence on consumer product judgments (e.g. Brown et al. 2005, Herr et al. 1990), the high volume of WOM seems to be beneficial to sales (Yong 2006). Having a powerful effect on consumers' attitudes and behavior (Sweeney et al. 2008), word-of-mouth is seen increasingly as part of firm's marketing efforts, especially viral and referral marketing campaigns (e.g. Phelps et al. 2004, Ryu & Feick 2007). Although, both concepts function more effectively on the online environment, viral and referral marketing should not be restricted in the computer mediated context (Vilpponen et al. 2006).

Viral marketing has allured marketers with its exponential growth potential in recent years, but there is not a clear understanding what it means or how it works (e.g. Eckler & Bolls 2011, Petrescu & Korgaonkar 2011). Phelps et al. (2004) view viral marketing as the process of encouraging an honest communication among consumer networks. This honest communication is easily perceived as a word-of-mouth activity. Cited by many scholarly reviewed articles, Modzelewski (2000) criticizes this generalization and believes that viral marketing differs from word-of-mouth because the value of the virus to the original consumer is directly related to the number of other users themessage attracts. Individuals are seen more as vehicles for spreading communication (José- Cabezudo & Camarero-Izquierdo 2012). By comparing the different definitions of viral marketing, Vilpponen et al. (2006) see the phenomenon as part of word-of-mouth communication when opinion leaders have a vital role in message delivery and the value of a recommended object increases as people use it. WOM seems to act both as a cause and effect of viral marketing campaigns (Petrescu & Korgaonkar 2011). Based on these notions, in specific circumstances, firms encouraging positive word-of-mouth behavior in consumer networks can be classified as viral marketing efforts. Top-level marketing journals started to publish research into electronic word-of-mouth (eWOM) only about ten years ago (Breazeale 2009). Since the late 1990s, the Internet has rapidly developed and enriched consumers' communication surface (Okazaki 2009). Particularly, the Internet's extensive reach, transparency, and accessibility have given new meaning to word-of-mouth, which is why marketers are especially interested in getting involved in WOM (Kozinets et al. 2010).

Due to the fact that it is a recent research phenomenon, the definition of electronic word-of-mouth is not yet established. Recent developments in peer-to-peer communication technologies have aroused scholarly interest in the enigmatic process of electronic word-of-mouth (Sohn 2009). Hennig-Thurau et al. (2004) see eWOM communication "as any positive or negative statement made by potential, actual, or former customers about a product or company, which is made available to a multitude of people and institutions via the Internet". Thorson and Rodgers (2006) add that peer-to-peer online communication can occur on other levels as well. It is possible that the communicator is not a consumer at all but it can provide a positive word of mouth (Breazeale 2009). Table 1 represents a summary of research conducted in the field of eWOM.

RESEARCH METHODOLOGY

The main purpose of this chapter is to investigate factors affecting electronic Word-of-Mouth. For this purpose the following methodology was adopted:

Research Design

The research design used is in accordance with the empirical study requirements. As such, it covers the type of data collected, the methodology of data collection and the various statistical tools and techniques used for analysis of data and hypotheses - testing. Being empirical study, it is completely based on primary data

Table 1. Research on eWOM

Author (Year)	Research Area
Brown (2007)	Word-of-mouth communication within online communities: conceptualizing the online social network
Godes (2004)	Using online conversations to study word-of-mouth communication
Dellarocas (2003)	The digitization of word of mouth: Promise and challenges of online feedback mechanisms.
Wirtz (2002)	The effects of Incentives deal proneness, satisfaction and tie strength on word-of-mouth behaviour.
Bickart (2002)	Expanding the scope of word of mouth: Consumer-to-consumer information on the internet.
Gremler (2001)	Generating positive word-of-mouth communication trough customer-employee relationships.
Berger (1988)	Word-of-mouth reputations in auto insurance markets.
Richins (1987)	Multivariate analysis of responses to dissatisfaction.
Gumpert (1986)	Interpersonal communication in a media world
Richins (1983)	Negative word of mouth by dissatisfied consumers
Arndt (1968)	Selective processes in word of mouth
Arndt (1967)	Role of product-related conversations in the diffusion of a new product
Dichter (1966)	How word-of-mouth advertising works
Brooks (1957)	Word-of-mouth advertising in selling new products

Data Collection

The research study is based on the Primary data which has collected through a structured questionnaire that was filled up by the students who are the customers of online companies. As per the objective of the study, in order to identify the factors explaining the eWOM, 6 constructs(Information sharing desire, Market satisfaction, Self-presentation desire, Market reward, Market Loyalty and Product perception) were identified through review of literature. These 6 constructs formed the independent variables and eWoM was treated as independent variable. The constructs were measured through scale items adopted from previous research. The data were collected from the 291 students of college level in various colleges of south Rajasthan on five point Likert scale to analyse and identify the factors influencing the impact over eWOM. To analyse the same following hypothesis were developed:

H_{1a}: Information sharing desire has a positive effect on eWOM.
H_{1b}: Market Satisfaction has a positive effect on eWOM.
H_{1c}: Self-presentation Desire has a positive effect on eWOM.
H_{1d}: Market reward has a positive effect on eWOM.
H_{1e}: Market loyalty has a positive effect on eWOM.
H_{1f}: Product perception has a positive effect on eWOM.

The proposed research model which depicts the factors affecting eWOM is shown in Figure 1 as under: The variables shown identified for conducting the study with the reference is shown in Table 2.

Figure 1. Factors effecting eWOM

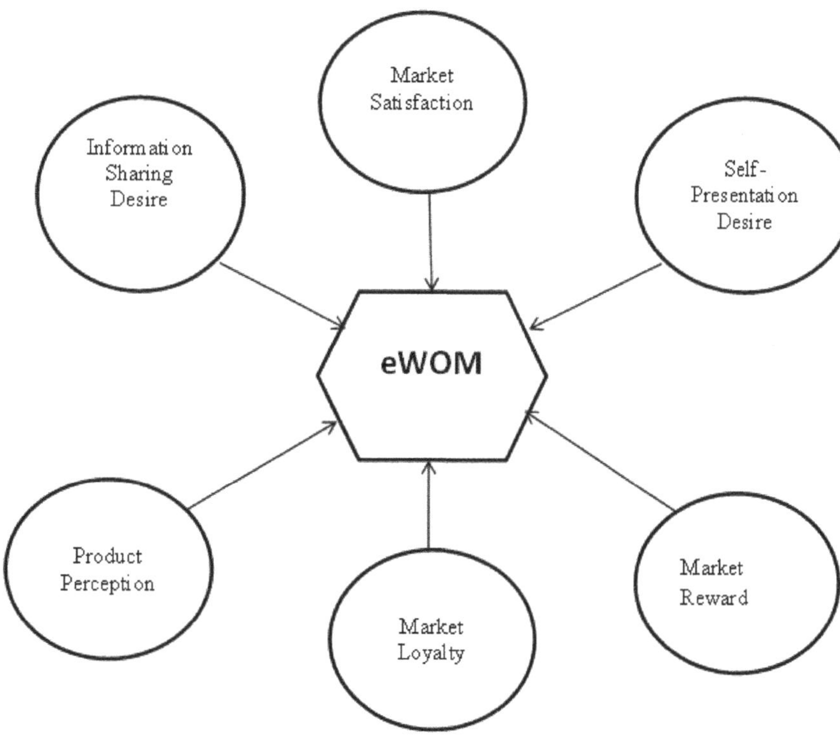

Table 2. Variables of eWOM

Construct	Variable	Variable Name	Reference
Information sharing desire	I want to share information that enables transaction to be sensible	IS_1	Son, kim and Jang (2012)
	I hope to share product information purchased online	IS_2	
	I wish to share service information that I had purchased online	IS_3	
	I want to share information about the seller from which online product was purchased.	IS_4	
Market satisfaction	I am Unsatisfied / Satisfied with my transaction in this market.	OMS_1	Spreng et al. (1996).
	I am Frustrated/ Contented with my transaction in this market.	OMS_2	
	I am Annoyed / Pleased with my transaction in this market.	OMS_3	
Self-presentation Desire	I hope to leave a good impression in the online market.	SP_1	Kim et al. (2014)
	I want to present a good image in the online market.	SP_2	
	I wish to make a good image in the online market.	SP_3	
Market reward	There are rewards according to sharing information to others in the online market.	OMR_1	Malhotra & Galletta (1999)
	In the online market, sharing information enables us to get a lot of benefits.	OMR_2	
	There are incentives according to sharing information to others in the online market.	OMR_3	
Market loyalty	I am a regular customer in this online market.	OML_1	Garbarino & Johnson (1999)
	I have a strong attachment in this online market.	OML_2	
	I hope that this online market will succeed in internet business.	OML_3	
Product perception	I understand a product better after receiving relevant information about that product from my contacts	PP_1	Park et al. (2007); Wangenheim & Bayon, (2004); Arndt, (1967)
	A former comment or update about a product on from my contacts has had an influence on how I consider that product.	PP_2	
	I can change my views about a product, after viewing a positive or negative comment about that product.	PP_3	
eWOM	I often tell so many things about transaction in the online market to others.	E_1	Thomas et al. (2006)
	I often introduce experience of previous dealing in the online market.	E_2	
	I often tell the features of products or services in the online market to others.	E_3	
	I frequently communicate with others contacts	E_4	Chu & Kim, (2011); Park et al., (2007).
	I tend to pass along my product-related opinions to my contacts.	E_5	
	I tend to seek for opinions from my contacts regarding a product that I intend to purchase.	E_6	
	I am likely to recommend a product to others, after receiving relevant comments about that product on social networking sites from my contacts.	E_6	

DATA ANALYSIS

To identify key variables in eWOM, multivariate regression analysis has been used with SPSS-19 software and results are shown in Table 3 and Table 4.

The final Regression model with two constructs namely Product perception and Market loyalty explains almost 86% of the variance in eWOM. Also, the standard errors of the estimate has been reduced

Table 3. Multiple Regressions (variables and Correlation)

Variables	Mean	Std. Deviation	N
eWOM	3.4032	.62090	291
ML	3.2428	.58968	291
MR	3.2784	.56123	291
SP	2.9324	.80588	291
MS	3.0401	.69723	291
IS	3.0696	.78406	291
PP	3.1512	.96373	291

Correlations		eWOM	ML	MR	SP	MS	IS	PP
Pearson Correlation	eWOM	1.000	.623	.576	.561	.686	.607	.924
	ML	.623	1.000	.425	.734	.789	.651	.595
	MR	.576	.425	1.000	.419	.536	.589	.623
	SP	.561	.734	.419	1.000	.840	.773	.562
	MS	.686	.789	.536	.840	1.000	.737	.682
	IS	.607	.651	.589	.773	.737	1.000	.618
	PP	.924	.595	.623	.562	.682	.618	1.000
Sig. (1-tailed)	eWOM	.	.000	.000	.000	.000	.000	.000
	ML	.000	.	.000	.000	.000	.000	.000
	MR	.000	.000	.	.000	.000	.000	.000
	SP	.000	.000	.000	.	.000	.000	.000
	MS	.000	.000	.000	.000	.	.000	.000
	IS	.000	.000	.000	.000	.000	.	.000
	PP	.000	.000	.000	.000	.000	.000	.
N		291	291	291	291	291	291	291

Model	Variables Entered	Variables Removed	Method
1	PP	.	Stepwise (Criteria: Probability-of-F-to-enter <= .050, Probability-of-F-to-remove >= .100).
2	ML	.	Stepwise (Criteria: Probability-of-F-to-enter <= .050, Probability-of-F-to-remove >= .100).

Stepwise (Criteria: Probability-of-F-to-enter <= .050, Probability-of-F-to-remove >= .100).
a. Dependent Variable: Ewom

Table 4. Model Summary, ANOVA and Coefficients

Model	R	R Square	Adjusted R Square	Std. Error of the Estimate	Change Statistics				
					R Square Change	F Change	df1	df2	Sig. F Change
1	.924[a]	.853	.852	.23857	.853	1675.292	1	289	.000
2	.928[b]	.861	.860	.23197	.009	17.678	1	288	.000

Model		Sum of Squares	df	Mean Square	F	Sig.
1	Regression	95.352	1	95.352	1675.292	.000[a]
	Residual	16.449	289	.057		
	Total	111.801	290			
2	Regression	96.304	2	48.152	894.825	.000[b]
	Residual	15.498	288	.054		
	Total	111.801	290			

Model		Unstandardized Coefficients		Standardized Coefficients	t	Sig.	Correlations			Collinearity Statistics	
		B	Std. Error	Beta			Zero order	Partial	Part	Tolerance	VIF
1	(Constant)	1.528	.048		31.909	.000					
	PP	.595	.015	.924	40.930	.000	.924	.924	.924	1.000	1.000
2	(Constant)	1.275	.076		16.747	.000					
	PP	.551	.018	.855	31.348	.000	.924	.879	.688	.647	1.547
	ML	.121	.029	.115	4.204	.000	.623	.240	.092	.647	1.547

a. Predictors: (Constant), PP
b. Predictors: (Constant), PP, ML
c. Dependent Variable: eWOM

to .23197, which means that at 95% level, the margin of errors for any predicted value of eWOM items can be calculated as ± .4546612 (1.96 X . 23197). The two regression coefficients, plus the constraints are significant at 0.05 levels. The impact of multi colinerarity in the two constructs is substantial. They all have the tolerance value less than 0.647, indicating that only over 35% of the variance is accounted for by the other variables in the equation.

The ANOVA analysis provides the statistical test for overall model fit in terms of F Ratio. The total sum of squares (111.801) is the squared error that would accrue if the mean of constructs has been used to predict the dependent variable (eWOM). Using the values of Product perception and Market loyalty these errors can be reduced by 86.14% (96.304/111.801). This reduction is deemed statistically significant with the F ratio of 894.825 and significance at level of 0.000. With the above analysis it can be concluded that two variables i.e., Product perception and Market loyalty explains the variance of eWOM in student consumers' online purchase behaviour.

On the basis of above data, Table 5 gives a list of hypotheses that are accepted / rejected.

Table 5. Status of hypotheses

Hypothesis	Construct	Beta	t	Sig.	VIF	Status
H_{1a}:	IS	.058	.228	.082	2.025	Rejected
H_{1b}:	MS	.106	1.040	.299	3.252	Rejected
H_{1c}:	SP	.061	-.296	.767	2.288	Rejected
H_{1d}:	MR	.001	-.325	.745	1.647	Rejected
H_{1e}:	ML	.115	4.204	.000	1.547	Accepted
H_{1f}:	PP	.855	31.348	.000	1.547	Accepted

CONCLUSION

This study was conducted to identify the factors effecting students behaviour on eWOM, by taking data from 291 college students, and applying multiple regression analysis with SPSS-19 software. The study was conducted with 26 items under 7 constructs (1 dependent construct and 6 independent constructs) out of which two constructs which have reduced the standard errors were selected. These final solutions with two constructs presented the views of the online students customers and reflect their online purchase behaviour. The final results suggest towards rejection of null hypothesis because of selection on two constructs in the model. Results also revealed that online customers with strong and positive product perception and high loyalty towards online market tend to share their experiences more aggressively on Internet. Future studies can be undertaken to understand the inter-dependence of these two factors, since product perception and market loyalty can be inter-related. Marketers can utilize this significant finding in planning their marketing strategies that focus towards creating a positive brand image and product perception in the minds of customers.

REFERENCES

Arndt, J. (1967). Role of Product-Related Conversations in the Diffusion of a New Product. *JMR, Journal of Marketing Research*, *4*(3), 291–295. doi:10.2307/3149462

Arndt, J. (1968). Selective Processes in Word of Mouth. *Journal of Advertising Research*, *8*(3), 19–22.

Azar, O. H. (2008). *Incentives and Service Quality in the Restaurant Industry: The Tipping – Service Puzzle.* Working Paper. Department of Business Administration, Ben-Gurion University of Nagev.

Bearden, W. O., & Teel, J. E. (1983). Selected determinants of consumer satisfaction and complaint reports. *JMR, Journal of Marketing Research*, *20*(1), 21–28. doi:10.2307/3151408

Berger, L. A. (1988). Word-of-Mouth Reputations in Auto Insurance Markets. *Journal of Behavior and Organization*, *10*(2), 225–234. doi:10.1016/0167-2681(88)90046-7

Bickart, B., & Schindler, R. M. (2002). Expanding the scope of word of mouth: Consumer-to-consumer informations on the internet. *Advances in Consumer Research. Association for Consumer Research (U. S.)*, *29*, 428–430.

Bolton, R. N., & Drew, J. H. (1991). A longitudinal analysis of the impact of service changes on customer attitudes. *Journal of Marketing*, *55*(1), 1–10. doi:10.2307/1252199

Brooks, R. C. Jr. (1957). 'Word-of-Mouth' Advertising in Selling New Products. *Journal of Marketing*, *22*(2), 154–161. doi:10.2307/1247212

Brown, J., Broderik, A. J., & Lee, N. (2007). Word of Mouth Communication within online communities: Conceptualizing the online social network. *Journal of Interactive Marketing*, *21*(3), 2–20. doi:10.1002/dir.20082

Chu, S. C., & Kim, Y. (2011). Determinants of consumer engagement in electronic word-of-mouth (eWOM) in social networking sites. *International Journal of Advertising*, *30*(1), 47–75. doi:10.2501/IJA-30-1-047-075

Cohen, B. (1997). The 'Wow' Effect: How One Restaurateur Continues to Delight Customers. *The Cornell Hotel and Restaurant Administration Quarterly*, *38*(2).

Cordell, V. (1991). Competitive Context and Price as Moderators of Country of Origin Preference. *Journal of the Academy of Marketing Science*, *19*(Spring), 123–128. doi:10.1007/BF02726004

Dellarocas, C. (2003). The Digitization of Word of Mouth: Promise and Challenges of Online Feedback Mechanisms. *Management Science*, *49*(10), 1407–1424. doi:10.1287/mnsc.49.10.1407.17308

Dichter, E. (1966). How word-of-mouth advertising works. *Harvard Business Review*, *44*(6), 147–160.

Elliot, G., & Cameron, A. (1994). Consumer Perception of Product Quality and the Country of Origin Effect. *Journal of International Marketing*, *2*(2), 49–62.

Forges, T. (2007). Valuing Customers. *Journal of Database Marketing & Customer Strategy Management*, *15*, 20–57.

Garbarino, E., & Johnson, M. S. (1999). The Different Roles of Satisfaction, Trust, and Commitmentin Customer Relationships. *Journal of Marketing*, *63*(2), 70–87. doi:10.2307/1251946

Godes, D., & Mayzlin, D. (2004). Using Online Conversations to Study Word-of-Mouth Communication. *Marketing Science*, *34*(4), 545–560. doi:10.1287/mksc.1040.0071

Gremler, D. D., Gwinner, K. P., & Brown, S. W. (2001). Generating Positive Word-of-Mouth Communication Trough Customer-Employee Relationships. *International Journal of Service Industry Management*, *12*(1), 44–59. doi:10.1108/09564230110382763

Gumpert, G., & Cathcart, R. (1986). *Inter/Media: Interpersonal Communication in a Media World*. New York: Oxford University Press.

Holjevac, I. A., Marković, S., & Raspor, S. (2000), *Customer Satisfaction Measurement in Hotel Industry: Content Analysis Study*. Working paper.

Jones, P., & Dent, M. (1994). Improving Service: Managing Response Time in Hospitality Operations. *International Journal of Operations & Production Management*, *14*(5), 52–58. doi:10.1108/01443579410056795

Kim, H. W., Chan, H. C. & Kankanhalli, A. (2014). *What motivates people to purchase digital items on virtual community websites? The desire for online self-presentation.* Information Systems Research (ISR).

Lee, H., Kim, C., & Miller, J. (1992). The Relative Effects of Price, Warranty and Country of Origin on Consumer Evaluations. *Journal of Global Marketing*, *6*(1/2), 55–80.

Lee, J., Lee, J., & Feick, L. (2006). Incorporating Word-of-Mouth Effects in Estimating Customer Lifetime Value, *Journal of Database Marketing & Customer Strategy Management, 14.*

Liljander, V., & Strandvik, T. (1997). Emotions in service satisfaction. *International Journal of Service Industry Management*, *8*(2), 148–169. doi:10.1108/09564239710166272

Malhotra, Y., & Galletta, D. F. (1999). Extending the technology acceptance model to account for social influence: Theoretical bases and empirical validation. *Proceedings of the 32nd Hawaii International Conference on System Sciences.* doi:10.1109/HICSS.1999.772658

Malthouse, E. C., Oakley, J. L. & Iacobucci, D. (2003). *Customer Satisfaction Across Organizational Units.* Working Paper. Northwestern University.

Martin, D., O'Neill, M., Hubbard, S., & Palmer, A. (2008). The role of emotion in explaining consumer satisfaction and future behavioural intention. *Journal of Services Marketing*, *22*(3), 224–236. doi:10.1108/08876040810871183

Nusair, K., Yoon, H. J., Naipaul, S., & Parsa, H. G. (2010). Effect of Price Discount Frames and Price Discount Levels on Consumers' Perceptions. *International Journal of Contemporary Hospitality Management*, *22*(9).

Okechucu, C. (1994). The Importance of Product Country of Origin. *European Journal of Marketing*, *28*(4), 5–19. doi:10.1108/03090569410061150

Oliver, R. L. (1980). A cognitive model of the antecedents and consequences of satisfaction decisions. *JMR, Journal of Marketing Research*, *17*(4), 460–469. doi:10.2307/3150499

Oliver, R. L. (1981). Measurement and evaluation of satisfaction processes in retail settings. *Journal of Retailing*, *57*(3), 25–48.

Oliver, R. L. (1997). *Satisfaction: a behavioral perspective on the consumer.* New York: McGraw-Hill.

Oliver, R. L., & Westbrook, R. A. (1993). Cognitive, affective, and attribute bases of the satisfaction response. *The Journal of Consumer Research*, *20*(3), 418–430. doi:10.1086/209358

Park, D. H., Lee, J., & Han, I. (2007). The effect of on-line consumer reviews on consumer purchasing intention: The moderating role of involvement. *International Journal of Electronic Commerce*, *11*(4), 125–148. doi:10.2753/JEC1086-4415110405

Rahimi, R. (2007), *Feasibility Study of Customer Relationship Management (CRM) Application in Hotel Industry: Case of Hamgame Arya Group Hotels.* (Master Thesis). Lulea University of Technology.

Ranaweera, C., & Prabhu, J. (2003). On the relative importance of customer satisfaction and trust as determinants of customer retention and positive word of mouth. *Journal of Targeting, Measurement and Analysis of Marketing*, *12*(1), 82–90. doi:10.1057/palgrave.jt.5740100

Richins, M. L. (1983). Negative word-of-mouth by dissatisfied consumers: A pilot study. *Journal of Marketing*, *47*(1), 68–78. doi:10.2307/3203428

Richins, M. L. (1983). Negative Word-of-Mouth by Dissatisfied Consumers: A Pilot Study. *Journal of Marketing*, *47*(1), 68–78. doi:10.2307/3203428

Richins, M. L. (1987). A multivariate analyses of responses to dissatisfaction. *Journal of the Academy of Marketing Science*, *15*(3), 24–31. doi:10.1007/BF02722168

Shang, W., & Hooker, N. H. (2006). *Scales or Stars? Consumer Preferences for Food Quality Signals.* Working Paper. American Agricultural Economics Association Annual Meeting.

Sirdeshmukh, D., Singh, J., & Sabol, B. (2002). Consumer trust, value, and loyalty in relational exchanges. *Journal of Marketing*, *66*(1), 15–37. doi:10.1509/jmkg.66.1.15.18449

Son, J.-E., Kim, H.-W., & Jang, Y.-J. (2012). Investigating Factors Affecting Electronic Word-Of- Mouth In The Open Market Context: A Mixed Methods Approach. In *Proceedings of Pacific Asia Conference on Information Systems* (PACIS). Association for Information Systems, AIS Electronic Library (AISeL).

Spreng, R. A., MacKenzie, S. B., & Olshavsky, R. W. (1996). A re-examination of the determinants of consumer satisfaction. *Journal of Marketing*, *60*(3), 15–32. doi:10.2307/1251839

Straus, B., & Neuhaus, P. (1997). The qualitative satisfaction model. *International Journal of Service Industry Management*, *8*(3), 236–249. doi:10.1108/09564239710185424

Sutanto, J. E. (2009), Dimension Quality of Service Influence Customer Satisfaction in the Hotel: A Case study and examination of the transaction model in service industry. In *Proceeding of the International Seminar on Industrial Engineering and Management.* Academic Press.

Thomas, W. G., Talai, O., & Andrew, J. C. (2006). eWOM: The impact of customer-to-customer online know-how exchange on customer value and loyalty. *Journal of Business Research*, *59*(4), 449–456. doi:10.1016/j.jbusres.2005.10.004

Wangenheim, F. V., & Bayón, T. (2004). The Effect of Word-of-Mouth on Services Switching: Measurement and Moderating Variables. *European Journal of Marketing*, *38*(9–10), 1173–1185. doi:10.1108/03090560410548924

Westbrook, R. A., & Oliver, R. L. (1991). The dimensionality of consumption emotion patterns and consumer satisfaction. *The Journal of Consumer Research*, *18*(1), 84–91. doi:10.1086/209243

Wirtz, J., & Chew, P. (2002). The Effects of Incentives, Deal Proneness, Satisfaction and Tie Strength on Word-of-Mouth Behaviour. *International Journal of Service Industry Management*, *13*(2), 141–162. doi:10.1108/09564230210425340

KEY TERMS AND DEFINITIONS

Brand Loyalty: It is the preferential, attitudinal and behavioral response toward one or more brands in a product category expressed over a period of time by a consumer.

e-Business: E-business, is the application of information and communication technologies (ICT) in support of all the activities of business.

Loyalty: Loyalty is an approach to marketing, based on strategic management, in which a company focuses on growing and retaining existing customers through incentives.

Perception: Perception is the organization, identification, and interpretation of sensory information in order to represent and understand the environment.

Satisfaction: Fulfillment of one's wishes, expectations, or needs, or the pleasure derived.

Section 3
Capturing and Analysing Electronic Word of Mouth

Chapter 8
Network Text Analysis and Sentiment Analysis:
An Integration to Analyse Word-of-Mouth in the Digital Marketplace

Veronica Ravaglia
Catholic University of the Sacred Heart, Italy

Luca Zanazzi
University of Bologna, Italy

Elvis Mazzoni
University of Bologna, Italy

ABSTRACT

Through Social Media, like social networking sites, wikis, web forums or blogs, people can debate and influence each other. Due to this reason, the analysis of online conversations has been recognized to be relevant to organizations. In the chapter we introduce two strategic tools to monitor and analyze online conversations, Sentiment Text Analysis (STA) and Network Text Analysis (NTA). Finally, we propose one empirical example in which these tools are integrated to analyze Word-of-Mouth regarding products and services in the Digital Marketplace.

INTRODUCTION

The Social Web environment is an important and free public space in which, virtually, everyone may express his or her impressions, opinions and beliefs against a product, an event or a cause. More and more people, of every age, use the social web before they make any kind of decision, could it be to buy something, change something in their lives or make a difficult choice. Through Social Web tools, i.e. social networking sites, wikis, web forums or blogs, people can debate and influence each other's opinion. This kind of User Generated Content is very important for every organization because people interact

DOI: 10.4018/978-1-4666-9449-1.ch008

with each other and generate, on their own, a topic of discussion. This is the major advantage, compared to the other traditional forms of assessment that an organization can set. Most of the User Generated Contents on the web are public, which means that they are free to view. These contents and commentaries, therefore, represent a valuable and accessible resource to assess people's ideological positions. But, at the same time, people play an important role in influencing each other about a specific brand, product, service or something else (a film, an actor and so on) that has attracted the online debate. From this point of view, we can refer to the public and free online debate that arose around the choice of the actor for the second episode of Spider-Man, which seems to have influenced a lot the production of the film.

There is no doubt about the direct effect of the word-of-mouth on the digital marketplace and for this reason it is clear how these phenomena have to be taken into account for an efficient market strategy. Monitoring and intervening on brands and products' social perception is nowadays very important for all organizations. How organizational marketing campaign affects the consumption of the products, how the brand is perceived by the users and non-users, are there any differences in the sentiment against the product based on the characteristics of the users are some of the questions that need to be answered.

Many tools can be used to analyze these data, but one of the most valuable is the Sentiment Text Analysis (STA). Once the most relevant or important words are identified or specified, this technique allows, not only, to understand the polarity of the feelings undergoing a comment (positive, neutral, negative), but also to identify the single emotion involved. Moreover, the STA is based on a conventional Text Analysis (TA) and, therefore, there are also other several text analyses that can be performed at once. Some of these analyses are, for instance, counting the contingency of two single words (how much they appear close and linked in the text), some others perform the grammatical analysis of a word (nouns, adjectives or verbs), or simply their number in the text and their relevance amongst all comments.

To get a better understanding of these types of data, a complementary methodology that can be integrated with the STA is the Social Network Analysis (SNA) applied to text, i.e. the Network Text Analysis (NTA). Traditionally the SNA is a set of methods for analyzing the structure of whole social entities as well as a variety of theories explaining the patterns observed in these structures (Wasserman & Faust, 1994). Within this chapter, the SNA is mixed with STA to analyze the network and connections of the most used words about a specific topic, brand, service or organization. Each word will be a node in the network and each node may have several properties, such as type, (noun, adjective, verbs), speaker, location (where the word has been spoken) or sentiment (positive, neutral or negative) of the various words.

The aim of this chapter is to give a theoretical framework about Sentiment Analysis and Network Text Analysis and some concrete examples of their use to better understand the word-of-mouth effect in the digital marketplace.

BACKGROUND

Content Analysis and Sentiment Analysis

The term Big Data is often invoked to describe the overwhelming volume of information produced by and about human activity, made possible by the growing ubiquity of mobile devices, tracking tools, always-on sensors, and cheap computing storage. "In a digitized world, consumers going about their day – communicating, browsing, buying, sharing, searching – create their own enormous trails of data" (Manyika et al., 2011).

Social media today have become very popular communication tools among Internet users. Millions of messages are appearing daily in popular websites for social interaction such as Twitter, Tumblr, Facebook, blogs or forums. In these User Generated Contents, people write about their life, share opinions on variety of topics and discuss current issues. Moreover, because of a free format of messages and an easy accessibility of platforms, Internet users tend to post more and more comments about products and services they use, or express their opinion about brands. Thus, social media websites become valuable sources of people's topics of conversation, opinions and sentiments, particularly for business intelligence units.

For example, companies may be interested in the following questions:

- Which ones of our products are more discussed?
- What do people think about our products (or brand)?
- How positive (or negative) are people about our products (or brand)?
- What would people prefer our products (or brand) to be like?

Technological advances have made easier than ever to harness, organize, and scrutinize massive repositories of these digital traces; while once computational techniques required supercomputers to perform large-scale data analysis, now it can be deployed on a desktop or laptop computer (Manovich, 2011).

Within the context of mass communication, Content Analysis is one of the most familiar methods (Berelson, 1952; Krippendorff, 2012; Riff, Lacy, & Fico, 2014). The classical definition of content analysis is "a research technique for the objective, systematic, and quantitative description of the manifest content of communication" (Berelson, 1952, p. 18). Content analysis is generally conformed to the following procedure: 1) the research questions and/or hypotheses are formulated; 2) the sample is selected; 3) categories are defined for coding; 4) coders are trained, the content is coded, and reliability is assessed; 5) the coded data are analyzed and interpreted (McMillan, 2000; Riff et al., 2014). For content analysts in particular, the development of digital media's architecture has led to a fast-changing array of new structural features associated with communication, such as the hashtag on Twitter, as well as the development of socio-cultural contexts around those new features – both representing virgin terrain for content-analysis exploration. This opportunity has attracted all manner of content analysis work. In one small but flourishing branch of this research, there are content analyses of Twitter use by journalists (Bruns, 2012; Herrera & Requejo, 2012; Lasorsa, Lewis, & Holton, 2012), news organizations (Blasingame, 2011; Greer & Ferguson, 2011; Messner, Linke, & Eford, 2011; Newman, 2011), foreign correspondents (Bruno, 2011; Cozma & Chen, 2013; Heinrich, 2012), nonprofit organizations (Waters & Jamal, 2011), and even the homeless (Koepfler & Fleischmann, 2012).

Nevertheless, although Content Analysis seems appropriate for Big Data Analytics, much of the scholarly literature does not agree whether classical approaches are adequate for studying online content. McMillan (2000) and Weare & Lin (2000), for example, identify a number of challenges to applying content analysis to the Web, including difficulties in obtaining a representative sample because of the vastness of the Web; in defining the unit of analysis; and in ensuring that coders are presented with the same content for purposes of reliability. However, ultimately both conclude that minor adaptations to traditional approaches of content analysis are sufficient, such as using lists to help generate sampling frames and using software to capture snapshots of websites.

Frequently, researchers and stakeholders are not fully satisfied in the detection of contents in online conversations and, frequently, insights about opinion and sentiment associated to these topics are required.

Sentiment analysis, also called opinion mining, is the field of study that analyzes people's opinions, sentiments, evaluations, appraisals, attitudes, and emotions towards entities such as products, services, organizations, individuals, issues, events, topics, and their attributes.

With the growing availability and popularity of opinion-rich resources such as online review sites (like Trip Advisor) and personal blogs, new opportunities and challenges arise as people now can, and do, actively use information technologies to seek out and understand the opinions of others (Pang & Lee, 2008). A very broad overview of the existing work was presented by Pang & Lee (2008). In their survey, the authors describe existing techniques and approaches for an opinion-oriented information retrieval. Yang, Lin, & Chen (2007) use web-blogs to construct corpora for sentiment analysis and use emotion icons assigned to blog posts as indicators of users' mood. The authors applied support vector machine (SVM) and conditional random field (CRF) learners to classify sentiments at the sentence level and then investigated several strategies to determine the overall sentiment of the document. As the result, the winning strategy is defined by considering the sentiment of the last sentence of the document as the sentiment at the document level.

Read (2005) used emoticons such as ":-)" and ":-(" to form a training set for the sentiment classification. For this purpose, the author collected texts containing emoticons from Usenet newsgroups. The dataset was divided into "positive" (texts with happy emoticons) and "negative" (texts with sad or angry emoticons) samples. Emoticons-trained classifiers: SVM and Naive Bayes, were able to obtain up to 70% of accuracy on the test set.

Go and colleague (Go, Huang, & Bhayani, 2009) used Twitter to collect training data and then to perform a sentiment search. The approach is similar to that of Read (2005). The authors construct corpora by using emoticons to obtain "positive" and "negative" samples, and then use various classifiers. The Naive Bayes classifier obtained the best result with a mutual information measure for feature selection. The authors were able to obtain up to 81% of accuracy on their test set. However, the method showed a bad performance with three classes ("negative", "positive" and "neutral").

Interest in using both Content and Sentiment Analysis as a marketing research tool is due to many reasons. Firstly, not only academics but even marketers have recognized the profound influence of social communities on consumer behavior (Gruen, Osmonbekov, & Czaplewski, 2006; Park, Lee, & Han, 2007). Secondly, recent developments in technology have enhanced classification accuracy, and user friendliness. Marketers can collect large body of data in real time, unobstructed or contaminated by the presence of external researchers. Therefore, through online data analysis, market research cost and sampling error are reduced and validity and reliability of research findings are enhanced (Rambocas & Gama, 2013).

Because of all the possible applications, there are a good number of companies, large and small, that have opinion mining and sentiment analysis as part of their mission. Besides reputation management and public relations, one might perhaps hope that by tracking public viewpoints, one could perform trend prediction in sales or other relevant data. Yet, this Internet development is also vexing because "the glittering promise of online data abundance too often proves to be fool's gold" (Karpf, 2012, p. 652). Firstly, researchers struggle to anticipate when and how to "trap" such data streams, given that most objects of study (e.g., tweets, web traffic data, online news homepages) go un-archived (Karlsson & Strömbäck, 2010). Additionally, public data often pales in quality to proprietary data, which is rarely available to scholars. As Boyd and Crawford (2012, p. 669) note, even while scholars are able to access vast numbers of tweets via Twitter's public Application Programming Interface (API), many researchers are not getting the "firehose" of the complete content stream, but merely a "gardenhose" of very limited numbers of public tweets – the randomness of which is entirely unknown, raising questions about the representativeness of such data to all tweets, let alone to all users on the service. Finally, controversial questions about consumer privacy, research ethics, and the overall quantification of social life should never be left out (Boyd & Crawford, 2012; Oboler, Welsh, & Cruz, 2012).

THE SOCIAL NETWORK ANALYSIS

We are not alone. Everyone, in the everyday life, is connected with someone else. These ties may be represented e.g. by the family, a group of friends or a team of colleagues that create our personal network. In a social network, the actors and their actions are viewed as interdependent rather than independent, autonomous units. Relational ties (linkages) between actors are channels for transfer or "flow" of resources (either material or nonmaterial). For these reasons, the data describe the connections, the contacts and the ties between all the entity (individuals or organizations) in a defined group (people, family, society, enterprises, country). Network models focusing on individuals view the network as a structural environment that provides opportunities for or constraints on individual actions. On the contrary, network models focusing on structures (social, economic, political, and so forth) are lasting patterns of relations among actors (Gaggioli, Riva, Milani, & Mazzoni, 2012; Riva, Banos, Botella, Wiederhold, & Gaggioli, 2012; Scott & Amaturo, 1997; Wasserman & Faust, 1994).

From this brief introduction, it is clear that the focus of attention of the SNA is the relation between a set of entities rather than their attributes, even though, as it will be more clear in the following of this chapter, attributes are important to better describe and analyze the structure of relations. In this definition, the actor is a social entity, a discrete individual, corporate or collective social units, for instance people, departments, agencies. The relational ties are social ties, such as the evaluation or the selection of one person by another, the transfer of resources, association, behavioral interaction, formal relations, or biological relationships.

In the SNA each individual is a node and has its own attributes (gender, age, work position, etc.), while the relationships between individuals are represented by ties.

These social relations vary along three dimensions – direction, strength, content:

- **Direction:** Who originates the communication and/or receives a contact. Ties may be "MAN" – mutual, asymmetric, null. Asymmetric ties are called directed ties, in contrast to undirected or non-ties.
- **Strength:** The frequency of interaction. Simplest strength measure is binary (present/absent); other strength indicators may take discrete or continuous values (for instance, class attendance is binary; talking duration is continuous).
- **Relational Content:** A specific substantive connection among actors. Relations are multiplex when actors are connected by more than one type of tie (e.g., friendship and business). Some of the relations are forcibly biunivocal (brother-brother), others exclusive (wife-husband) and others not exclusive (teacher-alumni) with all the possible combinations.

The power of social network analysis stems from its difference from traditional methods in social scientific studies, which assume that attributes of individual actors define whether they are friends or not, how many friends or acquaintances they have, but also how old they are, and other psycho-social dimensions (such as self-esteem, life satisfaction, job satisfaction, etc.). This approach has turned out to be useful for explaining many real-world phenomena, but leaves less room for individual agency, the ability for individuals to influence their success, because so much of it rests within the structure of their network. Social networks have been used to examine e.g. how organizations interact with each other, characterizing the many informal connections that link executives together, as well as associations and connections between individual employees at different organizations. For example, power within organizations often comes more from the degree to which an individual within a network is at the center of many relationships, rather than actual job title. Social networks play also a key role in hiring, in business success, and in job performance. Networks provide ways for companies to gather information, deter competition and collude in setting prices or policies (Kilduff & Brass, 2010).

Metrics (Measures) in Social Network Analysis

SNA is a corpus of analysis that allows to describe and examine the relational structure of a specific context by means of some metrics (indexes) and the related sociograms (graphs). Each analysis allows to focus the attention at two levels: the whole network of relations (whole network or full network analysis) or the individuals (ego-network analysis) (Scott, 2000; Wasserman & Faust, 1994). Not all analysis are good for any setting: the type of analysis and the index to calculate is determined by the context and the aims of the study (Gaggioli, Milani, Mazzoni, & Riva, 2011). Examples of the most relevant types of analysis, and the related network and individual indexes, are the following:

- **Neighborhood Analysis:** Density/inclusiveness I nodes degree. In this type of analysis, two nodes are 'adjacent' (connected) if there is a line (connection) between them. A node is 'incident' to a line if the node is one of the pair of nodes defining the line. Nodal 'degree' (of connection) is the number of lines that are incident with it. It measures the size of its direct neighborhood. Two types of measurements are present: In-Degree and Out-Degree. The nodal 'In-Degree' is the number of lines to which the node is incident as target (receiver); the'Out-Degree' is the number of lines to which the node is incident as source. Density is the ratio of the number of present lines (connections) with respect to the maximum possible, i.e. how much the network of relations approaches the situations in which all possible relations are activated (complete graph). Inclusiveness is the number of connected nodes expressed as a proportion of the total number of nodes.
- **Cohesion Analysis:** Cliques I cliques participation index. Clique is a maximal complete sub graph composed of three or more nodes. We can briefly summarize this concept as a subset of nodes connected. A node can be a member of more than one cliques, therefore the cliques in a network may overlap. Cliques participation index (CPI) describes the average number of cliques each participant is involved in (Gaggioli, Riva, Milani, Mazzoni, 2012).

Nevertheless, one of the most famous and important SNA measures, particularly relevant for the scope of this chapter, is the centrality analysis and the related indexes of centralization (network) and of centrality (individual). This type of analysis tells us how central or peripheral is a specific entity (centrality index) and how the network is centralized on its more central entities (centralization index). In other terms, the centrality is a measure of the relevance, prestige, power or status characterizing a set of entities of a specific context (Scott, 2000; Wasserman & Faust, 1994). There are many types of centrality (and centralization) indexes based on the type of relational dynamic on which the attention is focused. For instance, the degree centrality describes the relevance of the nodes of a network based on the quantity of relations: e.g., the more an actor receives connections, the more the actor has a high status. The betweenness centrality focus the attention on nodes that lie between other nodes in the network, since they have a power (more relevance) in controlling the transmission of information between the networks: e.g., the more an actor acts as bridge between many nodes, the more the actor has the power to "control" the flow of information. A further interesting centrality index is the eigenvector centrality. It is similar to the degree centrality, but the centrality of a node is determined also by the centrality of its adjacent nodes (directly connected): e.g., the more an actor is connected to nodes with a high relevance, the more it becomes relevant.

NETWORK TEXT ANALYSIS AND THE ANALYSIS OF WORD-OF-MOUTH IN THE DIGITAL MARKETPLACE

The SNA is a very solid and specific method of quantitative analysis. It can be used in several contexts and has many positive aspects such as handling big data and complex networks. However, focusing on the mere communication exchange or similarities between nodes, it considers neither the context in which the conversations took place nor the quality (content) of the exchange. Take for example a conversation about a product on a blog. This particular conversation could be very dense (many communication exchanges are present). It is the extent to which all possible relationships between the elements are in fact present, and is evaluated on a scale ranging from 0 (absence of aggregation) to 1 (maximum aggregation)) from an SNA point of view. Moreover, the centrality index could be meaningful. However, the conversation could have many topics and could also treat other areas of interest.

Starting from this issue, as anticipated before, the aim of this chapter is to create an integration between the content analysis (CA) and the social network analysis (SNA). It is, indeed, possible to use SNA on qualitative data and not only in the relations and exchanges within a network of individuals (Mangione, Mazzoni, Orciuoli, & Pierri, 2011). There are several examples of an integration between CA and SNA, especially as regards the study of ontology (Hoser, Hotho, Jäschke, Schmitz, & Stumme, 2006; Yu, 2008) and the semantic aspect of a network (Erétéo, Gandon, Corby, & Buffa, 2009; Mika, 2005).

From this original idea, a new type of analysis joins the traditional SNA: the Network Text Analysis (NTA). The NTA is based on the content and the quality of the data, considering, at the same time, the relations between the nodes (lemmas) in the dimensions of time, space, conditions of the communicational exchange. The basic assumption of the NTA is that a given text is a genuine network, formed by different words. The words, as in a traditional SNA, are the nodes of the network, but unlike in the latter, each words has a specific property (it can be a noun, a verb or an adjective). However this property is not intrinsic but, rather, based on more or less explicit rules (grammar and logic). Functionality and relations between words can also be based on the content of the sentence.

The purpose of this methodology is to explore the nature of the relationships between words to achieve a deeper understanding that goes beyond the simple numerical data of the SNA. In particular, the NTA allow us to have a deeper understanding about the central and peripheral arguments of a speech, the strengths and weaknesses of a message or conversation, which arguments are more or less central in real or virtual conversations about the same topic, etc..

Similar to SNA, NTA has several fields of application; however, the choice of the correct indexes is subject to what you need to get from the text (Gaggioli, Riva, Milani, Mazzoni, 2012). The same index has different meanings: in the SNA, the adjacency matrix shows the relational information among the nodes, while, in the NTA, it shows the co-occurrence between the topic or words in a given User Generated Content. An interesting field of application is that of the *knowledge graphs*, i.e. schemas representing the graphical synthesis of a particular construct (e.g. a theory) by means of keywords (Popping and Strijker, 1997; Popping, 2003). To construct these types of graphs, NTA is needed to extract information about the relations between the lemmas of a given text. Starting from the relations detected by the NTA, in a knowledge graph such relations are enriched by indication of the type of relation: CAU describes a relation of cause and effect; PAR indicates the relation "is part of"; AKO indicates the relation "a kind of", etc.

One of the most interesting and promising field of application of the NTA, which could have important implication for the analysis of the word-of-mouth in the digital marketplace, is its use to understand the social representations characterizing a given topic (Gaggioli, Riva, Milani, Mazzoni, 2012). A theoretical framework can be useful to understand how the NTA may be exploited as driving force of the social representations change. In order to answer to this need Abric's point of view about social representations turns out to be particularly interesting and effective (Abric, 1989). He describes social representations based on a double system:

- The central system, which corresponds to the core of the representation and is fixed socially, as it is linked to historic, sociological, and ideological conditions. The central core is fundamental for the stability and coherence of each representation, guaranteeing that it will endure in time. This system specifies the fundamental elements around which representations are generated, and constitutes the social and collective basis of the representations, which defines the degree of consensus and homogeneity of a group, independently of each individual.
- The peripheral system, which depends strictly on characteristics of the individuals and the context in which they are positioned. Such a system therefore makes a differentiation within the group of individuals and is able to adapt itself to specific situations and to explore certain everyday experiences. It is much more versatile than the central system, and it enables the integration of information and practices of varying types, thus showing the heterogeneity of behavior and contents. The peripheral system is essential in the identification of the changes and transformations underway in the representations, which indicate their evolution and likely future modifications.

Therefore, stability and rigidity of representations depend on the core, strongly linked to the value systems shared by members of the group, while the richness and variety of individual experiences and the evolution of everyday practices determine a representation's mutability and flexibility.

Since the central system creates and organizes the representation, Abric avers that it is also its most stable element, that which more than any other resists to change. This means that a representation's evolution will begin from the modification of its peripheral and less central elements. A transformation of the central nucleus would indeed bring about a modification in the structure and the totality of the representation. Therefore, we can presume that the change and evolution of a representation will only be superficial if it comes about through the modification of the meaning, or the nature, of the peripheral elements, while the involvement of the core would radically alter the representation itself. There are therefore two interesting aspects, which relate to the use of NTA in the analysis of the representations, which characterize a network of individuals:

- The possibility to differentiate between elements of the central core and peripheral elements in a social representation;
- The possibility to carry out a longitudinal analysis of the representation's evolution, paying particular attention to the transition of certain aspects from peripheral to central, and vice versa.

NTA in Practice

In practice, the NTA can be very useful in order to analyze User Generated Contents like conversations or discussion about products, policies or events, particularly in online contexts in which data collection is easy and could be automatized. An example of data collection and elaboration to perform a network text analysis is the following.

The first step is identifying a meaningful conversation on the web. It can be taken directly from a blog, a forum or even from a social network site. The data collected have to be "clean" from unnecessary words, such as time line of the conversation, name of the speaker or number of the post etc. Part of the analysis preparation is also the selection of the keywords. The keywords are the words that have a high incidence in the given text. Most of the text analysis software have a built-in dictionary and algorithms to safely identify keywords. You have to pay attention to not include in the keywords the self-referred words (for instance, when a speaker starts a post using the name of another speaker), the pronouns, the auxiliary verbs, the prepositions, the articles or the conjunctions. Moreover, some words have to be treated as identical, if they share the same meaning, even if they have different grammatical properties: pear = pears or write = wrote = writing.

Secondarily, the collected data have to be processed with specific text analysis application (like software for text mining or content analysis) in order to obtain the co-occurrence matrix (it indicates the amount of times that two words are matched within a text). The co-occurrence matrix is formed by the words that are more central in the discussions analyzed, namely those which not only have a greater amount of co-occurrences than other entries, but which would also be given greater weight by the interlocutors for their relevance in terms of centrality. From an operative point of view, the co-occurrence matrices are square matrices similar to typical SNA adjacency matrices and show, at the crossing of two terms, the strength of the link (the amount of times in which they match within the text). It is therefore possible to transpose the data of this matrix onto an adjacency matrix and then perform the SNA on nodes represented by lemmas, i.e. the Network Text Analysis. The index of eigenvector centrality, for instance, allows to discriminate the concepts which are most central and peripheral in a speech. The cohesion analysis describes how much a principal conversation is composed by many sub-conversations having specific topics. The connectivity analysis shows which parts of a speech are more solid and which arguments are weaker (peripheral in terms of centrality index).

At the conclusion of this chapter, we propose a purely demonstrative example of an analysis of the conversations held on an online blog by a group of users about the controversial (and elusive) case of the Pink Beer made by one of the most famous brand.

THE PINK BEER CASE STUDY

This case concerns a Danish brand producing beer since 1856, traditionally a Strong Ale with low fermentation and a robust and bitter taste. In March 2014 a lot of information appears online (more or less officials) announcing a new product, the Soft Ale: a light, kitschy, pink beer made with raspberry and ginger. The new product was advertised on a website, accompanied with a video-spot and the official trademark of the brand. Eventually the advertisement has proven to be an April fool, but during the days before the discovery, many conversations took place, triggering a flaming debate on the taste of the future beer.

More than a mere April fool, this advertising campaign may be an attempt by the brand to understand, in advance, the reaction of consumers about a new product. We believe that, although consumers, did not appreciate overall rose beer after careful analysis, a meaningful interpretation of the data and a conscious changing of the unpopular peripheral topics, the brand's new product could have a positive review. We took one of those conversations with the purpose of finding the general sentiments and topics about the Pink Beer.

The first step was to clean the text-file from all the unusual words. This has been done through a Text Mining Software (like T-Lab) and a subsequent human check intervention. The plain text-file was then analyzed with the same software and several keywords emerged. They were obtained starting from the occurrences of the same words in the text-file. As anticipated before, words with the same semantic meaning were considered the same word (for instance: beer = beers). Secondarily the co-occurrence matrix was obtained and transformed in the adjacency matrix. By comparing the keywords with the sentences in which these words were present, a topic and a sentiment were assigned to each sentence. An expert of the field made the sentiment analysis manually. Operatively, a sentiment (negative, neutral or positive) and a topic were given to each sentence. Each keyword was related to all the sentences in which it was included and to the respective sentiment and topic. For instance, if a keyword is included in five sentences, the keyword is also associated to five sentiments and topics. Eventually, the most recurrent topic and sentiment related to the keyword was chosen and attributed as the main ones.

These tags became the node attribute in the following NTA. Several analyses were conducted, but for explanatory purposes, we only report the neighborhood analysis (Figure 1) and the degree centrality (Figure 2).

As it is shown in the picture (Figure 1), each node is a keyword and the ties indicate the co-occurrences. The shape stands for the topic of the sentence in which the keyword existed (if it concerns the trademark or the product, i.e. beer), while the color indicates the general sentiment of the sentence (positive, neutral or negative). It is quite evident that the discussion concerns principally the product (beer) and in negative way (red color). Particularly interesting is that while the discussion is much focused on the product (beer), see also the next picture (Figure 2), it also influences the brand that has a high frequency (dimension) becoming one of the focus of the negative sentiment.

Further, by looking on the left of the picture, we have a representation of the "beer" such as something concerning industrial or artisanal fields in which it is characterized by procedures such as filtering and tasting. But the upper side of the picture shows the relations between the most negative keywords that characterized the discussion: raspberry (the taste of the beer), Lambic (the type of beer obtained by spontaneous fermentation), passion (described as something that will decrease) and finally the trademark (that has principally an undirected negative sentiment determined by the negativity of the other keywords with which it co-occurs).

The second pictures (Figure 2) shows with more detail the relative ranking (centrality) among the various most important lemmas. While in the previous picture (Figure 1) the relations between lemmas were evident, in this second the centrality of both trademark and product in the discussion is clearer. But since the product and the trademark were the focus of the discussion, for a better understanding of the

Figure 1.

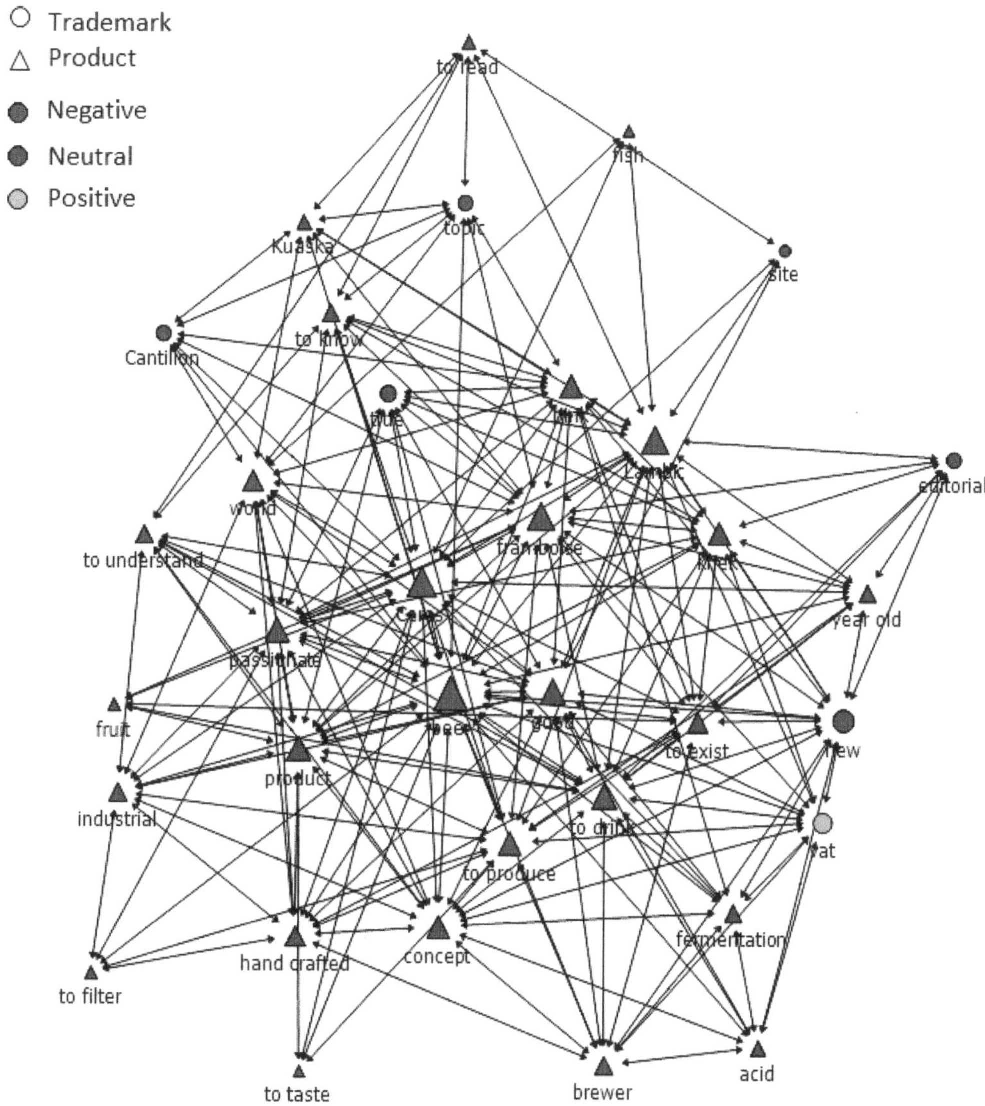

central and peripheral lemmas characterizing the discussions, it could be useful to eliminate the focus of the discussion (product and trademark) and concentrate on the remaining lemmas (the arguments connected to the principal product and the trademark)(Figure 3).

Now the focus of the negative sentiment characterizing the discussion about the "pink beer" is clear. The production and the existence of a Lambic pink beer produced by raspberries does not meet the positive sentiment of people involved in the discussion. Strangely, the "kriek bier", a sort of beer originally obtained by adding fresh black cherries to a Lambic beer, has a positive sentiment. Probably the fact that this is an historical type of beer, already well known and conceptualized in people's "beer representation", play an important role in its acceptance. While the new one, is probably seen as a mere copy of the other and it does not encounter the same sentiment.

Figure 2.

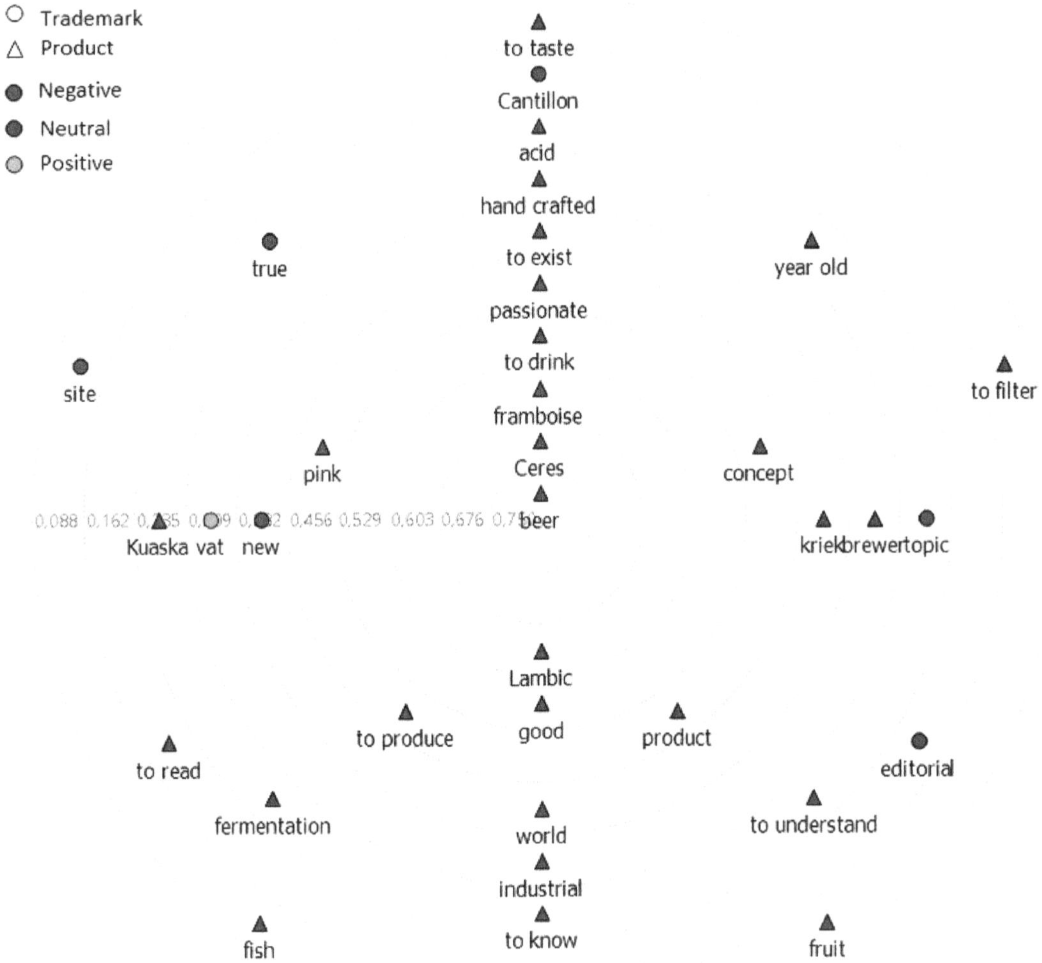

CONCLUSION

The existence of a vast, publicly accessible reservoir of observable peer-to-peer communications is unprecedented. There is meaningful information in these conversations which can be accessed at minimal cost. Compared with the more costly survey-based methods typically employed, this data source is significantly more efficient and may offer an easy and cost-effective opportunity to gain the flow, drivers and sentiment associated to a specific product or brand

In this chapter, we have described three types of analysis that could be very useful to analyze Word-of-Mouth in the Digital Marketplace: Content Analysis, Sentiment Analysis and Network Text Analysis. While all the three types of analysis have interesting potentiality to analyze dialogues, conversations,

Figure 3.

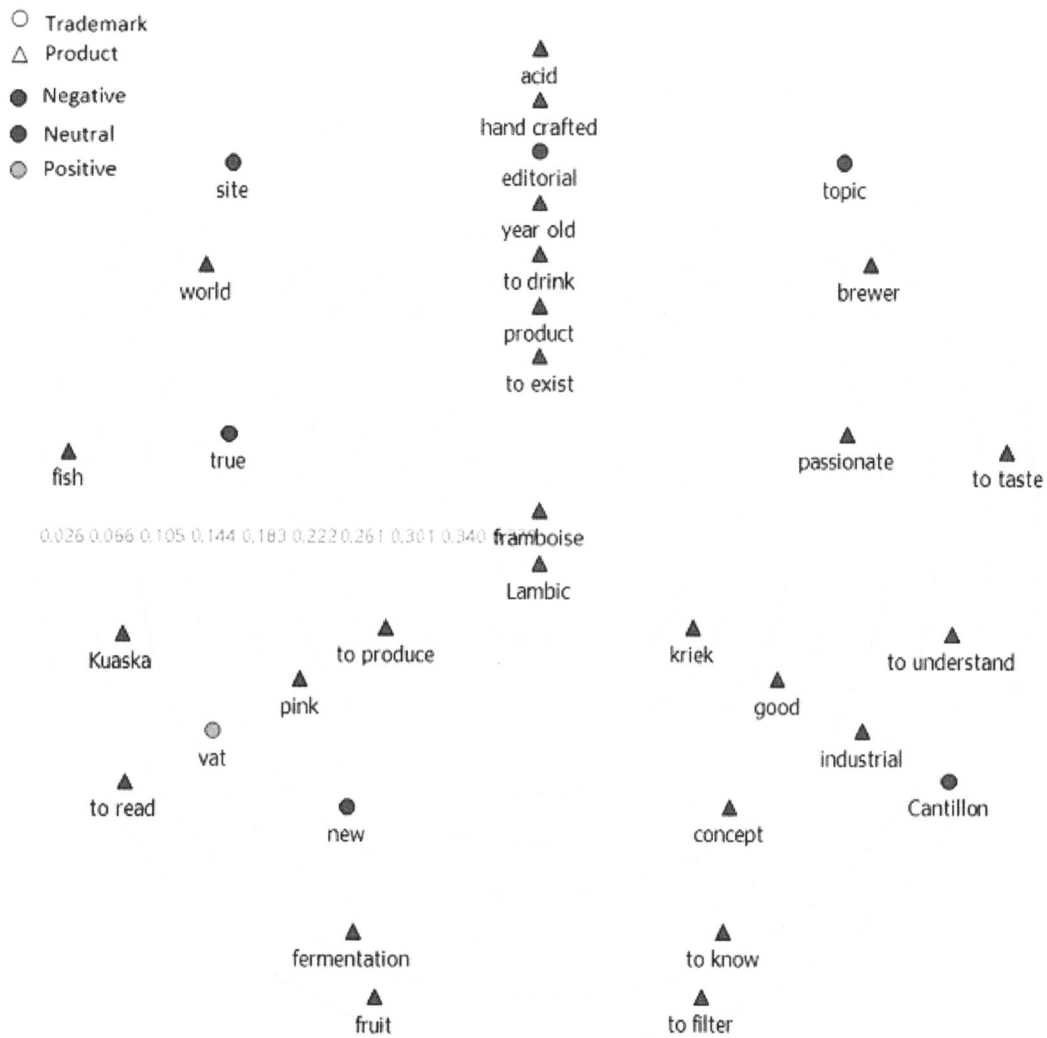

commentaries in online contexts, we would suggest an integration of the three to have a deeper understanding of the arguments, sentiment and structures that characterize people's representations about a given product or brand.

From this point of view, the Network Text Analysis (integrated with SA information) seems to have important margins of progress since it could be associated with the classic Social Network Analysis to have a double level of analysis: the first on the relations between people and the second on the structural representation of their discussions. This could be very interesting to analyze the influence processes such as emotional contagion and virtual influence in online contexts.

From a brand perspective, the integrated exploration of these elements could help in improving brand engagement and brand image in many ways. Firstly, the detection of people's arguments about products or brands – and sentiment associated to these – helps in the construction of a brand image more syntonic with the consumer's desiderata.

Secondly, the understanding of the topics, sentiment and structures of brand's representations in online conversation is extremely useful when it comes to customer relationship management. The most efficient way to create consumer engagement is to create a brand-consumer exchange relationship. This particular relationship is highly consistent with the Web 2.0 and SNSs environments, where both players within an environment can be active content creators and the communication is immediately characterized by bidirectional flows. The detection of the drivers and the sentiment of conversations favour the brand in creating engaging conversations with its customers. Moreover, the study of the network helps in individualizing brand's ambassadors, what they care most about, the strength and the weakness in their brand's representation.

Finally, the analysis of online user generated content generate insights relevant in product improvement.

However, this study is not without limitations; indeed, if online conversations provide a huge range of useful elements in managing brand online presence, brand image and product improvement, the relationship between the online and the offline worlds should be investigated, too. Future research is needed to explore the match between insights hidden in online conversation and offline behavior of consumers.

REFERENCES

Abric, J. C. (1976). *Jeux, conflits et représentations sociales [thèse]*. Marseille: Université de Provence.

Abric, J.-C. (1989). L'étude expérimentale des représentations sociales. *Les Représentations Sociales*, *4*, 187–203.

Berelson, B. (1952). *Content Analysis in Communication Research*. Glencoe, IL: Free Press.

Blasingame, D. (2011). Gatejumping: Twitter, TV news and the delivery of breaking news. *#ISOJ Journal: The Official Research Journal of the International Symposium on Online Journalism*, *1*(2). Retrieved from http://online.journalism.utexas.edu/ebook.php

Boyd, D., & Crawford, K. (2012). Critical questions for big data: Provocations for a cultural, technological, and scholarly phenomenon. *Information Communication and Society*, *15*(5), 662–679. doi:10.1080/1369118X.2012.678878

Brass, D. J. (1984). Being in the right place: A structural analysis of individual influence in an organization. *Administrative Science Quarterly*, *29*(4), 518–539. doi:10.2307/2392937

Brass, D. J. (2011). A social network perspective on industrial/organizational psychology. In S. W. J. Kozlowski (Ed.), *The Oxford handbook of organizational psychology* (pp. 667–695). New York: Oxford University Press.

Bruno, N. (2011). Tweet first, verify later? How real-time information is changing the coverage of worldwide crisis events. Oxford, UK: Reuters Institute for the Study of Journalism, University of Oxford. Retrieved from http://reutersinstitute.politics.ox.ac.uk/fileadmin/documents/Publications/

Bruns, A. (2012). Journalists and Twitter: How Australian news organisations adapt to a new medium. *Media International Australia Incorporating Culture and Policy*, (144), 97–107.

Cozma, R., & Chen, K.-J. (2013). What's in a tweet? Foreign correspondents' use of social media. *Journalism Practice*, *7*(1), 33–46. doi:10.1080/17512786.2012.683340

Erétéo, G., Gandon, F., Corby, O., & Buffa, M. (2009). Semantic social network analysis. In B. K. Daniel (Ed.), *Handbook of Research on Methods and Techniques for Studying Virtual Communities: Paradigms and Phenomena* (pp. 122–156). Academic Press.

Gaggioli, A., Milani, L., Mazzoni, E., & Riva, G. (2011). Networked flow: A framework for understanding the dynamics of creative collaboration in educational and training settings. *The Open Education Journal*, *4*(1), M3. doi:10.2174/1874920801104010041

Gaggioli, A., Riva, G., Milani, L., & Mazzoni, E. (2012). *Networked flow: Towards an understanding of creative networks*. Berlin, Germany: Springer.

Go, A., Huang, L., & Bhayani. R. (2009). *Twitter sentiment analysis*. Final Projects from CS224N for Spring 2008/2009 at The Stanford Natural Language Processing Group.

Greer, C. F., & Ferguson, D. A. (2011). Using Twitter for promotion and branding: A content analysis of local television Twitter sites. *Journal of Broadcasting & Electronic Media*, *55*(2), 198–214. doi:10.1080/08838151.2011.570824

Gruen, T. W., Osmonbekov, T., & Czaplewski, A. J. (2006). eWOM: The impact of customer-to-customer online know-how exchange on customer value and loyalty. *Journal of Business Research*, *59*(4), 449–456. doi:10.1016/j.jbusres.2005.10.004

Heinrich, A. (2012). Foreign reporting in the sphere of network journalism. *Journalism Practice*, *6*(5-6), 766–775. doi:10.1080/17512786.2012.667280

Herrera, S., & Requejo, J. L. (2012). 10 Good Practices for News Organizations Using Twitter. *Journal of Applied Journalism & Media Studies*, *1*(1), 79–95. doi:10.1386/ajms.1.1.79_1

Hoser, B., Hotho, A., Jäschke, R., Schmitz, C., & Stumme, G. (2006). *Semantic network analysis of ontologies*. Berlin, Germany: Springer. doi:10.1007/11762256_38

IEEE. (2007). *WI '07: Proceedings of the IEEE/WIC/ACM International Conference on Web Intelligence*. Washington, DC: IEEE Computer Society.

Karlsson, M., & Strömbäck, J. (2010). Freezing the flow of online news: Exploring approaches to the study of the liquidity of online news. *Journalism Studies*, *11*(1), 2–19. doi:10.1080/14616700903119784

Karpf, D. (2012). Social science research methods in Internet time. *Information Communication and Society*, *15*(5), 639–661. doi:10.1080/1369118X.2012.665468

Kilduff, M., & Brass, D. J. (2010). Organizational social network research: Core ideas and key debates. *The Academy of Management Annals*, *4*(1), 317–357. doi:10.1080/19416520.2010.494827

Koepfler, J. A., & Fleischmann, K. R. (2012). Studying the values of hard-to-reach populations: Content analysis of Tweets by the 21st Century homeless. *Proceedings of the 2012 iConference*, *7*(1), 48-55.

Krippendorff, K. (2012). *Content analysis: An introduction to its methodology*. Thousand Oaks, CA: Sage Publications; doi:10.1145/2132176.2132183

Lasorsa, D. L., Lewis, S. C., & Holton, A. E. (2012). Normalizing Twitter: Journalism practice in an emerging communication space. *Journalism Studies*, *13*(1), 19–36. doi:10.1080/1461670X.2011.571825

Mangione, G. R., Mazzoni, E., Orciuoli, F., & Pierri, A. (2011). *A pedagogical approach for collaborative ontologies building*. Berlin, Germany: Springer. doi:10.1007/978-3-642-19814-4_7

Manovich, L. (2012). Trending: The Promises and the Challenges of Big Social Data. Debates in the Digital Humanities. In M. K. Gold (Ed.), *Debates in the Digital Humanities* (pp. 460–475). Minneapolis, MN: The University of Minnesota Press.

Manyika, J., Chui, M., Brown, B., Bughin, J., Dobbs, R., Roxburgh, C., & Byers, A. H. (2011). *Big data: The next frontier for innovation, competition, and productivity*. Technical report. McKinsey Global Institute.

McMillan, S. J. (2000). The microscope and the moving target: The challenge of applying content analysis to the World Wide Web. *Journalism & Mass Communication Quarterly*, *77*(1), 80–98. doi:10.1177/107769900007700107

Messner, M., Linke, M., & Eford, A. (2011, April). *Shoveling tweets: An analysis of the microblogging engagement of traditional news organizations*. Paper presented at the 12th International Symposium for Online Journalism, Austin, TX.

Mika, P. (2005). *Ontologies are us: A unified model of social networks and semantics*. Berlin, Germany: Springer.

Newman, N. (2011). *Mainstream media and the distribution of news in the age of social discovery*. Oxford, UK: Reuters Institute of Journalism.

Oboler, A., Welsh, K., & Cruz, L. (2012). The danger of big data: Social media as computational social science. *First Monday*, *17*(7).

Pang, B., & Lee, L. (2008, February). *Using Very Simple Statistics for Review Search: An Exploration*. Poster presented at the International Conference on Computational Linguistics, Haifa, Israel.

Park, D.-H., Lee, J., & Han, I. (2007). The effect of on-line consumer reviews on consumer purchasing intention: The moderating role of involvement. *International Journal of Electronic Commerce*, *11*(4), 125–148. doi:10.2753/JEC1086-4415110405

Popping, R. (2003). Knowledge graphs and network text analysis. *Social Sciences Information. Information Sur les Sciences Sociales*, *42*(1), 91–106. doi:10.1177/0539018403042001798

Popping, R., & Strijker, I. (1997). Representation and integration of sociological knowledge using knowledge graphs. *Social Sciences Information. Information Sur les Sciences Sociales*, *36*(4), 731–747. doi:10.1177/053901897036004006

Rambocas, M., & Gama, J. (2013). Marketing Research: The Role of Sentiment Analysis. *FEP Economics and Management*, 1-24.

Read, J. (2005). Using emoticons to reduce dependency in machine learning techniques for sentiment classification (pp. 43–48). In *Proceedings of the ACL-2005 Student Research Workshop*. Ann Arbor, MI: ACL. doi:10.3115/1628960.1628969

Riff, D., Lacy, S., & Fico, F. (2014). *Analyzing media messages: Using quantitative content analysis in research*. London, UK: Routledge.

Riva, G., Banos, R. M., Botella, C., Wiederhold, B. K., & Gaggioli, A. (2012). Positive technology: Using interactive technologies to promote positive functioning. *Cyberpsychology, Behavior, and Social Networking*, *15*(2), 69–77. doi:10.1089/cyber.2011.0139 PMID:22149077

Scott, J. (2000). *Social network analysis: A handbook*. London, UK: Sage.

Scott, J., & Amaturo, E. (1997). *L'analisi delle reti sociali*. Roma, Italy: La Nuova Italia Scientifica.

Wasserman, S., & Faust, K. (1994). *Social network analysis: Methods and applications* (Vol. 8). Cambridge, UK: Cambridge University Press. doi:10.1017/CBO9780511815478

Waters, R. D., & Jamal, J. Y. (2011). Tweet, tweet, tweet: A content analysis of nonprofit organizations' Twitter updates. *Public Relations Review*, *37*(3), 321–324. doi:10.1016/j.pubrev.2011.03.002

Weare, C., & Lin, W.-Y. (2000). Content Analysis of the World Wide Web Opportunities and Challenges. *Social Science Computer Review*, *18*(3), 272–292. doi:10.1177/089443930001800304

Yang, C., Lin, K. H.-Y., & Chen, H.-H. (2007). Emotion classification using web blog corpora. Academic Press.

Yu, E. (2008). *Social Network Analysis Applied to Ontology 3D Visualization.* (Doctoral dissertation). Miami University, Miami, FL.

KEY TERMS AND DEFINITIONS

Consumer-Brand Engagement (CBE): The cognitive, emotional, behavioral factors, which connect a brand with its followers.

Content Analysis (CA): The study and analysis of the text contained within the various types of human (cultural) artifacts such as writing, images and recordings.

Digital Marketplace: A kind of e-commerce that engages the stakeholder with the multimedia device and the web technologies, protocols and tools.

Network Text Analysis (NTA): A set of methodologies, supported by software, that allow to extract networks of concepts" from texts and to discern the "meaning" represented or encoded therein.

Online Conversation Monitoring: A group of tools and activity aimed to check the customers believes through online channels.

Sentiment Analysis: A type of analysis that aims to determine an attitude, a judgment, a belief or an evaluation toward a given topic.

Social Network Analysis (SNA): A methodology that allows studying and visualizing the ties between the nodes of a given network.

Word of Mouth: A spontaneous and free oral or written recommendation by a satisfied customer to the prospective customers of a good or service.

Chapter 9
Developing a Research Framework to Assess Online Consumer Behaviour Using Netnography in India:
A Review of Related Research

Gautam Deka
Sir Padampat Singhania University, India

Sumangla Rathore
Sir Padampat Singhania University, India

Avinash Panwar
Sir Padampat Singhania University, India

ABSTRACT

Netnography is a specialized form of ethnographic research that has been adapted to the unique contingencies of various types of computer-mediated social interaction. With the tremendous growth in the number of Internet users in India, the potential of utilizing netnography to study various aspects of management and business has also increased. Several e-Commerce companies have started operating in India since 2007. Over time, the number of online consumers has also increased in India. Therefore it is important to know the online consumer behaviour towards e-Commerce companies operating in India. Keeping the above facts in view, this chapter proposes Netnogrpahy as an effective research method to assess online consumer behavior. The chapter not only helps in providing future agenda for research, but also presents a framework that may be adopted to carry out Netnogrpahy of e-commerce related websites in India.

DOI: 10.4018/978-1-4666-9449-1.ch009

INTRODUCTION

Market research is the cornerstone that supports the marketing machines of every company. For consumer-facing companies, it is absolutely necessary to be tapped into the thoughts and pulses of current customers, as well as prospective ones, in order to uncover market segments and needs and better position products for consumer adoption.

Traditionally companies used to conduct surveys and studies with a goal to create data to analyze and act upon as per their objectives. Companies have traditionally relied on a range of qualitative and quantitative market research techniques conducted in parallel or serially, such as focus groups, surveys, interviews and ethnographies, the direct observance of human behavior. Such approaches are usually biased, costly and time-intensive (slow). It has been argued that companies pour in resources only to get mediocre results.

Ethnography is an anthropological approach that has gained popularity in sociology, cultural studies, marketing and consumer research, and many other fields in the social sciences. The term refers both to the act of doing ethnographic fieldwork and to the representations based on such a study. Dick Hobbs (2011) provides a cogent definition of ethnography, defining it as: a cocktail of methodologies that share the assumption that personal engagement with the subject is the key to understanding a particular culture or social setting.

While in the past such methods were the only means for gathering this kind of data, today internet has provided another approach to obtain the desired information. With the rapid emergence of blogs, forums, social networks and plethora of information posted on the internet, huge amount of information (data) is now available, which needs to be collected and analyzed. This has opened a new approach to understanding consumer behavior, by collection and analysis of data from the internet. This approach is called "netnography" (Kozinets 2002). Basically netnography is an ethnographic study using the internet as a proxy for the voice of the consumer.

The literal implementation of ethnography on the internet, netnography is the process of accessing and analyzing sentiments and opinions expressed by consumers chatting in blogs, forums and online discussion groups. This method is much quicker, cheaper and results are arguably more authentic expressions of opinion and need.

A netnography study can also be a very valuable first step in a larger research programme. Performing a netnograph study before launching into more expensive and time-consuming methods can expedite the research cycle by providing researchers with preliminary information that enables them to immediately dive into more focused and valuable tasks. Netnography can make it possible to leverage the vast quantities of data on the internet of all kinds, in providing much more deep and meaningful way.

Netnographic research has its shortcomings and challenges also. First, the researchers, as nonparticipant observers, cannot direct the content of participants' text. Secondly, the researchers cannot verify the authenticity of participants' claim (e.g. regarding their age and place of residence). As a result, researchers might inadvertently find themselves engaged with data contributed by child participants masquerading as adults, in studies that are age-range specific. Furthermore, netnography researchers have no access to nonverbal communications, and have to rely entirely on written text, a condition that may limit the thickness of data. There are also legitimate concerns that some website content might be manipulated for various ends, as in the case of, for example, where corporate-owned sites are administered in a manner that portrays a desired business image, so that negative customer reviews, for instance, deleted by website administrators. These limitations pose significant challenges for web-based research (Mkono 2012).

A major concern in all research is the honesty of the responses upon which a researcher bases her or his conclusions. In netnographic research, this concern is amplified by the uncertain nature of the interactions and respondents. Virtual communities are composed of people who rarely meet face to face, who are largely (but probably not totally) unaccountable for the information they share, and whose identities may be kept permanently anonymous. Because the virtual self is separate from the physical body, and thus apparently from "material" consequences, it might be assumed that this self-simulation is more likely to engage in self-dissimulation.

A key consideration is the ethical issues that arise when research is conducted online (Beven and Laws 2007, Dwivedi 209, Ismail 2010, Janta and Ladkin 2009, Kozinets 1997, 1998, 2002, 2006, Langer and Beckman 2005, Morgan 2008, Woodside et al. 2007). Key among these is the informed consent dilemma. However, most authors agree that where data are collected from pseudonymous/ anonymous public-type forums, with the researcher acting as nonparticipant observer, the requirement for informed consent of individual participants falls away, although researchers might still need to negotiate access from gatekeepers (e.g. website administrators) (Mkono 2012). However, in the case of private membership forums, researchers might need to disclose their intentions before participating in the online exchanges. In relation to sensitive topics, however, revealing researchers identity might comprise the quality of data, as the observer effect begins to operate (Mkono 2012).

Kozinets (1998) observed that the ways in which virtual identities interacts visual communities (and, on the large stage, in a virtual world) is at a very early stage of understanding. He further stated that there is a tradeoff effect at work: the same freedom which inspires people to mischievously construct deliberate falsehood about themselves and their opinions also allows them and others the freedom to express aspects of themselves, their ambitions and inner conflicts, that they would otherwise keep deeply hidden (Tyrkle 1995, Kozinets 1998).

Devoid of the kinesthetic clues of body language, netnographs may be blinded in a way that in-person researchers are not. Netnography do not judge veracity, nor depends on it, so much as they study interpretations.

Beginning in 2000, and continuing thereafter, netnography has been tested and adapted with a variety of real-world business problems. One form of application of netnography takes the form of working with organizations such as for-profit and non-profits in a number of practical marketing research consulting assignments. Netnography has also been used in consulting and research work with a variety of different companies in the finance, entertainment, pharmaceutical, consumer packaged goods, retail, and technology industries, as well as with industry associations, small and medium-sized enterprises (SEMs) and non-profits (Kozinets 2010). These experiences have led to some adaptation and refinement of the method.

Bengry-Howell et al. (2011) assessed the netnography's academic impact and provided some evidence of the relative impact of these 'marketing' style methods. Since the early publications on netnography there has been a steady increase in citations referring to the method, with the majority of citations located broadly within the field of management and business studies. They found some evidence of uptake or interest in netnography from wider social science disciplines but declared this to be 'relatively limited' (Bengry-Howell et al. 2011). They also found that most of the citations are from authors from North America, although citations from authors from Europe (mainly UK), Australia and Hong Kong were also available. This indicates some amount of global spread of the approach, although mostly within the specific disciplines from which it originated (Bengry-Howell et al, 2012). They also reported that netnography was the most-cited method during the last decade.

At this stage, process, paradigmatic, ethical, and conceptual issues relating to netnography are still under debate (Mkono 2012). However it appears that this methodology will become more important as the cyberspace continues to permeate everyday life.

It has been shown that netnography can be successfully utilize to determine consumer bahaviour in various fields like: advertising, tourism, boycotting of specific products, introduction of innovations, product development, market research, cyberculture, brand communities, web-based teaching etc. etc. However, netnographic studies have remained confined mainly to North America and Europe. Researchers in India still using traditional ethnology for such studied. With the tremendous growth in the Internet users in India, the potential of utilizing netnography to study various aspects involved in management and business has also increased. Several e-Commerce companies have started operating in India since 2007. Over time, the number of online consumers has also increased in India. Therefore it is important to know the online consumer behaviour towards e-Commerce companies operating in India. Keeping the above facts in view, the present study has been designed to propose a research framework to assess online consumer behavior through netnography of e-Commerce related websites in India.

REVIEW OF LITERATURE

Netnography can be defined as a specialized form of ethnographic research that has been adapted to the unique contingencies of various types of computer-mediated social interaction. Developed in 1995 in response to rapid changes in online social interaction, the novelty of the approach lies in the view that the online world is a social and cultural world, and that scientists can benefit from understanding online interactions using a cultural frame of reference (Kozinets 1996, 1997, 1998). However, it also recognizes that these social worlds are so different in their manifestation that they require specific new approaches to data collection and research engagement, and that, as a consequence, having a common understanding and a common set of standards for such online ethinographic, or netnographic, studies will confer stability, consistency, and legitimacy (Kozinets 2010b). Netnography was not intended as a new brand, but as a distinct set of procedures intended to provide some reliability and confer some consistency on a new field of research.

Netnography differs from methods such as focus group, surveys, interviews, data mining, and content mining in that it is naturalistic, immersive, contextually driven, and observational as well as participative, these are also characteristics of ethnography (Fetterman 2009). To distinguish netnography from embodied face-to-face ethnography, Kozinets (2010b) identifies four critical differences between online and face-to-face cultural and social interactions. First, the nature of the social and cultural interaction is altered-both constrained and liberated- by the specific nature and rules of the technological medium in which it is carried. Netnographies must work with technological artifacts in a way that ethnographies do not. Next, the interaction can be optimally anonymous or pseudonymous and even 'real' identities can be suspect. This has implications for the conduct of ethical and effective research, as well as for data collection and analysis. Third, is the wide accessibility of many of the relevant forums of social interaction. This accessibility also alters the research approach and often radically transforms the data collection process from one of relative scarcity and difficulty to one of abundance. Finally, nothing in the physical world compares to the automatic archiving of conversations and data that we see in online social worlds and this facet also transforms data collection and analysis. These differences in the nature of the culture, the nature of the communications, and the nature of the researcher interaction complicated and rendered less relevant prior elements of the ethnographic approach, such as making entrée, collecting data, analyzing data, ensuring a trustworthy interpretation, and following ethical research standards. Netnography offered researchers a new standard approach for working within this new cultural setting, a setting which is constantly evolving and changing the approaches available to social scientific researchers (Giglietto and Rossi 2012, Das 2012).

Traditionally, more qualitative field research, such as participant observation, requires the researchers to interact with their informants in a real physical setting (Taylor and Bogdan 1984). Interestingly, with the rise of Internet use and its popularity among consumers, evidence shows that individuals may be more open online than they are in real life (Reid 1996, Chuldress and Asamen 1998). But how con researchers develop insight derived from face-to-face encounters in online settings? There is a lack of consensus on this issue. Lee and Broderick (2007) argue that netnography researchers employ 'static' words' used by online consumers but do not interact with them. Puri (2007) refutes this by suggesting that, by its very nature, the netnography method requires researchers to 'live' in the virtual space in the same way as ethnographers.

There has been little systematic investigation of currently available netnographic techniques. Like approaches used in conventional ethnographic studies, participate observation, non-participant observation and interview are common methods that can be employed by netnographic researchers. However, the choice of methods is essentially an epistemological issue and is grounded in the philosophical assumptions made. Kozinets (2002) suggests that netnography is 'based primarily on the observation of textual discourse.' This non-participant stance has greatly affected the practice of subsequent work (Langer and Beckman 2005, Hamilton and Hewer 2009). But it is worth pointing out that netnography is by no means restricted to non-participants observation in studying the online phenomenon. Participant observation and email-based interviewing are also equally relevant and potentially powerful tools, particularly when used in a 'mixed-method' fashion to capitalize on the interactive nature of Internet (Morgan and Symon 2003). Therefore, many researchers switch among participant observation, non-participant observation and email/instant messaging interviews at different stages of their research in order to improve the accuracy of accounts and acquire data representative of the whole context of online interactions (Xun 2010).

Netnography has several distinctive strengths for markets. A combination of the Internet's substantial information-carrying capacity and the removal of individual social cues (Gramtz and Ward 1996, Watt et al 2002), means that researcher is provided with 'a goldmine of information' (Childress and Asamen 1996).

Kozinets (1998) stated that the aspiring netnographers to immerse themselves not only in "virtual field" but in the history and methods of cultural anthropology. Kozinets (2002) used netnography to explore and analyze some of the meanings and symbol systems that surround contemporary coffee consumption for the posters to an online community that is dedicated to coffee related discussion. He concluded that netnography can be useful, flexible, ethically sensitive, and unobtrusive method adapted to the purpose of studying the language, motivation, consumption linkages, and symbol of consumption-oriented online communities.

Langer and Beckman (2005) used netnography to study cross-consumer online-communication about cosmetic surgery on Danish internet message board. He observed that owing to the relevance of studying sensitive research topic like cosmetic surgery, netnography was useful as it is difficult to obtain information offline. He further observed that the opportunity to masquerade and to cover their identities allow them to express attitudes, opinions, and expenses freely, and hence provide deeper insights into consumers' opinion, motives, and concerns.

Kozinets (2006) suggested that rigorous application of netnography could be helpful to advertisers and copywriters as they seek this enhanced understanding. He further stated that because it is unelicited, it is more naturalistic and unobtrusive than focus groups, surveys, or interviews. However, it is still largely text-based, anonymous, poses ethical issues, is often overwhelming, can invite superficial and decontexualized interpretation, and requires considerable researcher acuity (Kozinets 2006).

Cova and Pace (2006) recommend netnography as an ideal qualitative research approach for understanding virtual consumer community behavior.

Puri (2007) describes the online interaction amongst customers in online forums as "spontaneous consumer talk that is more natural and more 'real'; 'heartfelt' data that is more vivid and textured".

Riegner (2007) suggested that pricy tech-electronics is the number one product category consumers bought, after reading related eWord-of-Mouth (eWOM). In addition, market analyst eMarketer (2009) suggested that 44.4 percent of American electronics consumers are mostly influenced by WOM in marketing their purchase decisions. eWOM is a modified online extension of traditional-word-of-mouth (WOM). It is often used in the literature interchangeably with 'word-of-mouse' (Helm 2000), 'word-online' (Atkinson 2005), and 'online-word-of-mouth' (Edwards 2006) as well as being associated with 'user generated media' (ACNeilsen 2007), or 'used generated content' (Riegner 2007). Henning-Thurau et al (2004) defined eWOM as 'any positive or negative statement made by potential, actual, or former customers about a product or company, which is made available to a multitude of people and institutions via the Internet.' Although, WOM has also been defined as 'peer consumers' statements made online' (Edwards 2006), which is a dynamic and ongoing information exchange process.

Black (2007) examined a set of consumer demographics, values, attitudes and personality traits to assess these variables' impact on eBay participation by consumers. He found that consumer's family size and consumption motivation have an impact on their participation in eBay. Further, eBay consumers have a more positive attitude towards eBay than do eBay nonconsumers.

Rokka (2010) suggested that netnography can be used to study the constantly transforming consumption practices and cultural forms that transnational online environment may bring about.

To examine the gap between consumer motivation as revealed through online conservation and hospital communication managers' models about motivations, Jayanti (2010) conducted a content analysis of 40 cancer-center websites. The results demonstrated a gap. While the patients in online conversations emphasize physician partnership and personal outcome, the majority of hospital communications emphasize reputation, expertise, and compassion.

Osofsky (2011) used netnography to study the consumer sentiment towards Swatch watches, the largest watch company in the world, owning famous watches including Breguet, Omega, Rado, Longines, Tissot and Hamilton. Through this study they obtained useful insight about how the brand is positioned and perceived.

Karin and Brian (2011) used netnography to investigate boycott motivations and perceived boycott participation costs by analyzing consumer comments submitted to an online boycott petition. They found that consumers have the power to impact the boycott target's bottom line and/or behavior as well as the belief that the boycott will succeed in forcing the target to cease its egregious behavior.

Brodie et al (2011) adopted netnographic methodology to explore the nature and scope of consumer engagement in an online brand community environment. The study revealed the complex multidimensional and dynamic nature of consumer engagement, which may emerge at different levels of intensity over time, thus reflecting distinct engagement states. Further, the consumer engagement process comprises a range of sub-processes reflecting consumers' interactive experience within online communities, and value co-creation among community participation. Engaged consumers exhibit enhanced consumer loyalty, satisfaction, empowerment, connection, emotional bonding, trust and commitment. The author states that virtual communities are becoming increasingly prevalent. However, the virtual community prevalence does not imply the substitution of online, for offline, activity (Ward 1999). Thus, there is the need for comparative research, which focuses both on consumer engagement in offline, "physical world", and in online "virtual" settings (Brodieer al 2011).

Cruz (2012) used netnography to study consumer behavior in boycotting a Brazalian company Arezzo. He found that social networking websites were used by the consumers to express their feeling (positive or negative) towards the companies responsibilities, for the product they purchase. His study found that there were two dimensions of the boycott, economical and ideological. The first dimension is due to disagreement with the company's position regarding economical values (price, imperfection in the market- monopoly, economic crisis). In the second dimension, psychological motivations such as belonging to a group, peer pressure, and the personal values of the consumer are involved. Through this study the author could understand the consumer behavior for boycott, and advocated that netnography is a better tool for such kind of studies, especially in Brazil, where research funding is difficult to acquire.

Chen (2012) used netnography to study the consumer motivation with online group buying behavior in CC2B e-commerce, a popular group buying community website in Taiwan (lhergo.com), which is designed to aggregate the power of buying to gain volume discounts. They found four types of motivations for online group buying – profit, value, emotion, and achievement.

Kretz (2012) used netnography to study to understand consumer behavior of the community using fashion and luxury blogs. He observed that purchase decision depends not anymore on the brands advertised but on the quality of relationship held between the blogger and the readers. Bloggers, however, are expected to abide by a tacit initial contact, that is to remain true to their initial content and to their relationships with the audience.

Mkono (2012) argues that netnography could become more useful in tourism research as the Internet is increasingly normalized as part of everyday lifestyle. However, in the field of tourism research, every researcher has embraced netnography techniques as alternatives or compliments to traditional field methods such as face-to-face interviews and surveys. It is envisaged that in tourism research, more researchers will adopt Internet-based fieldwork as the volume and traffic of online posting relating to tourism experiences around the world continues to grow (Mkono 2012).

Nimrod (2012) after performing a netnographic study on adult tourism reported that online communities serve as a resource in older adults' tourism both before and after travelling. However he observed several limitations while applying netnography. First there was inherent bias in the sample, as only those who use the Internet and more specifically those who are interested in engaging with others concerning their travel. Secondly, since the study was carried out on English-based communities, it does not represent all older tourists.

Wu and Philip (2013) used netnography to analyze the choice of recreational vehicle by Chinese tourists visiting Australia, with a view to understand rapidly changing tourist market, the growing of new markets and the perspective of culturally distinctive groups. Issues that arose from the case study include the value of the detail inherent the posting, the attendant ability to consider the material using conceptual schemes, the practicality of getting additional information, the need to fully address ethical concerns and the value of supplementary perspectives.

Jalilvand et al (2013) studied the interrelationship among electronic word of mouth (eWOM), tourist' attitudes towards Islamic destinations, and travel intentions in Iran. A structural equation model test with maximum likelihood estimation was performed to test the relationship among the research variables using 189 participants. The empirical results from the structural model suggest that eWOM positively influences tourists' attitudes toward Islamic destinations and travel intentions. In addition, tourists' attitudes towards Islamic destinations are significantly associated with intension to travel (Jalilvandet al 2013).

Loanzon (2013) reported that netnography can be effectively applied during Phase 1 and 2 of the product development process as a Fuzzy Front End tool. Although netnography may prove valuable in the opportunity identification phase, it is not a sufficient tool to replace conventional FFE tools. Netnography has expanded to include more automated and passive application and will continue to evolve as a tool as long as the online consumer environment and respective behavior continue to change.

Kulavuz-Onal et al (2013) compared the multi-site online community of practice of English language teachers, known as Webheads in Action and ethnographic fieldwork practices. They found that the field, participant observation, interviews, and researcher survival skills are experienced in fundamentally different ways in netnography as opposed to in-person ethnography, which calls for reconceptualisation of fieldwork practices in online communities because of the dynamics of online environments and the use of web-based technologies.

Zaglia (2013) investigated through netnography the existence and functionality of different types of brand communities within social networks, which can influence consumer behavior differently. He found strong evidence of this existence, leading to a better understanding of such embedded brand communities, their peculiarities, and motivational drivers for participation. He further stated that due to the advantages of social networks, brand management is now able to implement brand communities with less time and financial effort; however, choosing the appropriate brand community type, cultivating consumers' interaction, and staying tuned to this social engagement are critical factors to gain anticipated brand outcomes.

Ricolfe and Perez (2014) applied netnography to determine the positioning for the food distributing companies in Spain, and concluded that netnography can be a source of information to determine brand image and positioning of companies.

INDIAN CONTEXT

India is a heterogeneous market and access to products is limited. Research firm Forrester estimates that India's e-commerce market will touch US$8.8 billion in 2016. Others estimate this to be as high as US$16 billion by then. India's internet users have risen to 200 million with over 20 million of them transacting online (Dhamija and Phadnis, 2014). The Indian online retail industry witnessed a considerable growth in 2007. Thereafter several e-Commerce companies have been established in India. Important among them are: Flipkart, Snapdeal, Jabong, Myntra, HomeShop18, eBay and the recent market entrant, Amazon India.

With the growing popularity of B2C e-commerce in India, there is a surge in customers' participation at the online forums related to Internet shopping on various social networking platforms. Customers are openly sharing their experiences, grievances and opinions on these online forums. Moreover, a new social phenomenon is emerging on Internet, with the help of social networking sites and online communities, which has not been explored and observed in its natural live setting to develop its understanding. Netnographic methodologies have not been utilized to study consumer behavior in India. Although there exists tremendous scope for its application to study consumer behavior, Indian researchers are still confined to traditional survey based methods, which are prone to bias and social desirability i.e.

answering questions according to the beliefs of what attitudes are socially most acceptable to uphold (Shaughnessy, Zechmeister and Jeanne, 2011). The netnography approach makes use of the information that is publicly available in online forums, in a naturalistic and unobtrusive setting and is entirely free of any fabrication by the researcher. Therefore, netnographic methodologies may be deployed to study the consumer behavior towards leading e-commerce companies in India such as Flipkart, Snapdeal and Amazon India. A comparative assessment of these companies may be done to determine whether customer perception and behavior is different for each of these companies.

RESOLVING ISSUES THROUGH NETNOGRAPHY

Some of the research questions that have emerged from the review of literature in the present chapter and which may be answered through netnographic studies in India are as follows:

1. How opinions and attitudes are formed in online shopping context?
2. What are the differences in customer perceptions of different e-commerce sites in India?
3. What are the socio-cultural aspects of online consumer behavior?
4. How participative are e-commerce companies on discussion forums?
5. To what extent does online word of mouth influence the decision making process of consumers?
6. What are the consumer motivations for buying online?
7. What are the major considerations related to customer services offered by online sellers?

RESEARCH METHODOLOGY

The netnographic studies are qualitative in nature, which are known by several names such as *naturalistic, ethnographic, subjective, or postpositivistic* (Borg and Gall, 1989).

Strauss and Corbin (1990) have opined that qualitative method is better suited for studies related to understanding a phenomenon about which little is yet known or to gain new perspectives on things about which much is already known, or to gain more in-depth information that may be difficult to convey quantitatively. The variables that are identified through qualitative research might be applied to test using a quantitative research as the next step. A qualitative research may begin with framing of research problems in the form of open-ended questions that will support discovery of new information.

Designing a qualitative research study is quite different from designing a quantitative study (Savenye and Robinson, 2004). As suggested by Jacob (1987), the initial choice of methods, depends upon the research questions to be addressed; however, the questions, issues, and topics of the study themselves may change as the researcher's conception of the reality of the "world" being studied changes. Lincoln and Guba (1985) have also suggested that it is contradictory to completely "design" a naturalistic study prior to beginning the study.

Considering the various definitions and descriptions of ethnographic research methods, netnography falls in the category of non-verbal, non-interactive observation method, where the observer does not interact to a great degree with those he or she is observing. The researcher's role is mainly confined to observe and record, and not to actively participate. Patton (1990) also recommends observation as the most relevant method of data collection in naturalistic research. He further adds that observation also provides knowledge of the context in which events occur, and may help the researcher to see things which are not even known to the participants, or which they are unwilling to share in an interview.

The following methodological steps are proposed to be used for netnography to assess online customer behavior in India:

1. **Identification and Selection of Online Communities:** The communities to be involved in the research are to be identified in the first step. Examples include Facebook, YouTube channel, Twitter accounts, Blogs and Forums (both professional and amateur).
2. **Community Observation and Data Collection:** Individuals who are active in different social media pertaining to the research area should be identified and various parameters associated with personalities should be examined. All comments, feedbacks, reviews available in the social media sites should be collected and critically examined.
3. **Data Analysis and Aggregation of Consumer Insights:** Iterative Interpretation of Findings.

Data thus collected should be analyzed by using appropriate statistical procedures.

CONCLUSION

The present chapter provides a detailed analysis of netnography as a research approach to study customer behaviour in online context. A review of previous research suggests that it has been applied in various contexts and as the methodology continues to develop, it is possible that the netnographic technique may evolve to become a useful tool of twenty-first century consumer research.

REFERENCES

ACNeilsen. (2007). *Best Selling Tool is Word of Mouth Says Nelson Global Survey*. Retrieved from http://asiapacific.acneilsen.com/news/20071002.sctml

Atkinson, C. (2005). TV Networks Snap Up Key Words Online to Draw Views. *Advertising Age*, *76*, 4–21.

Bengry-Howell, A., Wiles, R., Nind, M., & Crow, G. (2011). *A Review of the Academic Impact of Three Methodological Innovations: Child-Led Research and Creative Research Methods. NCRM Hub*. University of Southampton.

Beven, Z., & Laws, C. (2007). Never let me down. Loyal Customer Attitude Towards Ticket Distribution Channels for Live Music Events: A Netnographic Exploration of the Us Leg of the Depeache Mode 2005-2006 World Tour. *Managing Leisure*, *12*(2-3), 120–142. doi:10.1080/13606710701339322

Black, G. S. (2007). A Comparison of the Characteristics of Ebay Consumers and Ebay Nonconsumers. *Journal of Direct. Data and Digital Marketing Practice*, *9*(1), 16–29. doi:10.1057/palgrave.dddmp.4350066

Borg, W. R., & Gall, M. D. (1989). *Educational Research: an Introduction, 5*th (N. York, Ed.). London.

Brodie, R. J. A llic, B Juric and L Hollebeek. (2011). Consumer Engagement in Virtual Brand Community: An Exploratory Analysis. *Journal of Business Research*. doi:10.1016/j.jbusres.2011.07.029

Chen, C. P. (2012). Online Group Buying Behaviour in CC2B E-Commerce: Understanding Consumer Motivations. *Journal of Internet Commerce*, *11*(3), 254–270. doi:10.1080/15332861.2012.729465

Chuldress, C. A., & Asamen, J. K. (1998). The Emerging Relationship of Psychology and Internet: Proposed Guidelines for Conducting Research. *Ethics & Behavior*, *1*, 19–35. doi:10.1207/s15327019eb0801_2 PMID:11655352

Cova, B., & Stefano, P. (2006). Brand Community of Convenience Products: New Forms of Customer Empowerment—The Case "My Nutella The Community". *European Journal of Marketing*, *40*(9/10), 1087–1105. doi:10.1108/03090560610681023

Cruz, D. B. P. A. (2012). The Netnography in the Consumers' Boycott Studies: The Brazilian Company Arezzo Case. *Revista de Administracaodo Gestor*, *2*, 119–146.

Das, M. (2012). Innovation in Online Data Collection for Scientific Research: The Dutch MESS Project. *Methodological Innovations Online*, *7*, 7–24.

Derya, K. O., & Camilla, V. (2013). Reconceptualising Fieldwork in a Netnography of an Online Community of English Language Teacher. *Ethnography and Education*, *8*(2), 224–238. doi:10.1080/17457823.2013.792511

Dhamija, A., & Phadnis, S. (2014, April 1). Internet users in India. *Times of India*, p. 11.

Dwivedi, M. (2009). Online Destination Image of India: A Consumer Based Perspective. *International Journal of Contemporary Hospitality Management*, *21*(2), 226–232. doi:10.1108/09596110910935714

Edwards, S. (2006). Special Issue on Electronic Word-Of-Mouth and its Relationship with Advertising, Marketing and Communication. *Journal of Interactive Advertising*, *6*, 1–2. doi:10.1080/15252019.2006.10722113

eMarketer. (2009). Why people go online. *eMarketer*. Retrieved from http://www.emarker.com/Article.aspx?R=1007184&N_{tt}=Why+People+Go+Online&No=4&xsrc=article_head_sitesearchx&N=0&N_tk=basic.access

Fetterman, D. M. (2009). *Ethnography: Step By Step*. London: Sage. doi:10.4135/9781483348858.n17

Giglietto, F., & Rossi, L. (2012). Ethics and Interdisciplinarity in Computational Social Science. *Methodological Innovations Online*, *7*, 25–36.

Gramtz, N. A., & Ward, J. C. (1996). Virtual Community: A Social-cognitive Analysis. *Advertising Consumer Research*, *23*, 161–166.

Hamilton, K., & Hewer, P. (2009). Salsa Magic: An Exploratory Netnography Analysis of the Salsa Experience. *Advertising Consumer Researc.*, *36*, 502–510.

Helm, S. (2000). Virtual Marketing- Establishing Customer Relationships By 'Word Of Mouth'. *Electronic Markets*, *10*(3), 158–164. doi:10.1080/10196780050177053

Henning-Thurau, T., Gwinner, K. P., Walsh, G., & Gremler, D. D. (2004). Electronic Word-Of-Mouth Via Consumer-Opinion Platforms: What Motivates Consumers to Articulate Themselves on the Internet? *Journal of Interactive Marketing*, *18*(1), 38–52. doi:10.1002/dir.10073

Hobbs, D. (2011). *Ethnography in Context*. SAGA. doi:10.4135/9781446261583

Ismail, A. R. (2010). *Investigating British Customers' Experience to Maximize Brand Loyalty Within the Context of Tourism In Egypt: Netnography And Structural Modeling Approach*. Retrieved from http://bura.brunel.ac.uk/handle/2438/4461

Jacob, E. (1987). Qualitative Research Traditions: A Review. *Review of Educational Research*, *57*(1), 1–50. doi:10.3102/00346543057001001

Jalilvand, M. R., Ebrahimi, A., & Samiei, N. (2013). Electronic Word Of Mouth Effects on Tourist' Attitudes Towards Islamic Destinations and Travel Intentions: An Empirical Study in Iran. *Procedia: Social and Behavioral Sciences*, *81*, 484–489. doi:10.1016/j.sbspro.2013.06.465

Janta, H., & Ladkin, A. (2009). Polish Migrant Labour in the Hospitality Workforce: Implications for Recruitiment and Retention. *Tourism Culture and Communication*, *9*(1), 5–15. doi:10.3727/109830409787556693

Jayanti, R. K. (2010). Anetnographic Explanation: Listing to Online Consumer Conversations. *Journal of Advertising Research*, *50*(2), 181–196. doi:10.2501/S0021849910091348

Karin, B., & Brian, B. (2011). What Motivates Consumers to Participate in Boycotts: Lessons from the Ongoing Canadian Seafood Boycott. *Journal of Business Research*, *64*(1), 96–102. doi:10.1016/j.jbusres.2009.12.008

Kozinet, R. V. (2012). Marketing Netnography: Promoting a New Research Method. *Methodological Innovations Online*, *7*, 37–45.

Kozinets, R. V. (1997). I Want to Believe: A Netnography of the X-Philes' Subculture of Consumption. Advances in Consumer Research, 24, 470-475.

Kozinets, R. V. (1998). On Netnography: Initial Reflection on Consumer Research Investigations of Cyberculture. Advances in Consumer Research, 25, 366-371.

Kozinets, R. V. (2002). The Field Behind The Screen: Using Netnography for Marketing Research in Online Communities. *JMR, Journal of Marketing Research*, *39*(1), 61–72. doi:10.1509/jmkr.39.1.61.18935

Kozinets, R. V. (2006). Click to Connect. Netnography and Tribal Advertising. *Journal of Advertising Research*, *46*(3), 279–288. doi:10.2501/S0021849906060338

Kozinets, R. V. (2010a). Netnography: The Marketer's Secret Ingredient. *MIT Technology Review*. Retrieved from http://www.technologyreview.com/business/26434/

Kozinets, R. V. (2010b). *Netnography: Doing Ethnographic Research Online*. London: Sage.

Kretz, G. (2012). Consuming Branded Stories: A Netnography of Fashion and Luxury Blog Consumption. *Advances in Consumer Research. Association for Consumer Research (U. S.)*, *40*, 1057–1058.

Langer, R., & Beckman, S. C. (2005). Sensitive research topics: Netnography revisited. *Qualitative Market Research*, *8*(2), 189–203. doi:10.1108/13522750510592454

Lee, N., & Broderick, A. J. (2007). The past, present and future of observational research in marketing. *Qualitative Market Research*, *10*(2), 121–129. doi:10.1108/13522750710740790

Lincoln, Y. S., & Guba, E. G. (1985). *Naturalistic Enquiry*. Beverly Hills, CA: Sage.

Loanzon E. (2013). Netnography: evolution, trend, and implications as a fuzzy front end tool. In *Proc. Technology Management in the IT-Driven Services-13* (PICMET'13) (pp. 1572-1593). Academic Press.

Mkono, M. (2012). Netnographic tourist research: The Internet as a virtual fieldwork site. *Tourism Analysis*, *17*(4), 553–555. doi:10.3727/108354212X13473157390966

Morgan, M. (2008). What makes a good festival? Understanding the event experience. *Event Management*, *12*(2), 81–93. doi:10.3727/152599509787992562

Morgan, S. J., & Symon, G. (2003). Electronic interviews in organizational research. In *Essential Guide to qualitative methods in organizational research.* London: SAGE.

Nimrod, G. (2012). Online communities as a resource in older adult tourism. *The Journal of Community Informatics.*, *8*, 56–67.

Osofsky, M. (2011). Swatch netnography: A look at consumer sentiment in social media. *Social Media*, *9*, 31–35.

Patton, M. Q. (1990). Qualitative Evaluation and Research Methods (2nd ed.). Newbury Park, CA: Sage Publications, Inc.

Puri, A. (2007). The web of insights: The art and practice of webnography. *International Journal of Market Research*, *49*, 384–408.

Reid, E. (1996). Informed consent in the study of online communities: A reflection on the effects of computer-mediated social research. *The Information Society*, *12*(2), 119–127. doi:10.1080/713856138

Ricolfe, J. S., & Perez, C. E. (2014). Applying netnography to the obtaining of the map of positioning for companies of food. *Cuadernos de Gestion*, *14*(1), 57–74. doi:10.5295/cdg.110322jc

Riegner, C. (2007). Word of mouth on the web: The impact of web 2.0 on consumer purchase decisions. *Journal of Advertising Research*, *47*(4), 436–447. doi:10.2501/S0021849907070456

Rokka, J. (2010). Netnographic inquiry and new translocal sites of the social. *International Journal of Consumer Studies*, *34*(4), 381–387. doi:10.1111/j.1470-6431.2010.00877.x

Shaughnessy, J., Zechmeister, E., & Jeanne, Z. (2011). *Research methods in psychology* (9th ed.). New York, NY: McGraw Hill.

Strauss, A., & Corbin, J. (1990). *Basics of qualitative research: Grounded theory procedures and techniques. Newbury Park*, CA: Sage Publications, Inc.

Taylor, S. J., & Bogdan, R. (1984). *Introduction to qualitative research methods: the search for meaning*. New York: John Willey & Sons.

Ward, K. J. (1999). The cyber-ethnographic (re)construction of two feminist online communities. *Sociological Research Online*, *4*(1). doi:10.5153/sro.222

Watt, S. E., Lee, M., & Spears, R. (2002). How social is Internet communication? A reappraisal of bandwidth and anonymity effect. In S. Woolgar (Ed.), *Virtual Society*. Oxford, UK: Oxford University Press.

Woodside, A. G., Cruickshank, B. F., & Dehuang, N. (2007). Stories visitors tell about Italian cities as destination icons. *Tourism Management*, *28*(1), 162–174. doi:10.1016/j.tourman.2005.10.026

Wu, M., & Yand, P. L. Pearce. (2013). Appraising netnography: Towards insight about new markets in the digital tourist era. *Current Issues in Tourism*. doi:10.1080/13683500.2013.833179

Xun, J., & Reynolds, J. (2010). Applying netnography to market research: The case of the online forum. *Journal of Targeting. Measurement and Analysis for Marketing.*, *18*(1), 17–31. doi:10.1057/jt.2009.29

Zaglia, M. E. (2013). Brand communities embedded in social networks. *Journal of Business Research*, *66*(2), 216–223. doi:10.1016/j.jbusres.2012.07.015 PMID:23564989

KEY TERMS AND DEFINITIONS

E-Commerce: Buying or selling of products and services using electronic networks such as Internet.

Ethnogrpahy: A systematic study of human races and cultures.

Netnography: The branch of ethnography that analyses the free behaviour of individuals on the Internet by accessing and analyzing sentiments and opinions expressed by consumers chatting in blogs, forums and online discussion groups.

Qualitative Research: Research method that aims at providing insights of the target audience's range of behavior and perceptions or at exploring a problem setting by using un-structured data.

Social Media: Internet-based tools and applications that allow users to generate, share or exchange information, ideas, and data in online social communities and groups.

Chapter 10
An Application of Text Mining to Capture and Analyze eWOM: A Pilot Study on Tourism Sector

Taşkın Dirsehan
Marmara University, Turkey

ABSTRACT

Marketing concept has progressed through different phases of evolution in the past. At the moment, customer relationship management is considered as the last era of marketing development. The main purpose of this approach is to build long-term oriented profitable relationships with customers. So, companies should know better their customers. This knowledge can be created through a deeper analysis of companies' data with data mining tools. Companies which are able to use data mining tools will gain strong competitive advantages for their strategic decisions. Hotel industry is selected in this study, since it provides a warehouse of customer comments from which precious knowledge can be obtained if text mining as a data mining tool is used appropriately. Thus, this study attempts to explain the stages of text mining with the use of Rapidminer. As a result, different approaches according to the customer satisfaction/dissatisfaction are discussed to build competitive advantages.

INTRODUCTION

The rapid growth of web 2.0 applications directed consumers to communicate their experiences online and to read these reviews before choosing new experiences. By this way, huge volumes of textual data -called eWOM- are created by them and these data keep precious information for businesses. A useful tool to reach this kind of information from large data sets is data mining. When the data is in textual form, text mining as an extension of data mining can help them to uncover hidden patterns existing in large data sets. Moreover, these hidden patterns may lead a company to create unique competitive advantages in today's information era.

DOI: 10.4018/978-1-4666-9449-1.ch010

Without a strong data analysis tool, an abundance of data is still poor in information. Data gathering over time are like raw ore, and the gap between data and information requires systematic data mining tools to pan that ore for gold (Han & Kamber, 2001).

The most common functions of data mining are association rules, artificial neural networks, decision trees, and clustering analysis. Researchers may gather significant information from raw data by using these functions, gaining competitive advantage from it. For instance, new customer segments may be explored and studied with data mining techniques (Köktürk and Dirsehan, 2012).

On the other hand, as a data mining tool, text mining enumerates words and number of repeats in a basic view. This methodology is appropriate for texts in the online environments, and especially for electronic word-of-mouth (eWOM).

Consumers perceive WOM as more trustworthy and persuasive than traditional media (Cheung & Thadani, 2012). The advent of the Internet has given birth to eWOM. Consumers post their opinions, comments and reviews on weblogs, discussion forums, websites and social networks (Cheung & Lee, 2012). In the tourism industry, Jalilvand et al. (2012) indicate that eWOM positively influences the destination image, tourist attitude and travel intention. Moreover, increasing consumer opinion portals on travel services shows that eWOM will continue to play an ever more vital role in travelers' purchasing decisions. Thus, eWOM becomes an important focus of research in marketing, e-commerce, and e-tourism studies (Filieri & McLeay, 2013). The shift of WOM to the electronic environment has made it also easier for companies to reach raw data. Tweets, online reviews, and blogs have become "Big Data" sources of real sharing behavior (Berger, 2014). Content of texts in such communication is a challenge for researchers to extract meaningful information from the unstructured data to enhance customer relationship management and marketing (Leong et al., 2004). Since a company may know its customers by revealing the knowledge from these data sets.

This study aims to show the application of text mining to analyze eWOM in a fundamental way. A practical tool for this purpose is RapidMiner, which can be downloaded from the website rapidminer.com freely, with some limitations. Among many functions, the "Text Processing" application has been used in this study. The comments have been retrieved from "booking.com", one of the famous hotel booking websites. All the steps have been explained in details with screenshots of RapidMiner.

After dividing the comments in two (high satisfaction levels and low satisfaction levels) according to the stars of visitors, the keywords determined for the tourism sector such as "price" have been analyzed for these groups. At the end, a general guideline is provided for researchers and practitioners, to enable them to perform basic text mining by themselves.

BACKGROUND

Text Mining as an Innovative Research Tool

Technological advancements enable new techniques in marketing research. In today's digital information environment, customer data are recorded and stored in digital data warehouses. A data warehouse is defined by Hair et al. (2009) as a "logical aggregation of information stored in a single location." A digital one can be defined as an aggregation of customer information collected in digital environments stored in a digital location. The purpose of a single data storage area is that managers may use such data for further analysis and decision making. This process of analyzing data to extract patterns and relationships not easily visible from simply looking is called data mining (Hair et al., 2009). Herein, one should see that meaningful information is tried to be extracted from lots of crowded data. So, what is the difference between these two poles? The main distinction between data and information is that, information emerges when data are combined with interpretation and meaning, in other words, information formats, filters and summarizes data. Furthermore, when information is combined with action and application, it becomes knowledge (Chen, 2001). However, companies face more competition and are overloaded with more information than ever before (Leong et al., 2004). So, turning information into knowledge with emerging techniques such as data mining will create competitive advantages for them. Data mining is defined as "a process of searching through computerized data files to detect patterns and it focuses on identifying relationships not obvious to marketers-in a sense, answering questions that marketing researchers may not even have thought to ask" (Kurtz & Boone, 2010). While conventional methods rely on a set of predefined hypotheses, researchers let the data reveal patterns in Big Data analytics (Xiang et al., 2015). Brachman et al. (1993) call this process "data archaeology" in which the analyst can discover interesting knowledge through an iterative, exploratory process. Dr. Penzias, a Nobel Prize winner interviewed in ComputerWorld in January 1999, states (Groth, 1999, p.5):

"Data mining will become much more important, and companies will throw away nothing about their customers because it will be so valuable. If you're not doing this, you're out of business."

This statement from around 15 years ago explains clearly the importance of data mining techniques to companies' survival, since these techniques and approaches (such as clustering, visualization, association, prediction, and estimation) provide competitive advantages for organizations. However, it's believed that some of these techniques are not used enough yet and need to be explained in more detail.

One of them is text mining (TM) which is a natural extension of data mining (Hearst, 1999). TM can be called also as Intelligent Text Analysis, Text Data Mining (TDM) or Knowledge-Discovery in Text (KDT) (Gupta & Lehal, 2009). It refers to a "computer-driven automated technique used to discover significant and non-trivial patterns of information from the unstructured texts" (Liau & Tan, 2014, p. 1345). One needs to revisit theoretical origins of content analysis to better understand the foundations of text mining (Leong et al., 2004).

Content analysis is used as a research technique, when the phenomenon to be observed is communication, rather than behavior or physical objects. It is defined as "the objective, systematic, and quantitative description of the manifest content of a communication" (Malhotra, 2007). It can be also used together with other qualitative research techniques. For instance, it can be defined as "a systematic procedure of taking individual responses and grouping them into larger theme categories or patterns" (Hair et al., 2009). Kassarjian (1977) provides some different definitions and indicates that the characteristics of content analysis are that it must be objective, systematic, and quantitative. While it was originated from text materials, it is extended to include non-linguistic materials such as visual art, body language, facial expressions, or cultural materials (Shapiro & Markoff, 1997). On the other hand, text analysis is a narrower term to include only the investigation of text materials (Stone, 1997). The research procedures of text analysis are used by text mining to uncover useful information hidden in large data sets (Leong et al., 2004).

Through the use of text analysis research techniques, text mining attempts to reveal useful information buried in text documents (Leong et al., 2004). Discussions in newsgroups and online boards may provide sources for market intelligence (e.g., consumer preferences, evaluation of existing services, and customer complaints) (Lau et al., 2005). So, text mining can be applied on these data to extract useful information for marketing strategies such as optimization of customer relationship management (Chang et al., 2009), social media competitive analysis (He et al., 2013), evaluation of consumers' sentiment towards brands (Mostafa, 2013), knowledge of a tourism destination (Gassiot & Coromina, 2013) and understanding consumers' needs (Liau & Tan, 2014).

In the 19th century, machines revolutionized the industrial age. Now text mining tools have the potential to revolutionize the information age and provide innovative solutions in the 21st century (Yang et al., 2008). However, unlike humans' language capabilities to comprehend unstructured data, computers still need to be developed for their ability to process text in large volumes or at high speeds (Gupta & Lehal, 2009). There are many tools available for text mining, however to get started with basic text analysis, one can use Voyant Tools, TAPoRware and Orange Text Mining. Their characteristics are summarized in Table 1. In this table, the tools are classified according to their cost, license, usability, tool type, import formats and export formats. However, these criteria may change according to the usage aims. For instance, a big company may consider how much space do these tools occupy in their servers.

On the other hand, there are other alternatives for text mining such as Juxta. KNIME integrates well with Weka (Tseng, 2014). Some other text mining, text analyzing or database provider tools include Clear Forest Text Analytics, Gold Fire Innovator, Inxight Smart Discovery, Omniviz, and TEMIS, which are flexible and capable of handling unstructured text; Quosa, RefViz, STN AnaVist, VantagePoint, and Thomson Data Analyzer which work best with structured text; and Aureka, M-Cam Doors, Wisdomain, and PatAnalyst which handle partially structured data (Yang et al, 2008). Yet, there are much more text-mining softwares presented by well-known vendors such as SAS, SPSS, and IBM to develop and customize them for industry uses (Lau et al., 2005). So, organizations may choose software according to their specific needs.

Text mining programs are very expensive; this is why adoption of text mining is slow (Chen, 2009). To overcome this problem, this study chose RapidMiner's Text Mining Extension because it was free and easy to use. Rapidminer involves an extensive set of operators for text processing and text mining (Ertek et al., 2013). More documentation of it can be found on RapidMiner's Documentation web site. In order to conduct text mining, one should follow these steps (Köktürk & Dirsehan, 2012):

1. Listing all the words with text mining,
2. Removing non-significant words,
3. Conducting the analysis for significant words,
4. Removing again the words which are not significant according to the results,

Table 1. Table of comparisons for basic text analysis

	Voyant Tools	TAPoRware	Orange Text Mining
Cost	Free	Free	Free
License	Closed Source	Closed Source	GPL/GNU General Public License
Usability	Easy	Easy	Easy
Tool Type	Web Application	Web Application	Desktop Application
Import Formats	TXT, CSV, HTML, XML, PDF, RTF, URL	TXT, CSV, HTML, XML, URL	TXT, CSV
Export Formats	TXT, CSV, XML	TXT, CSV, HTML, XML	CSV, TAB

(Source: Tseng, 2014)

5. Grouping the words that will be used in further researches,
6. Listing special words (according to the period, sector, product, etc.),
7. Finding the chosen words in the databases,
8. Revising the words periodically and tracking the changes.

The first four steps aim to clarify data warehouse, the following three steps aim to reveal the hidden patterns, and the last step is about the sustainability of the process.

Hotel Guests' Electronic Word of Mouth (eWOM)

As online commerce has grown rapidly worldwide, electronic communication becomes a more important platform. Businesses may interact with their customers via: (1)Face-to-face interaction with retail personnel; (2)Calls to customer service centers and conversations with customer service representatives; (3)Comments on company websites; and (4)Opinions expressed through e-mail (Chang et al., 2009).

Beyond this direct business-customers interaction types, firms may learn from customer networks too. Moreover, consumer generated websites and social network sites allow consumers to share information and experiences with other people online (Mauri & Minazzi, 2013). So, consumers learn about product quality by using online consumer reviews (Filieri, 2015).

Electronic Word of Mouth (eWOM) is developed in parallel with the adoption of the Internet. Christodoulides et al. (2012) indicates that eWOM has experienced significant growth due to the proliferation of user-generated content (UGC) which is content created by people through the internet. Now, consumers can post their opinions, comments and reviews on weblogs, discussion forums, websites and social networks (Cheung & Lee, 2012). So, eWOM refers to online reviews, online recommendations or online opinions, and has gained importance with the advancement of new technology tools (Cantallops & Salvi, 2014). Hennig-Thurau et al. (2004) define eWOM as "any positive or negative statement made by potential, actual, or former customers about a product or company, which is made available to a multitude of people and institutions via the Internet". There are two poles in online communication; sender/narrator and recipient/receiver. Sender who provides an online recommendation (eWOM) might be opinion leaders, close friends, family, relatives or strangers who can be anonymous (Sotiriadis & van Zyl, 2013). This anonymity allows consumers to share their opinions more comfortably (Goldsmith & Horowitz, 2006). Thus, even though eWOM is generated from strangers for whom there is no indication of expertise, such eWOM is used as a source of product information, particularly if experience with the product is a valuable evaluative cue (Gupta & Harris, 2010). On the other hand, the anonymous nature of eWOM can result in difficulties to determine the credibility of information by consumers (Chatterjee, 2001). According to the "Consumer Trust in Advertising" research results of Nielsen (2009), in the first place, 90% of the people rate "recommendations from people they know" and in the second place, 70% of them rate "consumer opinions posted online". In addition as trust towards online consumer reviews has increased 9% compared to the respective study in 2007, one may infer that an increasing number of users globally share information about products and brands (Christodoulides et al., 2012).

Liang et al. (2013) indicate that eWOM is more influential than traditional WOM, since eWOM messages reach larger audiences, recipients seek a broader range of comments, eWOM can be accessed immediately, and anonymity encourages its use.

The valence (positive or negative) of online reviews influences purchasing intentions in the hospitality industry (Mauri & Minazzi, 2013). Negative ones deserve special attention, since they are spread to more people for a longer period of time than the positive contents (Hornik et al., 2015). In addition, consumer complaints are precious sources of information, since they help marketers to identify sources of dissatisfaction and therefore should be encouraged (Nyer, 2000).

This study is conducted in tourism sector, since it represents an important part of Turkish economy. The ratio of tourism revenue in GNP is increasing (3.4 in 2010, 3.6 in 2011, and 3.7 in 2012). In addition, tourism revenue, number of visitors and average expenses are also increasing as can be seen in Table 2.

Online reviews and eWOM are increasingly used in tourism services that are high involvement services (Sotiriadis & van Zyl, 2013). In addition, they are important since this industry represents intangible products that are difficult to evaluate prior to the consumption (Litvin et al., 2008).

Cantallops and Salvi (2014) identify two main lines of research based on their review on eWOM and hotels; review-generating factors (previous factors that cause consumers to write reviews) and impacts of eWOM (impacts caused by online reviews). From the consumers' side, many potential tourists check previous' guests opinions online before making their booking decisions. Moreover, these reviews have a significant impact on online hotel bookings (Ye et al., 2011). Thus, tourism companies desire to eliminate negative comments and hold positive ones (Melián-González et al., 2013). Actually, strategies for managing eWom in tourism can be classified in two categories; informational and revenue generating. Informational perspective consists of establishment of procedures to harvest discussion and feedback created online as information sources. On the revenue generation side, the efforts should be directed toward spreading good WOM (Litvin et al., 2008). For these reasons, firms should analyze eWOM and determine the positive and negative aspects of customers' stay. So, text mining tools are essential for this purpose, because the increasing customer-generated content creates big warehouses of textual data and these data include hidden knowledge to gain a competitive advantage (He et al., 2013). As indicated by Tang and Guo (2013), the linguistic indicators generated by text analysis are predictive of eWOM communicators' attitudes toward a product or service.

AN APPLICATION OF TEXT MINING IN THE TOURISM SECTOR

Research Problem

The aim of this chapter is to conduct text mining to find out the factors that drive customers to be happy or unhappy about their stays in Antalya. Located on the Mediterranean coast of Turkey, the Antalya metropolitan region is the leading tourism destination of the country, hosting 9 million tourists every year (Erkuş-Öztürk & Eraydin, 2011).

Table 2. Tourism statistics in Turkey

	Tourism Revenue ('000$)	Number of Visitors	Average Expense ($)
2010	24 930 997	33 027 943	755
2011	28 115 692	36 151 328	778
2012	29 007 003	36 463 921	795
2013	32 310 424	39 226 226	824
2014	34 305 904	41 415 070	828

(Source: http://www.tursab.org.tr)

In this study, it is aimed to detect the keywords in positive and negative comments. For this purpose, the comments on "booking.com" are collected in two separate files, named as positives and negatives, and then they are analyzed with RapidMiner's text mining tool.

Preparing the Data

Data are collected from the website "booking.com". First, Antalya is searched as a destination and the results are filtered by choosing hotels. Then, 13 hotels are selected randomly among the ones which have enough comments. One of the comments is presented in Figure 1.

The comments provide the customers' name, nationality, and traveling type. They include also the average rating of the customers and the date of the comments. The important part is they are separated as positives and negatives in two separate folders. Then all the positive comments are aggregated in a "positives" text file and the negative ones in a "negatives" text file. These files' extensions are ".txt." Some comments written in different languages are translated into English using Google Translate. Even though the translations are not always adequate to the language structure, they can provide the adjectives, which are enough to capture the customers' general sentiments in text mining.

Downloading RapidMiner's Free Trial

RapidMiner tool can be downloaded freely from the website "rapidminer.com" after completing a short signup form. After logging in the system, the user can select "RapidMiner Studio (v6)" and the download begins when the user clicks on the operating system. When starting a new process on RapidMiner Studio, two windows appear on the left, "Operators" and "Repositories." One may realize the text mining tool is not available among the operators. An extension should be downloaded for it through the "Updates and Extensions (Marketplace)" command, available under the "Help" button on the top of the window as indicated in Figure 2.

In the RapidMiner Marketplace, "Text Mining Extension" can be easily found under the "Top Downloads" tab. This extension can be downloaded after accepting the terms and conditions. Then the "Text Processing" will be available in the "Operators" window.

Figure 1. Traveler's comment (Taken from booking.com)

Figure 2. "Help" menu (Screenshot from RapidMiner)

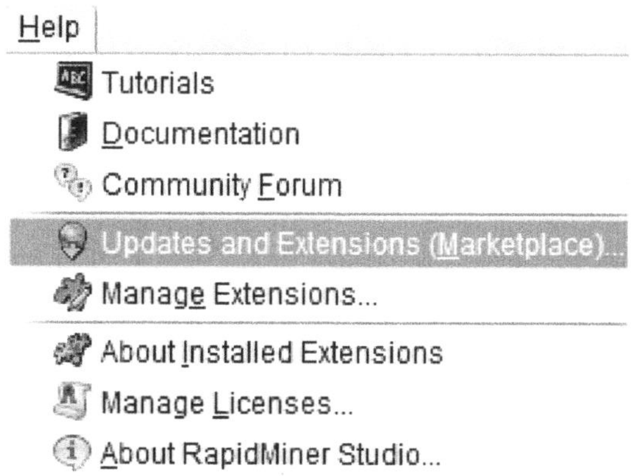

Analyzing Data with Text Mining

First, the system should indicate where to find the data. Hence, the operator "Process Documents from Files" under the "Text Processing" folder should be placed on the "Main Process" screen. Then, "Edit List" should be clicked to indicate the text directories (Figure 3). The directories can be selected in the "Edit Parameter List" dialogue box (Figure 4). Two text files were prepared to be analyzed in this study and saved under two different folders. The locations of these folders are indicated in the directory parts and their names are written in the class name boxes. A new directory can be added with the "Add Entry" button or deleted with the "Remove Entry" button. The "Apply" button can be clicked after indicating the locations of the directories.

Second, the texts should be divided word by word for the software to analyze. Thus, the operator "Process Documents from Files" should be clicked twice and a new empty window named "Vector

Figure 3. "Process documents from files" operator (Screenshot from RapidMiner)

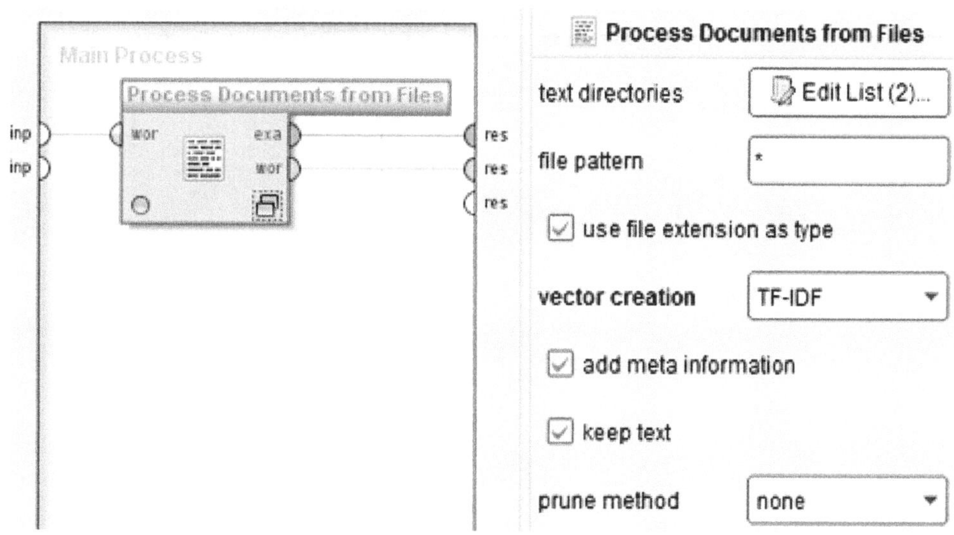

Figure 4. "Edit parameter list" dialogue box (Screenshot from RapidMiner)

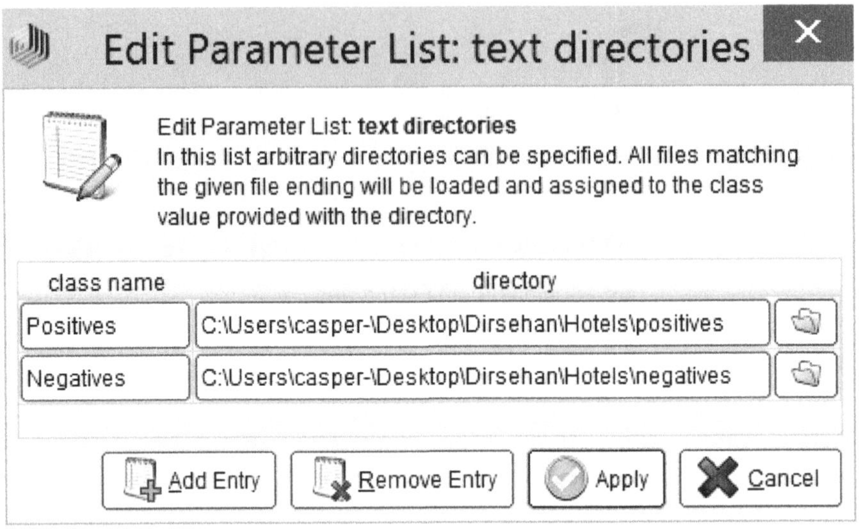

Creation" will appear. The operator "Tokenize" should be placed on this window and the "doc" parts should be connected as can be seen in Figure 5. Then, the upper-directed arrow should be clicked to return to the main process, which will then be ready for analysis.

Third, to conduct the analysis, the "Run" button above the process should be clicked. After analyzing the process, a word list appears in the results section as in Figure 6. When clicking on the "Design" on top right or touching simply on F8, the main process window will appear, to allow some changes. When clicking on the "Results" on top right or touching simply on F9, the results window will appear again.

Figure 5. "Tokenize" operator (Screenshot from RapidMiner)

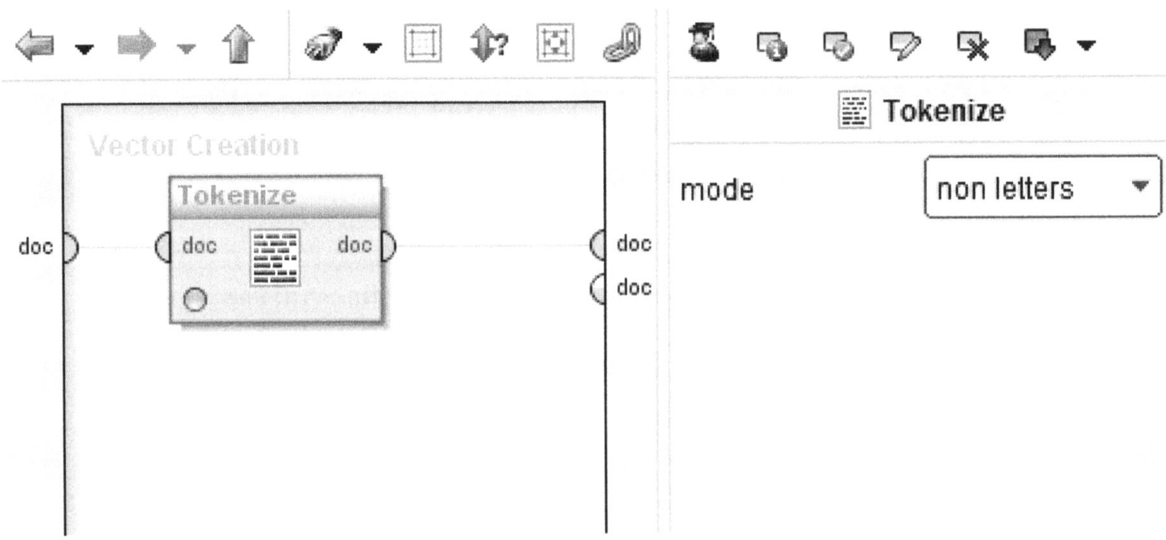

Figure 6. Word list to be interpreted (Screenshot from RapidMiner)

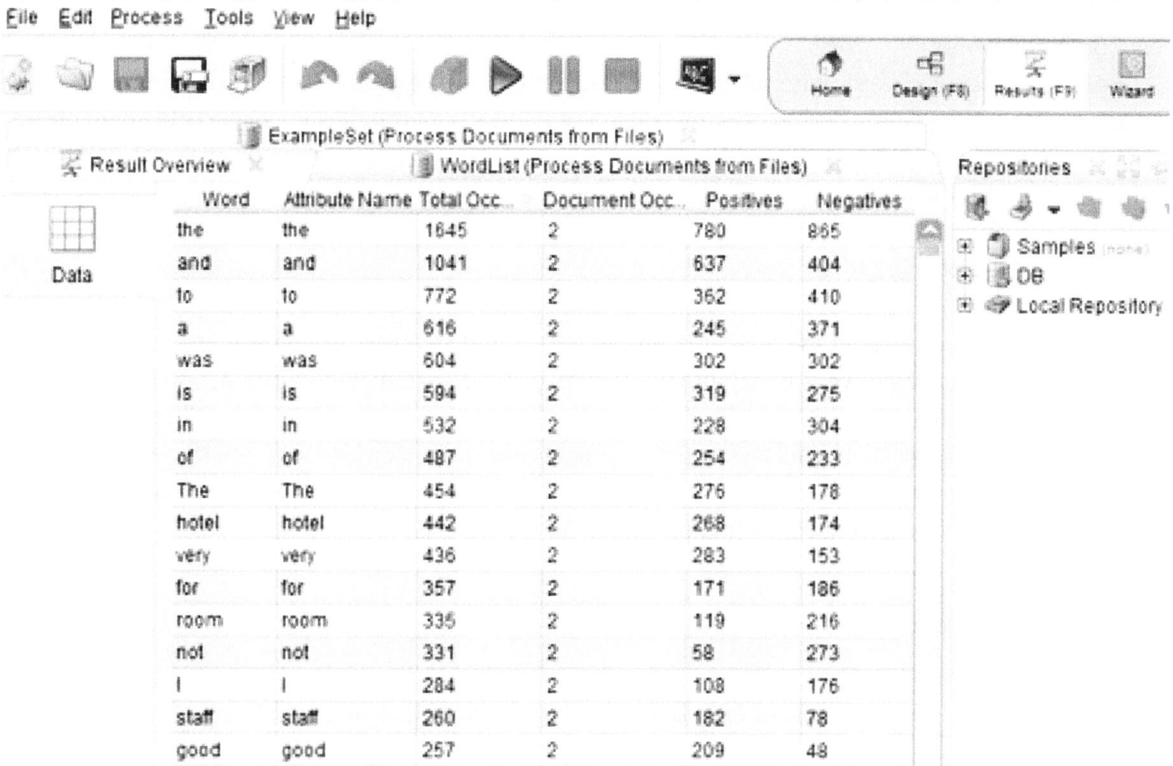

Word	Attribute Name	Total Occ...	Document Occ...	Positives	Negatives
the	the	1645	2	780	865
and	and	1041	2	637	404
to	to	772	2	362	410
a	a	616	2	245	371
was	was	604	2	302	302
is	is	594	2	319	275
in	in	532	2	228	304
of	of	487	2	254	233
The	The	454	2	276	178
hotel	hotel	442	2	268	174
very	very	436	2	283	153
for	for	357	2	171	186
room	room	335	2	119	216
not	not	331	2	58	273
I	I	284	2	108	176
staff	staff	260	2	182	78
good	good	257	2	209	48

The "WordList" window lists the words of the two documents. "Total Occurrences" column indicates how many times the word occurs in these documents. "Document Occurrences" column shows in how many documents the word exists. "Positives" column represents how many times the word occurs in the document, named as "Positives" and "Negatives" column for the document named as "Negatives." The words can be listed according to these titles, such as from most to least frequently occurring.

Revising the Results

After conducting the analysis, the researcher should carefully investigate the results. He or she may then revise the data or the analyzing process. For instance, the researcher may want to also see the results according to traveling type to determine the differences, so the data should be revised.

On the other hand, the researcher may add or change operators in the process. For instance, when the words are listed according to their total occurrences, it's easy to see that some words are repeated many times (such as "the" 1645 times, "and" 1041 times, "to" 772 times, and "a" 616 times). To eliminate these words from the analysis, it's possible to place the operator "Filter Stopwords" after the operator "Tokenize" on the vector creation window. By this way, these commonly used words will be eliminated.

As another example, the results provide the occurrences of words one by one. However the researcher may desire to analyze the occurrences of combined words, such as "Internet connection" instead of

"Internet" and "connection." In this case, an operator called "Generate n-Grams (Terms)" should be placed after the operator "Tokenize" on the vector creation window, making results available for different combined words.

Still another case is words with suffixes. The researcher may see the number of occurrences of a word together with all the words derived from it, such as clean-, instead of clean, cleaner, cleaning, cleanliness, etc. To allow this, the operator "Stem (Porter)" should be placed after the operator "Tokenize" on the vector creation window.

Interpreting the Results

After analyzing and revising the texts, the researcher should interpret the results and report them. In this study, the main objective is to explore the factors driving customers to write positive and negative comments. After analyzing the words in the texts, these factors are summarized in Table 3.

Accordingly, the most cited factors in the comments are staff-related words. So, how staff members approach customers attracts their attention. They are the crucial part of customer satisfaction. Thus, hotel managers should organize education and programs for staffs.

Table 3. Word occurrences in positive and negative comments

Words	Occurrences in Positive Comments	Occurrences in Negative Comments	% of Change
Staff-	216	98	-54.6
Locat-	215	27	-87.4
Breakfast	175	97	-44.6
Friendli-	124	9	-92.7
Beach	115	52	-54.8
Help-	103	19	-81.6
Clean	94	74	-21.3
Pool	88	49	-44.3
Food	78	38	-51.3
View	73	21	-71.2
Sea	70	22	-68.6
Servic-	59	52	-11.9
Comfort-	53	7	-86.8
Price	51	27	-47.1
Garden	33	3	-90.9
Valu-	24	4	-83.3
Small	19	65	242.1
Bathroom	15	58	286.7
Nois-	9	47	422.2
Wifi	8	41	412.5
Shower	3	28	833.3

It's also possible to group the words taking place in the comments. First, there are some words cited in positive comments, such as *garden,* comfort-related words, and friendliness-related words. These words can be considered as important in only positive cases. If a hotel has a garden, it's indicated in the positive comments. If it does not, customers don't mention gardens. Secondly, some words occur commonly in negative cases such as *bathroom, shower, wifi,* and noise-related words. These words can be considered as the standards of customers. When they are provided, customers do not indicate them in positive comments. When there is a problem with them, customers indicate their absence or problems in the negative comments. A third group of words are two-sided, appearing in both positive and negative comments. These factors include *price, clean*, and service-related words. If hotels provide good quality of services to their customers, these are indicated in positive comments, but a weak service presentation conducts people to negative comments. This kind of word grouping is important for hotel managers to determine the factors to be improved and the potential risks.

However, other grouping alternatives are possible. For instance, behavior-related words can be extracted from this list such as friendliness-related and help-related words. Such groups may be useful for managers to see the customers' desires about behavior.

Another grouping alternative may be used to make clear the difference between positive and negative comments. For instance, price-related words occur 51 times in positive comments, 27 times in negative comments. To make the difference more clear, one can analyze related words such as *money, worth, cost,* and value-related words. This increases the difference is increased to 48 (86-38) from 24 (51-27). The occurrences of these words are listed in Table 4.

Repeating the Process for Sustainability

The results used by marketing managers may create competitive advantage for the company. However, this advantage is temporary because the competition is dynamic. In order to create sustainable competitive advantages, the text mining process should be repeated periodically and strategies should consider any changes without losing time.

FUTURE RESEARCH DIRECTIONS

Data mining tools can be used by academicians and practitioners. From the practitioners' side, human resources department may use data mining to choose better candidates to the work, to determine wages

Table 4. Occurrences of price related words

Words	Occurrences in Positive Comments	Occurrences in Negative Comments
Price-	51	27
Money	2	2
Valu-	24	5
Worth	4	0
Cost	5	4
Total	86	38

and to organize training programmes in an efficient way. Finance department may use it for financial forecasting, risk analysis, managing new investments, etc. Marketing department may benefit from data mining to reveal information about customers, to organize shelves in retailing, etc. The need for experts will increase in professions such as;

- Data mining experts,
- Data scientists do work on data arrangement,
- Data visualization experts,
- Data analysts,
- Data warehouse builders,
- Database managers.

Businesses retaining these experts to produce and use information will gain competitive advantages in today's information era (Köktürk and Dirsehan, 2012). Particularly, managers of services companies will need "text archaeologists" to analyze customer reviews on the web, since in the near future, these reviews will reach to such a number that reading and analyzing them manually will be impossible. Businesses capable to "understand" the hidden patterns will survive.

From the academicians' side, this study provides an alternative research methodology that can be adapted easily to different service sectors. The methodology presented in this research can be applied to other sectors too.

In this chapter, RapidMiner is used as a text mining tool to determine the differences and underlying factors of online positive and negative customer comments. Alternatively, researchers may divide the comments according to nationalities and the comments of national and foreign tourists may be compared. As another alternative, comments may be divided according to customers' types, for instance solo travelers and families. Then, the factors can be analyzed to revise the segmentation criteria. As another option, the texts on social media can be extracted for analysis. It's also to conduct text mining for web sites of the companies too.

In sum, text mining is a useful tool to uncover information from large textual data sets to help managers making marketing decisions.

CONCLUSION

Relationship marketing is considered as emerging field in the 20th century and improving in the last era of marketing history (Kurtz and Boone, 2010). The main purpose of this approach is to build long-term, profitable relationships with customers. The strategy to build this relationship should be based on customer data. These raw data can produce information if it's analyzed with some data mining tools. One of these tools is text mining.

How does text mining create competitive advantage for companies? This process can be illustrated in Figure 7. So, the process can be summarized as:

1. A business offers its services to consumers. (In this study, a hotel offers vacation to visitors.)
2. Consumers receive these services and share his/her experiences to other consumers. (In this study, visitors write the experiences on a web site.)

Figure 7. An overview of text mining process (based on the relevant literature review)

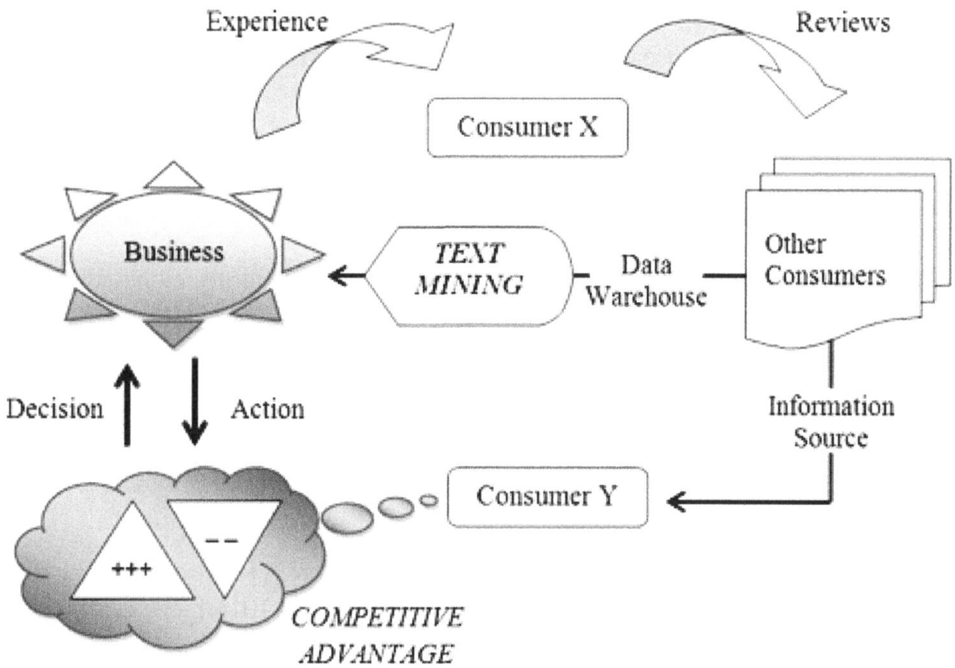

3. Other consumers are informed about these experiences and they evaluate alternative companies. (In this study, other tourists evaluate the stories of tourists previously visited the hotel.)
4. On the business side, these reviews can be used as data to reveal information about customers' opinions. (In this study, hotels should find a research tool to analyze visitors' opinions.)
5. Companies may use text mining to reveal meaningful information from customer reviews. (In this study, hotel managers may use text mining on visitor comments that exist on the web site.)
6. By using text mining, firms may see the hidden patterns in negative and positive customer comments. (For instance, hotel managers may see which characteristics' presence results in satisfaction and their absence in dissatisfaction.)
7. Businesses can take actions according to information provided by customer data and create competitive advantages. For instance, they can offer new improved services. (For instance, hotel managers should focus firstly on characteristics for which their presence results in satisfaction and their absence in dissatisfaction.)
8. Customers can decide to choose businesses according to these new improved services.
9. If this process is repeated over time, a strong relationship between business and consumers can be created providing a strong competitive advantage for the firm.

The main purpose of this study was to present RapidMiner as a text mining tool and show its practical use. Data collected from a booking web site were analyzed through text mining technique and a classification was suggested in the hospitality marketing area.

1. Some hotel characteristics' presence results in satisfaction but their absence does not result in dissatisfaction.
2. Other characteristics' absence results in dissatisfaction but their presence does not result in satisfaction.
3. Still other characteristics' presence results in satisfaction and their absence in dissatisfaction. Additional classifications can also be suggested such as characteristics depending on the hotel management (e.g., *staff*) and not depending on them (e.g., *sea*).

With different grouping options, the results may provide important information for hotel managers for their strategic marketing decisions such as segmentation and marketing mix tools. In terms of academic implications, this study is expected to encourage new "data archaeologists" to conduct researches with the use of text mining in marketing research.

REFERENCES

Berger, J. (2014). Word of Mouth and Interpersonal Communication: A Review and Directions for Future Research. *Journal of Consumer Psychology*, *24*(4), 586–607. doi:10.1016/j.jcps.2014.05.002

Booking.com. (n.d.). Retrieved from www.booking.com

Brachmann, R. J., Selfridge, P. G., Terveen, L. G., Altman, B., Borgida, A., Halper, F., & Resnick, L. A. et al. (1993). Integrated Support for Data Archaeology. *International Journal of Intelligent and Cooperative Information Systems*, *2*(2), 159–185. doi:10.1142/S0218215793000083

Cantallops, A., & Salvi, F. (2014). New Consumer Behavior: A Review of Research on eWOM and Hotels. *International Journal of Hospitality Management*, *36*, 41–51. doi:10.1016/j.ijhm.2013.08.007

Chang, C.-W., Lin, C.-T., & Wang, L.-Q. (2009). Mining the Text Information to Optimizing the Customer Relationship Management. *Expert Systems with Applications*, *36*(2), 1433–1443. doi:10.1016/j.eswa.2007.11.027

Chatterjee, P. (2001). Online Review: Do Consumers Use Them? *Advances in Consumer Research. Association for Consumer Research (U. S.)*, *28*, 129–133.

Chen, H. (2001). *Knowledge Management Systems: A Text Mining Perspective*. Arizona: Knowledge Computing Corporation.

Chen, K. C. (2009). Text Mining e-Complaints Data From e-Auction Store With Implications For Internet Marketing Research. *Journal of Business & Economics Research*, *7*(5), 15–24.

Cheung, C., & Lee, M. (2012). What Drives Consumers to Spread Electronic Word of Mouth in Online Consumer-Opinion Platforms. *Decision Support Systems*, *53*(1), 218–225. doi:10.1016/j.dss.2012.01.015

Cheung, C., & Thadani, D. (2012). The Impact of Electronic Word-of-Mouth Communication: A Literature Analysis and Integrative Model. *Decision Support Systems*, *54*(1), 461–470. doi:10.1016/j.dss.2012.06.008

Christodoulides, G., Michaelidou, N., & Argyriou, E. (2012). Cross-National Differences in e-WOM Influence. *European Journal of Marketing*, *46*(11/12), 1689–1707. doi:10.1108/03090561211260040

Erkuş-Öztürk, H., & Eraydin, A. (2011). Factors of Global Connectivity in Antalya's Tourism. *Annals of Tourism Research*, *38*(4), 1300–1321. doi:10.1016/j.annals.2011.03.002

Ertek, G., Tapucu, D., & Arın, I. (2013). Text Mining with RapidMiner. In M. Hofmann & R. Klinkenberg (Eds.), *RapidMiner: Data Mining Use Cases and Business Analytics Applications*. Chapman and Hall/CRC.

Filieri, R. (2015). What Makes Online Reviews Helpful? A Diagnosticity-Adoption Framework to Explain Informational and Normative Influences in e-WOM. *Journal of Business Research*, *68*(6), 1261–1270. doi:10.1016/j.jbusres.2014.11.006

Filieri, R., & McLeay, F. (2013). E-WOM and Accommodation: An Analysis of the Factors That Influence Travelers' Adoption of Information from Online Reviews. *Journal of Travel Research*, *53*(1), 44–57. doi:10.1177/0047287513481274

Gassiot, A., & Coromina, L. (2013). Destination Image of Girona: An Online Text-Mining Approach. *International Journal of Management Cases*, *15*(4), 301–314.

Goldsmith, R. E., & Horowitz, D. (2006). Measuring Motivations For Online Opinion Seeking. *Journal of Interactive Advertising*, *6*(2), 1–16. doi:10.1080/15252019.2006.10722114

Groth, R. (1999). *Data Mining: Building Competitive Advantage*. Prentice Hall PTR.

Gupta, P., & Harris, J. (2010). How e-WOM Recommendations Influence Product Consideration and Quality of Choice: A Motivation to Process Information Perspective. *Journal of Business Research*, *63*(9-10), 1041–1049. doi:10.1016/j.jbusres.2009.01.015

Gupta, V., & Lehal, G. S. (2009). A Survey of Text Mining Techniques and Applications. *Journal of Emerging Technologies in Web Intelligence*, *1*(1), 60–76. doi:10.4304/jetwi.1.1.60-76

Hair, J., Robert, B. R., & Ortinau, D. (2009). Marketing Research in a Digital Information Environment (4th ed.). New York: McGraw Hill/Irwin.

Han, J., & Kamber, M. (2001). *Data Mining: Concepts and Techniques*. Morgan Kaufmann Publishers.

He, W., Zha, S., & Li, L. (2013). Social Media Competitive Analysis and Text Mining: A Case Study in the Pizza Industry. *International Journal of Information Management*, *33*(3), 464–472. doi:10.1016/j.ijinfomgt.2013.01.001

Hearst, M. (1999). Untangling Text Data Mining. In *Proceedings of ACL'99: the 37th Annual Meeting of the Association for Computational Linguistics,* University of Maryland. Available at http://people.ischool.berkeley.edu/~hearst/pape rs/acl99/acl99-tdm.html

Hennig-Thurau, T., Gwinner, K. P., Walsh, G., & Gremler, D. D. (2004). Electronic Word-of-Mouth Via Consumer-Opinion Platforms: What Motivates Consumers to Articulate Themselves On The Internet? *Journal of Interactive Marketing*, *18*(1), 38–52. doi:10.1002/dir.10073

Hornik, J., Satchi, R. S., Cesareo, L., & Pastore, A. (2015). Information Dissemination Via Electronic Word-of-Mouth: Good News Travels Fast, Bad News Travels Faster! *Computers in Human Behavior*, *45*, 273–280. doi:10.1016/j.chb.2014.11.008

Jalilvand, M., Samiei, N., Dini, B., & Manzari, P. (2012). Examining the Structural Relationships of Electronic Word of Mouth, Destination Image, Tourist Attitude Toward Destination and Travel Intention: An Integrated Approach. *Journal of Destination Marketing & Management*, *1*(1-2), 134–143. doi:10.1016/j.jdmm.2012.10.001

Kassarjian, H. H. (1977). Content Analysis in Consumer Research. *The Journal of Consumer Research*, *4*(1), 8–18. doi:10.1086/208674

Köktürk, M., & Dirsehan, T. (2012). *Veri Madenciliği ile Pazarlama Etkileşimi (Interaction between Data Mining and Marketing)*. Ankara: Nobel.

Kurtz, D., & Boone, L. (2010). Principles of Contemporary Marketing (14th int. ed.). South-Western.

Lau, K.-N., Lee, K.-H., & Ho, Y. (2005). Text Mining for the Hotel Industry. *The Cornell Hotel and Restaurant Administration Quarterly*, *46*(3), 344–362. doi:10.1177/0010880405275966

Leong, E. K. F., Ewing, M. T., & Pitt, L. F. (2004). Analysing Competitors' Online Persuasive Themes with Text Mining. *Marketing Intelligence & Planning*, *22*(2), 187–200. doi:10.1108/02634500410525850

Liang, S.-J., Ekinci, Y., Occhiocupo, N., & Whyatt, G. (2013). Antecedents of Travellers' Electronic Word-of-Mouth Communication. *Journal of Marketing Management*, *29*(5-6), 584–606. doi:10.1080/0267257X.2013.771204

Liau, B., & Tan, P. (2014). Gaining Customer Knowledge in Low Cost Airlines Through Text Mining. *Industrial Management & Data Systems*, *114*(9), 1344–1359. doi:10.1108/IMDS-07-2014-0225

Litvin, S. W., Goldsmith, R. E., & Pan, B. (2008). Electronic Word-of-Mouth in Hospitality and Tourism Management. *Tourism Management*, *29*(3), 458–468. doi:10.1016/j.tourman.2007.05.011

Malhotra, N. (2007). Marketing Research: An Applied Orientation (5th ed.). Pearson Prentice Hall.

Mauri, A., & Minazzi, R. (2013). Web Reviews Influence on Expectations and Purchasing Intentions of Hotel Potential Customers. *International Journal of Hospitality Management*, *34*, 99–107. doi:10.1016/j.ijhm.2013.02.012

Melián-González, S., Bulchand-Gidumal, J., & López-Valcárcel, B. (2013). Online Customer Reviews of Hotels: As Participation Increases, Better Evaluation Is Obtained. *Cornell Hospitality Quarterly*, *54*(3), 274–283. doi:10.1177/1938965513481498

Mostafa, M. (2013). More Than Words: Social Networks' Text Mining for Consumer Brand Sentiments. *Expert Systems with Applications*, *40*(10), 4241–4251. doi:10.1016/j.eswa.2013.01.019

Nielsen. (2009). *Trust, value and engagement in advertising: Nielsen Global Online Consumer Survey*. The Nielsen Company. Retrieved from http://www.nielsen.com/content/dam/corporate/us/en/newswire/uploads/2009/07/trustinadvertising0709.pdf

Nyer, P. U. (2000). An Investigation Into Whether Complaining Can Cause Increased Consumer Satisfaction. *Journal of Consumer Marketing*, *17*(1), 9–19. doi:10.1108/07363760010309500

Rapid Miner Documentation. (n.d.). Retrieved from https://rapidminer.com/documentation/

Shapiro, G., & Markoff, J. (1997). A Matter of Definition. In C. W. Roberts (Ed.), *Text Analysis for the Social Sciences* (pp. 9–31). Mahwah, NJ: Lawrence Erlbaum Associates.

Sotiriadis, M. D., & van Zyl, C. (2013). Electronic Word-of-Mouth and Online Reviews in Tourism Services: The Use of Twitter by Tourists. *Electronic Commerce Research*, *13*(1), 103–124. doi:10.1007/s10660-013-9108-1

Stone, P. J. (1997). Thematic Text Analysis: New Agendas for Analyzing Text Content. In C. W. Roberts (Ed.), *Text Analysis for the Social Sciences* (pp. 35–54). Mahwah, NJ: Lawrence Erlbaum Associates.

Tang, C., & Guo, L. (2013). Digging for Gold with a Simple Tool: Validating Text Mining in Studying Electronic Word-of-Mouth (eWOM) Communication. *Marketing Letters*, *26*(1), 67–80. doi:10.1007/s11002-013-9268-8

Translate, Google. (n.d.). Retrieved from https://translate.google.com.tr/

Tseng, A. (2014). *Text Mining Tools*. Retrieved from http://blogs.unimelb.edu.au/23researchthings/2014/08/04/ thing-18-text-mining-tools/

TÜRSAB (Association of Turkish Travel Agency). (n.d.). Available at http://www.tursab.org.tr/

Xiang, Z., Schwartz, Z., Gerdes, J. Jr, & Uysal, M. (2015). What Can Big Data and Text Analytics Tell Us About Hotel Guest Experience and Satisfaction? *International Journal of Hospitality Management*, *44*, 120–130. doi:10.1016/j.ijhm.2014.10.013

Yang, Y., Akers, L., Klose, T., & Yang, C. (2008). Text Mining and Visualization Tools – Impressions of *Emerging Capabilities. World Patent Information*, *30*(4), 280–293. doi:10.1016/j.wpi.2008.01.007

Ye, Q., Law, R., Gu, B., & Chen, W. (2011). The Influence of User-Generated Content on Traveler Behavior: An Empirical Investigation on The Effects of e-Word-of-Mouth to Hotel Online Bookings. *Computers in Human Behavior*, *27*(2), 634–639. doi:10.1016/j.chb.2010.04.014

ADDITIONAL READING

Chisholm, A. (2013). *Exploring Data with RapidMiner*. UK: Packt Publishing.

Hofmann, M., & Klinkenberg, R. (Eds.). (2014). *RapidMiner: Data Mining Use Cases and Business Analytics Applications (Chapman & Hall/CRC Data Mining and Knowledge Discovery Series)*. USA: Taylor & Francis Group.

Kotu, V., & Deshpande, B. (2014). *Predictive Analytics and Data Mining: Concepts and Practice with RapidMiner*. USA: Morgan Kaufmann.

Miner, G., Elder, I. V. J., Hill, T., Nisbet, R., Delen, D., & Fast, A. (2012). *Practical Text Mining and Statistical Analysis for Non-structured Text Data Applications*. UK: Academic Press.

Provost, F., & Fawcett, T. (2013). *Data Science For Business: What You Need To Know About Data Mining and Data-Analytic Thinking*. USA: O'Reilly Media.

Weber, C. (2013). *An Application of Text Mining: A Practical Approach to Manage Account Feedback Using Text Mining Algorithms*. AV Akademikerverlag.

KEY TERMS AND DEFINITIONS

Artificial Neural Networks: They are an example of most common functions of data mining. They are biologically inspired computer programs and their main purpose is to estimate functions from a complex set of data.

Association Rules: They are an example of most common functions of data mining. They are used to uncover relationships in large databases.

Big Data: It refers to analytical capabilities that can be extracted from data.

Clustering Analysis: It's a technique to group objects or variables based on data.

Data Mining: It refers to the process of analyzing large data sets and extracting hidden patterns. The main purpose of data mining is to discover knowledge from data sets.

Data Mining Tools: They are analyses used to examine large databases.

Decision Trees: They are an example of most common functions of data mining, used to choose between different courses of action.

Electronic Word-of-Mouth (eWOM): It represents personal communication such as complaints, recommendations through electronic means.

RapidMiner: Is a software to conduct several data mining analyzes.

Social Networking Sites (SNSs): They are web sites used to create public profiles and to communicate with other users, in other terms, to build social networks.

Text Mining (TM): It is an extension of data mining, useful to produce information and discover knowledge from unstructured textual data.

Text Processing: It is an application in RapidMiner to start conducting text mining.

User Generated Content (UGC): It refers to content created by people/users on the Internet.

Section 4
Studies in Indian Context

Chapter 11
Facebook Experience Is Different:
An Empirical Study in Indian Context

Punita Duhan
Meera Bai Institute of Technology, India

Anurag Singh
Banaras Hindu University, India

ABSTRACT

Though the concept of experience was propounded decades ago, the terms such as Customer Experience Management, Brand Experience etc. have started gaining currency only recently. Renewed focus on the concept is the result of positive impacts of brand experience as evidenced by researches. Emergence of Social Media has provided the organizations with supplementary platforms to enhance customer experiences. The experiences of customers with various social media platforms may rub on to their experiences with the brands being promoted through these. Accordingly, present research studies the experience of select social media platforms in Indian context. Result revealed that the experience of Facebook was significantly favorable in comparison to the rest three platforms; however, a scope of improvement is evident. Result is important for platform developers as it helps them to improve their platforms and for Marketing managers as it guides them to associate their brands with the more favourable platforms in order to reap concomitant benefits.

INTRODUCTION

Bifurcation between buying and consumption of products and services brought to the fore various mental activities associated with the act of consumption. Though, the need to focus on multisensory experiences related to consumption had become evident decades back (Alderson, 1957; Boyd & Levy, 1963), yet the subjective aspects of consumption were sacrificed on the altar of logical and bounded rationality till very late (Olshavsky & Granbois, 1979; Sheth, 1979; Holbrook & Hirschman, 1982). Termed as "experiential view" by Holbrook & Hirschman (1982), these conscious and subjective aspects of consump-

DOI: 10.4018/978-1-4666-9449-1.ch011

tion essentially explore the emotional responses of the consumers inherent in the act of consumption (Holbrook et al., 1982). Consumers attribute certain symbolic (Levy, 1959), syntactic (structure and style of message content), hedonic, psychotemporal, psychobiological meanings to the products they consume and these attributed subjective meanings facilitate researchers and marketers to explore the multisensory relationships in consumer behavior (Levy, 1959; Holbrook et al., 1982). Researches on customer's brand experiences and the antecedent impact of positive experiences on brand attitude, brand loyalty, brand commitment, brand performance, brand satisfaction, brand trust and brand attachment has led the focus of marketers on managing and enhancing Customers' Experience. All this has resulted in the incorporation of the terms like Experience Marketing, Experiential Marketing, Customer Experience Management, Experience Economy and Brand Experience in marketing glossary.

Dawn of era of digital economy is another factor, which has necessitated the study of brand experience (Chui, Manyika, Bughin, Dobbs, Sarrazin, Sands & Westergen, 2012). Digitization, by leveraging the power of Internet, has paved way for new business models, in which business communications, interactions and transactions between Consumers and marketers are carried over web (Kalakota & Robinson, 2001), facilitated by new media channels in the form of Social Media or Web 2.0 (Edelman, 2010). Absence of temporal and geographic boundaries in virtual experiences warrants for ongoing, real time analysis of customers' expectations, experiences (Kalakota et al., 2001) and effective handling of web experience, as inept web experiences can severely influence online as well as offline reputation of the firm (Constantinides, 2004). Web 2.0 has led to the emergence of new influencers in consumer decision journey such as strong online advocacy and discussions in brand communities (Edelman, 2010).

Social media's propagation and acceptance among masses across the globe is unprecedented (Stanley, 2009; Hughes, 2010; Nielsen, 2012; Vehr, 2012). Level of realism provided by an experience leads to more enduring attitudes towards the experience. Characteristics such as "telepresence" and "flow experience" have enabled Internet to exhibit a higher level of realism even in comparison to television. Researchers have indicated that enhanced interactivity and vividness of digital media leads to stronger perceptions of simulated experience (Schiffman, Kanuk& Kumar, 2010). This has prompted the organizations to use Social media platforms for variety of marketing purposes (Stelzner, 2012; Stelzner, 2013). Moreover, as per the Congruity theory of attitudes, changes in the evaluations of a source and a concept can be linked together by an associative assertion (Osgood & Tannenbaum, 1955). Hence, the experiences of customers with various social media platforms may rub on to their experiences with the products and services being promoted through these platforms.

Accordingly, present chapter is an attempt in this direction as to comprehend the customers' experience in relation to four popular social media platforms *viz.* Facebook, Google+, LinkedIn and Twitter in the Indian context. This comprehension of brand experience of given social media platforms will help marketers to devise effective marketing strategies to enhance the experience of these platforms for customers and in turn will help them to derive more value from these platforms. These media channels though not in entire control of manufacturers and retailers (Edelman, 2010), but can be utilized by organizations as the supplementary platforms to influence and enhance customer experiences. The objectives, which study attempts to explore, are to assess Facebook, Google+, LinkedIn and Twitter's experience, to assess Facebook, Google+, LinkedIn and Twitter's sensory experience, to assess Facebook, Google+, LinkedIn and Twitter's affective experience, to assess Facebook, Google+, LinkedIn and Twitter's behavioral experience and to assess Facebook, Google+, LinkedIn and Twitter's intellectual experience.

The Chapter has been structured around six sections. First section deals with the conceptual framework detailing the concept and advantages of the brand experience. Second section gives the literature review about brand experience in the wake of digitization and the need of the present research. This section also deals with the research questions, objectives and hypotheses of the research. Third section elaborates on the research methodology undertaken by the researchers. Focus of the fourth section is on analysis and interpretation of the results. Fifth section caters to the implications of the research and the concluding section of the chapter talks about limitations and future research possibilities.

CONCEPTUAL FRAMEWORK

Brand Experience

Concept of customer experience is not a novel concept as researchers have emphasized upon it since long time (Pine & Gilmore, 1998; Pine & Gilmore, 1999; Carbone & Haeckel, 1994; Johnston, 1999). Renewed focus on the concept is the result of the need for standardization for both products as well as services, as commoditization leaves lesser scope for competing in market on the basis of features alone (Pine et al., 1998). Experienced utility, subjective notions of value accorded to the brands, is a better differentiator than expected utility, the utilitarian notions of value, in today's highly competitive markets (Zaichkowsky, 1985; Schmitt, 2011).

In marketing parlance, two meanings have been attributed to the term "Experience". One meaning connotes the accumulated knowledge and experiences over time, whereas the other connotes the ongoing perceptions and feelings and direct observation. However, for the present chapter researchers go by the second connotation i.e. the perceptions, feelings and thoughts consumers attribute to the brands they encounter and consume.

Braunsberger and Munch (1998) define experience as *"displaying a relatively high degree of familiarity with a certain subject area, obtained through some type of exposure."* According to Brakus, Schmitt and Zarantonello (2009), "*Brand experience refers to subjective, internal consumer responses (sensations, feelings, and cognitions) and behavioral responses evoked by brand-related stimuli that are part of a brand's design and identity, packaging, communications, and environments.*"

Any interaction – direct or indirect, of the customer with the brand results in brand experience (Aaker & Maheswaran, 1997). It is the sum total of the various experiential aspects resulting from all the points of contact with the brand (wikipedia.com). Various stimuli related to the brand, such as unique identifications (viz. name, logo, symbols, signs), colors, shapes, packaging, typefaces, background design elements, slogans, mascots and brand characters communication (viz. print, electronic, audio, visual, audio-visual) and marketing environments (viz. stores, events, social media, websites) have symbolic meanings for the customers (Ha & Perks, 2005; Brakus et al., 2009; Ofir & Simonson, 2007; Bellizzi & Hite 1992; Meyers-Levy & Peracchio 1995; Joy & Sherry, 2003;Mandel & Johnson, 2002; Johar, Sengupta, & Aaker, 2005). These symbolic meanings assist consumer in brand evaluation through the formation of subjective and internal responses towards the brand. (Arnold, Reynolds, Ponder & Lueg, 2005; Chinomona, 2013).

ADVANTAGES OF POSITIVE BRAND EXPERIENCE

Although the concept of experience is novel and research on the concept is in nascent stages, yet it has emerged as a powerful and exciting concept in marketing (Schmitt, 2011). The statement that "Benefits are not in the products but in consumer experiences" underlines this importance (Zaichkowsky, 1985). As per Berry (2000), it is the most vital and powerful aspect of branding strategy. Unique brand experiences become unique selling propositions and help the brand stay ahead of competition (Pine et al., 1998; Pine et al., 1999; Voss 2003; Prahalad & Ramaswamy, 2004; Meyer & Schwager, 2007). Positive brand experiences lead to favorable brand image, customer satisfaction and loyalty (Yulianti & Tung, 2013; Chinomona, 2013). Satisfied customers repurchase the brands and repurchases, in turn, result in brand trust, brand loyalty and brand attachment (Koufaris, 2002; Kim, 2005; Wang & Emurian, 2005; Ercis, Unal, Candan & Yildrinm, 2012;Chinomona, 2013).

Satisfaction, trust, loyalty, and attachment with the brand influences repurchases and results in enhanced sales and profits (Chinomona, 2013; Liljander & Strandvik 1997; Yu & Dean, 2001; Pullman & Gross, 2004). Brand experience thus influences expectations (Johnson & Mathews 1997), brand perception (Cliffe & Motion, 2005), instills confidence (Flanagan, Johnston & Talbot, 2005), supports the brand (Berry & Carbone, 2007) and creates emotional bonds with customers (Pullman et al., 2004). As the Brand experience tends to become a prior as well as personal source of information for future purchase decisions of consumer (Brakus, Schmitt & Zhang, 2008; Sahin, Zehir & Kitapç, 2011), it becomes imperative for marketers to analyze and comprehend brand experience in order to frame effective marketing strategies (Smith & Wheeler, 2002;Schmitt, 2003; Yulianti et al., 2013). Advantages of the positive brand experience have been summarized in the Figure 1.

LITERATURE REVIEW

Brand Experience in the Era of Digitization

Induction of information technology in the organizations has mandated e-based structural reconfigurations, as e- business is the new path to profitability (Kalakota et al., 2001). "Virtual Trendsetters" (Guadagni & Tommaso, 2007) are adding new dimensions to the purchases and influencing consumers through virtual networks and informed groups (Bellini, Ascenzo, Ghi, Spagnoli & Traversi, (n. d.)). Digitization has altered the consumer decision journey by adding new touch points such as Web, Internet channels, Blogs, Forums and Social Networks (Edelman, 2010). This has mandated organizations to keep a tab on the opinions of the "netizens" about their brand by combing through the "voice of customers" to gain competitive advantages. New digital analytical tools such as "Opinion mining", "Sentiment Analysis", "Social media monitoring and analysis" are enabling the organizations to comprehend the types of interactions- quantitative and qualitative, emotional valence - positive or negative and emotional intensity for their brands in an unprecedented manner. Analysis and comprehension of unadulterated consumer sentiments can be instrumental in creating unforgettable customer experiences (Schmitt, 2003; Bellini et al., (n. d.))

Due to digitization, it has become obligatory on the part of organizations to interact and correlate with the market (Morace, 2002; Bellini et al., (n. d.)). Traditional 4P (Product, Price, Place & Promotion) marketing model is making way for 4E (Engagement, Experience, Enhance and Emotion) model of "ex-

Figure 1. Advantages of Brand Experience

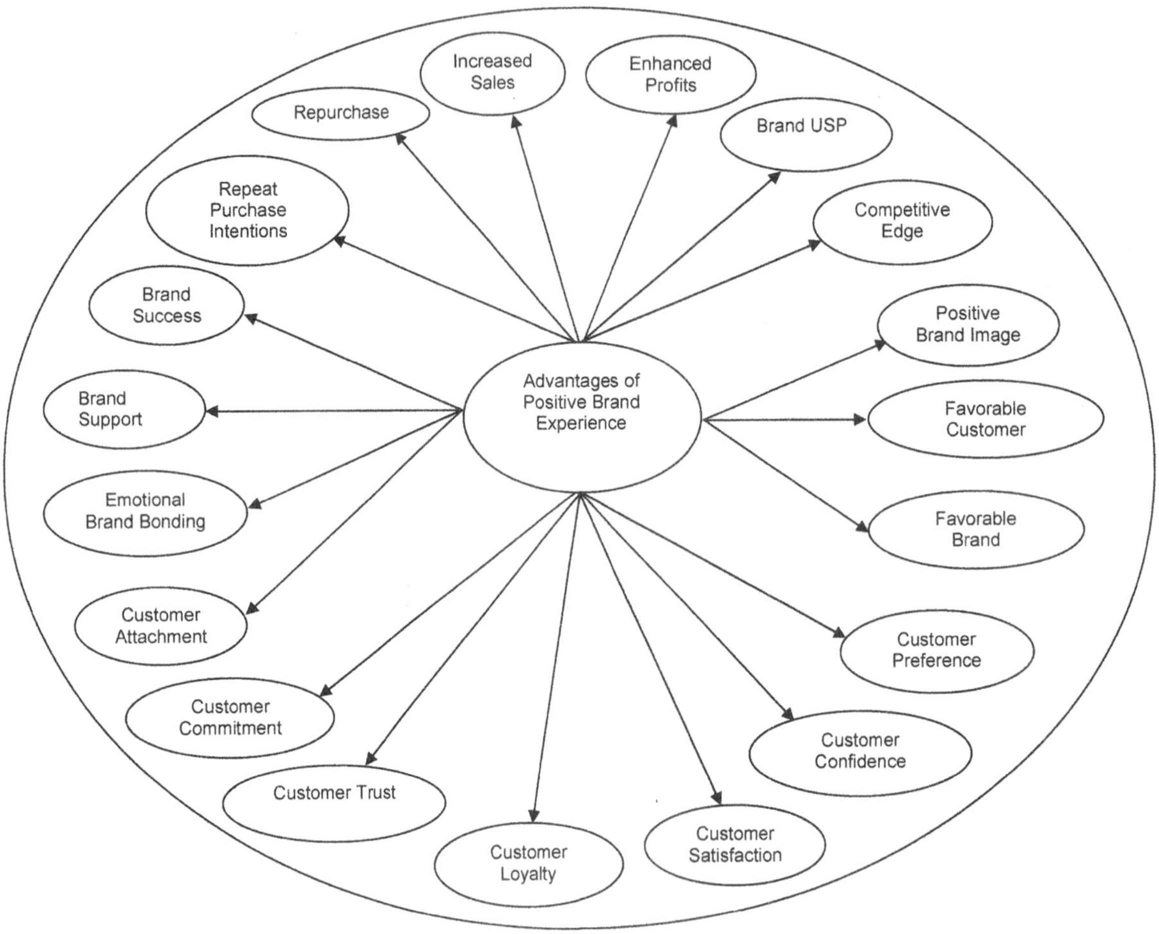

perience economy" (Gelter, 2007a) in order to deliver meaningful experiences to the customers (Bellini et al., (n. d.)).Customer Experience Management (CEM) being a concurrent approach with emotional dimensions is gaining currency over Customer Relationship Management (CRM) to manage customer encounters with the organizations (Schmitt, 2003; Meyer et al., 2007). "Strategic Experiential Module" is being advocated in order to provide "hybrid" and "holistic" experiences to customers (Schmitt, 2003; Ferraresi & Schmitt, 2006). Concomitant benefits of brand experience such as brand familiarity, customer satisfaction and brand trust has necessitated the creation and delivery of customer experience in case of e-brands as well (Reichheld & Schefter, 2000; Kenny & Marshall, 2000; Mcwilliam, 2000; Shankar et al., 2000; Ha, 2004; Kania, 2001; Ha et al., 2005). Brand trust is one of the most important factors in Internet based transactions (Quelch & Klein, 1996; Corbitt, Thanasankit & Yi, 2003) and positive brand experience can play a crucial role in inculcating trust in e-transactions and can ensure the participation of the individuals (Ha et al., 2005).

Dynamic digital arena demands a bottom-up approach to customer experience management- an approach based on detailed road map of customer's end-to-end journey in which customer experiences are managed at multiple touch points across multiple channels in a cumulative fashion (Rawson, Duncan &

Jones, 2013). One such touch point facilitated by Internet is website brand experience, which has been defined as "*a consumer's positive navigations (i.e. using web-based communities and participating in events) and perceptions (i.e. the attractiveness of cookies, variety and uniqueness of visual displays and value for money) with a specific website*" (Ha et al., 2005). A website, which delivers relevant, well-organized and engaging information, offers positive experience (Chen &Wells, 1999) to the users and is successful in luring the customer to stay for a longer period, to explore further (Menon& Kahn, 2002) and in retaining the customer traffic (Ha et al., 2005). Most consumers on Internet are price seekers and positive brand experiences have a positive reaction to pricing as well. Hence, positive brand experiences on Internet can turn such price seekers into loyal customers (Ha et al., 2005). As such, there is a need for organizations to invest in community-building infrastructure (*viz.* chat rooms, bulletin boards and interactive events) to facilitate the interactions and support the brand experiences. Amazon's 'customer recommendation' content page is an oft quoted and successful instance in the case. Understanding customer's virtual experience is vital as it only influences virtual interactions but also the online and offline decision making of the customer (Constantinides, 2004).

RESEARCH GAP

Literature review has evidenced that brand experience- both offline as well as online, is a critical aspect of brand marketing strategy due to its wide-ranging concomitant impacts. However, the number of studies undertaken to study customer's brand experience is limited. Number of researches looking into the web experiences is even lesser and such studies in Indian context are hard to find. Added to this is the fact that despite the augmented usage of social media worldwide, there is almost nil research available exploring the experience concomitant to various social media platforms, same being true in Indian context. Hence, this study is an attempt to explore and comprehend customers' overall experience as well to study their experiences along the four dimensions *viz.* Sensory, Affective, Behavioural and Intellectual in relation to select social media platforms in Indian context and thereby fill the research void on this academic and research turf.

Research Questions

1. What ratings customers give to the experience of some select brands of social media platforms *viz.* Facebook, Google+, LinkedIn and Twitter?
2. Are the experiences related to these brands different from each other?
3. What ratings customers give to the four dimensions of experience *viz.* Sensory, Affective, Behavioral and Intellectual- in relation of Facebook, Google+, LinkedIn and Twitter?
4. Are the experiences of four dimensions different from each other for Facebook, Google+, LinkedIn and Twitter?

OBJECTIVES

In accordance with the research questions the objectives of the study are:

1. To assess Facebook, Google+, LinkedIn and Twitter's experience
2. To assess Facebook, Google+, LinkedIn and Twitter's sensory experience
3. To assess Facebook, Google+, LinkedIn and Twitter's affective experience
4. To assess Facebook, Google+, LinkedIn and Twitter's behavioral experience
5. To assess Facebook, Google+, LinkedIn and Twitter's intellectual experience.

RESEARCH AND STATISTICAL HYPOTHESES

$\mathbf{H}_{01:}$ There is no significant difference between Facebook, Google+, LinkedIn and Twitter's experience
$\mathbf{H}_{a1:}$ There is a significant difference between Facebook, Google+, LinkedIn and Twitter's experience
$\mathbf{H}_{01:}$ $\mu_{FB} = \mu_{GL} = \mu_{LN} = \mu_{TW}$
$\mathbf{H}_{a1:}$ $\mu_{FB} \neq \mu_{GL} \neq \mu_{LN} \neq \mu_{TW}$

where

$\boldsymbol{\mu}_{\mathbf{FB}}$: Mean value of FaceBook Experience
$\boldsymbol{\mu}_{\mathbf{GL}}$: Mean value of Google+ Experience
$\boldsymbol{\mu}_{\mathbf{LN}}$: Mean value of LinkedIn Experience
$\boldsymbol{\mu}_{\mathbf{TW}}$: Mean value of Twitter Experience
$\mathbf{H}_{02:}$ There is no significant difference between Facebook, Google+, LinkedIn and Twitter's Sensory experience
$\mathbf{H}_{a2:}$ There is a significant difference between Facebook, Google+, LinkedIn and Twitter's Sensory experience
$\mathbf{H}_{02:}$ $\mu_{FBSD} = \mu_{GLSD} = \mu_{LNSD} = \mu_{TWSD}$
$\mathbf{H}_{a2:}$ $\mu_{FBSD} \neq \mu_{GLSD} \neq \mu_{LNSD} \neq \mu_{TWSD}$

where

$\boldsymbol{\mu}_{\mathbf{FBSD}}$: Mean value of FaceBook's Sensory Experience
$\boldsymbol{\mu}_{\mathbf{GLSD}}$: Mean value of Google+'s Sensory Experience
$\boldsymbol{\mu}_{\mathbf{LNSD}}$: Mean value of LinkedIn's Sensory Experience
$\boldsymbol{\mu}_{\mathbf{TWSD}}$: Mean value of Twitter's Sensory Experience
$\mathbf{H}_{03:}$ There is no significant difference between Facebook, Google+, LinkedIn and Twitter's affective experience
$\mathbf{H}_{a3:}$ There is a significant difference between Facebook, Google+, LinkedIn and Twitter's affective experience
$\mathbf{H}_{03:}$ $\mu_{FBAD} = \mu_{GLAD} = \mu_{LNAD} = \mu_{TWAD}$
$\mathbf{H}_{a3:}$ $\mu_{FBAD} \neq \mu_{GLAD} \neq \mu_{LNAD} \neq \mu_{TWAD}$

where

$\boldsymbol{\mu}_{\mathbf{FBAD}}$: Mean value of Facebook's affective Experience
$\boldsymbol{\mu}_{\mathbf{GLAD}}$: Mean value of Google+'s affective Experience

μ_{LNAD}: Mean value of LinkedIn's affective Experience
μ_{TWAD}: Mean value of Twitter's affective Experience
$H_{04:}$ There is no significant difference between Facebook, Google+, LinkedIn and Twitter's behavioural experience
$H_{a4:}$ There is a significant difference between Facebook, Google+, LinkedIn and Twitter's behavioural experience
$H_{04:}$ $\mu_{FBBD} = \mu_{GLBD} = \mu_{LNBD} = \mu_{TWBD}$
$H_{a4:}$ $\mu_{FBBD} \neq \mu_{GLBD} \neq \mu_{LNBD} \neq \mu_{TWBD}$

where

μ_{FBBD}: Mean value of Facebook's behavioural Experience
μ_{GLBD}: Mean value of Google+'sbehavioural Experience
μ_{LNBD}: Mean value of LinkedIn's behavioural Experience
μ_{TWBD}: Mean value of Twitter's behavioural Experience
$H_{05:}$ There is no significant difference between Facebook, Google+, LinkedIn and Twitter's intellectual experience
$H_{a5:}$ There is a significant difference between Facebook, Google+, LinkedIn and Twitter's intellectual experience
$H_{05:}$ $\mu_{FBID} = \mu_{GLID} = \mu_{LNID} = \mu_{TWID}$
$H_{a5:}$ $\mu_{FBID} \neq \mu_{GLID} \neq \mu_{LNID} \neq \mu_{TWID}$

where

μ_{FBID}: Mean value of FaceBook's intellectual Experience
μ_{GLID}: Mean value of Google+'s intellectual Experience
μ_{LNID}: Mean value of LinkedIn's intellectual Experience
μ_{TWID}: Mean value of Twitter's intellectual Experience.

RESEARCH METHODOLOGY

Both primary as well as secondary data have been used in the research. Secondary data were used majorly for literature review, to develop the theoretical concept, to identify the research gap and to corroborate the research findings. Secondary sources of the data used were the available and published literature, such as research papers published in journals (both offline and online), other proprietary data in the form of reports, whitepapers etc. available at their websites and the relevant books.

For primary data collection, an online questionnaire was developed on Google docs. The questionnaire consisted of Brand Experience scale developed by Brakus, Schmitt & Zarantonello (2009). Items used in the scale for measuring various components of the experience as well as the overall brand experience are as under:

Sensory Dimension:

1. This brand makes a strong impression on my visual senses or other senses.
2. I find this brand interesting in a sensory way.
3. This brand does not appeal to my senses.

Affective Dimension:

4. This brand induces feelings and sentiments.
5. I do not have strong emotions for this brand.
6. This brand is an emotional brand.

Behavioral Dimension:

7. I engage in physical actions and behaviors when I use this brand.
8. This brand results in bodily experiences.
9. This brand is not action oriented.

Intellectual Dimension:

10. I engage in a lot of thinking when I encounter this brand.
11. This brand does not make me think.
12. This brand stimulates my curiosity and problem solving.

(The word "this brand" in each statement was replaced by the words Facebook, Google+, LinedIn and Twitter respectively in order to obtain responses for all the four brands of social media platforms)

The scale measured Brand experience of the respondents on a seven- point (with "1" for Strongly Agree and "7" for Strongly Disagree) Likert scale. Data were collected by means of an online national survey using snowball-sampling technique. Online survey instrument was distributed among Indian Social Media users via e-mail, Face Book, Twitter and other social media platforms. Collected data were analyzed using One-Way Repeated Measures ANOVA.

ANALYSIS AND INTERPRETATION

Reliability Testing of the Scale Items

The value of the Cronbach's alphas for the entire scale of Facebook, Google+, LinkedIn and Twitter are .830, .874, .724 and .841 respectively for 12 items in each scale. The values of α for the four platforms indicated the scale to be highly reliable.

BASIC SAMPLE ANALYSIS

Out of the received 117 responses, 09 were not using Social Media Platforms and excluded from the analysis. Out of the remaining 108 responses, all 108 were using Facebook, while 89, 87 and 87 were active on Google+, LinkedIn and Twitter respectively. As the One-Way Repeated Measures ANOVA was used for comparing means, only those respondents who were active on all the four platforms were selected, in order to control for individual differences (Field, 2009). Accordingly, 87 responses, which remained for the final analysis, were checked for data duplication and missing values. 04 numbers of missing values in the data were replaced by average response for that particular field. Demographic composition of the sample has been summarized in Table 1.

Table 1. Summary of Demographic Details of Respondents

Demographic Variable	Classifications	Frequency	Valid Percent	Cumulative Percent
Gender	Male	64	73.6	73.6
	Female	23	26.4	100.0
Marital status	Married	41	47.1	47.1
	Unmarried	46	52.9	100.0
Age (in Years)	18-24	5	5.7	5.7
	24-30	44	50.6	56.3
	30-36	11	12.6	69.0
	36-42	13	14.9	83.9
	42 and above	14	16.1	100.0
Education	Diploma	1	1.1	1.1
	Graduate	7	8.0	9.2
	Post- Graduate	49	56.3	65.5
	Ph. D. & higher	30	34.5	100.0
Profession	Student	19	21.8	21.8
	Private Job	29	33.3	55.2
	Govt. Job	33	37.9	93.1
	Self-employed	5	5.7	98.9
	Homemaker	1	1.1	100.0
Annual household income (in Rupees)	1- 4 Lakhs	36	41.4	41.4
	4-7 Lakhs	29	33.3	74.7
	7 lakhs & above	22	25.3	100.0
Net use per day (in Hours)	1-4 Hrs	31	35.6	35.6
	4-7 Hrs	33	37.9	73.6
	7 Hrs & above	23	26.4	100.0
Social Media usage per day (in Hours)	1-4 Hrs	69	79.3	79.3
	4-7 Hrs	16	18.4	97.7
	7 Hrs & above	2	2.3	100.0

ONE-WAY REPEATED MEASURES ANOVA

Analysis for H_{01}:$\mu_{FB} = \mu_{GL} = \mu_{LN} = \mu_{TW}$

As Mauchly's test was non-significant, χ^2 (5) = 8.031, p > .05, hence data did not violate the assumptions of sphericity and indicated that the variances of differences are homogenous. F (3, 258) = 30.41, p < .05, for the Tests of Within-Subjects Effects, indicated that there is a significant difference between Facebook, Google+, LinkedIn and Twitter's experience. In addition, multivariate tests also support the result as the Pillai's Trace V = 0.489, F (3, 84) = 26.840, p < .05, ω^2 = .16, the value of ω^2 indicates large effect (Field, 2009). Hence, H_{01} is rejected and H_{a1} is accepted that there is a significant difference between Facebook, Google+, LinkedIn and Twitter's experience.

As the experience of select social media platforms was statistically significant, repeated contrast results were interpreted to determine which platforms contributed to the overall difference. First contrast between Level 1 (FB) vs. Level 2 (GL) was significant, F (1, 86) = 72.926, *p<.05*, $r_{FBvs.GL}$= .68 (Medium Effect explaining 46.2% of the total variance), meaning thereby that there is a significant difference between Facebook experience and Google+ experience. Second contrast between Level 2 (GL) and Level 3(LN), F (1, 86) = 6.980, *p<.05*, $r_{GLvs.LN}$= .27 (small effect explaining 7.3% of the total variance) again indicates thatthere is a significant difference between Google+ experience and LinkedIn experience. However, the third contrast between Level 3 (LN) and Level 4(TW), F (1, 86) = 0.828, *p>.05*, $r_{LNvs.TW}$ = .10 (small effect explaining 0.95% of the total variance) was not significant and only difference in means is due to chance. Same was also indicated by the Bar Graph (Figure 2) of the Mean values of various social media

Figure 2. Mean Values of Experience of Different Platforms

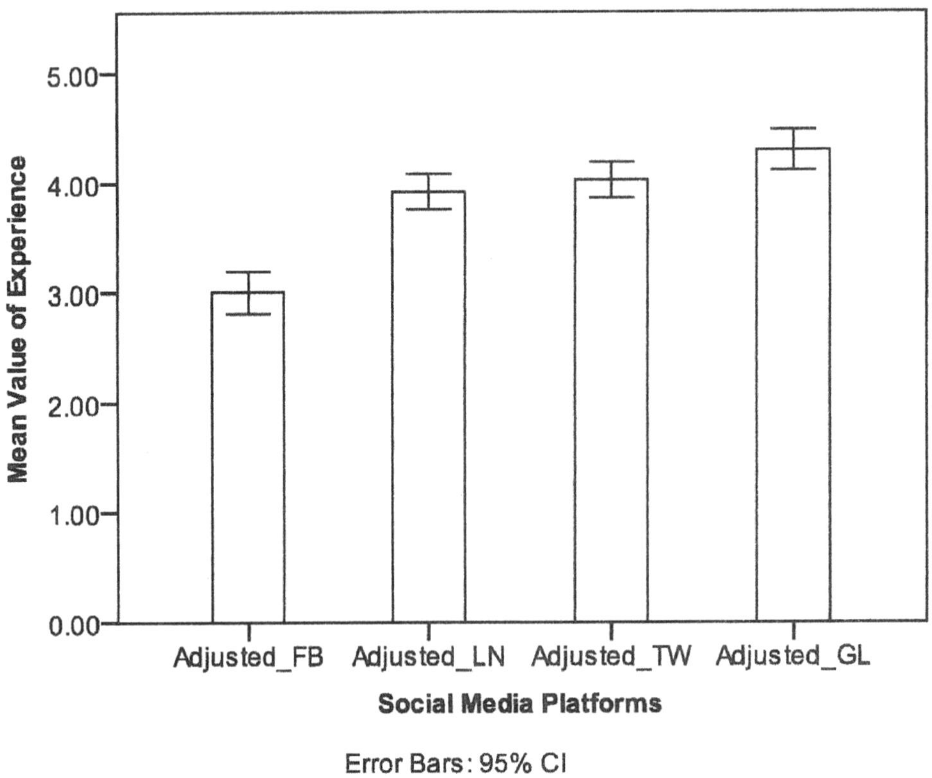

platforms, which evidences that respondents find FaceBook experience (μ_{FB} = 3.00) best and Google+ experience (μ_{GL} =4.30) worst out of the four. LinkedIn experience (μ_{LN} = 3.92) and Twitter experience (μ_{TW} = 4.03) are somewhat similar to each other.

Post-hoc analysis for Pairwise Comparison (with Bonferroni correction) indicated that the Facebook Experience is significantly different and better in comparison to Google+ (μ_{FB} - μ_{GL} = -1.299, p<.05), LinkedIn (μ_{FB} - μ_{LN} = -0.918, p<.05) and Twitter experience (μ_{FB} - μ_{TW} = -1.027, p<.05). Other Experiences i.e. of Google+ from LinkedIn (μ_{GL} - μ_{LN} =0.380, p>.05), of Google+ from Twitter (μ_{GL} - μ_{TW} =0.271, p>.05) and of LinkedIn from Twitter (μ_{LN} - μ_{TW} =-0.109, p>.05) though were different from each other, were not significant. Pairwise analysis too corroborated the above conclusion that Facebook experience is significantly better in comparison to Google+, LinkedIn and Twitter experience. Other three platforms, though differ in the experience, mean values being different from each other, the difference is not significant.

Analysis for H_{01}:$\mu_{FBSD} = \mu_{GLSD} = \mu_{LNSD} = \mu_{TWSD}$

Results from analysis of Mauchly's test, χ^2 (5) = 2.376, p > .05, being non-significant, data did not violate the assumptions of sphericity. F (3, 258) = 18.52, p < .05, for the Tests of Within-Subjects Effects, and multivariate test -Pillai's Trace V = 0.400, F (3, 84) = 18.673, p < .05, ω^2 = .12 (Large effect), indicated that there is a significant difference between Facebook, Google+, LinkedIn and Twitter's sensory experience. Hence, H_{02} is not supported and H_{a2} is supported that there is a significant difference between Facebook, Google+, LinkedIn and Twitter's sensory experience.

Interpretation of repeated contrast results revealed that first contrast between Level 1 (μ_{FBSD}) vs. Level 2 (μ_{GLSD}) was significant F (1,86) = 41.634, *p<.05*, $r_{FBSDvs.GLSD}$= .57 (Medium Effect explaining 32.62% of the total variance) meaning thereby that there is a significant difference between Facebook sensory experience and Google+ sensory experience. Second contrast between Level 2 (μ_{GLSD}) and Level 3(μ_{LNSD}), F (1, 86) = 3.304, *p>.05*, $r_{GLSDvs.LNSD}$= .19 (small effect explaining 3.7% of the total variance) and the third contrast between Level 3 (μ_{LNSD}) and Level 4 (μ_{TWSD}), F (1,86) = 1.738, *p>.05*, $r_{LNSDvs.TWSD}$= .14 (small effect explaining 1.98% of the total variance) were not significant. This means that there is not a significant difference between Google+ sensory experience and LinkedIn sensory experience and between LinkedIn sensory experience and Twitter sensory experience. Differences in mean values are purely coincidental.

Same was pointed out by the Bar Graph (Figure 3) of the Mean values of sensory experiences of various social media platforms. Graph evidenced that respondents find Facebook sensory experience (μ_{FBSD} = 2.57) best, LinkedIn sensory experience (μ_{LNSD} = 3.56) second best, Twitter sensory experience (μ_{TWSD} = 3.81) third best and Google+ sensory experience (μ_{GLSD} =3.93) has been rated worst out of the four.

Post-hoc analysis for Pairwise Comparison (with Bonferroni adjustment) indicated that the Facebook sensory experience is statistically significant and better in comparison to Google+ (μ_{FBSD} - μ_{GLSD} = -1.367, p<.05), LinkedIn (μ_{FBSD} - μ_{LNSD} = -0.988, p<.05) and Twitter's sensory experience (μ_{FBSD} - μ_{TWSD} = -1.241, p<.05). Other sensory experiences i.e. of Google+ from LinkedIn (μ_{GLSD} - μ_{LNSD} =0.380, p>.05), of Google+ from Twitter (μ_{GLSD} - μ_{TWSD} =0.126, p>.05) and of LinkedIn from Twitter (μ_{LNSD} - μ_{TWSD} =-.253, p>.05) though were different from each other, were not significant. Pairwise analysis too corroborated the above conclusion that Facebook sensory experience is significantly better in comparison to Google+, LinkedIn and Twitter's sensory experience. Differences between the sensory experiences of other three platforms are not significant.

Figure 3. Mean Values of Sensory Experience of Different Platforms

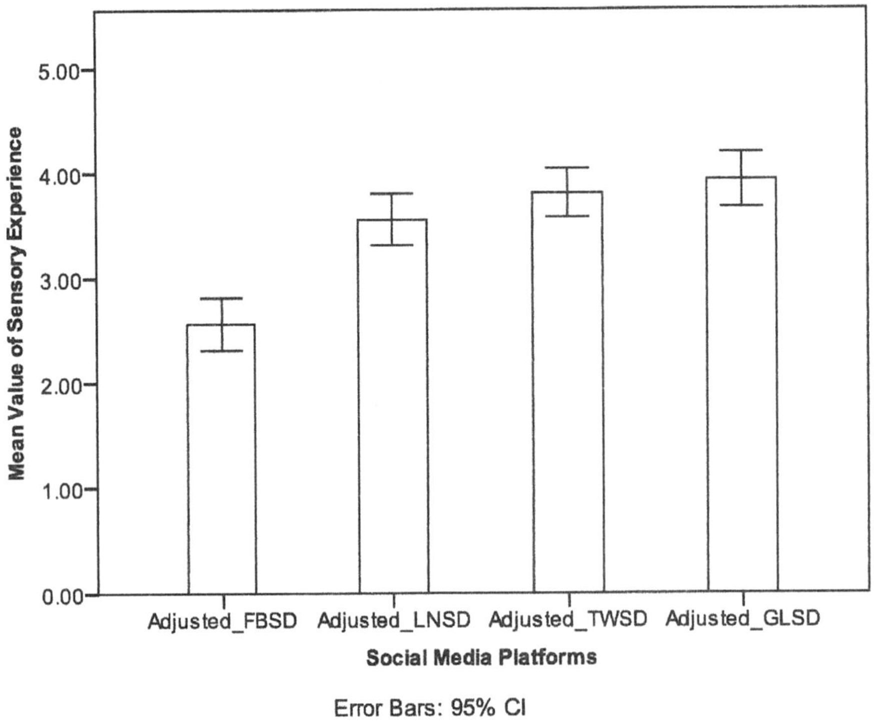

Analysis for H_{03}:$\mu_{FBAD} = \mu_{GLAD} = \mu_{LNAD} = \mu_{TWAD}$

χ^2 (5) = 10.927, $p > .05$, being non-significant, assumptions of sphericity was not violated. F (3, 258) = 36.74, $p < .05$, for the Tests of Within-Subjects Effects, along with multivariate test -Pillai's Trace V = 0.504, F(3, 84) = 28.461, $p < .05$, $\omega^2 = .18$ (Large effect), indicated that there is a significant difference between Facebook, Google+, LinkedIn and Twitter's affective experience. Hence, H_{03} is not supported and H_{a3} is supported that there is a significant difference between Facebook, Google+, LinkedIn and Twitter's affective experience.

Interpretation of repeated contrast results exhibited that first contrast between Level 1 (μ_{FBAD}) vs. Level 2 (μ_{GLAD}) is significant F (1, 86) = 78.710, $p<.05$,$r_{FBADvs.GLAD}$= .69 (Medium Effect explaining 47.80% of the total variance) meaning thereby that there is a significant difference between affective experience of Facebook and Google+. Second contrast between Level 2 (μ_{GLAD}) and Level 3(μ_{LNAD}), F (1, 86) = 0.502, $p>.05$, $r_{GLADvs.LNAD}$= .08 (small effect explaining 0.64% of the total variance) and the third contrast between Level 3 (μ_{LNAD}) and Level 4(μ_{TWAD}), F (1, 86) = 0.495, $p>.05$,$r_{LNADvs.TWAD}$= .08 (small effect explaining 0.64% of the total variance) are not significant. This means that there is not a significant difference between affective experience of Google+ and LinkedIn and between affective experience of LinkedIn and Twitter, and any differences in mean values of affective experience are purely by chance.

Bar Graph (Figure 4) of the mean values of affective experiences of various social media platforms, also evidences that respondents find affective experience of Facebook (μ_{FBAD} = 2.51) better than the rest three. Affective experience of Google+ (μ_{GLAD} =4.17) once again is last in experience ratings. Affective experience of Twitter (μ_{TWAD} = 3.94) is only marginally better than LinkedIn (μ_{LNAD} = 4.05).

Figure 4. Mean Values of Affective Experience of Different Platforms

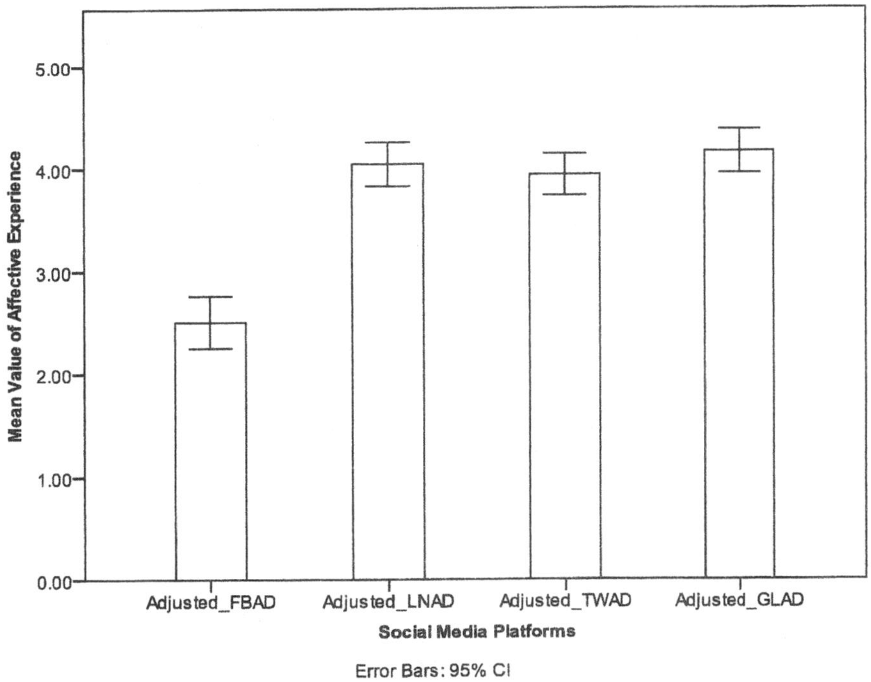

Post-hoc analysis for Pairwise Comparison (with Bonferroni adjustment) indicated that the affective experience of Facebook is statistically significant and better in comparison to Google+ ($\mu_{FBAD} - \mu_{GLAD} = -1.662$, $p<.05$), LinkedIn ($\mu_{FBAD} - \mu_{LNAD} = -1.541$, $p<.05$) and Twitter's affective experience ($\mu_{FBAD} - \mu_{TWAD} = -1.433$, $p<.05$). Other affective experiences i.e. of Google+ from LinkedIn ($\mu_{GLAD} - \mu_{LNAD} = 0.122$, $p>.05$), of Google+ from Twitter ($\mu_{GLAD} - \mu_{TWAD} = 0.229$, $p>.05$) and of LinkedIn from Twitter ($\mu_{LNAD} - \mu_{TWAD} = 0.107$, $p>.05$) though were different from each other, were not significant. Hence, Pairwise analysis too supported the above conclusion that affective experience of Facebook is significantly better in comparison to Google+, LinkedIn and Twitter's affective experience. Other three platforms, though differ in the affective experience from each other, these differences are not statistically significant.

Analysis for H_{04}:$\mu_{FBBD} = \mu_{GLBD} = \mu_{LNBD} = \mu_{TWBD}$

As Mauchly's test, χ^2 (5) = 33.564, $p < .05$, was significant, hence data violated the assumptions of sphericity and the variances of the differences between behavioural experience of the four social media platforms were not equal. However, the value of Greenhouse-Geisser's epsilon being .835 that is away from the lower bound limit i.e. .333 and closer to upper limit 1; data were closer to being spherical. Value of Huynh-Feldt epsilon .862 was also high, which reaffirmed that variance of differences are homogenous.

The Tests of Within-Subjects Effects F (2.505, 215.403) = 11.102, $p < .05$ for Greenhouse-Geisser correction, and F (2.586, 222.384) = 11.102, $p < .05$ for Huynh-Feldt correction, indicated that there is a significant difference between Facebook, Google+, LinkedIn and Twitter's behavioural experience. In addition, multivariate tests also support the result as the Pillai's Trace $V = 0.255$, F (3, 84) = 9.599, p<

.05, ω^2 =.01, the value of ω^2 indicates small effect. Hence, H_{04} is rejected and H_{a4} is accepted that there is a significant difference between Facebook, Google+, LinkedIn and Twitter's behavioural experience.

Interpretation of repeated contrast results revealed that first contrast between Level 1 (μ_{FBBD}) vs. Level 2 (μ_{GLBD}) is significant F (1, 86) = 26.278, $p<.05$, $r_{FBBDvs.GLBD}$= .48 (small effect explaining 23.04% of the total variance) meaning thereby that there is a significant difference between Facebook behavioural experience and Google+ behavioural experience. Second contrast between Level 2 (μ_{GLSD}) and Level 3(μ_{LNSD}), F (1, 86) = 2.725, $p>.05$, $r_{GLSDvs.LNSD}$= .18 (small effect explaining 3.24% of the total variance) and the third contrast between Level 3 (μ_{LNSD}) and Level 4(μ_{TWSD}), F (1,86) = 0.650, $p>.05$, $r_{LNSDvs.TWSD}$= .09 (small effect explaining 0.81% of the total variance) are not significant. Hence, there is not a significant difference between behavioural experience of Google+ and LinkedIn and between behavioural experience of LinkedIn and Twitter.

Bar Graph (Figure 5) of the mean values of behavioural experiences of various social media platforms also supported the above assertion as respondents rated behavioural experience of FaceBook (μ_{FBBD} = 3.82) highest and once again, behavioural experience of Google+ (μ_{GLBD} =4.53) is rated least. Behavioural experience of LinkedIn (μ_{LNBD} = 4.31) and Twitter (μ_{TWBD} = 4.38) marginally differ from each other.

Pairwise Comparison (with Bonferroni correction) evidenced that the Facebook behavioural experience is statistically significant and better in comparison to Google+ (μ_{FBBD} - μ_{GLBD} = -0.705, p<.05), LinkedIn (μ_{FBBD} - μ_{LNBD} = -0.490, p<.05) and Twitter's behavioural experience (μ_{FBBD} - μ_{TWBD} = -0.558, p<.05). Other behavioural experiences i.e. of Google+ from LinkedIn (μ_{GLBD} - μ_{LNBD} =0.214, p>.05), of Google+ from Twitter (μ_{GLBD} - μ_{TWBD} =0.147, p>.05) and of LinkedIn from Twitter (μ_{LNBD} - μ_{TWBD} =-0.068,

Figure 5. Mean Values of Behavioural Experience of Different Platforms

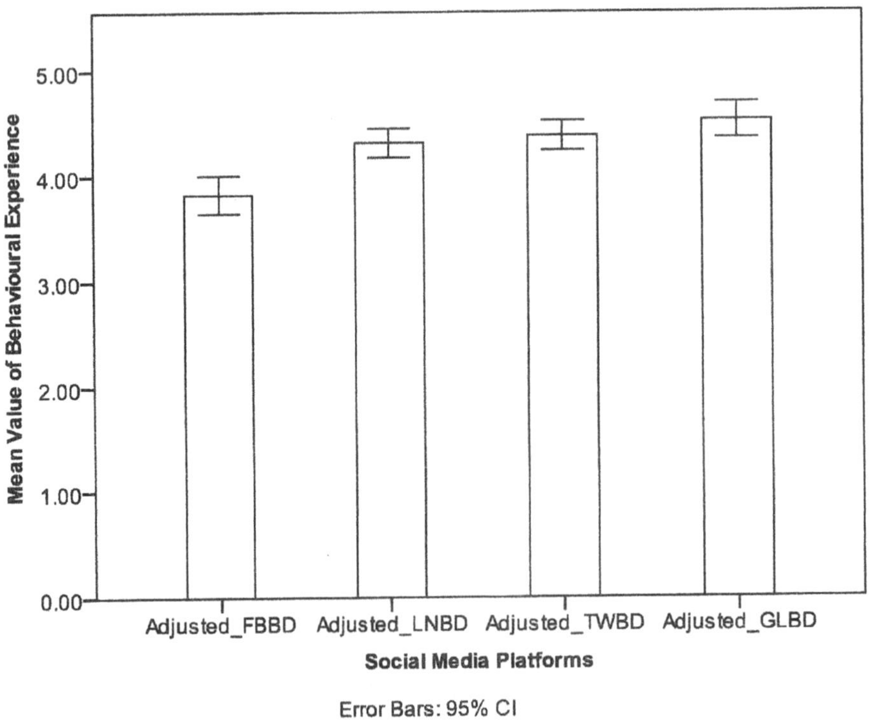

p>.05) though were not significantly different from each other. Pairwise analysis too substantiated the conclusion that Facebook's behavioural experience is significantly better in comparison to Google+, LinkedIn and Twitter's behavioural experience.

Analysis for H_{05}:$\mu_{FBID} = \mu_{GLID} = \mu_{LNID} = \mu_{TWID}$

As Mauchly's test, $\chi^2(5) = 10.266, p > .05$, was non-significant, hence data does not violate the assumptions of sphericity and the variances of differences are homogenous. The results for the Tests of Within-Subjects Effects indicated that there is a significant difference between Facebook, Google+, LinkedIn and Twitter's intellectual experience, $F(3, 258) = 13.37, p < .05$. In addition, multivariate tests also supported the result as the Pillai's Trace $V = 0.301$, $F(3, 84) = 12.053$, $p < .05$, $\omega^2 = .08$, the value of ω^2 indicates medium effect. Hence, H_{05} is not supported and H_{a5} is supported that there is a significant difference between Facebook, Google+, LinkedIn and Twitter's intellectual experience.

Tests of Within-Subjects repeated contrast demonstrated that first contrast between Level 1 (μ_{FBID}) vs. Level 2 (μ_{GLID}) was significant, $F(1, 86) = 27.916$, $p<.05$,$r_{FBIDvs.GLID}= .49$ (small effect explaining 24.01% of the total variance), meaning that there is a significant difference between Facebook intellectual experience and Google+ intellectual experience. Second contrast between Level 2 (μ_{GLID}) and Level 3(μ_{LNID}), $F(1, 86) = 5.081$, $p<.05$, $r_{GLIDvs.LNID}= .24$ (small effect explaining 5.83% of the total variance), being significant indicate that there is a significant difference between intellectual experience of Google+ and LinkedIn. The third contrast between Level 3 (μ_{LNID}) and Level 4(μ_{TWID}), $F(1, 86) = 2.215$, $p>.05$,$r_{LNIDvs.TWID}= .16$ (small effect explaining 2.56% of the total variance) is not significant i.e. there is not a significant difference between intellectual experience of LinkedIn and Twitter.

Significant difference between Facebook, Google+, LinkedIn and Twitter's intellectual experience necessitated post-hoc analysis (with Bonferroni's correction). Pairwise comparisons evidenced that the Facebook intellectual experience is statistically significant and better in comparison to Google+ ($\mu_{FBID} - \mu_{GLID} = -1.092$, p<.05), LinkedIn ($\mu_{FBID} - \mu_{LNID} = -0.652$, p<.05) and Twitter's intellectual experience ($\mu_{FBID} - \mu_{TWID} = -0.878$, p<.05). Other intellectual experiences i.e. of Google+ from LinkedIn ($\mu_{GLID} - \mu_{LNID} = 0.440$, p>.05), of Google+ from Twitter ($\mu_{GLID} - \mu_{TWID} = 0.215$, p>.05) and of LinkedIn from Twitter ($\mu_{LNID} - \mu_{TWID} = -0.225$, p>.05) were not significantly different from each other.

Bar Graph (Figure 6) of the mean values of intellectual experiences of various social media platforms too substantiated that intellectual experience of Facebook ($\mu_{FBID} = 3.12$) is better than the intellectual experience of the other three platforms *viz.* Google+ ($\mu_{GLID} = 4.21$), LinkedIn ($\mu_{LNID} = 3.77$) and Twitter ($\mu_{TWID} = 4.00$).

Result at a Glance

Results of the One-way Repeated Measure ANOVA have been summarized in the Table 2 for a quick glimpse.

IMPLICATIONS OF RESEARCH

Obtained results are important for social media platform developers as the results indicate how Indian Social Media users rate the experience of select platforms. Results demonstrate that Facebook is a clear

Figure 6. Mean Values of Intellectual Experience of Different Platforms

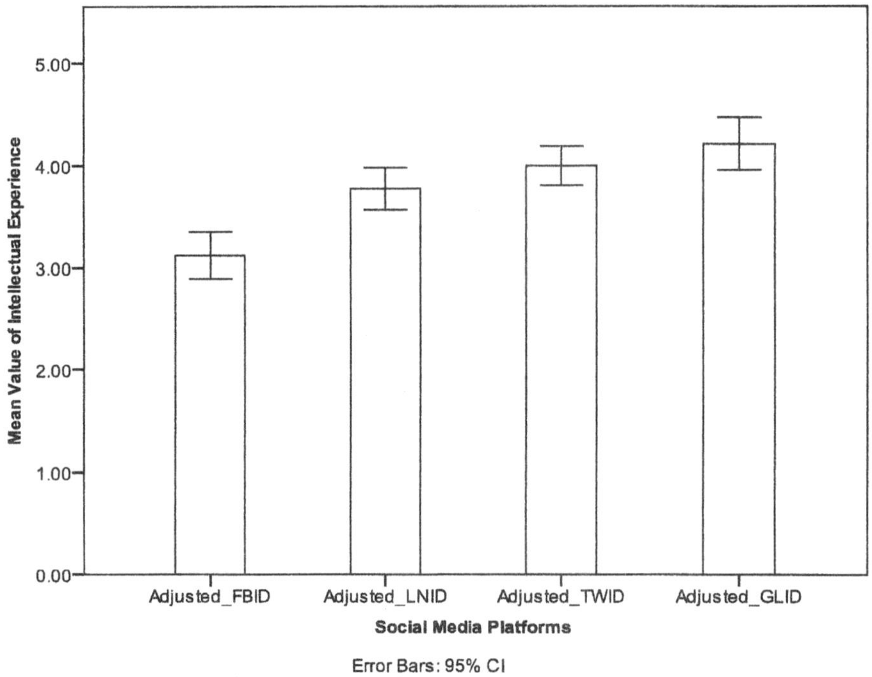

Table 2. Summary of One-way Repeated Measure ANOVA

Hypotheses	Result
H_{01}	Not Supported
H_{02}	Not Supported
H_{03}	Not Supported
H_{04}	Not Supported
H_{05}	Not Supported

winner as far as overall experience and experiences along various dimensions *viz*. Sensory, Affective, Behavioural and Intellectual are concerned. Higher absolute number of people using Facebook in India is a testimony to the fact that people prefer Facebook to other platforms (Kemp, 2014). However, this should not make developers of Facebook complacent. All the mean values i.e. of overall experience ($\mu_{FB} = 3.00$) and of various dimensions ($\mu_{FBSD} = 2.57$, $\mu_{FBAD} = 2.51$, $\mu_{FBBD} = 3.82$, $\mu_{FBID} = 3.12$) lie between almost 3.00 and 4.00, which when interpreted result in ratings between Somewhat agree and neither agree nor disagree along a continuum of 1-Strongly agree to 7- strongly disagree. This is a clear indication to the developers of Facebook that they have miles to go before they sleep.

Developers of remaining three social media platforms have more reasons to worry as not only their platforms have been rated lower, results indicate that experiences of these platforms do not differ significantly from each other. Hence, they not only need to incorporate the features that lead to better user experiences, but also must take steps to differentiate their experiences from the others. Though the developers are adding new features such as Facebook facility of video calling using Skype, social games, facility to the organizations to have their Facebook pages (Pogue, 2012), enabling local language feature, messaging products like Whatsapp (Thomas, 2014) and Google+'s 'circles', facility to integrate with other Google products, 'huddle' and Hangout'(Pogue, 2012). However, as the results of the study indicate, a lot is yet to be achieved in Indian market. Continuous up gradation of features is mandated by the fact that better and unique experiences will not only keep one ahead of the competition by attracting more "virtual footfalls", it will also attract more advertisers/marketers to the platform. More number of visitors to the platform will result in enhanced access to demographic data in the shape of virtual footprints that can be diced and sliced (Sarkar, 2014) variously for behavioral targeting (Schiffman et al., 2010). All this will ensure more revenue generation for the platforms on one hand and the marketers on the other hand.

Customer experience production is all about engaging a customer (Pine et al., 1999) and it may be facilitated by Social Media in a very effective way as social web represents an increasingly important point of interaction between businesses and consumers (Fauser, Wiedenhofer & Lorenz, 2011). Opinion seekers are willing to accept and adopt online consumer reviews. e-Word of mouth communication can be treated as the extension of traditional interpersonal communication into this era of Web-based technologies and it is a great impact on the purchasing decisions of online Consumers (Cheung, Lee &Rabjohn, 2008). Marketers can employ advanced analytical techniques like "Opinion mining", "Sentiment Analysis", "Social media monitoring and analysis" to comb through the "voice of customers", available at these new generation touch point (Web, Internet channel, Blog, Forum and Social Network). This will help them to track the emotional valence (positive or negative) and emotional intensity for their brands that can be used for effectively managing the customer experiences (Bellini et al., (n.d.)).

Various activities undertaken by organizations on social media (Zailskaite-jakste & Kuvykaite, 2012) produce experience for the customers, which in turn lead to either Watching or Sharing or Commenting or Producing or Curating stage of Engagement pyramid (Owyang, 2010; Zailskaite-jakste et al., 2012). Depending upon the stage of engagement pyramid, either Involvement or Interaction or Intimacy or Influence is generated (Haven, 2007), which further results in benefits such as brand awareness, brand associations, brand loyalty, brand trust, brand advocacy etc. for the brands (Zailskaite-jakste et al., 2012).

Marketing managers can take a cue from here and can advertise, communicate and associate their products, services and brands with those platforms, which consumers rate high on brand experience scale in order to reap concomitant benefits. This is advantageous from various facets:

1. The platforms, which are better rated, will attract more "netizens" and will result in more exposure for the brands being advertised on these platforms.
2. Comprehension of experiences of social media platforms is important as Customer's virtual experience influences the virtual interaction and online as well as offline decision-making process of the customer (Constantinides, 2004), meaning thereby that better the experience, favourable the impression on the customer and favorable decision making.
3. Associations with favored platforms (in terms of experience) may result in positive attitude towards the products and services that have been advertised through these platforms (Duhan & Singh, 2013) as per the Congruity theory of attitudes (Osgood et al., 1955)
4. As many of the consumers on the Internet are price seekers, positive experience of social media platform together with the positive brand experience might lead to a affirmative reaction to the pricing (Ha et al., 2005).

Last, but not the least, research may prove to be a value addition to the existing body of knowledge, as there is a paucity of literature, more specifically in Indian context, in the area of brand experience, online brand experience and social media brand experience.

LIMITATIONS, FUTURE RESEARCH AVENUES, AND CONCLUSION

Limitations

The major limitations of the study encompass the possibilities of self-reported bias, repeat responses and most responses from more active social media users. The study may have given better and probably different results with a larger sample size selected using non-random sampling. Similarly, controlled experimental design may have yielded different results.

Future Research Avenues

As, the study is possibly the first of its kind in Indian perspective, it opens abundant research opportunities like exploring the experiences of Indian consumers with various brands of social media platforms across different age groups, different income groups, different genders, different marital status and different social media usage in order to formulate more competitive strategies to woo the customers. As the Indian consumers and markets, in comparison to other developed nations, are still warming up to the usage of ever evolving social media platforms, longitudinal research can aid marketers and social media marketing firms to keep track of the emerging development in this market. In addition, qualitative research such as Focus group interviews may result in better insights regarding consumer preferences. Future research focus can be on studying the impact of favourable experience on loyalty, satisfaction, commitment, future purchase intentions, repurchases etc.

Conclusion

Observing the significance of positive consumer experiences in today's dynamic digital business environment and the paucity of research in the area, more specifically in the Indian context, researchers undertook the study. Research attempted to study over all brand experience of consumers as well as the experience along the four dimensions (viz. Sensory, Affective, Behavioural and Intellectual) of experience with respect to select social media platforms. Results of One-way Repeated Measure ANOVA indicated that Indians consumers find Facebook experience, overall as well as along the four dimensions, significantly better and different from the other social media platforms. Obtained results are important for social media platform developers, as the results guide them to possibilities for improvement in brand experiences. The similarities and dissimilarities of one platform vis-a-vis the others reveal the potential and scope for differentiating one platform from others. Research may be useful guide to the marketing managers by helping them to select the most appropriate platform for promoting their products, services and brands.

REFERENCES

Aaker, J. L., & Maheswaran, D. (1997). The effect of cultural orientation on persuasion. *The Journal of Consumer Research*, *24*(3), 315–328. doi:10.1086/209513

Alderson, W. (1957). *Marketing Behavior and Executive Action*. Homewood, Illinois: Richard D. Irwin, INC.

Arnold, M. J., Reynolds, K. E., Ponder, N., & Lueg, J. E. (2005). Customer Delight in a Retail Context: Investigating Delightful and Terrible Shopping Experiences. *Journal of Business Research*, *58*(8), 1132–1145. doi:10.1016/j.jbusres.2004.01.006

Bellini, F., Ascenzo, F. D., Ghi, A., Spagnoli, F., & Traversi, V. (n.d.). *The Role of the Prosumer in Social Networks and the Sentiment Analysis for the Customer Experience Management*. Retrieved on January 10, 2014 from http://www.cersi.it/itais2012/pdf/066.pdf

Bellizzi, J. A., & Hite, R. E. (1992). Environmental Color, Consumer Feelings, and Purchase Likelihood. *Psychology and Marketing*, *9*(5), 347–363. doi:10.1002/mar.4220090502

Berry, L. L. (2000). Cultivating service brand equity. *Journal of the Academy of Marketing Science*, *28*(1), 128–137. doi:10.1177/0092070300281012

Berry, L. L., & Carbone, L. P. (2007). Build Loyalty Through Experience Management. *Quality Progress*, *40*(9), 26–32.

Boyd, Harper W., J., & Levy, S.J. (1963). New Dimensions in Consumer Analysis. *Harvard Business Review*, *41*(November-December), 129–140.

Brakus, J. J., Schmitt, B. H., & Zarantonello, L. (2009). Brand Experience : What Is It? How Is It Measured? Does It Affect Loyalty? *Journal of Marketing*, *73*(May), 52–68. doi:10.1509/jmkg.73.3.52

Brakus, J. J., Schmitt, B. H., & Zhang, S. (2008). Experiential Attributes and Consumer Judgments. In Handbook on Brand and Experience Management. Northampton, MA: EdwardElgar

Braunsberger, K., & Munch, J. M. (1998). Source expertise versus experience effects in hospital advertising. *Journal of Services Marketing*, *12*(1), 23–38. doi:10.1108/08876049810202348

Carbone, L. P., & Haeckel, S. H. (1994). Engineering Customer Experience. *Marketing Management*, *3*(3), 8–19.

Chen, Q., & Wells, W. D. (1999). Attitude toward the site. *Journal of Advertising Research*, *39*(5), 27–37.

Cheung, C. M. K., Lee, M. K. O., & Rabjohn, N. (2008). The impact of electronic customer communities. *Internet Research*, *18*(3), 229–247. doi:10.1108/10662240810883290

Chinomona, R. (2013). The Influence of Brand Experience on Brand Satisfaction, Trust And Attachment In South Africa. *International Business & Economics Research Journal*, *12*(10), 1303–1316.

Chui, M., Manyika, J., Bughin, J., Dobbs, R., Sarrazin, H., Sands, G., & Westergen, M. (2012). *The social economy: Unlocking value and productivity through social technologies.* McKinsey Global Institute Report. Retrieved on January 1, 2014 from http://www.mckinsey.com/insights/high_tech_telecoms_internet/the_social_economy

Cliffe, S. J., & Motion, J. (2005). Building contemporary brands: A sponsorship-based strategy. *Journal of Business Research, 58*(8), 1068–1077. doi:10.1016/j.jbusres.2004.03.004

Constantinides, E. (2004). Influencing the online consumer's behavior: The Web experience. *Internet Research, 14*(2), 111–126. doi:10.1108/10662240410530835

Corbitt, B., Thanasankit, T., & Yi, H. (2003). Trust and e-commerce: A study of consumer perception. *Electronic Commerce Research and Applications, 2*(3), 203–215. doi:10.1016/S1567-4223(03)00024-3

Duhan, P., & Singh, A. (2013). Impact of Usefulness, Ease of Use, Enjoyment, Attitude and Subjective Norms on Behavioural Intentions and Adoption Of Virtual Communities: An Empirical Study. *Journal of IMS Group, 10*(02), 19–31.

Edelman, D. C. (2010). Branding in the digital age. *Harvard Business Review, 88*(12), 62–69.

Erciş, A., Ünal, S., Candan, F. B., & Yıldırım, H. (2012). The effect of brand satisfaction, trust and brand commitment on loyalty and repurchase intentions. *Procedia: Social and Behavioral Sciences, 58*, 1395–1404. doi:10.1016/j.sbspro.2012.09.1124

Fauser, S. G., Wiedenhofer, J., & Lorenz, M. (2011). "Touchpoint social web": An explorative study about using the social web for influencing high involvement purchase decisions. *Problems and Perspectives in Management., 9*(1), 39–45.

Ferraresi, M., & Schmitt, B. H. (2006). *Marketing esperienziale*. Milano: FrancoAngeli.

Field, A. (2009). *Discovering statistics using SPSS* (3rd ed.). New Delhi: Sage Publications India Ltd.

Flanagan, P., Johnston, R., & Talbot, D. (2005). Customer confidence: The development of a "pre-experience" concept. *International Journal of Service Industry Management, 16*(4), 373–384. doi:10.1108/09564230510614013

Gelter, H. (2007a). Towards an understanding of experience production. In Articles on Experiences 4 Digital Media & Games. University of Lapland Press.

Gelter, H. (2007b). Experience production in digital media and games. In Articles on Experiences 4 Digital Media & Games. University of Lapland Press.

Guadagni, P., & De Tommaso, V. (2007). *Ilnuovopoteredeiconsumatorisul web*. Hoepli.

Ha, H., & Perks, H. (2005). Effects of consumer perceptions of brand experience on the web : Brand familiarity, satisfaction and brand trust. *Journal of Consumer Behaviour, 4*(6), 438–452. doi:10.1002/cb.29

Ha, H.-Y. (2004). Factors influencing consumer perception on brand trust on the online. *Journal of Product and Brand Management, 13*(5), 329–342. doi:10.1108/10610420410554412

Haven, B. (2007). *Marketing's New Key Metric: Engagement*. Marketing. Retrieved on February, 07, 2013 from http://www.adobe.com/engagement/pdfs/marketings_new_key_metric_engagement.pdf

Holbrook, M. B., & Hirschman, E. C. (1982). The Experiential Aspects of Consumption: Consumer Fantasies, Feelings, and Fun. *The Journal of Consumer Research*, *9*(2), 132–140. doi:10.1086/208906

Hughes, R. (2010). *Enterprise Social Networking: Don ' t Be Afraid*. Retrieved on February 14, 2014 from http://www.clearvale.com/clearvale/mkt-nav/en/whitepapers/Enterprise_Social_Networking-Dont_Be_Afraid_2010_02_24.pdf

Johar, G. V., Sengupta, J., & Aaker, J. L. (2005). Two roads to updating brand personality impressions: Trait versus evaluative inferences. *JMR, Journal of Marketing Research*, *42*(4), 458–469. doi:10.1509/jmkr.2005.42.4.458

Johnson, C., & Mathews, B. P. (1997). The influence of experience on service expectations. *International Journal of Service Industry Management*, *8*(4), 290–305. doi:10.1108/09564239710174381

Johnston, R. (1999). Service transaction analysis: Assessing and improving the customer's experience. *Managing Service Quality*, *9*(2), 102–109. doi:10.1108/09604529910257876

Joy, A., & Sherry, J. F. Jr. (2003). Speaking of art as embodied imagination: A multisensory approach to understanding aesthetic experience. *The Journal of Consumer Research*, *30*(2), 259–282. doi:10.1086/376802

Kalakota, R., & Robinson, M. (2001). e-Business 2.0 Roadmap for Success (2nd ed.). New Delhi: Pearson Education.

Kania, D. (2001). *Branding. com*. Lincolnwood, IL: NTC Business Books.

Kemp, S. (2014). *Digital in India*. Retrieved on October 12, 2014 from http://www.slideshare.net/wearesocialsg/social-digital-mobile-around-the-world-january-2014

Kenny, D., & Marshall, J. F. (2000). Contextual marketing: The real business of the Internet. *Harvard Business Review*, *78*(6), 119–125. PMID:11184966

Kim, H. S. (2005). Consumer profiles of apparel product involvement and values. *Journal of Fashion Marketing and Management*, *9*(2), 207–220. doi:10.1108/13612020510599358

Koufaris, M. (2002). Applying the technology acceptance model and flow theory to online consumer behavior. *Information Systems Research*, *13*(2), 205–223. doi:10.1287/isre.13.2.205.83

Levy, S. J. (1959). Symbols for sale. *Harvard Business Review*, *37*(4), 117–124.

Liljander, V., & Strandvik, T. (1997). Emotions in Service Satisfaction. *International Journal of Service Industry Management*, *8*(2), 148–160. doi:10.1108/09564239710166272

Mandel, N., & Johnson, E. J. (2002). When web pages influence choice: Effects of visual primes on experts and novices. *The Journal of Consumer Research*, *29*(2), 235–245. doi:10.1086/341573

Mayfield, A. (2008). *What is Social Media*. Retrieved on May 06, 2013 from http://www.icrossing.com/ebooks

Mcwilliam, G. (2000). Building strong brands through online communities. *Sloan Management Review*, *41*(Spring), 43–54.

Menon, S., & Kahn, B. (2002). Cross-category effects of induced arousal and pleasure on the internet shopping experience. *Journal of Retailing*, *78*(1), 31–40. doi:10.1016/S0022-4359(01)00064-1

Meyer, C., & Schwager, A. (2007). Understanding customer experience. *Harvard Business Review*, *85*(2), 116–126. PMID:17345685

Meyers-Levy, J., & Peracchio, L. A. (1995). Understanding the effects of color: How the correspondence between available and required resources affects attitudes. *The Journal of Consumer Research*, *22*(2), 121–138. doi:10.1086/209440

Morace, F. (2002). *European Asymmetries*. Milano: Scheiwiller.

Nielsen nmIncite. (2012). *State of the Media: The Social Media Report 2012*. Retrieved on May 5, 2013 from http://postmediavancouversun.files.wordpress.com/2012/12/nielsen-social-media-report-20122.pdf

Ofir, C., & Simonson, I. (2007). The effect of stating expectations on customer satisfaction and shopping experience. *JMR, Journal of Marketing Research*, *44*(1), 164–174. doi:10.1509/jmkr.44.1.164

Olshavsky, R. W., & Granbois, D. H. (1979). Consumer decision making-fact or fiction? *The Journal of Consumer Research*, *6*(2), 93–100. doi:10.1086/208753

Osgood, C. E., & Tannenbaum, P. H. (1955). The Principle of Congruity in the Prediction of Attitude Change. *Psychological Review*, *62*(1), 42–55. doi:10.1037/h0048153 PMID:14357526

Owyang, J. (2010). *Socialgraphics Help You to Understand Your Customers: Slides and Webinar Recording*. Retrieved on September 04, 2013 from http://www.web-strategist.com/blog/category/socialgraphics/

Pine, B. J. II, & Gilmore, J. H. (1998). Welcome to the Experience Economy. *Harvard Business Review*, *1998*(July-August), 97–105. PMID:10181589

Pine, B. J. II, & Gilmore, J. H. (1999). *The Experience Economy: Work is Theatre and Every Business a Stage*. Cambridge, MA: Harvard Business School Press.

Pogue, D. (2012, July 18). Why Face Book should begin to worry. *Economic Times*, p. 8

Prahalad, C. K., & Ramaswamy, V. (2004). *The Future of Competition - Co-Creating Unique Value with Customers*. Boston: HarvardBusinessSchool Press.

Pullman, M. E., & Gross, M. A. (2004). Ability of experience design elements to elicit emotions and loyalty behaviors. *Decision Sciences*, *35*(3), 551–578. doi:10.1111/j.0011-7315.2004.02611.x

Quelch, J. A., & Klein, L. R. (1996). The Internet and International Marketing! *Sloan Management Review*, *37*(3), 60–75.

Rawson, A., Duncan, E., & Jones, C. (2013). The truth about customer experience. *Harvard Business Review*, *91*(9), 90–98. PMID:23593770

Reichheld, F. F., & Schefter, P. (2000). E-loyalty: Your secret weapon on the web. *Harvard Business Review*, *78*(4), 105–113.

Sahin, A., Zehir, C., & Kitapçı, H. (2011). The effects of brand experiences, trust and satisfaction on building brand loyalty; an empirical research on global brands. *Procedia: Social and Behavioral Sciences*, *24*, 1288–1301. doi:10.1016/j.sbspro.2011.09.143

Sarkar, R., (2014, October 8). Mobile doing to e-Commerce what e-Commerce did to retail, *Business Standard,* p. 1.

Schiffman, L. G., Kanuk, L. L., & Kumar, S. R. (2010). Consumer Behaviour (10th ed.). New Delhi: DorlingKindersley (India) Pvt. Ltd.

Schmitt, B. (2011). Experience marketing: Concepts, frameworks and consumer insights (Vol. 5, No. 2). Now Publishers Inc.

Schmitt, B. H. (2003). Customer Experience Management: A Revolutionary Approach to Connecting with Your Customers. John Wiley & Sons, Inc.

Shankar, V., Smith, A. K., & Rangaswamy, A. (2003). Customer satisfaction and loyalty in online and offline environments. *International Journal of Research in Marketing*, *20*(2), 153–175. doi:10.1016/S0167-8116(03)00016-8

Sheth, J. N. (1979). The Surpluses and Shortages in Consumer Behaviour Theory and Research. *Journal of the Academy of Marketing Science*, *7*(4), 414–427. doi:10.1007/BF02729689

Smith, S., & Wheeler, J. (2002). *Managing the customer experience: Turning customers into advocates*. Pearson Education.

Stanley, M. (2009). *Mobile Internet Report*. Retrieved on December 24, 2012 from www.ms.com/techresearch

Stelzner, M. A. (2012). Social Media Marketing Report, 2012. *Social Media Examiner*. Retrieved on January 3, 2013 from http://www.socialmediaexaminer.com/SocialMedia MarketingIndustryReport2012.pdf

Stelzner, M. A. (2013). *2013 social media marketing industry report: How marketers are using Social Media to Grow Their Businesses*. Retrieved on August 2, 2013, from http://www.socialmediaexaminer.com/SocialMedia MarketingIndustryReport2013.pdf

Thomas, T. K. (2014, October 10). Benefits of bringing connectivity to India are going to be profound: Zuckerberg. *The Hindu*, p. 11.

Vehr, N. J. (2012). *Vehr Communications, 2012 Social Media Usage Survey*. Retrieved on May 05, 2013 from http://www.vehrcommunications.com/wp-content/uploads/2012/02/2012-Social-Media-Usage-Survey-PRINT-FINAL.pdf

Voss, C. A. (2003). Rethinking paradigms of service - service in a virtual environment. *International Journal of Operations & Production Management*, *23*(1), 88–104. doi:10.1108/01443570310453271

Wang, Y. D., & Emurian, H. H. (2005). An overview of online trust: Concepts, elements, and implications. *Computers in Human Behavior*, *21*(1), 105–125. doi:10.1016/j.chb.2003.11.008

Yu, Y.-T., & Dean, A. (2001). The contribution of emotional satisfaction to customer loyalty. *International Journal of Service Industry Management*, *12*(3), 234–251. doi:10.1108/09564230110393239

Yulianti, I., & Tung, W. (2013). The Relationship Among Brand Experience, Brand Image and Customer Satisfaction of Facebook Users in Indonesia. *World Applied Sciences Journal, 28*, 100–113. doi:10.5829/idosi.wasj.2013.28.efmo.27017

Zaichkowsky, J. L. (1985). Measuring the involvement construct. *The Journal of Consumer Research, 12*(3), 341–352. doi:10.1086/208520

Zailskaite-jakste, L., & Kuvykaite, R. (2012). Consumer Engagement in Social Media by Building the Brand. In *Electronic International Interdisciplinary Conference 2012* (pp. 194–202). Academic Press.

KEY TERMS AND DEFINITIONS

Brand Experience: Refers to sum total of the perceptions, feelings and thoughts, resulting from all the points of contact, which consumers attribute to the brands they encounter and consume. Various responses such as emotional, subjective, internal and behavioural of the customer due to his/her interaction with the brand through various touch points are collectively termed as Brand experience.

Customer Experience Management: Refers to the management of customer experiences, in a cumulative manner, at multiple touch points across multiple channels based on a detailed road map of customer's end-to-end journey. The approach is based on, the hitherto largely ignored, emotional and internal aspects of the consumer behavior to manage customer encounters with the organizations.

Digitized Business Model: A Business model, leveraging the power of internet and characterized by business communications, interactions and transactions between Consumers and marketers being carried over web.

Expected Utility of the Brand: Refers to the value accorded to the brand by the customers based on their utilitarian and functional evaluations of the brand.

Experience: Refers to the familiarity, with some object/subject/area of interest, generated due to knowledge acquired and accumulated through some exposure to the object/subject/area of interest.

Experienced Utility of Brand: Refers to the value accorded to the brand by the customers based on their subjective and emotional evaluations of the brand.

Experiential View of Consumer Behavior: Refers to the exploration of the symbolic, syntactic, hedonic, psycho-temporal, and psychobiological meanings attributed to the products/brands by the consumers based on their conscious and subjective evaluations of the products/brands.

Web 2.0: Can be termed as the ideological and technical architecture, result of participatory and collaborative tools such as Adobe Flash, Really Simple Syndication (RSS), and Asynchronous Java Script (AJAX), of social media.

Website Brand Experience: Encompasses a consumer's navigational experiences and perceptions about the various features such as attractiveness of cookies, variety, currency, quality and uniqueness of visual display and/or graphical user interfaces of a specific website.

Chapter 12
Investigating impact of Electronic Word of Mouth on Consumer Purchase Intention

Shubham Goswami
Sir PadampatSinghania University, India

ABSTRACT

The domination of Word of mouth (WOM) has been applauded for many years as key influence on consumer purchases. Associating WOM with the internet usually called electronic-WOM (e-WOM) makes transmission of messages much easier, wider and faster. As e-WOM is not restricted to strong social tie groups thus the message itself plays a critical role in building purchase intention. The present study, first attempts to investigate messages efficacy on identified constructs. The study recognized credibility of message as a sole component that could moderate the discord between level of involvement and expected intention for online purchase.

INTRODUCTION

Earlier researcher of word-of-mouth, Arndt (1967) defined it as informal, noncommercial, oral, person-to-person communication about a brand, a product or a service between two or more consumers and also identified Word-of-Mouth (WOM) as one of the most effective marketing source for consumers. WOM can be more influential than print sources and is more important than advertising in raising awareness of an innovation and purchase decision (Sheth, 1971). WOM which provide pre-purchase information is known as input WOM and sharing information after the purchase like consumption experience is known as output WOM. Richins (1983) associated word-of-mouth with price and stated that the higher prices are likely to attract negative messages, if product fails to satisfy the needs.

The World Wide Web (WWW) is providing unprecedented opportunities for consumers to voice their opinions on brands, products and services in a written format, structured in the form of product reviews, complaints, discussion threads, or chats. In current scenario, customers often search for product information and features before making purchase decisions and use online reviews as primary sources

DOI: 10.4018/978-1-4666-9449-1.ch012

that influence their decision. Opinion leaders are also present online, however they are not considered as significant contributor to the decision making process for online purchases. Yet they also act as good transmitting agents of market information and in diffusion of business information. Opinions in form of messages present on internet are called electronic Word of Mouth (e-WOM), which need not be face-to-face or direct. Associating WOM with the internet makes transmission of word of mouth much easier, wider and faster. With the advent of web 2.0, e-WOM is getting more universal and important in purchase decision making. Online communities have become a popular place for online users to search and gather information on other consumers' shopping experiences, evaluations, and opinions (Kozinets, 2002). E-WOM can be in the form of electronic bulletin boards, review websites, posted-views, discussion boards, community websites, personal e-mails, chat rooms, instant messaging, blogging, twittering and others which perform in similar functions as to face-to- face WOM.

For company'sperspective, e-WOM can also serve as a feedback mechanism that helps to improve the quality of product and in acquiring new customers. Companies even offer consumer opinion forums on their own web sites to strengthen customer loyalty and reduce service costs (Dellarocas, 2003). But it was found that product information provided by companies is less influential among consumers than information provided on consumer opinion sites or discussion boards (Bickart, B. and Schindler, R.M., 2001). Further, if not enough information about the product is available from offline sources like family, friends and colleagues; then the risk involved in purchase for the buyer becomes high. Hence the influence of e-WOM on consumers' purchasing decisions also becomes higher.

The similar condition is true for the purchase of technology products like mobile phone, desktop computer, laptop, digital camera etc. People buying technology products are not having enough experience of true features of product and insufficient knowledge about a product category hence raises difficulties in making the correct purchasing decision, this scenario gives importance to pre-purchase searches of opinions and product reviews. The internet provides both opinion leaders and opinion seekers with efficient ways to spread and search information online. For these reasons, e-WOM is an important product information source as they provide potential customers with an extensive source of customer and expert opinions about the product. In addition, since opinions are gathered from many customers, the process supports impartiality, truthfulness and information richness.

Word-of-mouth communication is considered as a type of social influence that affects consumers' belief, attitude, and purchase intention (Arndt, 1967). Purchase intention, which is the willingness to purchase a product in the future, is the most widely studied outcome variables of e-WOM communication model (Hovland, 1948). Past studies also support that customers purchase intentions increase when they are exposed to high quality messages which include information that is specific, objective, and logical. In current internet arena, although the sender and the receiver of messages are independent to each other, therefore message characteristic have significant influence on e-WOM and subsequently on purchase intention (Senecal and Nantel, 2004). But, little has been researched on impact of quality of e-WOM messages on purchase intention.

Against this backdrop, the present study attempts to investigate messages efficacy on identified constructs. It further analyzes the potency of constructs to abridge gap between the customers' level of involvement and predisposition towards online purchase. The first part of the paper being introductory, discusses about the significance of electronic word of mouth. Following the introduction, second section provides an extensive related literature review related to e-WOM, message characteristics and its influence on purchase intention. The next section deals with the research methodology and data source which chiefly includes development of hypotheses, identification of survey pool & administration of questionnaire. The following section focuses on the data analysis and results of the study. The final section concludes the paper.

LITERATURE REVIEW

Electronic Word of Mouth

Sociologists and psychologists have examined the impact of interpersonal communications on attitudes and behaviour for many years. Hovland (1948) noted that social communication involved four factors, which he termed the communicator (sender), the stimuli (message), the receiver and the response. Hovland (1948) further noted that the receiver and their responses were the most difficult to study, while Hovland and Weiss (1951) highlighted the difficulty in measuring or controlling such diffusion. Nonetheless, given the well-established importance of WOM, it is surprising that so little research has been conducted on the topic compared with the more extensive domain of interpersonal influence, which was particularly prominent in psychology from the last 3 decades.

The important role WOM plays has been long recognized by diffusion of innovation researchers (Ryan and Gross, 1943), and has been acknowledged as the most important communication source between consumers. Further, little past research has focused on what happens when WOM is received (Bansal and Voyer, 2000). Since WOM is known to convey vivid novel experiences that are pleasant when positive and complaining when negative (Anderson, 1998), WOM receivers may be affected emotionally as well as rationally. WOM has a strong influence on product and service perceptions, leading to changes in judgments, value ratings and the likelihood of purchase (Arndt, 1967).

Positive WOM reduces risk during the evaluation stage of the consumer purchase cycle (Woodside and Delozier, 1976). WOM has been recognized as a key risk reducer for various forms of risk, including functional, time, financial, psychological and social. These risk types can usefully be classified into functional or financial risk, which is product-focused and social or psychological risk, which is consumer-focused (von Wangenheim and Bayo´n, 2004). Thus, as already noted, WOM is likely to be more important in service contexts. Other outcomes are also likely. Research has suggested electronic WOM (eWOM), such as online customer forums, generates greater empathy, credibility and relevance, than does information generated by the organisation itself, such as through a corporate webpage, apparently because eWOM relates personal experiences and stories (Bickart and Schindler, 2001).

In an online environment in which there has been a reduction in consumer trust on both organization promotion and advertising efforts, word of mouth (WOM) offers a way to obtain a significant competitive advantage HennigThurau et al. (2004, p .39) define e-WOM communication as "any positive or negative statement made by potential, actual, or former customers about a product or company, which is made available to a multitude of people and institutions via the Internet" and consumers will probably adapt their buying behavior after reading a positive or negative comment on-line. Moreover, Dellarocas(2003) suggested that information posted by the consumer is more credible and trustworthy than information given by the marketers.

Word-of-mouth provides potential customers with user experience to reduce purchase risk and shows influence on variety of conditions: awareness, expectations, perceptions, attitudes and behavioral intentions (Silverman, 1997). Day (1971) identified reliability and flexibility of interpersonal communication as one of key strength of WOM. From a marketing perspective, WOM can be either positive or negative, but studies suggest that negative WOM has more potent impact than positive WOM (Arndt, 1967). Two key motivations to the acceptance of WOM are the perceived interest of the giver in the receiver and the expertise of the giver (Dichter, 1966). These aspects include the importance of the credibility of the messenger. Opinion leadership research has highlighted the impact of source expertise on interpersonal influence. Curiously, the characteristics of the e-WOM activity itself have not been widely considered. E-WOM has been suggested as vivid, which relates to whether information is emotionally interesting, concrete and imagery provoking and "proximate in a sensory, temporal or spatial way". However, little research has investigated the impact these aspects have on electronic WOM influence, although Gremler (1994) suggested messages have more impact when delivered enthusiastically. Further, the power of the message delivery may impact on people's ability to recall WOM. This suggests WOM outcomes might be influenced by the vividness of the information, with negative WOM likely to be more easily remembered as it is more vivid.

E-WOM communication has some differences with traditional WOM communication. Unlike traditional WOM, e-WOM communications possess unparalleled scalability and speed of diffusion (Li &Hitt 2008, Dellarocas 2003). Being of web, these messages are persistence and accessible for a longer period of time (Hennig-Thurau et. al., 2004; Park & Lee, 2009). Further, e-WOM communications are more measurable than traditional WOM (Lee, Park and Hen, 2008). Therefore, it is easier to measure its strength on the extent to which the message receiver find the argument as convincing or valid in supporting its position. (Cheung et al, 2009). Traditional WOM involve the credibility of the communicator but on the contrary, e-WOM in most occasions eliminates the receiver's ability to judge the credibility of the sender. It is obvious that these online messages affect consumers' information search (Jepsen, 2006). But being a relatively new concept, e-WOM is in an early stage of research and its impact is still to be determined.

Message Characteristics

E-WOM allows consumers to more comfortably share their opinions without revealing their identities; this increases the volume of e-WOM over the Internet. But the strength of the relationship between the communicators and the receivers of e-WOM is usually considered weak because anyone can post their opinions about a product to various online platforms (Chatterjee, 2001). Therefore in present study, author only concentrates in examining the impact of online WOM messages on purchase intention. This study investigates how particular motivations are associated with different eWOM message characteristics. This is examined from the sender's perspective in both positive and negative eWOM contexts.

A number of authors have emphasised the importance of the message characteristics on the message persuasiveness, including both rational and emotional aspects. Anderson (1998) recognised the importance of examining WOM content and suggested positive WOM can vary in its intensity, appeal and novelty, as well as the extent to which it conveys a sender's experiences. Semin (2000, p.597) stated: ''. . . talk does not simply involve producing words. It requires choosing words from a lexicon to create sentences. . . with the purpose of communicating an intention to someone else. It is a production with a social end''. The importance of words, content, body language, and expressiveness has been emphasised in WOM messages (Dichter, 1966; East et al., 2008). In this study we specifically explore the cognitive and affective characteristics of eWOM since these are core communication dimensions. In this study, we define cognitive characteristics as the rational component of a message that typically refers to product attributes including performance, response to problems, and price-value perceptions. Affective characteristics refer to the message's depth, intensity and vividness and reflect the language. eWOM messages can be described in terms of cognitive and/or affective characteristics.

Many literatures have referred message as stimulus also (Hovland, 1948). With the literature survey, following factors are selected to measure the message characteristics.

- **Credibility:** As e-WOM is not restricted to strong social tie groups (e.g., family and friends), any consumer can post product information to geographically dispersed group of people who are largely strangers. This could raise receivers' concern about the credibility of information as trust-building online is perceived to be very difficult (Evans and Volery, 2001).
- **Consistency:** It can be expressed as the extent to which the current e-WOM recommendation is consistent with other contributors' experiences concerning to the same product or service evaluation (Zhang & Watts 2003).
- **Timeliness:** It concerns whether the messages are current, timely, and up-to-date. It also refers to the availability of the information at a suitable time (Bailey and Pearson, 1983) and plays an important role in information quality (Cheung et al., 2008)
- **Accuracy:** It concerns with reliability of the message or arguments. It also represents user's perception that the information is correct (Wixom and Todd, 2005)
- **Completeness:** It refers to message comprehensiveness. Cheung et al. (2008) found that comprehensiveness exhibited significant impact on perceived information usefulness.
- **Relevance:** It refers to the extent to which the messages are applicable and useful for decision making (Cheung et al., 2008).
- **Valence:** It is a concept adapted from emotion research which describes the positive or negative emotional tone of e-WOM, it is also called message sentiment. It was found that impact is greater for negative e-WOM than for positive e-WOM (Park and Lee, 2009) and it also affects product sales (Chintagunta et. al, 2010).
- **Volume:** It measures the total number of posted reviews on a topic. Researchers noted that more number of reviews impact the purchase intention (Park, Lee and Han, 2008; Park and Kim, 2008; Park and Lee, 2009).

Purchase Intention

In order to understand why consumers purchase safe vegetable, we will firstly look at the two very basic behaviour theories called Theory of Reasoned Action (TRA) and Theory of Planned Behaviour (TPB). The TRA is developed by Ajzen and Fishbein in 1980, and after that the TPB is developed by Ajzen in 1991. Both the two theories explain how a person leads to certain behaviour. The central factor in the theories is the individual's intention to perform a given behaviour. According to Ajzen (1991) "intentions are assumed to capture the motivational factors that influence a behaviour, they are indications of how hard people are willing to try, of how much of an effort they are planning to exert, in order to perform the behaviour". And he makes further emphasis that "when people have the stronger intention to engage in the behaviour, they will more likely to perform the behaviour" (Ajzen, 1991, p.181). Added by Samin et al. (2012) that "intention is the person's motivation in the sense of his or her intention to perform behaviour. Purchase intention can also be defined as the decision to act or physiological action that shows an individual's behaviour according to the product. Dodds et al. (1991) suggested that purchase intention represents the possibility for consumers to buy a product. Long and Ching also conclude "purchase intention stands for what we would like to buy in future" (Long and Ching, 2010, p.20).

According to the TRA, a person's behavioural intention is determined by the two basis components which are attitude toward behaviour and subjective norm. These two factors will directly affect an individual's behavioural intention and then consequently affect his or her behaviour (Sudin, Geoffrey and Hanudin, 2009). Ajzen (1991, p.188) defines attitude toward the behaviour as "the degree to which a person has a favourable or unfavourable evaluation or appraisal of the behaviour in question". A person will hold a favourable attitude toward performing the behaviour if he or she believes that positive outcomes will be mostly achieved if performing a given behaviour and vice versa. The more favourable attitude toward performing a behaviour a person is holding, the stronger intention he or she will make to perform the behaviour (Ajzen, 1991, p.181). Sudin et al. (2009, p.68) terms the beliefs that underlie a person's attitude toward the behaviour are behavioural beliefs. Ajzen also refers subjective norm as "the perceived social pressure to perform or not to perform the behaviour" (Ajzen, 1991, p.188). Teresa, Bonnie and Yingjiao (2005, p.407) makes more explanation for subjective norm as "a function of an individual's beliefs that specific individuals or groups think he/she should or should not perform the behaviour". To solve the TRA's limitation, Ajzen develops another theory called Theory of Planned Behaviour. "Theory of Planned Behaviour (TPB) is an extension of the theory of reasoned action (TRA) made necessary by the original model's limitations in dealing with behaviours over which people have incomplete volitional control" (Ajzen, 1991, p.181). The TPB is developed by adding one more component which is called perceived behavioural control to the TRA. Then in the TPB model, an individual's behavioural intention is a function of three basis components which are attitude toward the behaviour, subjective norm and perceived behavioural control. The TPB solves the limitation of the TRA by its ability to explain why in some scenarios, people hold a great favourable attitude toward performing behaviour as well as perceive strong social pressure to perform the behaviour but they still don't perform the behaviour. Those scenarios are explained by the TPB that because people perceive obstacles or difficulty in performing the behaviour. Or the perception of having low capacity to perform the behaviour also lowers a person's behavioural intention and consequently makes him or her not performing the behaviour. Those TPB calls perceived behavioural control.

Previous researchers have explained how offline word of mouth (WOM) influences consumer behavior. But as increasingly, consumers are turning to online WOM, especially online forums. Grounded in social comparison theory, the theory of reasoned action and TPB, a mall intercept survey of consumers were taken a user's interests and a forum's topic and user attitudes towards the forum strongly predict purchase intentions. Theoretical implications are discussed as well as practical implications for marketers and recommendations for further research.Scholars studied e-WOM influence on consumer shopping behaviors and also receiver's perceived value of a company's products and their loyalty intentions (Bickart et al., 2001; Gruen et al., 2005). Authors have also confirmed that e-WOM is likely to play an increasingly important role in the consumer decision-making process (Litvin et al., 2005). Park et al. (2008) examined the effects of both the quality and the quantity of e-WOM messages and found that customers purchase intentions increase when they are exposed to messages which are specific and logical as compared when they are exposed to low quality messages which are vague and emotional. Huang et al. (2009) reveal that the presence of product reviews from other consumers enhances consumer search and purchase behavior. Most of research has focused on factor analysis of electronic word-of-mouth and the comparison of traditional and online word-of-mouth. However, there are fewer studies related to measuring effectiveness of e-WOM messages and its impact on online purchase intention of customers.

Studies of e-WOM related effectiveness can be classified into two research types: market-level and individual-level (Lee et al. 2009). The difference lies in how the information is viewed. At market-level, e-WOM is considered to be related to parameters, such as average rating, dispersion of ratings and sales (Clemons, 2006). In this, a group of post-purchase customers must rate the target product information as integers representing their quality. As e-WOM systems mature and more customers participate, ratings are accumulated. On the other hand, at the individual level, identification of customer's decision-making process is performed by viewing the e-WOM as informational tool and parameters such as trust and purchase intention are considered. With the inferred product information, the customer estimates the product value and makes a purchase decision (Lee et al. 2009). More specifically, consumers develop the prevention system to identify useful information for avoiding undesirable outcomes. It was evident from literature survey that the customer's perception of the product is more important than the actual rating levels in the e-WOM systems (Ba, S. et. al, 2002). With these reasons the present study measures the effectiveness of e-WOM at the individual level.

Despite of rapid growth of e-WOM and the recent interest in this area, a significantly fewer research studies were published regarding the effect of e-WOM messages on online purchase intentions of consumers and how it is perceived by consumers. Therefore, the purpose of this study is to measure the influence of online messages and reviews on consumer purchase intention.

RESEARCH METHODOLOGY AND DATA SOURCE

Research Methodology and Data Source

This section discusses a phase-wise development of comprehensive methodology, which chiefly involves selection of variables, development of hypotheses, identification of survey pool, designing and pretesting of questionnaire, and scale reliability.

Phase I: Selection of Attributes

The measures were borrowed from previous studies and were modified to fit the present context. The pertinent details are explained in Table 1.

Phase II: Hypotheses Development and Research Model

The following hypotheses were developed and further subjected to empirical testing:

H_1: The variables configuring characteristics of e-WOM message significantly explain consumers' level of involvement for product information search process.

H_2: The variables configuring characteristics of e-WOM message significantly explain consumers' purchase intention for product.

Table 1. Construct Table

	Construct	Measures	Authors
Seeker characteristics	Level of involvement	I frequently visit review sites and internet to gather information about the product.	Zaichkowsky (1985)
Message Characteristics	Credibility	I trust on the information provided online.	Evans and Volery (2001)
	Consistency	I find online recommendations consistent with others' experiences	Zhang & Watts (2003); Cheung et al. (2008)
	Timeliness	Internet offers updated information.	Bailey and Pearson (1983); Kim et al. (2008)
	Accuracy	I believe that product information provided online is correct	Wixom and Todd, (2005)
	Completeness	Online messages provide complete and comprehensive information about the product	Cheung et al. (2008)
	Relevance	I believe that information provided online about the products is relevant and necessary.	Venkatesh and Davis (1996); Kim et al. (2008); Cheung et al. (2008)
	Valence	I often find negative things about the product	Park and Lee (2009); Chintagunta et. al. (2010)
	Volume (Number of review)	I believe that more number of reviews on a product gives more power to recommendation	Park, Lee and Han, (2008); Park and Kim (2008); Park and Lee (2009)
Purchase Intention	Influence on decision making	Online messages influence my decision to purchase the product	Park et al. (2008); Huang et al. (2009); Lee et al. (2009)

Based upon the literature review, the present study develops a framework of e-WOM functioning method. The level of consumer involvement has been considered as a significant input stimulus that achieves attention and stimulates search process at the initial level for any given product.

Zaichkowsky (1985) based upon a study observed that low involvement leads to a relative lack of information-seeking on brands and little comparison between product attributes; on the other hand high involvement consumers are more interested in acquiring information about the products and evaluating alternatives. The knowledge acquisition process is further mediated by the factors configuring message characteristics which include credibility, consistency, timeliness, accuracy, completeness, relevance, valence, volume which, inturn, influence buyers' predispositions. This finally leads to the development of online purchase intention. The process view of the proposed model has been shown in the Figure 1. Arrows in the model depict major directions of influence that specific variables exert.

Phase III: Survey Pool and Data Collection

In order to examine the hypotheses a final questionnaire was developed followed by pilot study before finally advancing to field study. The reliability of the developed questionnaire was tested by deploying the statistical test 'Cronbach's alpha' which has come out to be 0.699, considered a good sign of reliability of the questionnaire. A survey pool comprising of students pursuing higher education which includes undergraduate and postgraduate students of selected higher educational institutions in Udaipur

Figure 1. Research model dynamics

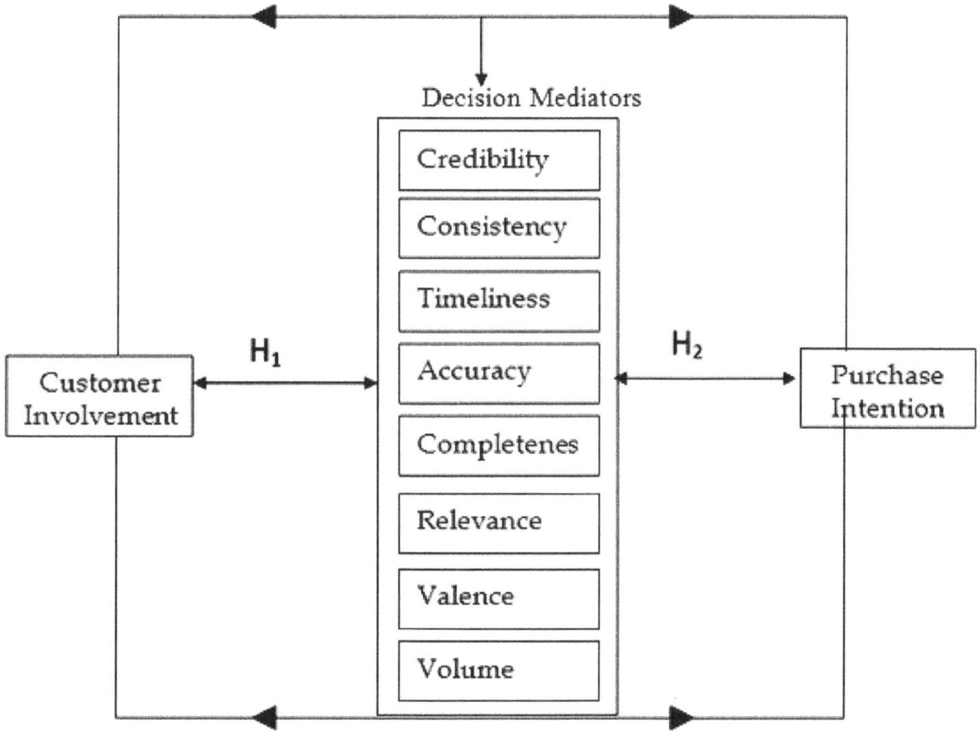

city of Rajasthan state. Initially, a sample size of one hundred was selected by applying convenience and judgmental sampling technique, and data was collected through internet. Through an email invitation, respondents received hypertext link of an online survey. Finally, seventy two of them had responded which gives a response rate of 72%. Despite the fact that internet surveys have the poorest response rates, even lower than e-mail surveys (Malhotra, 2007), a high rate of response in this study can be attributed to two factors: (1) The questionnaires were directed to educated students and such people are generally motivated to respond in studies of academic interest (Boyd et al., 1998). (2) The respondents were repeatedly reminded through phone calls and emails to fill the questionnaire

RESULT

Testing of H1

H_1: The variables configuring characteristics of e-WOM message significantly explain consumers' level of involvement for product information search process.

To test the hypothesis H1, two questions were developed on a five-point Likert rating scale. The respondents were asked to display their degree of agreement/disagreement on the statements. The scale categories have been allotted numerical values ranging from 1(extremely disagree) to 5 (extremely agree). The first question attempted to gain the respondents' overall level of involvement in online search process for any given product. The second set of questions dealt with the perceptions of respondents on the constructs configuring characteristics of e-WOM message. Multiple regression analysis has been performed to investigate the explanatory power of constructs configuring message characteristic on the customers' level of involvement in the search process for online purchase.

As shown in Table 2, the final regression model with two independent variables (Accuracy, and Credibility) explains 8.4% of the variance of customers' level of involvement in the search process (Adjusted R^2= .084, F= 4.022, p= .049<.05) . Also, the standard error of the estimate has been reduced to 0.79719, which means that at the 95% confidence level, the margin of error for any predictable value of 'customer involvement' can be calculated at ±1.56. The ANOVA analysis provides the statistical test for the overall model fit in terms of the F ratio. The values of two predictors reduce the error by 11.01 percent. This reduction is deemed statistically significant with F ratio of 4.270 and a significance level .018. The two regression coefficients, plus the constant, are all significant at the .05 level ($B_{constant}$= 4.475, t=8.389, p=.000<.05; $B_{accuracy}$= -.235, t= -2.114, p= .038<.05; $B_{Credibility}$= .203, t= 2.005, p= .049<.05). The effect of multicollinearity is nullified as both the predicted variables in the final model have tolerance of 1.000 respectively, explaining no variance of each predicted variable by others.

Testing of H2

H_2: The variables configuring characteristics of e-WOM message significantly explain consumers' purchase intention for product.

To test the hypothesis H2, two questions were developed on a five-point Likert rating scale. The first question attempted to gain the respondents' online purchase intention for any given product. The second set of questions dealt with the perceptions of respondents on the constructs configuring characteristics of e-WOM message. Multiple regression analysis has been performed to investigate the explanatory power of constructs configuring message characteristic on the customers' intention for online purchase.

As revealed in data presented in tables 3.1 to 3.4, the final regression model with two independent variables (Credibility, and Volume) explains 17.5% of the variance of customers purchase intention (Adjusted R^2= .175, F= 5.571, p= .021<.05). Also, the standard error of the estimate has been reduced to

Table 2. Multiple Regression Analysis- Customer Involvement Descriptive Statistics

	Mean	Std. Deviation	N
Level of involvement	4.3056	.83310	72
Credibility	3.3333	.93447	72
Consistency	3.3611	.98303	72
Timeliness	4.3056	.57259	72
Accuracy	3.5972	.85018	72
Completeness	3.3611	.99726	72
Relevance	3.5139	.80479	72
Valence	3.4306	.81925	72
Volume	3.7222	.75475	72

Table 3. Model Summary

Model	R	R Square	Adjusted R Square	Std. Error of the Estimate	Change Statistics				
					R Square Change	F Change	df1	df2	Sig. F Change
1	.241[a]	.058	.045	.81422	.058	4.331	1	70	.041
2	.332[b]	.110	.084	.79719	.052	4.022	1	69	.049

Table 4. ANOVA[c]

Model		Sum of Squares	Df	Mean Square	F	Sig.
1	Regression	2.871	1	2.871	4.331	.041[a]
	Residual	46.406	70	.663		
	Total	49.278	71			
2	Regression	5.427	2	2.714	4.270	.018[b]
	Residual	43.851	69	.636		
	Total	49.278	71			

a. Predictors: (Constant), Accuracy
b. Predictors: (Constant), Accuracy, Credibility
c. Dependent Variable: Level of involvement

Table 5. Coefficients[a]

Model		Unstandardized Coefficients		Standardized Coefficients	t	Sig.	95.0% Confidence Interval for B		Collinearity Statistics	
		B	Std. Error	Beta			Lower Bound	Upper Bound	Tolerance	VIF
1	(Constant)	5.156	.420		12.278	.000	4.319	5.994		
	Accuracy	-.237	.114	-.241	-2.081	.041	-.463	-.010	1.000	1.000
2	(Constant)	4.475	.533		8.389	.000	3.411	5.539		
	Accuracy	-.235	.111	-.240	-2.114	.038	-.457	-.013	1.000	1.000
	Credibility	.203	.101	.228	2.005	.049	.001	.405	1.000	1.000

a. Dependent Variable: Level of Involvement

1.13745, which means that at the 95% confidence level, the margin of error for any predictable value of 'customer purchase intention' can be calculated at ±2.23. The ANOVA analysis provides the statistical test for the overall model fit in terms of the F ratio. The values of two predictors reduce the error by 19.80 percent. This reduction is deemed statistically significant with F ratio of 8.521 and a significance level .000. The two regression coefficients except the constant are significant at the .05 level ($B_{constant}$= .129, t=.163, p=.871>.05; $B_{Credibility}$= .429, t= 2.927, p= .005<.05; B_{Volume}= .429, t= 2.360, p= .021<.05). The effect of multicollinearity is nullified as both the predicted variables in the final model have tolerance of .970 respectively, explaining 3% variance of each predicted variable by others.

Table 6. Multiple Regression Analysis- Purchase Intention Descriptive Statistics

	Mean	Std. Deviation	N
Purchase intention	3.1528	1.25215	72
Credibility	3.3333	.93447	72
Consistency	3.3611	.98303	72
Timeliness	4.3056	.57259	72
Accuracy	3.5972	.85018	72
Completeness	3.3611	.99726	72
Relevance	3.5139	.80479	72
Valence	3.4306	.81925	72
Volume	3.7222	.75475	72

Table 7. Model Summary

Model	R	R Square	Adjusted R Square	Std. Error of the Estimate	Change Statistics				
					R Square Change	F Change	df1	df2	Sig. F Change
1	.365[a]	.133	.121	1.17400	.133	10.767	1	70	.002
2	.445[b]	.198	.175	1.13745	.065	5.571	1	69	.021

a. Predictors: (Constant), Credibility
b. Predictors: (Constant), Credibility, Volume

Table 8. ANOVA

Model		Sum of Squares	Df	Mean Square	F	Sig.
1	Regression	14.841	1	14.841	10.767	.002[a]
	Residual	96.479	70	1.378		
	Total	111.319	71			
2	Regression	22.048	2	11.024	8.521	.000[b]
	Residual	89.272	69	1.294		
	Total	111.319	71			

a. Predictors: (Constant), Credibility
b. Predictors: (Constant), Credibility, Volume
c. Dependent Variable: purchase_intention

Based upon the results obtained from the analysis of both hypotheses, it has been observed that the credibility of eWOM message emerged as an exclusive component that could preserve potency to abridge discord between the consumers' level of involvement in the search process to the final online purchase intention.

Table 9. Coefficients

Model		Unstandardized Coefficients		Standardized Coefficients	t	Sig.	95.0% Confidence Interval for B		Collinearity Statistics	
		B	Std. Error	Beta			Lower Bound	Upper Bound	Tolerance	VIF
1	(Constant)	1.522	.516		2.950	.004	.493	2.551		
	Credibility	.489	.149	.365	3.281	.002	.192	.787	1.000	1.000
2	(Constant)	.126	.774		.163	.871	-1.418	1.671		
	Credibility	.429	.147	.320	2.927	.005	.137	.722	.970	1.031
	Volume	.429	.182	.258	2.360	.021	.066	.791	.970	1.031

a. Dependent Variable: purchase_intention

CONCLUSION

The advent of internet has brought paradigm shift in the consumer purchase behaviour. Now, the consumers have alternative to access the products online. Moreover, the accessibility is not merely confined to the existing products acquaintance but extends to the information about the consumers' experience about the products. Consequently, consumers gain enough space to communicate among acquaintances in a new communication format, namely electronic word-of-mouth (eWOM). Traditional WOM involve the credibility of the communicator but on the contrary, e-WOM in most occasions eliminates the receiver's ability to judge the credibility of the sender. In addition, as e-WOM is not restricted to strong social tie groups thus the message itself plays a critical role in building purchase intention. E-WOM allows consumers to more comfortably share their opinions without revealing their identities, thus increasing the volume of e-WOM over the Internet. But the strength of the relationship between the communicators and the receivers of e-WOM is usually considered weak because anyone can post their opinions about a product to various online platforms (Chatterjee, 2001). Therefore, the present study concentrates exclusively on examining the impact of online WOM messages initially on consumers' involvement in search process to final purchase intention. The study deciphers that the credibility and accuracy of message are cardinal to engage consumers initially in online search process. It further reveals that credibility and amount of reviews are pivotal in developing online purchase intention. Finally, the study recognized credibility of message as a sole component that could mitigate discord between level of involvement and expected intention for online purchase.

FUTURE RESEARCH

In conclusion, we can confirm that although e-WOM has not replaced WOM and is still not as powerful, but in near future it can be predicted to influence consumers' purchase intentions and may be considered as a more trusted information source. The area is likely to provide a rich and interesting stream of exploration. Future research related to the application of eWOM strategies should require more focus. Experimental studied should be designed to measure the cognitive, affective, and behavioral implications upon consumer behavior. Researchers will have to devise new methods to study online interpersonal influence so that they can test theoretical propositions derived from the existing literature on social influence. Studies should be made of what kind of information consumers seek online and how they actually use the information they acquire online to make purchase decisions.

REFERENCES

Ajzen, I. (1991). The theory of planned behaviour. *Organizational Behavior and Human Decision Processes*, *50*(2), 179–211. doi:10.1016/0749-5978(91)90020-T

Anderson, E. W. (1998). Customer satisfaction and word of mouth. *Journal of Service Research*, *1*(1), 5–17. doi:10.1177/109467059800100102

Arndt, J. (1967). *Word of Mouth Advertising: A Review of the Literature*. New York, NY: Advertising Research Foundation, Inc.

Arndt, J. (1967). Role of product- related conversations in the diffusion of a new product. *JMR, Journal of Marketing Research*, *4*(3), 291–295. doi:10.2307/3149462

Ba, S., & Pavlou, P. A. (2002). Evidence of the effect of trust in electronic markets: Price premiums and buyer behavior. *Management Information Systems Quarterly*, *23*(4), 243–268. doi:10.2307/4132332

Bailey, J. E., & Pearson, S. W. (1983). Development of a tool for measuring and analyzing computer user satisfaction. *Management Science*, *29*(5), 530–545. doi:10.1287/mnsc.29.5.530

Bansal, H. S., & Voyer, P. A. (2000). Word-of-mouth processes within a service purchase decision context. *Journal of Service Research*, *3*(2), 166–177. doi:10.1177/109467050032005

Bickart, B., & Schindler, R. M. (2001). Internet forums as influential sources of consumer information. *Journal of Interactive Marketing*, *15*(3), 31–40. doi:10.1002/dir.1014

Bickart, B., & Schindler, R. M. (2001). Internet Forums as Influential Sources of Consumer Information. *Journal of Interactive Marketing*, *15*(3), 31–40. doi:10.1002/dir.1014

Boyd, H. W., Jr., Westfall, R., & Stasch., S. F. (1998). Marketing research (7th ed.). Richard D. Irwin Inc.

Chatterjee, P. (2001). Online review: Do consumers use them? *Advances in Consumer Research. Association for Consumer Research (U. S.)*, *28*, 129–133.

Cheung, C. M. K., Lee, M. K. O., & Rabjohn, N. (2008). The impact of electronic word-of-mouth: The adoption of online opinions in online customer communities. *Internet Research*, *18*(3), 229–247. doi:10.1108/10662240810883290

Cheung, M., Luo, C., Sia, C., & Chen, H. (2009). Credibility of Electronic Word-of- Mouth: Informational and Normative Determinants of On-line Consumer Recommendations. *International Journal of Electronic Commerce*, *13*(4), 9–38. doi:10.2753/JEC1086-4415130402

Chintagunta, P. K., Gopinath, S., & Venkataraman, S. (2010). The Effects of Online User Reviews on Movie Box Office Performance: Accounting for Sequential Rollout and Aggregation across Local Markets. *Marketing Science*, *29*(5), 944–957. doi:10.1287/mksc.1100.0572

Clemons, E. K., Gao, G., & Hitt, L. M. (2006). When online reviews meet hyperdifferentiation: A study of the craft beer industry. *Journal of Management Information Systems*, *23*(2), 149–171. doi:10.2753/MIS0742-1222230207

Day, G. S. (1971). Attitude change, media and word of mouth. *Journal of Advertising Research*, *11*(6), 31–40.

Dellarocas, C. (2003). The Digitization of Word of Mouth: Promise and Challenges of Online Feedback Mechanisms. *Management Science*, *49*(10), 1407–1424. doi:10.1287/mnsc.49.10.1407.17308

Dichter, E. (1966). How word of mouth advertising works. *Harvard Business Review*, *44*(6), 147–160.

Dodds, W. B., Monroe, K. B., & Grewal, D. (1991). Effects of price, brand, and store information on buyers' product evaluations. *JMR, Journal of Marketing Research*, *28*(3), 307–319. doi:10.2307/3172866

East, R., Hammond, K., & Lomax, W. (2008). Measuring the impact of positive and negative word of mouth on brand purchase probability. *International Journal of Research in Marketing*, *25*(3), 215–224. doi:10.1016/j.ijresmar.2008.04.001

Evans, D., & Volery, T. (2001). Online business development services for entrepreneurs: An exploratory study. *Entrepreneurship & Regional Development*, *13*(4), 333–350. doi:10.1080/08985620110052274

Gremler, D. D. (1994). Word-of-mouth about service providers: an illustration of theory development in marketing. In C. W. Park & D. Smith (Eds.), *AMA Winter Educators' Conference: Marketing Theory and Applications* (pp. 62–70). Chicago, IL: American Marketing Association.

Gruen, T. W., Osmonbekov, T., & Czaplewski, A. J. (2005). eWOM: The impact of customer-to-customer online know-how exchange on customer value and loyalty. *Journal of Business Research*, *59*(4), 449–456. doi:10.1016/j.jbusres.2005.10.004

Hennig-Thurau, T., Gwinner, K. P., Walsh, G., & Gremler, D. D. (2004). E- word of mouth via consumer-opinion platforms: What motivates consumers to articulate themselves on the Internet? *Journal of Interactive Marketing*, *18*(1), 38–52. doi:10.1002/dir.10073

Hovland, C. I. (1948). Social Communication. *Proceedings of the American Philosophical Society*, *92*(5), 371–375.

Hovland, C. I., & Weiss, W. (1951). The influence of source credibility on communications effectiveness. *Public Opinion Quarterly*, *15*(4), 635–650. doi:10.1086/266350

Huang, P., Lurie, N., & Mitra, S. (2009). Searching for Experience on the Web: An Empirical Examination of Consumer Behavior for Search and Experience Goods. *Journal of Marketing*, *73*(2), 55–69. doi:10.1509/jmkg.73.2.55

Jepsen, A. L. (2006). Information Search in Virtual Communities: Is it Replacing Use of Off-Line Communication? *Journal of Marketing Communications*, *12*(4), 247–261. doi:10.1080/13527260600694308

Kim, D. J., Ferrin, D. L., & Rao, R. H. (2008). A trust-based consumer decision-making model in electronic commerce: The role of trust, perceived risk, and their antecedents. *Decision Support Systems*, *44*(2), 544–564. doi:10.1016/j.dss.2007.07.001

Kotler, P., & Armstrong, G. (2006). *Principles of Marketing*. Pearson Education.

Kozinets, R. V. (2002). The field behind the screen: Using netnography for marketing research in online communities. *JMR, Journal of Marketing Research*, *39*(1), 61–72. doi:10.1509/jmkr.39.1.61.18935

Lee, J., & Lee, J. N. (2009). Understanding the product information inference process in electronic word-ofmouth: An objectivity–subjectivity dichotomy perspective. *Information & Management*, *46*(5), 302–311. doi:10.1016/j.im.2009.05.004

Lee, J., Park, D.-H., & Han, I. (2008). The effect of negative online consumer reviews on product attitude: An information processing view. *Electronic Commerce Research and Applications*, *7*(3), 341–352. doi:10.1016/j.elerap.2007.05.004

Li, X., & Hitt, L. (2008). Self-Selection and Information Role of Online Product Reviews. *Information Systems Research*, *19*(4), 456–474. doi:10.1287/isre.1070.0154

Litvin S.W., Goldsmith R., Pan B., (2005). E-WOM in Hosptitaly and Tourism. *Tourism Management*, 1-30

Long, Y. L., & Ching, Y. L. (2010). The influence of corporate image, relationship marketing, and trust on purchase intention: The moderating effects of word ofmouth. *Emerald Group Publishing Limited*, *65*(3), 16–34. doi:10.1108/16605371011083503

Malhotra, N. (2007). *Marketing Research- an applied orientation* (5th ed.). Pearson Education.

Park, C., & Lee, T. (2009). Information direction, website reputation and eWOM effect: A moderating role of product type. *Journal of Business Research*, *62*(1), 61–67. doi:10.1016/j.jbusres.2007.11.017

Park, D. H., & Kim, S. (2008). The effects of consumer knowledge on message processing of electronic word-of-mouth via online consumer reviews. *Electronic Commerce Research and Applications*, *7*(4), 399–410. doi:10.1016/j.elerap.2007.12.001

Richins, M. L. (1983). Negative word-of-mouth by dissatisfied customers: A pilot study. *Journal of Marketing*, *47*(1), 68–78. doi:10.2307/3203428

Ryan, B., & Gross, N. (1943). The diffusion of hybrid seed corn in two Iowa communities. *Rural Sociology*, *8*(1), 15–24.

Samin, R., Goodarz, J. D., Muhammad, S. R., Firoozeh, F., Mahsa, H., & Sanaz, E. (2012). A Conceptual Study on the Country of Origin Effect on Consumer Purchase Intention. *Canadian Center of Science and Education*, *8*(12), 205–215.

Schiffman, L., & Kanuk, L. L. (2007). *Consumer Behavior*. Pearson Prentice-Hall.

Semin, G. R. (2000). Agenda 2000—Communication: Language as an implementational device for cognition. *European Journal of Social Psychology*, *30*(5), 595–612. doi:10.1002/1099-0992(200009/10)30:5<595::AID-EJSP23>3.0.CO;2-A

Senecal, S., & Nantel, J. (2004). The Influence of Online Product Recommendations on Consumers' Online Choices. *Journal of Retailing*, *80*(2), 156–169. doi:10.1016/j.jretai.2004.04.001

Sheth, J. N. (1971). Word of mouth in low risk innovations. *Journal of Advertising Research*, *11*, 15–18.

Silverman, G. (1997). Harvesting the Power of Word of mouth. *Potentials in Marketing*, *30*(9), 14–16.

Suddin, L., Geoffrey, H. T., & Hanudin, A. (2009). Predicting intention to choose halal products using theory of reasoned action. *Journal of Islamic and Middle Eastern Finance and Management*, *2*(1), 66–76. doi:10.1108/17538390910946276

Venkatesh, V., & Davis, F. D. (1996). A model of the antecedents of perceived ease of use: Development and test. *Decision Sciences*, *27*(3), 451–481. doi:10.1111/j.1540-5915.1996.tb01822.x

Von Wangenheim, F., & Bayo'n, T. (2004). The effect of word of mouth on service switching. *European Journal of Marketing*, *38*(9/10), 1173–1185. doi:10.1108/03090560410548924

Wixom, B. H., & Todd, P. A. (2005). A theoretical integration of user satisfaction and technology acceptance. *Information Systems Research*, *16*(1), 85–102. doi:10.1287/isre.1050.0042

Woodside, A. G., & Delozier, M. W. (1976). Effect of word of mouth advertising on consumer risk taking. *Journal of Advertising*, *5*(4), 12–19. doi:10.1080/00913367.1976.10672658

Zaichkowsky, J. L. (1985, December). Measuring the Involvement Construct. *The Journal of Consumer Research*, *12*(3), 341–352. doi:10.1086/208520

Zhang, W., & Watts, S. A. (2003). Capitalizing on Content: Information Adoption in Two Online communities. *Journal of the Association for Information Systems*, *9*(2), 73–94.

KEY TERMS AND DEFINITIONS

Electronic Word-of-Mouth: Word-of-mouth often takes a form of objective product information and subjective personal opinions and experiences. These same WOM principles have spread in the field of internet. On-line WOM practices are referred to as electronic or e-word-of-mouth (e-WOM).

Likert Rating Scale: Likert (1932) developed the principle of measuring attitudes by asking people to respond to a series of statements about a topic, in terms of the extent to which they agree with them, and so tapping into the cognitive and affective components of attitudes. Likert-type scales use fixed choice response formats and are designed to measure attitudes or opinions.

Multicollinearity: Multicollinearity (also collinearity) is a statistical phenomenon in which two or more predictor variables in a multiple regression model are highly correlated, meaning that one can be linearly predicted from the others with a non-trivial degree of accuracy.

Purchase Intention: Purchase intention is the implied promise to one's self to buy the product again whenever one makes next trip to the market.

Valence: The term used in psychology, especially in discussing emotions, means the intrinsic attractiveness (positive valence) or averseness (negative valence) of an event, object, or situation. However, the term is also used to characterize and categorize specific emotions.

Chapter 13

E-WOM Issues and Challenges: A Study with Respect to the FMCG Sector

Dhiraj Jain
Symbiosis Centre for Management Studies, India

Yuvraj Sharma
Cognus Technology Ltd., India

ABSTRACT

In the global era, Electronic Word of Mouth (E-WOM) has become an important emerging business strategy in the marketing and consumer environment. Along with the growth of digital connectivity and E-WOM, new ongoing challenges have also emerged for online users, businesses, and services. The chapter mainly aims to look closer upon how Electronic Word of Mouth faced challenges related to social, personal, psychological and human appeal in FMCG sector which influence customers as well as firms. The study used survey method to approach the respondents. The primary data was collected from 250 respondents and descriptive statistics and F-test ANOVA were used to test the significant of the association / non-association between variables. It was found that mostly customers have positive attitude towards E-WOM phenomenon. The study could help the FMCG Company in taking such steps that could make improvements in their business processes and expand their business without spending lot of money.

INTRODUCTION

Electronic word-of-mouth (e-WOM) is a method of communicating with the customers to share their opinions and experiences on goods and services with a multitude of other consumers. It focuses on person to person contacts happening on the Internet (Hung, 2007). Marketers are also searching for low cost alternatives compared to other advertising media such as television and radio. More and more customers are sharing their online views and opinions regarding products and also exchange product experiences with other customers. E-WOM and social media have revolutionized the way in which information and experience is shared with each other in an effective manner. It has become an emerging business strat-

DOI: 10.4018/978-1-4666-9449-1.ch013

Table 1. Characteristics of Traditional WOM and e-WOM

Traditional Word of Mouth Publicity	E-WOM
Interpersonal communication sets apart from mass communication.	It makes traditional word of mouth more powerful. Information can be passed online in a quick manner with help of Internet such as text, images or even movies.
Main focus is on promoting commercial entities such as products, brands and services.	It has a greater potential to reach a multitude of people at the same time in an effective manner.
Communication between the parties is perceived as unbiased and genuine.	Allows people to share comments online, shape consumers' attitudes towards a product; people's trust on other people and the right connection and knowledge features make e-WOM more powerful (Hung, 2007).
Receivers are familiar with senders and high trust is established between them.	Receivers are not always familiar with the senders and lack trust. It is informal and inorganic in spreading information among the customers about goods and services.
	It provides a window of opportunity for companies to monitor and analyze word of mouth responses and enables them to share information by deploying the social sharing button compared to the traditional marketing methods (Hung, 2007).

egy in the evolving marketing environment. It has created a worldwide publically accessible network that is in the form of communication channels and platforms. Significant differences exist between the traditional word-of-mouth and the e-WOM.

The global community is able to access both positive and negative e-WOM comments about countless number of products and services offered by FMCG sector companies. Kavitha (2012) has opined in a study that FMCG companies in India have enjoyed a large potential market and offer a variety of products to consumers, namely soaps, detergents, healthcare products, grooming and personal care products etc. It comes fourth in terms of employment generation for more than 3 million people .The market was estimated to grow to over Rs 185,000 crore (around $37 billion) by 2014 (Kavitha, 2012).

E-WOM for FMCG Brands

E-WOM opens a new and diverse channel for FMCG companies to promote their brands while engaging and influencing consumers by effectively utilizing the medium. Major FMCG companies such as Procter & Gamble, Emami, Marico Ltd, Colgate Palmolive, Godrej Consumers Pvt. Ltd. and Nestle India etc. in India have been effectively using e-WOM and social media to interact with customers to solve their queries regarding their products and services. These companies are including e-WOM in their marketing functions to reap the market opportunities in order to humanize their brands, communicate with the customers (listen and monitor), connect with the consumers emotionally and build customers response platform to influence consumers towards their brands and grab their attention for a long time. Several studies have also indicated the impact of e-WOM on customer purchase intentions and their perceptions towards brands. The words internet and social media are preferred as a communication channel that flashes many images upon the canvas of the human mind (Yildirim, 2011).Several social media marketing tactics are used worldwide that make use of the social networking platforms such as Twitter, Facebook, Google+, LinkedIn, Yelp, Foursquare, You tube, Blogs and Instagram etc. Thomas(2006) investigated the effect of e-WOM on the customer loyalty and the perception of the brand on the customers' mind. They found that e-WOM activities have an influence on customer perceptions towards brands.

REVIEW OF LITERATURE

Overview of E-WOM

E-WOM has been defined as an online communication between receivers and communicators who receive products or services of the firms and post reviews about the products. It is working as a tool that moves ideas and information in an efficient & an effective manner and also influence the marketing tactics and strategies of respective companies (Javornik, 2012). As a part of the economic reformation, the information technology has been deregulated and made more competitive. IT revolution has made it possible to provide easy and flexible operations to communicate with customers. It has been observed that consumer motivation towards reading online reviews and other related characteristics (Involvement, demographics) are the major factors affecting consumer purchasing decisions.

Benefits and Drawbacks of E-WOM from Company and Customers' Perspectives

Seeberger, Schwarting and Meiners (2010) focused on the benefits of e-WOM publicity for firms in order to reach the consumers. They described that firms rely on the electronic media to tell others about their goods and services than broadcasting transformed communications and other traditional media channels. It is an important marketing tool for FMCG companies in terms of creating trust and organizations can easily reach to their customers through social networking and referral programs. Products or services based on a referral are more appropriate for companies to retain the existing customers and attract the new ones towards the brands. It is an inexpensive marketing tool and referral costs almost nothing. So FMCG enterprises use this tool to build a positive image about their products and services in the minds of the customers. It also provides an easy means of sharing information about company and its products with other people. Parka (2009) examined the contribution of e-WOM towards firm performance and suggested that it would be helpful for the organizations to understand information direction (positive vs. negative) which contributed in creating brand reputation. It was found that e-WOM positively affected the source of social capital, brand choice facilitation, persuasion knowledge development and their reflexivity.

Customer satisfaction, trust and emotional appeal in e-WOM based passive or active recommendations provided by other people were the major factors which provided guidance to consumers and influenced their buying behaviors regarding FMCG products. Peer group and relatives shared trust worthy information on social networking sites (SNS) which influenced purchasing decisions.

Buyers' purchasing intention is also influenced by their involvement in e-WOM activities but sometimes get irritated when too much information is overloaded on websites. Park and Lee(2008) found that positive reviews attract customers toward products and services offered. However, while consumers have more favorable attitude towards a product as a greater number of positive reviews are offered, they may be confronted with too much information in the process which results in information overload. Casalo(2008) found that positive word-of-mouth enhanced the satisfaction level of customers and was beneficial for the firm as well as the customers . Chu(2011) examined how social relationship factors relate with e-WOM which was transmitted via SNS . It was found that trust, normative and informational factors were positively associated with users and attract customers towards products and services of the firm. Wu and Wang (2011) explored that high degree of firm involvement in e-WOM activities indicated a better brand attitude. To attract customers towards their products, higher credibility towards the message source was required. Lee, Rodgers, and Miyoung (2009) conducted a study to examine the influence of customers' product reviews on their attitude towards brands and websites and found that extremely positive reviews increased consumer's preference towards brands while negative reviews towards products had a stronger influence on their attitudes and de-motivated them to purchase products from online sources. They found that negative influence of e-WOM was more effective as compared to positive e-WOM. Reputation of established websites also influenced customer perception towards brands in an appropriate manner. Hwang (2009) explored how consumers evaluated e-WOM messages about products and took decisions regarding brands. They showed that the credibility of web sites and e-WOM messages had created a great impact in the customers' mind for a long time. Hung (2007) examined the effectiveness of e-WOM in the product brand communications, consumer learning's and their behavior. Javornik (2012) investigated the willingness of customers towards engagement with three Swiss premium online and offline food brands and found that customers were not willing to engage with FMCG brands if they were not being offered a unique value proposition.

Challenges Faced by the FMCG Sectors

In the modern era, with the emergence of new technology, challenges are also arising. Different types of issues and challenges are creating problems for FMCG companies in promoting their products and gain wider customers' base in an effective manner. Along with the growth of digital connectivity and e-WOM, new ongoing challenges have also emerged for users, businesses, and service providers alike (Marketing Chart, 2013).Companies are still trying to understand the new, massy and the ever-changing e-WOM phenomenon. The idea is new and differentiates from other information sharing methods like storytelling and makes person to person network offline (Labsomboonsiri, 2012).According to Kavita(2012), FMCG sector companies are facing several problems while promoting their products in the rural as well as urban India such as the media problem (non-availability of power in the rural area), lower literacy rates (leads to communication related problems and misinterpreted information) and cultural factors (religion, caste, occupation, income, age, education and politics).

e-WOM has provided a mechanism through which information relating to ownership, usage, characteristics of particular goods exchanges on the internet(Jalilvand, 2008). E-WOM is a fast medium of customer-to-customer information exchange in the ever increasing competitive market as compared to the other traditional mass-media commercial advertisements like newspapers, TV etc. However, the reliability of e-WOM sources remains an important concern for the marketers as well as the consumers. Gaitan (2013) explored the e-WOM mechanisms that were helpful for organizations to promote the transmission and reception of online opinions in the context of social network services in a reliable manner. They found that social identification is beneficial for SNS and its users. It played an important role in the transmission of information.

McConnell and Huba (2003) recommended that companies could enhance customer satisfaction and create a positive image of their products by applying various strategies such as building the buzz (gaining expertise and build intelligent word-of-mouth networks), making bite-size chunks (smaller offerings to get customers to bite) and napsterize knowledge (sharing knowledge freely with consumers about products) etc. They suggested that FMCG companies could encourage communities of customers to share their perceptions towards products usage and services offered by firms. By continuously gathering customer feedback, firms could be able to better understand needs of customers and make the world of the FMCG industry better (McConnell and Huba, 2003).

Research Gap

The above literature has tried to understand the various e-WOM issues but the understanding of the respondent's behavior towards online posting of comments by users and challenges faced by the FMCG sector related to social, personal, psychological and human appeal were missing. It is important for FMCG organizations to understand the opinion and awareness of customers towards e-WOM and hence helped in framing the below objectives for the study.

Objectives of the Study

The study focuses on the challenges in the adoption of e-WOM such as the lack of awareness about this new concept and the problems relating to trust and authenticity of the customer feedback. The study tries to investigate the challenges faced by the FMCG companies due to improper use of e-WOM in their business operations. The study also focuses on understanding its effects on purchasing behavior of the customers. The objectives could be framed as under:

- To determine the association between the demographic factors of the users and their engagement with e-WOM
- To investigate specific issues and challenges regarding the use of e-WOM in creating social space and attracting customers towards FMCG brands

RESEARCH METHODOLOGY USED IN THE STUDY

The main aim of the study is to look closer as to how e-WOM creates challenges like social, personal, psychological and human appeal in the FMCG sector and influence respondent's behavior and propose solutions to overcome these problems. Primary data collection technique was used to collect the information from the customers to know their perception towards e-WOM. With the help of validated statistical tools an attempt has been made to explore the relationship between demographic factors and the perception towards the challenges faced by the FMCG firms. The survey method was used to approach

Table 2. Hypothesis framed for the study

H_{01}	There is no significant influence of the age of the respondents on their perception towards the social challenges created due to e-WOM.
H_{02}	There is no significant influence of the occupation of the respondents on their perception towards the social challenges created due to e-WOM.
H_{03}	There is no influence of the frequency of posting comments online on the personal challenges created due to e -WOM.
H_{04}	There is no significant influence of the human appeal on the consumers' perception towards FMCG brands
H_{05}	There is no significant influence of the consumers' perceptions on the peer group created due to e –WOM
H_{06}	There is no significant influence of the e -WOM related activities on consumers' engagement
H_{07}	There is no significant influence of the frequencies of posting comments online on the human appeal challenges created due to e- WOM

the respondents. A pre-tested and a well- structured questionnaire were sent on-line to collect the data related to the subject matter. The study shows the impact of peer product reviews on the internet and other social media on the individual or the society. For this purpose, a sample of 250 respondents was selected who had written on-line reviews or had been taking decisions on the basis of on-line reviews. Secondary data was collected from different published sources including journals, articles, and websites of FMCG companies.

Research Approach

The deductive approach was employed in the study as it was concerned with testing and conforming the hypothesis framed (Panneerselvam, 2004). A quantitative technique has been used to identify the factors that force customers and organizations to engage in e-WOM activities (Goddarad and Melville, 2004). This approach would help in understanding the respondents' behavior towards comments posted online by its users.

Research Philosophy

The positivism theory was used to understand the methodology and the supporting statistical methods to quantify observations (Taylor et. al, 2011). Positivism philosophy is beneficial for firms to understand the factors which influenced their performance and to identify e-WOM challenges that influenced the performance of FMCG sector (Daniel and Aroma, 2011).

Research Design

A research design is a blue print of the research and it helps an individual or an organization to take rational decisions related to sample size selection, sources of data collection and analysis of data (Wu and Wang, 2011). In the following context a descriptive study was employed as it was beneficial for the researcher to understand the e-WOM challenges faced by the FMCG sector.

Research Type

Both qualitative and quantitative approach has been used in the study. With the help of quantitative data, the hypothesis was tested and the results interpreted. This method was used for considering the relationship between demographic factors and user engagement with e-WOM. The qualitative data helped to understand the theories and factors affecting social, personal, psychological and human appeal that created challenges for the FMCG companies and influenced customers towards their brands.

Data Collection

Both primary and secondary research methods were considered. Primary data collection method was used to collect data from customers and it helped to know their perception towards e- WOM publicity. While the secondary research technique was useful to attain better results and identify the concept of e-WOM and its impact on consumers in an appropriate manner.

DATA ANALYSIS AND INTERPRETATION

This process contains activities related to collection, inspection, transformation and modeling of information. The data was collected and tabulated. The major factors identified were related to social, personal, psychological and human appeal which influence the buying behavior of the customers and created challenges for the FMCG organizations. This understanding could help the FMCG companies to survive in the market and perform better than their competitors (Hung, 2007). The review of literature helped to determine how internet and e-WOM publicity influenced the respondents' behavior towards the frequency of commenting online (Fowler, 2009). On the other side descriptive statistics and one way ANOVA was used to understand the influence between demographic factors and user engagement with e-WOM activities and recognized the respondents' behavior towards the frequency of posting online comments by the users (Brown, 2003). Respondents were requested to submit their assessments based on a five -point likert scale. All items were used to measure the level of agreement of respondents with statements, ranging from 1(strongly Disagree) to 5(Strongly Agree). The cronbach alpha value was found to be .812 confirming the reliability of the responses for the study.

Table 3 Interpretation: Most of the respondents were male, in the age group between 21-30 years, majority of them were intermediate and belonged to the private sector and had salaries ranging from Rs 10001-20000.

Table 3. Demographic profile of the respondents

Demographic Factors		Frequency	Percent
Age (in Years)	< 20 years	61	24.4
	21- 30 years	77	30.8
	31- 50 years	58	23.2
	> 50 years	54	21.6
Gender	Male	170	68.0
	Female	80	32.0
Education	High School	25	10.0
	Intermediate	92	36.8
	Graduation	76	30.4
	PG and Above	57	22.8
Occupation	Public Sector	15	6.0
	Private Sector	99	39.6
	Professional	73	29.2
	Business	45	18.0
	Student	18	7.2
Income (in Rs.)	<10000	53	21.2
	10001-20000	73	29.2
	20001-50000	45	18.0
	Above 50000	79	31.6
	Total	250	100.0

Table 4 Interpretation: Table 4 shows data regarding demographic factors and the respondents association with social media gives a clear picture that the respondents within the age group 21- 30 years have more engaged with social media. Respondents who had an intermediate qualification and who worked for the private sector were highly associated with social media from more than five years.

Table 5 Interpretation: Most of the respondents who were professional, in the age group of 31- 50 years and graduates had posted online comment only 2-4 times in a week. Respondents in the public sector were the least interested in posting online comments. And professionals and those employed in the private sector were the most active in sharing their view online about FMCG products.

Table 6 Interpretation: From Table 6 it is clear that most of the respondents who were working in the private sector and in the age group of 21-30 years and income level between Rs 10001-20000 were highly engaged in e-WOM activities. They used it for social purposes & increasing brand awareness among the people. They were also using the electronic publicity medium for marketing purpose and by doing so were promoting their products online and were reaching out to more customers to create awareness towards their brands. They also used this tool for social purposes to share their view about the products or services offered by the firms and used by them or the experience they had with the products. Most of the male candidates were using this technique for marketing purposes while female respondents were using them for sharing their opinions about the products.

$\mathbf{H}_{01:}$ There is no significant influence of the age of the respondents on their perception towards the social challenges created due to e-WOM.

Table 4. Respondents' association with social media

Respondents' Association with Social Media		<1 Year	2-3 Years	4-5 Years	>5 Years	Total
Age (in Years)	< 20 years	10	13	23	15	61
	21- 30 years	16	26	19	16	77
	31- 50 years	3	17	25	13	58
	> 50 years	3	21	10	20	54
	Total	32	77	77	64	250
Education	High School	2	6	13	4	25
	Intermediate	22	18	18	34	92
	Graduation	4	20	29	23	76
	PG and Above	4	33	17	3	57
	Total	32	77	77	64	250
Occupation	Public Sector	5	0	10	0	15
	Private Sector	8	33	19	39	99
	Professional	11	30	22	10	73
	Student	8	14	26	15	63
	Total	32	77	77	64	250

Table 5. Frequency of posting comments online

Frequency of Posting Comments Online		< 2 Times / Week	2-4 Times / Week	4-10 Times / Week	> 10 Times / Week	Total
Age (in years)	< 20 years	8	26	9	18	61
	21- 30 years	14	20	31	12	77
	31- 50 years	9	30	6	13	58
	> 50 years	6	23	17	8	54
	Total	37	99	63	51	250
Education	High School	1	4	9	11	25
	Intermediate	14	28	24	26	92
	Graduation	17	36	15	8	76
	PG and Above	5	31	15	6	57
	Total	37	99	63	51	250
Occupation	Public Sector	5	10	0	0	15
	Private Sector	7	37	33	22	99
	Professional	7	39	19	8	73
	Student	18	13	11	21	63
	Total	37	99	63	51	250

Table 6. Engagement of consumers towards e-WOM activities

Demographic Factors/ Engagement with e-WOM Activities		Social Purpose and Increasing Awareness among the People	Marketing and Utilize Option	Sharing Opinion And experiences	Fun and Entertainment
Age (in Years)	< 20 years	29	32	34	20
	21- 30 years	46	53	43	36
	31- 50 years	32	29	26	24
	> 50 years	20	29	30	29
Gender	Male	87	105	94	73
	Female	40	38	39	36
Education	High School	10	15	19	7
	Intermediate	42	57	53	38
	Graduation	49	39	27	41
	PG and Above	26	32	34	23
Occupation	Public Sector	7	10	6	5
	Private Sector	57	57	54	45
	Professional	29	50	37	38
	Student	34	26	36	21
Income level	<10000	32	29	27	25
	10001-20000	25	41	39	32
	20001-50000	24	22	32	14
	Above 50000	46	51	35	38

Table 7 Interpretation: When studied across the age it was found that the respondents did feel that a few companies used software that automatically posted comments to increase their sales which influenced the consumers' perception towards the social challenges created due to e- WOM. They also felt that age had an influence on the perception that the posted content had a memorable impact. But in all the other cases the null hypothesis was accepted indicating no significant association between age and the perception towards the social challenges due to e- WOM.

$H_{02:}$ There is no significant influence of the occupation of the respondents on their perception towards the social challenges created due to e- WOM.

Table 8 Interpretation: Table 8 shows that the occupation of the respondents had no influence on the perception that posting content had a memorable impact in the long term, on the perception that few companies were using software that automatically posted comments to increase sales and that false comments were posted by unethical persons on blogs and social media websites to promote products / services. In all the other cases the null hypothesis was rejected indicating a significant influence on the perception that rivals gave payments to individuals to promote unethical activity and use e-WOM wrongly, on believing on unsolicited emails without properly identifying their sources and on the perception that the issues that could not be solved online decreased satisfaction.

H_{03}**:** There is no influence of the frequency of posting comments online on the personal challenges created due to e -WOM.

Table 7. Influence of age of the respondents on their perception towards the social challenges

Social Factors		Sum of Squares	Mean Square	F	Sig.
Posted content has a memorable impact in the long term	Between Groups	7.641	2.547	1.459	.226
	Within Groups	429.35	1.745		
	Total	436.99			
Few companies use software that automatically posts comments to increase their sales	Between Groups	.399	.133	.088	.967
	Within Groups	373.425	1.518		
	Total	373.824			
False comments are posted by some unethical persons on blogs and social media websites to promote a product or service	Between Groups	17.455	5.818	4.043	.008
	Within Groups	354.021	1.439		
	Total	371.476			
Rivals give payments to individuals to promote unethical activity and use e-WOM wrongly	Between Groups	65.751	21.917	9.070	.000
	Within Groups	594.473	2.417		
	Total	660.224			
People easily believe on unsolicited emails without properly identifying their sources	Between Groups	82.364	27.455	10.222	.000
	Within Groups	660.712	2.686		
	Total	743.076			
Some issues that cannot be solved online decreases satisfaction.	Between Groups	94.991	31.664	12.485	.000
	Within Groups	623.893	2.536		
	Total	718.884			

Table 8. Influence of occupation of the respondents on their perception towards the social challenges

Social Factors		Sum of Squares	Mean Square	F	Sig.
Posted content has a memorable impact in the long term	Between Groups	15.663	3.916	2.277	.062
	Within Groups	421.333	1.720		
	Total	436.996			
Few companies use software that automatically posts comments to increase their sales	Between Groups	6.446	1.612	1.075	.370
	Within Groups	367.378	1.500		
	Total	373.824			
False comments are posted by some unethical persons on blogs and social media websites to promote a product or service	Between Groups	4.184	1.046	.698	.594
	Within Groups	367.292	1.499		
	Total	371.476			
Rivals give payments to individuals to promote unethical activity and use e-WOM wrongly	Between Groups	37.636	9.409	3.703	.006
	Within Groups	622.588	2.541		
	Total	660.224			
People easily believe on unsolicited emails without properly identifying their sources	Between Groups	29.615	7.404	2.542	.040
	Within Groups	713.461	2.912		
	Total	743.076			
Some issues that cannot be solved online decreases satisfaction	Between Groups	40.376	10.094	3.645	.007
	Within Groups	678.508	2.769		
	Total	718.884			

Table 9 Interpretation: From Table 9 it could be interpreted that the frequency of posting comments online had no significant influence on the difficulty of identifying online identities as they are changeable and the perception that bad reviews from unsatisfied visitors had a detrimental impact on the image/brand. In all the other cases there was a significant influence.

$H_{04:}$ There is no significant influence of the human appeal on the consumers' perception towards FMCG brands.

Table 10 Interpretation: The null hypothesis was rejected only in one of the cases indicating that there is significant influence of the negative comments about various FMCG products on the purchasing decisions of the respondents. In all the other cases the null hypothesis was accepted indicating no significant influence on the perception towards FMCG brands .The above shows that trust, comments posted by colleagues and other customers, comments and social relationships and customized offers had no influence on the purchasing decisions of the respondents .

H_{05}: There is no significant influence of the peer group created due to e –WOM on the consumers' perceptions towards FMCG products.

Table 11 Interpretation: The null hypothesis was accepted in three of the cases indicating that there is no significant influence of the perception that encouraging friends and relatives to share trustworthy information on SNS, e-WOM and lucrative marketing techniques being used by companies to

Table 9. Influence of the frequency of posting comment online on the personal challenges created due to e-WOM

		Sum of Squares	Mean Square	F	Sig.
It is difficult to identify the online identities as they are changeable	Between Groups	7.248	1.812	.595	.666
	Within Groups	745.652	3.043		
	Total	752.900			
Lack of transparency in information influences buying behavior	Between Groups	18.651	4.663	3.266	.012
	Within Groups	349.785	1.428		
	Total	368.436			
Information exchange through e-WOM has a positive impact on trust	Between Groups	25.006	6.252	3.583	.007
	Within Groups	427.494	1.745		
	Total	452.500			
Most reviews are anonymous and are difficult to reach out.	Between Groups	28.934	7.233	5.860	.000
	Within Groups	302.442	1.234		
	Total	331.376			
Bad reviews from unsatisfied visitors can have a detrimental impact on the image/brand.	Between Groups	6.545	1.636	1.144	.336
	Within Groups	350.479	1.431		
	Total	357.024			

Table 10. Influence of the human appeal on the consumers' perception towards FMCG brands

		Sum of Squares	Mean Square	F	Sig.
Trust on advice of other customers regarding use of FMCG products	Between Groups	4.830	1.207	.747	.561
	Within Groups	396.066	1.617		
	Total	400.896			
Posted comments of colleagues or other customers on SNS attracts me to purchase products	Between Groups	3.191	.798	.538	.708
	Within Groups	363.245	1.483		
	Total	366.436			
Mystery of the communicators and views of other users influence me to use specific FMCG products	Between Groups	9.912	2.478	1.943	.104
	Within Groups	312.488	1.275		
	Total	322.400			
Negative comments about various FMCG products influence purchasing decisions.	Between Groups	20.587	5.147	3.532	.008
	Within Groups	357.017	1.457		
	Total	377.604			
Consumers' comments and social relationships have affected me towards the consumption of FMCG products	Between Groups	4.446	1.111	.879	.477
	Within Groups	309.954	1.265		
	Total	314.400			
I was always attracted towards customized offers that is not accurate in many circumstances	Between Groups	10.845	2.711	2.166	.073
	Within Groups	306.659	1.252		
	Total	317.504			

Table 11. Influence of the peer group created due to e –WOM on the consumers' perceptions towards FMCG products

		Sum of Squares	Mean Square	F	Sig.
My peer group and their WOM influence me to purchase FMCG products.	Between Groups	14.504	4.835	2.945	.034
	Within Groups	403.896	1.642		
	Total	418.400			
I encourage my friends and relatives to share trust worthy information on SNS	Between Groups	5.153	1.718	.813	.488
	Within Groups	519.743	2.113		
	Total	524.896			
e-WOM and lucrative marketing techniques are used by companies to attract customers towards brands.	Between Groups	8.699	2.900	1.560	.200
	Within Groups	457.317	1.859		
	Total	466.016			
e-WOM is more credible, reliable and trustworthy if effectively used	Between Groups	5.193	1.731	.772	.511
	Within Groups	551.643	2.242		
	Total	556.836			
e-WOM has become a significant part of online consumers' interactions.	Between Groups	29.864	9.955	6.199	.000
	Within Groups	395.036	1.606		
	Total	424.900			
Most of my friends and relatives rely on e-WOM before buying FMCG products	Between Groups	37.156	12.385	7.609	.000
	Within Groups	400.444	1.628		
	Total	437.600			

attract customers and e-WOM being credible, reliable and trustworthy had any influence on the consumers' perception towards FMCG products. In all the other cases the null hypothesis was rejected indicating a significant influence.

H_{06}: There is no significant influence of the e -WOM related activities on consumers' engagement.

Table 12 Interpretation: The null hypothesis was accepted in all the cases indicating that the e-WOM related activities have no influence on consumer engagement.

H_{07}: There is no significant influence of the frequencies of posting comments online on the human appeal challenges created due to e- WOM.

Table 13 Interpretation: The null hypothesis was accepted in two of the cases indicating that there is no significant influence of the frequency of posting comments online on the perception that the mystery of the communicators and views of other users influence one to use specific FMCG products and on the perception that consumers' comments and social relationships affects one towards the consumption of FMCG products. In all the other cases the null hypothesis was rejected indicating a significant influence.

Table 12. Influence of e -WOM related activities on consumers' engagement

		Sum of Squares	Mean Square	F	Sig.
Social purpose & increasing awareness among people	Between Groups	5.567	1.392	1.006	.405
	Within Groups	339.109	1.384		
	Total	344.676			
Marketing & utilizing the options available	Between Groups	2.395	.599	1.371	.245
	Within Groups	107.049	.437		
	Total	109.444			
Sharing opinions & experiences	Between Groups	7.199	1.800	1.197	.313
	Within Groups	368.497	1.504		
	Total	375.696			
Fun and entertainment	Between Groups	3.241	.810	.543	.704
	Within Groups	365.623	1.492		
	Total	368.864			

Table 13. Influence of the frequencies of posting comments online on the human appeal challenges created due to e- WOM

		Sum of Squares	Mean Square	F	Sig.
Trust on advice of other customers regarding use of FMCG products	Between Groups	17.159	4.290	2.619	.036
	Within Groups	401.241	1.638		
	Total	418.400			
Posted comments of colleagues or other customers on SNS attracts me to purchase products	Between Groups	25.673	6.418	3.150	.015
	Within Groups	499.223	2.038		
	Total	524.896			
Mystery of the communicators and views of other users influence me to use specific FMCG products	Between Groups	3.177	.794	.420	.794
	Within Groups	462.839	1.889		
	Total	466.016			
Negative comments about various FMCG products influence purchasing decisions.	Between Groups	23.384	5.846	2.685	.032
	Within Groups	533.452	2.177		
	Total	556.836			
Consumers' comments and social relationships have affected me towards the consumption of FMCG products	Between Groups	9.168	2.292	1.351	.252
	Within Groups	415.732	1.697		
	Total	424.900			
I was always attracted towards customized offers that is not accurate in many circumstances	Between Groups	31.403	7.851	4.735	.001
	Within Groups	406.197	1.658		
	Total	437.600			

FINDINGS AND CONCLUSION

It is assumed that E-WOM changes the overall business circumstances and shifts the power from business to the consumers. It has provided opportunities to consumers to share information in real time with others. The result of the study explored that there was a positive relationship between demographic factors and their association with social and other online media. It was found that most of the customers were influenced by seeing the online comment posted by other people. It could be articulated that e-WOM communication has become a main part of online consumers' interactions and most of customers rely on e-WOM before deciding whether to buy a product/service of FMCG brands (Linda and et.al. 2014). Sometimes it could create challenges for the FMCG organizations because negative comments about products and services could manipulate clients' purchasing decisions as well as brand image of the firms is also affected by it.

FMCG Organizations were failing to identify the online identities which are simply changeable. Some business entities were misusing electronic media and giving payments to individuals to promote such kinds of activity on the internet and social media. These kinds of issues were creating challenges for the FMCG enterprises. Few companies also used technology and software that can automatically post comments to increase their sales and to generate positive image of products in customer mind for long time perspective. This created a lot of issues for the FMCG brands. It can be said that e-WOM positively influences the purchasing decision of the buyer when it is properly used. However, when the e-WOM facilities used in a wrong manner would create negative image of the product/brand in the minds of the customers and their confidence level was also decreasing towards purchasing of the products. Hence, it could be concluded that social, psychological, personal and human appeal factors were important constraints and FMCG companies should consider them during making their business policies to effectively use of e-WOM in product promotion.

The professionals and employees in the private sector had a maximum association with the social media. They have been posting comments online. The people in the government sector were the ones who were the ones who were the least aware and interested in posting comments. The e-WOM activities have been used for many reasons like socializing and increasing awareness among the people for marketing and utilizing the options available for sharing opinion and experiences and lastly for fun and entertainment .

Many of the respondents were of the opinion that e-WOM was being used for various marketing activities and many companies used automated software to post positive comments and increase their sale as these posted comments had influenced consumer perception. They felt that e-WOM had created various social challenges and also had a memorable impact. But the age of the respondents did not have an influence on the perception that rivals gave payments to individuals to promote unethical activities and use e-WOM wrongly, on the belief that people believed on unsolicited e-mails without properly identifying their sources and that some issues could not be solved on line and thereby decreased satisfaction. But the occupation of the respondents influenced the perception that rivals gave payments to individuals to promote unethical activities and used e-WOM wrongly and also the fact that people believed on unsolicited e-mails without properly identifying their sources.

The frequency of posting comments online did not influence the difficulty of identifying the identities online as they were changeable and the fact that bad reviews from unsatisfied visitors had a detrimental impact on the overall image of the product / brand. But the frequency of posting comments influenced the perception towards the lack of transparency, the perception towards the positive impact that information exchange through e-WOM had on trust and that most of the reviews was anonymous and was difficult to reach out. So online posting of comments influenced some aspects of personal challenges.

Human appeal like trust on advice of the customers regarding the use of FMCG products, posting comments of colleagues or other customers on SNS, consumer comments and social relationships and inaccurate customized offers have had no influence on the perception towards the consumption of FMCG brands .

Peer groups created by e-WOM also influences consumer perception towards FMCG products in different ways and aspects. There is a contrasting perception regarding the influence of e-WOM on consumer purchasing decisions. Some accept that e-WOM is a significant part of online consumers' interactions and agree that friends and relatives rely on e-WOM before buying FMCG products. But there are also certain e-WOM perceptions which are not influenced by the peer groups created. E-WOM also does not influence consumers' engagement in any way which implies that consumer engagement is completely free from e-WOM thereby engaging freely without any influence.

RECOMMENDATIONS AND FUTURE DIRECTIONS

- FMCG companies should take the help of professionals in monitoring and tracking online reviews of customers on the basis of the collected data so that corrective actions could be taken appropriately.
- Enterprise should try to solve customer queries related to the products and services at the earliest so that they will not post negative comments online.
- Other ways such as encouraging them by rewarding for the right comments about the products and giving response on time to consumers' and handling feedback might help firms to overcome negative impact of e-WOM (Thompson, 2005).
- FMCG brands should offer platforms to users so that they can share their views about products so that it could be beneficial for organizations to sense the consumer perception.
- FMCG organizations should try to increase transparency in their business operations as well as provide feedback to their clients on the company website so that they could be motivated to share their ideas and views about products on the company website.
- By identifying the online identities of users which were simply changeable it could be beneficial for the companies to better understand the needs and fulfill them in a proper manner.

This study would be helpful for all types of people such as entrepreneurs, research scholars and students etc. to understand the concept of e-WOM. By doing this, FMCG companies could survive for a long term and attract the customers towards the products. By properly using e-WOM techniques, organizations would be able to increase confidence of their customers in the services / products offered by them as well as motivate them to share positive comments towards the brands. Future research could be to consider the impact of other demographic variables on economic, legal, moral and ethical issues related to e-WOM.

Research Limitations

While gathering information, analyzing and representing them some limitations did exist. Majority of the data was collected from the customers who knew their views about FMCG companies. The study was not focused on the other sectors and their problems. Impact of privacy policies, security, privacy and public concerns played an important role but could not be considered into the study. Secondary data was not easily available and this created a lot of problems. Money and time were the other barriers of the research that emerged as impediments to the study. In future, researches could be conducted by considering other factors also such as developing transparent system to monitor online views of the users, rewarding increased customers motivation and link of CRM, mobile and new technology with e-WOM to improve the performance of the present system and better communicate with the consumers.

REFERENCES

Alllsop, T., Bassett, R. and Hoskins, A., (2007). Word -of - mouth Research: Principles and Applications. *Journals of Advertising Research.*

Bettina, L., & Simon, K. (2013). *DigitalesEmpfehlungsmarketing: Konzeption, Theorien und DeterminantenzurGlaubwürdigkeit des Electronic Word-of-Mouth (EWOM).* Springer-Verlag.

Brown. (2003). *Proceedings of the 2nd European Conference on Research Methodology for Business and Management Studies.* Academic Conferences Limited.

Casalo, V. A. (2008). *The role of satisfaction and website usability in developing customer loyalty and positive word-of-mouth in the e-banking services.* Spain: Emerald Group Publishing Limited.

Chu, S. A. (2011).Determinants of consumer engagement in electronicword-of-mouth (eWOM) in social networking sites. International Journal of Advertising, 47–75.

Daniel, P. S., & Aroma, G. S. (2011). *Research Methodology.* Gyan Publishing House.

Fowler, G. (2009). Survey Research Methods. *Sage (Atlanta, Ga.).*

Gabriella, B. (2006). *Imagery and Spatial Cognition: Methods, models and cognitive assessment.* John Benjamins Publishing.

Gaitan, A. C. (2013). *Social identity, electronic word-of-mouth and referrals in social network services.* Spain: Emerald Group Publishing Limited.

Goddarad, W., & Melville, S. (2004). *Research Methodology: An Introduction.* Juta and Company Ltd.

Hung, H. A., (2007). The Influence of Ewom on Virtual consumer communities:Social capital,Conusmer Learning and Behavioral outcomes. *Journal of Advertising Research.*

Hussain, P. T. (2011). *Research Methodology in physical education.* Pinnacle Technology.

Hwang, S.J., (2009). How Consumers Evaluate eWOM (Electronic Word-of-Mouth) Messages. *Cyber-Psychology & Behavior*, 193-197.

Javornik, A.A., (2012). Behavioral perspectives of customer engagement: An exploratory study of customer engagement with three Swiss FMCG brands. *Journal of Database Marketing & Customer Strategy Management*, 300–310.

Kavita. (2012). A Comparative Study of Growth, Challenges and Opportunities in FMCG of Rural Market. *Interscience Management Review, 2*(3).

Kuada, J. (2012). *Research Methodology: A Project Guide for University Students*. Samfundslitteratur.

Lee, M., Rodgers, S. & Miyoung, K. (2009). Effects of Valence and Extremity of eWOM on Attitude toward the Brand and Website. *Journal of Current Issues & Research in Advertising, 31*(2).

Linda et.al. (2014). Exploring the impact of customer feedback on the well-being of service entities: A TSR perspective. *Journal of Service Management*, *25*(4), 531 - 555.

Marie, C. & Lindsey, I. C. (2014). Sustainable, hedonic and efficient: Interaction effects between product properties and consumer reviews on post-experience responses. *European Journal of Marketing*, *48*(7/8), 1375 - 1394.

Marketing Chart. (2014). *Satisfaction with Word mouth and social media tactics*. Retrieved from http://www.marketingcharts.com/online/marketers-most-effective-word-of-mouth-tactics-42250/attachment/wommaama-satisfaction-w-o-m-social-tactics-apr2014/

Meiners, N. H., Schwarting, U., & Seeberger, B. (2010). The Renaissance of Word-of-Mouth Marketing: A 'New' Standard in Twenty-First Century Marketing Management?! *International Journal of Economic Sciences and Applied Research*, *3*(2), 79.

Panneerselvam, R. (2004). *Research methodology*. PHI Learning Pvt. Ltd.

Park, D. H., & Lee, J. (2008). eWOM overload and its effect on consumer behavioral intention depending on consumer involvement. *Electronic Commerce Research and Applications*, *7*(4), 386–398. doi:10.1016/j.elerap.2007.11.004

Parka, C.L., (2009). *Information direction, website reputation and eWOM effect: A moderating role of product type*. Elsevier.

Ronvran. (2013). *EWOM marketing*. Retrieved from http://www.marketingfacts.nl/berichten/de-6-nieuwste-wetten-van-word-of-mouth-marketing

Seong, N.Y, (2008). *The Effects of Electronic Word-of-mouth Systems (EWOMS) on the Acceptance of Recommendation*. The University of Nebraska - Lincoln.

Sven, T., (2010). Frequent (flier) frustration and the dark side of word-of-web: exploring online dysfunctional behavior in online feedback forums. *Journal of Services Marketing*, *24*(6), 446 – 457.

Taylorand et al. (2011). Research Methodology: A Guide To For Researchers. In *Management and Social Sciences*. PHI Learning Pvt. Ltd.

Thomas, W.G. (2006). eWOM: *The impact of customer-to-customer online know-how exchange on customer value and loyalty*. Elsevier.

Thomopsan. (2005). eWOM: The impact of customer-to-customer online know-how exchange on customer value and loyalty. *Journal of Business Research*, *59*(4), 459-466.

Thor, S., (n.d.). *Electronic Word-of-Mouth: Increasing the Velocity and Reach of Traditional Word-of-Mouth*. George Fox University.

Wu, P. C. S., & Wang, Y.-C. (2011). The influences of electronic word-of-mouth message appeal and message source credibility on brand attitude. *Asia Pacific Journal of Marketing and Logistics*, *23*(4), 448–472. doi:10.1108/13555851111165020

Yildirim, D. (2011). *The Effect of Social Capital and Outcome Expectations on Product recommendations in Social Networks: An Empirical Comparison of Facebook*. Academic Press.

Yoon, N. S. (2008). *The Effects of Electronic Word-Of-Mouth Systems (Ewoms) on the Acceptance of Recommendation*. UMI Microcrome, ProQuest LLC.

KEY TERMS AND DEFINITIONS

Consumer Engagement: Consumer engagement is the engagement of customers / consumers with one another, with a brand or a company. The initiative could be either consumer- or company-led and the medium of engagement could be online or offline.

Consumer Perception: Consumer perception is a concept that encompasses customer's impression, awareness and/or consciousness about a company or its offerings. Customer perception is typically affected by advertising, reviews, public relations, and social media.

E-WOM: Electronic word of mouth (e-WOM) refers to statements that consumers share via the Internet (e.g., web sites, social networks, instant messages, etc.) about an event, product, service, brand or a company. When the underlying message spreads from user to user and presumably resonates as it appears to come from a trusted, third-party source, as opposed to the brand or the company itself. This form of marketing results in earned media rather than paid media.

Online Comments: Comments given by users of information and products online using various sources are called online comments. Today they are becoming significant influencers for online decision making.

Social Media: Social media could be defined as a group of internet-based applications that build on the ideological and technological foundations and that allow the creation and exchange of user-generated content. They are computer system mediated tools that allow people to create, share / exchange information, ideas, and pictures/videos in virtual communities and networks. They depend on mobile and web-based technologies to create highly interactive platforms through which individuals and communities share, co-create, discuss, and modify user-generated content.

Chapter 14

Is It Worth Sharing?

Evaluating the Role of Content and Emotions in Viral Marketing

Moumita Roy
IIM Calcutta, India

ABSTRACT

Social media has been found to have created a paradigm shift in the digital marketplace by giving a new technological face to marketing, highlighting on brand awareness and effectiveness. In this digital marketplace, emotions lead users to like or dislike, share or not to share messages, thus evoking, influencing and shifting public opinions on everything from political parties to corporate reputations, brands, products etc. It is important to understand how emotions and content relevance make these messages go viral. To explore this relationship, in-depth interviews with people of Generation Y were conducted, who were shown two videos that have gone viral. Findings focus on how the content of these videos and emotions generated will lead the respondents to share them online. Further this study helped design a Emo-Cog (emotion –cognition) induced decision tree model which the generation Y consumers might frequently be using to decide on whether to share the videos or not. The discussion unveils future avenues highlighting emotions in viral marketing.

INTRODUCTION

Long since the advent of Internet, it has been seen that an organization's environment consists of a plural network of stakeholders in which many-to many communication allows individuals to be either the sender or receiver of messages, while also modifying and elaborating information (Illia, 2002). This results in the formation of an interconnected network where a huge influx of messages, content and information in the form of texts, pictures, videos and audios get passed on from one stakeholder to the next with immense speed and reach. Messages, spread through the online social networks, become viral. A very prominent example of viral communication through the medium of viral messaging, would be the protest of 2011 in Egypt where online protests towards a strong feeling for an idea was converted into a mass movement, say the protesters and the analysts (Choudhary, Hendrix, Lee, Palsetia& Liao, 2012).

DOI: 10.4018/978-1-4666-9449-1.ch014

The speed of viral communication has its roots in the concept of WOM (word of mouth phenomenon) which was the only way to market one's goods before the advent of the printing press, broadcast media and the Internet. An analogy of cause and effect relationship can be drawn between viral marketing and WOM. Viral marketing, a term first introduced by Knight in 1996 (Phelps, 2004) is like a virus that spreads across the social media .It may be defined as the 'cause' because it might take the form of influencing marketing programs, community-building portals, viral videos and street-level guerilla campaigns thus building awareness and buzz. Whereas positive WOM might be the 'effect' because theoretically it leads to trial and acquisition (Ferguson, 2008). The publication of Fred Reichheld's, The Ultimate Question and one of the top viral promotional campaigns like Dove's 'Real Beauty Sketches' convince even the most stubborn marketers to pursue viral marketing, in other words to leverage the potential of a product to a greater extent than it would have reached otherwise. Thus conversations between stakeholders can now reach the global audience within seconds by communicating, sharing and forwarding messages through viral communication.

Although Viral marketing campaigns have attracted huge attention due to the fact that it can connect and reach people disregarding their geographical locations, but lack of success can be attributed to the fact that there is lack of understanding in what contributes to the success of viral marketing (Phelps, 2003), despite the fact that several efforts have been used to understand what leads to the sharing of videos online. Content sharing plays a very vital role here. Content sharing is the fastest growing activity among Facebook users, with 7 billion pieces of content shared each week (Unruly Media, 2012). This is in part the result of increasing growth and popularity of social media in the recent years, and in part due to the emergence of the 'Connection generation' who crave interaction and connection with vast networks like never before (Pintado, 2009).Thus online video sharing that has risen due to the video sharing giant 'YouTube', combined with improved sharing functionality across most social networking sites, has successfully cemented one of the most important roles in viral marketing (Cashmore, 2009; Eckler& Bolls, 2011). If a viral video campaign is executed properly with precision, a viral video campaign is said to offer the marketer many benefits that ranges from extended mass reach of the campaign, publicity of the brand as well as reduced advertising costs (Dobele, Lindgreen, Beverland, Vanhamme, Wijk, 2007; Eckler& Bolls, 2011). Thus there are some videos which are shared thousand times in a few hours while others may suffer a miss and what leads to this kind of content sharing, many a times remains unknown. This research tries to highlight on these aspects of content sharing in viral marketing.

Some authors have tried to explain that emotions play a role in making messages go viral (Dobele et al., 2007; Phelps., 2003).An investigation was done with viral campaigns which explained that it is the emotions experienced by the viewer (and the strength with which they are felt) and not creative elements that are used within the content, that triggers forwarding behavior (Dobele et al., 2007). There is an important part played by emotional resonance that users experience which might be a cause behind forwarding behavior, to be explained in the later part of the study

Previous studies have tried to integrate and generalize an understanding of what role these video messages intend to play in the mind of the users and how the consecutive forwarding behavior takes place; however this study tries to bring out a relation between the role of user's ability to relate to the video as well as share it based on the emotional reaction to it. An important aspect of this study is that, firstly it gives a better understanding of what leads to online content sharing. Secondly it tries to highlight on the relational importance between the role of emotional reaction (based on relevance to the user) and online content sharing in the domain of viral marketing. Thirdly it also proposes the Emotion-Cognition induced decision tree the users may use which acts as an aid to help them decide on what content should be shared unlike previous studies which tried to model out the spread of viral messages as a means to explain this phenomenon (Nelson-Field, Riebe & Newstead, 2013; Phelps., 2003).

The present study in this chapter tries to elaborate on the importance of emotions by reviewing literature on it. It also highlights on how content sharing and emotions play a role in viral marketing. Emotions play a very dominant role in marketing and this study starts by taking a glimpse on the marketing literature that focus on the usage of social media and viral videos that revolve around emotions. This study tries to analyze how emotions are felt and shared due to content (videos) viewing with the help of emotional contagion and its applicability in the sphere of social media and viral marketing. Then the methodology is discussed and findings are provided on the basis of in-depth interviews taken. In the discussion area, focus is given on managerial aspects with limitations of the study and avenues for future research at the end.

LITERATURE REVIEW

Emergence of Viral Marketing

Word of Mouth: Defined

For the past decade one of the most remarkable developments in marketing communication has been highlighted on the understanding of how internet is used in creating word of mouth phenomenon. Johan Arndt (1967), the pioneer word-of-mouth researcher offered the following definition: "Oral, person-to-person communication between a receiver and a communicator whom the receiver perceives as non-commercial, concerning a brand, product, or a service." Thus in marketing literature it has been found that WOM or word of mouth phenomenon has been employed to illustrate advice from other experienced people. It has been found that WOM has actively influenced human behavior pertaining to many conditions like attitudes, perceptions, awareness, expectations, behavioral intentions and behavior as a whole. It has been seen that the interactivity, lack of communication bias and speed characterize WOM, making it a very prominent and effective choice for consumers. Thus WOM has emerged to be a very dominant forum for consumer choices (East, Hammond & Wright, 2007). On the other hand there has been the emergence of the electronic word of mouth (eWOM) that has eased the process of customer to customer interaction thus replacing the traditional word of mouth with the digital network, creating a domain for communication online, called electronic word of mouth (Golan &Zaidner, 2008). Therefore eWOM has been defined as "any positive or negative statement made by potential, actual, or former customers about a product or company which is made available to multitude of the people and institutes via the Internet" (Hennig-Thurau, Gwinner, Walsh, Gremlar, 2004).

E-Wom and Its Relation to Viral Marketing

Very few studies have been done on eWOM; existing literature on eWOM has been found only in the domain of viral marketing which can be defined as customer communication, a means of multiplying a brands popularity by spreading the brand's name of a product or the name of company (Hennig-Thurau *et al.*, 2004) (Figure 1). But a lot of theoretical contributions have been seen in the context of online articulations made by customers who come online to interact in order to share their passions and interests as well (Granitz & Ward, 1996). Focusing on eWOM, Phelps, Lewis, Mobilio, Perry & Raman (2004), conducted an important early study where consumer responses and motivations are examined as to what causes to pass along emails. Through focus groups, a content analysis and intensive interviews, these researchers recommended that advertisers focus on "desires for fun, entertainment and social connections". Thus in the marketing sphere eWOM has been converted into viral marketing which posits a very important role when it comes to online videos as a critical function of the recipients forwarding behavior (Chiu, Hsieh, Kao & Lee, 2007). E marketers are constantly in a process to exploit this feature of social media marketing because the trends in viral marketing relies on the evolution of streaming video technology as well as the popularity of video-sharing websites such as YouTube and Google Video (Lian, S, 2011). Thus Figure 1 appropriately explains the transition of how word of mouth phenomenon and social media leads to viral marketing.

Use of Videos as Means of Viral Marketing

Online video viewing has consumed most of the time that people used to spend on watching television. Based on you tube statistics (Youtube, 2014), with over 100 hours of videos uploaded to YouTube every minute, more than 1 billion unique users visit YouTube each month and over 6 billion hours of video are watched each month on YouTube which is almost an hour for every person on earth. Thus online video viewing has been the most frequent activity for all Internet users. Due to this activity of Internet, users videos are becoming viral i.e. some videos are so good that the consumers are driven to share it, promote it, discuss it or hunt it down - all of which generates voluntary video viewings. Viral video as a tool has a great potential value to the marketers. Firstly, viewings of a video are effectively 'free' advertising. Other than that, online viewing gives opportunities for a deeper and better brand engagement. Viewers are watching out of their own free will which leads to further interaction playing and replaying the video, rating it, adding a comment and even forwarding it to another friend leading to a viral cycle. Marketers may also believe that their videos will be viewed favorably if they have been recommended

Figure 1.

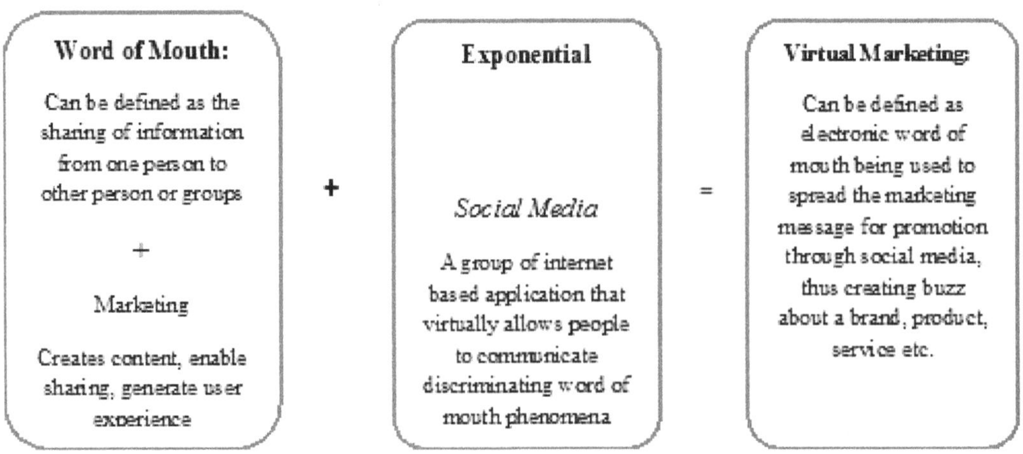

by a friend or online source (Southgate, Westoby, & Page, 2010). Despite the popularity of viral videos, there is little empirical research on the reasons as to why some videos become viral and spread across the Internet. Researchers have suggested various factors behind the videos which go viral, including the emotional connection between the viewer and the video (Phelps et al., 2004; Dobele et al., 2007).

Emotions in Viral Marketing

Definition and Nature of Emotions

According to Desmet (2003), it is important to understand that emotion should be firstly characterized and distinguished from the other states. Various states of affect are generalized as emotions in most of the studies. For e. g a feeling of sadness for not being able to reach a desired goal may be termed as a negative emotion while a feeling of joy for attaining it would be termed as positive emotion. Given this situation Desmet (2003) suggests that emotion be best treated as a "multifaceted phenomenon" consisting of: behavioral reactions, both expressive and physiological reactions topped by subjective feelings. An apt definition, that seems to best suit the needs of the existing study is the one that is offered by Bourne and Russo (1998, p. 364), who defined emotion as a "subjective internal state that has biological, cognitive and social components". In other words a sudden exposure to any stimulus would give rise to a state of positive or negative autonomic arousal, provoking a perception or a kind of cognitive analysis of the stimuli, which then provokes a physiological reaction that leads to a feeling best described as emotion. Usually these feelings are very strong and uncontrollable, triggered by outside events (Haksever, Render, Russell, &Murdick, 2000). Literatures on emotion have explained two different types of emotions, emotions explained on the basis of a continuum and emotions that are discrete in nature. The discrete approach states that emotions can be put into a number of distinct regions that represent basic emotions where each emotion is different from the other whereas emotions on a continuum can be defined as positive and negative emotions (Lawler &Thye, 1999).

Humans tend to perceive the nature of stimuli, in terms of emotions, as pleasant or unpleasant. Bradley and Lang (2007) advocate this view of the nature of human emotion as the 'dimensional theoretical perspective of emotion'. It is important to note that this theory of emotion draws a conceptual distinction among emotion, affective feelings (e.g., fear, guilt, happiness), and attitudes. While on one hand it is emotion which is goal- focused motivational in nature on the other hand affective feelings reflect a more exact cognition based emotion and attitudes tend to be relatively stable, affectively oriented with a more object-focused evaluation. In this study we are concerned about the emotion and affective feelings. Over the years many theories of emotion have been made which would also explain the nature of emotions. The theory developed by James- Lange views emotion as a feeling of physiological bodily change; the Cannon-Bard theory advocates that we perceive a stimulus and experience both emotion and physiological body changes at the same time, emotion is felt when we react to it; and there is more widely accepted Weiner's (1985) Two-factor Theory of Emotion. This theory proposes that emotional experience can be divided into two parts; namely, general arousal (physiological) and cognitive appraisal (psychological). While arousal refers to the energizing aspect of emotion, appraisal refers to the analyzing part of emotion. Further Zajonc (1980) adds that appraisal might precede arousal and vice- versa depending on the situations. (Martin, O'neill, Hubbard & Palmer, 2008). According to Russell's (1980) circumplex model of affect, the interrelationships between different emotions can be best described by a spatial model consisting of eight affective components that are organized in a circular arrangement of pleasure-displeasure (misery), arousal-sleepiness, excitement-depression and contentment- distress. Two of these pairs, pleasure-displeasure (misery) and arousal-sleepiness are the main bipolar dimensions. According to Russell, all words of affect can be defined as a combination of degree of pleasure and degree of arousal. Though it is debatable, as to what the dimensions of the circumplex of emotions should be, the majority of authors endorse a dimensional approach to the study of emotion as opposed to defining emotions as discrete feelings (Poels & Dewitte, 2006). Researchers have their agreements and disagreements on the basic characteristics of emotions, the terms emotion and affect would be used interchangeably in this study (Bagozzi, 1999), implying emotionality.

The Sharing of Emotions among and between People

Rimé, Philippot, Boca and Mesquita (1992) reviewed data in support of the anticipation that emotion would be socially shared, essentially relying upon a sort of a recall procedure. Respondents were instructed to recall and describe an emotional episode that elicited a specified basic emotion (e.g., joy, anger, fear...). Further they were asked questions about their sharing of this emotional episode: Did they talk about the particular episode with others? If yes then with whom? How long did they talk after the emotion and how frequently or often? (Rimé, Noël, &Philippot, 1991). From this piece of research it can be elaborated that the success behind the videos going viral depends primarily on the active participation of the consumers in forwarding messages to others, so campaigns focus more on the emotional impact of the message than the product itself (MindComet, 2006). A viral video could be built around a nondescript product which can go on to becoming popular because of a “wow factor” in the message (MindComet, 2006) Emotionality of the message is the driver or motivating force which leads to consumer participation thus forwarding behavior is often a consequence of the strong emotional appeals employed by the viral videos. Phelps et al. (2004) said that “messages that spark strong emotional feelings-humor, fear, sadness, or inspiration-are likely to be forwarded.” A message consisting of highly emotional message gets forwarded by people who were infrequent senders of pass-along e-mail. Similarly, Lindgreen and Vanhamme (2005) also argue that “emotions are key drivers of viral marketing campaigns”. They also admitted that surprise as an emotion plays a very important role when messages are forwarded leading to viral success. In this regard, Bradley and Lang (2007) explained that emotion and motivation may walk hand in hand when it comes to forwarding behavior online. Dobele et al. (2007) argued that it is emotions experienced by the viewer not creative elements used within the content that trigger forwarding behavior. Dobele et al. (2007) examined six primary emotions (surprise, fear, sadness, joy, disgust and anger), with sub-emotions used to capture the total strength with which primary emotions were felt. For example, discouraged, mad and enraged were the sub-emotions that were used to describe the total strength with which the primary emotion of anger was felt. Similarly, amazement and astonishment were classified as sub-emotions of surprise. They considered nine commercial viral campaigns, which varied in their use of delivery mechanism (i.e. eNewsletter, video, etc.). They concluded that an emotional response to the viral campaign alone was not sufficient to trigger sharing and that content that includes an element of surprise is the key to diffusion. It can be suggested that this can be generated through strongly felt feelings such as amazement and astonishment. Thus they concluded on the backdrop of social sharing of messages, most emotional experiences are shared shortly or instantaneously after they have occurred and that the extent of sharing with other people is directly related to the strength of the emotion felt. Though studies have suggested probable reasons leading to sharing, much still needs to be done.

Experience: A Summation of Positive and Negative Emotions

Humans tend to share experiences immediately or after days, months or years –following an emotional episode or event. Thus experience comes to us from the Latin term experientia, meaning 'knowledge gained by repeated trials'. Thus, experience could be called as something that comes out all by itself when one tries to do something for oneself. Experience is more about something that is direct and not imitated. Experiences can range from social to spiritual and from material to mental (Chakrabarti & Berthon, 2012, p. 157). In marketing literature, experience draws its significance from product experience (Hoch & Ha, 1986), shopping and service experience (Hui& Bateson, 1991), consumption experience (Holbrook & Hirschman, 1982) to brand experience (Brakus, Schmitt & Zarantonello, 2009). Evidence states that mentally or socially retrieving the memory of an emotional experience rekindles and reactivates response components of that experience, in the form of mental images, feelings, physiologic arousal and bodily sensations, (Rimé et al., 1991). Experiences are affected by both positive and negative emotions (Rimé, 2009). According to Carver & Scheier (1990), negative emotions occur when interference towards an activity is blocked. If the pursuit of a goal is paced down, or if it is blocked, this results in a negative emotional state (e.g., sadness, anger, fear, shame, etc).Negative emotions can lead to social interaction in many forms: social comparison, story- telling and narration, conversation and a search for any kind of emotional support through contact (Rimé, 2009). On the other hand positive emotions emerge when goal reaching activities are facilitated or they develop when the pursuit of a goal is paced up and is attained sooner than anticipated (Carver & Scheier, 1990,).

It is clear that negative emotional experiences result in social communication of those experiences despite the fact that talking about a negative episode would invoke an aversive experience. On the contrary the research explains that positive emotions are 'savored' and 'capitalized' upon (Langston, 1994), a good way to achieve this capitalization (letting others know of the event) is to talk about them, thus sharing experience and enhancing positive bonds. Thus it is predictable that positive and negative emotions apart from facilitating social interaction, work independently to deliver an emotional experience eliciting the "social sharing of such experience" (Rimé, 2009). Such social sharing of experience questions the nature of emotions involved in this process. Emotions majorly invested in the social sharing process relate its significance with social emotions (Parkinson, 1996).

Social Emotions: A Social Phenomenon Ruling the Social Media

Some emotions vary according to the social contexts, thus are different than the general or basic emotions. William and Happé (2010) in a study on autistic children found that these children were able to make responses to stimuli that elicited happiness or may be fear, however they couldn't do the same for emotions like guilt or shame or jealousy because the former emotions involved others. Thus to get a clarity on these themes of emotions, theorists and practitioners have conducted studies to differentiate social emotions from more 'basic' emotions (Hareli and Parkinson, 2008). Leary (2004) defines social emotions as emotions aroused by actual, imagined, anticipated, or recalled encounters with others, whereas Bennett and Mathews (2000) argue that social emotions are those emotions which are dependent on the perceptions of other's actual or imagined view of the self (Chakrabarti & Berthon, 2012).The social emotions share attributes with basic emotions (i.e. with happiness, anger, sadness etc.) in the sense that they elicit a more or lesser kind of automatic, hard-wired responses to contextual or situational input, but unlike basic emotions, the social emotions are able to coordinate and adjust people's responses so that they are able to fit in better into the social relations and groups in which they seem to exist. Since social emotions are experienced as a result of self- appraisal of situations and contexts with other people's thoughts and feelings, social emotions can be pride, envy, excitement etc. Social emotions can further be broken down into moral emotions like pride, guilt or contemplation and self-conscious emotions. According to Bagozzi (2006), to date social emotions have been playing a major role in the marketing. These emotions are different than goal directed or anticipatory emotions. Goal directed emotions are utilitarian in nature and expectation oriented as well. But on the other hand social emotions are more self-conscious in nature and are dependable on social relationships and different in content and function.

Social emotions have been found to function in a more complicated way because it assumes that there can be ontogeny or phylogeny developments later, also because of the cognitive dependence on high level functions like self-reflection i.e. reading of someone's mind (e.g. Bennett & Gillingham, 1991) or attribution (Graham & Weiner, 1986), while other approaches have been found to emerge from the combination of evolutionary forces and processes from where the social life of people emerges. For e.g., Parkinson, Fischer & Manstead (2005), have explained that social emotions serve functions affecting others reactions. Social emotions have been found to primarily relate to its most important function of influencing other people. But the most important question that rises here is, if all emotions are social in nature. For e.g. Storm and Storm (1987), in their taxonomic study of the vocabulary of emotions, found that only certain positive emotions are used in an interpersonal manner, but Parkinson (1996) on the other hand argued that all emotions are social. Therefore, due to such contradictory studies concerning emotions, there is much debate in this context as to which emotions are social, and if social emotions even exist.

Emotional Contagion or 'Caught between the Emotions'

If emotions are called a consequence of the social phenomenon then in that case social emotions arise out of social contact within the social contexts and situations. A very interesting concept that churns from here is emotional contagion. The emotional contagion phenomenon was originally defined by McDougall (1920) as "the principle of direct induction of emotion by way of the primitive sympathetic response" and more recently by Sullins (1991) as "the process by which individuals seem to catch the "mood" of those around them". The proposed underlying mechanism for the occurring of this mood is a continuous and automatic human tendency to analyze and synchronize voices, facial expressions, postural expression with others who are in their immediate environment (Hatfield, Cacioppo & Rapson 1993). According to their theory emotional contagion primarily constitutes of three stages namely mimicry, feedback, and contagion. Firstly people tend to automatically mimic the facial expressions, vocal expressions, postures, and instrumental behaviors of those who are around them. Secondly, to feel a paler reflection of other people's emotions as a result of such kind of feedback and thirdly it ends with people trying to catch other's emotions. It can be taken into an understanding that, when people automatically tend to mimic their companion's fleeting facial, vocal, and postural expressions of emotion; they often come to feel a pale reflection of their companion's actual emotions. Thus in every emotion taking place in every moment, people are able to feel the emotions undergone by others. They can track the intentions and feelings of other's emotions, even when they are not explicitly attending to this information. Thus emotional contagion is a process in which a person or group influences the emotions or behavior of another person or group through the conscious or unconscious induction of emotion states and behavioral attitudes (Schoenewolf, 1990).When people enter a group, they are exposed to the emotions of others in the groups, which can be characterized by the valence (positive or negative) of the emotion that are being displayed and the energy level with which the emotion is expressed. The choice of these two factors is based on the circumplex model of emotion (Russell, 1980). It has been seen that attention also has been seen to have influence on emotional contagion, which is the spread of mood and affect through populations by simple exposure (Hatfield et al, 1993). Researchers have shown that emotional contagion can lead emotions to spread through different kinds of social networks in various contexts, for e.g. between people who are in frequent close contact such as families (Larson et al, 1999), in the workplace interactions (e.g., Barsade, 2002), or in leadership contexts (e.g.). Emotional contagion may in turn have an influence on individual and group-level communication behavior in terms of information coordination and sharing (Barsade, 2002.,Sy, 2005). Thus emotional contagion has been explained to have relevant impact on sharing behavior among people with emotions working in the background. The present study tries to understand the importance of this sharing behavior in the context of online social media and how forwarding such content leads to the spread of the content making it viral.

Emotions in Social Media

Social Sharing of Experience Is Social Sharing of Emotions?

The concept of 'social sharing of emotions' holds relevance with the definition which says that it is "a phenomenon involving 1) the evocation of emotion in a socially shared language 2) at least at the symbolic level at some addressee" (Rimé, Noël, & Philippot, 1992) in a diary. People who experience everyday life emotions initiate communication process during which they share parts about their private experiences with social partners (i.e. friends, family etc) and only 10% of the private experiences are never socially shared (Rimé, Noël, & Philippot, 1992). It has also been seen that the more loud and disruptive an event is the faster is it shared. Social sharing is directly proportional to the intensity of the emotions. The social sharing process doesn't stop after the first sharing because another round of social sharing sparks off which again is dependent on the intensity of the emotion i.e. the louder or intense the emotion, more frequent and rapid the sharing is (Christophe &Rimé, 1997). Thus "the social sharing of emotion occurs in discourse, when individuals communicate openly with one or more persons about the circumstances of the emotion- eliciting event and about their own feelings and emotional reactions. In attenuated forms, it consists of latent or indirect communications in which the addressee is present only at a symbolic level, as is the case with letters or diaries." (Rimé, 2009).

While Chakrabarti and Berthon (2012) argued that social emotions are important in various exchanges on social media, they also argued that consumers have climbed up from the production of services to the production of experiences and online experience of value is an emotional one. Today, the consumption of viral videos in the social media is perceived and accepted as something that should lead to consumption of experiences. Nelson et al. (2013) posited that 'arousal', an established construct of emotion, might be the key to driving viral diffusion. For e.g. while anger and despair are both negative emotions, the degree of sensory alertness (or arousal) that seem to be associated with them differs (e.g. feeling anger may lead to an increased heart rate, while despair may not). They suggested that high arousal content will be linked positively to virality, while low arousal content will be linked negatively to virality. They found that content with more arousal (be it positive or negative) was shared more than those that had less arousal, and that articles that were of a positive nature were shared more than negative ones. Here still very little is known about the characteristics of successful viral video content, a deeper analysis into the kind of emotions that go into making a video content viral is important.

Dobele et al. (2007), selected nine viral marketing campaigns to study why people pass messages to others making it viral; in their study respondents had to reveal one or more of the six primary emotions that they experienced. They were asked to evaluate the level to which each of the six emotions was experienced and the emotions were a) joyful, delighted, and happy (emotion of joy); b) disgusted, distaste, and revolted (emotion of sadness); c) afraid, scared, and fearful (emotion of fear); and d) discouraged, mad, and enraged (emotion of anger); e) disgusted, distaste, and revolted (emotion of disgust) and f) emotion of surprise. Two themes were generated from the study; firstly it is important to capture the imagination of the study as well as to cleverly target them towards the right people who would react to it effectively. The main interpretation of this study was that messages are passed on to others because they connected to them emotionally which again states that messages should be emotionally viable. Here they argued that viral marketing messages should establish an emotional connection between the viewer and the campaign so that it is ensured that the message gets spread. According to them, it is because viral marketing campaigns can be equated with social sharing of emotions. This statement was not tested however; an empirical research in this domain is needed to gain a deeper understanding of the role of emotions in viral marketing.

Phelps et al. (2004) proposed that a typical viral message transmission process usually consists of four different stages: receiving the message, the decision of whether to open or not to open the message, the understanding of the message, and the decision of whether to forward or not to forward the message to others. This study illustrates the importance of selecting targets who will find the relevance in the advertiser's information and pass it along. This study highlighted on what emotions led Internet users to forward emails when they experienced the following emotions: 'happy', 'brightens', 'excited', 'connected', and 'inspired'. On the other hand, participants also experienced negative emotions when receiving 'pass-along' emails, like being 'irritated' or disgusted or 'disappointed', as well as 'thrash it now' kind of feeling. They therefore found that emotions did play an integral role in passing along emails to friends and family. But once again this model doesn't throw light on why videos go viral and what emotion causes this virality. Kibby (2005) suggests that the 'persuasive appeal of the sender' and an accompanying form of emotional response are two important factors that influence the forwarding of a viral message. Yet both Dobele et al. (2007) and Kibby (2005) agree on the fact that emotional connection is necessary to elicit a viable response. But the key drivers need to be investigated through more empirical researches. Norman and Russell (2006) investigated and empirically were able to determine that involvement with the survey topic, size of a participant's social connectivity and network, and tie strengths have a significant impact on what they called 'the pass-along effect'. But unfortunately they still couldn't establish the work of relevant mechanisms like tie strengths between the sender and the receiver. Harvey et al. (2011) studied the forwarding behavior with relevance to the peer to peer message propagation across social networks where 173 questionnaires were administered on a population of generation Y. He found out four predominant themes: sender involvement with the You Tube videos, tie strength, knowledge of You Tube videos online and amount of online communication across the tie. This study highlights on the positive relationship between the involvement ties of both the sender and the receiver, the strength of the tie, and a significant interaction effect on the impact of sender's involvement and likelihood of forwarding behavior. Though this study focused on relative variables like involvement and intimacy between sender and receiver, it did not highlight on the emotions and its connection in the context of viral marketing .Also the videos included in this study were concentrated on one particular emotion i.e. humor, other emotional appeals and their relevance with respect to forwarding behavior were not tested. Phelps et al. (2004) provided reasons as to why people did not feel it important or necessary to forward emails; it was evident that many participants in the study did mention the relevance of the content that they received. Participants also expressed their feelings by stating that they were 'uninterested' in the emails because they felt irritated perceiving or thinking that either the 'message is irrelevant' or sometimes it seemed that the 'content is offensive or shocking' (p. 339). Therefore, they not only gave emotional explanations as to why emails were not forwarded, they also commented on the content in the emails. There have been ample studies trying to explore the importance of concept of referral behavior and the emotional responses following therewith (for e.g. Dobele et al, 2007), and if it would make them forward a pass-along email (Phelps et al, 2004), but few have studied its impact on viral behavior, specifically why videos go viral.

The present chapter would focus on the role of emotions and content in viral marketing within the context of social media where videos are shared or forwarded by Internet users. This study highlights not only on the interplay between content relevance and emotion in viral videos but it also answers the question as to how relevant and what role does emotion play in determining why some videos go viral through sharing while others don't.

Research Questions (RQ)

RQ1(a): What kind of emotions are elicited that lead to sharing videos online (viral behavior)?
RQ1(b): What kind of content(specific, generic) loaded with positive affect leads to sharing videos online?
RQ2: Is viral behavior (sharing videos online) facilitated by both emotions and content?

Research Methodology

Sample: Generation Y Were the Respondents for the Study

To have a clear understanding of the aforementioned research questions, an exploratory study was conducted with 38 respondents in the form of in- depth, semi-structured interviews, until saturation was reached (Calder, 1977). The interviews ranged from 25-40 minutes with respondents who were the members of 'Generation Y', i.e. those born between 1978 and 1994 (Sheahan, 2005).Most of the respondents for the present study were college and university students and the rest were professionals working in different domains. Gen Y, also called the 'Internet generation', is considered an emerging market of potential customers with an incredible purchasing power (Sullivan, 2003). This group is raised in a consumption-oriented environment and it has more money available to them than any such young group in history (Morton, 2002). From 2005 onwards, this demographic has consistently been increasing their use of the Internet, while simultaneously decreasing their use of television and radio (Bridge Ratings, 2007). In addition, Gen Y is increasingly prone to 'multitasking' in terms of their media use as found in one of the studies which concluded that this generation is savvy in terms of both media and technology (Noble, Haytko & Phillips, 2009) A challenge crops up here in the form of capturing the attention of these consumers by contemporary approaches, as they spread their attention across multiple media at any given time; these consumers are also the major drivers and consumers of social media and viral messages (Berthon, Pitt & DesAutels, 2011).

Process: Semi-Structured Interviewed Suited Well for the Study

Hirsjärvi and Hurme (2006) found that the concept of semi-structured interview has been broadly recognized in research methodology literature, having many definitions. A semi-structured interview is something that is between an unstructured interview, where open-ended questions are asked, and a structured interview, where a set of predetermined questions are used. Hirsjärvi and Hurme (2006) explained that in a semi-structured interview, while the themes of discussion remain constant from one interview to the next, the questions tend to vary. There are possible reasons for selecting the interview method, two of which are particularly relevant for this study: first of all, the purpose of the study is to know the role of emotions and content sharing in viral marketing and secondly, insights regarding these themes will branch out from and to many different directions (Hirsjärvi et al. 2004).

The participants were shown both the videos discussed later and were then interviewed with reference to them. The interview guidelines followed an approach of asking open-ended questions to gain an in-depth understanding of the emotions generated by the videos they watched as well as the likelihood and reasons that they would or would not share these videos with others. The first interview was considered as the pilot interview to get an overview as to how the questions and what kind of questions should be asked to get a desired response. Questions asked to the respondents were like how did you find the video, what did you feel when you were watching the videos, would you like to watch these videos again, would you like to forward these videos etc. They were asked to elaborate on the reasons and factors as to why they think they should/shouldn't forward the videos to others. The participants were encouraged to talk freely and express their opinions and views with focus on the feeling part. The participant's initial reply and our probing for elaboration determined the direction of the interviews. Importance was given to the elaboration of emotional experiences followed by the probing after watching each of the two videos. These self-described emotions were carefully noted down in the form of transcripts. Lastly the participants were also probed to answer the question what kind of videos they like to watch and would like to share with others. Such a direct question not only stimulated a thoughtful response but it delivered answers which can serve as a key component to describe what emotions should be anchored within the viral marketing campaigns so that they become viral.

The Videos Chosen

Two videos were chosen from You Tube for the present study, to be shown to the respondents before starting the process of interview. Both the videos have been carefully selected. The rationale behind selecting these two videos are, firstly they have received high views (Table 1).

Secondly they have been talked about and discussed frequently in different websites and social media (Oh, Lim, Koh, Seo, & Suh, 2014; Kruitbosch & Nack, 2008).The most important reason that distinguishes these two videos from each other is the kind of content they have. While the first video (referred to as 'Star Wars' for ease of discussion) has specific content, the second video (referred to as 'Amaya peacefully sleeping' for ease of discussion) is more generic in content. Specific content could be defined here as the content which might be applicable to a specific group of the population. For e.g. videos that comment and depict movies or some political events should be more relevant to people who have watched the movie or are aware of the political event. The assumption with the specific content here is that the viewer should be having a background knowledge or past experience so that they can link or associate with the video. While the generic content is for all viewers with the assumption that

Table 1. Videos chosen; number of views as on 3rd October 2014 (when the data was taken)

Videos	Contain of Videos	url	Number of Views
Star Wars according to a 3 years old	Specific: should have some background knowledge about what star wars is	https://www.youtube.com/watch?v=EBM854BTGL0	22149816
My little girl Amaya peacefully sleeping...until her favorite song come on! Original	Generic: consist of baby singing and dancing to a song	https://www.youtube.com/watch?v=_Z_y3y5yqDQ	16656786

one can view, comment or like and associate even if they don't have any background knowledge about it. Several studies have suggested that either only positive affect or only negative affect can be used in researches investigating emotions (Sutton & Rafaeli, 1988., .Gountas & Ewing, 2003) According to Berger and Milkman (2010), 'while more positive *or* more negative content is more viral than content that does not evoke emotion, positive content is more viral than negative content'. In the video on Star Wars a three year old girl speaks on the characters and story-line of the movie, and 'this particular video was viewed by more than 5 million times after it was linked extensively across weblogs and social aggregation sites' (Kruitbosch & Nack, 2008). The other video shows footage of a baby who reacted to the song with Korean lyrics (Oppan Gangnam Style) by waking up from sleep and dancing with joy (Oh, Changhoon, et al. 2014). This video has featured on innumerable websites and blogs. Thus to conduct a more detailed investigation on the relationship between content and emotions in understanding virality of videos, videos were selected based on content specificity and positive affect. Henceforth finding highlighted on the role of different emotions felt by the respondents and the subsequent sharing of these videos i.e. analyzing the viral behavior pushed forward by these emotions. Care was taken while selecting the candidate's previous exposure to these videos i.e. those participants who had already seen these videos were eliminated from the study.

DATA ANALYSIS

Based on the literature review it was necessary to first understand the types of emotions that drive a video viral (which also answers RQ1(a)). To do so, three studies have been considered. These studies have been selected keeping in mind the number of Google citations, huge amount of data sets as well as the congruency in research themes that have been analyzed. In the study by Dobele et al. (2007), 6 emotions have been identified by conducting a research on nine viral marketing campaigns namely surprise (Lindgreen & Vanhamme, 2005), joy, fear, sadness, disgust and anger (Oatley & Jenkins, 1996; Plutchik, 1980). Similarly another research study by Berger and Milkman (2010) analysed and coded 2566 articles and found out 7 emotions namely awe, anger, sadness, interest, practical utility, surprise and anxiety. Lastly Nelson-Field et al. (2013) carried out an extensive research on the emotions that are most likely to trigger video sharing. One of the largest studies of its kind, Nelson-Field analyzed two data sets consisting of 400 non-commercial and 400 commercial videos provided by Unruly. She used psychological determinants to identify 16 potential emotions that each video could elicit and double-coded each of the videos to ensure objectivity. The emotions are hilarity, exhilaration, inspiration, astonishment, amusement, calmness surprise, happiness, disgust, sadness, shock, anger, discomfort, boredom, irritation, frustration. Combining these three studies a total of 21 emotions have been identified which excludes the emotions that are common or have already been identified by one of the authors. To add to this body of literature while coding interviews, the author was able to find out four new emotions which are funny, annoy, confusion and excitement felt by respondents while watching a video before deciding on to share or not to share (explained in detail in the Findings section).

To analyze the responses of the participants, coding was done for all the transcripts with the help of two coders to assist in the process who were educated about the respective broad themes but were kept blind to the specific themes of the study. Coding helped to not just code interviews which were mainly in the form of words or texts; it also helped generate a list of common emotions, which makes this study quintessentially a different one. The coders were given the transcripts to read, capture and note the major emotions, repeated emotional words and sentences describing certain emotions, in the codebook. The interview transcripts were studied extensively to have an elaborated category of meanings that came up in the form of words and texts. The coders along with the author worked together throughout the coding process. The author worked alongside the coders so that the factors like fatigue and altering the meaning of coding categories etc are being checked. Differences in coding categories were discussed and sorted out. The interview transcripts were content coded and also a list of mostly or frequently occurring emotions were listed. As this process continued, labels for codes emerged that were reflective of more than one key thought. Codes which evolved from the study then were sorted into categories based on how different codes are related and linked. These emergent categories were used to format and group codes into an organized list, thus exemplars from the codes were developed, some were words while some came out to be texts. It was noted that if a particular word or text (mostly emotion related, thoughts etc.) was mentioned by 12 or more than 12 participants then that word or text made its place in the list. From the whole list of codes the most frequently occurring emotions were also noted down. In this way a final list of 11 emotions evolved from the present study. It has been mentioned earlier that 21 emotions were already mentioned by the three aforementioned studies (Dobele et al., 2007, Berger & Milkman., 2010, Nelson- Field et al., 2013); 7 emotions identified through this study belonged to the group of 21 which were already identified while four more emotions made it new to the list, making the total to 25 (21+4). The inter rater reliability was found to be high on all the dimensions ($\alpha > 0.70$ it means that though there were definite differences for e.g. between instances of the emotion of hilarity or something which is funny, raters coded them similarly i.e. had agreements, which also means people tend to be evoked with similar emotions). The identification of the emotions through the process of interviewing followed by coding helped not just to prepare a list of 25 (11) emotions that lead videos to become viral but it also helped to understand the relevance of content, the role of these emotions along with the content in understanding the online sharing behavior and lastly the impact of online sharing behavior within the context of viral marketing.

FINDINGS

Which Emotions Drive People to Share Online?

During the interviews, it was extremely necessary to understand participants' emotions around the video. It was also witnessed that even if participants had an emotional reaction to the videos, it did not make the participants feel or think that they should share the video to their friends and/or family. One of the most important hurdles here was to understand why in spite of the fact that the videos were being liked by the participants; it didn't lead them to share the videos or elicit the intent to forward these videos. Therefore, an understanding of the answers of these people was required when they were asked whether they would be forwarding the video to their friends, family, relatives etc. The first set of findings relates to the question posed to participants on how the respective videos made them feel. It has been found from the present study as well as from past three studies (as mentioned in the data analysis section) that 25 vital emotions are aroused that lead to the intent of forwarding videos to others and four new emotions evolved from the present study. Two positive namely funny and excitement and two negative namely annoy and confusion have come up. They have been discussed in brief below.

'Funny' videos have been studied with respect to viral behavior or what lead to sharing videos online (Shamma, Yew., Kennedy, & Churchill, 2011., Yew, Shamma, .& Churchill, 2011). In both the studies social sharing behavior have been analyzed in the context of sharing videos based on content, funny has been mentioned along with other emotions. 'Funny' as an emotion has never been explained as one of the key emotions that characterizes the sharing behavior but has been suggested as one of the characteristic of the videos leading to sharing behavior. Indeed funny videos have been shown to explain comedy (Yew et al, 2011) and humor (Bergh, Lee, Quilliam& Hove, 2011; Shifman et al, 2012) in forwarding videos leading to virality but not as a construct of emotion leading to virality. In the light of the present study, Funny can be defined as an emotion that is quirky in nature which leads to a light laugh, enjoyment and a feel -good feeling within a given context.

The emotion of 'annoy' has been explained as one of the emotions in a study by Izawa (2010) in the forwarding of videos online leading to virality. In some studies it has been used to imply negativity of a particular strategy like prankvertising in social media (Duffy, 2014) while in others it has been used to imply a phenomenon like 'earworm' (Singhal, 2011). But annoy as a construct of emotion having an impact on forwarding of videos has not been explained before. From the present context annoy can be defined as any emotion that is disturbing and irrelevant and random in nature within a given context.

Confusion has been associated with having no emotional effect (Bardzell, J,& Bardzell, S, & Pace, 2008). In one of the studies that spoke about the importance of emotions in sharing viral cosmetic videos, it was found that confusion was associated with being tricked to as well as it was latched on to the usage of words like controversy and opaque (Drozdz, & Kanerva, 2014). Thus this study doesn't adequately define confusion as a construct of emotion having impact on forwarding behavior, it mentions confusion along with other emotions like annoy or shock i.e. emotion with a negative valence. From the present context confusion can be defined as any emotion that elicits the feeling of having no clarity or not being able to decipher the meaning of something within a given context.

While Brown (2009) explains that excitement works hand in hand with surprise in making videos viral, excitement is what makes viral marketing thrive (Kaplan &Haenlein, 2011). Excitement has also been associated with energy of getting involved in watching the video (Stephens, 2007); it is mentioned as an emotion that most viral marketing campaigns target amongst the consumers. But excitement as a construct of emotion has not been examined and studied which leads to the forwarding of videos making it viral. From the present study excitement can be defined as any emotion that explains anticipation of enthusiasm added with eagerness. Four emotions as constructs were established adding to the 21 emotions. The emotions are surprise, fear, disgust, joy, sad, anger, interest, practical utility, awe, anxiety, hilarity, exhilaration, inspiration, astonishment, amusement, calmness, shock, discomfort, boredom, irritation, frustration, confusion, annoy, funny and excitement. These emotions were identified as primary factors that lead to the sharing of videos online making them viral, and this finding also answers RQ1 (a).

Positive Affect Laden Content Is a Driver of Viral Behavior

When the responses were analyzed against the content of the videos it was quite interesting to find out that increased positivity and a latch of association works as an adhesive leading to sharing the video. In star wars video, the respondents had a mixed reaction regarding age. While some called her conversation as 'blabbing', many appreciated the kind of smartness with which she sipped into the glass while conversing. The most frequent emotions attached with this video were confusion, funny and joy. 'Confusion' elicited as an emotion because most of the respondents couldn't associate with the movie as they didn't watch it. While some said 'I don't watch supernatural movie', some also said that 'It was difficult to understand the language, so I was pretty confused'. Some respondents also showed disgust as a prime emotion all throughout the video saying 'I didn't like the continuous probing being done to the child who seemed she was not very excited about the movie but was made to narrate it'. Some found it incredibly funny because they said 'I have watched star wars and I liked the kid's idea about the movie and its characters. The most fascinating part of this video was the fact that a 3 year old child was talking about a movie called Star Wars which made the respondents 'curious' and secondly the 'cute' facial expressions of her which made people continue to watch it even when many of the respondents didn't quite understand it or had an interest to listen to it. Here due to specific content there was a greater disparity between the responses for some who related to the video due to some reason or the other. While some were calling it 'entertaining', 'very enjoyable', 'loved it' etc others commented 'inappropriate', 'cannot understand her language but she is cute'; 'confusion' as an emotion was mentioned most often alongside the emotions of excitement, surprise, joy etc. While most of them felt the emotion of joy and happiness, others felt it to be 'unrelated' and simply 'dragged on'. Thus the content, being specific in nature seemed to draw towards it a very specific group of people who seemed to link with it.

The second video namely 'Amaya peacefully sleeping' is a video that was enjoyed by most of the participants. The most often used emotion was 'funny' followed by 'excitement'. In this video, emotions were expressed at a wider range with almost all of them as positive. Compared to Star Wars video this video gained more brownie points because it had a content that everyone could watch and understand, as well as it aroused high emotional reactions.

Texts stating words like 'I had a laughing riot', 'I felt very happy', 'It is so funny', and 'laughter was always predominating' (indicating emotions of happiness or joy) emerged as key concepts. Most of the connectivity was explained by the emotion 'funny'. The term 'feel' emerged as a strong theme as participants experienced strong emotions while watching this video. Some comments to illustrate this are 'I was flooded with emotions when watching the video' 'it did lift my mood indeed'. Most people loved the little girl who kept on laughing instead of the child dancing. Words like 'attractive', 'hilarious', 'awesome', 'thrilled' were found which were positive, on the other hand ' the song was not a decent one', 'this is careless parenthood and I don't like such parents', 'such a video is very annoying', ' why are they commercializing a baby' etc. seemed negative.

Thus content had an impact on people while watching the video which could be understood from comments like ' I too wanted to dance' or ' I felt so happy and glad' . This answers our RQ1(b).

Would You Like to Share These Videos? –Is Viral Behavior!!

For the first video named Star Wars, when people were asked if they would like to share the video online, a mixed reaction was obtained, though most would want it to share online, some also expressed their disinterest in doing so. When a rationale was applied to this behavior, it seemed that content and emotional connection added to the forwarding behavior. Since Star Wars was an example of specific content, people who found it either familiar, relating or relevant gave statements like 'I would forward it to my friends and relatives who love supernatural movies', 'I think the child is too cute and I would share it on Facebook so that people can enjoy it', 'I think this video is interesting and everyone should watch it '. The most prominent positive themes were cute, surprise and amusing. Responses indicating these sentiments include 'I would forward this to my sister—she would think it's cute', 'I would probably forward this—they would think it's funny and amusing', etc. Facebook was mentioned by most of the candidates as the easiest platform to connect. Negative emotions emerged from statements like, 'I felt it was annoying to make a small child talk about movies, 'I don't watch star watch or any such movie and I will not forward this video, 'I don't think my friends or relatives would be curious enough to watch this video because they probably don't watch Star Wars, 'It's nonsense and useless totally and I will not share it'. Prominent negative words like annoy, and irritating were found while speaking about sharing behaviour. Thus sharing the emotions totally based on content was not a priority in most of the cases, what came into focus was, if a video's content seemed to be emotionally connecting, it was shared or probably led to being shared, whereas if it failed to connect emotionally, it was less likely to be shared or not at all.

Similarly for the video, 'Amaya peacefully sleeping', emergent positive themes for sharing behaviour that cropped up were funny, hilarious, laugh and Facebook. The participants explained their sentiments by saying, 'This video is funny and seemed hilarious to me and I think others would laugh too, ' I would share this because it caused a laugh riot in me,' 'This video can make anyone happy, ' I think others would enjoy it because it was hilarious'. Facebook emerged once again as the easily accessible medium to share and let others know. Intention of sharing was mainly expressed by most respondents when they stated that they would forward this video to friends, relatives or others as it made them laugh/happy or made them feel disgusted/irritated and that their friends were likely to have the same reaction. The content here was generic, sending behaviour was more determined and inclined towards emotions (arousal and stimulating). Negative themes emerged from statements like, 'I didn't find it something that is funny or something that I should forward to others, 'It was shockingly foolish and mindless and I don't think my friends would like it', 'it's horrible and I cannot share this video online'.

Here two more themes also popped up in relation to the sharing videos online namely Facebook which was mentioned often, was considered by respondents as the most stable and easy mode to share online while videos with good editing, animation, colours and video quality also seemed important as the respondents would like to forward a good quality video with clear picture than a bad one.

Thus viral behaviour needs to be backed by content and emotions in order to be forwarded or shared online which also answers our RQ2.

DISCUSSION

The present study tried to focus and analyze the combined effect of content and emotions on the sharing behavior of people throughout the social media. Content is very important when a decision to forward is to be made. For specific content, this study brings into the context that a video would gain the potential to be forwarded to others when it is perceived as familiar, the sender is able to relate to the video as well as they think it to be relevant. These three relative terms when combined, lead to an emotional reaction i.e. the video gets shared. Here it can be seen that an emotional connectivity with the video becomes a mandate before it is forwarded or shared by the sender to the recipients.

While in case of generic videos it has been seen nothing is targeted in specific. If the video is eliciting an emotional reaction then it is forwarded while if it is eliciting no emotional reaction and/or mixed or confused emotional reaction then it loses on the potential required to forward it. Here two relative terms pop out in the context of emotional reaction, arousal (Nelson-Field et al, 2013; Berger & Milkman, 2012) and stimulation both of which are necessary for the video to be forwarded. The more intense are the emotions while watching the video, the faster it is forwarded, making it a viral message (Dobele et al., 2007)

From this study a very important phenomenon gets noticed i.e. emotional contagion which is one of the major factors working as a sub set of emotion in forwarding behavior. As Hatfield et al (1993) rightly points out that emotional contagion can be defined as the "tendency to automatically mimic and synchronize expressions, vocalizations, postures and movements with those of another person's and, consequently to converge emotionally" and this definition works exactly when a video is forwarded to other. While this definition points out a face to face interaction, the present study puts forth an argument stating that emotional contagion can occur through the spread of content across social media by the process of forwarding or sharing it. Thus emotional arousal arises by an emotion eliciting content leading to the sharing behavior, consequently it leads people to "converge emotionally" as defined by Hatfield et al (1993).

Another theme that came up was the intermingling collaboration of emotion and experience that also acts actively in forwarding behavior. In the present study while interviewing the respondents it was found that they wanted to magnify and elaborate their experiences while feeling the emotions. This is specific characteristic of positive affect inducing feelings and positive affect laden videos. There is also a want or an urge to make others feel the same emotions and go through the same feelings. This is an impact brought about by social emotions as spoken earlier, thus social emotions play a vital role in forwarding behavior.

The present study helped design a decision tree that describes the decision making process that the respondents might have gone through in the study. While Fader Hardie&Lee (2005) conclude that consumer's past experience is an important predictor of the consumer's future behaviour and intentions, a decision tree model can help in understanding and predicting why people in a certain group do what they do, take decisions and what criteria they use in this decision making process (Gladwin, 1989). Decision trees have been defined as a graph that uses a branching method to illustrate every possible outcome of a decision; they have also been found to deliver a higher degree of prediction in a wide variety of choice contexts (Gladwin, 1989).The decision tree prepared by the following study focuses on the importance of both emotion and cognition. On one hand respondents viral behavior is driven by emotions, decision to forward the video gets mapped cognitively, thus elicits an intent to forward the video or not. As mentioned earlier this decision tree too works as with emotional contagion during the interplay and consequent evoking of emotional responses while and after watching the video. (Figure 2)

Figure 2.

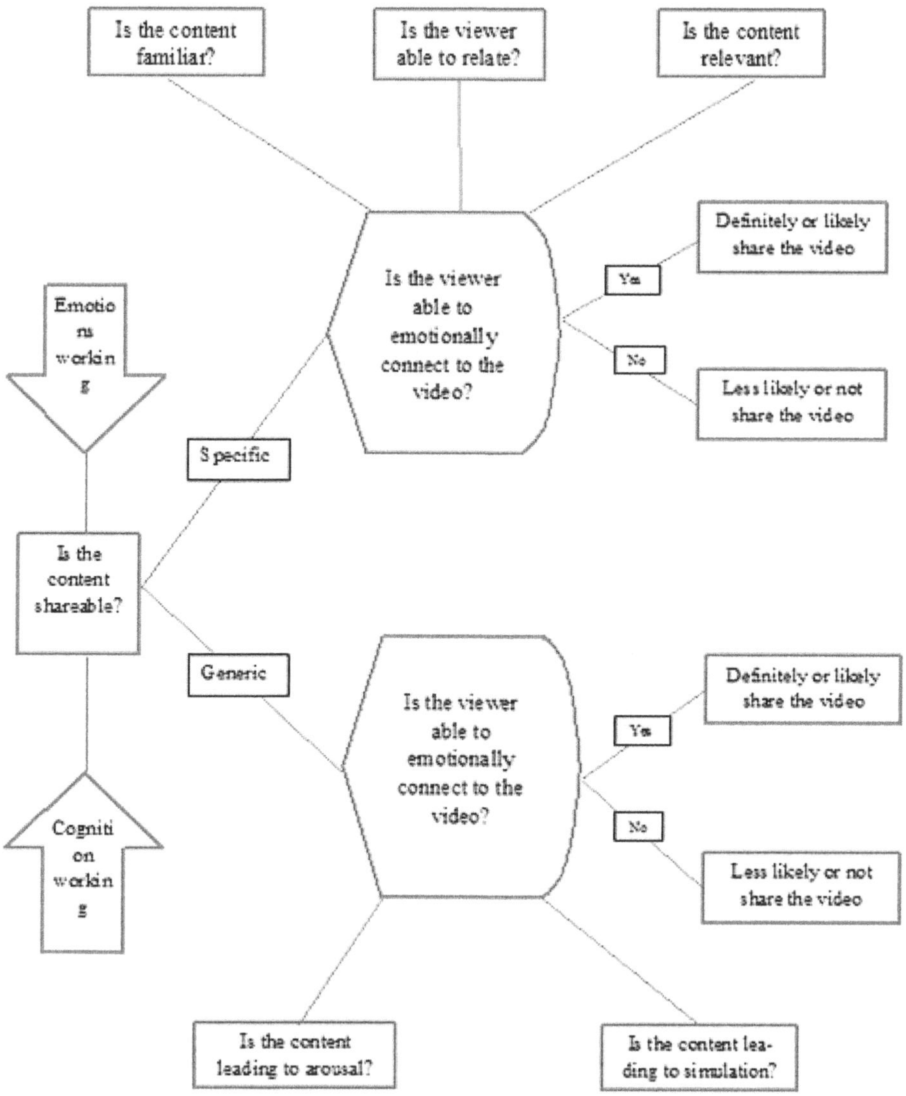

MANAGERIAL IMPLICATIONS

The present study purposefully tries to suggest that to make brands work effectively and efficiently it is necessary to create and prioritize shareable video content. While the statement seems easy the task is daunting too. Some of the considerations towards designing successful viral marketing campaigns based on current context can be the following:

1. Emotions are technically the most important facilitators, thus viral marketing campaigns should focus on a handful of emotions which arouse positive emotional reactions, keeping the videos simple but "stimulating" (as discussed before). This applies universally to all shareable content.
2. If it is being designed for a specific group of people or target segment like a particular age range, gender etc., then familiarity, easy to 'relate' and association should be important characteristics when the campaign designing is relatively at it planning stage.
3. One thing that has to be always remembered is that people, due to easy access to videos (all thanks to You Tube) tend to skip television advertisements which come randomly and watch them online. It is a serious aspect to consider because the viewers are intentionally and actively plugging on to them which again means they would view them with complete attention. Thus the campaign has to be minutely detailed, catchy and eliciting. It also means 'tell me or show me what you want to' which implies that marketers have to make use of this opportunity to create impression.
4. Audience or viewer engagement has to be taken care of. For e.g. emotions take some time to build in and then opinions are formed. So very small clips might create no emotional reaction while longer clips might help boredom creep in which means the video clip should be 'proactive' and 'do what it intends to do' from the beginning because sharing is an instant phenomenon and people don't think about it whole night and then share the next day or come back later to do it.
5. Positive affect laden content is shared more and tends to become viral as also argued by past studies on viral marketing.
6. Noncommercial videos are equally prone to become viral as commercial videos (Nelson- Field et al, 2013). So novelty, out of the box thinking and strong in emotional reaction should be the core of every viral marketing campaign to hold on to the level of attention of the viewer. The deeper the attention, the more intense are the emotions.
7. While emotions are the most sensitive counterpart of human psychology, they need to be tendered well because if a content appears to be a threat to the viewer's emotions, back lashing the video on social media can lead to serious injuries to the company.
8. Social media like Facebook can also be used to pilot study a newly designed marketing campaign video before releasing it on television or on You Tube or radio etc. to evaluate people's reaction, re-frame it and officially launch it.
9. Lastly social media thrives with Generation Y users. Thus it is essential to understand them and the trends they live with while making viral video campaigns.

These implications would be helpful for marketers (analysts) while creating viral video campaigns. It is essential to know that the brand building now depends immensely on viral marketing campaigns which are finding its place in every field, be it strategic planning or public policy domains.

LIMITATIONS

While interviews were the most important tool to analyze viral behavior, interview method also has certain limitations. These limitations are mentioned and include issues surrounding generalizability that it is difficult to reproduce and is subject to researcher bias (Malhotra, 2010). But the present study tried to gain a deeper understanding of what leads to viral behaviour rather than to generalize on the results.

Though concrete evidence still lacks in understanding what really drives viral behaviour this study takes into consideration the role of content and emotions in viral marketing as there might be other factors like personality, thought processes, perceptions, time constraints, liking, choices etc. to name a few. What and how exactly they think that drives them to forward and share content online still requires further research.

As mentioned by Dobele et al. (2007), culture is an important determinant in influencing forwarding behavior. Since this study takes place within the Indian context, ethnicity, values, customs and thought processes would definitely act as intervening variables when applied to other culture, thus further research can be carried out in this regard.

This study also doesn't take into consideration the role played by motivation and attitude as constructs because its main focus was to understand the role of emotion and content in viral behaviour. An extended research that is designed to incorporate both motivation and attitude in understanding the role of emotion and content should give a better understanding in getting a deeper analysis of the forwarding intentions in the viral behaviour.

AVENUES FOR FUTURE RESEARCH

As discussed earlier, studies on emotional contagion by Hatfield et al, (1993) and social emotions by Parkinson (1996) and Rimé` (2009) can be used as essential phenomenon while studying viral behavior and can be extended for further research.

While it has been seen that negative emotions like anger and anxiety do elicit positive responses (Milkman & Berger, 2012), it would not be justified to limit making of viral videos for positive emotional reactions only. Thus further research avenues should contribute to the understanding of these negative emotions and how to make use of these negative emotions that can lead to virality (for e.g. designing mixed emotion videos like starting with anger and crying and subsequently settling down with smiles and cheers and praises).

Lastly the "Emo-Cog (emotion- cognition) induced decision tree model" can be developed as a better equipped tool that would not only help marketers in doing perceptual mapping process to understand the perceptions of present and future consumers but it would also help them to enhance their marketing strategies. Thus future studies can use this tool as proposed by this study to develop a better understanding of how consumers are driven towards the viral behavior online.

CONCLUSION

The present chapter gives a detailed analysis of the role of emotion and content in viral marketing while trying to uncover the latent processes that lead to forwarding videos online. While many studies have been reviewed all throughout the chapter, focus has been mainly on generating clarity in understanding emotions, sharing and virality. The chapter helped generate two differently new things to broaden the understanding i.e. firstly, a list of common emotions that lead to viral behavior and secondly, the Emo-Cog induced decision tree model that would help graphically interpret how emotions and content influence individuals while forwarding videos online. An understanding of these two findings can lead to success in viral marketing campaigns.

REFERENCES

Arndt, J. (1967). Role of product-related conversations in the diffusion of a new product. *JMR, Journal of Marketing Research*, *4*(3), 291–295. doi:10.2307/3149462

Bagozzi, R. P. (2006). The role of social and self-conscious emotions in the regulation of business-to-business relationships in salesperson-customer interactions. *Journal of Business and Industrial Marketing*, *21*(7), 453–457. doi:10.1108/08858620610708948

Bardzell, J., Bardzell S., & Pace, T (2008). Emotion, Engagement and Internet Video. *Report: One to One Interactive*.

Barsade, S. G. (2002). The ripple effect: Emotional contagion and its influence on group behavior. *Administrative Science Quarterly*, *47*(4), 644–675. doi:10.2307/3094912

Bennett, M., & Gillingham, K. (1991). The role of self focused attention in children's attributions of social emotions to the self. *The Journal of Genetic Psychology*, *152*(3), 303–309. doi:10.1080/00221325.1991.9914688

Bennett, M., & Mathews, L. (2000). The role of second-order belief understanding in children's self-attribution of social emotions: A short note. *Social Development*, *9*, 126–130. doi:10.1111/1467-9507.t01-1-00115

Berger, J., & Milkman, K. (2010). Social transmission, emotion, and the virality of online content. *Wharton Research Paper*, 1-53.

Berger, J., & Milkman, K. (2012). What makes online content viral? *JMR, Journal of Marketing Research*, *49*(2), 192–205. doi:10.1509/jmr.10.0353

Bergh, B. V., Lee, M., Quilliam, E. T., & Hove, T. (2011). The multidimensional nature and brand impact of user-generated ad parodies in social media. *International Journal of Advertising*, *30*(1), 103–131. doi:10.2501/IJA-30-1-103-131

Berthon, P., Pitt, L., & DesAutels, P. (2011). Unveiling videos: Consumer-generated ads as qualitative inquiry. *Psychology and Marketing*, *28*(10), 1044–1060. doi:10.1002/mar.20427

Bourne, L. E., & Russo, N. F. (1998). *Psychology: Behavior in Context*. New York, NY: W.W. Norton and Co.

Bradley, M., & Lang, P. J. (2007). Emotion and Motivation in Handbook of Psychophisiology (3rd ed.). New York: Cambridge University Press.

Brakus, J., Schmitt, B., & Zarantonello, L. (2009). Brand experience: What is it? How is it measured? Does it affect loyalty? *Journal of Marketing*, *73*(3), 52–68. doi:10.1509/jmkg.73.3.52

Brown, M. (2009). Creative determinants of viral video viewing. *International Journal of Advertising*, *29*(3), 349–368.

Calder, B. J. (1977). Focus groups and the nature of qualitative research. *JMR, Journal of Marketing Research*, *14*(3), 353–364. doi:10.2307/3150774

Carver, C. S., & Scheier, M. F. (1990). Origins and functions of positive and negative affect:A control-process view. *Psychological Review*, *97*(1), 19–35. doi:10.1037/0033-295X.97.1.19

Cashmore, P. (2009). YouTube: Why Do We Watch? *CNN Tech*. Retrieved from http://www.cnn.com/2009/TECH/12/17/cashmore.youtube/index.html

Chakrabarti, R., & Berthon, P. (2012). Special Issue Paper: Gift giving and social emotions: experience as content. *Journal of Public Policy Affairs*, *12*(2), 154–161. doi:10.1002/pa.1417

Chiu, H.-C., Hsieh, Y.-C., Kao, Y.-H., & Lee, M. (2007). The determinants of email receivers' disseminating behaviors on the Internet. *Journal of Advertising Research*, *47*(4), 524–534. doi:10.2501/S0021849907070547

Choudhary, A., Hendrix, W., Lee, K., Palsetia, D., & Liao, W. (2012). Social media evolution of the Egyptian revolution. *Communications of the ACM*, *55*(5), 74–80. doi:10.1145/2160718.2160736

Christophe, V., & Rimé, B. (1997). Exposure to the social sharing of emotion: Emotional impact, listener responses and the secondary social sharing. *European Journal of Social Psychology*, *27*(1), 37–54. doi:10.1002/(SICI)1099-0992(199701)27:1<37::AID-EJSP806>3.0.CO;2-1

Desmet, P. (2005). Measuring emotion: Development and application of an instrument to measure emotional responses to products. In Funology (pp. 111-123). Springer Netherlands.

Dobele, A., Lindgreen, A., Beverland, M., Vanhamme, J., & Wijk, R. (2007). Why pass on viral messages? Because they connect emotionally. *Business Horizons*, *50*(4), 291–304. doi:10.1016/j.bushor.2007.01.004

Drozdz, C., & Kanerva, M. (2014). *The Importance of Emotions in the Dynamics of Sharing Viral Cosmetic Videos*. Retrieved from http://lup.lub.lu.se/student-papers/record/4499507/file/4499511.pdf

Duffy, S. (2014). *Prankvertising, a new strategy for Viral Marketing in movie industry–Thinkmodo as a case study*. Retrieved from http://www.brandba.se/blog/viral-marketing-prankvertising-movie

East, R., Hammond, K., & Wright, M. (2007). The relative incidence of positive and Negative word of mouth: A multi category study. *International Journal of Research in Marketing*, *24*(2), 175–184. doi:10.1016/j.ijresmar.2006.12.004

Eckler, P., & Bolls, P. (2011). Spreading the Virus: Emotional tone of viral advertising and its effect on forwarding intentions and attitudes. *Journal of Interactive Advertising*, *11*(2), 1–11. doi:10.1080/15252019.2011.10722180

Fader, P. S., Hardie, B. G. S., & Lee, K. L. (2005). RFM and CLV: Using iso-value curves for customer base analysis. *JMR, Journal of Marketing Research*, *62*(4), 415–430. doi:10.1509/jmkr.2005.42.4.415

Ferguson, R. (2008). Word of mouth and viral marketing: Taking the temperature of the hottest trends in marketing. *Journal of Consumer Marketing*, *25*(3), 179–182. doi:10.1108/07363760810870671

Gladwin, C. H. (Ed.). (1989). *Ethnographic decision tree modeling* (Vol. 19). Beverly Hills, CA: Sage Publication.

Golan, G. J., & Zaidner, L. (2008). Creative Strategies in Viral Advertising: An Application of Taylor's Six-Segment Message Strategy Wheel. *Journal of Computer-Mediated Communication*, *13*(4), 959–972. doi:10.1111/j.1083-6101.2008.00426.x

Gountas, S., & Ewing, M. (2003). The softer side of services: exploring the effect of sincerity and emotional contagion on satisfaction. *Conference Proceedings. Adelaide: ANZMAC '03'.*

Graham, S., & Weiner, B. (1986). From attribution theory to developmental psychology: A round-trip ticket? *Social Cognition*, *4*(2), 152–179. doi:10.1521/soco.1986.4.2.152

Granitz, N. A., & Ward, J. C. (1996). Virtual Community: A Socio-cognitive Analysis. *Advances in Consumer Research. Association for Consumer Research (U. S.)*, *23*, 161–166.

Haksever, C., Render, B., Russell, R. S., & Murdick, R. G. (2000). *Service Management and Operations* (2nd ed.). London: Prentice-Hall International.

Hareli, S., & Parkinson, B. (2008). What's social about social emotions? *Journal for the Theory of Social Behaviour*, *38*(2), 131–156. doi:10.1111/j.1468-5914.2008.00363.x

Harvey, C. G., Stewart, D. B., & Ewing, M. T. (2011). Forward or delete: What drives peer-to-peer message propagation across social networks? *Journal of Consumer Behaviour*, *10*(6), 365–372. doi:10.1002/cb.383

Hatfield, E., Cacioppo, J. L., & Rapson, R. L. (1993). Emotional contagion. *Current Directions in Psychological Science*, *2*(3), 96–99. doi:10.1111/1467-8721.ep10770953

Hennig-Thurau, T., Gwinner, K. P., Walsh, G., & Gremler, D. D. (2004). Electronic word-of-mouth via consumer-opinion platforms: What motivates consumers to articulate themselves on the Internet? *Journal of Interactive Marketing*, *18*(1), 38–52. doi:10.1002/dir.10073

Hennig-Thurau, T., & Walsh, G. (2004). Electronic word-of-mouth: Motives for and consequences of reading customer articulations on the Internet. *International Journal of Electronic Commerce*, *8*(2), 51–74.

Hirsjärvi, S., & Hurme, H. (2006). *Research Interview: The theme of the interview theory and practice.* Helsinki: Helsinki University Press.

Hirsjärvi, S., Remes, P., & Sajavaara, P. (2004). *Examine, and type*. Helsinki: Tammi.

Hoch, Y., & Ha, Y.-W. (1986). Consumer Learning: Advertising and the ambiguity of product experience. *The Journal of Consumer Research*, *13*(2), 221–233. doi:10.1086/209062

Holbrook, M. B., & Hirschman, E. C. (1982). The experiential aspects of consumption: Consumer fantasies, feelings, and fun. *The Journal of Consumer Research*, *9*(2), 132–140. doi:10.1086/208906

Hui, M. K., & Bateson John, E. G. (1991). Perceived Control and the Effects of Crowding and Consumer Choice on Service Experience. *The Journal of Consumer Research*, *18*(2), 174–184. doi:10.1086/209250

Illia, L. (2002). Passage to cyberactivism: How dynamics of activism change. *Journal of Public Affairs*, *3*(4), 326–337. doi:10.1002/pa.161

Izawa, M. (2010). What makes viral videos viral? Roles of emotion, impression, utility, and social ties in online sharing behavior. Baltimore, MD: The Johns Hopkins University. Retrieved from http://advanced.jhu.edu/media/files/communication/Izawa-Thesis-Final.pdf

Kaplan, A. M., & Haenlein, M. (2011). Two hearts in three-quarter time: How to waltz the social media/viral marketing dance. *Business Horizons*, *54*(3), 253–263. doi:10.1016/j.bushor.2011.01.006

Kibby, M. D. (2005). Email forwardables: Folklore in the age of the internet. *New Media & Society*, *7*(6), 770–790. doi:10.1177/1461444805058161

Kruitbosch, G., & Nack, F. (2008,). Broadcast yourself on YouTube: really? In *Proceedings of the 3rd ACM international workshop on Human-centered computing* (pp. 7-10). ACM. doi:10.1145/1462027.1462029

Langston, C. A. (1994). Capitalizing on and coping with daily-life events: Expressive responses to positive events. *Journal of Personality and Social Psychology*, *67*(6), 1112–1125. doi:10.1037/0022-3514.67.6.1112

Larson, R. W., & Almeida, D. M. (1999). Emotional transmission in the daily lives of families: A new paradigm for studying family process. *Journal of Marriage and the Family*, *61*(1), 1, 5–20. doi:10.2307/353879

Lawler, E. J., & Thye, S. R. (1999). Bringing emotions into social exchange theory. *Annual Review of Sociology*, *25*(1), 217–244. doi:10.1146/annurev.soc.25.1.217

Leary, M. R. (2004). Digging deeper: The fundamental nature of 'self-conscious' emotions. *Psychological Inquiry*, *15*, 129–131.

Lian, S. (2011). Innovative Internet video consuming based on media analysis techniques. *Electronic Commerce Research*, *11*(1), 75–89. doi:10.1007/s10660-010-9066-9

Lindgreen, A., & Vanhamme, J. (2005). Viral Marketing: The Use of Surprise. In I. Clarke & T. B. Flaherty (Eds.), *Advances in Electronic Marketing* (pp. 122–138). Hershey, PA: Idea Group Publishing. doi:10.4018/978-1-59140-321-0.ch007

Malhotra, N. K. (2010). Marketing Research: An Applied Orientation (6th ed.). Pearson.

Marsden, P. (1998). *Memetics and Social Contagion: Two Sides of the Same Coin? Journal of Memetics*. Evolutionary Models of Information Transmission.

Martin, D., O'neill, M., Hubbard, S., & Palmer, A. (2008). The role of emotion in explaining consumer satisfaction and future behavioural intention. *Journal of Services Marketing*, *22*(3), 224–236. doi:10.1108/08876040810871183

Media, U. (2012,). *Viral video charts*. Available: http://viralvideochart.unrulymedia.com

MindComet. (2006). *Viral Marketing: Understanding the Concepts and Benefits of Viral Marketing*. Retrieved from http://cmginteractive.com/uploads/viral_marketing.pdf

Morton, L.P. (2002, June). Targeting Generation Y. *Public Relations Quarterly,* 46–48.

Nelson-Field, K., Riebe, E., & Newstead, K. (2013). The emotions that drive viral video. *Australasian Marketing Journal, 21*(4), 205–211. doi:10.1016/j.ausmj.2013.07.003

Noble, S. M., Haytko, D. L., & Phillips, J. (2009). What drives college-age Generation Y consumers? *Journal of Business Research, 62*(6), 617–628. doi:10.1016/j.jbusres.2008.01.020

Norman, A. T., & Russell, C. A. (2006). The Pass-Along Effect: Investigating Word-of-Mouth Effects on Online Survey Procedures. *Journal of Computer-Mediated Communication, 11*(4), 1085–1103. doi:10.1111/j.1083-6101.2006.00309.x

Oatley, K., & Jenkins, J. M. (1996). *Understanding emotions*. Boston: Blackwell Publishers.

Oh, C., Lim, H., Koh, K., Seo, J., & Suh, B. (2014). *Oppan Internet Meme Style. 2014: A Case Study of Internet Memes through Digital Artifacts on Social Media.* Retrieved from http://www.kylekoh.com/s/2014Gangnam.pdf

Parkinson, B. (1996). Emotions are social. *British Journal of Psychology, 87*(4), 663–683. doi:10.1111/j.2044-8295.1996.tb02615.x PMID:8962482

Parkinson, B., Fischer, A. H., & Manstead, A. R. (2005). *Emotion in Social Relations: Cultural, Group, and Interpersonal Processes*. New York: Psychology Press.

Phelps, J. E. (2003). *Viral Marketing or Electronic Word-of-Mouth Advertising : Examining Consumer Responses and Motivations to Pass Along Email.* doi:10.1017/S0021849904040371

Phelps, J. E., Lewis, R., Mobilio, L., Perry, D., & Raman, N. (2004). Viral marketing or electronic word-of-mouth advertising: Examining consumer responses and motivations to pass along email. *Journal of Advertising Research, 44*(04), 333–348.

Pintado, I. (2009). *Connection Generation; How Connection Determines Our Place in Society and Business*. Charleston, SC: BookSurge Publishing.

Plutchik, R. (1980). *Emotion: A psychoevolutionarysynthesis* (2nd ed.). New York: Harper and Row.

Poels, K., & Siegfried, D. (2006). How to capture the heart? Reviewing 20 years of emotion measurement in advertising. *Journal of Advertising Resources, 46*(1).

Bridge Ratings. (2007). *A Bridge Ratings Analysis – The Digital Media Generation Gap*. Author.

Rimé, B. (2009). Emotion Elicits the Social Sharing of Emotion: Theory and Empirical Review. *Emotion Review, 1*(1), 60–85. doi:10.1177/1754073908097189

Rime, B., Mesquita, B., Philippot, P., & Boca, S. (1991). Beyond the emotional event: Six studies on the social sharing of emotion. *Cognition and Emotion, 5*(5-6), 435–465. doi:10.1080/02699939108411052

Rimé, B., Philippot, P., Boca, S., & Mesquita, B. (1992). Long-lasting cognitive and social consequences of emotion: Social sharing and rumination. *European Review of Social Psychology*, *3*(1), 225–258. doi:10.1080/14792779243000078

Russell, J. A. (1980). A circumplex model of affect. *Journal of Personality and Social Psychology*, *39*(6), 1161–1178. doi:10.1037/h0077714

Schoenewolf, G. (1990). Emotional contagion: Behavioral induction in individuals and groups. *Modern Psychoanalysis*, *15*, 49–61.

Shamma, D. A., Yew, J., Kennedy, L., & Churchill, E. F. (2011). Viral Actions: Predicting Video View Counts Using Synchronous Sharing Behaviors. In ICWSM. ICWSM.

Sheahan, P. (2005). *Generation Y: Surviving (and Thriving) with Generation Y at Work*. Victoria, Australia: Hardy Grant Publishing.

Shifman, L. (2012). An anatomy of a YouTube meme. *New Media & Society*, *14*(2), 187–203. doi:10.1177/1461444811412160

Singhal, D. (2011). *Why this Kolaveri Di: Maddening Phenomenon of Earworm*. Available at SSRN 1969781.

Southgate, D., Westoby, N., & Page, G. (2010). Creative determinants of viral video viewing. *International Journal of Advertising*, *29*(3), 349. doi:10.2501/S0265048710201221

Stephens, M. (2007). Chapter 5: Social Video: Videoblogging& YouTube. *Library Technology Reports*, *43*(5), 52–57.

Sullins, E. S. (1991). Emotional contagion revisited: Effects of social comparison and expressive style on mood convergence. *Personality and Social Psychology Bulletin*, *17*(2), 166–174. doi:10.1177/014616729101700208

Sullivan, D. P. (2003). *A Profile of Generation Y Online Shoppers and its Application to Marketing*. (Unpublished Doctoral Dissertation). Capella University, Ann Arbor, MI.

Sutton, R. I., & Rafaeli, A. (1988). Untangling the relationship between displayed emotions and organizational sales: The case of convenience stores. *Academy of Management Journal*, *31*(3), 461–487. doi:10.2307/256456

Sy, T., Côté, S., & Saavedra, R. (2005). The contagious leader: Impact of the leader's mood on group members, group affective tone, and group processes. *The Journal of Applied Psychology*, *90*(2), 295–305. doi:10.1037/0021-9010.90.2.295 PMID:15769239

YouTube. (2014). Retrieved from https://www.youtube.com/yt/press/statistics.html

Williams, D., & Happé, F. (2010). Representing intentions in self and other: Studies of autism and typical development. *Developmental Science*, *13*(2), 307–319. doi:10.1111/j.1467-7687.2009.00885.x PMID:20136927

Yew, J., Shamma, D. A., & Churchill, E. F. (2011). Knowing funny: genre perception and categorization in social video sharing. In *Proceedings of the SIGCHI Conference on Human Factors in Computing Systems* (pp. 297-306). doi:10.1145/1978942.1978984

Zajonc, R. B. (1980). Feeling and thinking: Preferences need no inferences. *The American Psychologist*, *35*(2), 151–175. doi:10.1037/0003-066X.35.2.151

KEY TERMS AND DEFINITIONS

Brand Awareness: Brand awareness is related to the functions of brand identities in consumers' memory and can be reflected by how well the consumers can identify the brand under various conditions.

Content and Emotions: In media production and publishing, content is information and experiences that provides value for an end-user or audience. Content can be delivered via many different media including the internet, television, and audio CDs, books, magazines, live events, such as conferences and stage performances.

Decision Tree Model: A decision tree is a flowchart-like structure in which each internal node represents a "test" on an attribute (e.g. whether a coin flip comes up heads or tails), each branch represents the outcome of the test and each leaf node represents a class rules. label (decision taken after computing all attributes). The paths from root to leaf represent classification.

Emotional Contagion: Emotional contagion is the tendency for two individuals to emotionally converge. It is the tendency to feel or express emotions similar to and influenced by those of others, also the phenomenon of one person's negative thoughts or anxiety affecting another's mood.

Emotions: Are a complex state of feeling that results in physical and psychological changes that influence our behavior. The physiology of emotion is closely linked to arousal of the nervous system with various states and strengths of arousal relating, apparently, to particular emotions. Emotion is also linked to behavioral tendency.

E-WOM: Social media marketing programs usually center on efforts to create content that attracts attention and encourages readers to share it across their social networks. The resulting electronic word of mouth (eWoM) refers to any statement consumers share via the Internet (e.g., web sites, social networks, instant messages, news feeds) about an event, product, service, brand or company.

Generation Y: Generally refers to the generation of people born between the early 1980s and the early 2000s, is also known as Generation Y, because it comes after Generation X — those people who are born between the early 1960s and the 1980s.

Positive and Negative Affect: Affect is the experience of feeling or emotion. Affect is a key part of the process of an organism's interaction with stimuli.

Social Emotions: Are emotions that require the representation of the mental states of other people. Examples are embarrassment, guilt, shame, jealousy, envy, empathy, and pride. In contrast, basic emotions such as happiness and sadness only require the awareness of one's own somatic state.

Social Media Marketing: It refers to a technique that takes advantage of social networking to help a company increase brand exposure and broaden customer reach. The goal is usually to create content compelling enough that user will share it with their social networks.

Social Media: A term that is used to refer to websites and applications that enable users to create and share content or to participate in social networking.

Viral Marketing: Viral marketing, viral advertising, or marketing buzz are buzzwords referring to marketing techniques that use pre-existing social networking services and other technologies to try to produce increases in brand awareness or to achieve other marketing objectives (such as product sales) through self-replicating viral processes, analogous to the spread of viruses.

Viral Messages: Refer to marketing messages that are passed from person to person through their social networks. Viral messages can defined as a Communication of information in media that can be easily forwarded such as Internet videos, text messages (SMS) can effectively augment word of mouth transmission of the information throughout social networks.

Viral Videos: Videos that have the ability to spark feelings –humour, happiness, fear etc thus trigger forwarding behavior.

Virality: A tendency of an image, video, or piece of information to be circulated rapidly and widely from one Internet user to another; the quality or fact of being viral.

Chapter 15
Impact of Online Reviews on Purchasing Decisions:
An Empirical Study among Indian Academicians

Dhiraj Jain
Symbiosis Centre for Management Studies, India

Lovish Bhansali
Pacific University, India

K. Sanal Nair
Pacific Institute of Management, India

ABSTRACT

Internet has enabled today's consumer to transform himself from passive to an active and an informed consumer who can share his experiences, opinions about product or services with an infinite number of consumers around the globe. These reviews or opinions are further used by potential buyers of that particular product or service via electronic Word of Mouth (e-WOM). The study on the impact of e-WOM on online sales has gradually emerged but a number of questions still remain unanswered. The aim of this study is to assess the impact of one type of e-WOM i.e., the online consumer reviews, on purchasing decisions of electronic products. This empirical study also focuses on the relationship between reviews and purchasing behaviour. An instrument was prepared to measure the proposed constructs, with questionnaire items taken from prior studies but adapted to fit the context of e-commerce. The survey was applied to academicians in India through internet. The results show that consumer reviews have a causal impact on consumer purchasing behaviour and they have an effect on choosing the products by consumer. Finally, the results and their implications are discussed.

DOI: 10.4018/978-1-4666-9449-1.ch015

INTRODUCTION

The primary source of information about any product is the internet. In this digitized world, most of the consumers have opted for it and it has drastically impacted their buying behaviour. With the introduction of the electronic platform like the internet, the information has not remained the puppet of the media of large conglomerate business houses. In the past the consumer was always less informed because of the limited source of information but because of digitization and online shopping the consumer has been able to transform himself from a passive consumer to an active and an informed consumer. Potential customers always tend to buy those products about which an existing data of its use, quality and other details are available from other consumers who have already bought and used the product. In traditional times people used to ask a person about a product and its reputation in the market and on that basis made their decisions of either buying the product or not. This was the first developed concept of the so called Traditional Word of Mouth. But today's world lives in the era of digitization where people neither have the time nor do they want to put in an effort to ask people the required information on their demand. In order to increase the sale of any product the sellers offering their products to be sold via internet have developed a free marketing tool and have given its control in the hand of the consumers. The word of mouth is not a modern concept as stated earlier. But in the age of digitization people have started to understand its meaning and importance and this concept being given a new name for and by generation X that is Electronic Word of Mouth (e-WOM). The e-wom is network user's information exchange and discussions on some products or services by the network media. In simple words e-wom could be defined as all kinds of informal communications present for the potential consumers by the previous consumers through Internet-based technology related to the usage of particular goods and services, or their sellers. Review of a product plays a vital role in the sale of a product. If a consumer finds that a product he is about to buy is as per the specification and his expectation, he gains confidence but if buys the opposite and finds a negative review he might not only lose the confidence in that product but also won't buy the product for himself and would also not let others buy it by using his word of mouth. Not surprisingly, several firms are becoming interested in leveraging this phenomenon, proactively and trying to induce consumers to "spread the word" about their products online (Godes, 2005). There is very little known data to know how certain types of e-WOM, such as numerical ratings or online text reviews, affect purchasing decisions, and by how much. The study adds to the knowledge pool of marketers by making them aware of the possible attitudes and behaviour of the consumer, which marketers can use to better segment and target them.

Review of Literature

(Yali, 2010) showed that consumer reviews had only a causal impact on consumer purchasing behaviour and they also had an effect on choosing the products by the consumer. Park (2009) showed that the type of reviews can be a key to explain the inconsistent relationship between consumer expertise and WOM in previous researches. They examined the type of reviews that cognitively fitted consumers with a high (low) level of expertise. Using the elaboration likelihood model (ELM), they also investigated the effects of the type of reviews and the number of reviews. They showed that the effect of cognitive fit (the type of reviews) on purchase intention was stronger for experts than for novices while the effect of the number of reviews on purchase intention was stronger for novices than experts. Park D. H.(2007) found that the quality of on-line reviews has a positive effect on consumers' purchasing intention, purchasing intention increased as the number of reviews increased and low-involvement consumers were affected by the quantity rather than the quality of reviews, but high-involvement consumers were affected by review quantity mainly when the review quality was high. Park D. H. (2009) found that online consumer reviews involving experiences, evaluations and opinions on products from previous consumers played two roles as an informant and as a recommender. These two roles affected a consumer's intention. However, there was a conflict between the two roles when large number of reviews were offered. From the perspective of the recommender role, consumers had a more favorable attitude towards a product as a greater number of positive reviews were offered while consumers were confronted with too much information, which resulted in information overload. Park C. a. (2009) showed that the e-WOM effect was greater for negative e-WOM than for positive e-WOM, greater for established websites than for un-established websites, and greater for experience goods than for search goods. Author's results supported the moderating effects of product type on the e-WOM information direction-website reputation-e-WOM effect relationship. The impact of negative e-WOM on the e-WOM effect was greater for experience goods than for search goods. Similarly, the impact of website reputation on the e-WOM effect was greater for experience goods than for search goods. Cheung (2008) found comprehensiveness and relevance to be the most effective components of the argument quality construct of the research model, making them key influencers of information adoption. They outlined ways to effectively promote one's business or cause through online customer communities, as well as general tips for web site and forum moderators for facilitating such presentation in a manner useful to the members of their online communities. Litvin(2008) described online interpersonal influence, or e-WOM, as a potentially cost-effective means for marketing hospitality and tourism, and discussed some of the nascent technological and ethical issues facing marketers as they sought to harness emerging e-WOM technologies. Interpersonal influence and word-of-mouth (WOM) were ranked the most important information source while a consumer was making a purchase decision. When WOM becomes digital, the large-scale, anonymous, ephemeral nature of the Internet induced new ways of capturing, analyzing, interpreting, and managing the influence that one consumer had on the other. Hennig-Thurau (2004) suggested that consumers' desire for social interaction, economic incentives, their concern for other consumers, and the potential to enhance their own self-worth were the primary factors leading to e-WOM behavior. Further, e-WOM providers could be grouped based on what motivated their behavior, suggesting that firms needed to develop different strategies for encouraging e-WOM behavior among their users. Jansen (2009) found that 19% of the micro-blogs mention the brand. Of the branding micro-blogs, nearly 20% contained some expression of brand sentiments. Of these, more than 50% were positive and 33% were critical of the company or product. They also found that micro-blogging was an online tool for customer word of mouth communications and discussed the implications for corporations using micro-blogging as a part of their overall marketing strategy. Doh(2009) explored how consumers evaluate electronic word-of-mouth (e-WOM) messages about products and showed significant differences across various sets of e-WOM messages. Although more positive sets showed higher scores in many cases, it was not true in all situations, especially for the case of credibility. Involvement and prior knowledge partially moderated the relationship between the ratio of messages and the e-WOM effect. The credibility of Web sites and e-WOM messages could be damaged in the long run if all the e-WOM messages were positive. Zhang (2010) showed that consumer-generated ratings about the quality of food, environment and service of restaurants, and the volume of online consumer reviews were positively associated with the online popularity of restaurants; whereas editor reviews had a negative relationship with consumers' intention to visit a restaurant's webpage. Goldsmith (2006) found that consumers sought the opinion of others online to reduce their risk as others did it to secure lower prices, to get information easily, by accident (unplanned), because it was cool, because they were stimulated by off-line inputs such as TV, and to get pre-purchase information. Their second study showed that: (1) the scales measuring these motivations were free from social desirability response bias and acquiescence, (2) other consumers' information was more important than advertising, and (3) consumers were likely to continue to seek WOM online, thereby confirming its importance in ecommerce. Lee (2009) examined the actions of a customer when inferring product information from e-WOM material at a website and developed a customer purchase intention model and simulated various e-WOM levels within this, adopting an objectivity–subjectivity dichotomy, and considered quality and preference as the major antecedents of customer purchase intention. They inferred the information that the customers had obtained from the e-WOM by categorizing the customers' responses. The e-WOM was parameterized using mean and variance; products that were categorized into quality and preference goods. They considered four cases in which customers inferred different product information and exhibited different reactions. Items for quality and preference goods were developed by using a card-sorting method. The hypotheses were partially supported using a Partial Least Squares path comparison method. Overall, their study provided guidance to firms in their managing e-WOM systems by identifying how customers reacted to them at various levels. Khammash (2011) offered new insights on the motives and antecedents of the reading behaviour of consumer reviews in online opinion platforms. They highlighted four different types of motives that drove customers to read online reviews: decision-involvement, product-involvement, social-involvement and economic-involvement motives. The outcomes also demonstrated four different types of motives: self-involvement motives, consumer-empowerment motives, new social-involvement motives and site-administration motives. Several related themes were also investigated, such as the preference for reading or writing online reviews and the reasons for choosing one over the other. They tested the relevance of online reading motives and their influence on consumer buying and communication behaviour. Cheung M. Y. (2009) extended to the on-line context (e-WOM) by examining the informational and normative determinants of the perceived credibility of on-line consumer recommendations. A survey of users of an on-line consumer discussion forum in China substantiated the effects of the determinants, although post-hoc analyses revealed that prior knowledge and involvement level moderated some of them. Amblee (2011) studied the effect of e-WOM communication among a closed community of book readers. They studied the entire market of Amazon Shorts e-books, which were digital microproducts sold at a low and a uniform price. With the minimal role of price in the buying decisions, social discussion via e-WOM becomes a collective signal of reputation, and ultimately a significant demand driver. Their empirical study suggested that e-WOM could be used to convey the reputation of the product (e.g., the book), the reputation of the brand (i.e., the author), and the reputation of complementary goods (e.g., books in the same category). Until newer social shopping technologies gained acceptance, e-WOM technologies could be considered by both e-tailers and shoppers as the first and perhaps the primary source of social buying experience. Lee J. P. (2011) investigated the effects of two types of (OCRs vs OEAs) on consumers' purchase intention from an informational influence perspective and secondly investigated the effects of OCRs from a credibility perspective. They showed that OCRs were more influenced by trust in online shopping malls than OEAs. The greater the perceived credibility of OCRs among potential consumers, the higher was the purchase intention. When the trust in online shopping malls is high, consumers' purchase intentions influenced by OCRs were more favorable than those influenced by OEAs. Fan (2012) used the extended Elaboration Likelihood Model and purchasing decisions in e-commerce virtual communities and showed that involvement had the most significant effect on perceived e-WOM credibility. They also found that perceived e-WOM credibility had a significant effect on e-WOM acceptance and intention to purchase. They showed that the male customers had different e-commerce shopping behaviors than female customers. Cheung C. M. (2012) used the social communication framework to summarize and classify prior e-WOM studies. They identified key factors related to the major elements of the social communication literature and built an integrative framework explaining the impact of e-WOM communication on consumer behavior. Zhang J. Q.(2010) examined the persuasiveness of e-WOM and proposed that the consumption goals that consumers associate with the reviewed product moderate the effect of review valence on persuasiveness. Data from lab experiments and actual online retailers suggested that consumers who evaluate products associated with promotion consumption goals perceive positive reviews to be more persuasive than negative ones (i.e., a positivity bias). Conversely, consumers who evaluate products associated with prevention consumption goals perceive negative reviews to be more persuasive than positive ones (i.e., a negativity bias).

Research Gap

The impact of online communication though were studied among various other groups and communities, their patterns understood and their persuasiveness examined, their positive and negative impact studied but no studies were found which tried to understand the impact of online consumer reviews on purchasing decisions of the Indian academicians thereby leading to the objective of the study . The online reviews were used to understand the buying behavior as well as their post sales perception .The academicians being relatively more qualified tend to take decisions after a proper review and hence it is important to understand their purchasing behavior after reading the online reviews which today has become a major influencer for purchase decisions .

Objective of the Study

- To study the perception towards the websites presenting the online reviews;
- To study and identify various elements relating to online reviews that affect purchase decisions.

Methodology Adopted

A structured questionnaire was designed to collect data for the study. Before conducting the field study, the questionnaire was pre-tested. A few modifications were made as a result of the pretest exercise. All the questions were analyzed on the nominal and ordinal scale. Likert scale was used to collect the responses. The scale was calibrated from 1 to 5 where 1 represented strongly disagree and 5 represented strongly agree. A total of 1200 questionnaires were sent to college academicians from across India and the first question raised was whether they purchased goods online or not. Of the total questionnaires sent, 342 responded positive and hence were selected. Of the total positive responses received, a total of 243 were completely filled in all respects and were hence used for the study. The research design used was descriptive in nature and convenient sampling method was used to select the responses from the target population. The questionnaire consisted of two parts –first the demographic profile of the academicians and the second consisted of the perception of the respondents towards the effect of online reviews on purchase decisions. Thereafter factor analysis was run in order to condense the variables relating to online reviews affecting purchase decisions.

DATA ANALYSIS AND INTERPRETATION

Table 1 Interpretation: Table 1 shows that both male and female academicians were equally participative after looking on their rate of responses. Most of the respondents were below the age of 40 years. As the age of the responses increased, the participation level decreased indicating greater purchasing among the younger academicians. The participation among the lower income group was higher than those who had higher income. Most of the respondents were graduates and most of the respondents accessed the internet for less than 5 hours a week.

Table 2 Interpretation: As seen from Table 2, most of the responses were seen to have an above average score and at the same time the deviations of the responses was also equally high indicating influence but at the same time a high level of variation.

Table 1. Demographic profile of the respondents

		Frequency	Percent
Gender	Male	128	52.7
	Female	115	47.3
	Total	243	100.0
Age	21-30 years	114	46.9
	31-40 years	91	37.4
	>=41 years	38	15.6
	Total	243	100.0
Monthly income (In Rupees)	<= Rs 20000	58	23.9
	20000- 40000	95	39.1
	40001- 60000	43	17.7
	60001-80000	21	8.6
	80001- 100000	3	1.2
	>=100000	23	9.5
	Total	243	100.0
Educational qualification	Graduate	105	43.2
	Post-graduate	99	40.7
	Ph.d	39	16.0
	Total	243	100.0
Frequency of internet usage (Weekly)	< 1 hour	70	28.8
	1-5 hours	85	35.0
	5-10 hours	20	8.2
	10-20 hours	32	13.2
	> 20 hours	36	14.8
	Total	243	100.0

Table 2. Effect on Purchase decision

Reviewers' Demographic Profile	Mean	Std. Deviation
The reviewer's frequency of posting reviews affect your purchase decision	3.20	1.073
The reviewer's age affect purchase decision	3.30	1.010
The reviewer's residence affects your purchase decision	3.07	1.052
The reviewer gender affect your purchase decision	3.53	1.111
If web site that present the reviews concern to company whose product you want to buy, affect your purchase decision	3.46	1.013

Table 3 Interpretation: Table 3 shows that the average score for all questions raised were found to be more than three indicating an influence on various aspects of purchasing. The deviations of most of the responses were found to be high. Positive reviews had a lesser positive influence than negative reviews influencing negatively. The number of positive reviews also had a significant positive influence on purchase decisions.

Table 4 Interpretation: Table 4 shows that most of the respondents agreed to the fact that online reviews did have an impact on purchase decisions and the reviews posted by the consumers were useful for taking purchasing decisions irrespective of their names. The deviation among the respondents is also high.

Table 5 Interpretation: As seen from Table 5, most of the respondents felt that the reliability of the websites that presented the reviews was above average. But the deviation was high with respect to the perception that the website presenting the reviews impacted purchase decisions. Deviation was comparatively low with respect to the perception that the internationality of the websites and their popularity affected purchase decisions.

Table 3. Consumer reviews

Statements about Consumer Reviews	Mean	Std. Deviation
You read the reviews presented on the website when buying a product online and are worried about your decision	3.61	.940
Consistency of other reviews posted on the website affect your purchase decision.	3.45	1.157
Reviews presented on the website were helpful are helpful for your purchase decision making	3.35	1.054
Attribute-value recommendations are specific, clear and having reasons for arguments.	3.60	1.088
Earlier the product review posted on the website higher(lower) the impact on your purchase decision	3.48	1.122
The reviews presented on the website makes you confident on purchasing the product.	3.78	1.056
The impact of negative reviews on the web has a greater affect for purchasing decision for electronic goods	3.48	1.018
The impact of positive reviews on the web has a greater affect for purchasing decision for electronic goods	3.37	1.218
Simple-recommendation reviews are subjective, emotional and have no support for arguments	3.60	1.021
High (low) ratings for product affects your purchase decision.	3.46	1.161
The number of online product reviews affect your purchase decision	3.44	1.195
Spelling or grammar mistakes in product review affect your purchase decision	3.40	.976

Table 4. Effect of reviewers

Statements About the Reviewer	Mean	Std. Deviation
Other reviewers' ratings of usefulness of the review affect your purchase decision	3.55	1.021
The reviewers using nick names or their real names also affect your purchase decision	3.52	1.073

Table 5. Effect of website

Statements About website that Present the Reviews	Mean	Std. Deviation
Reliability of the site that present the reviews affect your purchase decision	3.42	1.097
Internationality of the web site that present the reviews affect your purchase decision	3.56	.931
Popularity of the web site that present the reviews affect your purchase decision	3.29	.983

Tables 5 and 6 Factor Analysis: It is a general name denoting a class of procedures primarily used for data reduction and summarization. Relationship among set of many interrelated variables are examined and represented with the help of factor analysis. The approach used in the factor analysis is "Principle Component Analysis". In this analysis, the total variance in the data is considered. The diagonal of the correlation matrix consists of unities and full variance is brought in to the factor matrix. It determines the minimum number of factors that will account for maximum variance in the data for use in subsequent multivariate analysis. The factors are also called principal components. Although the initial or un-rotated factor matrix indicates the relationship between the factors and individual variables, it seldom results in factors that can be interpreted, because the factors are correlated with many variables. Hence the variance explained by each factor is redistributed

Table 6. Variables

V_1	Consistency of other reviews posted on the website affect your purchase decision
V_2	You buy a product online and the reviews presented on the website are helpful for decision making
V_3	Attribute-value recommendations are specific, clear and having reasons for arguments
V_4	Recency of product reviews posted on the website affect your purchase decision
V_5	When you buy a product online, the reviews presented on the website makes you confident in purchasing the product
V_6	When you buy a product online, the impact of negative reviews on the web for purchasing decisions is greater for electronic goods
V_7	When you buy a product online, the impact of positive reviews on the web for purchasing decisions is greater for electronic goods than other products
V_8	Simple-recommendation reviews are subjective, emotional and have no support for arguments
V_9	High ratings received for products affect your purchase decision
V_{10}	The numbers of product reviews affect your purchase decision
V_{11}	You read the reviews presented on the website when you buy a product online and are worried about your decision
V_{12}	Spelling or grammar mistakes in product review affect your purchase decision

by rotation. The method used for rotation in this study is "Varimax". It is a method of factor rotation that minimizes the numbers of variables with high loading on a factor, thereby enhancing the interpretability of the factors. The variables were defined as shown in Table 6.

Before the application of factor analysis the reliability of the scale items were tested by applying cronbach's alpha. The value of all factors ranges between 0.71 and 0.91 indicating the presence of internal consistency. Further to test the sampling, Kaiser-Meyer-Oklin measure of sampling adequacy is computed which is found to be 0.79 indicating that sample was good enough for sampling. Moreover the overall significance of correlation matrices has been tested with Bartlett Test which provided as well a support for the validity of data for factor analysis. All this gave the way for proceeding with factor analysis and the result of factor analysis over 12 factors showed that there were 5 key factors, which were determined by clubbing the similar variables & ignoring the rest, The below table shows the respective percentage of variance of these factors derived from factor analysis.

The total variances explained by the factors are as shown in Table 7.

Table 7 Interpretation: From Table 7 it is observed that 5 factors have an eigen value more than one and accordingly we proceed with the factors. The above table shows that around 59% of the variations is contributed by these six components. The total variance is explained by these factors (V_1, V_2, V_3, V_4 & V_5) 12.4%, 12.12%, 12.02%, 11.233% and 11.01% of the total variance, whereas the cumulative variance explained by these factors was around 59% and the rest of the variance was due to those factors beyond the scope of the study.

Table 7 Extraction Method: Principal Component Analysis. Rotation Method: Varimax with Kaiser Normalization. a. Rotation converged in 11 iterations

Table 7. Component matrix

Component	Initial Eigenvalues			Extraction Sums of Squared Loadings			Rotation Sums of Squared Loadings		
	Total	% of Variance	Cumulative %	Total	% of Variance	Cumulative %	Total	% of Variance	Cumulative %
V_1	1.743	14.529	14.529	1.743	14.529	14.529	1.489	**12.408**	12.408
V_2	1.623	13.528	28.057	1.623	13.528	28.057	1.454	**12.120**	24.528
V_3	1.531	12.760	40.818	1.531	12.760	40.818	1.442	**12.020**	36.548
V_4	1.098	9.148	49.966	1.098	9.148	49.966	1.348	**11.233**	47.781
V_5	1.060	8.833	58.799	1.060	8.833	58.799	1.322	**11.017**	58.799
V_6	.997	8.311	67.110						
V_7	.882	7.346	74.456						
V_8	.845	7.043	81.499						
V_9	.732	6.099	87.599						
V_{10}	.653	5.442	93.041						
V_{11}	.487	4.059	97.100						
V_{12}	.348	2.900	100.000						

Table 8 Interpretation: Table 8 shows each statement corresponding to the highlighted factor loading which is correlated with the factors corresponding to that factor loading. Higher the factor loading, stronger is the correlation between the factors and statement. On the basis of rotated component matrix the factor extraction table has been prepared which is as under.

Factor Extraction (Table 6) showing the variables in each factor with corresponding loading and percentage of variance is given in Table 9.

Table 9 Interpretation: The stated factors in Table 9 are in the order of degree of importance i.e. F1 is more important than F2; F2 is more important than F3 and so on. The factors F1 and F2 have the highest variance (12.408, and 12.12) and then followed by factor 3, 4, 5 where % of variance was 12.02, 11.233, 11.017. Hence it is concluded that product reviews, timeline and accuracy of reviews, Self-assessment after reading the reviews, Consistency of the reviews and the recommendations given were the most important factors relating to online reviews which were affecting online purchase decisions.

Table 8. Rotated component matrix

Statements about Consumer Reviews	Component				
	1	2	3	4	5
Consistency of other reviews posted on the website affect your purchase decision(V_1)	.053	.079	-.335	**.609**	-.024
You buy a product online and the reviews presented on the website are helpful for decision making(V_2)	**.745**	.088	-.250	.012	.003
Attribute-value recommendations are specific, clear and having reasons for arguments(V_3)	-.030	-.117	-.622	.077	**.125**
Recency of product reviews posted on the website affect your purchase decision(V_4)	-.283	**.505**	.268	.210	.156
When you buy a product online, the reviews presented on the website makes you confident in purchasing the product(V_5)	.480	**.565**	.010	-.114	.080
When you buy a product online, the impact of negative reviews on the web for purchasing decisions is greater for electronic goods (V_6)	.033	-.093	.252	**.625**	-.134
When you buy a product online, the impact of positive reviews on the web for purchasing decisions is greater for electronic goods than other products (V_7)	-.142	.259	-.048	**.589**	.316
Simple-recommendation reviews are subjective, emotional and have no support for arguments(V_8)	.228	-.279	-.237	.361	**.689**
High ratings received for products affect your purchase decision(V_9)	-.170	.186	.208	-.195	**.791**
The numbers of product reviews affect your purchase decision(V_{10})	**.713**	-.089	.446	.051	-.109
You read the reviews presented on the website when you buy a product online and are worried about your decision (V_{11})	-.075	.054	**.666**	.036	.202
Spelling or grammar mistakes in product review affect your purchase decision(V_{12})	.066	**.809**	.043	.065	-.063

Table 9. Factor Extraction

Factors	% of Variance	Loading
F1(Product reviews)	12.408	
You buy a product online and the reviews presented on the website are helpful for decision making (V_2)		.745
The numbers of product reviews affect your purchase decision(V_{10})		.713
F2 (Timeline and accuracy)	12.12	
Recency of product reviews posted on the website affect your purchase decision(V_4)		.505
When you buy a product online, the reviews presented on the website makes you confident in purchasing the product(V_5)		.565
Spelling or grammar mistakes in product review affect your purchase decision(V_{12})		.809
F_3(Self –assessment)	12.02	
You read the reviews presented on the website when you buy a product online and are worried about your decision (V_{11})		.66
F4 (Consistency)	11.233	
Consistency of other reviews posted on the website affect your purchase decision(V_1)		.609
When you buy a product online, the impact of negative reviews on the web for purchasing decisions is greater for electronic goods (V_6)		.625
When you buy a product online, the impact of positive reviews on the web for purchasing decisions is greater for electronic goods than other products (V_7)		.589
F5 (Recommendations)	11.017	
Attribute-value recommendations are specific, clear and having reasons for arguments(V_3)		.125
Simple-recommendation reviews are subjective, emotional and have no support for arguments(V_8)		.689
High ratings received for products affect your purchase decision(V_9)		.791

Table 10. Frequency Distribution

	1	2	3	4	5
Reviewer's frequency of posting reviews affect your purchase decision	17(7)	45(18.5)	78(32.1)	79(32.5)	24(9.9)
Reviewer age affect your purchase decision	10(4.1)	43(17.7)	80(32.9)	85(35)	25(10.3)
Reviewer residence affect your purchase decision	24(9.9)	34(14)	106(43.6)	59(24.3)	20(8.2)
The reviewer gender affect your purchase decision	18(7.4)	16(6.6)	78(32.1)	82(33.7)	49(20.2)
Web site that present the reviews concern to company whose product one wants to buy, affect purchase decision	11(4.5)	29(11.9)	73(30)	98(40.3)	32(13.2)

(1 – Strongly Disagree, 2- Disagree, 3- Neutral, 4- Agree, 5- Strongly Agree)
(Figures in parenthesis represent are in percentage)

From the tables presented it is also found that the frequency of posting reviews, age, place of residence gender and the websites presenting the reviews were also the other demographic factors affecting the purchase decisions online.

CONCLUSION AND DISCUSSION

Purchasing online has become the order of the day and organisations have been sourcing these new sources and medium to market their products. Online reviews have become great influencers and provide a platform to give feedback relating to products and services offered. The study clearly revealed that product reviews, timeline and accuracy of reviews, Self-assessment after reading the reviews, Consistency of the reviews and the recommendations given were the most important factors relating to online reviews which were affecting online purchase decisions among academicians . Though their demographic profile also had a significant role to play in influencing online purchase decisions, the above mentioned factors relating to online reviews were the most important influencers of online purchases. The present study had adopted limited variables and tried to explore into the factors relating to online reviews. The study could therefore be further expanded to include larger number of variables.

REFERENCES

Amblee, N., & Bui, T. (2011). Harnessing the influence of social proof in online shopping: The effect of electronic word of mouth on sales of digital microproducts. *International Journal of Electronic Commerce*, *16*(2), 91–114. doi:10.2753/JEC1086-4415160205

Cheung, C. M., Lee, M. K. O., & Rabjohn, N. (2008). The impact of electronic word-of-mouth: The adoption of online opinions in online customer communities. *Internet Research*, *18*(3), 229–247. doi:10.1108/10662240810883290

Cheung, C. M., & Thadani, D. R. (2012). The impact of electronic word-of-mouth communication: A literature analysis and integrative model. *Decision Support Systems*, *54*(1), 461–470. doi:10.1016/j.dss.2012.06.008

Cheung, M. Y., Luo, C., Sia, C. L., & Chen, H. (2009). Credibility of electronic word-of-mouth: Informational and normative determinants of on-line consumer recommendations. *International Journal of Electronic Commerce*, *13*(4), 9–38. doi:10.2753/JEC1086-4415130402

Doh, S. J., & Hwang, J.-S. (2009). How consumers evaluate eWOM (electronic word-of-mouth) messages. *Cyberpsychology & Behavior*, *12*(2), 193–197. doi:10.1089/cpb.2008.0109 PMID:19072076

Fan, Y. W. (2012). Effect of electronic word-of-mouth on consumer purchase intention: The perspective of gender differences. *International Journal of Electronic BusinessManagement*, *10*(3), 175.

Faulds, W. G. (2009). Social media: The new hybrid element of the promotion mix. *52*(4), 357-365.

Godes, D. M. (2005). The Firm's Management of Social Interactions. *Marketing Science*, 415–428.

Goldsmith, R. E. (2006). Measuring motivations for online opinion seeking. *Journal of Interactive Advertising*, *6*(4), 2-14.

Hennig-Thurau, T. G., Gwinner, K. P., Walsh, G., & Gremler, D. D. (2004). Electronic word-of-mouth via consumer-opinion platforms: What motivates consumers to articulate themselves on the Internet? *Journal of Interactive Marketing*, *18*(1), 38–52. doi:10.1002/dir.10073

Jansen, B. J., Zhang, M., Sobel, K., & Chowdury, A. (2009). Twitter power: Tweets as electronic word of mouth. *Journal of the American Society for Information Science and Technology*, *60*(11), 2169–2188. doi:10.1002/asi.21149

Khammash, M., & Griffiths, G. H. (2011). 'Arrivederci CIAO. com, Buongiorno Bing. com'—Electronic word-of-mouth (eWOM), antecedences and consequences. *International Journal of Information Management*, *31*(1), 82–87. doi:10.1016/j.ijinfomgt.2010.10.005

Lee, J., & Lee, J.-N. (2009). Understanding the product information inference process in electronic word-of-mouth: An objectivity–subjectivity dichotomy perspective. *Information & Management*, *46*(5), 302–311. doi:10.1016/j.im.2009.05.004

Lee, J. P., Park, D.-H., & Han, I. (2011). The different effects of online consumer reviews on consumers' purchase intentions depending on trust in online shopping malls: An advertising perspective. *Internet Research*, *21*(2), 187–206. doi:10.1108/10662241111123766

Litvin, S. W., Goldsmith, R. E., & Pan, B. (2008). Electronic word-of-mouth in hospitality and tourism management. *Tourism Management*, *29*(3), 458–468. doi:10.1016/j.tourman.2007.05.011

Park, C., & Lee, T. M. (2009). Information direction, website reputation and eWOM effect: A moderating role of product type. *Journal of Business Research*, *62*(1), 61–67. doi:10.1016/j.jbusres.2007.11.017

Park, D. H., & Kim, S. (2009). The effects of consumer knowledge on message processing of electronic word-of-mouth via online consumer reviews. *Electronic Commerce Research and Applications*, *7*(4), 399–410. doi:10.1016/j.elerap.2007.12.001

Park, D. H., & Lee, J. (2009). eWOM overload and its effect on consumer behavioral intention depending on consumer involvement. *Electronic Commerce Research and Applications*, *7*(4), 386–398. doi:10.1016/j.elerap.2007.11.004

Park, D. H., Lee, J., & Han, I. (2007). The effect of on-line consumer reviews on consumer purchasing intention: The moderating role of involvement. *International Journal of Electronic Commerce*, *11*(4), 125–148. doi:10.2753/JEC1086-4415110405

Yali, A. a. (2010). eWom: The effects of online consumer reviews on purchasing decision of electronic goods. In *Proceedings of the International Marketing Trends Conference*. Venice: Academic Press.

Zhang, J. Q., Craciun, G., & Shin, D. (2010). When does electronic word-of-mouth matter? A study of consumer product reviews. *Journal of Business Research*, *63*(12), 1336–1341. doi:10.1016/j.jbusres.2009.12.011

Zhang, Z. Y., Ye, Q., Law, R., & Li, Y. (2010). The impact of e-word-of-mouth on the online popularity of restaurants: A comparison of consumer reviews and editor reviews. *International Journal of Hospitality Management*, *29*(4), 694–700. doi:10.1016/j.ijhm.2010.02.002

KEY TERMS AND DEFINITIONS

Consumer Behavior: It is the study of individuals, groups, or organizations and the processes they are used to select, secure, use, and dispose of products/services/experiences/ ideas to satisfy needs and the impacts that these processes have on the consumers and the society. It blends elements from various streams like psychology, sociology, social anthropology, marketing and economics. It tries to understand the decision-making processes of buyers, both individually and in groups as to how emotions affect buying behaviour. It also tries to assess influences on the consumer from groups such as family, friends, sports, reference groups, and society in general.

E-WOM: Electronic word of mouth (e-WOM) refers to statements that consumers share via the Internet (e.g., web sites, social networks, instant messages, etc.) about an event, product, service, brand or a company. When the underlying message spreads from user to user and presumably resonates as it appears to come from a trusted, third-party source, as opposed to the brand or the company itself. This form of marketing results in earned media rather than paid media.

Internet Marketing: Internet marketing or online marketing, refers to the marketing efforts that use the internet and email to drive direct sales via e- commerce, in addition to sales leads from websites or emails. They are (Internet marketing / online advertising) efforts are typically used in conjunction with traditional types of advertising like radio, television, newspapers and magazines.

Online Reviews: Views and perceptions which the users of products and services share online with others or express their feelings about products / services are called online reviews.

Compilation of References

Aaker, J. L., & Maheswaran, D. (1997). The effect of cultural orientation on persuasion. *The Journal of Consumer Research*, *24*(3), 315–328. doi:10.1086/209513

Abric, J. C. (1976). *Jeux, conflits et représentations sociales [thèse]*. Marseille: Université de Provence.

Abric, J.-C. (1989). L'étude expérimentale des représentations sociales. *Les Représentations Sociales*, *4*, 187–203.

ACNeilsen. (2007). *Best Selling Tool is Word of Mouth Says Nelson Global Survey*. Retrieved from http://asiapacific.acneilsen.com/news/20071002.sctml

Addley, E. (2014, March 7). *Ellen's Oscars selfie most retweeted ever – and more of us are taking them*. Retrieved August 30, 2014, from http://www.theguardian.com: http://www.theguardian.com/media/2014/mar/07/oscars-selfie-most-retweeted-ever

Ajzen, I. (1991). The theory of planned behaviour. *Organizational Behavior and Human Decision Processes*, *50*(2), 179–211. doi:10.1016/0749-5978(91)90020-T

Alderson, W. (1957). *Marketing Behavior and Executive Action*. Homewood, Illinois: Richard D. Irwin, INC.

Alllsop, T., Bassett, R. and Hoskins, A., (2007). Word -of - mouth Research: Principles and Applications. *Journals of Advertising Research.*

Amblee, N., & Bui, T. (2011). Harnessing the influence of social proof in online shopping: The effect of electronic word of mouth on sales of digital microproducts. *International Journal of Electronic Commerce*, *16*(2), 91–114. doi:10.2753/JEC1086-4415160205

Amichai-Hamburger, Y., Kaynar, O., & Fine, A. (2007). The effects of need for cognition on Internet use. *Computers in Human Behavior*, *23*(1), 880–891. doi:10.1016/j.chb.2006.03.002

Anderson, E. W. (1998). Customer satisfaction and word of mouth. *Journal of Service Research*, *1*(August), 5–17. doi:10.1177/109467059800100102

Andreassen, T. W., & Streukens, S. (2009). Service innovation and electronic word-of-mouth: Is it worth listening to? *Managing Service Quality*, *19*(3), 249–265. doi:10.1108/09604520910955294

Are marketers spending wisely on social media ? (n.d.). Retrieved Sept 18, 2014, from http://economictimes.indiatimes.com/slideshows/advertising-marketing/are-marketers-spending-wisely-on-social-media/slideshow/17956181.cms

Armstrong, S. (2006). Bloggers for hire. *New Statesman (London, England)*, *135*(4807), 26–27.

Arndt, J. (1967). Word of Mouth Advertising: A Review of the Literature. *Advertising Research Foundation*, 3.

Arndt, J. (1967). The role of product related conversasions in the diffusion of a new product. *JMR, Journal of Marketing Research*, *4*(3), 291–295. doi:10.2307/3149462

Arndt, J. (1967). *Word of Mouth Advertising: A Review of the Literature*. New York, NY: Advertising Research Foundation, Inc.

Arndt, J. (1968). Selective Processes in Word of Mouth. *Journal of Advertising Research*, *8*(3), 19–22.

Arnold, M. J., Reynolds, K. E., Ponder, N., & Lueg, J. E. (2005). Customer Delight in a Retail Context: Investigating Delightful and Terrible Shopping Experiences. *Journal of Business Research*, *58*(8), 1132–1145. doi:10.1016/j.jbusres.2004.01.006

Atkinson, C. (2005). TV Networks Snap Up Key Words Online to Draw Views. *Advertising Age*, *76*, 4–21.

Awad, N. F., & Ragowsky, A. (2008). Establishing Trust in Electronic Commerce Through Online Word of Mouth: An Examination Across Genders. *Journal of Management Information Systems*, *24*(4), 101–121. doi:10.2753/MIS0742-1222240404

Azar, O. H. (2008). *Incentives and Service Quality in the Restaurant Industry: The Tipping – Service Puzzle*. Working Paper. Department of Business Administration, Ben-Gurion University of Nagev.

Azim, R., & Hassan, A. (2013). Impact analysis of wireless and mobile technology on business management strategies. *Journal of Information and Knowledge Management*, *2*(2), 141–150.

Bagozzi, R. P. (2006). The role of social and self-conscious emotions in the regulation of business-to-business relationships in salesperson-customer interactions. *Journal of Business and Industrial Marketing*, *21*(7), 453–457. doi:10.1108/08858620610708948

Bailey, A. A. (2004). Thiscompanysucks. com: The use of the Internet in negative consumer-to-consumer articulations. *Journal of Marketing Communications*, *10*(3), 169–182. doi:10.1080/1352726042000186634

Bailey, A. A. (2005). Consumer Awareness and Use of Product Review Websites. *Journal of Interactive Advertising*, *6*(1), 90–108. doi:10.1080/15252019.2005.10722109

Bailey, J. E., & Pearson, S. W. (1983). Development of a tool for measuring and analyzing computer user satisfaction. *Management Science*, *29*(5), 530–545. doi:10.1287/mnsc.29.5.530

Balasubramanian, S., & Mahajan, V. (2001). The Economic Leverage of the Virtual Community. *International Journal of Electronic Commerce*, *5*(Spring), 103–138.

Bansal, H. S., & Voyer, P. A. (2000). Word-of-mouth processes within a service purchase decision context. *Journal of Service Research*, *3*(2), 166–177. doi:10.1177/109467050032005

Bardzell, J., Bardzell S., & Pace, T (2008). Emotion, Engagement and Internet Video. *Report: One to One Interactive*.

Barker, V. (2009). Older adolescents' motivations for social network site use: The influence of gender, group identity, and collective self-esteem. *Cyberpsychology & Behavior*, *12*(2), 209–213. doi:10.1089/cpb.2008.0228 PMID:19250021

Barnes, N. G., & Jacobsen, S. L. (2014). Missed eWOM opportunities: A cross-sector analysis of online monitoring behavior. *Journal of Marketing Communications*, *20*(1-2), 147–158. doi:10.1080/13527266.2013.797788

Barsade, S. G. (2002). The ripple effect: Emotional contagion and its influence on group behavior. *Administrative Science Quarterly*, *47*(4), 644–675. doi:10.2307/3094912

Ba, S., & Pavlou, P. A. (2003). Evidence of the Effect of Trust Building Technology in Electronic Markets: Price Premiums and Buyer Behavior. *Management Information Systems Quarterly*, *26*(3), 243–268. doi:10.2307/4132332

Batson, C. D. (1994). Why act for the public good? Four answers. *Personality and Social Psychology Bulletin*, *20*(5), 603–610. doi:10.1177/0146167294205016

Baumeister, R. F. (1998). The Self. In S. Giblert, T. Fiske, & G. Lindzey (Eds.), *The Handbook of Social Psychology* (Vol. 1, pp. 680–740). NJ: John Wiley & Sons.

Bearden, W. O., & Teel, J. E. (1983). Selected determinants of consumer satisfaction and complaint reports. *JMR, Journal of Marketing Research*, *20*(1), 21–28. doi:10.2307/3151408

Beliclove, M. E. (2012). *8 Do's and Don'ts for Marketing on Online Forums and Message Boards*. Retrieved from http://www.entrepreneur.com/article/223900

Belk, R. W. (1988). Possessions and the extended self. *The Journal of Consumer Research*, *15*(2), 139–168. doi:10.1086/209154

Bellini, F., Ascenzo, F. D., Ghi, A., Spagnoli, F., & Traversi, V. (n.d.). *The Role of the Prosumer in Social Networks and the Sentiment Analysis for the Customer Experience Management*. Retrieved on January 10, 2014 from http://www.cersi.it/itais2012/pdf/066.pdf

Bellizzi, J. A., & Hite, R. E. (1992). Environmental Color, Consumer Feelings, and Purchase Likelihood. *Psychology and Marketing*, *9*(5), 347–363. doi:10.1002/mar.4220090502

Benefits of Social Media. (n.d.). Retrieved from http://rlcomputing.com/Blog/TabId/112/ArtMID/491/ArticleID/8/Benefits-of-Social-Media.aspx

Bengry-Howell, A., Wiles, R., Nind, M., & Crow, G. (2011). *A Review of the Academic Impact of Three Methodological Innovations: Child-Led Research and Creative Research Methods. NCRM Hub*. University of Southampton.

Bennett, M., & Gillingham, K. (1991). The role of self focused attention in children's attributions of social emotions to the self. *The Journal of Genetic Psychology*, *152*(3), 303–309. doi:10.1080/00221325.1991.9914688

Bennett, M., & Mathews, L. (2000). The role of second-order belief understanding in children's self-attribution of social emotions: A short note. *Social Development*, *9*, 126–130. doi:10.1111/1467-9507.t01-1-00115

Berelson, B. (1952). *Content Analysis in Communication Research*. Glencoe, IL: Free Press.

Berger, J., & Milkman, K. (2010). Social transmission, emotion, and the virality of online content. *Wharton Research Paper*, 1-53.

Berger, J. (2014). Word of Mouth and Interpersonal Communication: A Review and Directions for Future Research. *Journal of Consumer Psychology*, *24*(4), 586–607. doi:10.1016/j.jcps.2014.05.002

Berger, J., & Heath, C. (2007). Where consumers diverge from others: Identity signaling and product domains. *The Journal of Consumer Research*, *34*(2), 121–134. doi:10.1086/519142

Berger, J., & Milkman, K. (2012). What makes online content viral? *JMR, Journal of Marketing Research*, *49*(2), 192–205. doi:10.1509/jmr.10.0353

Berger, J., & Schwartz, E. (2011). What drives immediate and ongoing wordof- mouth? *JMR, Journal of Marketing Research*, *48*(5), 869–880. doi:10.1509/jmkr.48.5.869

Berger, J., Sorensen, A. T., & Rasmussen, S. J. (2010). Positive Effects of Negative Publicity: When Negative Reviews Increase Sales. *Marketing Science*, *29*(5), 815–827. doi:10.1287/mksc.1090.0557

Berger, L. A. (1988). Word-of-Mouth Reputations in Auto Insurance Markets. *Journal of Behavior and Organization*, *10*(2), 225–234. doi:10.1016/0167-2681(88)90046-7

Bergh, B. V., Lee, M., Quilliam, E. T., & Hove, T. (2011). The multidimensional nature and brand impact of user-generated ad parodies in social media. *International Journal of Advertising*, *30*(1), 103–131. doi:10.2501/IJA-30-1-103-131

Berry, L. L. (2000). Cultivating service brand equity. *Journal of the Academy of Marketing Science*, *28*(1), 128–137. doi:10.1177/0092070300281012

Berry, L. L., & Carbone, L. P. (2007). Build Loyalty Through Experience Management. *Quality Progress*, *40*(9), 26–32.

Berthon, P., Pitt, L., & DesAutels, P. (2011). Unveiling videos: Consumer-generated ads as qualitative inquiry. *Psychology and Marketing*, *28*(10), 1044–1060. doi:10.1002/mar.20427

Bettina, L., & Simon, K. (2013). *DigitalesEmpfehlungsmarketing: Konzeption, Theorien und DeterminantenzurGlaubwürdigkeit des Electronic Word-of-Mouth (EWOM)*. Springer-Verlag.

Beven, Z., & Laws, C. (2007). Never let me down. Loyal Customer Attitude Towards Ticket Distribution Channels for Live Music Events: A Netnographic Exploration of the Us Leg of the Depeache Mode 2005-2006 World Tour. *Managing Leisure*, *12*(2-3), 120–142. doi:10.1080/13606710701339322

Bickart, B., & Schindler, R. M. (2001). Internet forums as influential sources of consumer information. *Journal of Interactive Marketing*, *15*(3), 31–40. doi:10.1002/dir.1014

Bickart, B., & Schindler, R. M. (2002). Expanding the scope of word of mouth: Consumer-to-consumer informations on the internet. *Advances in Consumer Research. Association for Consumer Research (U. S.)*, *29*, 428–430.

Black, G. S. (2007). A Comparison of the Characteristics of Ebay Consumers and Ebay Nonconsumers. *Journal of Direct. Data and Digital Marketing Practice*, *9*(1), 16–29. doi:10.1057/palgrave.dddmp.4350066

Blasingame, D. (2011). Gatejumping: Twitter, TV news and the delivery of breaking news. *#ISOJ Journal: The Official Research Journal of the International Symposium on Online Journalism*, *1*(2). Retrieved from http://online.journalism.utexas.edu/ebook.php

Blood, R. (2002). *The weblog handbook: Practical advice on creating and maintaining your blog*. Basic Books.

Bolar, K. P. (2009). Motives behind the use of social networking sites: An empirical study. *The ICFAI Journal of Management Research*, *8*(1), 75–84.

Bolton, R. N., & Drew, J. H. (1991). A longitudinal analysis of the impact of service changes on customer attitudes. *Journal of Marketing*, *55*(1), 1–10. doi:10.2307/1252199

Booking.com. (n.d.). Retrieved from www.booking.com

Borg, W. R., & Gall, M. D. (1989). *Educational Research: an Introduction, 5th* (N. York, Ed.). London.

Bourdieu, P., & Wacquant, L. (1992). *An invitation to reflexive sociology*. Chicago: University of Chicago Press.

Bourne, L. E., & Russo, N. F. (1998). *Psychology: Behavior in Context*. New York, NY: W.W. Norton and Co.

Boyd, H. W., Jr., Westfall, R., & Stasch., S. F. (1998). Marketing research (7th ed.). Richard D. Irwin Inc.

Boyd, D. M., & Ellison, N. B. (2008). Social network sites: Definition, history, and scholarship. *Journal of Computer-Mediated Communication*, *13*(1), 210–230. doi:10.1111/j.1083-6101.2007.00393.x

Boyd, D., & Crawford, K. (2012). Critical questions for big data: Provocations for a cultural, technological, and scholarly phenomenon. *Information Communication and Society*, *15*(5), 662–679. doi:10.1080/1369118X.2012.678878

Boyd, Harper W., J., & Levy, S.J. (1963). New Dimensions in Consumer Analysis. *Harvard Business Review*, *41*(November-December), 129–140.

Brachmann, R. J., Selfridge, P. G., Terveen, L. G., Altman, B., Borgida, A., Halper, F., & Resnick, L. A. et al. (1993). Integrated Support for Data Archaeology. *International Journal of Intelligent and Cooperative Information Systems*, *2*(2), 159–185. doi:10.1142/S0218215793000083

Bradley, M., & Lang, P. J. (2007). Emotion and Motivation in Handbook of Psychophisiology (3rd ed.). New York: Cambridge University Press.

Brakus, J. J., Schmitt, B. H., & Zhang, S. (2008). Experiential Attributes and Consumer Judgments. In Handbook on Brand and Experience Management. Northampton, MA: EdwardElgar

Brakus, J. J., Schmitt, B. H., & Zarantonello, L. (2009). Brand Experience : What Is It? How Is It Measured? Does It Affect Loyalty? *Journal of Marketing*, *73*(May), 52–68. doi:10.1509/jmkg.73.3.52

Brass, D. J. (1984). Being in the right place: A structural analysis of individual influence in an organization. *Administrative Science Quarterly*, *29*(4), 518–539. doi:10.2307/2392937

Brass, D. J. (2011). A social network perspective on industrial/organizational psychology. In S. W. J. Kozlowski (Ed.), *The Oxford handbook of organizational psychology* (pp. 667–695). New York: Oxford University Press.

Braunsberger, K., & Munch, J. M. (1998). Source expertise versus experience effects in hospital advertising. *Journal of Services Marketing*, *12*(1), 23–38. doi:10.1108/08876049810202348

Bridge Ratings. (2007). *A Bridge Ratings Analysis – The Digital Media Generation Gap*. Author.

Brodie, R. J. A llic, B Juric and L Hollebeek. (2011). Consumer Engagement in Virtual Brand Community: An Exploratory Analysis. *Journal of Business Research*. doi:10.1016/j.jbusres.2011.07.029

Bronner, F., & de Hoog, R. (2011). Vacationers and eWOM: Who Posts, and Why, Where, and What? *Journal of Travel Research*, *50*(1), 15–26. doi:10.1177/0047287509355324

Brooks, R. C. Jr. (1957). 'Word-of-Mouth' Advertising in Selling New Products. *Journal of Marketing*, *22*(2), 154–161. doi:10.2307/1247212

Brown, T. (2014, Sept 8). *Are your tweets trusted or tainted? The realities of social media #fails*. Retrieved from http://www.theguardian.com/media/2014/sep/08/tweets-trusted-tainted-social-media-fails

Brown. (2003). *Proceedings of the 2nd European Conference on Research Methodology for Business and Management Studies*. Academic Conferences Limited.

Brown, J. J., & Reingen, P. H. (1987). Social ties and Word-of-Mouth referral behavior. *The Journal of Consumer Research*, *14*(3), 350–362. doi:10.1086/209118

Brown, J., Broderik, A. J., & Lee, N. (2007). Word of Mouth Communication within online communities: Conceptualizing the online social network. *Journal of Interactive Marketing*, *21*(3), 2–20. doi:10.1002/dir.20082

Brown, M. (2009). Creative determinants of viral video viewing. *International Journal of Advertising*, *29*(3), 349–368.

Bruno, N. (2011). Tweet first, verify later? How real-time information is changing the coverage of worldwide crisis events. Oxford, UK: Reuters Institute for the Study of Journalism, University of Oxford. Retrieved from http://reutersinstitute.politics.ox.ac.uk/fileadmin/documents/Publications/

Bruns, A. (2012). Journalists and Twitter: How Australian news organisations adapt to a new medium. *Media International Australia Incorporating Culture and Policy*, (144), 97–107.

Bruyn, A., & Lilien, G. L. (2008). A multi-stage of word of mouth influence through viral marketing. *International Journal of Research in Marketing*, *25*(3), 151–163. doi:10.1016/j.ijresmar.2008.03.004

Business Today. (n.d.). Retrieved from businesstoday.intoday.in/story/kolaveri-di-success-case-study/1/22957.htmlbusinesstoday.intoday.in/story/kolaveri-di-success-case-study/1/22957.html

Butler, R. W. (1980). The concept of a tourist area cycle evolution: Implications for management of resources. *Canadian Geographer*, *24*(1), 5–12. doi:10.1111/j.1541-0064.1980.tb00970.x

Buttle, F. A. (1998). Word of mouth: Understanding and managing referral marketing. *Journal of Strategic Marketing*, *6*(3), 241–254. doi:10.1080/096525498346658

Cacioppo, J. T., & Petty, R. E. (1982). The need for cognition. *Journal of Personality and Social Psychology*, *42*(1), 116–131. doi:10.1037/0022-3514.42.1.116

Cacioppo, J. T., Petty, R. E., & Morris, K. J. (1983). Effects of need for cognition on message evaluation, recall, and persuasion. *Journal of Personality and Social Psychology*, *45*(4), 805–818. doi:10.1037/0022-3514.45.4.805

Calder, B. J. (1977). Focus groups and the nature of qualitative research. *JMR, Journal of Marketing Research*, *14*(3), 353–364. doi:10.2307/3150774

Cantallops, A., & Salvi, F. (2014). New Consumer Behavior: A Review of Research on eWOM and Hotels. *International Journal of Hospitality Management*, *36*, 41–51. doi:10.1016/j.ijhm.2013.08.007

Carbone, L. P., & Haeckel, S. H. (1994). Engineering Customer Experience. *Marketing Management*, *3*(3), 8–19.

Carl, W. J. (2006). What's all the buzz about? Everyday communication and the relational basis of word-of-mouth and buzz marketing practices. *Management Communication Quarterly*, *19*(4), 601–634. doi:10.1177/0893318905284763

Carver, C. S., & Scheier, M. F. (1990). Origins and functions of positive and negative affect:A control-process view. *Psychological Review*, *97*(1), 19–35. doi:10.1037/0033-295X.97.1.19

Casalo, V. A. (2008). *The role of satisfaction and website usability in developing customer loyalty and positive word-of-mouth in the e-banking services*. Spain: Emerald Group Publishing Limited.

Cashmore, P. (2009). YouTube: Why Do We Watch? *CNN Tech*. Retrieved from http://www.cnn.com/2009/TECH/12/17/cashmore.youtube/index.html

Chakrabarti, R., & Berthon, P. (2012). Special Issue Paper: Gift giving and social emotions: experience as content. *Journal of Public Policy Affairs*, *12*(2), 154–161. doi:10.1002/pa.1417

Chaney, P. (2012). *Word Of Mouth Still Most Trusted Resource Says Nielsen; Implications For Social Commerce*. Retrieved in February 2015 from http://digitalintelligencetoday.com

Chang, C.-W., Lin, C.-T., & Wang, L.-Q. (2009). Mining the Text Information to Optimizing the Customer Relationship Management. *Expert Systems with Applications*, *36*(2), 1433–1443. doi:10.1016/j.eswa.2007.11.027

Chatterjee, P. (2001). Online review: Do consumers use them? *Advances in Consumer Research. Association for Consumer Research (U. S.)*, *28*, 129–133.

Chatterjee, P. (2001). Online Review: Do Consumers Use Them? *Advances in Consumer Research. Association for Consumer Research (U. S.)*, *28*, 129–133.

Chatterjee, P. (2001). Online reviews: Do consumers use them? *Advances in Consumer Research. Association for Consumer Research (U. S.)*, *28*(1), 129–133.

Chen, C. P. (2012). Online Group Buying Behaviour in CC2B E-Commerce: Understanding Consumer Motivations. *Journal of Internet Commerce*, *11*(3), 254–270. doi:10.1080/15332861.2012.729465

Chen, H. (2001). *Knowledge Management Systems: A Text Mining Perspective*. Arizona: Knowledge Computing Corporation.

Chen, K. C. (2009). Text Mining e-Complaints Data From e-Auction Store With Implications For Internet Marketing Research. *Journal of Business & Economics Research*, *7*(5), 15–24.

Chen, Q., & Wells, W. D. (1999). Attitude toward the site. *Journal of Advertising Research*, *39*(5), 27–37.

Chen, S.-C., Yen, D. C., & Hwang, M. I. (2012). Factors influencing the continuance intention to the usage of Web 2.0: An empirical study. *Computers in Human Behavior*, *28*(3), 933–941. doi:10.1016/j.chb.2011.12.014

Chen, Y., Liu, F., Fang, C.-H., & Lin, T. M. (2013). Understanding the effectiveness of word-of-mouth: An elasticity perspective. *Journal of Research in Interactive Marketing*, *7*(1), 57–77. doi:10.1108/17505931311316743

Chen, Y., & Xie, J. (2008). Online Consumer Review: Word-of-Mouth as a New Element of Marketing Communication Mix. *Management Science*, *54*(3), 477–491. doi:10.1287/mnsc.1070.0810

Cheun, & Thadani. (n.d.). Retrieved Oct 6, 2014, from https://domino.fov.uni-mb.si/proceedings.nsf/0/7d01f166eebae8e3c1257757003c5e98/$FILE/24_cheung.pdf

Cheung, C. M., & Thadani, D. R. (2010). The Effectiveness of Electronic Word-of-Mouth communication: A Literature Analysis. In *23rd Bled eConference eTrust: Implications for the Individual, Enterprises and Society*, 331.

Cheung, M. Y., Luo, C., Sia, C. L., & Chen, H. (2007). *How do People Evaluate Electronic Word-Of-Mouth? Informational and Normative Based Determinants of Perceived Credibility of Online Consumer Recommendations in China*. Paper presented at the 11th Pacific-Asia Conference on Information Systems, Auckland, New Zealand.

Cheung, C. M. K., Chui, P. Y., & Lee, M. K. O. (2011). Online social networks: Why do students use facebook? *Computers in Human Behavior*, *27*(4), 1337–1343. doi:10.1016/j.chb.2010.07.028

Cheung, C. M. K., Lee, M. K. O., & Rabjohn, N. (2008). The impact of electronic word-of-mouth: The adoption of online opinions in online customer communities. *Internet Research*, *18*(3), 229–247. doi:10.1108/10662240810883290

Cheung, C. M. K., & Thadani, D. R. (2012). The impact of electronic word-of-mouth communication: A literature analysis and integrative model. *Decision Support Systems*, *54*(1), 461–470. doi:10.1016/j.dss.2012.06.008

Cheung, C. M., Lee Mathew, K. O., & Rabjohn, N. (2008). The impact of electronic word-of mouth: The adoption of online opinions in online customer communities. *Internet Research*, 18.

Cheung, C., & Lee, M. (2012). What Drives Consumers to Spread Electronic Word of Mouth in Online Consumer-Opinion Platforms. *Decision Support Systems*, *53*(1), 218–225. doi:10.1016/j.dss.2012.01.015

Cheung, M. Y., Luo, C., Sia, C. L., & Chen, H. (2009). Credibility of Electronic Word-of-Mouth: Informational and Normative Determinants of On-line Consumer Recommendations. *International Journal of Electronic Commerce*, *13*(4), 9–38. doi:10.2753/JEC1086-4415130402

Chevalier, J. A., & Mayzlin, D. (2006). The Effect of Word-of-Mouth on sales: Online book reviews. *JMR, Journal of Marketing Research*, *43*(3), 345–354. doi:10.1509/jmkr.43.3.345

Chinomona, R. (2013). The Influence of Brand Experience on Brand Satisfaction, Trust And Attachment In South Africa. *International Business & Economics Research Journal*, *12*(10), 1303–1316.

Chintagunta, P. K., Gopinath, S., & Venkataraman, S. (2010). The Effects of Online User Reviews on Movie Box Office Performance: Accounting for Sequential Rollout and Aggregation across Local Markets. *Marketing Science*, *29*(5), 944–957. doi:10.1287/mksc.1100.0572

Chiu, H.-C., Hsieh, Y.-C., Kao, Y.-H., & Lee, M. (2007). The determinants of email receivers' disseminating behaviors on the Internet. *Journal of Advertising Research*, *47*(4), 524–534. doi:10.2501/S0021849907070547

Choi, S. M., Lee, W.-N., & Kim, H.-J. (2005). Lessons from the rich and famous: A cross-cultural comparison of celebrity endorsement in advertising. *Journal of Advertising*, *34*(2), 85–98. doi:10.1080/00913367.2005.10639190

Choudhary, A., Hendrix, W., Lee, K., Palsetia, D., & Liao, W. (2012). Social media evolution of the Egyptian revolution. *Communications of the ACM*, *55*(5), 74–80. doi:10.1145/2160718.2160736

Christodoulides, G., Michaelidou, N., & Argyriou, E. (2012). Cross-national differences in e-WOM influence. *European Journal of Marketing*, *46*(11/12), 1689–1707. doi:10.1108/03090561211260040

Christophe, V., & Rimé, B. (1997). Exposure to the social sharing of emotion: Emotional impact, listener responses and the secondary social sharing. *European Journal of Social Psychology*, *27*(1), 37–54. doi:10.1002/(SICI)1099-0992(199701)27:1<37::AID-EJSP806>3.0.CO;2-1

Chu, S. A. (2011).Determinants of consumer engagement in electronicword-of-mouth (eWOM) in social networking sites. International Journal of Advertising, 47–75.

Chui, M., Manyika, J., Bughin, J., Dobbs, R., Sarrazin, H., Sands, G., & Westergen, M. (2012). *The social economy: Unlocking value and productivity through social technologies.* McKinsey Global Institute Report. Retrieved on January 1, 2014 from http://www.mckinsey.com/insights/high_tech_telecoms_internet/the_social_economy

Chuldress, C. A., & Asamen, J. K. (1998). The Emerging Relationship of Psychology and Internet: Proposed Guidelines for Conducting Research. *Ethics & Behavior*, *1*, 19–35. doi:10.1207/s15327019eb0801_2 PMID:11655352

Chung, C., & Darke, P. (2006). The consumer as advocate: Self-relevance, culture, and word-of-mouth. *Marketing Letters*, *17*(4), 269–279. doi:10.1007/s11002-006-8426-7

Churchill, G. A. (1991). *Marketing research: Methodological foundations* (5th ed.). USA: Dryden Press.

Chu, S.-C., & Kamal, S. (2008). The Effect of Perceived Blogger Credibility and Argument Quality on Message Elaboration and Brand Attitudes: An Exploratory Study. *Journal of Interactive Advertising*, *8*(2), 1–31. doi:10.1080/15252019.2008.10722140

Cialdini, R. (2007). *Influence: The psychology of persuasion*. New York: HarperCollins.

Clemons, E. K., Gao, G., & Hitt, L. M. (2006). When online reviews meet hyperdifferentiation: A study of the craft beer industry. *Journal of Management Information Systems*, *23*(2), 149–171. doi:10.2753/MIS0742-1222230207

Cliffe, S. J., & Motion, J. (2005). Building contemporary brands: A sponsorship-based strategy. *Journal of Business Research*, *58*(8), 1068–1077. doi:10.1016/j.jbusres.2004.03.004

Cohen, B. (1997). The 'Wow' Effect: How One Restaurateur Continues to Delight Customers. *The Cornell Hotel and Restaurant Administration Quarterly*, *38*(2).

Cohen, E. (1972). Toward a sociology of international tourism. *Social Research*, *39*(1), 164–183.

Constantinides, E. (2004). Influencing the online consumer's behavior: The Web experience. *Internet Research*, *14*(2), 111–126. doi:10.1108/10662240410530835

Consumer Trust in Online Social and Mobile Advertising Grows. (2012) Retrieved from http://www.nielsen.com/us/en/insights/news/2012/ consumer-trust-in-online-social-and-mobile-advertising-grows.html

Corbin, J., & Strauss, A. (2008). Basics of Qualitative Research (3rd ed.). Thousand Oaks, CA: Sage.

Corbitt, B., Thanasankit, T., & Yi, H. (2003). Trust and e-commerce: A study of consumer perception. *Electronic Commerce Research and Applications*, *2*(3), 203–215. doi:10.1016/S1567-4223(03)00024-3

Corcoran, C. T. (2010, February17). 2010). Fashion's New Fever: Bloggers in Spotlight As They Aim for Fame. *Women's Wear Daily*, *199*, 18.

Cordelia Jenkins, S. A. (2011, December 8). *How 'Kolaveri Di' went viral.* Retrieved August 30, 2014, from http://www.livemint.com: http://www.livemint.com/Consumer/x7AZWkwVBjr7MbqrTyuChM/How-8216Kolaveri-Di8217-went-viral.html

Cordell, V. (1991). Competitive Context and Price as Moderators of Country of Origin Preference. *Journal of the Academy of Marketing Science*, *19*(Spring), 123–128. doi:10.1007/BF02726004

Cova, B., & Stefano, P. (2006). Brand Community of Convenience Products: New Forms of Customer Empowerment—The Case "My Nutella The Community". *European Journal of Marketing*, *40*(9/10), 1087–1105. doi:10.1108/03090560610681023

Cozma, R., & Chen, K.-J. (2013). What's in a tweet? Foreign correspondents' use of social media. *Journalism Practice*, *7*(1), 33–46. doi:10.1080/17512786.2012.683340

Crick, A. P. (2003). Internal marketing of attitudes in Caribbean tourism. *International Journal of Contemporary Hospitality Management*, *15*(3), 161–166. doi:10.1108/09596110310470202

Crotts, J. C., & Erdmann, R. (2000). Does national culture influence consumers' evaluation of travel services? A test of Hofstede's model of cross-cultural differences. *Managing Service Quality*, *10*(6), 410–419. doi:10.1108/09604520010351167

Cruz, D. B. P. A. (2012). The Netnography in the Consumers' Boycott Studies: The Brazilian Company Arezzo Case. *Revista de Administracaodo Gestor*, *2*, 119–146.

Cruz, D., & Fill, C. (2008). Evaluating viral marketing: Isolating the key criteria. *Marketing Intelligence & Planning*, *26*(7), 743–758. doi:10.1108/02634500810916690

Czepiel, J. A. (1974). Word-of-mouth process in the diffusion process of a major technological innovation. *JMR, Journal of Marketing Research*, *11*(2), 172–180. doi:10.2307/3150555

Daniel, P. S., & Aroma, G. S. (2011). *Research Methodology*. Gyan Publishing House.

Das, A. (2014, May). *How 'likes' bring votes – Narendra Modi's campaign on Facebook.* Retrieved August 30, 2014, from http://scroll.in/article/664756/How-%27likes%27-bring-votes-%E2%80%93-Narendra-Modi%E2%80%99s-campaign-on-Facebook

Das, D. (2013, May 20). *Evolution, rapid growth & future of research on electronic word of mouth (eWOM): A scientific review.* Retrieved from http://papers.ssrn.com: http://papers.ssrn.com/sol3/papers.cfm?abstract_id=2287134

Das, M. (2012). Innovation in Online Data Collection for Scientific Research: The Dutch MESS Project. *Methodological Innovations Online*, *7*, 7–24.

Daugherty, T., & Hoffman, E. (2014). eWOM and the importance of capturing consumer attention within social media. *Journal of Marketing Communications*, *20*(1-2), 82–102. doi:10.1080/13527266.2013.797764

Day, G. (1971). Attitude change, media, and word of mouth. *Journal of Advertising Research*, *11*(6), 31–40.

Day, G. S. (1971). Attitude change, media and word of mouth. *Journal of Advertising Research*, *11*(6), 31–40.

De Angelis, M., Bonezzi, A., Peluso, A. M., Rucker, D. D., & Costabile, M. (2012, August). On braggards and gossip: A self-enhancement account of word-of-mouth generation and transmission. *JMR, Journal of Marketing Research*, *XLXI*(4), 551–563. doi:10.1509/jmr.11.0136

De Bruyn, A., & Lilien, G. L. (2004). *A multi-stage model of word of mouth through electronic referrals.* eBusiness Research Center, Working Paper.

De Cristofaro, E. F. (2014). Paying for Likes?: Understanding Facebook Like Fraud Using Honeypots. In *Proceedings of the 2014 Conference on Internet Measurement Conference* (pp. 129-136). ACM.

Dearden, P., & Harron, S. (1992). Case study: Tourism and the Hilltribes of Thailand. In B. Weiler & B. M. Hall (Eds.), Special Interest Tourism. London: Belhaven Press.

Dellarocas, C. (2003). The digitization of word of mouth: Promise and challenges of online feedback mechanisms. *Management Science*, *49*(10), 1407–1424. doi:10.1287/mnsc.49.10.1407.17308

Dellarocas, C., & Narayan, R. (2006). A statistical measure of a population's propensity to engage in post-purchase online word-of-mouth. *Statistical Science*, *21*(2), 277–285. doi:10.1214/088342306000000169

Deloitte. (2014, September 11). *A new breed of brand advocates Social networking redefines consumer engagement.* Retrieved from: http://bit.ly/1tAnCrN

DeMers, J. (2014). *Forbes Top 10 Benefits Of Social Media Marketing.* Retrieved February 2015 from www. infused-digital.com

Dennen, V., & Myers, J. (2012). *Virtual Professional Development and Informal Learning via Social Networks.* IGI Global. doi:10.4018/978-1-4666-1815-2

Derya, K. O., & Camilla, V. (2013). Reconceptualising Fieldwork in a Netnography of an Online Community of English Language Teacher. *Ethnography and Education*, *8*(2), 224–238. doi:10.1080/17457823.2013.792511

Desmet, P. (2005). Measuring emotion: Development and application of an instrument to measure emotional responses to products. In Funology (pp. 111-123). Springer Netherlands.

Detterbeck, K., LaMoreaux, N., & Sciangula, M. (2012). Style and Substance: The Information Seeking Behavior of Fashion Bloggers. New-York: SUNNY.

Dhamija, A., & Phadnis, S. (2014, April 1). Internet users in India. *Times of India*, p. 11.

Dholakia, U. M., Bagozzi, R. P., & Pearo, L. K. (2004). A social influence model of consumer participation in network-and small-group-based virtual communities. *International Journal of Research in Marketing*, *21*(3), 241–263. doi:10.1016/j.ijresmar.2003.12.004

Díaz-Martín, A. M., Iglesias, V., Vázquez, R., & Ruiz, A. V. (2000). The use of quality expectations to segment a service market. *Journal of Services Marketing*, *14*(2), 132–146. doi:10.1108/08876040010320957

Dichter, E. (1966). How word of mouth advertising works. *Harvard Business Review*, *44*(6), 147–160.

Dierkes, E., Bichler, M., & Krishnan, R. (2011). Estimating the effect of word of mouth on churn and cross buying decisions in the mobile phone market with markov logic networks. *Decision Support Systems*, *51*(3), 361–371. doi:10.1016/j.dss.2011.01.002

Dobele, A., Lindgreen, A., Beverland, M., Vanhamme, J., & Wijk, R. (2007). Why pass on viral messages? Because they connect emotionally. *Business Horizons*, *50*(4), 291–304. doi:10.1016/j.bushor.2007.01.004

Dodds, W. B., Monroe, K. B., & Grewal, D. (1991). Effects of price, brand, and store information on buyers' product evaluations. *JMR, Journal of Marketing Research*, *28*(3), 307–319. doi:10.2307/3172866

Doh, S. J., & Hwang, J.-S. (2009). How consumers evaluate eWOM (electronic word-of-mouth) messages. *Cyberpsychology & Behavior*, *12*(2), 193–197. doi:10.1089/cpb.2008.0109 PMID:19072076

Drozdz, C., & Kanerva, M. (2014). *The Importance of Emotions in the Dynamics of Sharing Viral Cosmetic Videos.* Retrieved from http://lup.lub.lu.se/student-papers/record/4499507/file/4499511.pdf

Duan, W., Gu, B., & Whinston, A. B. (2008). Do online reviews matter?—An empirical investigation of panel data. *Decision Support Systems*, *45*(4), 1007–1016. doi:10.1016/j.dss.2008.04.001

Duffy, S. (2014). *Prankvertising, a new strategy for Viral Marketing in movie industry–Thinkmodo as a case study.* Retrieved from http://www.brandba.se/blog/viral-marketing-prankvertising-movie

Duhan, D., Johnson, S., Wilcox, J., & Harrell, G. (1997). Influences on consumer use of word-of-mouth recommendation sources. *Journal of the Academy of Marketing Science*, *25*(4), 283–295. doi:10.1177/0092070397254001

Duhan, P., & Singh, A. (2013). Impact of Usefulness, Ease of Use, Enjoyment, Attitude and Subjective Norms on Behavioural Intentions and Adoption Of Virtual Communities: An Empirical Study. *Journal of IMS Group*, *10*(02), 19–31.

Dwivedi, M. (2009). Online Destination Image of India: A Consumer Based Perspective. *International Journal of Contemporary Hospitality Management*, *21*(2), 226–232. doi:10.1108/09596110910935714

Dwyer, P. (2007). Measuring the value of electronic word of mouth and its impact in consumer communities. *Journal of Interactive Marketing, 21*(2), 63-79.

East, R., Hammond, K., & Lomax, W. (2008). Measuring the impact of positive and negative word of mouth on brand purchase probability. *International Journal of Research in Marketing*, *25*(3), 215–224. doi:10.1016/j.ijresmar.2008.04.001

East, R., Hammond, K., & Wright, M. (2007). The relative incidence of positive and Negative word of mouth: A multi category study. *International Journal of Research in Marketing*, *24*(2), 175–184. doi:10.1016/j.ijresmar.2006.12.004

Eckler, P., & Bolls, P. (2011). Spreading the Virus: Emotional tone of viral advertising and its effect on forwarding intentions and attitudes. *Journal of Interactive Advertising*, *11*(2), 1–11. doi:10.1080/15252019.2011.10722180

Edelman, D. C. (2010). Branding in the digital age. *Harvard Business Review*, *88*(12), 62–69.

Edwards, S. (2006). Special Issue on Electronic Word-Of-Mouth and its Relationship with Advertising, Marketing and Communication. *Journal of Interactive Advertising*, *6*, 1–2. doi:10.1080/15252019.2006.10722113

Elizabeth, S. (2015). *Online tech startups dumping direct marketing for content marketing*. Retrieved from http://articles.economictimes.indiatimes.com/2015-02-17/news/59232653_1_content-marketing-direct-marketing-customers

Elliot, G., & Cameron, A. (1994). Consumer Perception of Product Quality and the Country of Origin Effect. *Journal of International Marketing*, *2*(2), 49–62.

Ellison, N. B., Steinfield, C., & Lampe, C. (2007). The benefit of Facebook friends: Capital and college students use of online social network sites. *Journal of Computer-Mediated Communication*, *12*(4), 1143–1168. doi:10.1111/j.1083-6101.2007.00367.x

Elo, S., & Kyngäs, H. (2008). The qualitative content analysis process. *Journal of Advanced Nursing*, *62*(1), 107–115. doi:10.1111/j.1365-2648.2007.04569.x PMID:18352969

eMarketer. (2009). Why people go online. *eMarketer*. Retrieved from http://www.emarker.com/Article.aspx?R=1007184&N_{tt}=Why+People+Go+Online&No=4&xsrc=article_head_sitesearchx&N=0&N_tk=basic.access

Engel, J. B., & Miniard, P. (1993). *Cosnumer Behavior* (8th ed.). Fort Worth, TX: Dryden Press.

Engel, J. F., Blackwell, R. D., & Miniard, P. W. (1993). *Consumer behavior* (8th ed.). Fort Worth: Dryden-Press.

Engel, J. F., Kegerris, R. J., & Blackwell, R. D. (1969). Word of mouth communication by the innovator. *Journal of Marketing*, *33*(3), 15–19. doi:10.2307/1248475

Erciş, A., Ünal, S., Candan, F. B., & Yıldırım, H. (2012). The effect of brand satisfaction, trust and brand commitment on loyalty and repurchase intentions. *Procedia: Social and Behavioral Sciences*, *58*, 1395–1404. doi:10.1016/j.sbspro.2012.09.1124

Erétéo, G., Gandon, F., Corby, O., & Buffa, M. (2009). Semantic social network analysis. In B. K. Daniel (Ed.), *Handbook of Research on Methods and Techniques for Studying Virtual Communities: Paradigms and Phenomena* (pp. 122–156). Academic Press.

Erkuş-Öztürk, H., & Eraydin, A. (2011). Factors of Global Connectivity in Antalya's Tourism. *Annals of Tourism Research*, *38*(4), 1300–1321. doi:10.1016/j.annals.2011.03.002

Ertek, G., Tapucu, D., & Arın, I. (2013). Text Mining with RapidMiner. In M. Hofmann & R. Klinkenberg (Eds.), *RapidMiner: Data Mining Use Cases and Business Analytics Applications*. Chapman and Hall/CRC.

Evans, D., & Volery, T. (2001). Online business development services for entrepreneurs: An exploratory study. *Entrepreneurship & Regional Development*, *13*(4), 333–350. doi:10.1080/08985620110052274

Evans, M., Wedande, G., Ralston, L., & Hul, S. (2001). Consumer Interaction in the Virtual Era: Some Qualitative Insights. *Qualitative Market Research*, *4*(3), 150–159. doi:10.1108/13522750110393053

Fader, P. S., Hardie, B. G. S., & Lee, K. L. (2005). RFM and CLV: Using iso-value curves for customer base analysis. *JMR, Journal of Marketing Research*, *62*(4), 415–430. doi:10.1509/jmkr.2005.42.4.415

Fandrich, M. W. (2007). *La Dernière Mode: Blogging Fashion.* Paper presented at the extremefashion - Pushing the boundaries of design, technology and business, Ryserson University.

Fan, Y. W. (2012). Effect of electronic word-of-mouth on consumer purchase intention: The perspective of gender differences. *International Journal of Electronic BusinessManagement*, *10*(3), 175.

Farmer, T., & Atchison, S. (2014, September 10). *Yours is a very bad hotel*. Retrieved from: http://bit.ly/WPT7ni

Fattah, H. (2000). Viral marketing is nothing new. *Technology Marketing Intelligence*, *20*(10), 1–3.

Faulds, W. G. (2009). Social media: The new hybrid element of the promotion mix. *52*(4), 357-365.

Fauser, S. G., Wiedenhofer, J., & Lorenz, M. (2011). "Touchpoint social web": An explorative study about using the social web for influencing high involvement purchase decisions. *Problems and Perspectives in Management.*, *9*(1), 39–45.

Ferguson, R. (2008). Word of mouth and viral marketing: Taking the temperature of the hottest trends in marketing. *Journal of Consumer Marketing*, *25*(3), 179–182. doi:10.1108/07363760810870671

Ferraresi, M., & Schmitt, B. H. (2006). *Marketing esperienziale*. Milano: FrancoAngeli.

Fetterman, D. M. (2009). *Ethnography: Step By Step*. London: Sage. doi:10.4135/9781483348858.n17

Field, A. (2009). *Discovering statistics using SPSS* (3rd ed.). New Delhi: Sage Publications India Ltd.

File, K., Judd, B., & Prince, R. (1992). Interactive Marketing: The Influence of Participation. *Journal of Services Marketing*, *6*(4), 5–14. doi:10.1108/08876049210037113

Filieri, R. (2015). What Makes Online Reviews Helpful? A Diagnosticity-Adoption Framework to Explain Informational and Normative Influences in e-WOM. *Journal of Business Research*, *68*(6), 1261–1270. doi:10.1016/j.jbusres.2014.11.006

Filieri, R., & McLeay, F. (2013). E-WOM and Accommodation: An Analysis of the Factors That Influence Travelers' Adoption of Information from Online Reviews. *Journal of Travel Research*, *53*(1), 44–57. doi:10.1177/0047287513481274

Fiske, S. T. (2001), Five core social motives, plus or minus five, In S. Spencer, S. Fein, M. Zanna & J. Olsen (Eds.), *Motivated Social Perception:The Ontario Symposium*, vol.9, Psychology Press.

Flanagan, P., Johnston, R., & Talbot, D. (2005). Customer confidence: The development of a "pre-experience" concept. *International Journal of Service Industry Management*, *16*(4), 373–384. doi:10.1108/09564230510614013

Fong, J., & Burton, S. (2006). Electronic Word-of-Mouth: A Comparison of Stated and Revealed Behavior on Electronic Discussion Boards. *Journal of Interactive Advertising*, *6*(2), 61–70. doi:10.1080/15252019.2006.10722119

Fong, J., & Burton, S. (2008). A cross cultural comparison of electronic word-of-mouth and country-of-origin effects. *Journal of Business Research*, *61*(3), 233–242. doi:10.1016/j.jbusres.2007.06.015

Foon, Y. S., & Fah, B. C. Y. (2011). Internet banking adoption in Kuala Lumpur: An application of UTAUT model. *International Journal of Business and Management*, *6*(4), 161–167.

Forbes (2014, September 11). *Here's is how Facebook and Google might completely disappear in the next 5 years*. Retrieved from: http://onforb.es/WMjF8J

Forges, T. (2007). Valuing Customers. *Journal of Database Marketing & Customer Strategy Management*, *15*, 20–57.

Foster, M. K., Francescucci, A., & West, B. C. (2010). Why users participate in online social networks. *International Journal of Business and Management*, *4*(1), 3–19.

Fournie, S., & Lee, R. (2009). *Getting Brand Communities Right*. Retrieved 4 15, 2015, from https://hbr.org: https://hbr.org/2009/04/getting-brand-communities-right

Fournier, S. (1998). Consumers and their brands: Developing relationship theory in consumer research. *The Journal of Consumer Research*, *24*(4), 343–353. doi:10.1086/209515

Fowler, G. (2009). Survey Research Methods. *Sage (Atlanta, Ga.)*.

Gabriella, B. (2006). *Imagery and Spatial Cognition: Methods, models and cognitive assessment*. John Benjamins Publishing.

Gaggioli, A., Milani, L., Mazzoni, E., & Riva, G. (2011). Networked flow: A framework for understanding the dynamics of creative collaboration in educational and training settings. *The Open Education Journal*, *4*(1), M3. doi:10.2174/1874920801104010041

Gaggioli, A., Riva, G., Milani, L., & Mazzoni, E. (2012). *Networked flow: Towards an understanding of creative networks*. Berlin, Germany: Springer.

Gaitan, A. C. (2013). *Social identity, electronic word-of-mouth and referrals in social network services*. Spain: Emerald Group Publishing Limited.

Garbarino, E., & Johnson, M. S. (1999). The Different Roles of Satisfaction, Trust, and Commitmentin Customer Relationships. *Journal of Marketing*, *63*(2), 70–87. doi:10.2307/1251946

Gassiot, A., & Coromina, L. (2013). Destination Image of Girona: An Online Text-Mining Approach. *International Journal of Management Cases*, *15*(4), 301–314.

Gehl, D. (2006). *How to Harness the Marketing Power of Blogs*. Retrieved from http://www.entrepreneur.com: http://www.entrepreneur.com/article/84232

Gelter, H. (2007a). Towards an understanding of experience production. In Articles on Experiences 4 Digital Media & Games. University of Lapland Press.

Gelter, H. (2007b). Experience production in digital media and games. In Articles on Experiences 4 Digital Media & Games. University of Lapland Press.

Giglietto, F., & Rossi, L. (2012). Ethics and Interdisciplinarity in Computational Social Science. *Methodological Innovations Online*, *7*, 25–36.

Gladwin, C. H. (Ed.). (1989). *Ethnographic decision tree modeling* (Vol. 19). Beverly Hills, CA: Sage Publication.

Global digital music market to top $9 billion in 2014. (n.d.). Retrieved from http://articles.economictimes.indiatimes.com/keyword/digital-marketing/recent/3

Go, A., Huang, L., & Bhayani. R. (2009). *Twitter sentiment analysis*. Final Projects from CS224N for Spring 2008/2009 at The Stanford Natural Language Processing Group.

Goddarad, W., & Melville, S. (2004). *Research Methodology: An Introduction*. Juta and Company Ltd.

Godes, D. M. (2005). The Firm's Management of Social Interactions. *Marketing Science*, 415–428.

Godes, D., & Mayzlin, D. (2004). Using Online Conversations to Study Word-of-Mouth Communication. *Marketing Science*, *23*(4), 545–560. doi:10.1287/mksc.1040.0071

Godin, S. (2001). *Les secrets du marketing viral: le bouche- à- oreille à la puissance 10!* Paris Maxima Laurent Du Mesnil Éditeur.

Golan, G. J., & Zaidner, L. (2008). Creative Strategies in Viral Advertising: An Application of Taylor's Six-Segment Message Strategy Wheel. *Journal of Computer-Mediated Communication*, *13*(4), 959–972. doi:10.1111/j.1083-6101.2008.00426.x

Goldsmith, R. E. (2006). Measuring motivations for online opinion seeking. *Journal of Interactive Advertising, 6*(4), 2-14.

Goldsmith, R. E., & Horowitz, D. (2006). Measuring Motivations for Online Opinion Seeking. *Journal of Interactive Advertising*, *6*(2), 1–16. doi:10.1080/15252019.2006.10722114

Gordon, W. (1999). *Good Thinking: A Guide to Qualitative Research.* Henley-on-Thames, UK: Admap Publications.

Gountas, S., & Ewing, M. (2003). The softer side of services: exploring the effect of sincerity and emotional contagion on satisfaction.*Conference Proceedings. Adelaide: ANZMAC '03'.*

Goyette, I. R. (2010). e-WOM Scale: Word-of_Mouth Measurement Scale for e-Services Context. *Canadian Journal of Administrative Sciences/Revue Canadienne des Sciences de l'Administration, 27*(1), 5-23.

Goyette, I., Ricard, L., Bergeron, J., & Marticotte, F. (2010). e-WOM Scale: Word-of-Mouth Measurement Scale for e-Services Context. *Canadian Journal of Administrative Sciences, 27*(1), 5–23. doi:10.1002/cjas.129

Graham, S., & Weiner, B. (1986). From attribution theory to developmental psychology: A round-trip ticket? *Social Cognition, 4*(2), 152–179. doi:10.1521/soco.1986.4.2.152

Gramtz, N. A., & Ward, J. C. (1996). Virtual Community: A Social-cognitive Analysis. *Advertising Consumer Research, 23*, 161–166.

Granitz, N. A., & Ward, J. C. (1996). Virtual Community: A Socio-cognitive Analysis. *Advances in Consumer Research. Association for Consumer Research (U. S.), 23*, 161–166.

Greer, C. F., & Ferguson, D. A. (2011). Using Twitter for promotion and branding: A content analysis of local television Twitter sites. *Journal of Broadcasting & Electronic Media, 55*(2), 198–214. doi:10.1080/08838151.2011.570824

Gremler, D. D. (1994). Word-of-mouth about service providers: an illustration of theory development in marketing. In C. W. Park & D. Smith (Eds.), *AMA Winter Educators' Conference: Marketing Theory and Applications* (pp. 62–70). Chicago, IL: American Marketing Association.

Gremler, D. D., Gwinner, K. P., & Brown, S. W. (2001). Generating Positive Word-of-Mouth Communication Trough Customer-Employee Relationships. *International Journal of Service Industry Management, 12*(1), 44–59. doi:10.1108/09564230110382763

Grewal, D., Gotlieb, J., & Marmorstein, H. (1994). The Moderating Effects of Message Framing and Source Credibility on the Price-perceived Risk Relationship. *The Journal of Consumer Research, 21*(1), 145–153. doi:10.1086/209388

Groth, R. (1999). *Data Mining: Building Competitive Advantage.* Prentice Hall PTR.

Grubb, E. L., & Grathwohl, H. L. (1967). Consumer self-concept, symbolism and marketing behavior: A theoretical approach. *Journal of Marketing, 31*(4), 22–27. doi:10.2307/1249461

Guadagni, P., & De Tommaso, V. (2007). *Ilnuovopoteredeiconsumatorisul web.* Hoepli.

Gumpert, G., & Cathcart, R. (1986). *Inter/Media: Interpersonal Communication in a Media World.* New York: Oxford University Press.

Gupta, P., & Harris, J. (2010). How eWOM recommandations influence product consideration and quality of choice: A motivation to process information perspective. *Journal of Business Research, 63*(9-10), 1041–1049. doi:10.1016/j.jbusres.2009.01.015

Gupta, V., & Lehal, G. S. (2009). A Survey of Text Mining Techniques and Applications. *Journal of Emerging Technologies in Web Intelligence, 1*(1), 60–76. doi:10.4304/jetwi.1.1.60-76

Ha, H., & Perks, H. (2005). Effects of consumer perceptions of brand experience on the web : Brand familiarity, satisfaction and brand trust. *Journal of Consumer Behaviour, 4*(6), 438–452. doi:10.1002/cb.29

Ha, H.-Y. (2004). Factors influencing consumer perception on brand trust on the online. *Journal of Product and Brand Management*, *13*(5), 329–342. doi:10.1108/10610420410554412

Hair, J., Robert, B. R., & Ortinau, D. (2009). Marketing Research in a Digital Information Environment (4th ed.). New York: McGraw Hill/Irwin.

Hair, J. F., Black, W. C., Babin, B. B., & Anderson, R. E. (2006). *Multivariate data analysis*. New Jersey: Prentice Hall.

Haksever, C., Render, B., Russell, R. S., & Murdick, R. G. (2000). *Service Management and Operations* (2nd ed.). London: Prentice-Hall International.

Hamilton, K., & Hewer, P. (2009). Salsa Magic: An Exploratory Netnography Analysis of the Salsa Experience. *Advertising Consumer Researc.*, *36*, 502–510.

Han, J., & Kamber, M. (2001). *Data Mining: Concepts and Techniques*. Morgan Kaufmann Publishers.

Hansen, S. S., & Lee, J. K. (2013). What drives consumers to pass along marketer generated eWOM in social network games? Social and game factors. *Journal of Theoretical And Applied Electronic Commerce*, *8*(1), 53–68.

Hareli, S., & Parkinson, B. (2008). What's social about social emotions? *Journal for the Theory of Social Behaviour*, *38*(2), 131–156. doi:10.1111/j.1468-5914.2008.00363.x

Harris, J., & Gupta, P. (2008). You Should Buy This One! The Influences of Online Reccomandations on Product Attitudes and Choice Confidence. *Journal of Electronic Marketing and Retailing*, *2*(2), 176–189. doi:10.1504/IJEMR.2008.019816

Harrison-Walker, L. (2001). E-complaining: A Content Analysis of an Internet Complaint Forum. *Journal of Services Marketing*, *15*(5), 397–412. doi:10.1108/EUM0000000005657

Harvey, C. G., Stewart, D. B., & Ewing, M. T. (2011). Forward or delete: What drives peer-to-peer message propagation across social networks? *Journal of Consumer Behaviour*, *10*(6), 365–372. doi:10.1002/cb.383

Hatfield, E., Cacioppo, J. L., & Rapson, R. L. (1993). Emotional contagion. *Current Directions in Psychological Science*, *2*(3), 96–99. doi:10.1111/1467-8721.ep10770953

Haven, B. (2007). *Marketing's New Key Metric: Engagement*. Marketing. Retrieved on February, 07, 2013 from http://www.adobe.com/engagement/pdfs/marketings_new_key_metric_engagement.pdf

Haywood, K. (1989). Managing Word of Mouth Communications. *Journal of Services Marketing*, *3*(2), 55–67. doi:10.1108/EUM0000000002486

Hearst, M. (1999). Untangling Text Data Mining. In *Proceedings of ACL'99: the 37th Annual Meeting of the Association for Computational Linguistics,* University of Maryland. Available at http://people.ischool.berkeley.edu/~hearst/pape rs/acl99/acl99-tdm.html

Heinrich, A. (2012). Foreign reporting in the sphere of network journalism. *Journalism Practice*, *6*(5-6), 766–775. doi:10.1080/17512786.2012.667280

Helm, S. (2000). Virtual Marketing- Establishing Customer Relationships By 'Word Of Mouth'. *Electronic Markets*, *10*(3), 158–164. doi:10.1080/10196780050177053

Hennig-Thurau, T., Gwinner, K. P., Walsh, G., & Gremler, D. D. (2004). Electronic word-of-mouth via consumer-opinion platforms: What motivates consumers to articulate themselves on the Internet? *Journal of Interactive Marketing*, *18*(1), 38–52. doi:10.1002/dir.10073

Hennig-Thurau, T., & Walsh, G. (2003). Electronic Word-of-Mouth: Motives for and Consequences of Reading Customer Articulations on the Internet. *International Journal of Electronic Commerce*, *8*(2), 51–74.

Hennig-Thurau, T., & Walsh, G. (2004). Electronic word-of-mouth: Motives for and consequences of reading customer articulations on the Internet. *International Journal of Electronic Commerce*, *8*(2), 51–74.

Herrera, S., & Requejo, J. L. (2012). 10 Good Practices for News Organizations Using Twitter. *Journal of Applied Journalism & Media Studies*, *1*(1), 79–95. doi:10.1386/ajms.1.1.79_1

He, W., Zha, S., & Li, L. (2013). Social Media Competitive Analysis and Text Mining: A Case Study in the Pizza Industry. *International Journal of Information Management*, *33*(3), 464–472. doi:10.1016/j.ijinfomgt.2013.01.001

Heyne, L. (2009). *Electronic Word of Mouth - a New Marekting Tool? A Practical Approach to the Opportunities and Perils of Consumer Generated Online Content.* Academic Press.

Hill, J. (2005). *The voice of the blog: the attitudes and experiences of small business bloggers using blogs as a marketing and communications tool.* (MBA Thesis). The University of Liverpool, Liverpool, UK.

Hirsjärvi, S., & Hurme, H. (2006). *Research Interview: The theme of the interview theory and practice.* Helsinki: Helsinki University Press.

Hirsjärvi, S., Remes, P., & Sajavaara, P. (2004). *Examine, and type.* Helsinki: Tammi.

Hobbs, D. (2011). *Ethnography in Context.* SAGA. doi:10.4135/9781446261583

Hoch, Y., & Ha, Y.-W. (1986). Consumer Learning: Advertising and the ambiguity of product experience. *The Journal of Consumer Research*, *13*(2), 221–233. doi:10.1086/209062

Hofstede, G. (1991). *Cultures and organizations: Intercultural cooperation and its importance for survival: software of the mind.* London: McGraw-Hill.

Ho, J. Y., & Dempsey, M. (2010). Viral marketing: Motivations to forward online content. *Journal of Business Research*, *63*(9), 1000–1006. doi:10.1016/j.jbusres.2008.08.010

Holbrook, M. B. (2001). The millennial consumer in the texts of our times: Exhibitionism. *Journal of Macromarketing*, *21*(1), 81–95. doi:10.1177/0276146701211008

Holbrook, M. B., & Hirschman, E. C. (1982). The Experiential Aspects of Consumption: Consumer Fantasies, Feelings, and Fun. *The Journal of Consumer Research*, *9*(2), 132–140. doi:10.1086/208906

Holjevac, I. A., Marković, S., & Raspor, S. (2000), *Customer Satisfaction Measurement in Hotel Industry: Content Analysis Study.* Working paper.

Hollenbaugh, E. E. (2011). Motives for maintaining personal journal blogs. *Cyberpsychology, Behavior, and Social Networking*, *14*(1-2), 13–20. doi:10.1089/cyber.2009.0403 PMID:21329438

Hornik, J., Satchi, R. S., Cesareo, L., & Pastore, A. (2015). Information Dissemination Via Electronic Word-of-Mouth: Good News Travels Fast, Bad News Travels Faster! *Computers in Human Behavior*, *45*, 273–280. doi:10.1016/j.chb.2014.11.008

Hoser, B., Hotho, A., Jäschke, R., Schmitz, C., & Stumme, G. (2006). *Semantic network analysis of ontologies.* Berlin, Germany: Springer. doi:10.1007/11762256_38

Hovland, C. I. (1948). Social Communication. *Proceedings of the American Philosophical Society*, *92*(5), 371–375.

Hovland, C. I., & Weiss, W. (1951). The influence of source credibility on communications effectiveness. *Public Opinion Quarterly*, *15*(4), 635–650. doi:10.1086/266350

How IKEA uses social media to emerge a marketing success. (n.d.). Retrieved Sept 18, 2014, from http://articles.economictimes.indiatimes.com/2014-03-03/news/47859301_1_largest-home-furnishing-retailer-catalogue-own-friends-day

Hsu, Y., & Tran, T. H. C. (2013). Social relationship factors influence on eWOM behaviors in social networking sites: an empirical study: Taiwan and Vietnam. *International Journal of Business. Human Technology*, *3*(3), 22–31.

Huang, M., Cai, F., Tsang, A. S. L., & Zhou, N. (2011). Making your online voice loud: The critical role of WOM information. *European Journal of Marketing*, *45*(7/8), 1277–1297. doi:10.1108/03090561111137714

Huang, P., Lurie, N., & Mitra, S. (2009). Searching for Experience on the Web: An Empirical Examination of Consumer Behavior for Search and Experience Goods. *Journal of Marketing*, *73*(2), 55–69. doi:10.1509/jmkg.73.2.55

Hughes, R. (2010). *Enterprise Social Networking: Don ' t Be Afraid.* Retrieved on February 14, 2014 from http://www.clearvale.com/clearvale/mkt-nav/en/whitepapers/Enterprise_Social_Networking-Dont_Be_Afraid_2010_02_24.pdf

Hui, M. K., & Bateson John, E. G. (1991). Perceived Control and the Effects of Crowding and Consumer Choice on Service Experience. *The Journal of Consumer Research*, *18*(2), 174–184. doi:10.1086/209250

Hung, H. A., (2007). The Influence of Ewom on Virtual consumer communities:Social capital,Conusmer Learning and Behavioral outcomes. *Journal of Advertising Research.*

Hung, K. H., & Yiyan Li, S. (2007). The Influence of eWOM on Virtual Consumer Communities: Social Capital, Consumer Learning, and Behavioral Outcomes. *Journal of Advertising Research*, *47*(4), 485–495. doi:10.2501/S002184990707050X

Hussain, P. T. (2011). *Research Methodology in physical education.* Pinnacle Technology.

Hwang, S.J., (2009). How Consumers Evaluate eWOM (Electronic Word-of-Mouth) Messages. *CyberPsychology & Behavior*, 193-197.

IEEE. (2007). *WI '07: Proceedings of the IEEE/WIC/ACM International Conference on Web Intelligence.* Washington, DC: IEEE Computer Society.

Illia, L. (2002). Passage to cyberactivism: How dynamics of activism change. *Journal of Public Affairs*, *3*(4), 326–337. doi:10.1002/pa.161

Internet World Stats. (2014, Sept 24). Retrieved from http://www.internetlivestats.com: http://www.internetlivestats.com/internet-users/

Ionel, O. (2012). *Effective Online Marketing with Forums and Message Boards.* Retrieved from http://kikolani.com/effective-online-marketing-with-forums-and-message-boards.html

Ipsos, O. T. X. Ipsos Global @dvisor Survey (2012, June 26). *Socialogue.* Retrieved from http://www.ipsos-na.com/news-polls/pressrelease.aspx?id=5671

Ismail, A. R. (2010). *Investigating British Customers' Experience to Maximize Brand Loyalty Within the Context of Tourism In Egypt: Netnography And Structural Modeling Approach.* Retrieved from http://bura.brunel.ac.uk/handle/2438/4461

Izawa, M. (2010). What makes viral videos viral? Roles of emotion, impression, utility, and social ties in online sharing behavior. Baltimore, MD: The Johns Hopkins University. Retrieved from http://advanced.jhu.edu/media/files/communication/Izawa-Thesis-Final.pdf

Jacob, E. (1987). Qualitative Research Traditions: A Review. *Review of Educational Research*, *57*(1), 1–50. doi:10.3102/00346543057001001

Jalilvand, M. R., Ebrahimi, A., & Samiei, N. (2013). Electronic Word Of Mouth Effects on Tourist' Attitudes Towards Islamic Destinations and Travel Intentions: An Empirical Study in Iran. *Procedia: Social and Behavioral Sciences*, *81*, 484–489. doi:10.1016/j.sbspro.2013.06.465

Jalilvand, M. R., Esfahani, S. S., & Samiei, N. (2011). Electronic word-of-mouth: Challenges and opportunities. *Procedia Computer Science*, *3*, 42–46. doi:10.1016/j.procs.2010.12.008

Jalilvand, M., Samiei, N., Dini, B., & Manzari, P. (2012). Examining the Structural Relationships of Electronic Word of Mouth, Destination Image, Tourist Attitude Toward Destination and Travel Intention: An Integrated Approach. *Journal of Destination Marketing & Management*, *1*(1-2), 134–143. doi:10.1016/j.jdmm.2012.10.001

Jansen, B. J., Zhang, M., Sobel, K., & Chowdury, A. (2009). *Micro-blogging as online word of mouth branding*. Paper presented at the CHI'09 Extended Abstracts on Human Factors in Computing Systems. doi:10.1145/1520340.1520584

Janta, H., & Ladkin, A. (2009). Polish Migrant Labour in the Hospitality Workforce: Implications for Recruitiment and Retention. *Tourism Culture and Communication*, *9*(1), 5–15. doi:10.3727/109830409787556693

Javornik, A.A., (2012). Behavioral perspectives of customer engagement: An exploratory study of customer engagement with three Swiss FMCG brands. *Journal of Database Marketing & Customer Strategy Management*, 300–310.

Jayanti, R. K. (2010). Anetnographic Explanation: Listing to Online Consumer Conversations. *Journal of Advertising Research*, *50*(2), 181–196. doi:10.2501/S0021849910091348

Jeong, E., Cheong, S., & Jang, S. (2011). Restaurant experiences triggering positive electronic word of mouth (eWOM) motivations. *International Journal of Hospitality Management*, *30*(2), 356–366. doi:10.1016/j.ijhm.2010.08.005

Jepsen, A. L. (2006). Information Search in Virtual Communities: Is it Replacing Use of Off-Line Communication? *Journal of Marketing Communications*, *12*(4), 247–261. doi:10.1080/13527260600694308

Johar, G. V., Sengupta, J., & Aaker, J. L. (2005). Two roads to updating brand personality impressions: Trait versus evaluative inferences. *JMR, Journal of Marketing Research*, *42*(4), 458–469. doi:10.1509/jmkr.2005.42.4.458

Johnson, C., & Mathews, B. P. (1997). The influence of experience on service expectations. *International Journal of Service Industry Management*, *8*(4), 290–305. doi:10.1108/09564239710174381

Johnson, T. J., & Kaye, B. K. (2004). Wag the blog: How reliance on traditional media and the Internet influence credibility perceptions of weblogs among blog users. *Journalism & Mass Communication Quarterly*, *81*(3), 622–642. doi:10.1177/107769900408100310

Johnston, R. (1999). Service transaction analysis: Assessing and improving the customer's experience. *Managing Service Quality*, *9*(2), 102–109. doi:10.1108/09604529910257876

Jones, P., & Dent, M. (1994). Improving Service: Managing Response Time in Hospitality Operations. *International Journal of Operations & Production Management*, *14*(5), 52–58. doi:10.1108/01443579410056795

Joshi, P. (2009). *Approval by a Blogger May Please a Sponsor*. Retrieved from http://www.nytimes.com/2009/07/13/technology/internet/13blog.html?_r=0

Joy, A., & Sherry, J. F. Jr. (2003). Speaking of art as embodied imagination: A multisensory approach to understanding aesthetic experience. *The Journal of Consumer Research*, *30*(2), 259–282. doi:10.1086/376802

Kalakota, R., & Robinson, M. (2001). e-Business 2.0 Roadmap for Success (2nd ed.). New Delhi: Pearson Education.

Kaner, G. (2013). *Consumer as an Institution in the Fashion System and the Participatory Role of New Media Technologies*. (New Media and Digital Culture Academic Master Master thesis). Universitat Utrecht, Utrecht, The Netherlands.

Kania, D. (2001). *Branding. com*. Lincolnwood, IL: NTC Business Books.

Kanouse, D. E. (1984). Explaining Negativity Biases in Evaluation and Choice Beavior: Theory and Reserach. *Advances in Consumer Research. Association for Consumer Research (U. S.)*, *11*(1), 703–708.

Kaplan, A. M., & Haenlein, M. (2010). Users of the world, unite! The challenges and opportunities of Social Media. *Business Horizons*, *53*(1), 59–68. doi:10.1016/j.bushor.2009.09.003

Kaplan, A. M., & Haenlein, M. (2011). Two hearts in three-quarter time: How to waltz the social media/viral marketing dance. *Business Horizons*, *54*(3), 253–263. doi:10.1016/j.bushor.2011.01.006

Karin, B., & Brian, B. (2011). What Motivates Consumers to Participate in Boycotts: Lessons from the Ongoing Canadian Seafood Boycott. *Journal of Business Research*, *64*(1), 96–102. doi:10.1016/j.jbusres.2009.12.008

Karlsson, M., & Strömbäck, J. (2010). Freezing the flow of online news: Exploring approaches to the study of the liquidity of online news. *Journalism Studies*, *11*(1), 2–19. doi:10.1080/14616700903119784

Karpf, D. (2012). Social science research methods in Internet time. *Information Communication and Society*, *15*(5), 639–661. doi:10.1080/1369118X.2012.665468

Kassarjian, H. H. (1977). Content Analysis in Consumer Research. *The Journal of Consumer Research*, *4*(1), 8–18. doi:10.1086/208674

Kavita. (2012).A Comparative Study of Growth, Challenges and Opportunities in FMCG of Rural Market. *Interscience Management Review*, *2*(3).

Keep Social Honest. (n.d.). Retrieved from http://www.keepsocialhonest.com/: http://www.keepsocialhonest.com/

Keller Fay Group. (2014, September 11). *The social power of television: what's in it for television*. Retrieved from: http://bit.ly/1qMT4mT

Keller, E. (2007). Unleashing the power of word of mouth: Creating brand advocacy to drive growth. *Journal of Advertising Research*, *47*(4), 448–452. doi:10.2501/S0021849907070468

Kemp, S. (2014). *Digital in India*. Retrieved on October 12, 2014 from http://www.slideshare.net/wearesocialsg/social-digital-mobile-around-the-world-january-2014

Kenny, D., & Marshall, J. F. (2000). Contextual marketing: The real business of the Internet. *Harvard Business Review*, *78*(6), 119–125. PMID:11184966

Khammash, M., & Griffiths, G. H. (2011). 'Arrivederci CIAO. com, Buongiorno Bing. com'—Electronic word-of-mouth (eWOM), antecedences and consequences. *International Journal of Information Management*, *31*(1), 82–87. doi:10.1016/j.ijinfomgt.2010.10.005

Khosl, V. R. (2014). *Social media sites like Facebook, Twitter in grip of viral videos*. Retrieved 4 15, 2015, from http://articles.economictimes.indiatimes.com/2014-08-16/news/52873607_1_video-online-social-media-viral

Kibby, M. D. (2005). Email forwardables: Folklore in the age of the internet. *New Media & Society*, *7*(6), 770–790. doi:10.1177/1461444805058161

Kietzmann, J., & Canhoto, A. (2013). Bittersweet! Understanding and Managing Electronic Word of Mouth. *Journal Of Public Affairs*, *13*(2), 146–159. doi:10.1002/pa.1470

Kilduff, M., & Brass, D. J. (2010). Organizational social network research: Core ideas and key debates. *The Academy of Management Annals*, *4*(1), 317–357. doi:10.1080/19416520.2010.494827

Kim, H. W., Chan, H. C. & Kankanhalli, A. (2014). *What motivates people to purchase digital items on virtual community websites? The desire for online self-presentation.* Information Systems Research (ISR).

Kim, B. (2011). Understanding antecedents of continuance intention in social-networking services. *Cyberpsychology, Behavior, and Social Networking*, *14*(4), 199–205. doi:10.1089/cyber.2010.0009 PMID:21192764

Kim, D. J., Ferrin, D. L., & Rao, R. H. (2008). A trust-based consumer decision-making model in electronic commerce: The role of trust, perceived risk, and their antecedents. *Decision Support Systems*, *44*(2), 544–564. doi:10.1016/j.dss.2007.07.001

Kim, H. S. (2005). Consumer profiles of apparel product involvement and values. *Journal of Fashion Marketing and Management*, *9*(2), 207–220. doi:10.1108/13612020510599358

Kim, Y., Sohn, D., & Choi, S. M. (2011). Cultural difference in motivations for using social network sites: A comparative study of American and Korean college students. *Computers in Human Behavior*, *27*(1), 365–372. doi:10.1016/j.chb.2010.08.015

Kleine, S. S., Kleine, R. E., & Allen, C. T. (1995, December). How is a possession 'me' or 'not me?' characterizing types and an antecedent of material possession attachment. *The Journal of Consumer Research*, *22*(3), 327–343. doi:10.1086/209454

Knight, C. (1999). Viral marketing – defy traditional methods for hyper growth. *Broadwatch Magazine*, *13*(11), 50-3.

Koepfler, J. A., & Fleischmann, K. R. (2012). Studying the values of hard-to-reach populations: Content analysis of Tweets by the 21st Century homeless.*Proceedings of the 2012 iConference*, *7*(1), 48-55.

Köktürk, M., & Dirsehan, T. (2012). *Veri Madenciliği ile Pazarlama Etkileşimi (Interaction between Data Mining and Marketing).* Ankara: Nobel.

Kollock, P. (1999). The economies of online cooperation: Gifts, and public goods in cyberspace. In M. A. Smith & P. Kollock (Eds.), *Communities in Cyberspace* (pp. 220–239). New York: Routledge.

Kotler, K., & Jha. (2013). Marketing Management: A South Asian Perspective. Pearson.

Kotler, P., & Armstrong, G. (2006). *Principles of Marketing.* Pearson Education.

Koufaris, M. (2002). Applying the technology acceptance model and flow theory to online consumer behavior. *Information Systems Research*, *13*(2), 205–223. doi:10.1287/isre.13.2.205.83

Kozinet, R. V. (2012). Marketing Netnography: Promoting a New Research Method. *Methodological Innovations Online*, *7*, 37–45.

Kozinets, R. V. (1997). I Want to Believe: A Netnography of the X-Philes' Subculture of Consumption. Advances in Consumer Research, 24, 470-475.

Kozinets, R. V. (1998). On Netnography: Initial Reflection on Consumer Research Investigations of Cyberculture. Advances in Consumer Research, 25, 366-371.

Kozinets, R. V. (2010a). Netnography: The Marketer's Secret Ingredient. *MIT Technology Review.* Retrieved from http://www.technologyreview.com/business/26434/

Kozinets, R. V. (2002). The field behind the screen: Using netnography for marketing research in online communities. *JMR, Journal of Marketing Research*, *39*(1), 61–72. doi:10.1509/jmkr.39.1.61.18935

Kozinets, R. V. (2006). Click to Connect. Netnography and Tribal Advertising. *Journal of Advertising Research*, *46*(3), 279–288. doi:10.2501/S0021849906060338

Kozinets, R. V. (2010b). *Netnography: Doing Ethnographic Research Online*. London: Sage.

Kozinets, R. V., Valck, K., Wojnicki, A. C., & Wilner, S. J. S. (2010). Networked narratives: Understanding word-of-mouth marketing in online communities. *Journal of Marketing*, *74*(2), 71–89. doi:10.1509/jmkg.74.2.71

Kraeuter, S. G., & Waiguny, M. (2011). *Why users stay in online social networks: Perceptions of value, trust, subjective norm, and the moderating influence of duration of use. 11th AMA Winter Educators' Conference, Winter 2011*. Chicago: American Marketing Association.

Kretz, G. (2012). Consuming Branded Stories: A Netnography of Fashion and Luxury Blog Consumption. *Advances in Consumer Research. Association for Consumer Research (U. S.)*, *40*, 1057–1058.

Krippendorff, K. (2012). *Content analysis: An introduction to its methodology*. Thousand Oaks, CA: Sage Publications; doi:10.1145/2132176.2132183

Krishnamurthy, S., & Dou, W. (2008). Note From Special Issue Editors: Advertsing With User-Generated Content: A Framework and Research Agenda. Journal of Interactive Advertising, 8(2), 1-4.

Kruitbosch, G., & Nack, F. (2008,). Broadcast yourself on YouTube: really? In *Proceedings of the 3rd ACM international workshop on Human-centered computing* (pp. 7-10). ACM. doi:10.1145/1462027.1462029

Kuada, J. (2012). *Research Methodology: A Project Guide for University Students*. Samfundslitteratur.

Kumar, K. (2014, August 5). *The untold stories of Narendra Modi's social media plan in Lok Sabha polls*. Retrieved August 30, 2014, from http://articles.economictimes.indiatimes.com/2014-08-05/news/52471092_1_bjp-team-it-cell-the-bjp

Kurtz, D., & Boone, L. (2010). Principles of Contemporary Marketing (14th int. ed.). South-Western.

Lakoff, G., & Johnson, M. (2008). *Metaphors we live by*. University of Chicago press.

Lampel, J., & Bhalla, A. (2007). The role of status seeking in online communities: Giving the gift of experience. *Journal of Computer-Mediated Communication*, *12*(2), 434–455. doi:10.1111/j.1083-6101.2007.00332.x

Langer, R., & Beckman, S. C. (2005). Sensitive research topics: Netnography revisited. *Qualitative Market Research*, *8*(2), 189–203. doi:10.1108/13522750510592454

Langston, C. A. (1994). Capitalizing on and coping with daily-life events: Expressive responses to positive events. *Journal of Personality and Social Psychology*, *67*(6), 1112–1125. doi:10.1037/0022-3514.67.6.1112

Larson, R. W., & Almeida, D. M. (1999). Emotional transmission in the daily lives of families: A new paradigm for studying family process. *Journal of Marriage and the Family*, *61*(1), 1, 5–20. doi:10.2307/353879

Lasorsa, D. L., Lewis, S. C., & Holton, A. E. (2012). Normalizing Twitter: Journalism practice in an emerging communication space. *Journalism Studies*, *13*(1), 19–36. doi:10.1080/1461670X.2011.571825

Lasswell, Harold D. (1948). The structure and function of communication in society. *The Communication of Ideas, 37*.

Lau, K.-N., Lee, K.-H., & Ho, Y. (2005). Text Mining for the Hotel Industry. *The Cornell Hotel and Restaurant Administration Quarterly*, *46*(3), 344–362. doi:10.1177/0010880405275966

Lawler, E. I. (1984). The Strategic Desing of Reward Systems. *Strategic Human Resource Management*, 127-147.

Lawler, E. J., & Thye, S. R. (1999). Bringing emotions into social exchange theory. *Annual Review of Sociology*, *25*(1), 217–244. doi:10.1146/annurev.soc.25.1.217

Leary, M. R. (2004). Digging deeper: The fundamental nature of 'self-conscious' emotions. *Psychological Inquiry*, *15*, 129–131.

Lee, J., Lee, J., & Feick, L. (2006). Incorporating Word-of-Mouth Effects in Estimating Customer Lifetime Value, *Journal of Database Marketing & Customer Strategy Management, 14.*

Lee, M., Rodgers, S. & Miyoung, K. (2009). Effects of Valence and Extremity of eWOM on Attitude toward the Brand and Website. *Journal of Current Issues & Research in Advertising, 31*(2).

Lee, H., Kim, C., & Miller, J. (1992). The Relative Effects of Price, Warranty and Country of Origin on Consumer Evaluations. *Journal of Global Marketing*, *6*(1/2), 55–80.

Lee, J. P., Park, D.-H., & Han, I. (2011). The different effects of online consumer reviews on consumers' purchase intentions depending on trust in online shopping malls: An advertising perspective. *Internet Research*, *21*(2), 187–206. doi:10.1108/10662241111123766

Lee, J., & Lee, J. N. (2009). Understanding the product information inference process in electronic word-ofmouth: An objectivity–subjectivity dichotomy perspective. *Information & Management*, *46*(5), 302–311. doi:10.1016/j.im.2009.05.004

Lee, J., Park, D.-H., & Han, I. (2008). The effect of negative online consumer reviews on product attitude: An information processing view. *Electronic Commerce Research and Applications*, *7*(3), 341–352. doi:10.1016/j.elerap.2007.05.004

Lee, K. T., & Koo, D. M. (2013). Effects of Attribute and Valence of eWOM on message adaptation: Moderating roles of subjective knowledge and regulatory focus. *Computers in Human Behavior*, *28*(5), 1974–1984. doi:10.1016/j.chb.2012.05.018

Lee, M., & Youn, S. (2009). Electronic Word of Mouth (eWOM). *Journal of Advertising*, *28*(3), 473–499. doi:10.2501/S0265048709200709

Lee, N., & Broderick, A. J. (2007). The past, present and future of observational research in marketing. *Qualitative Market Research*, *10*(2), 121–129. doi:10.1108/13522750710740790

Leivadiotou, E., & Markopoulos, D. (2010). Cyber communities and Electronic Word-of-Mouth: The use of Facebook in the promotion of hospitality services. *MIBES Transactions*, *4*(1), 138–151.

Leong, E. K. F., Ewing, M. T., & Pitt, L. F. (2004). Analysing Competitors' Online Persuasive Themes with Text Mining. *Marketing Intelligence & Planning*, *22*(2), 187–200. doi:10.1108/02634500410525850

Levy, S. J. (1959, July-August). Symbols for sale. *Harvard Business Review*, *37*, 117–124.

Li, C. (2007, April 23). *Forrester's new Social Technographics report*. Retrieved from http://forrester.typepad.com: http://forrester.typepad.com/groundswell/2007/04/forresters_new_.html

Liang, S.-J., Ekinci, Y., Occhiocupo, N., & Whyatt, G. (2013). Antecedents of Travellers' Electronic Word-of-Mouth Communication. *Journal of Marketing Management*, *29*(5-6), 584–606. doi:10.1080/0267257X.2013.771204

Lian, S. (2011). Innovative Internet video consuming based on media analysis techniques. *Electronic Commerce Research*, *11*(1), 75–89. doi:10.1007/s10660-010-9066-9

Liau, B., & Tan, P. (2014). Gaining Customer Knowledge in Low Cost Airlines Through Text Mining. *Industrial Management & Data Systems*, *114*(9), 1344–1359. doi:10.1108/IMDS-07-2014-0225

Liljander, V., & Strandvik, T. (1997). Emotions in service satisfaction. *International Journal of Service Industry Management, 8*(2), 148–169. doi:10.1108/09564239710166272

Lin, C. H., Lee, S. H., & Horng, D. J. (2011). The effects of online reviews on purchasing intention: The moderating role of need for cognition. *Social Behavior and Personality, 39*(1), 71–82. doi:10.2224/sbp.2011.39.1.71

Lincoln, Y. S., & Guba, E. G. (1985). *Naturalistic Enquiry*. Beverly Hills, CA: Sage.

Linda et.al. (2014). Exploring the impact of customer feedback on the well-being of service entities: A TSR perspective. *Journal of Service Management, 25*(4), 531 - 555.

Lindgreen, A., & Vanhamme, J. (2005). Viral Marketing: The Use of Surprise. In I. Clarke & T. B. Flaherty (Eds.), *Advances in Electronic Marketing* (pp. 122–138). Hershey, PA: Idea Group Publishing. doi:10.4018/978-1-59140-321-0.ch007

Lin, K. Y., & Lu, H. P. (2011). Why people use social networking sites: An empirical study integrating network externalities and motivations theory. *Computers in Human Behavior, 27*(3), 1152–1161. doi:10.1016/j.chb.2010.12.009

Litvin S.W., Goldsmith R., Pan B., (2005). E-WOM in Hosptitaly and Tourism. *Tourism Management*, 1-30

Litvin, S. W., Goldsmith, R. E., & Pan, B. (2008). Electronic word-of-mouth in hospitality and tourism management. *Tourism Management, 29*(3), 458–468. doi:10.1016/j.tourman.2007.05.011

Liu, Y. (2006). Word of mouth for movies: Its dynamics and impact on box office revenue. *Journal of Marketing, 70*(3), 74–89. doi:10.1509/jmkg.70.3.74

Li, X., & Hitt, L. (2008). Self-Selection and Information Role of Online Product Reviews. *Information Systems Research, 19*(4), 456–474. doi:10.1287/isre.1070.0154

Loanzon E. (2013). Netnography: evolution, trend, and implications as a fuzzy front end tool. In *Proc. Technology Management in the IT-Driven Services-13* (PICMET'13) (pp. 1572-1593). Academic Press.

Long, Y. L., & Ching, Y. L. (2010). The influence of corporate image, relationship marketing, and trust on purchase intention: The moderating effects of word ofmouth. *Emerald Group Publishing Limited, 65*(3), 16–34. doi:10.1108/16605371011083503

López, M., & Sicilia, M. (2014). Determinants of E-WOM Influence: The Role of Consumers' Internet Experience. *Journal of Theoretical and Applied Electronic Commerce Research, 9*(1), 28-43.

Madhavan, N. (2012, April 1). *As if by Magic*. Retrieved August 30, 2014, from http://businesstoday.intoday.in/story/kolaveri-di-success-case-study/1/22957.html

Maher, G. (2014). *Breaking Tradition! Using Crowdsourcing As Part Of Your Social Media Marketing Strategy*. Retrieved 4 15, 2015, from http://www.business2community.com/social-media/breaking-tradition-using-crowdsourcing-part-social-media-marketing-strategy-01090556

Malhotra, N. (2007). *Marketing Research: An Applied Orientation* (5th ed.). Pearson Prentice Hall.

Malhotra, N. K. (2010). *Marketing Research: An Applied Orientation* (6th ed.). Pearson.

Malhotra, Y., & Galletta, D. F. (1999). Extending the technology acceptance model to account for social influence: Theoretical bases and empirical validation.*Proceedings of the 32nd Hawaii International Conference on System Sciences*. doi:10.1109/HICSS.1999.772658

Malthouse, E. C., Oakley, J. L. & Iacobucci, D. (2003). *Customer Satisfaction Across Organizational Units*. Working Paper. Northwestern University.

Mandel, N., & Johnson, E. J. (2002). When web pages influence choice: Effects of visual primes on experts and novices. *The Journal of Consumer Research, 29*(2), 235–245. doi:10.1086/341573

Manga, X. (2011). *Les blogs mode seraient-ils devenus des modèles d'inspiration pour ZARA?* Paper presented at the Colloque Web social, communautés virtuelles et consommation 79e congrès international ACFAS, Université Bishop's et Université de Sherbrooke.

Mangione, G. R., Mazzoni, E., Orciuoli, F., & Pierri, A. (2011). *A pedagogical approach for collaborative ontologies building*. Berlin, Germany: Springer. doi:10.1007/978-3-642-19814-4_7

Manovich, L. (2012). Trending: The Promises and the Challenges of Big Social Data. Debates in the Digital Humanities. In M. K. Gold (Ed.), *Debates in the Digital Humanities* (pp. 460–475). Minneapolis, MN: The University of Minnesota Press.

Manyika, J., Chui, M., Brown, B., Bughin, J., Dobbs, R., Roxburgh, C., & Byers, A. H. (2011). *Big data: The next frontier for innovation, competition, and productivity*. Technical report. McKinsey Global Institute.

Marie, C. & Lindsey, I. C. (2014). Sustainable, hedonic and efficient: Interaction effects between product properties and consumer reviews on post-experience responses. *European Journal of Marketing, 48*(7/8), 1375 - 1394.

Marketing Chart. (2014). *Satisfaction with Word mouth and social media tactics*. Retrieved from http://www.marketingcharts.com/online/marketers-most-effective-word-of-mouth-tactics-42250/attachment/wommaama-satisfaction-w-o-m-social-tactics-apr2014/

Marsden, P. (1998). *Memetics and Social Contagion: Two Sides of the Same Coin? Journal of Memetics*. Evolutionary Models of Information Transmission.

Martin, D., O'Neill, M., Hubbard, S., & Palmer, A. (2008). The role of emotion in explaining consumer satisfaction and future behavioural intention. *Journal of Services Marketing, 22*(3), 224–236. doi:10.1108/08876040810871183

Martosko, D. (2015). *More than 2 MILLION of Hillary Clinton's Twitter followers are fake or never tweet – and she's already under fire for 'buying' fake Facebook fans*. Retrieved from http://www.dailymail.co.uk/news/article-3038621/More-2-MILLION-Hillary-Clinton-s-Twitter-followers-fake-never-tweet.html

Marwick, A. (2011). *Conspicuous and Authentic: Fashion Blogs, Style, and Consumption* Paper presented at the 61st Annual ICA Conference, Boston, MA.

Marwick, A. E. (2013). *"They're really profound women, they're entrepreneurs": Conceptions of Authenticity in Fashion Blogging*. Paper presented at the 7th International AAAI Conference on Weblogs and Social Media, Boston, MA.

Mauri, A., & Minazzi, R. (2013). Web Reviews Influence on Expectations and Purchasing Intentions of Hotel Potential Customers. *International Journal of Hospitality Management, 34*, 99–107. doi:10.1016/j.ijhm.2013.02.012

Mayfield, A. (2008). *What is Social Media*. Retrieved on May 06, 2013 from http://www.icrossing.com/ebooks

McCracken, G. (1986). Culture and consumption: A theoretical account of the structure: A theoretical account of the structure and movement of the cultural meaning of consumer goods. *The Journal of Consumer Research, 13*(1), 71–84. doi:10.1086/209048

McCracken, G. (1989). Who is the celebrity endorser? Cultural foundations of the endorsement process. *The Journal of Consumer Research, 16*(3), 310–321. doi:10.1086/209217

McCroskey, J. C., & McCain, T. A. (1974). *The measurement of interpersonal attraction*. Academic Press.

McMillan, S. J. (2000). The microscope and the moving target: The challenge of applying content analysis to the World Wide Web. *Journalism & Mass Communication Quarterly, 77*(1), 80–98. doi:10.1177/107769900007700107

McNeal, G. S. (2014). *Facebook Manipulated User News Feeds To Create Emotional Responses*. Retrieved from http://www.forbes.com/sites/gregorymcneal/2014/06/28/facebook-manipulated-user-news-feeds-to-create-emotional-contagion/

Mcwilliam, G. (2000). Building strong brands through online communities. *Sloan Management Review*, *41*(Spring), 43–54.

Media, P. Q. (2014, September 11). *Word-of-mouth forecast 2009-2013*. Retrieved from: http://bit.ly/1unFPLX

Media, U. (2012,). *Viral video charts*. Available: http://viralvideochart.unrulymedia.com

Meiners, N. H., Schwarting, U., & Seeberger, B. (2010). The Renaissance of Word-of-Mouth Marketing: A 'New' Standard in Twenty-First Century Marketing Management?! *International Journal of Economic Sciences and Applied Research*, *3*(2), 79.

Melián-González, S., Bulchand-Gidumal, J., & López-Valcárcel, B. (2013). Online Customer Reviews of Hotels: As Participation Increases, Better Evaluation Is Obtained. *Cornell Hospitality Quarterly*, *54*(3), 274–283. doi:10.1177/1938965513481498

Mendoza, M. (2010). I Blog. You Buy. How bloggers are creating a new generation of product endorsers. *Digital Research & Publishing*, *7*, 114–122.

Menon, S., & Kahn, B. (2002). Cross-category effects of induced arousal and pleasure on the internet shopping experience. *Journal of Retailing*, *78*(1), 31–40. doi:10.1016/S0022-4359(01)00064-1

Messner, M., Linke, M., & Eford, A. (2011, April). *Shoveling tweets: An analysis of the microblogging engagement of traditional news organizations*. Paper presented at the 12th International Symposium for Online Journalism, Austin, TX.

Meyer, C., & Schwager, A. (2007). Understanding customer experience. *Harvard Business Review*, *85*(2), 116–126. PMID:17345685

Meyers-Levy, J., & Peracchio, L. A. (1995). Understanding the effects of color: How the correspondence between available and required resources affects attitudes. *The Journal of Consumer Research*, *22*(2), 121–138. doi:10.1086/209440

Mika, P. (2005). *Ontologies are us: A unified model of social networks and semantics*. Berlin, Germany: Springer.

Miller, R., & Lammas, N. (2010). Social media and its implications for viral marketing. *Asia Pacific Public Relations Journal*, *11*, 1–9.

MindComet. (2006). *Viral Marketing: Understanding the Concepts and Benefits of Viral Marketing*. Retrieved from http://cmginteractive.com/uploads/viral_marketing.pdf

Misra, B. (2014, February 22). *How IKEA uses social media to emerge a marketing success*. Retrieved August 30, 2014, from http://retail.economictimes.indiatimes.com/news/home-and-decor/furniture-and-decor/how-ikea-uses-social-media-to-emerge-a-marketing-success/30857725

Mkono, M. (2012). Netnographic tourist research: The Internet as a virtual fieldwork site. *Tourism Analysis*, *17*(4), 553–555. doi:10.3727/108354212X13473157390966

Morace, F. (2002). *European Asymmetries*. Milano: Scheiwiller.

Morgan, M. (2008). What makes a good festival? Understanding the event experience. *Event Management*, *12*(2), 81–93. doi:10.3727/152599509787992562

Morgan, N. J., Pritchard, A., & Piggott, R. (2003). Destination branding and the role of the stakeholders: The case of New Zealand. *Journal of Vacation Marketing*, *9*(3), 285–299. doi:10.1177/135676670300900307

Morgan, S. J., & Symon, G. (2003). Electronic interviews in organizational research. In *Essential Guide to qualitative methods in organizational research*. London: SAGE.

Morimoto, M., & Trimble, C. S. (2012). Consumer's Use of Blogs as Product Information Sources: From Nee-for-Cognition Perspective. *Marketing Management Journal*, *22*(2), 45–60.

Morin, S. (1983, February 28). Influentials advising their friends to sell lots of high-tech gadgetry. *Wall Street Journal*, 30.

Morton, L.P. (2002, June). Targeting Generation Y. *Public Relations Quarterly,* 46–48.

Mostafa, M. (2013). More Than Words: Social Networks' Text Mining for Consumer Brand Sentiments. *Expert Systems with Applications*, *40*(10), 4241–4251. doi:10.1016/j.eswa.2013.01.019

Mowen, J. C., Park, S., & Zablah, A. (2007). Toward a theory of motivation and personality with application to word-of-mouth communications. *Journal of Business Research*, *60*(6), 590–596. doi:10.1016/j.jbusres.2006.06.007

Murray, K. (1991). A Test of Services Marketing Theory: Consumer Information Acquisition Activities. *Journal of Marketing*, *55*(1), 10–25. doi:10.2307/1252200

Nardi, B. A., Schiano, D. J., Gumbrecht, M., & Swartz, L. (2004). Why we blog. *Communications of the ACM*, *47*(12), 41–46. doi:10.1145/1035134.1035163

Nelson-Field, K., Riebe, E., & Newstead, K. (2013). The emotions that drive viral video. *Australasian Marketing Journal*, *21*(4), 205–211. doi:10.1016/j.ausmj.2013.07.003

Nelson, M. R., & Otnes, C. C. (2005). Exploring cross-cultural ambivalence: A netnography of intercultural wedding message boards. *Journal of Business Research*, *58*(1), 89–95. doi:10.1016/S0148-2963(02)00477-0

Neter, J., Wasserman, W., & Kutner, M. H. (1985). *Applied linear statistical models: Regression, analysis of variance, and experimental design*. Homewood: Irwin.

Newcomb, T. (1953). An Approance to the Study of Communicative Acts. *Psycholigical Reveiw*, *60*(6), 393–404. doi:10.1037/h0063098 PMID:13112341

Newman, N. (2011). *Mainstream media and the distribution of news in the age of social discovery*. Oxford, UK: Reuters Institute of Journalism.

Nielsen nmIncite. (2012). *State of the Media: The Social Media Report 2012*. Retrieved on May 5, 2013 from http://postmediavancouversun.files.wordpress.com/2012/12/nielsen-social-media-report-20122.pdf

Nielsen. (2009). *Trust, value and engagement in advertising: Nielsen Global Online Consumer Survey*. The Nielsen Company. Retrieved from http://www.nielsen.com/content/dam /corporate/us/en/newswire/uploads/2009/07/trustinadvertising0709.pdf

Nielsen. (2014, September 11). *Why word-of- mouth is loudest in Africa*. Retrieved from: http://bit.ly/1lY1dG4

Nimrod, G. (2012). Online communities as a resource in older adult tourism. *The Journal of Community Informatics.*, *8*, 56–67.

Nine Big Reasons For Serious Womm. (n.d.). Retrieved from http://www.lithium.com/pdfs/infographic/lithium_nine_big_reasons_for_serious_WOMM.pdf

Noble, S. M., Haytko, D. L., & Phillips, J. (2009). What drives college-age Generation Y consumers? *Journal of Business Research*, *62*(6), 617–628. doi:10.1016/j.jbusres.2008.01.020

Norman, A. T., & Russell, C. A. (2006). The Pass-Along Effect: Investigating Word-of-Mouth Effects on Online Survey Procedures. *Journal of Computer-Mediated Communication, 11*(4), 1085–1103. doi:10.1111/j.1083-6101.2006.00309.x

Nusair, K., Yoon, H. J., Naipaul, S., & Parsa, H. G. (2010). Effect of Price Discount Frames and Price Discount Levels on Consumers' Perceptions. *International Journal of Contemporary Hospitality Management, 22*(9).

Nyer, P. U. (2000). An Investigation Into Whether Complaining Can Cause Increased Consumer Satisfaction. *Journal of Consumer Marketing, 17*(1), 9–19. doi:10.1108/07363760010309500

O'Neill, M., Palmer, A., & Charters, S. (2002). Wine production as a service experience – the effects of service quality on wine sales. *Journal of Services Marketing, 16*(4), 342–362. doi:10.1108/08876040210433239

Oatley, K., & Jenkins, J. M. (1996). *Understanding emotions.* Boston: Blackwell Publishers.

Oboler, A., Welsh, K., & Cruz, L. (2012). The danger of big data: Social media as computational social science. *First Monday, 17*(7).

OECD. (2007). *Participative web and user-created content: Web 2.0, wikis, and social networking*. Paris: Organisation for Economic Co-operation and Development.

Ofir, C., & Simonson, I. (2007). The effect of stating expectations on customer satisfaction and shopping experience. *JMR, Journal of Marketing Research, 44*(1), 164–174. doi:10.1509/jmkr.44.1.164

Oh, C., Lim, H., Koh, K., Seo, J., & Suh, B. (2014). *Oppan Internet Meme Style. 2014: A Case Study of Internet Memes through Digital Artifacts on Social Media.* Retrieved from http://www.kylekoh.com/s/2014Gangnam.pdf

Ohanian, R. (1991). The impact of celebrity spokespersons' perceived image on consumers' intention to purchase. *Journal of Advertising Research.*

Okazaki, S. (2009). Social influence model and electronic word of mouth PC versus mobile internet. *International Journal of Advertising, 28*(3), 439–472. doi:10.2501/S0265048709200692

Okechucu, C. (1994). The Importance of Product Country of Origin. *European Journal of Marketing, 28*(4), 5–19. doi:10.1108/03090569410061150

Oliver, R. L. (1980). A cognitive model of the antecedents and consequences of satisfaction decisions. *JMR, Journal of Marketing Research, 17*(4), 460–469. doi:10.2307/3150499

Oliver, R. L. (1981). Measurement and evaluation of satisfaction processes in retail settings. *Journal of Retailing, 57*(3), 25–48.

Oliver, R. L. (1997). *Satisfaction: a behavioral perspective on the consumer.* New York: McGraw-Hill.

Oliver, R. L., & Westbrook, R. A. (1993). Cognitive, affective, and attribute bases of the satisfaction response. *The Journal of Consumer Research, 20*(3), 418–430. doi:10.1086/209358

Oliver, R., & Swan, J. (1989). Consumer Perceptions of Interpersonal Equity and Satisfaction in Transactions: A Field Survey Approach. *Journal of Marketing, 53*(2), 21–35. doi:10.2307/1251411

Olshavsky, R. W., & Granbois, D. H. (1979). Consumer decision making-fact or fiction? *The Journal of Consumer Research, 6*(2), 93–100. doi:10.1086/208753

Online retailers ready to utilise social media's reach. (n.d.). Retrieved from http://articles.economictimes.indiatimes.com/2014-08-13/news/52768005_1_amazon-india-ravi-vora-social-media

Osgood, C. E., & Tannenbaum, P. H. (1955). The Principle of Congruity in the Prediction of Attitude Change. *Psychological Review*, *62*(1), 42–55. doi:10.1037/h0048153 PMID:14357526

Osofsky, M. (2011). Swatch netnography: A look at consumer sentiment in social media. *Social Media*, *9*, 31–35.

Owyang, J. (2010). *Socialgraphics Help You to Understand Your Customers: Slides and Webinar Recording*. Retrieved on September 04, 2013 from http://www.web-strategist.com/blog/category/socialgraphics/

Pande, S. (2014, June 8). *Just the Right Image*. Retrieved August 30, 2014, from http://businesstoday.intoday.in/story/case-study-strategy-tactics-behind-creation-of-brand-narendra-modi/1/206321.html

Pang, B., & Lee, L. (2008, February). *Using Very Simple Statistics for Review Search: An Exploration*. Poster presented at the International Conference on Computational Linguistics, Haifa, Israel.

Panneerselvam, R. (2004). *Research methodology*. PHI Learning Pvt. Ltd.

Parka, C.L., (2009). *Information direction, website reputation and eWOM effect: A moderating role of product type*. Elsevier.

Park, C., & Lee, T. (2009). Information direction, website reputation and eWOM effect: A moderating role of product type. *Journal of Business Research*, *62*(1), 61–67. doi:10.1016/j.jbusres.2007.11.017

Park, D. H., & Kim, S. (2008). The effects of consumer knowledge on message processing of electronic word-of-mouth via online consumer reviews. *Electronic Commerce Research and Applications*, *7*(4), 399–410. doi:10.1016/j.elerap.2007.12.001

Park, D. H., & Lee, J. (2008). eWOM overload and its effect on consumer behavioral intention depending on consumer involvement. *Electronic Commerce Research and Applications*, *7*(4), 386–398. doi:10.1016/j.elerap.2007.11.004

Park, D.-H., Lee, J., & Han, I. (2007). The Effect of On-Line Consumer Reviews on Consumer Purchasing Intention: The Moderating Role of Involvement. *International Journal of Electronic Commerce*, *11*(4), 125–148. doi:10.2753/JEC1086-4415110405

Parkinson, B. (1996). Emotions are social. *British Journal of Psychology*, *87*(4), 663–683. doi:10.1111/j.2044-8295.1996.tb02615.x PMID:8962482

Parkinson, B., Fischer, A. H., & Manstead, A. R. (2005). *Emotion in Social Relations: Cultural, Group, and Interpersonal Processes*. New York: Psychology Press.

Parry, M. E., Kawakami, T., & Kishiya, K. (2012). The Effect of Personal and Virtual Word-of-Mouth on Technology Acceptance. *Journal of Product Innovation Management*, *29*(6), 952–966. doi:10.1111/j.1540-5885.2012.00972.x

Patton, M. Q. (1990). Qualitative Evaluation and Research Methods (2nd ed.). Newbury Park, CA: Sage Publications, Inc.

Peeling, E. L., & White, K. M. (2009). The theory of planned behavior applied to young people's use of social networking web sites. *Cyberpsychology & Behavior*, *12*(2), 755–759. doi:10.1089/cpb.2009.0109 PMID:19788377

Pereira, P.A., Irene, C., Medina, G., Fabiola, Z., Romo, G., & Contreras-Espinosa, R.S. (2014). The importance of Facebook as an online social networking tool for companies. *International Journal of Accounting & Information Management*, *22* (4).

Pescher, C., Reichhart, P., & Spann, M. (2014). Consumer decision-making processes in mobile viral marketing campaigns. *Journal of Interactive Marketing*, *28*(1), 43–54. doi:10.1016/j.intmar.2013.08.001

Phelps, J. E. (2003). *Viral Marketing or Electronic Word-of-Mouth Advertising : Examining Consumer Responses and Motivations to Pass Along Email*. doi:10.1017/S0021849904040371

Phelps, J. E., Lewis, R., Mobilio, L., & Perry, D. (2004, December). Viral marketing or electronic word-of-mouth advertising: Examining consumer responses and motivations to pass along e-mail. *Journal of Advertising Research*, *44*(4), 333–348.

Phelps, J. E., Lewis, R., Mobilio, L., Perry, D., & Raman, N. (2004). Viral marketing or electronic word-of-mouth advertising: Examining consumer responses and motivations to pass along email. *Journal of Advertising Research*, *44*(04), 333–348.

Pine, B. J. II, & Gilmore, J. H. (1998). Welcome to the Experience Economy. *Harvard Business Review*, *1998*(July-August), 97–105. PMID:10181589

Pine, B. J. II, & Gilmore, J. H. (1999). *The Experience Economy: Work is Theatre and Every Business a Stage*. Cambridge, MA: Harvard Business School Press.

Pintado, I. (2009). *Connection Generation; How Connection Determines Our Place in Society and Business*. Charleston, SC: BookSurge Publishing.

Plog, S. C. (1974). Why destination areas rise and fall in popularity. *The Cornell H.R. AQ (Balmain, N.S.W.)*, *4*(4), 55–58.

Plutchik, R. (1980). *Emotion: A psychoevolutionarysynthesis* (2nd ed.). New York: Harper and Row.

Poels, K., & Siegfried, D. (2006). How to capture the heart? Reviewing 20 years of emotion measurement in advertising. *Journal of Advertising Resources*, *46*(1).

Pogue, D. (2012, July 18). Why Face Book should begin to worry. *Economic Times*, p. 8

Pollay, R. W. (1983). Measuring the cultural values manifest in advertising. In J. H. Leigh & C. R. Martin Jr., (Eds.), *Current Issues and Research in Advertising* (pp. 72–92). Ann Arbor, MI: Graduate School of Business, Division of Research, University of Michigan.

Popping, R. (2003). Knowledge graphs and network text analysis. *Social Sciences Information. Information Sur les Sciences Sociales*, *42*(1), 91–106. doi:10.1177/0539018403042001798

Popping, R., & Strijker, I. (1997). Representation and integration of sociological knowledge using knowledge graphs. *Social Sciences Information. Information Sur les Sciences Sociales*, *36*(4), 731–747. doi:10.1177/053901897036004006

Prahalad, C. K., & Ramaswamy, V. (2004). *The Future of Competition - Co-Creating Unique Value with Customers*. Boston: HarvardBusinessSchool Press.

Pruden, D. a. (2004). Controlling the grapevine: How to measure and manage word-of-mouth. *Marketing Management*, *13*(4), 24–30.

Pullman, M. E., & Gross, M. A. (2004). Ability of experience design elements to elicit emotions and loyalty behaviors. *Decision Sciences*, *35*(3), 551–578. doi:10.1111/j.0011-7315.2004.02611.x

Puri, A. (2007). The web of insights: The art and practice of webnography. *International Journal of Market Research*, *49*, 384–408.

Quelch, J. A., & Klein, L. R. (1996). The Internet and International Marketing! *Sloan Management Review*, *37*(3), 60–75.

Quinton, S., & March, S. H. (2010). Relationships in online communities. *Journal of Research in Interactive Marketing*, *4*(1), 59–73. doi:10.1108/17505931011033560

Quipp, J. (2008). *50+ Sites To Help You Bury Negative Posts About You or Your Company!* Retrieved from http://www.searchenginepeople.com/blog/50-sites-to-help-you-bury-negative-posts-about-you-or-your-company.html

Rahimi, R. (2007), *Feasibility Study of Customer Relationship Management (CRM) Application in Hotel Industry: Case of Hamgame Arya Group Hotels.* (Master Thesis). Lulea University of Technology.

Rambocas, M., & Gama, J. (2013). Marketing Research: The Role of Sentiment Analysis. *FEP Economics and Management*, 1-24.

Ranaweera, C., & Prabhu, J. (2003). On the relative importance of customer satisfaction and trust as determinants of customer retention and positive word of mouth. *Journal of Targeting,Measurement and Analysis of Marketing*, *12*(1), 82–90. doi:10.1057/palgrave.jt.5740100

Rapid Miner Documentation. (n.d.). Retrieved from https://rapidminer.com/documentation/

Raskin, R., & Terry, H. (1988). A principal-components analysis of the narcissisti personality inventory and further evidence of its construct validity. *Journal of Personality and Social Psychology*, *54*(5), 890–902. doi:10.1037/0022-3514.54.5.890 PMID:3379585

Ratchford, B. T., Talukdar, D., & Lee, M.-S. (2001). A model of consumer choice of the Internet as an information source. *International Journal of Electronic Commerce*, *5*, 7–22.

Rawson, A., Duncan, E., & Jones, C. (2013). The truth about customer experience. *Harvard Business Review*, *91*(9), 90–98. PMID:23593770

Read, J. (2005). Using emoticons to reduce dependency in machine learning techniques for sentiment classification (pp. 43–48). In *Proceedings of the ACL-2005 Student Research Workshop*. Ann Arbor, MI: ACL. doi:10.3115/1628960.1628969

Reichelt, J., Sievert, J., & Jacob, F. (2014). How credibility affects eWOM reading: The influences of expertise, trustworthiness, and similarity on utilitarian and social functions. *Journal of Marketing Communications*, *20*(1-2), 65–81. doi:10.1080/13527266.2013.797758

Reichheld, F. F., & Schefter, P. (2000). E-loyalty: Your secret weapon on the web. *Harvard Business Review*, *78*(4), 105–113.

Reid, E. (1996). Informed consent in the study of online communities: A reflection on the effects of computer-mediated social research. *The Information Society*, *12*(2), 119–127. doi:10.1080/713856138

Rejón-Guardia, F., & Martínez-López, F. J. (2014). *The Pervasive Influence of Electronic Word of Mouth (eWOM) on Today's Social Consumer Handbook of Strategic e-Business Management* (pp. 821–839). Springer.

Richins, M. L. (1983). Negative word-of-mouth by dissatisfied consumers: A pilot study. *Journal of Marketing*, *47*(1), 68–78. doi:10.2307/3203428

Richins, M. L. (1987). A multivariate analyses of responses to dissatisfaction. *Journal of the Academy of Marketing Science*, *15*(3), 24–31. doi:10.1007/BF02722168

Richins, M. L., & Root-Shaffer, T. (1988). The role of involvement and opinion leadership in consumer word of mouth: An implicit made explicit. *Advances in Consumer Research. Association for Consumer Research (U. S.)*, *15*(1), 32–36.

Ricolfe, J. S., & Perez, C. E. (2014). Applying netnography to the obtaining of the map of positioning for companies of food. *Cuadernos de Gestion*, *14*(1), 57–74. doi:10.5295/cdg.110322jc

Riegner, C. (2007). Word of mouth on the web: The impact of web 2.0 on consumer purchase decisions. *Journal of Advertising Research*, *47*(4), 436–447. doi:10.2501/S0021849907070456

Riesman, D., Glazer, N., & Denney, R. (1961). *The lonely crowd: A study of the changing American character.* New Haven, CT: Yale University Press.

Riff, D., Lacy, S., & Fico, F. (2014). *Analyzing media messages: Using quantitative content analysis in research*. London, UK: Routledge.

Rimé, B. (2009). Emotion Elicits the Social Sharing of Emotion: Theory and Empirical Review. *Emotion Review*, *1*(1), 60–85. doi:10.1177/1754073908097189

Rime, B., Mesquita, B., Philippot, P., & Boca, S. (1991). Beyond the emotional event: Six studies on the social sharing of emotion. *Cognition and Emotion*, *5*(5-6), 435–465. doi:10.1080/02699939108411052

Rimé, B., Philippot, P., Boca, S., & Mesquita, B. (1992). Long-lasting cognitive and social consequences of emotion: Social sharing and rumination. *European Review of Social Psychology*, *3*(1), 225–258. doi:10.1080/14792779243000078

Riva, G., Banos, R. M., Botella, C., Wiederhold, B. K., & Gaggioli, A. (2012). Positive technology: Using interactive technologies to promote positive functioning. *Cyberpsychology, Behavior, and Social Networking*, *15*(2), 69–77. doi:10.1089/cyber.2011.0139 PMID:22149077

Robert, L. P. Jr, Dennis, A. R., & Ahuja, M. K. (2008). Social capital and knowledge integration in digitally enabled teams. *Information Systems Research*, *19*(3), 314–334. doi:10.1287/isre.1080.0177

Rocamora, A. (2011). Personal fashion blogs: Screens and mirrors in digital self-portraits. *Fashion Theory*, *15*(4), 407–424. doi:10.2752/175174111X13115179149794

Rogers, T. B., Kuiper, N. A., & Kirker, W. S. (1977). Self-reference and the encoding of personal information. *Journal of Personality and Social Psychology*, *35*(9), 677–688. doi:10.1037/0022-3514.35.9.677 PMID:909043

Rokka, J. (2010). Netnographic inquiry and new translocal sites of the social. *International Journal of Consumer Studies*, *34*(4), 381–387. doi:10.1111/j.1470-6431.2010.00877.x

Ronvran. (2013). *EWOM marketing*. Retrieved from http://www.marketingfacts.nl/berichten/de-6-nieuwste-wetten-van-word-of-mouth-marketing

Rooney, J. (2012, September 25). *In Dell Social-Media Journey, Lessons For Marketers About The Power Of Listening*. Retrieved August 30, 2014, from http://www.forbes.com/sites/jenniferrooney/2012/09/25/in-dell-social-media-journey-lessons-for-marketers-about-the-power-of-listening/

Russell, J. A. (1980). A circumplex model of affect. *Journal of Personality and Social Psychology*, *39*(6), 1161–1178. doi:10.1037/h0077714

Ryan, B., & Gross, N. (1943). The diffusion of hybrid seed corn in two Iowa communities. *Rural Sociology*, *8*(1), 15–24.

Sachse, S. B., & Mangold, S. (2011). Brand equity dilution through negative online word-of-mouth communication. *Journal of Retailing and Consumer Services*, *18*(1), 38–45. doi:10.1016/j.jretconser.2010.09.003

Sahin, A., Zehir, C., & Kitapçı, H. (2011). The effects of brand experiences, trust and satisfaction on building brand loyalty; an empirical research on global brands. *Procedia: Social and Behavioral Sciences*, *24*, 1288–1301. doi:10.1016/j.sbspro.2011.09.143

Salzman, M., Matathia, I., & O'Reilly, A. (2004). *Buzz . . . Le marketing du bouche-à-oreille*. Paris: Village Mondial.

Samin, R., Goodarz, J. D., Muhammad, S. R., Firoozeh, F., Mahsa, H., & Sanaz, E. (2012). A Conceptual Study on the Country of Origin Effect on Consumer Purchase Intention. *Canadian Center of Science and Education*, *8*(12), 205–215.

Sarkar, R., (2014, October 8). Mobile doing to e-Commerce what e-Commerce did to retail, *Business Standard,* p. 1.

Schiffman, L. G., Kanuk, L. L., & Kumar, S. R. (2010). Consumer Behaviour (10th ed.). New Delhi: DorlingKindersley (India) Pvt. Ltd.

Schiffman, L., & Kanuk, L. L. (2007). *Consumer Behavior*. Pearson Prentice-Hall.

Schmitt, B. (2011). Experience marketing: Concepts, frameworks and consumer insights (Vol. 5, No. 2). Now Publishers Inc.

Schmitt, B. H. (2003). Customer Experience Management: A Revolutionary Approach to Connecting with Your Customers. John Wiley & Sons, Inc.

Schmitt, B. H. (1999). *Experiential marketing: How to get customers to sense, feel, think, act, and relate to your company and brands. NewYork.* Free Press.

Schoenewolf, G. (1990). Emotional contagion: Behavioral induction in individuals and groups. *Modern Psychoanalysis*, *15*, 49–61.

Scott, C. A., & Tybout, A. M. (1981). Theoretical perspectives on the impact of negative information: Does valence matter? *Advances in Consumer Research. Association for Consumer Research (U. S.)*, *8*, 408–409.

Scott, J. (2000). *Social network analysis: A handbook*. London, UK: Sage.

Scott, J., & Amaturo, E. (1997). *L'analisi delle reti sociali*. Roma, Italy: La Nuova Italia Scientifica.

Semin, G. R. (2000). Agenda 2000—Communication: Language as an implementational device for cognition. *European Journal of Social Psychology*, *30*(5), 595–612. doi:10.1002/1099-0992(200009/10)30:5<595::AID-EJSP23>3.0.CO;2-A

Senecal, S., & Nantel, J. (2004). The Influence of Online Product Recommendations on Consumers' Online Choices. *Journal of Retailing*, *80*(2), 156–169. doi:10.1016/j.jretai.2004.04.001

Seong, N.Y, (2008). *The Effects of Electronic Word-of-mouth Systems (EWOMS) on the Acceptance of Recommendation*. The University of Nebraska - Lincoln.

Sernovitz, A. (2009). *Word of mouth marketing: How smart companies get people talking*. New York: Kaplan.

Shamma, D. A., Yew, J., Kennedy, L., & Churchill, E. F. (2011). Viral Actions: Predicting Video View Counts Using Synchronous Sharing Behaviors. In ICWSM. ICWSM.

Shang, W., & Hooker, N. H. (2006). *Scales or Stars? Consumer Preferences for Food Quality Signals*. Working Paper. American Agricultural Economics Association Annual Meeting.

Shankar, V., Smith, A. K., & Rangaswamy, A. (2003). Customer satisfaction and loyalty in online and offline environments. *International Journal of Research in Marketing*, *20*(2), 153–175. doi:10.1016/S0167-8116(03)00016-8

Shanka, T., Ali-Knight, J., & Pope, J. (2002). Intrastate travel experiences of international students and their perceptions of Western Australia as a tourist destination. *Tourism and Hospitality Research*, *3*(3), 245–256.

Shapiro, G., & Markoff, J. (1997). A Matter of Definition. In C. W. Roberts (Ed.), *Text Analysis for the Social Sciences* (pp. 9–31). Mahwah, NJ: Lawrence Erlbaum Associates.

Shaughnessy, J., Zechmeister, E., & Jeanne, Z. (2011). *Research methods in psychology* (9th ed.). New York, NY: McGraw Hill.

Sheahan, P. (2005). *Generation Y: Surviving (and Thriving) with Generation Y at Work*. Victoria, Australia: Hardy Grant Publishing.

Shen, W., Maceli, K. M., Zhao, Y., Baack, D. W., & Bacon, D. R. (2014). *The Impact Of Gender and National Culture On Electronic Word Of Mouth Communication.* Paper presented at the Annual Meeting of the Association of Collegiate Marketing educators, Dallas.

Sher, P., & Lee, S. (2009). Consumer Skepticism and Online Reviews: An Elaboration Likehihood Model Perspective. *Social Behavior and Personality*, *37*(1), 137–144. doi:10.2224/sbp.2009.37.1.137

Sheth, J. N. (1971). Word of mouth in low risk innovations. *Journal of Advertising Research*, *11*, 15–18.

Sheth, J. N. (1979). The Surpluses and Shortages in Consumer Behaviour Theory and Research. *Journal of the Academy of Marketing Science*, *7*(4), 414–427. doi:10.1007/BF02729689

Shifman, L. (2012). An anatomy of a YouTube meme. *New Media & Society*, *14*(2), 187–203. doi:10.1177/1461444811412160

Shin, D. H. (2008). Understanding purchasing behaviors in a virtual economy: Consumer behavior involving virtual currency in Web 2.0 communities. *Interacting with Computers*, *20*(4), 433–446. doi:10.1016/j.intcom.2008.04.001

Shu-Chuan, C., & Yoojung, K. (2011). Determinants of consumer engagement in electronic word-of-mouth (eWOM) in social networking sites. *International Journal of Advertising*, *30*(1), 47–75. doi:10.2501/IJA-30-1-047-075

Silverman, G. (1997). Harvesting the Power of Word of mouth. *Potentials in Marketing*, *30*(9), 14–16.

Silverman, G. (2011). *Secrets of Word-of-mouth Marketing: How to Trigger Exponential Sales through Runaway Word-of-mouth.* New York: American Management Association.

Singhal, D. (2011). *Why this Kolaveri Di: Maddening Phenomenon of Earworm.* Available at SSRN 1969781.

Sirdeshmukh, D., Singh, J., & Sabol, B. (2002). Consumer trust, value, and loyalty in relational exchanges. *Journal of Marketing*, *66*(1), 15–37. doi:10.1509/jmkg.66.1.15.18449

Sirgy, M. J. (1982). Self-concept in consumer behavior: A critical review. *The Journal of Consumer Research*, *9*(3), 287–300. doi:10.1086/208924

Smith, S., & Wheeler, J. (2002). *Managing the customer experience: Turning customers into advocates.* Pearson Education.

Smudde, P. M. (2005). Blogging, ethics and public relations: A proactive and dialogic approach. *Public Relations Quarterly*, *50*(3), 34–38.

Social Media Marketing. (2015). In *Wikipedia*. Retrieved February, 2015, from http://en.wikipedia.org /wiki/Social_Media_Marketing

Social Media. (2014). Retrieved from http://westshoreconsultants.com/social-media/

Son, J.-E., Kim, H.-W., & Jang, Y.-J. (2012). Investigating Factors Affecting Electronic Word-Of- Mouth In The Open Market Context: A Mixed Methods Approach. In *Proceedings of Pacific Asia Conference on Information Systems* (PACIS). Association for Information Systems, AIS Electronic Library (AISeL).

Sotiriadis, M. D. (2013). Electronic word-of-mouth and online reviews in tourism services: The use of twitter by tourists. *Journal Electronic Research*, *13*(1), 103–124.

Sotiriadis, M. D., & van Zyl, C. (2013). Electronic Word-of-Mouth and Online Reviews in Tourism Services: The Use of Twitter by Tourists. *Electronic Commerce Research*, *13*(1), 103–124. doi:10.1007/s10660-013-9108-1

Spam: Internet menace on the prowl. (2013). Retrieved from http://economictimes.indiatimes.com/slideshows/tech-life/spam-internet-menace-on-the-prowl/spam-facts-and-figures/slideshow/20044279.cms

Spreng, R. A., MacKenzie, S. B., & Olshavsky, R. W. (1996). A re-examination of the determinants of consumer satisfaction. *Journal of Marketing*, *60*(3), 15–32. doi:10.2307/1251839

Stanbouli, K. (2003). Marketing Viral et Publicité. *Revue Française du Marketing*(192), 97-106.

Stanley, M. (2009). *Mobile Internet Report*. Retrieved on December 24, 2012 from www.ms.com/techresearch

Stauss, B. (1997). Global Word of Mouth. *Marketing Management*, *6*, 28–30.

Stauss, B. (2000). In T. Hennig-Thurau & U. Hansen (Eds.), *Relationship Marketing* (pp. 233–253). Berlin: Springer. doi:10.1007/978-3-662-09745-8_13

Stefanone, M. A., Lackaff, D., & Rosen, D. (2011). Contingencies of self-worth and social networking site behavior. *Cyberpsychology, Behavior, and Social Networking*, *14*(1-2), 41–49. doi:10.1089/cyber.2010.0049 PMID:21329442

Steffes, E. M., & Burgee, L. E. (2009). Social ties and online word of mouth. *Internet Research*, *19*(1), 42–59. doi:10.1108/10662240910927812

Steinkuehler, C., & Williams, D. (2006). Where everybody knows your (screen) name: Online games as "third places". *Journal of Computer-Mediated Communication*, *11*(4), 885–909. doi:10.1111/j.1083-6101.2006.00300.x

Stelzner, M. A. (2012). Social Media Marketing Report, 2012. *Social Media Examiner*. Retrieved on January 3, 2013 from http://www.socialmediaexaminer.com/SocialMedia MarketingIndustryReport2012.pdf

Stelzner, M. A. (2013). *2013 social media marketing industry report: How marketers are using Social Media to Grow Their Businesses*. Retrieved on August 2, 2013, from http://www.socialmediaexaminer.com/SocialMedia MarketingIndustryReport2013.pdf

Stephens, M. (2007). Chapter 5: Social Video: Videoblogging& YouTube. *Library Technology Reports*, *43*(5), 52–57.

Stöckl, R., Rohrmeier, P., & Hess, T. (2008). *Why customers produce user generated content Web 2.0* (pp. 271–287). Springer.

Stone, P. J. (1997). Thematic Text Analysis: New Agendas for Analyzing Text Content. In C. W. Roberts (Ed.), *Text Analysis for the Social Sciences* (pp. 35–54). Mahwah, NJ: Lawrence Erlbaum Associates.

Straus, B., & Neuhaus, P. (1997). The qualitative satisfaction model. *International Journal of Service Industry Management*, *8*(3), 236–249. doi:10.1108/09564239710185424

Strauss, A., & Corbin, J. (1990). *Basics of qualitative research: Grounded theory procedures and techniques. Newbury Park*, CA: Sage Publications, Inc.

Subramani, M. R., & Rajagopalan, B. (2003). Knowledge Sharing and Influence in Online Social Networks Via Viral Marketing. *Communications of the ACM*, *46*(12), 300–307. doi:10.1145/953460.953514

Suddin, L., Geoffrey, H. T., & Hanudin, A. (2009). Predicting intention to choose halal products using theory of reasoned action. *Journal of Islamic and Middle Eastern Finance and Management*, *2*(1), 66–76. doi:10.1108/17538390910946276

Sullins, E. S. (1991). Emotional contagion revisited: Effects of social comparison and expressive style on mood convergence. *Personality and Social Psychology Bulletin*, *17*(2), 166–174. doi:10.1177/0146167291017002008

Sullivan, D. P. (2003). *A Profile of Generation Y Online Shoppers and its Application to Marketing*. (Unpublished Doctoral Dissertation). Capella University, Ann Arbor, MI.

Sun, T., Youn, Y., Wu, G., & Kuntaraporn, M. (2006). Online word-of-mouth (or mouse): An exploration of its antecedents and consequences. *Journal of Computer-Mediated Communication, 11* (4). Retrieved from http://jcmc.indiana,edu/voll11/issue4/sun.html

Sundaram, D. S., Mitra, K., & Webster, C. (1998). Word of mouth communications: A motivational analysis. *Advances in Consumer Research. Association for Consumer Research (U. S.), 25*, 527–531.

Sundaram, D. S., Mitra, K., & Webster, C. (1998). Word-of-Mouth Communications: A Motivational Analysis. *Advances in Consumer Research. Association for Consumer Research (U. S.), 25*(1), 527–531.

Sutanto, J. E. (2009), Dimension Quality of Service Influence Customer Satisfaction in the Hotel: A Case study and examination of the transaction model in service industry. In *Proceeding of theInternational Seminar on Industrial Engineering and Management.* Academic Press.

Sutton, R. I., & Rafaeli, A. (1988). Untangling the relationship between displayed emotions and organizational sales: The case of convenience stores. *Academy of Management Journal, 31*(3), 461–487. doi:10.2307/256456

Sven, T., (2010). Frequent (flier) frustration and the dark side of word-of-web: exploring online dysfunctional behavior in online feedback forums. *Journal of Services Marketing, 24*(6), 446 – 457.

Svensson, A. (n.d.). *Facebook - the Social Newspaper that Never Sleeps. A Study of Facebook eWOM's persuasiveness on the receivers.* Academic Press.

Svensson, A. E. (n.d.). *Facebook - The Social Newspaper That Never Sleeps. A Study of Facebook eWOM's persuasiveness on the receivers.* Retrieved Sept 14, 2014, from https://gupea.ub.gu.se/bitstream/2077/26249/1/gupea_2077_26249_1.pdf

Sy, T., Côté, S., & Saavedra, R. (2005). The contagious leader: Impact of the leader's mood on group members, group affective tone, and group processes. *The Journal of Applied Psychology, 90*(2), 295–305. doi:10.1037/0021-9010.90.2.295 PMID:15769239

Taiwo, A. A., & Downe, A. G. (2013). The theory of User acceptance of information technology (UTAUT): A meta-analytic review of empirical findings. *Journal of Theoretical and Applied Information Technology, 49*(1), 48–58.

Tang, C., & Guo, L. (2013). Digging for Gold with a Simple Tool: Validating Text Mining in Studying Electronic Word-of-Mouth (eWOM) Communication. *Marketing Letters, 26*(1), 67–80. doi:10.1007/s11002-013-9268-8

Taylor, D. G. (2010). *I speak, therefore I am: Identity and self-construction as motivation to engage in electronic word of mouth.* (Unpublished doctoral dissertation). University of North Texas.

Taylorand et al. (2011). Research Methodology: A Guide To For Researchers. In *Management and Social Sciences.* PHI Learning Pvt. Ltd.

Taylor, D. G., Strutton, D., & Thompson, K. (2012). Self-enhancement as a motivation for sharing online advertisement. *Journal of Interactive Advertising, 12*(2), 13–28. doi:10.1080/15252019.2012.10722193

Taylor, S. J., & Bogdan, R. (1984). *Introduction to qualitative research methods: the search for meaning.* New York: John Willey & Sons.

The Ehrenberg-Bass Institute for Marketing Science. (2014, September 11). *News and press release.* Retrieved from: http://bit.ly/1pajBXi

Thomas, T. K. (2014, October 10). Benefits of bringing connectivity to India are going to be profound: Zuckerberg. *The Hindu*, p. 11.

Thomas, W.G. (2006). eWOM: *The impact of customer-to-customer online know-how exchange on customer value and loyalty*. Elsevier.

Thomas, W. G., Talai, O., & Andrew, J. C. (2006). eWOM: The impact of customer-to-customer online know-how exchange on customer value and loyalty. *Journal of Business Research*, *59*(4), 449–456. doi:10.1016/j.jbusres.2005.10.004

Thomopsan. (2005). eWOM: The impact of customer-to-customer online know-how exchange on customer value and loyalty. *Journal of Business Research*, *59*(4), 459-466.

Thor, S., (n.d.). *Electronic Word-of-Mouth: Increasing the Velocity and Reach of Traditional Word-of-Mouth*. George Fox University.

Thorson, K. S., & Rodgers, S. (2006). Relationships between Blogs as eWOM and Interactivity, Perceived Interactivity, and Parasocial Interaction. *Journal of Interactive Advertising*, *6*(2), 39–50. doi:10.1080/15252019.2006.10722117

Translate, Google. (n.d.). Retrieved from https://translate.google.com.tr/

Trust In Advertising. (2013). Retrieved from http://www.nielsen.com/us/en/insights/news/2013/under-the-influence-consumer-trust-in-advertising.html

Tseng, A. (2014). *Text Mining Tools*. Retrieved from http://blogs.unimelb.edu.au/23researchthings/2014/08/04/ thing-18-text-mining-tools/

TÜRSAB (Association of Turkish Travel Agency). (n.d.). Available at http://www.tursab.org.tr/

Tuten, T., & Bosnjak, M. (2001). Understanding differences in web usage: The role of need for cognition and the five factor model of personality. *Social Behavior and Personality: An International Journal*, *29*(4), 391–398. doi:10.2224/sbp.2001.29.4.391

Uboweja, S. (2015). *How to build a brand using social media*. Retrieved 4 15, 2015, from http://articles.economictimes.indiatimes.com/2015-04-08/news/60942975_1_social-media-brand-equity/2

US company says FB, Twitter ads fail to deliver. (n.d.). Retrieved from http://articles.economictimes.indiatimes.com/2014-04-16/news/49185111_1_ads-facebook-google

van Raaij, E. M., & Schepers, J. J. L. (2008). The acceptance and use of a virtual learning environment in China. *Computers & Education*, *50*(3), 838–852. doi:10.1016/j.compedu.2006.09.001

Vehr, N. J. (2012). *Vehr Communications, 2012 Social Media Usage Survey*. Retrieved on May 05, 2013 from http://www.vehrcommunications.com/wp-content/uploads/2012/02/2012-Social-Media-Usage-Survey-PRINT-FINAL.pdf

Venkatesh, V., & Davis, F. D. (1996). A model of the antecedents of perceived ease of use: Development and test. *Decision Sciences*, *27*(3), 451–481. doi:10.1111/j.1540-5915.1996.tb01822.x

Venkatesh, V., Morris, M. G., Davis, G. B., & Davis, F. D. (2003). User acceptance of information technology: Toward a unified view. *Management Information Systems Quarterly*, *27*(3), 425–478.

Voss, C. A. (2003). Rethinking paradigms of service - service in a virtual environment. *International Journal of Operations & Production Management*, *23*(1), 88–104. doi:10.1108/01443570310453271

Walsh, G., Gwinner, K. P., & Swanson, S. R. (2004). What makes mavens tick? Exploring the motives of market mavens' initiation of information diffusion. *Journal of Consumer Marketing*, *21*(2), 109–122. doi:10.1108/07363760410525678

Wang, Y., & Rodgers, S. (2011). Electronic Word of Mouth and Consumer Generated Content In Handbook of Research on Digital Media and Advertising: User Generated Content (pp. 212-231). Academic Press.

Wangenheim, F. V., & Bayón, T. (2004). The Effect of Word-of-Mouth on Services Switching: Measurement and Moderating Variables. *European Journal of Marketing*, *38*(9–10), 1173–1185. doi:10.1108/03090560410548924

Wang, Y. D., & Emurian, H. H. (2005). An overview of online trust: Concepts, elements, and implications. *Computers in Human Behavior*, *21*(1), 105–125. doi:10.1016/j.chb.2003.11.008

Ward, K. J. (1999). The cyber-ethnographic (re)construction of two feminist online communities. *Sociological Research Online*, *4*(1). doi:10.5153/sro.222

Wasserman, S., & Faust, K. (1994). *Social network analysis: Methods and applications* (Vol. 8). Cambridge, UK: Cambridge University Press. doi:10.1017/CBO9780511815478

Waters, R. D., & Jamal, J. Y. (2011). Tweet, tweet, tweet: A content analysis of nonprofit organizations' Twitter updates. *Public Relations Review*, *37*(3), 321–324. doi:10.1016/j.pubrev.2011.03.002

Watt, S. E., Lee, M., & Spears, R. (2002). How social is Internet communication? A reappraisal of bandwidth and anonymity effect. In S. Woolgar (Ed.), *Virtual Society*. Oxford, UK: Oxford University Press.

Weare, C., & Lin, W.-Y. (2000). Content Analysis of the World Wide Web Opportunities and Challenges. *Social Science Computer Review*, *18*(3), 272–292. doi:10.1177/089443930001800304

Weinberger, M. G., Allen, C. T., & Dillon, W. R. (1981). Negative Information: Perspectives and Research Directions. *Advances in Consumer Research. Association for Consumer Research (U. S.)*, *8*(1), 398–404.

Westbrook, R. A., & Oliver, R. L. (1991). The dimensionality of consumption emotion patterns and consumer satisfaction. *The Journal of Consumer Research*, *18*(1), 84–91. doi:10.1086/209243

Wetzer, I. M., Zeelenberg, M., & Pieters, R. (2007). "Never eat in that restaurant, I did!": Exploring why people engage in negative word-of-mouth communication. *Psychology and Marketing*, *24*(8), 661–680. doi:10.1002/mar.20178

Whitler, K. A. (2014). *Why Word Of Mouth Marketing is the Most Important Social Media*. Retrieved from http://www.forbes.com

Whyte, W. J. (1954). The web of Word of Mouth. *Fortune*, *50*(5), 140–143.

Williams, D., & Happé, F. (2010). Representing intentions in self and other: Studies of autism and typical development. *Developmental Science*, *13*(2), 307–319. doi:10.1111/j.1467-7687.2009.00885.x PMID:20136927

Williams, R., van der Wiele, T., van Iwaarden, J., & Eldridge, S. (2010). The importance of user-generated content: The case of hotels. *The TQM Journal*, *22*(2), 117–128. doi:10.1108/17542731011024246

Wilson, R. (2000). The six simple principles of viral marketing. *Wilson, R.F*, *70*, 1-3.

Wirtz, J., & Chew, P. (2002). The Effects of Incentives, Deal Proneness, Satisfaction and Tie Strength on Word-of-Mouth Behaviour. *International Journal of Service Industry Management*, *13*(2), 141–162. doi:10.1108/09564230210425340

Wixom, B. H., & Todd, P. A. (2005). A Theoretical Integration of User Satisfaction and Technology Acceptance. *Information Systems Research*, *16*(1), 85–102. doi:10.1287/isre.1050.0042

Wojnicki, A.C., & Godes, D. (2008). Word-of-mouth as self-enhancement. *Social Science Research Network*. Retrieved from http://ssrn.com/paper=908999

Wojnicki, A. C. (2006). Word-of-mouth and word-of-web: Talking about products, talking about me. *Advances in Consumer Research. Association for Consumer Research (U. S.)*, *33*(1), 573–575.

Wolny, J., & Mueller, C. (2013). Analysis of fashion consumers' motives to engage in electronic word-of-mouth communication through social media. *Journal of Marketing Management*, *29*(5-6), 562–583. doi:10.1080/0267257X.2013.778324

Woodside, A. G., Cruickshank, B. F., & Dehuang, N. (2007). Stories visitors tell about Italian cities as destination icons. *Tourism Management*, *28*(1), 162–174. doi:10.1016/j.tourman.2005.10.026

Woodside, A. G., & Delozier, M. W. (1976). Effect of word of mouth advertising on consumer risk taking. *Journal of Advertising*, *5*(4), 12–19. doi:10.1080/00913367.1976.10672658

Wright, P. (1974, October). The harassed decision maker: Time pressures, distractions, and use of evidence. *The Journal of Applied Psychology*, *59*(5), 555–561. doi:10.1037/h0037186

Wu, M., & Yand, P. L. Pearce. (2013). Appraising netnography: Towards insight about new markets in the digital tourist era. *Current Issues in Tourism*. doi:10.1080/13683500.2013.833179

Wu, P. C. S., & Wang, Y.-C. (2011). The influences of electronic word-of-mouth message appeal and message source credibility on brand attitude. *Asia Pacific Journal of Marketing and Logistics*, *23*(4), 448–472. doi:10.1108/13555851111165020

Wu, W., & Sukoco, B. M. (2010, Summer). Why should I share? Examining consumers' motives and trust on knowledge sharing. *Journal of Computer Information Systems*, 11–19.

Xiang, Z., Schwartz, Z., Gerdes, J. Jr, & Uysal, M. (2015). What Can Big Data and Text Analytics Tell Us About Hotel Guest Experience and Satisfaction? *International Journal of Hospitality Management*, *44*, 120–130. doi:10.1016/j.ijhm.2014.10.013

Xun, J., & Reynolds, J. (2010). Applying netnography to market research: The case of the online forum. *Journal of Targeting. Measurement and Analysis for Marketing.*, *18*(1), 17–31. doi:10.1057/jt.2009.29

Yali, A. a. (2010). eWom: The effects of online consumer reviews on purchasing decision of electronic goods. In *Proceedings of the International Marketing Trends Conference*. Venice: Academic Press.

Yang, C., Lin, K. H.-Y., & Chen, H.-H. (2007). Emotion classification using web blog corpora. Academic Press.

Yang, Y., Akers, L., Klose, T., & Yang, C. (2008). Text Mining and Visualization Tools – Impressions of *Emerging Capabilities. World Patent Information*, *30*(4), 280–293. doi:10.1016/j.wpi.2008.01.007

Ye, Q., Law, R., Gu, B., & Chen, W. (2011). The Influence of User-Generated Content on Traveler Behavior: An Empirical Investigation on The Effects of e-Word-of-Mouth to Hotel Online Bookings. *Computers in Human Behavior*, *27*(2), 634–639. doi:10.1016/j.chb.2010.04.014

Yew, J., Shamma, D. A., & Churchill, E. F. (2011). Knowing funny: genre perception and categorization in social video sharing. In *Proceedings of the SIGCHI Conference on Human Factors in Computing Systems* (pp. 297-306). doi:10.1145/1978942.1978984

Yildirim, D. (2011). *The Effect of Social Capital and Outcome Expectations on Product recommendations in Social Networks: An Empirical Comparison of Facebook*. Academic Press.

Yoon, N. S. (2008). *The Effects of Electronic Word-Of-Mouth Systems (Ewoms) on the Acceptance of Recommendation*. UMI Microcrome, ProQuest LLC.

You Tube. (2014). Retrieved from https://www.youtube.com/yt/press/statistics.html

Yu, E. (2008). *Social Network Analysis Applied to Ontology 3D Visualization*. (Doctoral dissertation). Miami University, Miami, FL.

Yulianti, I., & Tung, W. (2013). The Relationship Among Brand Experience, Brand Image and Customer Satisfaction of Facebook Users in Indonesia. *World Applied Sciences Journal, 28*, 100–113. doi:10.5829/idosi.wasj.2013.28.efmo.27017

Yu, Y.-T., & Dean, A. (2001). The contribution of emotional satisfaction to customer loyalty. *International Journal of Service Industry Management*, *12*(3), 234–251. doi:10.1108/09564230110393239

Zaglia, M. E. (2013). Brand communities embedded in social networks. *Journal of Business Research*, *66*(2), 216–223. doi:10.1016/j.jbusres.2012.07.015 PMID:23564989

Zaichkowsky, J. L. (1985). Measuring the involvement construct. *The Journal of Consumer Research*, *12*(3), 341–352. doi:10.1086/208520

Zailskaite-jakste, L., & Kuvykaite, R. (2012). Consumer Engagement in Social Media by Building the Brand. In *Electronic International Interdisciplinary Conference 2012* (pp. 194–202). Academic Press.

Zajonc, R. (1971). The Concepts of Balance, Congruity, and Dissocance. In Attitude Change (pp. 63-85). Chicago: Aldine-Atherton.

Zajonc, R. B. (1980). Feeling and thinking: Preferences need no inferences. *The American Psychologist*, *35*(2), 151–175. doi:10.1037/0003-066X.35.2.151

Zhang, W., & Watts, S. (2003). *Knowledge adoption in online communities of practice.* Paper presented at the 24th International Conference on Information Systems, Atlanta, GA.

Zhang, B. J. (2009). Twitter Power:Tweets as Electronic Word of Mouth. *Journal of the American Society for Information Science and Technology*, *60*(11), 2169–2188. doi:10.1002/asi.21149

Zhang, C. (2010). Fashion Blogs: The new member in fashion industry. *Journal of Digital Research & Publishing*, *3*(1), 25–32.

Zhang, J. Q., Craciun, G., & Shin, D. (2010). When does electronic word-of-mouth matter? A study of consumer product reviews. *Journal of Business Research*, *63*(12), 1336–1341. doi:10.1016/j.jbusres.2009.12.011

Zhang, W., & Watts, S. A. (2008). Capitalizing on Content: Information Adoption in Two Online communities. *Journal of the Association for Information Systems*, *9*(2), 72–93.

Zhang, Z. Y., Ye, Q., Law, R., & Li, Y. (2010). The impact of e-word-of-mouth on the online popularity of restaurants: A comparison of consumer reviews and editor reviews. *International Journal of Hospitality Management*, *29*(4), 694–700. doi:10.1016/j.ijhm.2010.02.002

About the Contributors

Sumangla Rathore is currently working as Assistant Professor in School of Management at Sir Padampat Singhania University, Udaipur, Rajasthan, India. She holds a PhD in e-commerce domain and a Post graduate degree in Computer Applications. Dr. Rathore has been an active participant in cross-cultural international experiences involving students and academic exchange. She has several national and international publications to her credit in the field of e-commerce and Information Technology. Her research interests are in the field of e-commerce, Social media, electronic Word of Mouth, online buying behavior, technology adoption and usability evaluation.

Avinash Panwar holds a PhD in e-commerce domain and a Master's degree in Computer Science and Applications. His interest areas in teaching and research include System Designing, application of IT for improvement of processes and public services, Social Network Analysis and electronic Word of Mouth. He has an experience of more than 14years in various administrative and academic positions. Dr. Panwar has had international exposure through his visit to University of Nebraska, USA as a faculty representative for a 15 day exchange programme which included 40 students from five different countries. He is also strongly associated with academic fraternity by means of guest lectures, collaborative research, conferences, meetings and other academic initiatives. He has several national and international publications to his credit.

* * *

Lovish Bhansali is a student of MBA (II) majoring in Finance and is actively involved in writing papers.

Arijit Bhattacharya is from India and is an MBA (Marketing) with 12 years of industry experience in customer service and marketing. He shifted to academics four years back where he found his true calling. Presently, he works as an Assistant Professor in Lala Lajpatrai Institute of Management, Mumbai where he teaches subjects in marketing domain to MBA students. His teaching interests include consumer behavior, retail marketing, marketing strategy and applied marketing research. He is also pursuing PhD in Management from Narsee Monjee Institute of Management Studies, Mumbai in the field of online consumer behavior. He has published and presented papers on different aspects of e-retailing.

Tuğçe Ozansoy Çadırcı has a PhD degree on marketing and a assistant prof. of marketing at Yıldız Technical University (YTU). Her particular area of interest is electronic mediums like online social networks, particularly their impact on online consumer behavior. Other research areas in her interest include consumer theory, fashion consumption and symbolic consumption. Currently she is lecturing at YTU on the subjects of e-commerce and digital marketing, direct marketing, consumption theory and marketing research.

Vineet Chouhan, having PhD in Commerce, MBA-FM and UGC-NET, RPSC-SLET qualification with over 13 years of experience, 6 book (including 1 reference book) to his credit. He has published over 30 research papers and participated and presented papers in 50 conferences/ seminars with 3 FDP programs.

Mohsen Debabi teaches Marketing and Distribution at the Ecole Supérieure de Commerce (University of Mannouba). He is the author of several publication and conference communication. His research interests are the communication, distribution, digital marketing and consumer behavior fields.

Gautam Deka hails from a small town in the far-eastern state of Assam, India. He did his schooling from Army School, Jorhat, and obtained bachelor and master degree in Commerce and Management from Amity University, Noida and OP Jindal Global University, Sonipat. At present serving in Gurgaon for the last 3 years and also pursuing his doctorate degree programme at Sir Padampat Singhania University, Udaipur. His area of specialization is Marketing, and has switched over or rather experimented with Digital Marketing. He desires to improve his skills for his future professional endeavours. Besides, he has a passion for travel and exploration, which he performs on a regular basis.

Taşkın Dirsehan joined the Faculty of Business Administration (lectured in English) in Marmara University as a marketing research assistant in February 2011. He received his BA in Business Administration from Galatasaray University in 2009, his MA in Production Management and Marketing from Marmara University and PhD in Marketing from Istanbul University. His research and teaching interests are in the areas of sustainability, international marketing, consumer behavior, brand management and marketing research. His research has been published in various national and international journals including Boğaziçi Journal Review of Social, Economic and Administrative Studies. He has also presented his research at various conferences including National Marketing Congress and International Strategic Management Conference.

Punita Duhan is a Doctoral Research Fellow in marketing area at Faculty of Management Studies, Banaras Hindu University, Varanasi and is pursuing her research in the area of Social Media. She is faculty in Business Administration with Department of Training And Technical Education, Govt. of Delhi for the last 14 years. Prior to this, she has worked as Faculty of Management with University Business School, Panjab University, Chandigarh and IMT, Faridabad.

Shubham Goswami is currently working as Assistant Professor, School of Management at Sir Padampat Singhania University, Udaipur. He holds doctoral degree in Computer Science and Masters in Business Administration. He has been involved in teaching and research for more than six years. He has also worked with Indian Institute of Management, Ahmedabad as Academic Associate in Information Systems Area. His area of research includes Technology adoption, Information Systems, ICT for development, Enterprise systems and electronic marketing. His research papers has been published in refereed conference proceedings of national and international repute and in refereed journals including Paradigm-IMT Ghaziabad, IUP Journal of Marketing Management (ICFAI press), Abhigyan- FORE School of Management, IPE Journal of Marketing Vistas (Institute of Public Enterprise),The Alternative-Journal of Management Studies and Research (BIT-Mesra).

Ayşegül Sağkaya Güngör has a PhD degree on marketing. Her particular area of interest is electronic mediums like online social networks, particularly their impact on online consumer behavior. Other research areas in her interest include consumer acceptance of technology, digital marketing methods and e-commerce. Currently she is lecturing in various universities on the subjects of e-commerce, e-business, digital marketing and marketing management.

Azizul Hassan is a member of the Tourism Consultants Network of the UK Tourism Society, and is currently working towards a PhD at Cardiff Metropolitan University. His main areas of research are: technology-supported marketing in tourism; innovative marketing dynamics; destination branding in tourism; cultural heritage tourism; heritage interpretation; and sustainable management/marketing alternatives for cultural heritage industries. He is a regular reviewer of the International Journal of Human Resource Management, the International Journal of Ecotourism and the eReview of Tourism Research (eRTR) and The International Interdisciplinary Business-Economics Advancement Journal.

Dhiraj Jain is an Associate Professor of Finance at SCMS Pune. He has qualified the UGC-NET, a Ph. D and an Associate Member of the Insurance Institute of India. He has worked for the industry for13 years and has been into academics since the past 9 years. His areas of interest include Security Analysis & Portfolio Mgt., Financial Derivatives & Financial Planning. He has been a corporate trainer for Reliance Mutual Fund, Pru-ICICI, HDFC Mutual Fund and many other AMCs & broking houses for the past 8 years and has conducted more than 100 training sessions for various corporate, bankers, brokers and investors. He has also been associated with BSE for content development. He has 87 papers published in various National and International Journals. He has presented papers in various conferences of National & International repute. Two students have already completed their PHD under his guidance.

Anne-Flore Maman Larraufie, SemioConsult and ESSEC, a Military Academy Engineer and PhD, Anne-Flore Maman Larraufie founded her own consulting business SémioConsult in 2010, whilst also pursuing academic research and teaching. SémioConsult is focused on managing brand image and identity, thanks to semiotics, along with getting consumer insights. She is a member of the editorial boards of The Luxury Research Journal, The Journal of Consumer Marketing, and of The International Journal of Marketing Research. She is also the Academic Director of the Advanced Master in Strategy & Management of International Business at ESSEC Business School (Paris, France).

Dipin Mathur is an Associate Professor and coordinator for the Masters in Business Administration program at Advent Institute of Management, Udaipur (India). He also serves as Principal (Officiating). He holds a PhD degree in commerce, Masters in Business Administration with specialization in Human resources and a Masters in Commerce. He teaches courses on General Management, Human Resource Management & Training and Development. He researches in areas of training needs assessment, organisational behaviour, etc. He has conducted several management development programs and training sessions. He holds a lifetime membership to Indian Society for Training and Development.

Disha Mathur works as an Assistant Professor in the School of Management, Sir Padampat Singhania University, Udaipur (India). She received her Doctoral Degree in the area of Advertising Management and a Master's Degree in Business Administration with Marketing as specialisation. She is UGC-NET qualified and teaches courses on Marketing, Consumer Behaviour and Advertising. Her research interests include branding issues, emerging trends in applications of advertising and consumer behaviour research. She is the member of Indian Society for Training and Development.

Elvis Mazzoni is a PhD researcher at the Department of Psychology of the ALMA MATER STUDIORUM - University of Bologna. His fields of study is Lifespan Development and Lifelong Learning. He's Managing Editor of the European Journal of Psychology of Education and member of the Editorial Board of Cyberpsychology, Behaviour and Social Networking. His research interests are focused on: Digital Natives; Education and Information and Communication Technologies (ICT); Co-evolution characterizing human activity systems (in the Activity Theory perspective) and the Information and Communication Technologies (ICT); analysis of the changes produced by ICT (specifically by Web Artifacts) on human activity systems involving educational training and knowledge construction; Human-robot interaction in educational context; Web Artifacts supporting lifespan development; and Networked Flow (the network creativity).

Sanal Nair is an avid writer and a researcher.

Veronica Ravaglia graduated in Psychology of Marketing from the University of Sacred Heard, Milan. She has been working as Social Media Research since 2013 in Duepuntozero DOXA, a digital research agency located in Milan.

Moumita Roy is working as a teaching associate at Indian Institute Of Management (IIM), Calcutta. She has completed her masters in Applied Psychology from University Of Calcutta and has also earned a bachelors degree in Education from University Of Pune. She has research interests in creativity and innovation, consumer behaviour and emotional intelligence.

Yuvraj Sharma is working as a business Associate at Cognus Technology Limited, Udaipur Rajasthan. He has completed his MBA from FMS Pacific University, Udaipur. His area of specializations includes IT and Finance. He completed his B-tech in computer science from Rajasthan Technical University. He had worked as a software associate in Sarayu Issue Management Pvt. Ltd, Mumbai. He has completed his MBA summer training in SAP FI/CO module from i-logic technologies, Hyderabad. His area of interest includes ERP & Database management system and research projects related to IT & its implementation into various fields. He has cleared Microsoft Certification Professional Exam [70-536] .Net Framework 2.0 Core Foundation.

Anurag Singh is a Faculty at Faculty of Management Studies, Banaras Hindu University, Varanasi, with fifteen years of academic and six years of research experience. He has authored one book and has to his credit thirty-five research papers in national and international journals. He is a former Assistant professor of Department of Business Administration, Assam University, Silchar.

Fabien Sommer, INSEEC, press relation agent in fashion and sport industry in Paris. Master degree in communication - INSEEC Bordeaux / Harrington College of Design – Chicago.

Rym Srarfi Tabbane is an assistant lecturer of marketing in the Ecole Supérieure d'Economie Numérique (ESEN) at the University of Manouba (Tunisia). She has published research articles in conferences, posters and also teaching materials such as case studies. Her research focuses mainly on the area of Online Marketing, Online Consumer Behavior, Online information processing, Mobile marketing and online Commerce. She is actually involved in different research about the moderating role of culture and gender on the buying intention. Over the years she has taught different courses in marketing, Online Consumer Behavior, Marketing Strategy and Direct Marketing.

Luca Zanazzi graduated on November 2012 in the Master Degree of Work, Organization, Personnel Psychology & Services, University of Bologna. Currently employed as HR Specialist, he is still working as a Researcher. Currently, he's working on some projects regarding Social Network Sites, Social Network Analysis and Text Analysis.

Index

F

G

I

L

M

N

O

P

Q

R

S

T

U

V

W

Lightning Source UK Ltd.
Milton Keynes UK
UKOW07n0141080116

266022UK00012B/172/P